International Handbook on Land Use Planning

Edited by
NICHOLAS N. PATRICIOS

Greenwood Press
New York • Westport, Connecticut • London

Library of Congress Cataloging in Publication Data
Main entry under title:

International handbook on land use planning.

Bibliography: p.
Includes index.
1. Land use—Planning—Case studies. I. Patricios,
Nicholas N.
HD108.6.I58 1986   333.73'17   84-29018
ISBN 0-313-23950-9 (lib. bdg.)

Library of Congress Catalog Card Number: 84-29018
ISBN: 0-313-23950-9

First published in 1986

Greenwood Press, Inc.
88 Post Road West
Westport, Connecticut 06881

Printed in the United States of America

The paper used in this book complies with the
Permanent Paper Standard issued by the National
Information Standards Organization (Z39.48-1984).

10 9 8 7 6 5 4 3 2 1

To Emily, Leon, and Lana

Contents

Part III: Africa

Part IV: Europe

Part V: North America

Part VI: Central and South America

Part VII: Australasia

Illustrations

Tables

Preface

This handbook presents basic information on land use planning in representative countries around the world. The concise descriptive accounts of each country will be of use to decisionmakers and administrators everywhere who are involved in development and land use planning at all levels, to planning practitioners, to those in various agencies concerned with physical development, to scholars and students in planning, geography, and other areas, and to anyone else with an interest in the land problems and planning approaches of individual countries or groups of countries.

In addition to information on land use planning in individual countries, comparisons of countries can be made because each contributor has followed a standard format. The results of a comparative study of the similarities and differences among countries are contained in chapter 1, "A Global Perspective of Land Use Planning." My guidelines to contributors were to provide a succinct, descriptive, and analytical account of land use planning in a specified country according to the established format. Accordingly, the chapters on individual countries present information on the historical development and current status of land use planning, the institutional and landownership framework, the major challenges as well as the approaches to land use planning; they conclude with future thrusts or discernible trends. This book presents only basic facts about each country. Those interested in further information will find of value the references and bibliography at the end of each chapter.

The countries included in this book are considered representative of "international" land use planning. Any omissions are due in most cases to the lack of comprehensive information about planning in a particular country and, to some extent, the unavailability of knowledgeable contributors, as well as the problem of international communications. The use of the term *international land use planning* is not meant to imply that there is an approach to planning called international, as there is city planning, regional planning, rural planning, and so forth. The connotation here is that the focus is on land use planning at the international level, that is, on planning in countries around the world and comparisons among countries.

A problem I wrestled with was the question on how to structure the book. The obvious answer was an alphabetical ordering of countries. I rejected this solution quickly because I felt this would not provide readers with a coherent and comprehensible picture of land use planning around the world. The other extreme was to impose an ordering system, but which one? It is possible to group countries according to economic systems—capitalist or socialist, developed or developing countries, East or West, and by means of other concepts. In the end I decided on a neutral but meaningful geographical sequence, one in which readers could devise their own structure if they so wished. This allows readers to make their own observations, over and above the basic information provided in the handbook. As the map shown here illustrates, the space-time sequence selected begins with the countries with the longest traditions in the planning of cities (China, Japan, India) and ends with a country where land use planning is recent (Australia). The sequence is not consistent in the time dimension, and is not meant to be. The controlling factor in the order is spatial, an imaginary journey to countries on the continents of, in sequence, Asia, Africa, Europe, North America, South America, and finally Australasia.

I thank all of the contributors for their fine efforts in preparing a chapter in this book and for their compliance with the guidelines. I am most grateful to Anita Angelica for her patience and accuracy in typing, and retyping, parts of this handbook. I am also grateful to Rafael Padilla for his drawing and redrawing some of the illustrations.

                                                                Nicholas N. Patricios

International
Handbook on
Land Use Planning

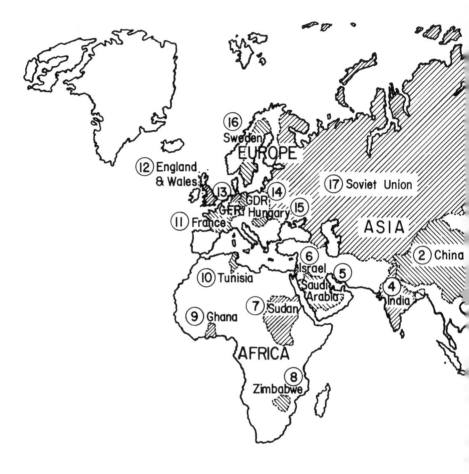

NOTES: * The sequence begins with ②(China) & ends with ㉓(Australia).

* GFR - German Federal Republic

* GDR - German Democratic Republic

Map Showing Sequence of Countries in Handbook, by Chapter Numbers

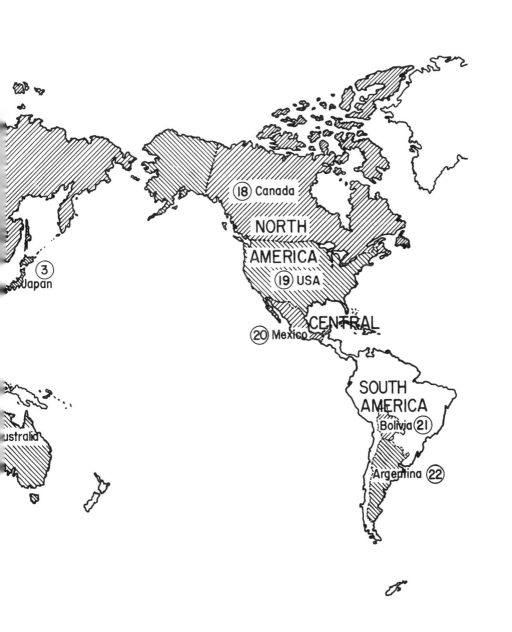

PART I

OVERVIEW

A Global Perspective of Land Use Planning

NICHOLAS N. PATRICIOS

APPROACH

This chapter presents an overview of land use planning from a global perspective based on the contributions in this book. The focus of the overview is on the similarities and the differences among countries. A comparative study of the countries in the handbook reveals predominant resemblances and noteworthy variations in land use issues and planning that are described in this global perspective of land use planning.

The difficulty in attempting to identify similarities across countries is the variability among nations. The difficulty was lessened somewhat by the adoption of a common framework by each contributor in·structuring and presenting information on land use planning for a particular country. It was found, consequently, that meaningful generalizations could be made at the ''continental'' level, both intra-continental and inter-continental. The parallels at these continental levels are described in this overview and apply to most of the continents. Resemblances in land use issues and planning that apply to a few countries only follow the continental comparisons. A brief account of distinctive and globally significant differences between countries then follows. The overview is concluded by a summary of a global perspective of land use planning.

The framework used in the comparative study is similar to that used by the contributors. It consists of a review of historical developments in land use, major challenges to the use of land, approaches to planning, and future thrusts in challenges and approaches to land use planning. Where appropriate, reference to institutional and landownership characteristics is also included. The framework is used not only for intra-continental and inter-continental comparisons but for analyzing international similarities and differences as well.

INTRA-CONTINENTAL COMPARISONS

Asia

The countries of eastern Asia have a somewhat similar historical background— a long tradition, over thousands of years, of planning cities. In this century the countries face high population and urbanization growth rates. The large increases in total population and the number and concentration of people living in cities are probably the major challenges in land use planning in the Far East. Other issues common to these countries are overcrowding in and the lack of low-income housing and the sprawl of cities into the surrounding countryside. The so-called urban periphery problem, where urban and rural fringes meet, is perhaps not even recognized by the authorities.

In Asia two major continental planning similarities are evident. First, a policy in virtually all the countries is the decentralization of population and industry from metropolitan areas to medium- and small-sized towns. To implement this policy of directing the flow of population and industry, the British program of satellite or independent new towns has been adopted to some extent. Second, all countries have a similar approach to planning in their use of a hierarchy of plans; from national to regional or provincial to local. In some cases there are also plans with a time horizon, the most common being five years.

Future development in countries of eastern Asia is likely to follow a parallel path—the emphasis on a regional approach, on the development of currently medium and small towns to reduce the concentration of population and industry in the few, huge metropolitan areas. The influence of the British new towns policy, the development of medium- and small-sized towns, and the future emphasis on rural development projects are also to be found in the countries of western Asia.

Africa

The countries of Africa share historical development patterns that are very much the same: the influence of colonial powers, the impact of the railway, and the emergence of primate cities are the predominant characteristics. The British, for example, appear to have adopted fairly extensively the use of the gridiron layout with segregated areas. Railway lines determined which parts of a country were developed, and stations determined which towns would become important. The railway network inevitably focused on what was to become the largest and dominant city of a country.

The major challenge in African countries is the high rate of urbanization.

There is some evidence that it may be out of control. This may be related to the issue of overlapping planning processes and numerous decision-making authorities and to the common problem of a lack of skilled manpower or adequate numbers of technically competent persons. Another major challenge is the provision of urban shelter for the large number of migrants from rural areas.

Institutional frameworks in African countries resemble one another in that decentralization of central government functions is being or has been attempted. Similarities in planning approaches are the hierarchy of plans and the increasing amount of public participation in the planning process, as well as the use of international agencies such as the World Bank and the United States Agency for International Development (US-AID). The resemblance in future thrusts is toward increasing the decentralization of decisionmaking accompanied by regional planning and development.

Europe

Industrialization in parallel with urbanization occurred in European countries during the nineteenth century and into the early twentieth century. This pattern contrasts with the process of urbanization, in many cases not accompanied by industrialization, that took place in Asia, Africa, and Central and South America during this century. The combined impact of industrialization and urbanization in Europe eventually brought about reactions that led to the development of modern city or town planning.

To varying extents, the countries of Europe are faced with the major challenges of loss of agricultural land, urban sprawl, and preserving historically important structures in the renewal of inner cities. Although European countries differ among themselves considerably in their economic and political systems, the loss of valuable agricultural land to urban development, industry, and mining is a common concern. The random and fragmented spread of urban peripheries into the countryside has led to countermeasures such as greenbelts, development of satellite settlements, and public acquisition of large tracts of land beyond the urban edge. Parallel problems in European cities are the clearing of slums from inner areas and improving the quality of the existing housing stock.

Similarities in approaches are the extensive application of land use planning and implementation measures, the employment of general and specific plans at national, regional, and local levels, and planned decentralization to achieve regional balances. In Europe planning is facilitated by the acceptance of the public ownership of land on a large scale, obviously most extensively in socialist countries.

In the future the deconcentration of metropolitan areas and the renewal of inner cities will remain major issues. Of increasing importance will be environmental concerns, both urban and rural.

North America

In North America urban development and planning are essentially twentieth century phenomena. In both Canada and the United States, they have occurred in the context of a federal system of government. The major common problem is the loss of high-productivity agricultural land or a perceived loss of farmland to suburbanization and rural and recreational developments. An international problem involving the jurisdictional issue of cross-national air pollution, highlighted in North America, is now drawing attention on other continents as well, where international water pollution is an additional problem. The management of coastal and other resources is another challenge in North America. Similarities in planning are in the comprehensive approach and use of new methods such as environmental impact statements, planned unit developments, and growth management. Parallel future developments are the slower growth of the large, metropolitan areas and the increased growth of the smaller urban settlements, as well as continued and intense public concern over environmental regulation.

Central and South America

In Central and South America colonial powers and the railway were determining factors in historical development, analogous to the development of Africa. In the case of the Americas, the Spanish were the dominant power. Their influence on the evolution of land use was twofold. First, under the Laws of the Indies, decreed by King Philip II in 1573, towns were to be founded and laid out according to a set of guidelines. Second, the Spanish *hacienda* (plantation) system of landholding is the root of Latin America's land and class structure problems.

Major challenges common to Central and South American countries are high population growth rates, high rates of migration of the rural poor and landless to large urban areas causing unbalanced distributions of population, and the consequent land shortage and shelter problems in metropolitan areas. Other problems are political instability and the lack of comprehensive and effective implementation of plans. The weight of the problem is apparently overwhelming the capacity to plan. High rates of population growth and urbanization are likely to continue into the future, as are land shortages and the provision of adequate shelter. Probably there will be pressure to decentralize government decision-making and to institutionalize and consolidate the democratic process.

INTER-CONTINENTAL COMPARISONS

There are fewer similarities in an inter-continental comparison than there are in the intra-continental case. There are, however, some striking resemblances in the historical development of land use, the issues related to the use of land, the approaches to planning, and future land use and planning thrusts. Some global parallels have already been alluded to.

Perhaps the most pervasive influence on the evolution of and changes to land use on all continents in the nineteenth and twentieth centuries has been the railway, followed by the building of highways for motor vehicles. These new means of transportation linked capital cities with ports and regional administrative centers. The Canadian Pacific Railway, for example, was the most influential agent in determining settlement locations and the physical form of towns in Canada. Following closely on the sway of the railway in the historical development of land use patterns were the activities of the colonial powers in Africa, North, Central, and South America, Australasia, and some countries in Asia. Direct British influence on land use is evident mainly in many African countries. The British established municipalities, regulations for public health, and building bylaws. They also created segregated areas, usually within gridiron type plans. The Spanish influenced cities in Central and South American by means of the Laws of the Indies and the rural areas through the *hacienda* system. The effect the French had on their few colonies in north Africa and North America was cultural rather than physical in nature.

Clearly urbanization is the major challenge to land use planning in Asia, Africa, and Central and South America, as it was in most of Europe and North America in the nineteenth and early twentieth centuries. The problem is exacerbated in many cases in that the flow of rural migrants is to a primate city, which becomes overwhelmed by the sheer numbers of people. The vast majority of countries have now become urbanized, with the population located in one, or a few, large cities. Urbanization is related to two other inter-continental challenges. First is the loss of valued agricultural land, in Europe and North America mainly, due to urban development, industrial activities, and mining. Second is the complex and competing demands of rural and urban interests that occur at the periphery of expanding cities. This problem of urban sprawl, fragmentation, and disorganization occurs across continents in such countries as India, Japan, Saudi Arabia, England and Wales, the Soviet Union, Canada, and Argentina.

From a global perspective, commonalities in the approach to planning are few. One similarity is hierarchical planning, the preparation of interrelated plans by, or for, authorities at the national, regional or provincial, and local levels. At the local level (whether metropolitan, city, or village) plans are usually of two types: general, guide, or policy plans and specific, detailed plans. In addition to their spatial characteristic, plans usually have a time dimension as well. Five-year national plans are particularly favored. Another inter-continental similarity in approach is, or rather has been to a large extent, the use of new towns to assist in the deconcentration of metropolitan areas, to deal with urban sprawl, and to act as countermagnets of attraction to the large cities. The approach was used most extensively in Europe, particularly in England and Wales, France, and Sweden, after World War II to accommodate increased population growth and urbanization. Israel's New Towns are an integral part of that country's national land use policy. China is now proceeding with New Towns in the face of an unprecedented rate of urbanization over the last few decades.

The most widespread inter-continental similarity is decentralization. In Asia, Africa, and Australia the decentralization of population and industry and regional development are generally interrelated. In many European metropolitan areas, the future thrust is the deconcentration and the revitalization of the inner cities, which is much the same concern in North American cities. In Central and South America in the coming years, there is likely to be more pressure to decentralize, specifically central government decisionmaking.

INTERNATIONAL SIMILARITIES

Truly "international" comparisons are also possible, but they are far more complex and do not readily produce the generalizations that may be deduced from a "continental" level of analysis. For example, Islamic religion and Marxist-Lenist ideology, as well as the Zionist system of ideas, influence one or more countries. Although Saudi Arabia, Sudan, and Tunisia share Islamic beliefs, the countries are very different from one another due to historical events and varying economic, social, and political systems. The socialist countries of China, the German Democratic Republic, Hungary, and the Soviet Union have in common state ownership of land (but with different allowances for some private ownership and the degree of cooperative and collectivist arrangements) but have dissimilar challenges and approaches to land use planning.

Some limited generalizations, however, can be made. The movement of people to cities is, or has been, a ubiquitous process internationally with land use planning in its various forms, and with different degrees of success, as the universal reaction in response to the consequences of urbanization. One effect of urbanization is land speculation and price hikes. The question of betterment—public benefit from the increase in land values—is a related issue. Countries that have dealt with these problems include Japan, India, Saudi Arabia, Israel, England and Wales, France, Bolivia, and Australia. Another effect is land and housing shortages, particularly for low-income families, as in Tunisia, Zimbabwe, and many Central and South American countries. There is also increased questioning of the rigid and rather high residential standards applied to low-income housing. A further result of urbanization is the concentration of people in the center of large cities and accompanying overcrowding and congestion. For countries such as China and Japan, in particular, these are major issues.

Internationally there are problems with the system of planning, including lack of data (China, Saudi Arabia), lack of adequate technical planners (Ghana, Sudan, Tunisia, Zimbabwe, Bolivia), and inadequate implementation or compliance measures (India, Israel, Ghana, Sudan, Soviet Union, Argentina, Bolivia, Mexico). A positive aspect of planning at the international level, though, is established public participation in the decisionmaking process (such as in Sudan,

Zimbabwe, Israel, German Federal Republic, Canada, the United States, and Australia) and the fact that it is on the increase (for example, in England and Wales, Sweden, and Argentina).

NOTEWORTHY INTERNATIONAL DIFFERENCES

Differences among countries are many and varied. Those of international significance and interest are identified and described here.

In China the Cultural Revolution, which took place between 1966 and 1976, had a dramatic impact on land use planning. This followed on changes made in the Rectification Campaign that began in 1957 when a new set of urban space utilization standards were adopted upon the withdrawal of Soviet advisers. Marxist ideology clearly is evident in the policies adopted during the period of the Cultural Revolution: eliminating urban-rural differences, de-emphasizing heavy industry, de-emphasizing large metropolitan cities, and giving priority to the building of small settlements in which residence, industry, and agriculture are spatially integrated. Daqing emerged as a city planned according to socialist ideals. In the Modernization Era, which began after 1978, functional zoning and cities as the centers of industrial development were reinstated, and the construction of satellite towns with self-contained residential neighborhoods was reinstituted.

In another part of the world, the national revolutions that occurred in Central and South America brought about many land reforms. In Mexico the Agrarian Reform initiated after 1910 that solved the legal aspects of rural land tenure was emulated throughout Latin America. Mexico was able to go on and solve three other important problems: establish orderly democratic political life, subordinate the military to civilian institutional order, and institutionalize the spirit of the revolution into the economic system. Besides the General Law on Human Settlements (1976) and the National Planning Law (1983), Mexico has the National Program for Ecological Development of Human Settlements (1981); it emphasizes the qualitative aspects of development and thus may be unmatched in the industrialized world. The Urban Reform decree of 1955 in Bolivia, significant in Latin America at that time, provided for expropriation and allocations of land by municipalities.

The policy of reducing urban-rural differences is also explicit in the German Democratic Republic (GDR). Central place theory is used as a basis to obtain balance by locating services in hierarchical fashion in order to minimize travel time. In the 1950s sixteen socialist principles of urban planning were established to eliminate the "defects" of capitalist cities. Overall the German Democratic Republic constitution allows for a centrally planned economy and management of land use. In Hungary, for administrative reasons, settlements are divided into inner built-up areas and outer, usually garden, areas. The approach in the Soviet Union is to categorize land according to economic purpose—agricultural, populated places, industry, forestry, water, land reserve, and so on. For each category there are land tenure, transfer, and development regulations, which were incorporated in 1977 into the Soviet constitution. The prominent characteristic of that country's urban land use planning is its normative nature. Central agencies lay down guidelines and norms, which urban and development decisions are expected to conform to.

Israel is very much a planned society. Its rural settlements and the innovative range of types of cooperative or communal arrangements are aspects of Zionist ideology. In Saudi Arabia Islamic religious teaching and Sharia law are the basis for ideas about the design of buildings and the relationship of a building to the surrounding area. Concerns include privacy, adequacy of light and ventilation, and the adequacy of spaces between buildings for the movement of pedestrians and loaded camels. The Vedic tradition in India emphasized the interdependency between locations and nature and strove for organic unity. The siting and positioning of buildings were to be considered very carefully.

The concept of universal landownership, of private property rights and freehold tenure, was developed in the United States during the fifteenth and sixteenth centuries. This was a major break with European experience where only the ruling classes owned land. Although the problem of land speculation is in evidence today in some countries (India, Saudi Arabia, and Bolivia, for example), it was a major issue in Japan in the early 1970s and is still a matter for concern. The response has been to announce land prices in order to establish a system of standard prices. In addition, Japan has enacted a series of taxes to control speculative land transactions. Part of the problem is the artificial shortage of urban land due to the separation of ownership and use of land. Other countries have dealt with land speculation through public control of potential urban land as with the *Zone d'Amenagement Concerte* (ZAD) in France, the active land policy in Sweden where municipalities are allowed ownership of peripheral urban land suitable for future development, or the nationalization of development rights (not the land itself) in England and Wales.

England and Wales are also noted for their universal and comprehensive planning system. Started piecemeal in 1909, it reached maturity in the planning act of 1947. Legislation in England and Wales in 1909 and 1947 influenced planning thinking in other countries, such as Canada, Israel, and Sudan. The distinguishing characteristic of the universal and comprehensive system is that planning permission is required for every development. Canada has an interesting mixture of this development control system and zoning instruments. In contrast, West German planning is underpinned by public law—that is, the principles of legal order. Administrative courts thus play an important role in planning in that country.

The internationally noteworthy characteristics of Ghana and Tunisia are their concentration on intermediate-sized or secondary cities and on channeling resources to and focusing development on medium-sized cities. In Ghana a land use programming concept and demonstration project has been established to build institutional capacities. It also has a national training program designed to produce skilled technicians. The framework of central government agencies in Tunisia that assemble and develop land for housing and industrial purposes and provide housing and services is notable. Urban land is developed to ensure the availability of land and to dampen speculation.

SUMMARY OF A GLOBAL PERSPECTIVE

Intra-continental analogies are those common to countries grouped geographically according to continent. Asian countries are characterized by a long tradition in planning cities, current high rates of urbanization and population growth, the challenges of urban shelter and urban sprawl, with present-day attempts at decentralization continuing into the future. African countries were very much influenced by colonial powers and the railway. Currently they face high rates of urbanization and population increase as well as problems of sheltering large numbers of people migrating from rural to urban areas. Planning of secondary cities, hierarchical plans, and public participation are fairly common. The involvement of international aid agencies is evident. Probably future emphasis will be on the decentralization of decisionmaking. European countries, and to some extent those in North America, are alike in their concerns for the loss of valuable agricultural land, urban sprawl, and inner-city renewal. Their approach to planning is comprehensive, and they show increasing concern over environmental issues. Central and South America are characterized by the influence of colonial Spanish approaches to rural landholdings and urban layouts. Major challenges are high rates of population growth and urbanization. The lack of political stability and planning implementation mechanisms is a common problem. There is likely to be pressure in the future to decentralize decisionmaking.

Inter-continental parallels are mainly the influence of the railway and colonial powers in the historical development of land use systems, the major challenge of urbanization and issues related to it, the use of hierarchical plans and new towns in approaches to planning, and the existing and future thrust of the decentralization of population, industry, and decisionmaking.

At the international level, which includes both intra-continental and inter-continental levels, the similarities that are identified are the influence of ideologies and religion, interrelated urbanization issues, the increase in public participation in the planning process, and the inadequacies of planning systems. Finally, many distinctive differences in individual countries concerning urban-rural issues, socialist principles, building-site relationships, land speculation, comprehensive planning, and planning for secondary cities are noted.

CONCLUSION

This overview has exposed numerous themes in land use planning viewed from a global perspective. The reason for the variety are, first, the fact that land use is determined or influenced by historical, institutional, political, socio-economic, and technological factors, among others. Second, each of these factors differs in the effect it has in each country. There are, consequently, numerous land use issues and planning responses around the world. Thus, even though the overview generalizes at the continental level, there are still a bewildering number and variety of themes.

PART II

ASIA

2

China

KA-IU FUNG

URBAN LAND USE PLANNING IN CHINA

Dynamic changes have taken place in urban development in China since the 1950s. On a national scale the increase in the number of cities is unprecedented in China's urban history. Urban places with populations exceeding 2,000 increased from 1,999 in 1953 to 3,450 in 1979. Significantly the number of metropolitan centers with a population over 1 million increased from nine in 1953 to 24 in 1982 (Ma and Hanten, 1981, 114). Furthermore, all of the traditional administrative and commercial centers have developed modern manufacturing industries, a goal the present government hoped to achieve when it first came to power in 1949.

Because China is a centrally planned socialist state, the planning and construction of cities have been intimately linked with the nation's economic policies and political ideology. Since 1950 changes in emphasis from industrial expansion to agricultural development have brought about a surge and decline pattern in the pace of urban development. In the First Five Year Plan (1953-57), Chinese economic planners concentrated their efforts on industrial development in designated urban centers known as key-point cities. As a result, growth of metropolitan cities was greatly accelerated. From the beginning of the Cultural Revolution in 1966 to the death of Mao Zedong in 1976, political ideology constituted the main driving force in promoting development of small settlements for the purpose of eliminating the differences between city and countryside. This period, therefore, saw very little activity in large cities. Since the introduction of the Four Modernizations in 1978, a new large city bias has emerged.[1] Major industrial projects and capital constructions have been located in metropolitan cities. To avoid excessive growth in large cities, emphasis has been placed on the development of small- and medium-sized cities, including satellite towns within the city regions of large metropolitan centers.

This chapter addresses the issues and problems of urban land use planning in China during the early phase of city building in the 1950s, mainly for three reasons. First, this period is significant in the discussion of city planning in the People's Republic of China (PRC) as socialist principles and concepts in city planning and development were first introduced. Second, within this period both qualitative and quantitative data of cities were relatively more available than those of later years. Third, despite a growing body of literature on urban China published in recent years (see Schenk, 1972; Towers, 1973; Buck, 1975; Pannell, 1977; Ma, 1970; Leung and Ginsburg, 1980; Pannell and Welch, 1980; Ma and Hanten, 1981), there is virtually nothing written that explores the important issue of urban land use planning during the period of rapid urbanization and urban growth in China. This study is intended to rectify the omission. Because of China's long urban history, a brief sketch of land use planning in cities of the Imperial Era and that of pre-1949 contemporary China is also presented in order to place the central theme of the chapter in perspective.

Historical Development of Urban Use Planning in Imperial China

Like other ancient civilizations, China has a long historical record of city building. By the Shang dynasty (c.1500 B.C.), walled settlements had already become part of the agricultural landscape in the western region of the Yellow River Plain and gradually spread toward east and south China. Both archaeological data and ancient Chinese literature have substantiated the long tradition of "planned development" of cities in dynastic China. Almost without exception, the early cities were built according to "plans" and did not grow spontaneously from villages.

One of the unique elements of ancient Chinese city planning was the spatial organization of various specialized quarters within the walled settlements. As early as the Shang dynasty, a rudimentary form of functional differentiation had already emerged. The excavation of Xiaotun, located on the southern bank of Huanghe (the Yellow River), about 3 kilometers to the northwest of Anyang, revealed three functional areas inside the settlement. The first area, which lay to the northeast of the city, consisted of fifteen rectangular houses arranged parallel to each other and built on stamped earth foundations. Immediately to the south was the second area, with 21 large square or rectangular-shaped houses, also built on stamped earth platforms. This group of buildings was arranged in three rows on a north-south axis. The central row consisted of three large houses and five gates. The third area, to the southwest of the excavation site, had seventeen individual stamped earth foundations, arranged according to a preconceived plan. The northeastern part of the city has been assessed to

be the residential area, the area immediately to its south to be the royal temples, and the area to the southwest to be the ceremonial quarter (Chang, 1963,
157). The famous Shang city of Anyang also seemed to have been planned.
One of the excavation sites, about 6.5 hectares in extent, was completely covered with foundations for buildings of considerable size, which suggested the
possible location of the royal palaces. Adjacent to this was a handicraft area,
including various kinds of specialized workshops that belonged to artisans
serving the royal family. At least three separate sections could be differentiated. One of these sections produced bronze articles; ash, crucibles, and broken molds were discovered at the site. A different section specialized in making
stone implements and jade products. Still another section produced bone implements and utensils, such as arrowheads, ladles, and hairpins (Creel, 1958,
68).

The basic components of Shang cities, including the aristocratic and ceremonial structures and the specialized handicraft quarters, persisted through the
entire span of the West Zhou dynasty (1050-770 B.C.). The traditional spatial
pattern of urban functions underwent some important changes after the beginning
of the East Zhou dynasty (770-211B.C.) when iron metallurgy was developed.
Introduction of this new technology, which greatly stimulated commercial activities, further intensified industrial specialization. From the late Chunchiu period new cities were developed over the north China plain. These fortified
strongholds served not only as administrative and religious centers but incorporated within them manufacturing and commercial districts, indicating the growing importance of these economic activities. The inclusion of commercial districts
in cities like Zhengzhou and Houmazhen and the widespread appearance of state
currency and the construction of roads is evident from the archaeological records,
which testify to the increasing importance of commerce in the urban economy
(Chang, 1963, 194).

Some post-1949 archaeological expeditions have shed new light on traditional
Chinese urban planning. Several archaeological sites of cities of the periods of
Chunchiu and Changuo (770-221 B.C.) were excavated during the 1960s, re-
vealing a considerable degree of spatial organization of various functional areas
in ancient Chinese cities. The royal palace, the ceremonial platforms, the commercial areas, the manufacturing section, and the residential areas of the com-
moners occupied specific locations within the cities, as if they were built according
to a city plan. In 1961 the archaeological team of the Hebei Bureau of Culture
excavated Yen Xiadu (the lower capital of the state of Yen), one of the seven
prominent states of Changuo time, located to the southeast of the present county
seat of Yi Xian in Hebei. Detailed investigations carried out on the remains of
the city enclosures, building foundations, tombs, and artifacts revealed that the
layout and functional specialization of the interior city were different from those
in cities of earlier periods. Most of the buildings, as well as the palace, protected
by an additional enclosure, were concentrated in the eastern part of the city.
North of Wuyang Terrace, the foundation for the central structure of the royal

palace, stood three groups of buildings, each centered around a main structure. The residential areas were located in the southeastern part of the city, which were both impressive and well planned. Surrounding the palace precinct once stood various types of handicraft workshops manufacturing iron implements, weapons, coins, pottery, and bone articles. The beds of several old streams and a canal were among some of the important findings of the expedition. The canal was connected with the central Yi River, which was believed to have been used for transporting tax grains to the capital. The geographical location of various functional areas in relation to the streams within the walled area seemed to have been carefully planned. One stream separated the workshops and the palace, providing a means of defense for the latter. Another stream isolated the cemetery from the rest of the city. All workshops were close to the streams, so that water could easily be obtained for manufacturing activities. The streams served other useful purposes: a means of transportation within the city or even a linkage with the areas outside the walls, domestic water supply as well as drainage (Hebei Bureau of Culture, 1965).

Another important early urban site was excavated just before the Cultural Revolution in 1966 by the archaeological team of Shandong. The excavation was undertaken at Linzi, the capital of the state of Qi (770-221 B.C.) during the late Changuo period. A ground plan quite different from that of cities in an earlier period was unveiled at the site. Besides a small enclosure, confirmed to be the seat of the Qi prince and other aristocrats, located at the southeastern corner of the walled city, there is a much larger area that, according to archaeological remains, consisted of discrete functional zones, including the industrial quarters, residential areas, and commercial streets (Guan, 1972).[2] Without doubt, these relatively recent archaeological discoveries have confirmed the early origin of a pragmatic approach to urban planning, though in only rudimentary form, throughout ancient China.

A more elaborate form of zoning approach, combining the principle of axiality of the ideal city, prevailed in later periods. It evolved into the concept of dividing the urban space into uniformly sized and shaped blocks that resembled a chessboard pattern. It was known that in both the dynasties of South Qi (479-501 A.D.) and North Wei (386-532 A.D.), the traditional spatial organization of the interior of Chinese cities remained more or less the same for over four hundred years. The walled area was divided into wards (*xiang*), forming units of functional areas. In Changan, the capital of the Han, there were as many as 160 such wards (Tuan, 1970, 108). This system remained when the city became the capital of Sui (589-618 A.D.) and Tang (618-905 A.D.). In Bianzhou, another Tang city, there were 24 wards, known as *li* or, later, *fang*. The inhabitants of each of the blocks seemed to be engaged in the same business; for example, prostitutes occupied an entire block, and instrument shops were in another block (Kato, 1952, 327). From mid-Tang times on, the ward system gradually became obsolete, but the chessboard street plan is still evident today in many Chinese cities despite some modifications due to subsequent rebuilding of part of the cities in an arbitrary way.

Apart from the ward system, the adoption of land use planning in cities and regulations in the urban development of metropolitan Loyang in the North Wei dynasty was noted by He Bingdi to have existed in literary records. Although the earliest plans and regulations had long been lost, certain restrictive land use clauses still existed in a long memorandum submitted by the grand minister of public works to Cheng, prince of Rencheng, in 517 A.D.. These regulations controlled the encroachment of Buddhist monasteries on the land originally planned for residential development. One of the ordinances stated, ''Within the walled city there shall be designated land only for the Yungning Monastery, that within the suburbs there shall be designated land for only one nunnery, and that the rest shall all be outside of the city and the suburbs.'' In the old capital city of Pingcheng, all residential wards were allowed to be built only to the south of the palace city, forming the most striking feature in the planned layout of the urban settlement. When North Wei moved its capital to Loyang, half of the city was a separate unit of palaces and imperial parks, while in the remainder were located 14 government offices, nine monasteries, and eight recorded wards (Ho, 1966, 78-79). To a remarkable extent these characteristics of planned spatial organization of urban functions have remained in cities of later dynasties. In Hangzhou, the capital of South Song (1127-1278 A.D.), the residential area of the rich was on the hills to the south of the imperial palace. High officials resided on the hills of the Ten Thousand Pines. Merchants who had made their fortune in maritime trade lived on Mount Phoenix, farther to the south, and commercial areas, artisans' workshops, and residential areas of the poorer people crowded in the highly congested northern half of the city (Gernet, 1962, 32-33). The functions of Fengtian (present-day Shenyang) of the Qing dynasty (1662-1911 A.D.) in relation to its internal physical layout were successfully reconstructed in a study using cartographic records and literary evidence as the major source of information (Leeming, 1970). The principal types of land use seem to have been designated within the urban space enclosed by the inner walls and outer walls of the regional capital. Like all other traditional Chinese capital cities, the palace was located in the inner city. The majority of government offices were concentrated near the approaches to the palace. The ammunition works, which adjoined the military hospital, was appropriately sited on the fringe of the northwest part of the outer city where vacant land prevailed. The main business districts were strategically located. They occupied the northern half of the inner city and were centered along the more northerly of the two east-west thoroughfares, in the vicinity of all the gates of the inner city, and on the two major intersections marked, respectively, by the Drum and Bell Towers.

This brief review of land use planning in traditional Chinese cities during the Imperial Era shows two distinct developments. At times land use zoning in cities

followed a rational approach, but there is evidence indicating that it was sometimes governed by the principle of social segregation established by the ruling
elites.

Urban Development in the Republican Era

The Republicans came to power in 1911. During the following 38 years, the
layout and physical characteristics of the traditional Chinese cities did not undergo
any major transformation. The ancient and medieval wall structures, which
defined the geometric morphology of the urban centers, generally remained
intact. The cardinal orientation of the original street patterns was modified in
varying degrees by unplanned reconstruction, however. Within the city walls
many urban structures became dilapidated. Modern urban development was confined to metropolitan Shanghai and other treaty ports where Western-style architecture and city layouts had been introduced by foreign settlers. Modern
concepts and approaches in city planning might have been brought back to China
by returning students who had been sent abroad under the Shimonoseki Indemnity
Agreement to receive foreign education and absorb Western experience during
the late Qing and early Republican periods. Many of them had hoped to adopt
these contemporary ideas to city building by remodeling Chinese traditional cities
and transforming them into bases for economic change.

Due mainly to the failure of the Guomindang to institute industrialization
throughout the nation, both the function and spatial structure of cities remained
unchanged, although there were plans for urban reconstruction and development.
In the late 1920s and early 1930s, literature concerning Western concepts of
urban development, building of garden cities, urban land use zoning, and urban
administration was available. These books provided general and comprehensive
plans for the urban renewal of Zhuangxing (Zhuangjiakou), Amoy, and Pengfou,
reconstruction of Beijing, development of the residential areas in Fengtian (Shenyang), transportation improvement in Hankou, and construction of modern harbor
facilities at Yuepu in the Greater Shanghai Municipality (Wu et al., 1929; Chen,
1933). Actual urban reconstruction work on a limited scale started in the 1920s,
due mainly to the impact of returning students from abroad, who deplored the
insanitary conditions, the narrow and winding streets impassable to modern
means of transportation, and the chaotic land use patterns in Chinese cities. A
movement to modernize the city of Chongqing in Sichuan, an ancient inland
city that became a treaty port in 1891, was launched under local initiative instead
of the effort of the Republican government. Because the city was built on difficult
terrain, the streets were narrow and winding, dark and dirty. Thus the first step
of the urban modernization scheme was to widen the streets for motor traffic,
followed by installation of electric lights, piped water, and an adequate telephone
exchange (Spencer, 1939, 53).

Overall, because of the shortage of public funds for urban reconstruction,
urban development plans in some cities were not implemented or new projects

that were underway were left incomplete. To alleviate the unsanitary living conditions of the urban poor in Shanghai, a local group of businessmen proposed a scheme to construct several "civilian villages" in the city. This plan involved the construction of housing estates near existing industrial areas to resettle the residents of the shack areas at Zhabei, a municipal district to the north of Shanghai. In order to launch such a project, a drive was conducted to solicit private donations to finance the purchase of land and the construction (Wu, 1929, 32). A plan was drawn up to develop an industrial district and a commercial area in Kunming, the provincial capital of Yunnan in southwest China. According to the plan, this large-scale urban project was to be sited in the open space to the south of the existing built-up area. A radial pattern was adopted for the layout of the streets. Unfortunately the feasibility of this plan was limited due to the shortage of capital (Wu, 1929, 10). The ambitious and comprehensive development scheme of Jiangwan to convert the northern suburb of Shanghai into the civic center for the entire metropolis also met the same fate.

These examples demonstrate the lack of progress in city building throughout the Republican period despite Sun Yatsen's great hope to modernize the nation. And during the Sino-Japanese War, which raged for eight years, many cities were heavily damaged. The open conflict between the GMD and the Communists that broke out soon after World War II prevented large-scale reconstruction of these war-torn settlements.

Post-1949 Urban Planning

Although China has a long record of city planning and building, the traditional administrative and commercial centers of the agrarian society were essentially a ritual and symbolic system, physically planned and sited according to ancient ritual laws and tradition of cosmology descended from the dynasties of Shang and Zhou, as well as the prescription of a common belief known as *feng-shui* (geomancy). During the early phase of urban development in the PRC, these religious-geomantic concepts in city design were rejected by urban planners who regarded them as irrelevant and unacceptable in the planning of socialist industrial cities. To Chinese city planners, the land use organization found in many traditional Chinese cities was a system of social segregation. Although modern Western concepts in city planning were utilized in the design of industrial cities in Manchuria by the Japanese and in the construction of foreign concessions in treaty ports by European powers, these models were not accepted because they failed to reflect socialist ideology. One of the most important characteristics of socialist city planning is that the organization of land use is based on the neighborhood concept, which emphasizes integration of functions and independence of interrelated units. Further, this planning concept creates uniformity and class-lessness in the socioeconomic characteristics of the society.

Landownership

Besides the adoption of socialist tenets for designing the spatial structure of cities, another important step was taken by the new political order to make land readily available for long-term urban land use planning. Two important land laws were enacted in 1950; the Urban Land Law placed all land within city limits under state ownership and administration, and the Suburban Agrarian Reform Law (Fung, 1979, 75-112) was promulgated to transform the pre-1949 socioeconomic patterns in suburban China and to utilize land resources in the vicinity of large urban centers for construction purposes and for developing agriculture to serve the needs of urban residents. Although the Suburban Agrarian Reform Law also dealt with redistribution of agricultural land, it was essentially a land acquisition policy. It provided municipal authorities with the power to nationalize land within delimited suburban areas, either by confiscating farmland previously owned by landlords (except experimental agricultural grounds, vegetable gardens, orchards, and farmland using machinery or other modern equipment for cultivation) or by expropriating other privately owned land. Thus, through implementation of the land laws, the government was able to assemble expeditiously large amounts of land within urban areas and delimited suburban districts, without siphoning off part of the scarce capital needed for industrialization and thinning out the limited administrative personnel to carry out its programs of city transformation and construction. Furthermore, state ownership of urban land eliminated conflicts in public and private development rights in cities.

MAJOR CHALLENGES

Planned development of cities requires not merely an adequate supply of land but also adequate manpower, sound urban plans and land use zoning control. In China, although land has been made available for municipal and industrial developments since 1950, there were no blueprints, zoning regulations, or building codes. As a result, the early 1950s witnessed a period of chaos in urban development in the PRC. Individual construction units of government departments, municipalities, and state enterprises freely built on whatever site they desired. Department stores, movie theaters, municipal offices, and other public buildings were erected at sites where there was very little or no residential housing because those areas had been designated for future municipal development (*Chengshi Jianshe*, 1957a). Also, because no comprehensive urban plans were available for building key-point industrial cities, there was no coordination between long-term planning of industrial construction and that of the development of various urban infrastructures, as exemplified by Anshan, a steel manufacturing center in northeast China. The Anshan experience was publicized to provide a lesson for planning personnel in other industrial cities:

Under the assistance of Soviet experts the long term plan for expansion of the Anshan Steel Complex was drawn up, but there was no plan for the city. Therefore when the Anshan Steel Plant built several hundred thousand square meters of workers' housing, the city had to use the "Capital Construction Plan" previously prepared by the Japanese during their occupation of the city in the "Manzhouguo Era." That urban plan was obviously unsuitable for our construction need: it divided the city into the Japanese residential district to the east of the railway, and the Chinese residential district to the west side of the track, while the commercial district was designed according to capitalistic planning methods. . . . Because there was no comprehensive urban plan, work on constructing sewerage and roads, and installing electric lights and gas lines could not be coordinated simultaneously with the construction work on residential housing . . . and large sums of money were wasted on installing a temporary supply of electricity and water and in building of temporary roads. (Ku, 1952)

The inability to draft plans for urban development was attributable to two reasons. First, at the beginning of the First Plan period, none of the cities in China possessed the physical, social, economic, and demographic data essential for the preparation of urban plans. Paradoxically, Shanghai, a city not initially designated for intensive industrial development, was the only urban center that initiated the collection of urban data by the end of 1951, and the preliminary plan for the city was not completed until September 1953 (Hsu, 1957). It was not until early 1954 that several cities in the Central South District, including Wuhan, Huangshi, Zhengzhou, Xinxiang, Zhuzhou, Guangzhou, and Zhanjiang, which had been designated important centers for industrial construction and the focus of urban expansion, announced the establishment of urban construction committees. The initial task of these organizations was to collect and analyze meteorologic, hydrologic, geologic, topographic, economic, and demographic data to provide the necessary basis for drafting comprehensive urban plans (*Wenhui Bao*, 1954). Second, China faced another severe handicap at the time when the program for urban reconstruction and industrialization was first introduced— an acute shortage of trained technical and engineering personnel in various specialized fields, including urban planning. The acute shortage of city planners was particularly serious regarding implementing the program of urban construction at key-point industrial cities, which had been assigned first priority for large-scale development. There were very few urban planners in the country at the time of liberation and even for several years after:

Five years ago, city planning in China was comparable to a blank piece of paper. The graduates in city planning today were illiterates. Nobody even knew what socialist urban planning was. Since the beginning of planning of the eight large key-point cities designated for industrial development such as Xian and Baotou, with the assistance of Soviet experts, [we] learned [about] urban planning while [we] worked. From "have not" to "have", from "point" to "area", and from "do not know" to "know," [we] established step by step this special field of science. Urban planning departments have been set up in some provinces and cities, and faculty of urban planning introduced in four universities.(Wang, 1958)

Although the number of town planners had risen to over 1,600 by 1958 (Qing, 1959), this number was still far from adequate for the urgent nationwide tasks of constructing large numbers of new industrial cities and reconstructing existing manufacturing centers during the First Five Year Plan period. Because of the general shortage of city planners during the First Plan period, when active urban development was taking place, plans of large Soviet cities such as Moscow, Leningrad, and Kiev were universally adopted for use in designing Chinese cities, despite wide variations between Russian and Chinese urban centers with regard to size, type, geographical location, and terrain characteristics. Consequently cities in China were not designed according to the conditions in the country or the geographical diversities of individual cities: "Regardless of large cities or small cities, northern cities or southern cities, old cities or new cities, the formulating method and contents of the urban plans were all exactly the same" (Wang, 1958, 3).

The plan for even a small workers' town of fewer than 20,000 inhabitants would include all the urban features and amenities of a large city: large municipal public squares with wide central boulevards and central axis road, emulating Tiananmen Square in the national capital, civic centers for municipal government buildings, district parks, three sports stadiums, cultural palaces, and a movie theatre (Wang, 1958). In another example, an extensive green area was unnecessarily included in the urban plan of Beidaihe, a seaside resort located in an already well-wooded environment and with very low population density (Wang, 1958, 4). Furthermore, public squares, typical features of Soviet cities, have become basic land use components in many plans for Chinese cities. These have included municipal central squares, district central squares, traffic squares, and other squares of special types.

Emulation of the Soviet Model

Under the Mutual Aid and Friendship Alliance Treaty of 1951, the Soviet Union agreed to provide China with over 825 large industrial projects to be installed and constructed during the First Five Year Plan period (Yang, 1957). Under the same agreement Soviet advisers provided direction on the selection of key-point cities where new industrial plants were to be located and assisted in selecting factory sites in cities of the northwest, central-south, and Inner Mongolian Autonomous Region. In addition, the Soviet experts participated in the general urban planning of the eight large key-point cities of Xian, Lanzhou, Baotou, Wuhan, Loyang, Taiyuan, Dadong, and Chengdu, as well as contributing ideas and suggestions to the planning and construction work of Beijing, Shanghai, Tianjin, Shenyang, Harbin, Anshan, Zhengzhou, and Shijiazhuang (*Chengshi Jianshe*, 1957b). Soviet aid played a vital role in China's initial industrial development effort, providing technical assistance, industrial equipment, and materials that China could not have obtained elsewhere at that time, although in the field of urban and suburban planning, the Russians themselves were plagued by difficulties in the 1950s.

During the 1950s, the Soviet Union was considerably behind many nonsocialist European countries, including the United Kingdom, France, Germany, the Netherlands, and Sweden, in urban planning and development. There is ample evidence indicating chaotic development in Soviet cities (Baranov, 1961; Kucherenko, 1959) and their suburban areas, as well as there being an acute shortage of urban planners. I. Nikolayev, a member of the U.S.S.R. Academy of Construction and Architecture, disclosed some grave problems in Soviet city planning. In 1958 several sputnik settlements, including Elektrostal, Khimki, Krasnogorsk, and Kryukovo, were built outside Moscow's city limits, based on a concept not dissimilar to that of Britain's new towns to channel industrial growth and population pressure from metropolitan cities. An unusual problem emerged in Kryukovo, Moscow's first satellite town located 29 kilometers northwest of the capital on the main railway line to Leningrad. There was no definite idea as to what new industrial enterprises should be built and where in the new town, even in its second year of construction (Nikolayev, 1960). This appears to be truly a case of putting the cart before the horse, a practice that seems to have been typical of Soviet city planning during the 1950s.

In examining the issues and problems relating to China's urban planning, it is relevant to discuss the indiscriminate acceptance of the Soviet standard of residential space utilization and its impact on urban land supply, an issue that invariably affects the long-term physical planning of cities. According to the Soviet system, residential land in urban areas was divided into two major categories: dwelling space, the area available within dwelling units, and living space, land for communal uses, public buildings, open space or parks, and roads or squares. In quantitative terms, the norms used by Soviet planners in the 1950s for dwelling space were 9 square meters per person and that for living space 76 square meters per person (*Chengshi Jianshe*, 1957c). It is true that the residential space utilization standard employed by Shanghai's urban planners was quite modest when compared to the Soviet standards. One of the housing projects, Zaoyang Xincun (Zaoyang New Village), which was built at the outskirts of Shanghai, provided an average dwelling space of 4 square meters per person.[3] It was not only higher than the national average of slightly less than 3 square meters per person and well above the average dwelling space standard of many large cities in 1956-57, including Shanghai itself (see Table 2.1). It is worth noting that the standard for dwelling space used for designing new dwellings in the key-point industrial centers of China surpassed, by a considerable amount, the 4.7 square meters per person the Soviets were able to reach in 1932 (Pan, 1957). More than two decades later, in 1955, the actual dwelling space per person in the Soviet Union was only 7.4 square meters (Pan, 1957). This implies that the urban planners in China's new industrial cities strived to achieve within the First Five Year Plan period what the Soviets had failed to attain within a period of over half a century since the Bolshevik revolution. By way of comparison, the dwelling space per capita in China's key-point industrial cities was higher than that of urban Japan's 7.5 square meters (Keizai, 1972, 72) and that of public housing in Singapore's new towns where the average was 6.2 square meters in the 1960s (Stephen, Yeh, and Lee, 1968).

In some cases the space utilization standard used by the Chinese exceeded that of the Soviets. An investigation disclosed that the state-owned Zhengzhou textile machinery factory employed 3,955 workers. Since its establishment, 50,659 square meters of workers' housing had been constructed, of which 39,361 square meters was for married workers and 11,298 square meters for single workers. If these dwellings were to house all the workers in the factory, each would have had to have 12.8 square meters of dwelling space (*Renmin Ribao*, 1957a). In Chongqing the norm for dwelling space per person exceeded 10 square meters, and that adopted for long-term residential development reached 12.6 square meters (Kung, 1958). Under such circumstances if the Chinese had been able to build high-rise structures, the pressure on China's scarce land resources would have been less intense. However, because of technical constraints and the shortage of reinforced building materials, most of the residential housing built during the First Five Year Plan period was either of one or two stories. The adoption of a generous dwelling space standard inevitably accelerated the horizontal spread of the built-up areas of cities into the surrounding countryside. In January 1957 the head of the Architectural Planning Bureau discussed the serious problem of land shortage and announced that in order to achieve more rational use of land, the construction of single-storied dwellings would be limited and multi-storied buildings encouraged (*Wenhui Bao*, 1957).

Another category of land use in Chinese cities that formed an important component of the urban plan was green space, which generally occupied at least 25 to 30 percent of the total urban living space (Cheng, 1957). In the process of city building, the new government placed great emphasis on improving the living environment of urban areas. In the early 1950s a nationwide program of afforestation was implemented in cities as well as in the countryside. Since 1949, public parks, outdoor recreation space, and other recreational facilities in urban areas have been expanded considerably. In Shanghai, for example, public parks underwent very rapid increase in both area and number within the seven years after liberation. In 1949 the city had fourteen parks occupying a total area of 988.2 *mou* (65.9 hectares). From 1868, when the first park was established, to 1949, the annual increase of park area was only 11.8 *mou* (0.8 hectares), whereas between 1949 and 1957, park space increased to 2,993.5 *mou* (119.7 hectares), representing an average annual increase of 374.2 *mou* (14.9 hectares). On a per capita basis the area of public parks increased from 0.12 square meter to nearly 0.33 square meter during the period (*Jiefang Ribao*, 1956). Most of these parks were developed on the urban fringe and in workers' housing estates outside the built-up areas.

The amount of open space allocated to each inhabitant in new industrial cities, and also to workers living in housing estates within existing urban centers, generally ranged from 10 to 12 square meters. It was a standard used by Soviet planners for cities located in regions of mixed forests, broadleaf-deciduous forests and treed steppes in the central Soviet Union, and with a population ranging from 50,000 to 500,000 (see Table 2.2). For China such a standard for open space in cities is unrealistic.[4] It compares more favorably with the island state of Singapore, which recorded in 1967 only 0.2 hectare per thousand population (2 square meters per person) for the island as a whole and 0.12 hectare per thousand population (1.2 square meters per person) for the Singapore city area. The goal of Singapore's planners was to achieve a long-term standard of 0.6 hectare per thousand population (6 square meters per person) (Chua, 1973, 71-73). The adoption of a standard of 10 square meters or more per person for open space by Chinese planners no doubt would exert a large impact on land consumption. In a city with 1 million people, for example, over 10.4 square kilometers of land must be set aside for this type of land use. Often because of a scarcity of land for large parks within the built-up areas of cities, it became a general practice to convert large amounts of suburban agricultural land to recreational purposes. Also, the total area of planned open space in cities was based on the projected population, which was generally overestimated by urban planners.[5]

Other Urban Planning Problems

The central government instructed municipal authorities of cities where urban construction was to take place to make necessary provisions for both short- and long-term urban development, with specific reference to spatial expansion:[6]

Urban construction is a matter of long term planning, and the scope of possible urban development must be examined in the light of the nation's plan for industrial development. . . . A unified plan must be formulated in order to fulfill current requirements while, simultaneously, to assure future needs. . . . Appropriate amount of land should be set aside to meet development needs in the distant future. (*Renmin Ribao*, 1954)

Soon after the decree came into effect, municipal government acquired and reserved vast suburban territories for future development, since land expropriation for such a purpose had already been endorsed by the state. Available evidence indicated that the amount of land acquired by cities for long-term use exceeded that actually needed. The municipal officials of Baoding, a city with a built-up area of nearly 12 square kilometers, expropriated and retained such a large amount of land that the city would never need it. According to the preliminary city plan, the built-up area would expand toward Diexi (literally meaning "west of the railway"; the present city was located to the east of the Beijing-Hankou Railway in Hebei province). The total area of the *Jihuachu* (planned district) occupied almost 14 square kilometers. The area reserved for the synthetic fiber factory, the textile factory, and the thermal power plant was only about 2 square kilometers. Even if the battery factory, machinery factory, and others to

Table 2.1

Average Dwelling Space per Person in Selected Large Cities, 1956–1957

Region No.		City Population ('000s)		
		5	5-20	20-50
II	Coniferous forests of European Russia and coastal areas of the Baltic Sea. Mixed forests and broadleaf-deciduous forests of the Amur River region and coastal areas of Eastern Siberia.	6	8	10
III	Mixed forests, broadleaf-deciduous forests and treed steppes of Central Russia	8	10	12
IV	Steppes	10	12	15

Sources: a. *Xinhuo Banyuekan* (*New China Semimonthly*) 1957, 24:63.
  b. Pan, Zeyun 1958. On the Schedule of Urban Construction and Prescribed Standard of Dwelling Space for our Nation, *Chengshi Jianshe* (*Urban Construction*) 8:22.
  c. *Ibid.*, 25.
  d. *Renmin Ribao* (*People's Daily*) 6 January 1957.
  e. Editorial: 1957. Learn the Ability to build Cities through Diligence and Frugality upon the Foundation of Seriously Undertaking Rectification. *Chengshi Jianshe* (*Urban Construction*) 7:2.
  f. *Changchun Ribao* (*Changchun Daily*), 30 December 1956.
  g. Sun, Guang 1956. The Pressing Need to Control Urban Population Growth. *Renmin Ribao* (*People's Daily*, 27 November 1957.
  h. Editorial: 1956. Lower the (Space Utilization) Standard for Buildings. *Jianzhu Ziebao* (*Journal of Architecture*), 8:13.

Table 2.2

Soviet Standard for Public Green Area (Number of Square Meters per Person)

Shanghai	2.97[a]	Luda	3.18[d]
Guangzhou	2.80[b]	Tianjin	2.50[e]
Taiyuen	1.90[b]	Changchun	3.40[f]
Beijing	4.20[c]	Wuhan	3.06[g]
Nanjing	3.20[c]	Nat'l Avg.	3.00[h]

Note: In permafrost area and forested permafrost area (Region I) desert and semi-desert (Region No. V) and in mountainous areas (including Caucasus and coastal area of southern Armenia) allocation of green area will be determined by local conditions, including climate, topography and irrigation practice.

Sources: Jian, Xifu 1957. On the Three Problems of the Green Area System, *Xinhua Banyuekan* (*New China Semimonthly*). Quoted Second Section of Second Chapter "Problems on Determining (Size of) Green Area in Cities," in: *Green Areas in Soviet Cities*, 1954, p. 22.

be constructed in future were to be located within the planned district, the total amount of land required would be only about 3 square kilometers, an equivalent of less than 20 percent of the land designated for long-term use. In other words, over 80 percent, or nearly 11 square kilometers, of the expropriated land would have to be filled by nonindustrial developments such as provincial and municipal offices and schools, which was impossible (Zhou, 1958). At the same time, public buildings and factories and even housing estates were being built sporadically over areas specified for long-term development use. Such chaotic and dispersed patterns of development emerged in the suburban areas of many cities in the interior. Xian was a case in point. The majority of factories in this new industrial city were scattered outside the existing built-up areas because the building sites for these factories had been randomly selected within the territory to be used for long-term development. The textile city of Xian was located on the bank of Chenhe, about 8 kilometers from the city, with over 20 large state enterprises scattered over the northern and the western suburban areas. As a result, new construction was dispersed in all directions within a radius ranging from 20 to 30 kilometers from the city (Cheng, 1957, 75). The newly constructed industrial districts of Xigu and Andingbao were located over 20 kilometers from the city center of Lanzhou and the industrial enterprises of Baotou and Taiyuan also over 10 kilometers from the urban area (Yun, 1957). These were not self-contained settlements like satellite industrial communities that possessed at least the basic amenities.

These sprawling urban developments had not been confined to key-point cities. They were also rife in the urban fringe areas of cities not specified for active industrial growth at the beginning of the First Five Year Plan period. A Polish delegation of architects and urban planners noted such phenomena while touring China, at all the six cities visited—including Beijing, Fushun, Anshan, Hangzhou, Suzhou, and Nanjing. The problem was particularly serious in the city of Nanjing. With the exception of the suburban areas to the south, where the terrain conditions were unfavorable for urban use, new construction was scattered throughout the northern, eastern, and western suburbs, although there was still ample empty space within the urban limits that could have been used for construction (*Jianzhu Xiebao*, 1956). These descriptions of and comments on sprawling cities were widely publicized in the official media, reflecting the persistence and seriousness of the problem that had already emerged soon after nationwide urban reconstruction began. The roots of the problems of excessive land expropriation by city authorities, absence of effective land use control measures, and the attitude of municipal officials and planning personnel were disclosed in an official publication:

In order that cities use land rationally, municipal construction departments should formulate regulations on the use of urban land, and exercise necessary control [over the use of land]. It was particularly important that the construction units must set out from reality, and the amount of land [required by] the enterprises in accordance with the need of the construction projects rationally calculated. *[We must] prevent dispersionism and departmentalism that have led to neglect of the entirety of city building.* [We must] oppose acquiring land excessively, expropriating land at one's will and proceeding with construction without official permission. (Shih, 1958)

APPROACHES

As the First Plan period came to an end, the central administration fully appreciated the weaknesses in the sector of urban planning and development. It also realized the serious impact of urban sprawl on suburban agricultural land resources. To rectify the grave situation, several measures were instituted as early as 1957.

Following the directive issued at a meeting of the Central Committee of the CCP held on 27 April, a rectification campaign (*Zhengfeng yundong*) was launched officially on 1 May.[7] The primary objective of this nationwide movement was to eradicate the bureaucratism, departmentalism, and dispersionism that prevailed among personnel engaged in urban planning and municipal construction work (*Renmin Ribao*, 1957b). At the end of May 1957, the National Planning Work Conference was held in Beijing, convened by the State Construction Commission, the State Planning Commission, and the State Economic Commission. The nine hundred delegates participating in this important meeting included all the renowned architects, senior administrative cadres from various branches of the Department of Economic Construction of the central administration, and the heads and chief engineers of more than one hundred planning and design institutes in China. The main theme of the nine-day conference centered on reviewing the problems of land use and errors committed in urban planning and construction work during the past five years and to devise means to avoid repeating similar mistakes in the Second Five Year Plan period, which was about to begin (*Renmin Ribao, 1957c*). In June 1957 the *People's Daily* published an editorial, "Urban Construction Work Must Conform to the Principle of Frugality," which severely attacked the attitude and thinking of urban planners who designed and built cities without taking into consideration the "real conditions" of the country:

In the past some comrades engaged in city planning work seldom reckoned with the current economic level and other existing conditions in the country. . . . Our nation is populous and economically backward. . . . Because of the large population and the scarcity of land, a lower standard for dwelling space and living space should be adopted, and land should be used economically . . . but in urban construction work some comrades blindly sought grandiosity and modernity, leading to unnecessary waste [of land and capital]. . . . Some other comrades placed too much emphasis on development for the future. Contemplating to build, once and for all, ideal large socialist cities by the end of the decade [the urban planners] unduly pursued "grand scale" and "high standard." Undoubtedly, in urban planning and construction, appropriate consideration should be given to future development of cities, but it is more important to set out in accordance with reality, and to carry out planning and construction work to suit present conditions.

The State Construction Commission and the State Urban Construction Department on 31 January 1958 jointly prescribed a set of urban space utilization standards for urban planning activities in the Second Plan period. The standard for living space per capita in cities was drastically reduced from 76 square meters to 18 to 28 square meters. For dwelling space, the standard was reduced to less than 4 square meters per person. For the first time, specifications were provided for the percentage of the total area residential areas in cities were to take up.

The proportions of one-, two-, three-, and four-storied dwellings were to range about 50 percent, over 35 percent, over 30 percent, and over 25 percent, respectively.[8] Not surprisingly, even the standards to be adopted for long-term (10 to 15 years) urban planning were well below those used in key-point cities during the First Five Year Plan period. For dwelling space each urban resident was to be allocated less than 5 square meters and for living space less than 35 square meters.[9]

Apart from substantially reducing the amount of dwelling and living space to be allocated to each city inhabitant, other means of augmenting the intensity of use of land were also adopted for both the built-up areas of cities and the agricultural hinterland of municipalities. In many large urban centers, additional structures (usually one or two stories) were added to existing buildings.

Post-1960 Urban Developments

Urban developments in China were seriously affected by the withdrawal of Soviet advisers in mid-1960. The construction of many urban projects was curtailed, and activities in urban planning were drastically reduced. For several years city planners became preoccupied with reviewing theories and techniques of city design and construction. The main objective of this effort was to develop China's own planning resources so as to be independent of foreign assistance in city building.

A shift in urban policies occurred during the Cultural Revolution (1966-76), influenced by the Marxist ideology of eliminating the differences between city and countryside. The central government de-emphasized development of heavy industry and building of large metropolitan cities, and it assigned top priority to the building of small settlements that integrated spatially residence, industry, and agriculture. As a result, urban planning in China took a new direction. The principle and practice of city planning based on functional zoning and concentration on heavy industries in nodal cities was abandoned. A new type of city, spatially planned according to socialist ideals, emerged. The best-known example was Daqing, located at China's largest oil field in the province of Heilongjiang, northeast China. The city was made up of a constellation of settlements arranged hierarchically. There were about thirty small oil refining towns, known as "living bases." Each of these settlements offered retail services, as well as health and educational facilities, for a population of about 5,000. Within a radius of between 1 and 2 kilometers from each living base were three to five habitation points with a population of about 1,200 each. The residents of these satellite communities were oil well workers and their families. Adjacent to the residential areas were large tracts of agricultural land where some members of the oil workers' families engaged in crop production, horticulture, and animal raising. These settlements at the lower end of the hierarchy also had education facilities, health services, and shops (Foreign Language Press, 1972). Such settlement design was emulated by other oil field cities such as Shengli and Dagang.[10]

The influence of political ideology on urban planning seemed to have lessened since the death of Mao late in 1976. From the beginning of the Modernization Era in 1978, urban planners have reintroduced functional zoning, which seeks to classify and develop various types of land use in cities, including residential, industrial, open space for recreation, and transportation. The location of these land use types is determined mainly by compatibility and environmental considerations. As China's new economic policies have strongly emphasized efficiency and profit of the industrial sector, cities once more are regarded as centers of active industrial development that play an important role in the process of national modernization. More large, modern factories have been built in cities at the upper levels of the hierarchy in order to take advantage of economy of scale. To avoid excessive spatial growth of central cities and to implement the functional zoning concept, all large industrial plants that are potential sources of pollutants have been built in satellite towns. For example, Shanghai recently built a huge, modern petrochemical plant at Jinshan and China's largest integrated steel mill at Baoshan. Both are satellite towns located about 70 kilometers from the central city. In 1982 several large synthetic textile mills were built in a satellite community south of Beijing.[11] As a general rule, residential neighborhoods are built within 1 to 2 kilometers from factories in order to keep commuting distance for workers as short as possible. These large housing estates are self-contained urban communities, generally including neighborhood-level administrative offices, health clinics, schools, cultural and recreational facilities, and general stores that serve the basic needs of the residents. To minimize the effects of industrial pollution, factories are often sited on the downwind side of residential areas. Tree belts are planted to serve as a buffer between industrial districts and residential areas.

Institutional Framework

In China the three special municipalities of Beijing, Shanghai, and Tianjin are under the direct jurisdiction of the central government. All other urban places are administered by a hierarchy of local governments. The central authorities formulate national urban planning policies to be carried out by an intricate network of urban administrations. Based on ideological principles, these policies outline the main objectives in urban land use planning within the socialist system. The state government also sets technical guidelines and regulations that municipal planning authorities must conform to. These regulations constitute the legal basis for land use planning in cities. There is no evidence that the central government participates in the decisionmaking process in designing land use zones in cities. The Bureau of Urban Construction and Management (*Chengshi guihua guanliju*), one of several major departments in city administration, is responsible for the physical planning of the city. The planners prepare three sets of plans: a long-term plan that serves to guide the general direction of growth of the city within a period of ten to fifteen years; a development plan for a five- to ten-year period; and detailed plans that are based on the development plan. Local residents do not participate in the planning process.[12]

Approaches to Land, Density, and Pollution Problems

The problem of land shortage for development in central cities has emerged. Two major factors contribute to this problem. First, in order to ensure that urban residents can grow their own vegetables, stringent regulations have been laid down by the state government to prevent encroachment on urban fringe horticultural land by urban development. Even if, under exceptional circumstances, acquisition of land within the market garden zone is approved by the municipal government, the Bureau of City Planning and Management has to pay a large sum of money to the suburban commune for the land.[13] Second, Chinese city planners have not altered the older core of cities (Pannell and Ma, 1983, 243), which otherwise would have provided additional land for redevelopment. Within these areas housing is overcrowded and often substandard, and the narrow, winding lanes are passable only by bicycles and pedestrian traffic. Because of the high cost of redevelopment, large-scale renewal of older areas is often not given a high priority. In order to cope with the land shortage problem, building of high-rise apartments of fifteen stories has been common in modern cities such as Beijing and Shanghai. Another significant consequence of the urban land shortage is the elimination of the much-needed green space in residential neighborhoods. Chinese cities are generally short of public parks and green space. Even in Beijing, the national capital, the amount of green space per capita is only 10 square meters. This compares quite unfavorably with London and Paris, where each urban resident has 22.8 square meters and 24.7 square meters, respectively (Zhao, 1982). Municipal planning authorities have made serious efforts to enhance the amenity of new housing estates, designating about 3 to 4 percent within the proposed site for green open space use. Often, however, the land originally planned for such a purpose is eventually used for dwelling construction (Wei, 1982). It is quite likely that the policy of providing more urban housing at the expense of environmental improvement will continue. This would ensure urban dwellers better housing and at the same time reduce the need for converting valuable urban fringe farmland for urban use.

Another serious problem that hinders planned urban development is the overcrowded condition of large urban centers and the slow growth of population in satellite communities. The population density of central Shanghai is 41,000 persons per square kilometer, and that of the western part of Huangpu District is as high as 100,000 per square kilometer (Li et al, 1983, 12-13). In Beijing, the most densely populated area, the Qianmen district in the central city, the density is 50,000 persons per square kilometer (Wu, 1983). Despite continuous efforts by municipal governments to disperse population to satellite towns in the urban region, population in these small communities has not grown as fast as planned. At the initial phase of development of the satellite towns in the city region of Shanghai in the late 1950s, it was planned that the population in each of the settlements would grow to 200,000 within two decades. The increase in satellite town population has been far short of the original target. For example, in Minhang, one of the best-known satellite towns, the population increased to only about 50,000 from 30,000 in a period of about twenty-five years. The inadequacy of cultural, educational, social, and recreational facilities, as well as services, in the satellite settlement has made it far less attractive than the central city to most Shanghai workers and their families.

Despite special emphasis in functional zoning, industrial location planning, and environmental control in cities, air pollution in some large urban areas has still remained a major problem. The main source of pollutants comes from the combustion of coal for industrial purposes and for domestic cooking and heating. In Beijing the consumption of 15.8 million tons of coal caused the emission of 268,00 tons of sulphur dioxide and nearly 400,000 tons of solid particles in 1980. Smog has become common in the national capital (Wu, 1983, 7). Solving the problem of industrial pollution poses a serious challenge to the city planners in Beijing.

FUTURE THRUSTS

The future trend in China's city planning will be a continuation of favoring development of small- and medium-sized central places and restraining the growth of large metropolises. In order to reduce congestion in Shanghai, Beijing, and Tianjin, continuous efforts will be made by the municipal governments and the Bureau of Urban Construction and Management of these cities to disperse population to satellite settlements. Instead of adopting the *Xiafang* method, which was used during the Mao era, particularly during the Cultural Revolution, to send large numbers of urban youths to the countryside, it is quite likely that the municipal authorities will provide workers and their families resettling in satellite towns with material incentives, such as higher wages and larger food rations. More capital investment for urban construction will be diverted to upgrade services, education facilities, and public amenities in suburban industrial satellites and to improve transport linkages between central cities and their satellite communities.

Within urban areas, more emphasis will be placed on developing functional areas to ensure compatibility of land use types. In particular, when locating obnoxious industries, urban planners will work closely with the Department of

Public Health and the Department of Environmental Protection so as to minimize the harmful effect of industrial pollution, which has been threatening public health in large urban centers. In addition, more small green spaces will be developed and more trees planted along roadsides to ameliorate the visually drab urban environment.

The development of multinodal and self-contained functional units will be continued in cities. These neighborhoods provide dwellings, places of employment, educational, cultural, and recreational facilities, and retail outlets and services. Such urban land use design will alleviate the problem of traffic congestion in the central city. Besides, development of such neighborhoods is in conformance with the socialist principles of city planning.

Few other developing countries in the world have accomplished as much as China in the field of urban planning and development within the relatively short time of three decades. Under difficult conditions, the planners have managed to clear the worst city slums, reorganized the intermixed and incompatible land uses that existed in old treaty ports and major urban centers, and greatly alleviated the problem of urban housing, despite the rapid rise in demand.

The Four Modernizations Program introduced in 1978 will certainly have some impact on the urban planning field. The major goal of this program of national development is to transform China into a modern and powerful socialist state by the end of the twentieth century. Quite contrary to the Mao era, the new pragmatic leadership under Deng Xiaoping has implemented an open door policy to encourage the inflow of foreign ideas, equipment, and capital (mainly from industrially advanced nations) for upgrading China's industry, agriculture, science and technology, and national defense capability. As a result, there has been a significant increase in the number of academic and professional exchange activities between Chinese experts and their foreign counterparts in various scientific and technological fields, including urban planning and development. Such contacts and exchanges will accelerate the absorption, assimilation, and adoption of foreign concepts and principles in urban land use planning. Thus, in the near future, although Chinese planners will continue to design cities according to socialist principles, it is quite probable that the existing austere urban landscape will be modified.

NOTES

1. The national drive for the Four Modernizations was proposed by Mao Zedong in 1973. The program aimed at achieving modernization of China's industry, agriculture, science and technology, and national defense by the year 2000. The theme was reiterated by Hua Guofeng, Mao's hand-picked successor and former chairman of the Chinese Communist party, at the First Congress on Industry Learning from Daqing, held in May 1977. The ambitious technological revolution eventually was launched in 1978 by Deng Xiaoping, the vice-premier.

The Four Modernizations Program originally included construction of 120 large-scale capital projects: 10 major iron and steel integrated plants, nine nonferrous metals manufacturing complexes, eight large coal mines, 10 major oil and gas fields, 30 hydropower stations, six trunk railways, five large deep-water harbor facilities, and others. The primary goal of the plan was to transform China into a major worldwide economic and military power by the end of the century.

2. This concept of a separate palace unit was widely adopted by many later dynasties; for example, the palace complexes of Changan and Loyang, the capitals of the Tang Dynasty, were well integrated and completed isolated from the rest of the city, as was the palace unit in Beijing, capital of the Yuan, Ming, and Qing dynasties.

3. The state's prescribed standard for dwelling space during the plan period was 4 square meters per person. See *Chengshe Jianshe (Urban Construction)*, 1957c.

4. In China open space in urban areas includes cultural-recreational parks, district parks, small district gardens, boulevard gardens, tree-lined roads, suburban green areas, special-purpose green areas, street green areas, neighborhood green areas, sports stadiums, and green open spaces.

5. In 1955 the director of the Bureau of Urban Construction criticized the overestimation of population in cities. See: Sun, Jingwen, 1955, Strengthen the Work of Urban Construction to Meet the Need of Industrial Construction, *Renmin Shouce (People's Handbook)*, 247.

6. This was probably an emulation of the Soviet city planning model. The long-term plans included municipal projects to be constructed within the next 10 to 15 years; short-term plans included developments to be completed within the next five years.

7. This was the fourth rectification campaign launched since the founding of the Chinese Communist party, reflecting the seriousness of the problem of urban sprawl the central government had to deal with near the end of the First Five Year Plan period.

8. "Notification Concerning Several Controlling Guidelines for Urban Planning," *Zhonghua Renmin Gongheguo Fakui Huipian (Compendium of Laws and Ordinances of the People's Republic of China*, Jan.-June, 1958), Beijing: Falu Chubanshe, 1958: 181-182.

9. Ibid., 182.

10. The author visited Shengli oilfield in July 1977.

11. Conversation with urban geographers at Beijing University, 11 August 1982.

12. Interview with Ke-ming Lin, city planner, Bureau of Urban Construction and Management, Guangzhou (Canton), 27 August 1982.

13. Meeting with production brigade leader of Evergreen Suburban Commune, Beijing, 12 August 1982.

BIBLIOGRAPHY

Baranov, N. 1961. The City of the Future Is Built Today. *Izvestia* 13, 20:15.
Buck, D. 1975. Directions in Chinese Urban Planning. *Urbanism Past and Present* 1: 24-35.
Chang, Kwang-chih. 1963. *The Archaeology of Ancient China*. New Haven: Yale University Press.
Chen, Yenlin. 1933. *Shanghai Dichan Dachuan (Comprehensive Account of Real Estate and Property in Shanghai Including the Concessions)*. Shanghai: Shanghai Dichan Yenjiuzu.
Cheng, Xifu. 1957. On the Three Problems of the Green Area System. *Xinhua Banyuekan (New China Semi-monthly)* 7:13.

Chengshi Jianshe (Urban Construction). 1957a. Editorial: Learning the Ability to Build Cities through Diligence and Frugality on the Foundation of Seriously Undertaking Rectification. 7:2.

Chengshi Jianshe (Urban Construction). 1957b. 10:11.

Chengshi Jianshe (Urban Construction). 1957c. 7:2.

Chengshi Jianshe (Urban Construction). 1957d. 16:12.

Chua, P. C. 1973. *Planning in Singapore: Selected Aspects and Issues*. Singapore: Chopmen Enterprises.

Creel, H. G. 1958. *The Birth of China*. London: Peter Owen.

Foreign Language Press. 1972. *Daqing, Red Banner on China's Industrial Front*. Beijing.

Fung, K. I. 1979. *City Regions of the People's Republic of China*. Ph.D. dissertation, University of London.

Gernet, J. 1962. *Daily Life in China on the Eve of the Mongol Invasion, 1250-1276* A.D.London: George Allen and Unwin.

Guan, Li. 1972. Essence of the Investigation of Lin Zi—Capital of Qi. *Wenwu (Cultural Relics)*, 45-54.

Hebei Bureau of Culture. Archaeological Team. 1965. Reconnaissance and Trial Excavations on the Site of Yen Xia Du (Lower Capital of the State of Yen) at Yixian, Hebei. *Kaogu Xuebao (Journal of Archaeology)*, 83-106.

Ho, P. T. 1966. Loyang, A.D. 495-534: A Study of Physical and Socio-economic Planning of a Metropolitan Area. *Harvard Journal of Asiatic Studies* 26:78-79.

Hsu, Shiping. 1957. Building Boom in Chinese Cities. *Chengshi Jianshe (Urban Construction)*. 1:7.

Jianzhu Xuebao (Architectural Journal), 1956. 1:103.

Jiefang Ribao (Liberation Daily). 1956. Shanghai, 11 August.

Kato, S. 1952. *Studies in Chinese Economic History* 1:327.

Keizai, Kikaku-cho. 1972. *Kokumin Seikatsu*.

Ku, Ming. 1952. City Construction Should Be Intimately Coordinated with Industrial Construction. *Dongbei Ribao (Northeast Daily)*. Shenyang, 19 December.

Kucherenko, V. A. 1959. The Future of Our Cities. *Pravda*, 29 October.

Kung, Talun. 1958. An Introduction to the Plan for a Small Urban Area in the Hilly Region of Chunking. *Jianzhu Xuebo (Architectural Journal)* 10:29.

Leeming, Frank. 1970. Reconstructing Late Ch'ing Feng-T'ien. *Modern Asian Studies* 4, 4:316-21.

Leung, C. K., and N. S. Ginsburg, eds. 1980. *China: Urbanization and National Development*. Chicago: University of Chicago Press.

Li, Chun-fen, et al. 1983. A Spatial Analysis of Shanghai's Economic Development. Paper presented at the China Canada Conference held at McMaster University, Hamilton, Canada, 3 November. *Hakusho (Economic Planning Agency: White Paper on People's Living Conditions)*. Tokyo: Keizai Kikaku-cho.

Ma, Laurence J. C. 1970. The Chinese Approach to City Planning: Policy, Administration, and Action. *Asian Survey* 19 (September) 838-55.

Ma, Laurence J. C., and E. W. Hanten, eds. 1981. *Urban Development in Modern China*. Boulder, Colo.: Westview Press.

Nikolayev, I. 1960. Industry and the City. Discussing Problems of Urban Development. *Izvestia*, 4 May: 4.

Pan, Zeyun. 1957. On the Standard for Dwelling Space and the Schedule for Urban Planning of Our Nation. *Chengshi Jianshe (Urban Construction)* 8:21.

Pannell, C. W. 1977. Past and Present City Structure in China. *Town Planning Review* 48 (April): 157-72.

Pannell, C. W., and Laurence J. C. Ma. 1983. *China: The Geography of Development and Modernization.* New York: Wiley.

Pannell, C. W., and R. Welch. 1980. Recent Growth and Structural Change in Chinese Cities. *Urban Geography* 1, 1:68-80.

Qing, Xin. 1959. Rapidly Developing Urban Construction in China. *Chengshi Jianshe (Urban Construction)* 10 (October): 13.

Renmin Ribao (People's Daily). 1954. 12 August.

Renmin Ribao (People's Daily). 1957a. 8 May.

Renmin Ribao (People's Daily). 1957b. 8 May.

Renmin Ribao (People's Daily). 1957c. 7 June.

Schenk, H. 1972. Notes on Urban Spatial Planning and Development in China. *Eastern Horizon* 11:34-41.

Shih, Tien. 1958. On the Study of the Scale of Urban Development. *Jihua Jingji (Planned Economy)* 1:26.

Spencer, J. E. 1939. Changing Chungking: The Rebuilding of an Old Chinese City. *Geographical Review* 29, 2:53.

Stephen, H. K. Yeh, and Y. S. Lee 1968. Housing Conditions in Singapore. *Malayan Economic Review* 13, 1:12.

Towers, G. 1973. City Planning in China. *Journal of the Royal Town Planning Institute* 59:125-27.

Tuan, Y. F. 1970. *China.* London: Longman.

Wang, Wenge. 1958. Campaign against Waste and Conservatism, Energetically Improve Urban Planning, Construction and Administration Work. *Jianzhu Xuebao (Architectural Journal)* 4:1.

Wei, Wenzhen. 1982. On the Reconstruction Project of the Guanyuan Neighbourhood, Beijing. *Jianzhu Xuebao (Architectural Journal)* 8:21.

Wenhui Bao (Cultural Contact Daily). 1954. Shanghai, 10 February.

Wenhui Bao (Cultural Contact Daily). 1957. Shanghai, 6 January.

Wu, Chuan-jun. 1983. Urban Planning Problems in Developing the Capital Beijing. Paper presented at the China Canada Conference held at McMaster University, Hamilton, Canada, 3 November.

Wu, Shan, et al. 1929. *Shizheng chuanshu (Handbook of Local Government).* Shanghai: Daolu.

Yang, Jingwen. 1957. Two Problems in Industrial Distribution. *Jihua Jingji (Planned Economy)* 8:13.

Yun, Cheng. 1957. The Problem of Coordinating among Municipal Construction, Residences and Service Facilities and Other Enterprises under Construction in New Industrial Districts. *Jihua Jingji (Planned Economy)* 4:13.

Zhao, Dongri. 1982. Planned Proportionate Development of Beijing. *Jianzhu Xuebao (Architectural Journal)* 5:12.

Zhou, Xuyu. 1958. Some Suggestions on the Preliminary Plan of Baoding. *Chengshi Jianshe (Urban Construction)* 5:19.

3

Japan

HIROSHI MATSUMOTO

CONTEXT

Japan's land problem is caused essentially by intensive development in limited habitable areas. Within this context, this chapter examines the land and urban problems Japan has faced since World War II. It divides the period into three important stages, beginning with 1960–70, when the Japanese economy experienced miraculous growth and its society experienced a drastic transformation of its industrial and employment structure. This change had profound effects on the demand for land in major metropolitan areas and led to such familiar land problems as confusion in land uses and a rise in land prices. Several factors are of special relevance to these land problems. First, land has always been a scarce resource in Japan; second, one of the unavoidable consequences of agricultural land reform enforced after World War II brought about extremely fragmented farmland ownership, making large-scale conversion of land from farm to nonfarm uses quite difficult; and third, the majority of urban dwellers were very eager to own a house on its own lot, even though small, which put immense demand on the urban land market.

The second stage, from 1971 to 1973, was characterized by the so-called land boom that shook the whole country. Stimulated primarily by an extremely relaxed capital market, large amounts of money flowed into the land market, which was then regarded as one of the most lucrative targets of investment. This led to an acute land price rise.

The third stage, from 1974 to the present, is characterized by low or moderate economic growth, resulting in a conspicuous reduction in population migration toward major metropolitan regions. The overall trend in the stabilization of socioeconomic activities has been reflected in the tapering off of the land price increases, and the supply of land in urban areas as a whole has registered a continuous decrease, particularly that derived from the private sector.

In each of the three stages, a number of policy measures have been employed to cope with these problems at the national, regional, prefectural, and local government levels. In the first stage, one of the main goals was to stabilize the rapid increase in land prices, especially by increasing the supply of land for housing. Compulsory purchase of land for large-scale housing developments was legislated for the first time. Also capital gains tax on the transfer of land was reduced in order to motivate landowners to sell their land. Other important legislation of the time was the City Planning Law, which introduced a new system that divided urban areas into urbanization promotion areas and urbanization control areas to promote orderly urban development.

In the second stage, the government developed and employed various interventions as a hedge against speculative activities. These included a series of legal measures relative to land administration represented by enactment of the National Land Use Planning Law (*Kokudo Riyo Keikaku Ho*). Land transactions were to be controlled, including the price, constituting an almost radical innovation of the City Planning Law (*Toshi Keikaku Ho*). In addition, there was a strengthening of various other existing land use control measures, such as forest conservation and the taxation system to discourage speculative land transactions.

In the third stage, policy has sought to ease the various restrictive measures introduced during the previous stage to deal with land speculation. There is also a concern to induce a large number of transactions in the land market, as exemplified by some new measures recently introduced, such as the promotion of urban facilities development and measures to facilitate planned conversion of land use (*Tochiriyo Tenkan Keikaku Seido*). Furthermore, amendments to the Urban Renewal Law have been made, and the District Planning Practice (*Chiku Keikaku Seido*) has been introduced in view of the importance of improving and renewing urban environments. These actions are in recognition of an urban age in which the majority of the Japanese people now live in cities.

Thus the crucial dimension of the urban land problem in Japan is gradually shifting from that of quantity (especially in the supply of land for housing) to that of quality (especially in land use). Accordingly, the following salient tasks need to be tackled immediately:

1. Restructuring of the land and urban development policies' institutional framework from that suited to the stage of drastic transformation to one more relevant to the age of a stabilized society
2. Introduction of measures designed to facilitate effective utilization of unused or inadequately used pockets engulfed in the already built-up areas
3. Adoption of measures conducive to a more equitable distribution of benefits accruing from development

EVOLUTION OF LAND AND URBAN POLICIES

Rapid Growth of the Economy and Rapid Urbanization

World War II ruined the Japanese economy, but the special procurement boom due to the Korean War provided a springboard for development. After 1960 heavy industries, such as iron and steel, shipbuilding, and petrochemical industries, provided the Japanese economy with remarkable growth. The average growth rate of the Japanese economy between 1960 and 1970 was 16.4 percent a year, compared to 6.7 percent in the United States, 7.2 percent in the United Kingdom, and West Germany's 8.6 percent. Clearly Japanese economic progress was rapid. With such great expansion in the economy came a rapid change in the industrial structure, that is, an increase in secondary (manufacturing) and tertiary (service) industries, which replaced primary (extractive) industry. The proportion of workers engaged in each industry was 32.6 percent for primary industry, 29.2 percent for secondary industry, and 38.2 percent for tertiary industry in 1960 compared to 19.3 percent, 34.2 percent, and 46.5 percent, respectively, in 1970.

In parallel with the change in the industrial and employment structure, population, industry, and the like concentrated gradually in cities, particularly metropolitan regions such as Tokyo, Osaka, and Nagoya. At the same time rural population decreased drastically. The number of people who moved into the three metropolitan regions from other provinces was 760,000 in 1955; it increased to 1.25 million in 1970 (see Figure 3.1). The total number of people in these three metropolitan regions was 30,850,000 in 1955 (34.6 percent of the total population in Japan) and 45,580,000 (43.9 percent) in 1970.

With such a rapid increase in population, especially in these three metropolitan regions, the urban areas expanded dramatically. Between 1960 and 1970, the densely inhabited district (DID) population increased by 45 percent; the DID area in the three metropolitan regions increased by 73 percent.[1] Within 15 years new urban areas were formed throughout the whole country.

Nationwide Land Boom and Countermeasures

The economic change came about due to the Nixon Shock of August 1971.[2] Money supply increased, and the outstanding balance reached a high of 20 to 30 percent over that of the previous year. The liquidity indexes of enterprises also rose sharply. While the balance in banks on the loans of real estate agencies had been less than 100 billion yen, occupying somewhat less than 1 percent of the entire balance of loans up to 1960, the scale of loans to real estate agencies expanded until by 1973 it surpassed 6 trillion yen, or was 7 percent of the entire balance of loans. Furthermore, the number of ownership transfers by transaction

Figure 3.1 Changes in Population Movement between Regions in Japan (in the Case of the Three Metropolitan Regions)

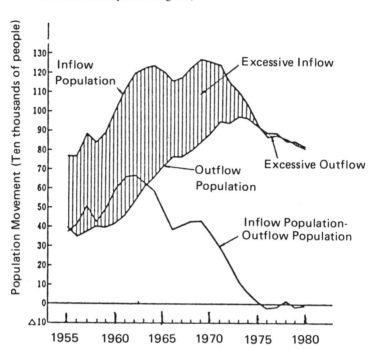

The White Paper on Construction, Ministry of Construction, 1982.

increased rapidly; it was 13.1 percent over that of the previous year and exceeded 3 million registrations in 1971. During fiscal 1972 the total value of landed property owned by corporations increased by 2.7 billion yen, about twice as much as that of the previous year. The investments in land by corporations covered every region in the country, especially forest areas. In this period not only corporations but also many individuals were interested in land transactions and were involved in them. This social phenomenon was called, somewhat cynically, "a hundred million real estate agents."

In this stage land prices at a national scale rose steeply: 25.1 percent in 1972 and 23 percent in 1973.[3] The main cause apparently was speculative demand triggered mainly by the overflow of currency. The government could not allow such demands to continue. The land taxation system, which included heavy taxation on corporate profit on alienation and a special land tenure tax was reinforced so as to manage land during a period of skyrocketing land prices. Also financial control policies for land transactions were introduced in 1973. In addition to the enactment of the National Land Use Planning Act, government officers now had the power to regulate land transactions directly in order to control land prices. These were powerful and unprecedented policies.

Stable Growth

When the first oil crisis was over at the end of 1973, the age of high Japanese economic growth, which had lasted for a considerable time, ended. For the periods 1965-73 and 1974-80 the average growth rate of the real gross national product (GNP) decreased from 9.8 percent to 4.6 percent, national income per person from 15.9 percent to 8.8 percent, private ultimate consumption expenditure from 15.4 percent to 11.1 percent, and private gross domestic fixed capital formation from 20.0 percent to 7.1 percent. The change in the basic economic condition of high-degree growth to steady growth is evident.

Additionally the excessive population inflow from the provincial regions to the metropolitan areas began to decrease rapidly after 1971. After the first oil crisis the out-migration population from the metropolitan regions exceeded the in-migration by a small margin. The rates of population growth in each prefecture, except Tokyo, leveled out between 1975 and 1980. Population tended to increase in smaller cities and their peripheral areas. On the other hand, the night-time population in the city centers and surrounding areas of the largest metropolitan areas decreased while the population in their peripheral areas increased, creating the so-called doughnut phenomenon. Thus a new pattern of population settlement came about.

LANDOWNERSHIP FRAMEWORK

National Land Use Characteristics

Japan has a relatively small land area, particularly plains. This is the main factor in the creation of land use problems. Urban and agricultural activities have to be conducted in very small, densely populated districts. Compared to other countries, the net population density per square kilometer in habitable areas is about nine times as high as that in France and about four times that of West Germany or the United Kingdom. Also the GNP per square kilometer in habitable areas of Japan is about seven times as much as that of France, about three times that of West Germany, and about four times that of the United Kingdom (see Figure 3.2). Another factor that makes land and city problems in Japan more complicated is the fact that major economic and social activities are concentrated in small regions. This distortion in land use is evident from the fact that the population density and the net product per square kilometer of open fields in the three metropolitan regions are 4.4 and 5.7 times higher, respectively, than in other provincial regions.

Figure 3.2 International Comparison of Population, GNP, etc. per km² of Habitable Area

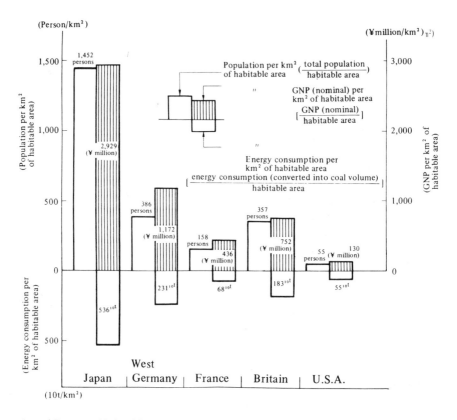

Annual Report on National Land Use, National Land Agency, 1982.

Efficient Land Use

In an ideal system in which private property rights are guaranteed, land should be owned by those who use the land in the way society desires. This is especially true in the large cities in Japan where small areas are overcrowded, there is a high density of socioeconomic activities, and land prices are high. In reality, however, the situation is complex. In order to realize good urban environments, it is essential to carry out desirable conversion of land use efficiently to meet various kinds of land use demands. For this purpose, it is essential to understand the specific characteristics of the situations unique to Japan and to devise practical measures suitable to such situations.

Landownership in Japan: Characteristics of Land Tenure and the Farmland Owner

At the end of the 1800s the right to use, make profits from, and dispose of land was legislated as the right of landownership in Japan. In rural areas generally, landlords possessed land and tenants used (cultivated) it; ownership and use were separate from each other. After World War II, the Agricultural Land Reform Act (*Nochi-Kaikaku Ho*) was promulgated to establish as the new rule of landownership that cultivators should possess agricultural land. However, problems such as the increase in the number of small landowners and the subdivision of agricultural management units emerged. Between 1945 and 1949 the ratio between farmland owned by cultivators and the total amount of cultivated farmland rose from 54 percent to 87 percent. Also the ratio of landed farm households (farm households owning more than 90 percent of the operational holding) to the total number of farm households rose from 31 percent to 62 percent between 1944 and 1950. In the period from 1941 to 1950, the number of farm households with 1 hectare or more of cultivated acreage decreased by 19 percent, while the number of farm households with less than 1 hectare increased by 28 percent.

After 1955 the Japanese economy grew very rapidly, and population and industry began to concentrate in metropolitan areas at an increased rate. Despite such rapid urbanization, the total number of farm households, including those in the largest metropolitan areas, decreased by only 12 percent from 1960 to 1970, while the number of people engaged in agriculture decreased by 30 percent during the same period. This was because more and more farm households began to engage in sideline businesses while continuing to cultivate their farmland. Population and industry from all over the country rushed to the limited metropolitan areas seeking sites for housing and production. The land suitable for such sites was owned by a great many small farm households in the form of small, subdivided farmlands. They were reluctant to sell their land. This was the most important factor in making postwar land and urban problems in Japan extremely difficult to solve. Four reasons account for the fact that farm households did not decrease as rapidly as did population engaged in agriculture:

1. Farmland ownership by cultivators was firmly protected by law.
2. In urban areas the price of farmland rose, more or less, to the same level as that of urban housing sites. This led to an increase in the value of farmland as property. Farmers were thus less motivated to sell quickly.
3. As the opportunities to gain income from jobs other than agriculture increased due to urbanization, farmland did not necessarily have to be sold by farmers.
4. Farmers were inclined to avoid abrupt changes in life-style that might be caused by the loss of farmland.

Before World War II the majority of workers in the urban areas lived in rented houses. But after the war people wanted their own home with a garden. Thus the number of homeowners increased rapidly, for the following reasons:

1. The workers in the cities, many of whom came from farm villages, were used to having their own home with a garden.
2. People became more highly conscious of living standards.
3. The prior land leasehold protection policies of the Land Lease Act (*Shakuchi-Ho*) had, ironically, prevented the improvement of rented houses.
4. Due to the increase in the income of workers, owning a home became a real possibility.
5. The continuous rise in both land prices and building construction costs drove urban households to owning a home as soon as possible.

One of the factors that had a decisive influence was that most of the land on the periphery of cities was owned by many small farm (or ex-farm) households who were given the land under the Agricultural Land Reform Act. Such farmland is not easily turned into housing sites despite the fact that a large part of it is already engulfed in the expansion of urban areas. Landowners are reluctant to let the land go. (In this connection, the situation could have been much more favorable if, at that time the reform act was legislated, the government had reserved the repurchase right in case of land conversion.)

Another major issue is whether the level of taxation imposed on farmland within urbanization promotion areas should be the same as that on housing sites. This question has been argued for years between the ''urban siders'' and the farmland owners. The former insist that the tenure tax on farmland (which is exceptionally light) should not be applied to farmlands in these areas since the lands are designated for urban development in the city master plan and these farmlands are exempt from the regular control of land use conversion prescribed by the Agricultural Land Act. The farmland owners, supported by strong political allies, insist that the exceptionally light taxation should be applied so long as farming is in fact continued there. A temporary compromise to this problem was arranged in 1982, frustrating many of the urban siders. It was agreed that a farmland owner in these areas must decide and declare whether he wants to continue to engage in agriculture for a given period (at least ten years). Under the new rule, the delineation of urbanization promotion and urbanization control areas will be re-examined at some time soon. Besides, in the near future it is also desirable to introduce amendments to the taxation system so that landowners will be induced to make their land available to those who need it.

Another obstacle to land use conversion is the problem of the land leasehold. If one looks out a window of a skyscraper at the downtown of Shinjuku in Tokyo, stretches of old, low, wooden houses can be seen at the bottom of the tall buildings. The land, although valued at as high as 2 million yen per square meter, has dilapidated low houses on it. One of the main reasons for this is the failure of negotiations between the tenants and the landowners. Even after the term of a land lease contract has passed (in the case of a wooden house, at least 30 years as a rule), a request for renewal of the lease by the tenants stands in the present legal system unless the landowner can show that he will use the land himself. According to a 1982 study of the National Land Agency, leased land covered 52 percent of the total land, and 52 percent of the leased land had low, detached houses on it. This takes into account only land larger than 500 square meters in area within the 11 central wards in Tokyo. A new rule of development is needed for the further reconstruction of urban areas.

Decisionmaking Structure in the Administration of Land Use Planning

The National Land Agency was established in 1974 as the administrative arm of the government responsible for formulating and implementing national and regional land use plans. At the national level, such plans include the National Land Use Plan and the National Comprehensive Development Plan, and at the regional level there is the National Capital Region Development Plan and others. Generally these plans have no more function than declaring principles and concepts and presenting general guidelines for local land use plans.

The Ministry of Construction is responsible for the administration of city planning and for the improvement of urban areas. The Ministry of Agriculture, Forestry and Fishery is in charge of the land use plan for agricultural land and forests. The City Planning Act of 1968 is the basic law that empowers local governments to make and implement land use plans, that is city plans. In principle, local public bodies (cities, towns, and villages) make plans, but at the same time the governors of the prefectures participate in making the plans to the extent that the plans are considered in terms of a larger region. The drafts of the local and prefectural government plans are subject to the approval of both the governor and the Ministry of Construction. Both plans are also subject to discussion by an administrative council and to public hearings. In principle a draft plan is not presented to the assembly of the local bodies for discussion directly, though it is practically impossible to neglect its opinions.

MAJOR CHALLENGES: LAND AND URBAN PROBLEMS CAUSED BY HIGH ECONOMIC GROWTH AND RAPID URBANIZATION

Confusion in Land Uses

A major problem was confusion in land uses, particularly on the periphery of large cities. Rapid urbanization caused disordered development of farmland and forest land, resulting frequently in urban sprawl, the formation of uncontrolled urban areas. These conditions lowered the quality of life and the environment and made public investments ineffective, which in turn led to social problems.

Because it was difficult to cope with the sharp increase needed in the supply of land to accommodate the rising housing and industrial demand, systematic development and conservation of land was not realized. The failure to coordinate various kinds of land use during that period is one of the most significant causes of subsequent urban land problems.

Land use confusion had several causes. First, as land prices rose, the demand for land was shifted to the periphery where land prices were comparatively cheaper. The demand for housing sites increased greatly even in areas without basic urban infrastructure, such as roads and sewerage. Second, the rapid and continuous rise in land prices discouraged landowners from selling their land in haste, which made the land shortage even more acute. Finally, the expansion of urban areas was so rapid that it was difficult to establish concrete policies for controlling and guiding it in a systematic way. The construction of public facilities could not keep up with the speed of expansion. It would be fair to say that the drastic and rapid change in the economy and society at that time was the fundamental cause of the confusion in land uses and other serious land problems today.

Sharp Rise in Land Prices

The second main problem was a sharp rise in land prices. If land prices had risen within the limits of improving land productivity, price would not have been an issue. The rise in prices, however, was so abnormal that it produced a chaotic land use pattern and brought about serious inequalities in the economic status of landowners and others. Between 1955 and 1970 land prices rose fourteenfold, with an average rate of increase of 19.2 percent a year. The rate of increase in land prices reached a high of 42.5 percent between 1960 and 1961. With respect to the increase in the rates of industrial sites and housing sites, the former exceeded the latter between 1955 and 1964, whereas after 1965 the latter tended to exceed the former. That is, from 1955 to 1964 the land prices of industrial sites rose due to the high growth of the Japanese economy, which was supported mainly by the remarkable increase in private plant and equipment investments. Since 1965, however, as housing investments increased, particularly due to population increase in the metropolises, land prices of residential sites rose substantially.

During the period 1955 to 1964 land prices in the largest six metropolises (Tokyo, Osaka, Nagoya, Yokohama, Kyoto, and Kobe) rose so sharply that the difference in land prices between these six metropolises and other provincial regions drew even further apart. Since 1965, however, the rate of increase in land prices in the urban areas of other provincial regions has been greater than in the six metropolises. Until 1965 the rate of increase in land prices of both farmland and forest was always lower than urban land. Since 1966, however, they have become almost the same as urban land.

Overpopulation and Depopulation

The third main problem was overpopulation of the metropolitan regions due to high concentration of population and industry and depopulation of provincial regions due to the outflow of young people. The concentration of population and industry in the larger urban areas brought about considerable economic benefits to those who lived there and to the companies engaged in economic activities there. The urban areas, however, expanded in a disorderly manner and lacked sufficient basic urban infrastructure such as roads, sewerage, and the like. This urbanization process caused housing shortages, the deterioration of residential environments, an increase in disaster risks, air and water pollution, noise, traffic jams, and a sharp rise in land prices. As large numbers of people, mainly young, moved into metropolises from provincial areas seeking job opportunities and higher incomes, the population in provincial areas decreased remarkably, and the proportion of aged people there rose. Consequently, community vitality declined, and economic potential weakened. Some rural communities in remote areas actually disappeared.

Land Speculation

Land prices continued to rise consistently through the period of high economic growth. In 1972 an overheating of the economy occurred due mainly to an overflow of currency triggered by the Nixon shock. During this period, land prices rose all over the country, not only in urban areas as before; speculative land transactions were made, particularly by private enterprises; prices of farmland and forests rose more rapidly than land in urban areas; and in urban areas the increase in land prices was especially evident in residential sections.

Due to the loose money policy, private enterprise could manage their funds in such a way as to make high profits through land transactions. Furthermore, this coincided with the social and economic circumstances that many large-scale housing and industrial undertakings were being developed, or being planned, all over the country.

New Needs for a Stabilized Society

After Japan's rapid economic growth ended, people's way of thinking and sense of values became more diversified. Increasingly people have come to value the quality of life. Recent social developments such as the rise in income, fulfillment of basic needs, increased leisure time, and increased proportion of aged and highly educated people, may be helping this tendency. People have also become more interested in health and security matters, self-fulfillment, public sector decisionmaking, and their roles in the community. The Third National Comprehensive Development Plan of 1976, reflecting these trends, emphasized the promotion of satisfactory environments for human habitation throughout the developed areas of the country, in contrast to the Second Plan that emphasized the promotion of industrial and economic development.

In 1974, after the first oil crisis, land prices decreased by 4.3 percent over the previous year for the first time since the end of the war.[4] After that, the rate of increase was low: 0.8 percent in 1975, 2.1 percent in 1976, and 2.8 percent in 1977. The rate then rose gradually to 4.6 percent in 1978, 8.5 percent in 1979, and 8.7 percent in 1980, but decreasing to 3.8 percent in 1982. Thus land prices seem to have stabilized. The supply of land for housing in new urban areas continued to decrease from a peak of 14,500 hectares in fiscal 1972 to 8,200 hectares in fiscal 1980, due partly to decreasing financial returns from housing development projects and the influence of negative development control policies adopted by local public bodies.

APPROACHES TO LAND AND URBAN MANAGEMENT

Balanced Distribution of Population and Industry

Japan is seeking to solve its land and urban problems by controlling the concentration of population and industry in the metropolises, promoting decentralization in order to increase industry and job opportunities in the provincial regions, and achieving balanced development nationally by reducing the income differences among regions. As far as the national capital region and Kinki region are concerned, various policies, including the National Capital Region Development Act (*Shutoken-Seibi Ho*), were adopted for the purpose of realizing balanced, systematic development.[5] This was to be achieved by restraining the excessive concentration of population and industry in the center of the cities.

At the national level, the first National Comprehensive Development Plan was prepared in 1962. A major aim was to establish a certain number of nationwide strategic bases for development, such as the new industrial cities and the special industrial development areas. The Second National Comprehensive Development Plan of 1969 was prepared specifically to promote improvements in nationwide networks such as transportation and communication services and to encourage large-scale development projects. These efforts have been successful to some extent, but in order to cope with the problems brought about by the heavy concentration of population and industry in urban areas, additional measures were needed.

Large-Scale Supply of Housing Sites

The rapid flow of population into the metropolitan areas created a great demand for houses and housing sites. Because supply could not meet the demand, land prices rose sharply and serious housing shortages occurred. The first measure taken to solve these problems was the land readjustment project undertaken by public bodies and private associations and supported by various national subsidies and special financial systems.[6] The project played a leading role in supplying housing sites of good quality during the 1950s and 1960s, particularly as at that stage in Japan private companies (called developers today) lacked adequate accumulation of capital and the capability to undertake large housing developments. Acknowledgment of the supply of housing sites and dwelling units as an important national task led to the second measure, establishment of the Japan Housing Corporation in 1955 as a national organization for supplying houses and housing sites. The corporation has played a pioneering role in the large-scale supply of houses and housing sites, particularly in the three largest metropolitan regions.

The third measure was the New Residential City Areas Development Act (*Shin-Jutaku-Shigaichi-Kaihatsu-Ho*) promulgated in 1963 to promote large-scale site development. This act included provision for land expropriation by local authorities or public corporations to provide land for housing sites. Some new towns such as Tama in Tokyo and Senri in Osaka were created under the provisions of this law.

The fourth measure was a policy of countermeasures to promote the improvement of public facilities and utilities for housing sites, such as roads, sewerage, parks, and schools. Adequate facilities are indispensable for the promotion of housing site development. If housing sites are developed on a large scale within a short time, however, the municipalities that are in a position to be responsible for providing the infrastructure would be required to develop extensive public facilities and utilities. With their weak financial basis, this would impose an excessive burden on them. These municipalities thus assumed a conservative attitude toward the supply of land for large-scale housing development. Since 1967, however, the Japan Housing and the Housing Finance Corporation have provided local public bodies with the financing for the improvement of public facilities and utilities.

Last, in the tax system affecting land use, some measures were taken in 1969. Above all, the capital gains tax on land sold by individuals was lowered in order to induce smoother transactions in the market.

Development of Good Urban Environments

Prior to the mid-1960s, the City Planning Act of 1919 had been considered the basic law for city planning. In conjunction with this act, various laws, such as the Urban Building Act (*Shigaichi Kenchikubutsu Ho*) of 1919, and the Building Standard Law of 1950, had been enacted that led to improvement in the basic urban infrastructure, primarily by public bodies, and control of land use activities by the private sector in accordance with comprehensive plans prepared by local governments. With respect to land use control, building activities (not including other types such as development of housing sites in advance of future building, which was the popular practice in those days) had been regulated by a rough classification of zoning only. Furthermore, the extent of control had been very limited and also could be applied only within the urban area of cities and towns. Thus, the development of farmland and forests on the periphery of cities had not been controlled in the development of housing. Because authorities could not cope with the rapid expansion of urban areas, disorderly development resulted.

Because of this situation the City Planning Act was overhauled in 1968. In this new City Planning Act, both urbanization promotion areas, which were intended to promote urbanization, and urbanization control areas, which were intended to control urbanization, were introduced with the belief that community improvement cannot be accomplished adequately without a systematic approach. At the same time the development permission system was introduced in order to realize the intentions of these two areas. Although the designation of urbanization promotion areas and urbanization control areas is a type of land use zoning, the aim was not only to control the rights concerning land use, as in the case of a static zoning system, but also to harmonize and synthesize various kinds of policies in accordance with the development objectives of each area; that is, a dynamic strategy was envisaged in which each area was designed to cope with urbanization by the synthesis of various kinds of policies for the urban edge, such as: (1) establishment of a public investments plan and the principle of who is to share the cost of development; (2) establishment of a land use plan to control individual rights on the urban side; (3) establishment of a public investments plan and control of farmland conversion on the agricultural side; and (4) establishment of a taxation system for both the urban and the agricultural sides.

One reason for establishing this strategy was that the city planning administration in a period of rapid urbanization could not function effectively without integrating related policies, such as public investment policies, a taxation system, and so on. Second, it was necessary to balance the interests of the regions in order to maintain impartiality and carry out administrative planning smoothly. It was inevitable, however, that the initial strategy did not work as expected at first because of the detailed examination that took place in the legislative process and the lack of coordination among the administrative bodies involved.

Public Announcement of Land Prices

A number of factors influence land prices: location, use pattern, shape, profitability, surrounding area, and so on. Price also is likely to be influenced by the price asked or offered for neighboring land and the speculation of those involved in land transactions. These factors prevented smooth and fair land transactions and caused the tremendous increases in land prices. To overcome this problem, the Real Estate Appraisal Act was enacted in 1963 to establish the real estate appraisal and evaluation system. The Land Price Publication Act was enacted in 1969 to provide for the public announcement of standard prices of land every year. These prices were to serve as guidelines for general land transactions so as to contribute to making land prices more reasonable.

National Land Use Planning Act

The National Land Use Planning Act is a basic law concerning land. It was promulgated in 1974 with the support of the four major political parties, including both ruling and opposition parties (rare in Japan). This was at the urging of strong public opinion that called for a cooling off of the land boom. In addition to price control, this law has two characteristics affecting land use. First, land use in large-scale private developments was to be checked prior to any transaction. Second, a land use master plan covering all parts of the country and all kinds of land use was institutionalized for the first time. Until then land use planning was carried out by various administrative bodies and from various viewpoints, such as city planning, promotion of agriculture, and forest improvement. Their objectives were not well coordinated. The governor of each prefecture was now empowered to draft a comprehensive land use master plan for the prefecture, to coordinate the various types of land use, and to comply with the national land use plan.

The National Land Use Planning Act consists of five components: (1) the national land use plan, (2) the land use master plan, (3) the land transaction permission system to control land transactions in designated areas, (4) the registration and recommendation system for land transactions through the nation, and (5) countermeasures against idle land. These components are briefly described in the following paragraphs.

1.   The national land use plan is a set of long-term plans for land use throughout the country prepared by the nation, prefectures, and municipalities.

2.   The land use master plan is prepared by each prefecture in compliance with the national land use plan. The plan is to contain future prospects for land use in five areas (urban area, agricultural area, forest area, natural park area, and nature conservation area).

3.   The permission system for land transactions is designed to cope with emergencies such as speculative land transactions and skyrocketing land prices. An area in which urgent measures need to be taken is designated a control area by the prefectural governor, and the permission system is enforced for each land use within the control area. The only land transaction permitted within the control area is that which fulfills one of the given purposes, such as for private residence or private business use. Also, the land price is to correspond to the standard at the time of the designation of the control area. Due to the special characteristics of this system, it has never been put into operation.

4.   The registration system is applied to those land transactions that involve larger areas than those prescribed. The prefectural governor is notified of the predetermined price and purpose for which the land is to be used. If the price

or purpose is judged inadequate, the governor may take measures such as recommending the cancellation of the contract.

5.   The purpose of the measures for idle land is to ensure the positive use of land not in use that is larger than a predetermined size. The measures supplement the permission and registration systems. They consist of such countermeasures as the notification of idle land, the registration of the plans for use by the owner, and advice, recommendations, and purchase negotiations proposed by the governor.

Revision and Reinforcement of Laws Concerning Land Use Control

Along with the enactment of the National Land Use Planning Act in 1974, laws for land use regulations such as the City Planning Act and the Forest Act were revised. These regulations were now applied to the development of almost all areas throughout the nation. At the same time, the subject matter of the regulations was reinforced. The Development Permission System was applied to all city planning areas. Land use controls provided under the Forest Act, which used to be applied only to the special reserved forests, were now to be applied to private forests as well.

Control of Speculative Land Transactions by the Taxation System

One of the main land management measures taken in the period of the land boom was to establish a series of strict, restraining taxation systems for controlling speculative land transactions and realizing better land use. A system of high taxes on a corporation's profit from the sale of land was adopted in order to control speculative land transactions by corporate enterprises, which had played a leading role in the nationwide land boom. A special measure of lower taxes on an individual's profit from selling land was established in 1969 in order to promote the supply of land for housing. Although the second measure had some effect on the supply of land, it became one of the factors that produced high profits and caused both social inequalities in income allocation and an abnormally high number of land transactions. Consequently, when the term of this special measure expired, the taxes on an individual's transfer of long-held land were increased considerably. Furthermore, in order to control speculative land transactions and to realize effective land uses, a special land tenure tax was established in 1973, imposed on both land tenure and on land acquisition. The tenure tax and the acquisition tax were combined with a view to controlling land speculation. A legal system to enable the imposition of property tax on farmland, similar to that on housing sites in an urbanization promotion area designated by the City Planning Act, was established in order to balance the tax liability and promote the supply of land for housing. This system, however, was opposed by farmers, and due to their political influence, the results were not satisfactory.

Turnabout from Restrictive Policies to Overcome the Stagnated Land Supply

The end of the age of high economic growth was triggered by the first oil crisis. After this, land prices began to stabilize, and Japan's land policies took a turn in a positive direction again. Several measures were adopted to promote the supply of housing sites, which had stagnated partly because of the negative effect of current restrictive policies on land transactions. The measures were seen as a means of stimulating home-building activities, which were considered essential as a way to combat the economic recession brought on by the first oil crisis.

1.   A Special Fund for the Improvement of Public Facilities related to Housing Development was established in 1978 in order to alleviate the financial burden on local governments, which often could not afford more than fulfilling the needs in built-up areas and were unable or unwilling to provide adequate infrastructure for the newly opened up urban areas.

2.   On the initiative of farmland owners in the urban peripheries, the Farmer's Housing Association Act was enacted in 1980 to encourage mixed and integrated land development for farming and housing. The purpose of the act was to bring about a favorable balance between urban and agricultural land use.

3.   The land taxation system was revised in 1973 and 1976 in order to control speculative transactions. After the land boom was over and the supply of land began to stagnate, due both to economic recession and restrictive policies, private developers in particular called for alleviation of the land tax. In 1982 a new set of taxation policies was established with a view to the promotion of the supply of urban land with adequate infrastructure, while at the same time controlling speculative transactions. These policies included easing the capital gains tax on long-held land and the establishment of a new tax system in which the tax imposed on the gains in transactions of residential property, is withheld for as long as the owner-occupier uses the revenue for purchasing a substitute residential property.

Promotion of Urban Renewal in the Age of Stabilized Growth

Even during the rapid urbanization in the 1950s and 1960s, urban renewal was an important issue. Now that an urban age has arrived—the majority of people reside in urban areas—urban renewal is becoming one of the greatest concerns of people for the improvement of their urban environment. When the original Urban Renewal Act was revised in 1979, local governments were required to prepare an urban renewal plan and to improve urban renewal projects by promoting efficient land use and revitalizing urban functions in built-up areas.

Furthermore, the district planning system (*Chiku Keikaku*) was introduced as a new approach to city planning practice. The intention was to prevent the formation of inferior residential areas caused by small, sporadic, and disorderly development and to preserve a favorable urban environment.

FUTURE ISSUES

Framework for Urban Improvements in a Stabilized Society

The most conspicuous policy to cope with the upheaval period when cities expanded rapidly due to high economic growth and rapid concentration of population in the cities was the strategy of delineating urbanization promotion areas and urbanization control areas. Now that the rapid expansion of cities has come to an end and land prices have stabilized, cities will be rebuilt and administered from a long-range point of view. The most important issue is how future city improvements should be conceived and carried out. Some steps have already been taken; for example, there has been a drastic revision of zone delineation in urban land use master plans in order to reflect a more realistic potential for development. On the assumption that the system of delineating the two types of areas will continue to exist, a comprehensive review is required of a number of related problems, taking into account the experiences and reflections of the past fifteen years. These problems are all difficult ones and are closely interrelated. Partial measures have been taken to solve these problems but most have been left to be solved in the future. The legislation underpinning this system, which was radical for those days, had to be devised in a hurry. Also the effect of sprawl was too powerful to be controlled effectively through statutory measures. In addition, the resources for infrastructure were insufficient at that time.

A number of major problems must be tackled:

1.   The objective and principle of urbanization promotion areas should be more clearly defined. A better measure needs to be established as to how seriously or urgently the land in an urbanization promotion area is required to be developed. Under the present system, development in urban promotion areas does not seem to be an obligation and sometimes is a mere hope. The function, now quite vague, of existing farmland in these areas should also be made clearer. The basic principles of tenure tax on idle land or farmland in these areas need to be determined.

2.   Adequate resources are needed for infrastructure improvements within urbanization promotion areas. The resources that local governments have for infrastructure improvement are more likely to be spent in already built up urban areas (naturally the center of concern of local politics), thus leaving the condition of newly developed areas inadequate. The political dimension of the problem is much more serious than the familiar constraint of lack of funds. In the future, it may be necessary to introduce a policy of permitting development applications on an alternative basis. That is, an applicant may choose either to wait until the

local government is ready or to obtain a permit with the condition that the necessary public facilities would be provided by the applicant.

3.   The program for the improvement of public facilities needs to be clarified. Furthermore, it is essential for municipalities to formulate land use plans at the earliest possible opportunity, despite recognition of the difficulties involved in the preparation of a land use plan in advance of actual development. It is desirable to relate as closely as possible development and the land use plan.

4.   The principle of determining the final sharing of costs for public facilities between central and local governments and private developers needs to be articulated realistically. A development permit request made within an urbanization promotion area is supposed to be approved as long as it conforms to the established planning standards; however, in order to close the gap between this legal principle and the actual capacity of local governments to supply infrastructure (and local political desire to restrain the increase in population), local governments have instituted a device that developers should contribute the expenses for infrastructure improvement according to the Guidelines for Land Development (*Takuchi-Kaihatsu Shido-Yoko*).

5.   The system of development permission should be revised to be more thorough and scrupulous. Under the present system, neither small-scale land development projects nor building activities that do not accompany land development are subject to control. The result has been the construction of small-sized poor quality buildings, haphazardly located and without proper public facilities. Their construction could not be prevented, and they damaged good urban environments. Because these small-sized developments are exempt from regulation, they do not share the burden of the social cost of infrastructure and are considered unjustly profitable. It is cheaper and more profitable for a person to buy a small lot and build a house on it without concern for public facilities than to buy a house supplied by a home builder. This means that farmland owners can sell their unserviced land at a considerably higher price than that which it ought to have been if such small developments were also subject to regulation. Ironically, the more stabilized land prices become, the less feasible it will be for home builders to carry out well-integrated housing projects under the present system.

Small-Scale Farmland

The Farmer's Housing Association system was established in 1981 for the purpose of the promotion of house building and the development of apartment houses by the landowners themselves. But so far the act has failed to offer attractive advantages to association members. An improvement of the system is required, including the extension of the applicable area in rural regions.

The Land Leasehold Act, enacted in 1921, has a marked disposition to protect the comparatively weak position of tenants. In the days of rapidly escalating land prices, landowners were unable to lease land without serious risk partially because it was difficult to negotiate an increase in rents. As a result, a practice has been established by which owners received premiums equal to a large percentage of the value of the land when leasing it. (Viewed from the other side, the lack of market prices for land rents has prevented the formation of reasonable land prices.) Recently a land lease method suitable to the present situation has been attempted by both public and private developers. Thus the need to revise the legal system related to land rent has become urgent.

Redevelopment and Rehousing

The nearer a ward is to the center of the city in Tokyo, the older the average age of households is, according to a housing survey. This tendency is evident only in the case of the households that own the house they occupy, illustrating the historic process of concentric expansion of urban areas due to population growth through the prewar and postwar periods rather than the difference in preferences for certain areas by each age group in a city. In order to promote redevelopment and land supply in the future, it is important to take into account the characteristics of such property owners, especially their attitude toward present and potential land use and disposal.

An onerous capital gains tax on land transactions is one of the major obstacles for those elderly people who wish to sell their residential properties. A new system of temporarily withholding imposition of transfer capital gains tax has been instituted in order to promote the construction of multistory buildings and renewal of residential properties. There have already been signs of a smoother conversion of land use due to this new system. To assist the aged, it has also been suggested that a system be established for the exemption from transfer capital gains tax once in a lifetime.

In order to ensure that urban land use takes the most satisfactory form, some advocate that efficient land use should be imposed by public authority. A far more detailed land use plan and more effective means for its implementation would then be required in order to improve living environments. As long as the free market economy system exists, however, the idea of land use imposed by public authorities over all landowners is neither relevant nor feasible, except for such extraordinary cases where expropriation can be justified. Accordingly the only way to approach the ultimate objective is a sustained effort of combining such policies as those of taxation and finance that may help motivate landowners to participate in realizing desirable land use.

Stabilization of Land Prices

Efficient land use is prevented primarily by speculative holding of land. Currently, however, such land speculation is virtually nonexistent because speculative investment in land is less profitable today, abnormal increases in land prices are restrained by the National Land Use Planning Act, and a heavy tax is imposed on profits from the sale of land.[7] In the future these policies should never be relaxed, though they might be strengthened.

Betterment

It is not peculiar to land that the rise in property prices brings unearned profits to the owner, thus expanding social inequity. Furthermore, holding land is not as safe or more profitable than other properties as before. And yet the restoration of betterment to society will be a more important issue in the future because land is unique in that profits accured from social investments and other activities are accumulated on it. This is especially true in Japan, where land is a scarce and precious resource.

Information on Land

The facts and suggestions related to land issues are generally not as well understood or persuasive as, for example, those related to economics. One reason is that the mechanisms have not been fully analyzed scientifically and the data on land are far from sufficient. Recently, however, processing of thorough, detailed, comprehensive land data systematized as digital information has been started. One such example is ''The Study on the Land Use of the National Capital Region,'' initiated by the Ministry of Construction. The study and development of such a land data system may be the most important step in the search for innovative and effective land policies in the future.

NOTES

1. DID (Densely Inhabited District) is a regional concept established in the Census of 1960 to clarify the characteristics of Japanese urban areas. DID is defined as the area of municipalities that have a population of 5,000 people or more and where the survey districts that have a high population density (more than about 4,000 people per square kilometer) are adjacent to one another.

2. On 16 August, 1971, President Richard Nixon of the United States announced a new economic policy in which convertibility of the dollar was to be suspended. Amid the international monetary confusion that followed, the previously fixed rate of the Japanese yen was replaced by a new system of floating rates. Speculative demand poured in for the Japanese yen. The government immediately adopted various policies designed to stimulate the stagnated economy, including an additional budget for investments in public facilities, tax reductions, and lowering of the official rate. Thus, overheating of the economy, with overflow of currency and high inflation, was brought about.

3. The fluctuating rates of land prices shown in this chapter are the price indexes of built-up areas throughout the country published by the Japan Real Estate Research Institute. The rate was 30.9 percent in 1972 and 32.4 percent in 1973 according to the Land Price Publication of the National Land Agency.

4. This figure is −9.2 percent according to the Land Price Publication of the National Land Agency.

5.   The following various laws for regional development and improvement were enacted in succession: the National Capital Region Development Act (*Shutoken Seibi Ho*)
(1956); the Act concerning Industry Restriction in the Built-up Area of the National
Capital Region (1959); the Act concerning the Development of the Suburban Development
Area and the Urban Development Area in the National Capital Region (1958); the Act
for the Development of the New Industrial Cities (1962); and the Act for the Development
of the Special Industrial Development Areas (1964).

6.   Land readjustment is a unique project method for urban development that has been
in use for more than sixty years in Japan. The local government or the public corporation
that undertakes this project is empowered to take a certain proportion of land—usually
from 30 to 50 percent—instead of buying it from the landowners in the project area for
the purpose of providing public facilities and financing the project. No compensation is
paid to the landowners as far as the total value of each property does not decrease after
the area is developed.

7.   On the assumption that the average rate of increase in land prices will not be more
than 7.4 percent a year, investment in land with an intention to hold it for less than 10
years (therefore the higher rate of capital gains tax on the "short-term-held" land is
applied on its transfer) would not be more profitable than that in, for example, a loan
trust for a term of five years as of the end of 1982. As for the recent rise in land prices,
the average rate was 8.4 percent in the past 10 years, 6.9 percent for the last five years,
and 3.8 percent in 1982.

BIBLIOGRAPHY

There are numerous publications in Japanese. Only the following are published with
summaries in English.

Ministry of Construction, *Annual White Paper on Construction.*
National Land Use Agency, *Annual Report (White Paper) on National Land Use.*

4

India

K. V. Sundaram and R. K. Wishwakarma

HISTORICAL DEVELOPMENT AND CURRENT STATUS OF LAND USE PLANNING

Population Growth, Distribution, and Density

India, with an area of 3.3 million square kilometers and a population of 658 million in 1981, is a subcontinent of great variety and contrasts. It is a federation consisting of 22 states and nine centrally administered territories. The states are autonomous units with legislatures of their own. The Indian Constitution has defined the functions of government under three lists: union, state, and concurrent. Local government is a state matter. The constitution, however, has recognized that local government institutions are an essential part of the national government (Article 12). The subject "Local Government" appears under entry 5 in the Seventh Schedule of the constitution.

The 658 million people of the country constitute about 14 percent of the world's population but occupy only about 2 percent of earth's land. They are distributed in 617,135 human settlements of varying types and sizes. Nearly 502 million people, or 76 percent of India's population, live in 613,890 villages, varying in size from 100 to 20,000 people each; the remainder (156 million, or 24 percent) are accommodated in 3,245 towns and cities varying in size from 5,000 to 5 million people each. The population of India is increasing at the rate of 2.48 percent per annum, resulting in a net addition of more than 13 million persons per year. Assuming a reasonable measure of success in the country's family planning efforts, the population of India is expected to be around 950 million by the end of the century.

The growth of population and the resultant increase in the pressure on land has not been uniform in all parts of India. The overall population density of India (216 persons per square kilometer) is lower than that of many countries in Europe. There are wide regional variations in density, with Kerala State having the highest density (more than 550 persons per square kilometer) and Arunachal Pradesh having the lowest (about 6 persons per square kilometer).

India is marked by a wide range of human settlements. They vary in size, structure, morphology, and economic base. Single-dwelling settlement units, such as homesteads in Kerala, coexist with high-density population cities like Calcutta and Bombay. There are, on the one hand, rural areas that show high social indexes of urban population and, on the other hand, pockets in metropolitan cities that show rural characteristics.

In absolute numbers, India has an urban population of 156 million, one of the largest in the world of population living in towns. This is more than the total population of any other developing country of the world, except China and Indonesia. Still, in terms of urbanization, India is one of the less urbanized countries, with less than 25 percent of the country's total population living in towns and cities. Even during the postindependence period, the growth of urban population has never been spectacular. During the period 1951–61, it increased by 26.4 percent as against 21.50 percent increase in the general population. The urban population during the decade 1961–71 increased by 37.9 percent, and during 1971–81, it increased by 46 percent (Table 4.1).

As far as growth of population in each size class of town is concerned, it has been observed that there has been an acceleration in the overall rate of growth of population in each class between each census year. Cities above 100,000 population have grown somewhat faster than the medium-sized towns. Small towns (below 10,000 population) also seem to have shown high-growth potential (Table 4.2).

These growth rates, however, did not operate uniformly in the different regions (states) of the country. As a result, urbanization is unbalanced in both space and structure. States such as Maharashtra and Gujarat, for example, have large cities that dominate the settlement structure, while in states such as Madhya Pradesh, Orissa, Assam, Bihar, West Bengal, Punjab, and Rajasthan, the pattern is one of urbanization of the countryside in which small towns predominate. The urban centers in the country each interact differently with the spatial structure of the economy and play widely different roles in transforming it. The concentration of population in areas of various density ranges may be seen in Table 4.3.

General Land Use Pattern

About 10 percent of the country's land surface is mountainous, 18.6 percent is under hilly tracts, 27.7 percent under plateaux, and 43 percent falls under plains. The usable area is estimated at about 62 percent of the total land area

Table 4.1
Growth of Urbanization in India

Census Year	Number of Urban Ag- glomerations and Towns	Urban Population (million)	Decadal Growth Rate	Cumulative Growth Rate
1901	1834	25.61	–	
1911	1776	25.58	-0.14	100
1921	1920	27.69	8.25	108
1931	2049	32.97	19.03	129
1941	2216	43.55	32.09	170
1951	2844	61.62	41.49	241
1961	2330	77.56	25.85	303
1971	2531	106.96	37.91	418
1981	3245	156.18	46.02	610

Source: Census of India, 1981.

(Census of India, 1951). The average per capita availability of land (based on the 1981 population count) is 0.480 hectare and that of arable land 0.205 hectare.

From the existing land use data for the year 1975–76, it is known that 92.5 percent of the geographical area has been put to some use; for the remaining 7.5 percent of the land area, no land use statistics are available. The land under forest and agricultural uses accounts for about 75 percent of the known used land area. The land under nonagricultural uses, which also includes land under urban uses, is 5.7 percent of the known used area (Table 4.4).

In a vast country like India, the land use pattern in the individual states and territories varies widely; no generalizations are possible. The issues of land use and population growth are linked. Most of the arable land in the country has

Table 4.2
Annual Growth Rate of Urban Population by Size of Town, 1971–1981

Size Class	No. of towns 1971	Total Population 1971 (in thousands)	Total Population 1981 (in thousands)	Growth Rate Percent per year	Growth Rate Percent over decade
Class I (100,000 and above)	145	60,122	85,801	3.62	42.7
Class II (50,000 to 100,000)	178	12,030	16,874	3.44	40.3
Class III (20,000 to 50,000)	560	17,170	23,712	3.28	38.1
Class IV (10,000 to 20,000)	818	11,656	16,107	3.29	38.2
Class V (Below 10,000)	594	4,300	6,264	3.83	45.6
Total:	2,295	105,278	148,758	3.52	41.3

Note: This Table takes towns according to their classification in 1971 and computes growth rates by comparing the total population of each class in 1971 with the total population of the same towns in 1981, irrespective of their classification in the later census.

Source: Rakesh Mohan, The strategy for housing and urban development: Some new perspectives (mimeograph, June 1982).

64

Table 4.3

Population Concentration and Density Ranges, 1971

Density Range per Square Kilometer	Number of Districts in each Category	Area in Square Kilometers	Percentage of Area in Col.3 to India Total Area	Population (in millions)	Percentage of Population
800 and above	14	17	0.58	28	5.28
501-800	22	101	3.43	60	11.19
201-500	110	740	25.06	232	43.31
101-200	118	1197	40.54	165	30.72
51-100	49	539	18.25	42	7.82
50 and below	26	358	12.14	9	1.68

Source: Census of India, 1971.

Table 4.4

India's Land Use Pattern

(Area million hectares)

Description	1950-51	1960-61	1970-71	1985	2000
1. Area under forest	40.5	54.0	66.0	70.0	70.0
2. Area not available for cultivation	47.5	50.7	45.0	54.0	56.0
(i) Area under non-agricultural uses	-	-	16.2	21.5	26.0
(ii) Barren and uncultivatable land	-	-	29.2	32.5	30.0
3. Other uncultivatable land excluding fallow land	49.4	37.6	33.8	32.5	29.0
(i) Permanent pastures and other grazing land	6.6	13.9	13.3	14.0	15.0
(ii) Land under miscellaneous trees, crops and groves not included	19.8	4.4	4.4	5.0	5.0
(iii) Cultivable wastes	22.9	19.2	16.1	13.5	9.0
4. Fallow land	28.1	22.8	19.7	16.5	13.0
(i) Current fallow	-	-	11.1	9.5	8.0
(ii) Other than current fallow	-	-	8.6	7.0	5.0
5. Net area sown	118.7	133.2	140.4	145.0	150.0
6. Total known used area	284.3	298.5	305.3	318.0	318.0
7. Unknown use area	-	-	22.7	10.0	10.0
Total Geographical Area	328.0	328.0	328.0	328.0	328.0

Sources: 1. National Commission on Agriculture 1976, Ministry of Agriculture & Irrigation, Government of India, for the year 1970-71, 1985 and 2000.
2. Government of India, Planning Commission, Basic Statistics, Relating to Indian Economy for the year 1950-51 and 1960-61.

already been put to use; as there is not much left to be added, the per capita availability of land has begun to decline. Population pressure in turn has brought ecological and environmental problems to the fore. There is a keen awareness of these problems, and India's current development plan is struggling to balance various considerations: economic needs, social goals, and environmental protection.

Urbanization and Land Use

With the growth of urban population, the urban centers have been expanding their physical boundaries. As a result, land use changes and population shifts have also been taking place within urban areas. During the decade 1961–71, for example, while the population added to urban areas was about 30 million, the addition to the total urban land was 0.531 million hectare; the total area under human settlements increased from 1.2 percent in 1961 to 1.8 percent in 1971 (Misra and Bhooshan, 1979). The urban areas have expanded their political limits by annexation of the peripheral areas and the suburbs. Since such annexation is a long process, the urban sprawl of big cities extends into the countryside, causing various problems for land use control (United Nations, 1977).

Land use within the built-up portions of the urban areas is no less problematic. By way of generalization on urban land use patterns, one may say that about 47 percent of the developed land in cities is under residential use, 13 percent under roads and streets, 12 percent in public or semipublic use, and nearly 10 percent under industry and commerce. Only 4 percent of the developed land consists of parks and playgrounds. Most of the towns have a large amount of undeveloped area. In medium and small towns this may account for more than 50 percent of the total area. Except in large cities and metropolitan areas, where segregation of land uses is characteristic, mixed land uses are characteristic in the other towns in the country (Misra and Bhooshan, 1979).

The cities with one million or more people stand apart from other cities in regard to the land use structure. Between 40 to 45 percent of their developed area is under residential uses, 4 to 5 percent under commercial uses, and 6 to 8 percent in industrial uses. Land devoted to public and semipublic uses is directly proportional to population size among the cities in general, and the million cities in particular, though the functional character of the city is important in this respect. Although there is some positive relationship between population size and land devoted to playgrounds and parks, the million cities do not conform to this rule. The reason is that in these cities, the scarcity and high value of land precludes the possibilities of apportioning larger areas for these purposes.

The rate of population growth is always greater than the rate of increase in the urban area, so that there is always an increase in population density within the urban area. In Bangalore city, for example, the city area increased from 53.6 square kilometers with a population of 159,000 in 1901, to 155.4 square kilometers with a population of 1.422 million in 1971. Within this overall population density of 91.4 persons per hectare, the intracity density varied from 4.9 persons to 882.1 persons per hectare (Prakasha Rao and Tewari, 1979). A sample study of 407 towns and cities of India undertaken by the government (Government of India, TCPO, 1979) revealed that more than 50 percent of these towns had an average gross density of fewer than 50 persons per hectare, and about one-third of these towns had densities ranging between 50 and 100 persons per hectare. Thus, for about 87 percent of towns and cities, the gross density is less than 100 persons per hectare. All the towns and cities taken together had an average gross density of 41 persons per hectare; the developed area had a density of 89 and the residential area a density of 249 persons per hectare, that is, a ratio of 1:2.2:6.0 (Table 4.5). Thus the range of variation in gross developed area and residential area densities is very wide. Although about one-fourth of the urban population is living under ward densities ranging from 250 to 1,000 persons per hectare, about 2.5 percent of the urban population is living under very high ward densities of about 1,000 persons per hectare. These averages sometimes hide more than they reveal. Some of the highest spot densities—more than 12,355 persons per hectare—have been reported in the metropolitan cities of Calcutta, Bombay, Delhi, and Ahmedabad.

The density gradient patterns in Indian cities differ considerably and it is not possible to make any simple generalizations on the subject. Four patterns have been identified (Brush, 1968). The first group comprises those cities where the highest density of population is found in a compact central area; examples are Ahmedabad and Poona. The second group has a density pattern resembling that of Western cities, where the density in central areas is low, as in Calcutta, Bombay, and Madras. The third group represents cities with dual city centers of high densities, such as Bangalore and Hyderabad. The fourth group comprises planned cities where the density is low throughout the urban area with little concentration in the central areas, as in Jamshedpur and Chandigarh.

Sharp differences exist among the core, intermediate, and peripheral areas of cities in terms of density, residential housing, and living conditions. In Bangalore city, it was observed that the population density in the core (368 persons per hectare) was more than five times that in the periphery (69 persons per hectare). The density of houses also declined in the same ratio from core to periphery. The other characteristics that showed a similar declining pattern from core to periphery were percentage of workers in trade and commerce, percentage of population in low-income and middle-income groups, percentage of Muslims, and percentage of rented houses. The percentage of population in the high-income group, percentage of Brahmins (high castes), rent per dwelling, percentage of households who used gas or electricity for cooking, percentage of households who owned a refrigerator, and percentage of households with independent toilet facilities were higher in intermediate and peripheral zones than in the core. It was observed that the city core acquired a special character by its centripetal pull and dominance over the periphery owing mainly to the high concentration of workplaces, financial institutions, higher-order shopping areas,

Table 4.5

Average Gross, Developed Area, and Residential Area Densities of Population by Size-Range of Towns and Cities

Size-range (Population in '000s)	Average Gross Density	Developed Area Density	Residential Area Density	Ratio of	
				Developed Area Density to Gross Density	Residential Area Density to Gross Density
1000 & above	75	118	414	1.6	5.5
500-1000	74	143	431	1.9	5.8
100-500	53	100	249	1.9	4.7
100 & above	58	108	286	1.9	4.9
50-100	37	64	172	1.7	4.6
20-50	21	61	190	2.9	9.0
Below 20	10	47	206	4.9	20.0
Below 100	23	60	183	2.6	8.0
All Size-Ranges	41	89	249	2.2	6.0

Source: Govt. of India, Town and Country Planning Organisation, Urban Land Use and Density Patterns in India, June, 1979 (Mimeograph).

educational institutions, transport terminals, hospitals, and recreational and cultural centers. On the other hand, the periphery was characterized by higher levels of good housing and living conditions than that in the core and intermediate zones (Prakasha Rao, 1983). Some typical residential densities in the central, intermediate, and peripheral sections in different size groups of selected Indian cities may be seen in Table 4.6.

Evolution of Land Use Goals and Planning Policies

The planning of towns, villages, and cities in India dates back to ancient times (Vedic times, as early as 3000 B.C.). A glance at the ancient treatises on town administration and architecture such as the Vastu Shastra, Manasara, and Kautilya's Artha Shastra indicates how scientifically, even in the early ages, the problems of town planning were studied. According to Lanchester, "It will probably be a revelation to modern architects to know how scientifically the problems of town planning are treated in the ancient Indian Architectural treatises. Beneath the great deal of mysticism, which may be scoffed at as pure superstition, there is a foundation of sound common-sense and a scientific knowledge which would appeal to the European" (1918, 63).

According to Patrick Geddes, the town planning principles laid down are "evidence of planned, organised and orderly life of all people in village, town and city alike" (Tyrwhitt, 1947, 22). It should be noted, however, that the traditional and hereditary character of the science did not prejudice its evolution and progress and grafting of new techniques and ideas. Knowledge of town planning was as extensive as it was intensive. Even the laymen knew something of the subject, as is evident from the descriptions of the towns contained in ancient literature. There was a strong civic pride and highly developed civic consciousness. The social status of civic architects was high.

The scope of Indian town planning included descriptions of markets, streets and lanes, ditches, temples, royal palaces and public buildings, housing for citizens, recreational centers, water supply for drinking and for cattle, and pleasure gardens. Descriptions of well-planned towns on record today include Ayodhya, Indraprastha, Pataliputra, Madura, Vamji (Karur), Kanchipuram, and Kaverippumpattinam. These towns were planned in a scientific manner, with specific areas earmarked for different trades and uses, such as markets, handicrafts, professions, and the military, and were provided with the necessary amenities for town life.

Village Planning

Although the general principles governing the planning of an Indo-Aryan house, village, and town are the same, the Vastu Shastra treats the village in a fuller way than even the towns. The difference between a village and a town is that the latter is artificial and the former is a natural unit. Hence, nature plays

Table 4.6

Typical Residential Densities in the Central, Intermediate, and Peripheral Areas of Selected Towns and Cities

Size of City Population	Name of the town/city	Density in Persons Per Hectare		
		Central Area	Intermediate Area	Peripheral Areas
1	2	3	4	5
1 million and above	Delhi	618-2471	123- 618	62-185
	Madras	370- 988	123- 370	49-123
	Bombay	1483-3459	247-1483	247-494
500,000 to one million	Bangalore	370-1730	185- 370	62-185
	Kanpur	370-1977	185- 370	37-185
	Howrah	618-1359	247- 618	148-247
200,000 to 500,000	Jaipur	247- 865	123- 247	49-123
	Luchiana	370-1235	123- 370	74-123
	Trivendrum	247- 432	123- 247	37-123
	Patna	247- 494	123- 247	49-123
100,000 to 200,000	Bhopal	247- 618	123- 247	49-123
	Gaya	247- 494	123- 247	49-123
	Mangalore	185- 247	62- 185	27-183
	Ranchi	123- 185	74- 123	37- 74
50,000 to 100,000	Junagarh	185- 370	62- 185	12- 62
	Broach	123- 247	62- 123	37- 62
	Trichur	74- 123	49- 74	27- 49
20,000 to 50,000	Kolar Town	185- 247	74- 185	49- 74
	Rajpipla	99- 148	74- 99	49- 74
	Wardha	247- 494	74- 123	27- 74
20,000 and below	Phaltan	185- 243	-	-
	Jharsignda	37- 74	-	-
	Devargh-Beria	5- 43	-	-

Source: Government of India, Ministry of Works & Housing, Report on Urban and Regional Planning in India, 1966.

Note: In the original source, the density was in persons per acre which has been converted into density in persons per hectare.

an important role in rural life. While a town can be composed of mainly congregated buildings, one next to another, the village can be like a garden interspersed with dwellings.

In the Manasara the following eight types of villages are described, classified according to shape, methods of street planning, folk planning, and temple planning (see figures 4.1 to 4.8, from Rame Gowda, 1972):

1. Dandaka
2. Chaturmukha
3. Nandyavarta
4. Padmaka
5. Sarvathobhadra
6. Swastika
7. Prastara
8. Karmuka

During the pre-Mughal and Mughal (1526–1857 A.D.) periods, the Muslim rulers had to establish a few new towns. Most of these bear the influence of traditional town planning in India. As such, this period makes no special contribution to the science of town planning, except the splendor that was associated with them can be emphasized. Mughal towns such as Delhi, Lucknow, and Lahore were built with spacious courts, pleasure gardens, water fountains, and rich decorations. The emphasis, however, was on the royal palaces, courts, and religious buildings; the town dwellers were left to themselves to get on as best as they could. Although the contribution of the Mughals to town planning was little, their contribution to architecture was substantial through the construction of such monuments as the famous Taj Mahal. Like the Romans, the Mughals wanted to show their power and pomp by constructing monumental structures for the use of the royal families, which was at the cost to other citizens.

During the last three centuries many new towns have been planned and built by the rulers of princely states. Examples are the cities of Jaipur, Udaipur, Hyderabad, Baroda, and Mysore.

Like the Mughals, the British concentrated more on the preservation of their power in India. Unlike the Mughals, they lived an exclusive life, quite separate from that of the local people. They built many cantonment towns on the basis of town planning principles practiced in England. They did not seriously address the town planning problems of and find solutions suitable to local conditions. The cantonments were built outside existing cities, such as Delhi, Agra, Ambala, Lahore, Poona, Hyderabad, Bangalore, and many others, keeping wide greenbelts between the native town and the British town.

Calcutta was developed as the capital of India before New Delhi was built as a new capital city by British planners, architects, and engineers. They introduced municipal regulations and constituted municipalities for the cities in India to improve the health and environment of the native towns. Although they did not

Figure 4.1 Dandaka Type of Town Plan

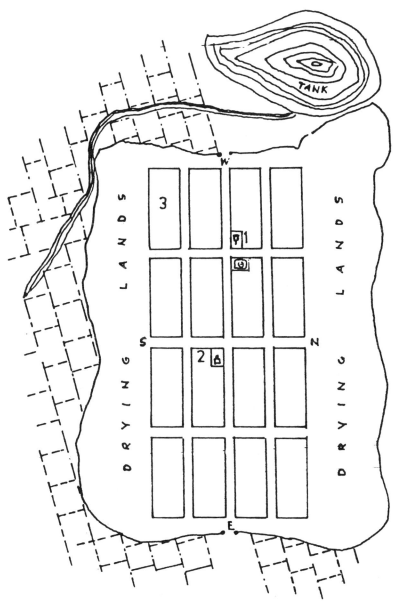

1) Vishnu Temple
2) Siva Temple
3) Monastery

Figure 4.2 Chaturmukha Type of Town Plan

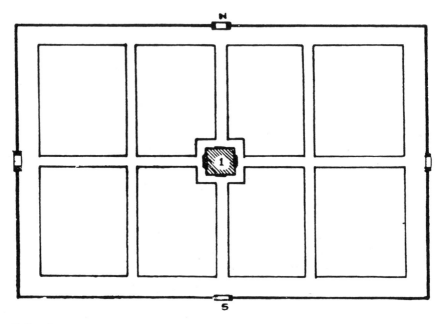

1) Temple

encourage large-scale industrial development, a few industrial towns grew during their times. They established new institutions such as universities, railways, and postal services, and organized water supply and sewerage systems in Indian cities. They introduced new methods of appraising a city's problems, but these were mostly copied from their experience back home (Rame Gowda, 1972).

In the early twentieth century, attempts were made by engineers, social administrators, and enlightened rulers to improve towns and villages with a view to providing adequate amenities and services. New Delhi, formerly the imperial capital, Baroda, and Mysore even now called the garden cities, are examples of improved towns planned in the early twentieth century.

The method of the military engineer was somewhat drastic: indiscriminate street widening or running straight roads through built-up areas, a practice that disrupted the social structure in the existing communities, so as to make the roads suitable for the movement of troops and other security personnel. It ignored almost wholly the human aspects of urban life.

It was under such circumstances that Sir Patrick Geddes (1854–1932) was invited to India in 1915 by Lord Pentland, the governor of Madras, to advise on the problems involved in the relationships between public improvements and recognized social standards, which appeared at first sight to be in conflict with each other. In his proposals for Indian towns, Geddes's practice was to reduce

Figure 4.3 Nandyavarta Type of Town Plan

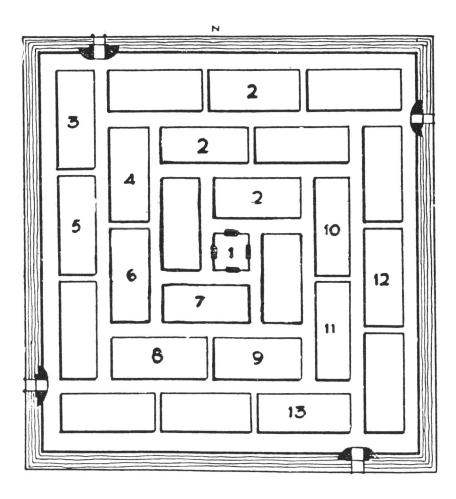

1) Siva or Vishnu Temple
2) Brahmin Quarters
3) School, college, etc.
4) Palace
5) Hospital
6) Court
7) Tank
8) Monastery
9) and 10) Residences for
   other castes
11) Artists Residences
12) Theatre, etc.
13) Quarters for fishermen and hunters

Figure 4.4 Padmaka Type of Town Plan

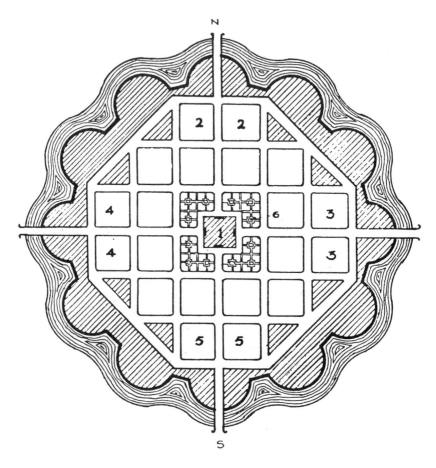

1) Temple
2) Palace
3) Shops and Vegetable Stalls
4) Meat Market
5) Shops for Other Articles
6) Tank

the number of street widenings and to reduce the amounts expended on elaborate mechanical sanitary facilities. With the money he saved, he proposed to increase the number of gardens and playgrounds, to plant fruit trees, and to retain in an effectively sanitary state the existing village water tanks. Patrick Geddes, through his teaching and the many illustrations he provided of ''folk-place-work'' planning following a proper diagnostic survey of the area, opened a new era of planning in India. This mode of planning challenged the ideals of officials; it was conceived in terms of primary human needs and not from current business

Figure 4.5 Sarvathobhadra Type of Town Plan

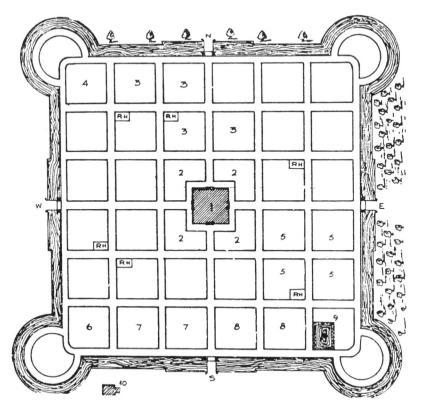

1) Temple
2) Brahmins
3) Sudras and Others
4) College
5) Weavers, cloth merchants, physicians, etc.

6) Hospital
7) Workmen's houses
8) Workshops
9) Monastery
10) Chamundi or Kali Temple
RH: Rest Houses

and engineering conventions. "Planning," Geddes wrote, "is not mere place-planning nor even work-planning. If it is to be successful, it must be folk planning" (Tyrwhitt, 1947, introduction). His method of diagnostic survey and application of conservative surgery is amply illustrated in the many improvement schemes he proposed for towns, which include Tanjore, Madura, Balrampur, Lucknow, and Indore.

The current efforts of town and country planners in the country are aimed toward establishing a happy and harmonious relationship between the urban and rural areas and providing in each of them an environment for living that is physically, emotionally, and aesthetically satisfactory to both the individual and the country. A stable economic hierarchy is being sought, with the village as

Figure 4.6 Swastika Type of Town Plan

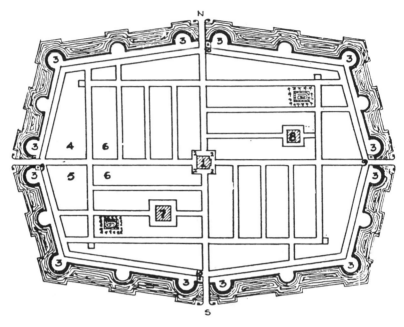

1) Siva or Vishnu Temple   6) Court and Office
2) Agraharam   7) Jain Temple
3) Armoury   8) Buddhist or Saraswati Temple
4) King's Palace   9) Ganesha Temple
5) Yuvaraja's Palace   10) Kali Temple

the basic primary unit and the metropolitan city at the apex of the hierarchy, with each unit complementing and supplementing others in social, economic, and physical relationships.

Evolution of Urban Land Use Planning

Prior to independence, the different states of the country had different provisions for town planning measures, either under the municipal acts or under special enactments such as City Improvement Trust Acts or Town Planning Acts. Only after independence did states think in terms of evolving a common policy on town and country planning matters.

With the growth of urban problems, the municipalities failed to respond to the changing situations. The work involved in planning, improvement, and extension of towns was so complex and great that the municipalities were unable to carry on this work effectively. It was in this context that certain enlightened states enacted special laws to tackle these problems more effectively. These special enactments give some idea of the measures taken and the efforts made

Figure 4.7 Prastara Type of Town Plan

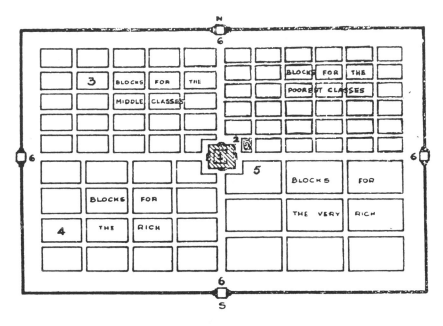

1) Siva or Vishnu Temple   4) Hospital
2) The Temple Tank   5) Monastery
3) College   6) Gates

by government, though in a limited way, to improve the living conditions of the people in urban areas and to guide the future growth of the urban centers in a planned manner.

Except for the states that had enacted special town planning acts, the other states in the country had to depend on the legal provisions contained in various city corporation acts, municipal acts, city improvement acts, village *panchayat* acts, cantonment board acts, and so on for the development of urban and rural areas.

The creation of improvement trusts in the cities of Bombay (1898) and Calcutta (1911) and some of the towns of the state of Uttar Pradesh in 1919 no doubt led to some improvements, such as the execution of remunerative schemes, for example, of markets and new expansions. But since the improvement trusts and so on were more concerned with the development of new areas, neglecting the development and redevelopment of older areas of the city, there was further deterioration in the urban environment.

In the preindependence period, no specific policies or strategies guided or influenced urban development or urbanization. The country was divided into presidency states, territories under the rule of the princes and centrally admin-

Figure 4.8 Karmuka Type of Town Plan

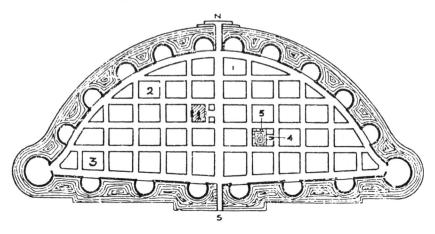

1) Siva or Vishnu Temple
2) College
3) Hospital

4) Monastery
5) Tank

istered areas. It was thus hardly possible to think of any overall policy for the growth of towns and cities. In some of the princely states, however, such as Mysore, Hyderabad, Jaipur, and Gwalior, the state administrations had a limited program for improving the cities, allowing them to expand on their peripheries, for which they undertook a number of town extension schemes. They also established new residential areas adjacent to industrial enterprises set up in the resource rich areas, such as the coal mines belt.

In the presidency states, a program for town improvement was underway, concentrating on town expansion and civic improvement. New industrial expansions did give rise to labor colonies near Bombay and Calcutta. The development of these colonies was not governed by any overall strategy, and it was mainly the economics of industry that decided the location and planning of such colonies. Although new industrial cities, for example, Jamshedpur and Kanpur, were built during this period, they were isolated instances and did not play any role in influencing the pattern of urbanization in the surrounding region. At the same time, they attracted uncontrolled slums in their immediate periphery, which even today pose a serious problem.

The period 1947–51 brought with it pressing problems of rehabilitation and settlement of displaced people from Pakistan. This initiated certain programs directed toward urban settlements. A number of refugee townships were built. Initially they were conceived as residential suburbs but subsequently planned as self-contained townships providing employment opportunities in industry, trade, and commerce.

India's first national plan (1951–56) placed emphasis on the rehabilitation of refugees by augmenting housing stock and linking housing to be on a sound footing with town and country planning principles. The second plan (1956–61), however, considered three problem areas: methods of securing planned development in urban areas, expansion of housing facilities, and development of civic administration along sound and progressive lines.

The third five year plan (1961–66) broadened the scope of urban planning. It considered urbanization as an important aspect of the process of economic and social development and closely connected with many other problems, such as the migration from villages to towns, standards of living in rural and urban areas, relative costs of providing economic and social services in towns of varying sizes, provision of housing for different sections of the population, and provision of facilities such as water supply, sanitation, transport, and power. The influence on the pattern of economic development of the location and dispersal of industries, the strengthening of civic administration, and the planning of land uses also received considerable attention. The plan was instrumental in the preparation of master plans for 72 major cities and their surrounding areas, including industrial centers and some of the rapidly growing regions of the country. It was during this period that the regional master plans for the metropolitan cities of Delhi, Calcutta, and greater Bombay were initiated. It is only since 1961 that a policy for guiding urbanization has taken deeper root at both the state and national levels. During the third plan period the policy of controlling urban land values through public acquisition of land, the physical planning of the use of land, the definition of minimum levels of services and standards, and the strengthening of urban administration were advocated and appropriate measures taken in this direction.

The fourth five year plan (1969–74) laid more emphasis on the dispersal of population to achieve a more even spatial distribution of economic activities. The stress was on controlling the growth of metropolitan cities and towns and evolving a national urban policy. There was also an emphasis on social housing, urban water supply and sanitation, land acquisition and development, and the preparation of master plans for selected towns and regions.

The fifth five year plan (1974–79) was aimed at augmenting civic services in urban areas, tackling the problem of metropolitan cities on a regional scale, promoting the development of smaller towns and new urban centers to ease the pressures of urbanization, assisting in the implementation of projects of national importance, and providing support for the enlargement of the functions of the industrial townships undertaken by central government bodies to make them self-contained.

The sixth five year plan (1980–85) recognized the problems of unregulated development and indiscriminate concentration of industries and amenities in small towns and rural areas, the problem of the migration to cities, and the problem of water pollution caused by cattle in urban areas. The plan introduced a policy for the integrated development of small and medium towns so as to provide a buffer against the large metropolitan areas and to act as growth centers for the rural hinterlands.

INSTITUTIONAL AND LANDOWNERSHIP FRAMEWORK

In India's Constitution, Article 19 guarantees certain fundamental rights to all citizens. Clause 1 (f) of this article guarantees the right "to acquire, hold and dispose of property," whereas clause 5 empowers the states to make any law imposing "reasonable restrictions" on the exercise of this particular right in the interest of the general public. There is another provision in Article 31 that no person "shall be deprived of his property save by authority of law" and that

no property shall be compulsorily acquired or requisitioned save for a public purpose and save by authority of a law which provides for compensation for the property so acquired or requisitioned and no such law shall be called in question in any court on the ground that the compensation provided by that law is not adequate.

But in spite of these articles and the explicit provision that no law relating to compulsory acquisition for a public purpose shall be questioned in any court on the grounds of the amount of compensation not being adequate, the highest courts in the country have either struck down payments that fall short of market value, or have granted stay orders.

Land Expropriation and Planning Laws

A number of central and state acts pertain to the acquisition of land for public use. The town and country planning law, which basically refers to land, is administered by the state. Suitable machinery at the state level has also been developed to administer it. Planning legislation in India had its beginning in the town planning and the improvement trust acts, municipal acts, peripheral ribbon development control acts, and restriction of land use acts and later from new legislation such as development authority acts, slum clearance and housing boards acts, regulation of building operations acts, water and sewerage board acts, prevention of water pollution acts, urban land ceiling acts, and urban arts commission acts (Balachandran and Haldipur, 1980).

Since the emergence of the Indian Republic in 1950, with a constitution that guaranteed every citizen the fundamental right to hold property, certain provisions in the early town and country planning acts required revision. Moreover, the old enactments were not sufficiently comprehensive. The Institute of Town Planners, India, the accredited professional body in the country, had drafted a model town planning act as early as 1957 and had circulated it among the states for adoption. The central government at this stage established the Town and Country Planning Organization, which scrutinised and further revised the model act. This act has guided the state governments in India since 1961 in making revisions in their respective enactments. The model act provided only for plan making and had no provisions for plan implementation. Later, it was supplemented by other model legislations, each providing for the acquisition of land for planning and development, and the setting up of development authorities to undertake large-scale urban development and work, relating to the provision of life-support systems for urban living.

Some of the states felt that common legislation providing for plan making and plan implementation, as well as land acquisition and development, was required immediately. This was realized in the Bombay Town Planning Act of 1954. But the Bombay act, like similar other acts, visualized the preparation of a city master plan by local authorities whose powers were limited to the area over which the authority had jurisdiction; unfortunately, some of the most serious planning problems existed not only within the city limits but outside its boundaries. Problems such as land development, transportation, and utilities and services transgress municipal boundaries. These discrepancies that exist between the legal city boundaries and the natural boundaries of communities that require planning have still to be remedied, particularly in metropolitan areas.

The Central Land Acquisition Act of 1894 is the oldest and by far the most important legislation; it forms the basis of land acquisition under almost all subsequent central or state acts. Under section 4 of this act, a notification in the official gazette is issued for acquisition for public purpose. The act, however, does not define public purpose but gives wide discretion to the executive to interpret this concept. The courts of the land have taken a liberal view of the concept. After notification is issued by the government, the collector makes the intent of acquisition known to the public through a notice displayed at a convenient place in the locality. Within 30 days of the issuance of the preliminary notification, the public may file objections to the intended acquisition. After considering the objections, the government declares its decision to acquire the notified land under section 6 of the Land Acquisition Act. Claims to rights and interests in the property and compensation from the affected parties are then invited. The collector conducts inquiries and assesses the amount of compensation, which is then awarded to the parties concerned. He subsequently takes possession of the land, which thereafter vests absolutely in the government. Under sections 23 and 24, compensation is determined as the market value of the land on the date of notification. The valuation generally becomes a matter of dispute until it is settled. In addition to the market value of the land, a *solatium* of 15 percent of the market value of the land in consideration of the compulsory nature of the acquisition has to be paid. This process of land acquisition up to the stage of final possession of land is time-consuming. It takes more than two years, provided there are no appeals or disputes taken to court. In the event of a dispute, the time is prolonged even more, which affects the purpose of land acquisition for public use.

Public participation in decisionmaking is involved only to the extent of inviting public objection to be made within 30 days of the first notification under section 4 of the Land Acquisition Act. No public opinion is gauged beforehand by the authorities entering in the process of land acquisition.

Several issues relating to urban land acquisition policy, including definition of public purpose, methods of expediting the acquisition process, and the payment of compensation, are under consideration by the central government.

Town Planning Legislation and Administration

Since the 1960s, the states have enacted their own town and country planning legislation more or less on the lines of the Model Act suggested by the Central Town and Country Planning Organisation. The Model Act provides for the establishment of a state town and country planning Board to advise the state government on matters relating to town planning and to guide, direct, and assist local planning authorities in the preparation and enforcement of development plans. It permits the designation of a local body as the planning authority. It requires that maps and a register of existing land use be prepared for each planning area. It provides for the preparation of an interim development plan to be followed by a comprehensive development plan. The act provides for public objection and hearings at each stage before the state government's final approval. After the enforcement of the plan, no change in land use is permitted, except with permission of the local authority. It also provides for a levy or development charge for the granting of planning permission. Other provisions have also been made for undertaking planning and control measures to regulate the development plan.

Decisionmaking Structures in the Administration of Land Use Planning

At the apex of the planning machinery is the National Economic Planning Commission, whose main function is to enunciate national policies and formulate five-year plans. The commission's Division of Housing and Urban Development deals with housing, water supply, and urban development. At the union government level, the subject of urban development is under the Ministry of Works, Housing and Urban Development. Within the ministry is the Town and Country Planning Organisation, a central technical advisory organization that advises the central ministries, departments, industrial undertakings, state governments, and local bodies on matters relating to town and country planning. Its other important function is to undertake research and to document urbanization and urban and regional planning problems.

The Town and Country Planning Organisation is gradually carving out its role by conducting studies to aid in major locational and planning decisions taken by various ministries and statutory corporations in the public sector. It prepared the master plan for Delhi and is also attempting to influence developments in the national capital region, which cut across the state boundaries of three states.

In states to which the constitution gave the prime responsibility for town planning, there is typically a town planning department. This department is generally under either the minister of local government or minister of public works. There are various other departments for economic development and planning, housing, public works, medical and public health, education, and so on, each of whose functions directly or indirectly affect urban development. In most states there are state statutory bodies such as housing boards, state electricity boards, and industrial development corporations. The town planning departments in the states are gradually expanding their role and are emerging as effective instruments to coordinate actions in the matters of urban planning and development.

At the local level, too, various organizational and administrative arrangements have emerged during the last decade. In metropolitan cities, special organizations or development authorities have been set up; for instance, the state of West Bengal has the Calcutta Metropolitan Development Authority and the Durgapur Development Authority, both statutory bodies. In Maharashtra the state government has established the City and Industrial Development Corporation to implement the new metro-center project in Bombay. In Delhi there is the Delhi Development Authority that was set up under the Delhi Development Act, enacted by parliament in 1957. This authority is statutorily responsible for the preparation, revision, and interpretation of the master plan and the zonal plans for Delhi and their implementation in development areas so declared under the act. This is one of the most active and viable urban development authorities in the country. Its plan is actually being enforced and, in addition, has been operating a massive land development and disposal program.

MAJOR CHALLENGES

The existing urban planning and development laws, numbering about 164, in force in India suffer from many gaps and deficiencies due to lack of proper linkages in various legal and juridical structures, overlapping of functions and jurisdictions, emphasis on plan preparation rather than implementation and execution, inadequacy of the effective provisions under the Land Acquisition Act of 1894, legal inadequacy for checking haphazard development, peripheral growth, and ribbon development, lack of provisions for organizing plan implementation, and lack of effective public participation.

The right to own property is one of the basic social values, as is the acquisition of land for public purpose. The various land control measures, which fall broadly under land use planning, land development, and taxation, suffer from the weakness of defective planning practices and/or administrative deficiencies, with the result that whatever plans or planning schemes are prepared never get implemented. During the last three decades as many as 615 development master plans have been prepared for various towns and cities in India, but hardly 1 or 2 percent of these plans has been executed. The emphasis has been solely on plan preparation. No attempts have been made to spell out the requisite tools of plan implementation (United Nations, 1977).

Apart from the gaps and deficiencies in legislation are other important challenges to be faced, as outlined in the following sections.

Urbanization Policy

There is no comprehensive urbanization policy to guide land use planning, with the result that locational coordination of investments is ineffective. There is no effective policy to control the population size of cities. Although there is some negative control on the further expansion of large metropolitan cities, there are no positive policies for guiding the location of major investments and the promotion of industrial agglomerations on sound lines. As part of the urbanization policy, it is also necessary to have policies to regulate migration. Solutions such as the development of countermagnets around fast-growing metropolitan cities and land reforms to encourage the rural population to stay in rural areas have not worked satisfactorily in India. The failure in the nonimplementation or partial implementation of land reforms and the wrong location of countermagnets may be cited as examples. Similarly in metropolitan areas, policies meant to improve slum conditions have not been adequate. Here both short-term (for improving housing and substandard living conditions) and long-term measures (for imparting education and improvement of skills) are necessary. In short, the absence of an effective and comprehensive urbanization policy has to be identified as a major constraint for effective land use planning.

Metropolitan Problems

Jurisdictional fragmentation with unequal levels in the administrative hierarchy has posed serious problems in planning and development in the metropolitan areas. The classic example is that of the Calcutta Metropolitan District, which has an area of 1,269 square kilometers and includes three municipal corporations, 31 municipal towns, 32 nonmunicipal towns, one notified area authority, and 450 rural *mauzas*, or small village clusters. An area-wide metropolitan governmental structure coupled with a second tier of service authorities to ensure a differentiation of tasks within an integrated administrative frame has been suggested as an approach to the solution. Problems in implementing such a structure remain.

Physical Planning Performance Standards

The problem of physical planning standards, both normative and regulatory, and the question of survival standards for housing and community facilities, particularly in squatter settlements and slums, have received considerable attention during the last two decades. The phase of master plan preparation without the parallel development of implementation machinery, which took place in the 1960s, brought to focus the need for developing indigenous standards close to human preferences. The need for approaching the standards problems in a variety of city frameworks in which a varying mix of factors are operating has been recognized. Separate sets of standards have evolved for (1) metropolitan cities, (2) medium and small towns, (3) industrial towns and new towns, (4) market towns, and (5) slum and squatter settlements. Additionally building bylaws have been standardized, and a national building code has emerged (Sundaram, 1977).

Rural-Urban Fringe

In metropolitan cities and rapidly developing cities, a new zone, the city fringe, is emerging, which is recognized neither by the city authority nor by the rural *panchayats*. This area has tended to become a problem zone. It is not only a zone of rapid population growth, consisting mainly of nonagricultural population employed in the city, but is also characterized by mixed land use and occupational structures. The introduction of broad-based regional planning covering both rural and urban areas and the creation of ''Rurban'' authorities to act as a buffer between the metropolitan authority and the rural *panchayats* will promote more orderly development in such areas (Naidu, 1979).

Urban Village

A majority of Indian cities and towns have sizable pockets of agricultural and vacant (undeveloped) land within them, where some cultivation is also carried on. Apart from this rural use characterizing the unbuilt areas, one also finds within the built-up areas of the Indian city relict villages, which were absorbed into the urban area during the course of urban expansion. The extension of the city engulfed these villages, taking away their agricultural land for urban use and bringing about a radical change in the economic base of their communities, though their physical patterns and social values have changed but little in a relative sense. Such urban villages pose serious problems in redevelopment planning and call for a policy of gradual assimilation and integration of physical and social development (Sundaram, 1977).

Urban Land and Property Values

The urban land and property market in India is so affected by a host of regulations, such as rent control legislation, building bylaws, and other controls, that it is highly segmented, and there are many temptations for concealing actual land and property values. The promulgation of an urban land ceiling has exacerbated this problem. There is also direct participation by the government in the urban land market through large-scale acquisition, development, and disposal of land. In this context, a large amount of unauthorized housing activity has occurred, which is characterized by a large number of illegal and unreported transactions.

APPROACHES TO LAND USE PLANNING

The organic interdependence of locations in harmony with nature, to maintain the human environmental balance, was stressed in the Vedic traditions of land use planning, which placed emphasis on spacing of buildings and siting. The organic unity of humans and nature in a pollution-free environment was the basic philosophy of Vedic tradition (Wishwakarma, 1981a). The formal concept of town planning that has developed initially as an instrument for the control of land use pattern has followed segregative and pathological approaches. The development of comprehensive plans and the regulation of land use are viewed as two separate, if not interdependent, activities.

Considerable thinking on land use planning to incorporate the goals of the communities has resulted from the preparation of the Delhi master plan (1961–81). It estimated population growth and propounded the idea of advance land acquisition for the probable growth of the city within urbanizable limits over a period of 20 years, housing needs, density standards, land use space requirements, development of Delhi as a multinodal city with 15 business centers, and restricting its growth by the development of ring towns around Delhi as countermagnets. The further growth of industries was to be restricted, and the old city was to be "decongested." These ideas have dominated the thinking on urban land use planning since they were first advanced. But these approaches are basically physical land use plans characterized by a relatively strict separation of land uses. Following British town planning, statutory plans had assumed high space standards beyond affordable limits. Also there was seldom a linking with investment planning, and hardly any statutory machinery was devised to link these plans with the national- and state-level plans.

The idea of developing ring towns as countermagnets has met with little success. In addition to the specific investment programs devoted to the development of state capital projects, substantial investment funds have also gone into the World Bank–aided urban development projects in Calcutta, Madras, and Kanpur. These projects are concerned merely with how far down the income distribution scale the projects were expected to reach and thus to provide improved housing for the urban poor. The earlier thinking on slum clearance and their rehabilitation has changed. State and city administrators all over India are now adopting an approach to preserve and develop this vast housing stock, albeit of poor quality, and to create conditions in which the slum communities themselves can upgrade their environment and integrate with the rest of the urban fabric. It is also being realized that slums are not merely places; slums involve people (Government of India, 1980). Associated with this are the sites and services projects for assisting the urban poor to obtain shelter. But these projects have been popular only in a few metropolitan cities such as Calcutta, Delhi, and Madras.

The gradual expansion of the capital base of towns and cities has resulted in more pressing demands for urban space for the location of offices, residential houses, factories and workshops, banks, insurance and financial institutions, airports, harbors, and a network of transport facilities, including parking sites. The capital budget programs incorporating these activities lack the effective controls of subdivision and zoning regulations to prevent further deterioration of the urban environment. The emphasis therefore has shifted from one plan to another, each introducing new approaches and innovations in the methods of urban development. The integrated approach is another offshoot of such developments. Integrated urban development projects that encompass many of the components of transport improvement, public utility systems, and provision of basic social services therefore are now the rule under the plans. The fifth five year plan contains an integrated urban development program, particularly for the cities of over 300,000 population. The idea has been extended to the integrated development of small and medium towns to cover the towns with less than 100,000 population, as enunciated in the sixth five year plan.

FUTURE THRUSTS

Attempts are being made to remove the deficiencies that arise out of a narrow definition and static conception of urban development by adopting a wider regional approach with an accent on integrated rural-urban development. But by and large, the physical approach to planning has been practiced in isolation from the mainstream of national and state social and economic planning. The need is to have an integrated outlook, preparing programs of capital budgets, and effective controls on subdivision and zoning regulations in order to prevent further deterioration of the urban environment and living conditions (Sah, 1971).

The growth of urbanization superimposes certain changes. The impact on economic development leads to the gradual expansion of the capital base of the towns and cities amid improvements in productivity, employment, and income levels. There is a chain reaction that leads to demand for office space, factories, workshops, banks and financial institutions, harbors, airports and communication systems, roads and transport, and parking (Sah, 1971). The existing methods of development planning, control measures, planning standards, and building bylaws/regulations with few exceptions do not cater to the growing needs of urbanization. Moreover, they are outdated, specification oriented, and lack uniformity in approach. They neither reflect the latest trends in building designs and construction techniques nor is there any scope for innovative experimentations. They are basically elitist in character.

In recent years some efforts have been made at the national level to rationalize and unify the existing provisions of development control rules, planning standards, and building bylaws with specific reference to housing for economically weaker sections. The 1978 National Building Code has become a model for various state governments, municipal corporations, and municipalities for revamping existing regulatory documents.

It has been observed that the approval of a large number of housing schemes is held up by the respective local bodies because of archaic and outdated provisions in the operative development control rules and building bylaws. This is more so in regard to minimum size of plots; the layout and subdivision requirements in terms of plotted development schemes (detached, semidetached, and row housing pattern), group housing schemes, and cluster planning in which a higher density of development is envisaged; and the requirements of technological changes in the design specifications and services for building.

It has also been felt that there is a need to revise the building bylaws and development control rules due to the specific problems of the old built-up areas. The control of housing construction and alterations in the existing built-up areas requires a separate strategy compared to the regulations for development activity in new areas.

It has been recognized that the planning of urban development should essentially be supportive of economic development to the nation, state, or subregion, whether it is in agriculture, extractive industries, manufacturing industry, or the service sectors. The provision of urban services and infrastructure resources is a constraint to the growth of these sectors. But the existing imbalance between resource availability and functions assigned to local bodies for providing services and infrastructure is a serious problem and needs to be corrected. The way to integrate master plans with economic plans is to bring the master plans within the framework of the regional resources development plans. These plans have not been effective tools of implementation because they lacked programming and budgeting linked to the availability of resources; thus they have acted more as negative instruments of control. Realizing these constraints, it is suggested that comprehensive legislation be enacted that could integrate economic development with settlement planning.

Zoning regulations that have found widespread acceptance as a means of providing public control over land development and subdivision regulations that prescribe minimum requirements to be met primarily through development on the fringe of urban areas are valid only when they help substantially in protecting health, safety, and welfare and providing amenities. The Model Act suggested by the central government, as well as the Delhi and Bombay acts, should be made to cater to the needs of zoning and subdivision regulations as part of statutory comprehensive development plans. In this way zoning and subdivision regulations can be integrated into development plans so that they can conform to the overall land use pattern. It is also necessary to dovetail building bylaws with other land use regulations. Thus, wherever the development functions of municipal authorities are taken over by development authorities, explicit relationships between varying life-styles and the set of building bylaws operating in the city should be established.

Land use planning could be made more effective by direct measures of allocating land to different groups and by indirect methods for curbing land speculation and encouraging the private supply of developed land. The policy could become more effective if, in land readjustment schemes, the original owners of the acquired land were compensated by returning a portion of the serviced developed land to them. The public authorities should also have the right of preemptive purchase in the cases of positive development. Although tools and techniques are essential, research needs to be promoted, and better training should be provided. More efficient mechanisms of implementation should be evolved through a sound framework of policies based on scientific knowledge and technological thinking ''without alienating people from their heritage and without de-spoiling nature of its beauty, freshness and purity so essential to our lives'' (India, Habitat–76).

BIBLIOGRAPHY

Ayyar, C. P. V. 1916. *Town Planning in Ancient Deccan*. Madras: Law Print House.
Balachandran, M. K., and R. N. Haldipur. 1980. Legislation Relating to Town Planning and Development Authorities. Mimeo.
Brush, J. E. 1968. Spatial Pattern of Population in Indian Cities. *Geographical Review* 58.
Census of India. 1951, 1971, 1981.
Datta, A., ed. 1980. *Municipal and Urban India*. New Delhi: Centre for Urban Studies, Indian Institute of Public Administration.
Dutt, B. B. 1925. *Town Planning in Ancient India*. Calcutta: Thacker, Spink & Company. (Second edition, 1977. New Delhi: New Asia Publishers.)
Government of India. 1980. Housing Stock—Third Session of the United Nations Conference held in Mexico. New Delhi: Department of Science and Technology.
Government of India. Ministry of Finance. Department of Economic Affairs. 1971. *Pocket Book of Economic Information*. New Delhi.
Government of India. Ministry of Works and Housing. 1982. Report of the Study Group on Town Planning and Building Regulations. New Delhi. Mimeo.
Government of India. Planning Commission. 1973. *Basic Statistics Relating to the Indian Economy, 1950–51 to 1970–71*. New Delhi.
Government of India. Planning Commission. 1983. Report of Task Forces on Housing and Urban Development, Planning of Urban Development. September. New Delhi. Mimeo.
Government of India. Town and Country Planning Organization. 1979. Urban Land Use and Density Patterns in India, New Delhi. June. Mimeo.
Government of India. Town and Country Planning Organization. 1962. *Town and Country Planning in India*. New Delhi: Ministry of Health.
Government of India. Town and Country Planning Organization. 1967. Land Use Pattern of India's Towns and Cities. New Delhi. Mimeo.
Habitat–76. 1976. India, The United Nations Conference on Human Settlements, Vancouver, 31 May–11 June.
Indian Society of Agricultural Economics. 1957. *Readings in Land Utilisation*. Bombay.

Indian Standards Institute. 1970. *National Building Code of India*. New Delhi: Manak Bhawan. Document No. UDC 969–001(540).

Indian Standards Institute. 1978. *National Building Code of India*. New Delhi: Manak Bhawan. Document No. 15:888.

Jagmohan. 1975. *Rebuilding Shahjahanabad: The Walled City of Delhi*. New Delhi: Vikas.

Kabra, K. N. 1976. *Urban Land and Housing Policies, Ceilings and Socialisátion*. New Delhi: Peoples Publishing House.

Lanchester, H. V. 1918. *Town Planning in Madras. A Review of Conditions and Requirements of the City Improvement and Development*. London: Constable Co.

Mandal, R. B. 1982. *Land Utilisátion: Theory and Practice*. New Delhi: Concept.

Misra, R. P., ed. 1978. *Million Cities in India*. New Delhi: Vikas.

Misra, R. P., ed. 1979. *Habitat Asia: Issues and Perspectives*. New Delhi: Concept.

Misra, R. P., and B. S. Bhooshan. 1979. *Human Settlements in Asia*. New Delhi: Public Policies and Programmes Heritage.

Misra, R. P., K. V. Sundaram, and V. L. S. Prakasha Rao. 1976. *Regional Development Planning in India: A New Strategy*, New Delhi: Vikas.

Naidu, Ratna. 1979. Organisational Structure of Hyderbad Urban Development Authority: Problems and Prospects. *Nagarlok* 11(2), April-June.

Prakasha Rao, V. L. S. 1983. *Urbanization in India: Spatial Dimensions*. New Delhi: Concept.

Prakasha Rao, V. L. S., and K. V. Sundaram. 1974. Delhi. *Encyclopaedia Brittanica* 15th edition.

Prakasha Rao, V. L. S., and Y. K. Tewari. 1979. *The Structure of an Indian Metropolis: A Study of Bangalore*. New Delhi: Allied Publishers.

Rame Gowda, K. S. 1972. *Urban and Regional Planning, Principles and Case Studies*. Mysore: Prasaranga University of Mysore.

Rangnathan, K. 1979. *Application of the Urban Lands (Ceilings and Regulation) Act, 1976 to Cantonments in India*. Harmondsworth: Penguin Books.

Report of Working Group. 1977. Appointed by the Government of India, Ministry of Works and Housing to assist the High Level Committee of Ministers on Urban Land Acquisition Policy. Mimeo.

Ronald, B. 1954. *The Art and Architecture of India*. New Delhi: Indian Institute of Public Administration.

Sah, J. P. 1971. Control and Planned Development of Urban Land: Urban Land Use Control Measures. Paper presented to the International Seminar on Urban Land Policies and Land Use Control Measures, Madrid, 12 November.

Sehgal. 1980. *Urban Land Policies in Cantonments*. New Delhi: Indian Institute of Public Administration.

Shafi, S. S. 1981. Planning the Indian Metropolis: Some Reconsideration in *Urban Problems and Policy Perspectives*, ed. Gopal Bhargava. New Delhi: Abhinavan Publications.

Sinha, M. M. P. 1980. *The Impact of Urbanisation on Land Use in the Rural Urban Fringe: A Case Study of Patna*. New Delhi: Concept.

Sundaram, K. V. 1975. Problems on Planning Standards in Metropolitan Cities of India (Ch. IV), and Planning Standards in Medium and Small Sized Towns in India (Ch. V) in R. P. Misra (ed.) *Shelter in Asia*, Volume IV. Mysore: Institute of Development Studies, University of Mysore.

Sundaram, K. V. 1977. *Urban and Regional Planning in India*. New Delhi: Vikas.

Tyrwhitt, Jacqueline, ed. 1947. *Patrick Geddes in India*. London: Lund Humphries.

United Nations. 1975. *Physical Planning Standards in Selected Countries in South East Asia*. ESA, HBP/AC/16/17. New York.

United Nations. 1977. *Urban Land Policies and Land Use Control Measures*. Vol. 2: *Asia and the Far East*. ST/CCA/167/Add.1. New York.

Vagale, L. R. 1958. Kotia Mubarakpur, An Urban Village, Urban and Rural Planning Thought. School of Planning and Architecture, New Delhi. January.

Vagale, L. R. 1964. Structure of Metropolitan Cities of India: Planning Problems and Prospects. New Delhi. Mimeo.

Vagale, L. R. 1972. *Local Government in Metropolitan Cities of India in Relation to Urban Planning and Development*. Institute of Administration, PFE: University Press, Nigeria.

Vagale, L. R. 1975. *Implementation of Master Plans and Planning Schemes: Fiscal Resources of Urban Local Authorities*. Ibadan, Nigeria. Mimeo.

Whittick, A., ed. 1974. *Encyclopaedia of Urban Planning*. New York: McGraw-Hill.

Wishwakarma, R. K. 1980. Land and Property Values: An Analysis of Environmental Impact, Centre for Urban Studies. New Delhi: Indian Institute of Public Administration, mimeographed report.

Wishwakarma, R. K. 1981a. *Urban and Regional Planning Policy in India*. New Delhi: Uppal Publishing House.

Wishwakarma, R. K. 1981b. Structural Dynamics of Urban Land Values. In *Urban Problems and Policy Perspectives*, ed. Gopal Bhargava. New Delhi: Abhinav Publications.

5

Saudi Arabia

ROBERT I. CHARD

HISTORICAL DEVELOPMENT AND CURRENT STATUS OF LAND USE PLANNING

Historical Development

Small towns have existed in Saudi Arabia since prehistoric times. There were market centers, ports, and religious centers scattered over wide areas, but most were very small and served also as places of assembly for nomadic tribes and traders. The town of Jars on the Red Sea, for example, is mentioned by classical authors, while Jeddah was founded or refounded by Persian merchants. Most of the ancient ruined towns have not been excavated yet, so it is possible that one day they may contribute to an understanding of urban development in the Middle East (DAM, 1975), but at present there is almost no evidence of town planning in Saudi Arabia before modern times. This is not to say that the idea of town planning was not accepted. On the contrary, the Arabs were responsible for some impressive town planning projects outside Saudi Arabia when they conquered more settled lands during the expansion of Islam in the seventh century A.D. The Round City of Baghdad founded by Al-Mansur in 762 A.D. is probably the most impressive example of Arab planning of this era (Creswell, 1940).

The Arabs also had concise ideas about the design of buildings and the relationship of a building to the surrounding area.[1] These customary rules for building were based on Islamic religious teaching and Sharia law and are still applicable today. Among other things they were concerned with privacy, adequate light and ventilation to buildings, and ensuring that roof spaces and internal courts were not overlooked. They required space between buildings adequate for the movement of pedestrians and loaded camels. Very often, however, each building, or a group of buildings in one family ownership, was built without reference to street lines or the orientation of other buildings. Streets were often merely areas left between buildings that were fronting in slightly different directions; however, such arrangements were capable of creating an attractive and varied sequence of narrow, irregular streets and informal open spaces. During the time of the Ottoman Empire, traditional building control codes of behavior were incorporated in written laws, which also applied to those parts of Arabia occupied by the Turks (Safak, 1980).

Socioeconomic Context

Saudi Arabia did not exist as a country at the beginning of the twentieth century. Neither was the area it now occupies influenced by the colonial rule of any European nation. Thus it was a country that until recently was little influenced by foreign social or economic pressures. It had a traditional agricultural and trading economy and a social structure based on Islam, which has remained unaltered in its fundamentals for over a thousand years. The country has one language, Arabic; one religion, Islam; and one culture; there are regional variations, but they are minimal. In rural areas a man's tribal origin, village, or family group may be of concern, but among Saudis in cities there is a uniformity of dress, language, and social customs not found in many other nations.

From being one of the more traditional and impoverished areas of the world, Saudi Arabia has rapidly become one of the more wealthy developed and cosmopolitan countries. In the last decade the GNP has grown by about 10 percent a year and there are now about 2 million temporary foreign workers, or over 20 percent of the population.[2] Although economic and technical change has been rapid, social change has been limited. The strong and continuing influences of the Islamic religions and the absence of any colonial influence have ensured that the present social values and laws are based firmly in the country's historic traditions. The state has sought to support, for example, the traditional importance of the extended family, the importance of religion in everyday life, and the traditional role and status of women. Nevertheless, there have been important social changes that the government has actively promoted. Nowhere has this been more so than in the development of education.[3]

Since the early 1960s there has been an enormous expansion of primary, secondary, and higher education. Apart from nomads and very remote villages, schooling is now available to all children, girls and boys, though some parents still choose not to educate girls. Adult literacy and vocational training programs have also been widely developed.

There has been a period of rapid modernization and urbanization since 1960 involving considerable changes in the prevailing rural life-style. Supermarkets, commuter traffic jams, home videos, soccer clubs, and fast food shops are now established features of urban life in Saudi Arabia.

Urbanization

In Saudi Arabia the process of urbanization first became noticeable in the early twentieth century. The period since 1960 has been one of rapid urbanization. Today about 60 percent of the population lives in urban areas. Data are difficult to obtain because no census or up-to-date population estimates have been published. About half the urban population is concentrated in three urbanized subregions, each of which has over 1 million population. These are the Jeddah-Makkah-Taif subregion on the Red Sea coast, the Riyadh region, and the Dammam-Dahran-Al-Khobar region of the oil fields on the gulf coast. Some planners believe that too much development has taken place in these primary urban areas in recent years. They have suffered from the classic symptoms of labor shortage, excessive in-migration, congestion, wage inflation, land speculation, and housing shortages. Efforts are now being made to develop some of the smaller towns and the new cities of Jubail and Yanbu.

In 1900 about 70 percent of the population were nomadic Bedouins. Their numbers have declined in parallel with the process of urbanization so that today they form only 20 percent of the population, and many who remain are only seminomadic. Some Budu have moved to the large cities where their most common occupations are traders, drivers, and army personnel; but a large proportion have settled in rural areas where they have become crop farmers on newly developed lands, or settled pastoralists, or they may be truck drivers and construction workers. The desire for better education, medical care, and housing has been among the main inducement to settlement, and the Bedouins have created many new villages in this century.[4]

The growth of towns and cities in the future is expected to slow because the population is now mainly urbanized.

Land Use

No exact figures are available on national land use. Resource development surveys indicate, however, that about 175,000 hectares are suitable for afforestation; about 385,200 hectares (0.3 percent) are currently under arable cultivation; and about 28 million hectares (25 percent) are semidesert used for grazing, while the remainder (about 75 percent) is sparsely used desert. Urban land area is less than 1 percent. Some land is used only occasionally for crops when rainfall and crop prices are favorable, and some potential arable land is not yet developed, so that the cultivated area could be greatly increased with more development expenditure.

Current Status of Planning: Central and Local Government

The first municipal authorities in Saudi Arabia were established in 1924, but their operations were very limited before the late 1960s. In 1947 Jeddah was still a traditional town enclosed within an ancient city wall. From the early

1970s, however, the rapid economic development and consequent urbanization and city growth required a corresponding increase in municipal operations and town planning.

The government of Saudi Arabia is centralized and operates in accordance with Islamic administrative procedures. The operation of municipalities is therefore different from countries with a federal structure or local democratically elected committees and councils. Local deviations from government policy are discouraged. Local planning bodies derive their powers by delegation of authority from central government and ultimately from the king. Delegation is through the Ministry of Municipal and Rural Affairs (MMRA) and also through the emirs and various executive ministries. In the regional capitals, the MMRA has offices that include planning and engineering affairs departments. The undersecretariat for town planning within the MMRA is responsible for initiating the preparation of local plans and supervising urban development in accordance with national standards. Municipal powers and responsibilities are defined in the Regulations for Municipalities and Rural Areas, issued in 1977.

National policy has stressed the formulation and implementation of common land development regulations pertaining to all municipalities. Land development regulations follow national standards, which are issued as royal decrees. The first Regulations on Roads and Buildings has been modified and added to by many subsequent supplementary decrees. Municipalities may adopt their own regulations, but such regulations must be compatible with national procedures and must incorporate national minimum standards. They are also subject to review by the higher authorities.

INSTITUTIONAL AND LANDOWNERSHIP FRAMEWORK

Landownership and Restrictions to Land Use

The ownership of land in Saudi Arabia normally is restricted to Saudi nationals, but foreigners can rent or lease private land. Traditionally Islamic law recognizes a variety of partial and limited rights to enjoy land and property, as well as private ownership. The law includes the concept that if rights are abused or exercised with unnecessary injury to other users or the community, it is legitimate for the courts to curtail or confiscate property rights.

As in all other Muslim countries, there are three basic categories of land-ownership. *Mulk* land is privately owned land and includes both cultivated land and private dwellings as well as most urban land. *Miri* land is owned communally, and its use is regulated by state control. This public land includes grazing land and semiwaste areas. *Waqf* land is land dedicated in perpetuity to communal and charity uses and is held in trust by the Ministry of Pilgrimage and Endowments. It includes mosques, cemeteries, and some open spaces and charity housing.

Private land can be sold, leased, or rented by written contract. Inheritance of land is normally arranged by agreement within a family group; however, most of the land in Saudi Arabia is semidesert and waste with no private owners; the ownership of this public land is vested in the king as the head of state who may make gifts of the land to persons or organizations with a particular need. Newly reclaimed arable land has been allocated in this way by the Ministry of Agriculture. Even so, people may have traditional rights to use public lands, especially near settlements, for grazing and other purposes, and when large areas are taken into private ownership, it may be necessary to compensate for loss of these rights.

Traditionally land also may be taken into private ownership by an individual reclaiming unused desert for arable land. If the occupier uses the land and remains unchallenged for a number of years, he may then claim title as a private owner. Persons can also claim plots for dwellings for themselves by reclaiming the desert, but the area allowed per claim is limited to one large dwelling plot. These traditional rights have been curtailed in recent years to reduce land speculation. Any person wishing to exercise the rights first needs to obtain permission from the Ministry of Agriculture, which has general jurisdiction over public lands outside settlements. Generally if land is allocated in this way, it is close to the claimant's village or town and given in accordance with local custom.

Today proof of ownership typically required for building permits is a written contract of purchase or a certificate issued by the Sharia court, which establishes the title. In the recent past, however, many contracts were made by verbal agreement and payment in the presence of two witnesses from adjacent properties. No written records were kept. These contracts are valid, but the parties concerned may be asked to make application to the Sharia court to obtain a certificate as proof of present ownership. The courts keep records of all transactions and ownerships.

One principle of private landownership is that land should be enclosed to establish the boundaries and the ownership claim. Urban land is enclosed by walls or fences and arable land by earth banks. Even in cities there is no cadastral survey, so boundaries have been established by landmarks, in addition to maps and specified dimensions. There have been some problems with overlapping land allocations, but they have mostly been resolved since accurate maps are being produced from air photos.

Acquisition of Public Land

The right of the state to take private property for public needs after payment of compensation has long been established in Islamic law. Today the government (and by delegation the ministries and municipalities) has powers to compulsorily acquire land for communal uses and projects. Private owners are compensated at market value for land and buildings. There is no independent valuation, but persons who are dissatisfied with the offer can pursue their grievances by bargaining and by appeals to higher authorities. As a general principle any person may make a written or verbal appeal against the action of a government department. In a very volatile land market, some owners inevitably feel they have been undercompensated, but with land prices so inflated they get little sympathy from the general public.

Islam attaches great importance to the idea that a family should enjoy its home without interference or entry by strangers. It has thus proved difficult to enforce the removal of illegal occupants of land and buildings in some cases. It is also a part of traditional land law that land in private ownership that is wantonly left unused can be reallocated to needy persons, who may thus become owners. Some squatters use this argument to justify their occupation of land. It is considered undesirable for bailiffs to enter homes and remove people or for bulldozers to be used on dwellings before public acquisition is accepted. Thus squatters have been allowed to continue occupying some private land and some public housing, while some road building is delayed by determined occupiers. In practice, however, the difference between Saudi Arabia and other countries is not great. In some squatter areas incentives and police persuasion have allowed bulldozers to demolish large areas of shanties.

Conservation and Resource Planning

Islamic law includes the concept that resources that are scarce and indispensable cannot be monopolized by individuals; they should be considered as free goods held in trust by the community leaders for the benefit of everybody (Llewellyn, 1980; Safak, 1980). This conservation principle applies to water, pasture land, forests, minerals, and wildlife. Although these concepts are upheld in disputes, they have not so far been developed into detailed codes of practice or regulations for resource management programs. Compared to North America or Western Europe rural resources, land management and pollution control in Saudi Arabia is less bureaucratic because of the lack of detailed regulations, codes, and standards and because the basic data are still being collected and evaluated. Nevertheless, the principles and concepts of limiting private rights to land and resources for the public good are accepted.

As the land boom slows, the more undesirable features of the Saudi Arabia urban land market are increasingly being brought under better control. Squatters, urban fringe land claims, and the abuse of land rights seem to be in decline.

Land Use Zoning

Although there are zoning plans for most towns, their exact legal status is not clear. Islamic law incorporates the idea of restrictions on the use of private land, but it also supports the individual's right to enjoy private property to the full without interference. Traditional law suggests the use of a piece of land can be restricted if it can be demonstrated that a particular use causes injury or disbenefit to somebody else or to the community. Where inconvenience or loss cannot be demonstrated, the presumption is that the owner's use should not be restricted. Often when an owner does not follow the zoning plan, it cannot be convincingly demonstrated that he is causing injury to others. The zoning plans may therefore be regarded as only advisory by some developers. For this reason, zoning has been ineffective in controlling shops and commercial development in towns and the construction of owner-occupier dwellings in semirural areas.

Public Participation

There is no public participation in planning of the type practiced in Western countries. Public meetings are not part of the general social system. Planning reports and master plans are not available to members of the public. Much of the background data, including the population census, are not published. Planning departments tend to give information only to people who have a specific and legitimate reason to know about a decision that affects them, and many documents can be consulted only after obtaining appropriate authorization. This does not mean that the planners and decisionmakers are not interested in knowing the wishes of the people, merely that according to traditional Saudi social and administrative customs, public participation operates in a different way.

Family heads, or the senior man in a group of families, give their opinions on local issues to the local head man—that is, the *sheikh* in a village or the *omdah* of an urban ward. These men are the lowest level of officials in the local government structure and hold a position equivalent to the part-time chairman of a village committee. They represent the people and put forward a summary of local opinion to technical planners or senior administrators after consultation with the people. When draft plans have been prepared or a consultant's report is submitted, it is the duty of the mayor or *emir* of a town to seek out local opinion and to hear the wishes of the people. He may do this with a formal committee or by invitation to hear the views of local citizens of importance and influence. Often he will make visits or initiate his own inquiries to be satisfied that he is aware of the views of particular groups. The senior government officials in Saudi Arabia also have an open door policy, which means that any citizen can seek audience and submit a suggestion or complaint. Also by tacit agreement the newspapers and television produce features and discussions on topics of interest.

Some people might be critical of this style of public participation, but it must be said that the central government makes its own investigations and is prepared to redeploy those local officials who unreasonably ignore the representations of local people, a solution not available in a democracy.

MAJOR CHALLENGES

Agricultural Land and Urban Growth

Most land in Saudi Arabia is public land. This includes most of the land with potential for development as arable, irrigated land. The Ministry of Agriculture is responsible for evaluating land resources and increasing the area of cultivation to achieve self-sufficiency in food production. After technical and economic evaluations, suitable areas of land are subdivided and allocated to approved applicants under the Public Land Distribution Ordinance (Royal Decree No. M/ 26 6/7/1388H) of 1968.[5] This ordinance replaced earlier allocation schemes and was accompanied by a number of other procedures for land allocation contained in reports and minutes. Land to be allocated must be free from any other claim to ownership, whether individual claims, the rights of groups of people to pastures, or water supplies, or any conflict of interests that might arise from the allocation. Any dispute must be clarified before allocation. Land to be allocated for cultivation must also be outside the boundaries of inhabited areas and any common grazing lands around towns or villages. Originally there was an idea of leaving a fixed distance of between 5 and 10 kilometers around settlements as village lands, but it was later decided that it would be unrealistic because of the different needs of various settlements. Therefore the town planning office has worked in collaboration with the Ministry of Agriculture to define arable lands outside urban areas and to define zones of future expansion around urban areas.[6] The zones of expansion are long term and widely defined. Land within the expansion zone that is not likely to be developed in the present plan period can be allocated for arable agriculture if there is agreement with the town planning office. The Ministry of Agriculture also considers urban development plans and proposals in deciding areas for allocation. Small settlements and groups of individuals have been given reserved zones around their private lands, which they hold in co-ownership and which can be used to meet the future needs of members of the group or community.

The areas of allocation of new arable lands are therefore nearly all some distance away from existing settlements. The boundaries of the allocation areas are defined by the Ministry of Agriculture, and the allocations are made after receiving recommendations from a local committee, which ensures the application of fair criteria in allocation. An allocation is between 5 and 10 hectares, and at first the recipient is a rent-free user for two to three years. If during this period the recipient shows serious intention to farm it by investing in equipment and irrigating the land so that at least 25 percent is under cultivation, he automatically becomes the owner of all the allocation. If he fails to use it, the gift of land will revert to its previous status as public land and can be reallocated. This is consistent with traditional Sharia law, which holds that private land that is wantonly left unused can be appropriated and reallocated by the ruler (Hajrah, 1982).

Land within the expansion zone and reserved zone also remains public if it has no private owners. Since 1968 attempts have been made to prevent squatters from settling on these public lands. An individual from the settlement concerned can make application to the Ministry of Agriculture to be given an allocation of land for any purpose, in accordance with local customs. In some cases public land has been subdivided and allocated as site and service plots to people who were nomads or had inadequate permanent dwellings. This is not a common practice because there is a large amount of private land and squatter land undeveloped around towns, and public lands often are too far from the present urban areas. Probably in the long term, town planners will define smaller areas within the zone of expansion and prepare plans for their development so that urban growth is limited to defined areas with a policy similar to the *zone d' urbanization priorité* in France.

Residential Areas

There is great variety in residential areas, not only in quality and appearance but also in planning, design, and control. This arises from the traditional desire of the individual to build his own dwelling as he wishes on any plot he can claim. Residential areas can occur alongside land of large developers who employ some of the best designers in the world to build luxury residential complexes. Some of the squatter settlements of Jizan and Khamis Mushayt, built of zinc sheets and plywood, look similar to shantytowns in underdeveloped countries. The inhabitants are mostly Bedouin, and many remain unconvinced of the value of spending money on better housing. To people who value independence and who traditionally did not own houses, government schemes for resettlement in rented housing may have little appeal.

In the larger towns and cities the majority of the dwellings are apartments in two- and three-story blocks. Land prices have dictated a fairly dense development, and although highway widths are generous, the space between adjacent blocks is usually the minimum necessary for light and ventilation. Some road patterns are grids, but most are more complex rectangular patterns of repeating modules, which can be equally monotonous. Although every town needs to have areas of apartment housing without gardens and some households prefer this housing type, it is generally agreed that Saudi cities have more than enough at present. Opinion surveys show that the preferred dwelling type for the majority is a detached dwelling on its own plot, called villas in Arabia.[7] In some cities apartments are 60 percent or more of the dwelling stock. They are becoming more difficult to rent, with vacancy rates rising over 10 percent.

It is clear that villas will increase as more Saudis are able to afford this type. By social custom, villas are enclosed by high screen walls. Despite this the variety of good architect-designed buildings with trees and gardens creates a visually attractive street scene in the more expensive neighborhoods. Saudi towns probably will now enter a phase of suburbanization in which low-density residential suburbs will be built in the peripheral areas of towns and in attractive villages and rural areas near cities.

It remains to be seen how far intermediate densities between apartments and villas will be developed. So far there are few medium- to low-density areas of row houses and semi-detached villas because these types are not familiar to local builders and purchasers. One possible alternative is attached one- or two-story patio and courtyard houses. This is a traditional dwelling type in Arabia, and many of the self-build and shanty areas aim for this type of dwelling. Ground-level living and outdoor private space is much appreciated. In many towns 20 to 40 percent of dwellings may be of this type.

Industrial Estates

At the beginning of the oil boom, Saudi Arabia had little modern manufacturing industry. Due to the labor shortage and wage inflation, most of the traditional craft industries of Arabia had been discontinued in favor of cheaper imports. Thus, in most towns in Saudi Arabia, there are few industries other than service industries, especially vehicle repairs, construction yards, food processing, and consumer durables repairs. In traditional Arabic cities, small workshops were interspersed within residential areas, and the new service industries have also grown up intermixed with housing and other land uses. It has proved difficult to enforce strict zoning regulation, though there has been some natural clustering of vehicle repairs. In this situation the planning authorities have developed two complementary strategies: they have tried to remove the most objectionable industries from residential areas and have developed in some towns large new industrial estates.

Large industrial estates have been created in Jeddah, Riyadh, and Dammam and smaller ones at Al-Qasim, Makkah, and Hoffuf. These were designed by foreign consultant planners and contain many ancillary facilities such as mosques, health clinics, emergency services, and their own power station and sewerage treatment works.[8] Employers are encouraged to build housing for their expatriate laborers within the boundaries of the estate. They can therefore operate as self-contained towns within their own boundary fence and are in fact called industrial cities. The purpose of these projects is to promote Saudi manufacturing and substitute home production for products currently imported. To this end, the government offers generous incentives, including 50 percent grants for buildings and machinery, serviced plots at low rentals, assistance with training schemes, and in some cases tariff protection or government purchases of the products. Because of these generous terms, the planners have been able to attract most of the new and larger industries into these estates. The demand for plots has been strong, and there have been several expansions of the larger estates. In many ways, they operate like industrial parks in the United States, with all the services, infrastructure, administration, and publicity run by a central management office, which leases plots to individual companies. The main difference is that 90 percent of the laborers at present are expatriates. The government policy is to train Saudis to take over many of these jobs; it seems, however, that most Saudis can find more attractive jobs elsewhere so the proportion of Saudis has not been increasing noticeably. Employers are expected to provide housing for workers, and at present most is rented outside the estates, and workers commute in company buses. It is not clear how the worker situation will evolve. More and better workers' housing could be built within the estate boundaries; however, if all the workers wanted to live outside and commute by car, there would be severe congestion problems.

In other parts of these cities, some existing industries are being encouraged to relocate to the industrial cities. There is a principle of Islamic law that states that the repelling of evil (or disbenefits) takes precedence over the acquisition of benefits (or profit) (Llewellyn, 1980). This is the legal basis for municipal policies to relocate undesirable industries. The principle also underlies the policy of upgrading some of the squatter housing and older mixed land use areas. The pace of change and expansion of the economy has been such that many of these industries were willing to move to obtain better sites. Many also had such flimsy temporary sheds that little capital was written off in abandoning their old buildings. In some cases there are policies to concentrate industrial land uses and especially vehicle repairers so that they are collected onto land zoned for industry and do not disturb residential areas.

Transport

In a country with enormous distances between cities and a scattered population, good transport links are important for economic development. The government has initiated many projects in all fields of transportation to ensure that networks keep ahead of demand. Measured by objective international standards of performance, Saudi Arabia now has some of the most efficient ports and airports in the world, and its intercity highway network will soon compare favorably with that of fully developed countries.[9] In the large cities, however, there are the familiar urban transport problems. Although women are not permitted to drive, car ownership rates are similar to Europe and are still rising rapidly. Paid drivers and more driving by other members of the family more than compensate for the absence of women drivers. In the late 1970s the increase in car registrations was reaching 20 percent a year.

The older areas of cities were not designed for full car usage and are now seriously congested and deficient in road space and car parking. The newer areas have been designed for high levels of car ownership with high-density residential areas. The way traffic generators and shops and offices are scattered along main roads and throughout residential areas means that almost any urban trip now requires a car journey. As more urban freeways and low-density residential suburbs are built, the cities will spread out, and the length of car journeys is likely to increase.

The government became concerned about the problem of traffic congestion in cities and established the national Saudi Arabian Public Transport Company (SAPTCO). SAPTCO runs a modern bus service in the larger towns and cities and the intercity bus services. After only three years of operation, SAPTCO has already had significant impact on urban journey-to-work movements. Buses now take many of the lower-paid workers to work, allowing the traffic police to remove many private buses and unlicensed passenger trucks from the streets. Most bus passengers, however, are foreign laborers, and only 10 percent are Saudis, a proportion that does not seem likely to increase. Women have a segregated section at the back of the bus, but only a few percentage of passengers are women; most are foreigners. In Saudi Arabia car ownership and car usage are probably cheaper than in any other country in the world, and the climate and social customs reinforce the preference for car use.

The largest cities seem destined to have the same transport problems as cities in developed, industrialized countries: massive expenditure on urban freeways, sophisticated but underused public transport systems, traffic congestion, urban sprawl, and petrochemical air pollution. Like Los Angeles the coastal areas of the Red Sea and the Persian Gulf have adverse climatic conditions for air pollution with frequent periods of minimal air movement, inversions, and high humidity. When these factors have been adequately evaluated, it is possible that with good planning the problems will be minimized because the cities are relatively small. Jeddah, the largest city, may reach 2 million people by the end of the century. There is now also more acceptance among planners and developers of the concept of neighborhood and district centers in cities. Also shopping centers and malls are being built, which may reduce the number and length of shopping and related trips.

National Parks and Recreation

Saudis are great tourists. By visiting many countries around the world, they have acquired a taste for modern recreation facilities. There are also about 2 million foreign workers in Saudi Arabia, some of whom like to take short holidays within the kingdom. The government therefore has adopted a program of development to provide major recreation facilities within the kingdom.

The first national park has been developed in Asir, covering areas of high mountains, forests, and some of the best beaches on the Red Sea, as well as some attractive villages and important wildlife habitats. The national park plan was developed with advice from the U.S. National Park Service, and developments clearly show the influence of American ideas on park management. (U.S./ Saudi Arabian CEC, 1976). The park area is nearly 500 hectares, but the park authority owns only a few small areas of land, the rest being farmland, semiwild scrub, and grazing land. The authorities have developed a number of picnic areas and outlooks on the edge of the spectacular cliffs of the mountain escarpments. There are two large camp sites with toilet blocks, vehicle standings, picnic tables, and playgrounds. There is a visitor education and interpretation center in Abha. Up to the present time the park has been well used, and there has been a steady increase in visitors, but they are mostly people from towns who come to picnic on weekends. Smaller camping and picnic areas are proposed for other mountain areas near Taif and Al-Baha. There are also plans to develop several tourist villages as hill stations for people to escape from the cities into the hills in the summer to enjoy the cooler weather.

Another large recreation project is the corniche development in Jeddah. When complete, this will provide a coastal parkway with lagoons, picnic areas, fishing piers, and play areas set in a landscape of palm trees and spectacular statues stretching along the coast for about 60 kilometers. Here again the main recreation is picnicking because Saudi custom and religion does not allow mixed bathing in public places. Similar corniche developments are planned for the gulf coast at Al-Khobar and Dammam.

So far the most ambitious project proposed is a plan to build a full-scale recreational park similar to Disneyland in a lagoon near Jeddah. The consultant's models illustrate a fantasia of small islands, pagodas, rotating restaurants, microtrains, and small boats. Like the other projects, if this proposal is adopted, it would get government backing.

Conservation of Historic Buildings

Arabia has been inhabited since the earliest times. This is the land where Abraham, Moses, and Mohammed lived. No doubt many interesting discoveries will be made when the numerous archaeological sites are investigated. Meanwhile the Department of Antiquities has a comprehensive program of protection, excavation, and restoration. The more important sites have military guards to deter treasure hunters and casual souvenir collectors so common in many other countries. It is possible to visit sites with prior permission, and museums are planned for each region of the country.

Although there is no formal system of conservation areas and listed buildings to be conserved, the conservation policy works along similar lines in an informal way. Some of the most important historic buildings in Riyadh and Jeddah have been carefully restored by their owners and will soon be open to the public. The owners of many other buildings are being encouraged to maintain and restore these. In the larger cities, detailed surveys and photographic records of all the older buildings have been completed.[10] Demolitions are actively discouraged, and most owners have been persuaded at least to maintain the outside appearance of the buildings. Well-known international firms of consultants have been employed to record, advise, and supervise restorations. To maintain economic confidence in areas like old Jeddah, there has been an extensive program of street improvements: paving, landscaping, and lighting and better vehicle access, car parking, and pedestrian routes.

It is only a few years since these conservation programs began, yet much has been achieved in a short time, especially changes of attitudes to old buildings. It is still, however, only a holding operation at this stage. In some small towns conservation work has not yet begun, and many old buildings are being allowed to fall into ruins or are being demolished. Saudi Arabia has an interesting vernacular architecture with a number of different rural dwelling types built in mud, stone, and wood. These are no longer being constructed and are rapidly disappearing; it is hoped that they will be recorded and some of the better examples preserved.

Major Development Projects

It is perhaps in the design and construction of major urban development projects that Saudi town planning has been most successful. In developed countries, the construction of airports, new towns, shopping centers, or hospitals inevitably involves compromises and adaptations to take account of existing buildings and transport links and the costs and complexities of land acquisition and site assembly. In underdeveloped countries, there may be no existing facilities to be incorporated in the design but limited finances. Also budget cutbacks often create a disjointed incrementalism, which inhibits comprehensive design.

Saudi Arabia is relatively free from these two common problems. Often the designers are given a more than adequate site and generous budget to design large complexes as total concepts from first principles. Fortunately, too, projects are built rapidly and do not suffer the modification and downgrading of later phases so common in many projects. The landscaping and architectural detailing of these projects are as important as their functional efficiency so they provide excellent oportunities for creative urban designers.

Among the more impressive projects that have been built so far are the new military cities (complete new minitowns), the Riyadh and Jeddah international airports, the diplomatic residential quarter in Riyadh (Kini, 1982), the National Guard Hospital complexes and associated residential areas, the Jeddah corniche parkway, the government office complexes and conference centers at Taif and Riyadh, as well as many smaller shopping plazas and residential compounds. Plans are also prepared for the university campuses at Riyadh, Jeddah, and Dammam, new neighborhoods and district centers at Jubail and Yanbu, and the kingdom's largest park at Taif.

Royal Commission for Jubail and Yanbu

The new industrial towns of Jubail and Yanbu deserve special consideration because in almost every respect the development of land and control of building development within their boundaries operates in a different way from other parts of the country.

The Royal Commission was established by royal decree M/75 in 1975. The purpose of the towns is to establish large new petrochemical and refinery complexes and associated downstream products industries. Jubail on the Persian Gulf has a target population of 300,000 and Yanbu on the Red Sea a target of 150,000.[11]

Within their designated areas, all land is owned by the Royal Commission. It is made available to selected developers by leases of different length depending on the type of development. Master plans were prepared in great detail for both towns before any permitted development took place. Since the Royal Commission is the landowner, as well as the controller of development, there has been complete and effective control of land use and development.

The master plans were prepared with assistance from foreign consultants, and technical experts were recruited from many countries. The plans thus include some of the best concepts in new town development with good development of neighborhoods, housing clusters, proper hierarchy of community facilities and subcenters, and segregation of vehicles and pedestrians.[12] They are not merely copies of foreign plans; a conscious effort has been made to design specifically for the culture of Saudi Arabia. The Jubail master plan, for example, features a detailed analysis of household size and structure and examples of house designs and housing clusters to illustrate the traditional room requirements, privacy, and segregation of the sexes. Saudi custom requires that schooling for children over six years of age is in separate boys' and girls' schools on nonadjacent sites. This requirement has led to a lively debate on how the neighborhood idea can be maintained, especially since many schoolgirls are brought to school by private car, and there are important traffic limitations to siting the schools. Also in the Arab tradition, the retail and commercial functions of the Jubail city center are separated from the government and administrative center so that the city does not have a Western-type central business district. Rather it has several separated areas for different centralized functions, such as retail, government, recreation, and cultural activities.

The master plans define the major highway network and the land use zonings. The subdivision plans for residential clusters, environmental areas, or various other projects are designed through architectural and planning competitions, competitive tenders from private firms, or by the developing organization. To ensure high standards, both cities have produced many detailed and comprehensive standards and design manuals against which proposals are judged before approval. At present, however, these documents have the status of internal working papers, which are subject to changes so they are not published or available outside the organizations that use them. They do, however, ensure that in the two Royal Commission cities, there is a system of land use control and building regulation that is as elaborate and comprehensive as anywhere else in the world. Some planners believe this sort of control should be extended to other parts of the country.

APPROACHES TO LAND USE PLANNING

Master Plans for Urban Areas

Master plans have been prepared for about 30 cities and towns.[13] They now cover all towns, as well as some that still have the character of large villages. Generally they have been prepared by foreign consultants to a fairly standard format. Because of the lack of any previous planning work and the need to produce them rapidly, they inevitably suffer from some deficiencies. There was no time for detailed comprehensive data collection exercises; indeed most municipalities lacked even the most basic data for their areas. The master plans therefore include sample surveys, estimates, and collections of professional opinions, which are adequate to give a general indication as to the scale of the problems but without any accuracy of the use of sophisticated quantitative analysis techniques.

The land use policies and proposals of the master plans are also at a fairly generalized level. In the circumstances, this was realistic. Many municipalities had no previous experience of town planning and no local planning staff. The pace of development has been so rapid that forecasts soon became outdated, and the scale and direction of future development was difficult to predict.

In one respect, however, the master plans are very precise. They conform to the stages of the five-year national plans. Saudi Arabia is one of the few countries in the world that can enjoy the luxury of preparing exact plans for government expenditure up to five years in the future, knowing that the budget will be available and the allocations to various sectors are unlikely to be changed by political changes. Various government projects in the five-year plan have therefore been incorporated in the master plans of the municipalities. Cooperation between the Ministry of Planning (responsible for the preparation of five-year national plans) and the Ministry of Municipal and Rural Affairs (responsible for authorizing the preparation of master plans) ensures integration between national and local levels of planning. The master plan preparation sometimes goes through two stages. The first stage is mainly a consultant's survey analysis and recommendations; stage 2 involves modifying the recommendations into policy objectives and adding detailed projects that conform to the national plan. The final plan is called a master directive plan since the municipality is required to make every effort to ensure all the projects are implemented. The projects in master plans are implemented by various ministries, but the sites are defined in the master plans. They include major roads, water, sewerage, electricity, schools, hospitals, and civic projects such as parks and markets.

The master plans also include land use zoning policies. Where the development is by government departments or involves government loans, these zoning policies have normally been adhered to, but where development is speculative and financed by the private sector, it has proved more difficult to keep to the land use zoning. The master plans have not been able to prevent continuous retail and commercial development along major highways or scattered industry and construction in semirural areas. Neither has it always been possible to confine residential development to areas that will be provided with roads, water, and electricity.

Land Subdivisions

Another way in which planning control is exercised is by the approval of land subdivisions and road layouts. In Saudi Arabia every landowner has the right to build a dwelling and other buildings on his own land for his own use, but if he wishes to sell portions of his land for development or divide it and develop it himself, the land subdivision must be approved by the municipality. This requirement has been quite vigorously enforced by the municipalities. Apart from squatter settlements, which have been in existence for some time, nearly all development now takes place on land with approved subdivisions. The municipalities apply strict rules to subdivisions. There are generous minimum widths for roads, minimum plot sizes, minimum frontage lengths, and so on, and a percentage of the land, usually 15 percent, has to be given to the municipality for public use such as parks, open space, or municipal buildings. The municipality may also require additional plots to be reserved for other public projects such as mosques and schools.

The requirement for approval of subdivision has secured many advantages in a period of rapid development. Especially important has been the reservation of land for roads and on-street car parking sufficient to cope with the explosive growth of car ownership. The design and approval of subdivisions, however, has suffered from the extreme pressure of land speculations, with unfortunate results. At the present time there is some critical re-evaluation of the hundreds of hectares of subdivisions that were approved in haste and are not yet developed. After 1973 the boom in the economy was so great and unexpected that the urban land market was ripe for speculation. Enormous fortunes were made by land speculators, and because sales of land or commencement of construction depended on approval of the subdivision, it was necessary for landowners to get approval as quickly as possible. In retrospect it is easy to criticize the municipalities for approving so many poor subdivisions. In reality, though, it is doubtful if realistically they could have done anything else. Nobody wished to hold up the process of development, and the central government would not tolerate bureaucratic delays. There were virtually no qualified Saudi town planners, and the limited expatriate staff of the municipalities were employed mainly as administrators and were not expected to develop policy. Subdivisions were therefore evaluated against lists of rules and requirements, but beyond these it was difficult for a municipality to hold out and refuse to approve a layout. Today the areas of approved subdivisions in many towns greatly exceed the requirements for the next twenty years. Some layouts have dangerous road junctions, excessive road areas, and monotonously repetitive geometrical patterns of streets. Possibly some of these will never be built, and others will be modified by mutual agreement between the landowner and the municipality, but some will remain. There are also some good layouts where developers have employed professional staff. Government departments often set a good example; the residential areas of the Ministry of Defense, for example, are of a high standard of design.

Development Control

The third way in which municipalities control development is by building permits. Before any building is commenced, the developer must submit detailed plans to the municipality and obtain approval for the building. The actual published building regulations in most municipalities are minimal, but building inspectors of the municipal architects' office also advise applicants to change plans and ask for changes in design when they think the design could be improved or if it is a policy to try to obtain certain improvements. In these situations the municipality often has a significant bargaining advantage. Many developers were in a great hurry to cash in on the property boom, and many had an inadequate understanding of modern planning and construction. For them any delay in approval could mean a significant loss of profit. Therefore many developers readily accepted any modifications the municipal inspectors suggested, whether the changes were to conform to building regulations or not. Contractors also rapidly got to know what was required and made sure the submitted plans conformed. Some municipalities have increased their advantage by vigorously demolishing the limited number of buildings being built without approval or differently from the approved plan. Building control in Saudi Arabia is not as effective as in many developed countries, but it is remarkable what has been achieved considering the enormous volume of construction and the limited numbers and expertise of local authority staff. Building approvals have been used to obtain planning improvements, as well as improving buildings, and have been used to promote advisory planning policies prepared by consultants and accepted by the municipalities. In fact, there has been no distinction between planning regulations and building regulations, and they are all enforceable by building permits.

The control of development is also made easier by the fact that the government is the financier of a large proportion of the development in Saudi Arabia. Although government policy is in favor of promoting private enterprises, the government also gives generous loans and grants. These are available for every Saudi national to build his own modern house or to develop industrial or some commercial properties. The government also finances hospitals, basic services, telephones, farms, bus companies, basic industries, and police and army projects, most of which also include housing for employees. Government projects often use foreign consultants, and wherever government finance is involved, the government has insisted on high standards of design. Many projects are designed to the highest international standards, which in practice means an amalgam of British, German, and U.S. building regulations and planning standards with appropriate modifications to cope with the extremes of climate. Thus the government has set an example that the private sector is being encouraged to emulate.

Some critics of Saudi planning policy have suggested that the government should control urban sprawl by refusing to provide urban services of water, electricity, and roads to developments that are outside approved layouts or the zonings of master plans. It is questionable, however, if such policies would be effective even if they were considered socially and legally reasonable. Much evidence suggests they would be less effective and less acceptable than in many other countries. There is the traditional right that any person may reclaim the desert and build his house on his own plot. Considering the cost of plots of land on some approved layouts, there is a great incentive for people to choose this course of action. To increase the attractions of the approved layouts, the government and municipalities have initiated large construction programs to build roads, water pipes, and electricity lines and substations. Today in most towns the provision of these services is often in advance of other development. Indeed in the larger cities, there are many hectares of subdivided land with surfaced roads, paved sidewalks, electricity, and water lines, street lights, and even trees and parks, which are ready and waiting for building to commence; however, many individuals have chosen the alternative option of a free house plot on reclaimed desert land as squatters. Although the journey to work may be longer, the costs of living outside the approved development area are not great. Many people use the type of vehicle that can travel easily off the road. Water can be delivered by tanker from a nearby well, and home generators are readily available and relatively inexpensive to run on cheap fuel. There is always the possibility that the town eventually will grow to encompass the plot within the urban area. Because the government is strongly committed to extending material benefits to all citizens, it is probable that main services and roads eventually will be provided.

The desire of many citizens to claim and build on their own plots of land has created unsightly sprawl and ribbon development along the main routes out of cities. It has been established that the minimum construction necessary to make a claim is a 10 square meter one-room dwelling of permanent materials and a surrounding wall. In areas of land speculation, these ugly little boxes of tin or blocks with many half-finished walls disfigure both villages and city fringes together with many other half-abandoned projects. In effect, there has been little control of development in rural areas, especially beyond the administrative boundaries of the larger municipalities. This is an area of concern where some improvements in planning control are urgently required. These will probably evolve if the land speculation boom suffers a permanent reversal.

Action Area Plans

To complement the master plans, especially in the larger cities, more detailed plans have been prepared for small areas. Called action area plans, they include plans for housing improvement areas, conservation and recreation areas, and plans for new neighborhoods. The intention is that they should cover parts of the urban area where government expenditure will be above average and where development is expected to be concentrated. The locations of the action area plans are defined in the master plans, and like the master plans their proposals and budget are derived from the five-year national plans so that their development objectives should be substantially achieved in five years.

Action area plans are being used especially to improve the existing unplanned areas of cities, and one plan can cover an area as large as 300 hectares. A typical improvement area will have a high proportion of land in residential use, sometimes nearly 70 percent, about 10 percent vacant, and about 18 percent road space of irregular roads, alleys, and open areas between buildings. Other land uses take up very little land, and schools and public open space may be completely absent. The housing is usually of mixed quality, ranging from single-story concrete block shanties to new four-story apartment blocks, but it is all at a high density, and the unplanned areas, which are 15 to 30 years old, appear similar. Improvement proposals are designed to increase the percentage of road area and improve minor roads, car parking, and pedestrian alleys so highway land is increased to about 30 percent of the total. Community facilities, including schools, mosques, health clinics, and government offices, may take another 8 to 12 percent of the land, which is obtained by acquisition and redevelopment of substandard property. Some nonconforming industry will be relocated, and commercial zoning is often increased to allow a modern shopping center to develop as a neighborhood center. Wherever possible public open space is increased, but it is not realistic at present to clear buildings for open space so the allocation may remain small, sometimes only 2 percent of the area.

Policy is to reduce population densities in these older areas, and the proportion of the land in residential use is reduced below 50 percent in most proposals. Currently there are no grants to improve dwellings or policies for internal improvements to dwellings. It is assumed that many of the worst will be acquired for roads or other land uses, and owners will soon redevelop most of the rest because of the increased rents that can be obtained from modern apartments. Redevelopment of residential plots usually involves a substantial increase in rooms on the plot, although occupancy rates are bound to fall from the high levels of 2 to 3 persons per habitable room existing before. Municipalities have contributed much to environmental improvements to complement private investment.

FUTURE THRUSTS

Rural Planning

Although there have been many important agricultural development projects, they have been concerned primarily with the distribution of arable land in newly irrigated areas (Hajrah, 1982). Most of the rural land and established villages have not had the benefit of planning and development studies because until recently work has been concentrated on cities. To restore the balance, rural development projects will become more important, and pilot projects are already in progress. Land resources management, settlement patterns and village plans, water resources management, afforestation, rural housing, coastal fisheries, local tourism, and recreation are areas for future rural development that are receiving increasing attention.

Land and Planning Law

In many Arab countries, the land laws and land use regulations have been derived from land laws of European countries based on Roman legal principles. The land laws of Algeria, Egypt, and Lebanon, for example, are influenced by French legal practice. Saudi Arabia is one of the few Islamic countries where foreign laws and legal concepts and regulations have not been incorporated in the land laws. The government policy is that the laws of Saudi Arabia should be strictly based on the established laws of Islam and the Sharia courts. This does not mean that there are no town planning regulations based on Western models; there are, but they are not published or formally adopted and do not always have full legal standing. They have been used as an interim arrangement and for guiding municipal employees who make decisions on specific cases. This conservative approach has encountered some difficulties with respect to town planning. The principles of the law are clear enough, and case law and legal tradition give clear guidance on traditional types of problems like disputes between neighbors. The difficulties arise because the newer ideas of modern town planning and development control were not considered by traditional jurists. Therefore there is a need for legal and religious academics to discuss and agree on the details of land laws and controls over the use of land; this is being done. Some observers believe that soon Saudi Arabia should be able to publish and implement comprehensive regulations for the control of development and the use of land in both urban and rural areas.

Development Control

Saudi Arabia has a good record for keeping construction projects according to the program and completing work on target. Many development projects also have excellent designs and are constructed to the highest international standards. There has been, however, some less satisfactory development in some private sector construction, especially in small towns and remote areas and on small projects where development control and advice inevitably has been less effective. There is now a large gap between the best development and the work of many small designers and builders. Some contractors, by giving overemphasis to speed and profit, have used hastily adapted and pirated plans to produce standardized and dull buildings, often constructed with inadequate technical supervision and poor workmanship. One of the challenges for future town planners will be to see how far it is possible to raise the standards of the less competent draftsmen, designers, and builders.

Updating Plans and Policies

The new fourth five-year development plan recognizes that after a period of exceptional economic expansion, the country needs to consolidate and reappraise the various development programs. It is a desirable prelude to further sustained growth and development. In the field of town planning, this should mean revision and updating of the master plans and reappraisal and refinement of policies. It is necessary to provide more accurate data by new surveys, more analysis of data already collected, and more systematic, continuous recording of data by government departments such as building inspectors and traffic police. Revisions of some zoning and land use allocations and the redesign of some minor road junctions are also desirable in many towns. Visually, parts of many Saudi towns are still an unattractive mixture of incomplete buildings, partly paved roads, advertisement signs, abandoned construction yards, haphazard car parking, and open storage. Landscaping and upgrading is making good progress, but much more could be done to improve the quality of urban areas.

Professional Training

The fourth five-year development plan has as one of its aims the training of Saudi manpower at all levels so that they will gradually be able to take over the many jobs currently performed by foreign experts. At present there are few Saudi town planners, and a large part of the town planning work is still done by foreigners. This is in contrast to architecture, where a larger proportion of the work is done by Saudis and Saudi companies. Town planning undergraduate courses exist at two universities, and the first students began to graduate a few years ago. Foreign consultants working with municipalities and ministries are also giving town planning training to local staff, including some qualified architects. Gradually the planning offices will be able to improve their staffing. Because the staff will be familiar with local traditions and cultural requirements, as well as good theory and practice in other countries, no doubt they will have a beneficial effect on land use planning.

NOTES

The opinions expressed in this chapter are the author's own and do not represent those of any organization in Saudi Arabia.

1. See, for example, International Symposium on Islamic Architecture, 1980; Serageldin and El Sadek, 1982; Fadan, 1983.
2. El Mallakh, 1982, contains many useful statistics.
3. Niblock, 1982, contains an analysis of social changes in recent years.
4. Katakura, 1977, has detailed sociological analysis of some Bedouin villages in Wadi Fatima.
5. Hajrah, 1982, contains a comprehensive account of the evolution of policy and major projects concerned with the development of new agricultural lands.
6. The Town Planning Office was a department of the Ministry of the Interior, which was replaced by the Ministry of Municipal and Rural Affairs in 1975.
7. Durrani, 1983, paper awaiting publication, Jeddah; working papers for Yanbu master plan.

8. For example, Binnie and Partners and Shankland Co. Partnership proposals for Al-Quasim and Al-Hofuf.

9. Kingdom of Saudi Arabia, Ministry of Communications, 1982, gives details of projects and proposals.

10. Among books of photographs published is Pesce, 1977.

11. Royal Commission for Jubail and Yanbu. The public relations departments of the two new towns produce many up-to-date brochures and fact sheets.

12. Jubail Industrial City Community Plan, 1978.

13. Mostly since 1975 when the Ministry of Municipal and Rural Affairs was created.

BIBLIOGRAPHY

Bindagji, Hussein H. 1980. *Atlas of Saudi Arabia*. Oxford: Oxford University Press.

Creswell, K. A. C. 1940. *Early Muslim Architecture*. Vol. 2. Oxford: Oxford University Press.

Department of Antiquities and Museums (DAM). Ministry of Education. 1975. *Saudi Arabian Antiquities*. Kingdom of Saudi Arabia.

Durrani, T. M. 1983. Saudi Norms for Neighborhoods and Housing Quality Expenditure: Jeddah. Paper presented to the first Saudi Engineering Conference, May 14–19, Jeddah.

El Mallakh, Ragaei. 1982. *Saudi Arabia, Rush to Development, Profile for an Energy Economy and Investment*. Baltimore: Johns Hopkins University Press.

Fadan, Yousef. 1983. Traditional Houses of Makka: The Influence of Socio-Cultural Themes upon Arab Muslim Dwellings. In A. German, ed. *Islamic Architecture and Urbanism*. Dammam: King Faisal University.

Hajrah, Hassan H. 1982. *Public Land Distribution in Saudi Arabia*. London: Longmans.

International Symposium on Islamic Architecture and Urbanism 1980. Report of Symposium. *Ekistics* 47(280), January-February.

Katakura, M. 1977. *Bedouin Village*. Tokyo: University of Tokyo.

Kingdom of Saudi Arabia. 1968. *Public Land Distribution Ordinance*. Royal Decree No. M/26, 6/7/1388H.

Kingdom of Saudi Arabia. 1980. *The Third Development Plan 1400–1404H*.

Kingdom of Saudi Arabia. 1984. *The Fourth Development Plan 1405–1409H*.

Kingdom of Saudi Arabia. Ministry of Communications. 1982. *Land and Marine Transportation*.

Kingdom of Saudi Arabia. Ministry of Finance and National Economy. Central Bureau of Statistics. *Statistical Year Book*.

Kingdom of Saudi Arabia. Royal Commission for Jubail and Yanbu. 1977. *Jubail and Yanbu Industrial Complexes*.

Kini, Devados. 1982. A New City in the Capital (Master Plan for Riyadh Diplomatic Quarter). *Saudi Business* 52, April.

Llewellyn, Othman B. 1980. The Objectives of Islamic Law and Administrative Planning. *Ekistics* 47(280):11–14. International Symposium on Islamic Architecture and Urbanism.

Looney, R. E. 1982. *Saudi Arabia's Development Potential*. Lexington, Mass.: D. C. Heath & Co.

Mathew, Johnson, Marshall and Ministry of Municipal and Rural Affairs. 1976–77.

Corniche, Vols. 1–3: Central, North, and South Action Areas. Edinburgh, U.K.: Consultant's Report to Ministry.

Niblock, T., ed. 1982. *State Society and Economy in Saudi Arabia*. London: Croom Helm Ltd.

Pesce, Angelo. 1977. *Jeddah: Portrait of an Arabian City*. New York: Olcander Press.

Royal Commission for Jubail and Yanbu. 1978. *Jubail Industrial City Community Plan*. Kingdom of Saudi Arabia.

Safak, Ali. 1980. Urbanism and Family Residence in Islamic Law. *Ekistics* 47(280):21-25. International Symposium on Islamic Architecture and Urbanism.

Saudi Arabian Parsons Ltd. 1978. *Master Plan for Madinat Yanbu Al Sanaiyah*. Kingdom of Saudi Arabia.

Serageldin, I., and S. El Sadek. 1982. *The Arab City: Its Character and Islamic Cultural Heritage*. Arab Towns Organization.

United States/Saudi Arabian Joint Commission on Economic Cooperation (CEC). 1976. *A Management and Development Plan for the Asir Kingdom Park*. Kingdom of Saudi Arabia.

6

Israel

RACHELLE ALTERMAN and MORRIS HILL

The history of land use planning in modern Israel is a mirror of changing ideologies and values. More than almost anywhere else, land in Israel is very much a symbol. The overriding goal of the Zionist movement of the past one hundred years has been the return of the Jewish people to their land. Land policy and land use planning have encapsulated both shared values and bitter controversies. These have encompassed both internal issues regarding social relations among the various groups in Israeli society and international issues pertaining to the Arab-Israeli conflict.

The term *land policy* can be construed both narrowly and broadly. Narrowly it can pertain to regulative, statutory land use planning, sometimes called negative land use controls. More broadly it can encompass positive or what we prefer to call initiatory planning and development, such as the actions of a public agency in the planning and implementation of a new town. In this chapter, we espouse the broader definition.

HISTORICAL DEVELOPMENT

History, Ideology and Planning Thought

Modern Israel is a planned society. Planning has figured prominently in the ideology and thinking of the Zionist movement since Theodore Herzl, the original visionary of the state, called for the return of the dispersed Jewish people to the then sparsely populated and partly derelict land of Palestine. In his landmark book, *Altneuland* (The Old-New Land) he outlined the contours of the new state, going into detail on the economic base of the future state and the desirable land policy (public control). He even outlined major public works, one of which is under discussion today, one hundred years later: a canal linking the Mediterranean to the Dead Sea that uses the difference in altitude for the generation of electric power. (For general orientation, see Figure 6.1)

From its inception, the Zionist movement gave planning a respectable place in its ideology, as befitted the needs of the chronically optimistic, large-scale social and political enterprise which the establishment of Israel certainly was. In the formative years, prior to the establishment of the state in 1948 and during the first decade of its existence, land use and physical planners occupied a position close to decisionmaking. At that time two phases of planning thought were identified (Law Yone and Wilkansky, 1984): the phase of the Grand Ideas (from the 1920s to about 1952) and the phase of Action (to the early 1960s).

During the phase of the Grand Ideas, a sizable proportion of Israel's rural settlements, with their innovative range of types of cooperative or communal arrangements, were established. In addition, long-range plans were formulated for various areas of land use and development. Although not all were implemented, they contained the seeds of many of Israel's major national land use goals, some of which persevere today. These include the goal of population distribution from the Mediterranean coast inward, which is still the major emphasis in Israel's national planning policy, as well as various regional development and transportation planning concepts.

The second phase, the phase of Action, has been called by Akzin and Dror (1966) high-pressure planning. During this time, Israeli society underwent turbulent social and economic change. The population grew 2.5-fold between 1948 and 1956 as waves of Jewish refugees from the Arab countries (56 percent) and from Europe (44 percent) arrived, often penniless, and became the responsibility of the prestate Jewish population of only 750,000 (Statistical Abstract of Israel, 1972). The existing population was already overburdened by an enormous security problem and by economic austerity. The phase of Action was a befitting response to the problem of planning under extreme turbulence (Hill, 1980). It was successful because of the general consensus on major goals. Its success was also due to considerable compromise with proper procedure and good planning and to uncoordinated action by separate government ministries, each acting in its own domain (Hill, 1980).

The achievements of the period of unmitigated Action are impressive. Most of Israel's 35 new towns were planned and established then; hundreds of thousands of new public housing units were constructed to house the new immigrants (Figure 6.2); extensive networks of public facilities, including schools and well-baby clinics, were set up; the model regional plan of the Lachish area was implemented; and Israel's major public work, the National Water Carrier, was constructed. In addition, the network of agricultural settlements was extended to the southern Negev desert and to other unoccupied areas. Yet this period of achievement also contained the seeds of many of Israel's current problems, such as the social cleavages between the residents of the New Towns and the long-

Figure 6.1 Map of Regions in Israel, within pre-1967 Borders

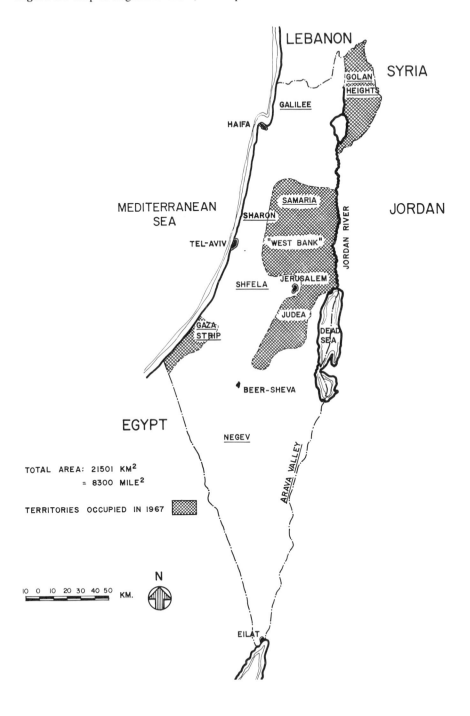

Figure 6.2 Map of New Towns in Israel, within pre-1967 Borders

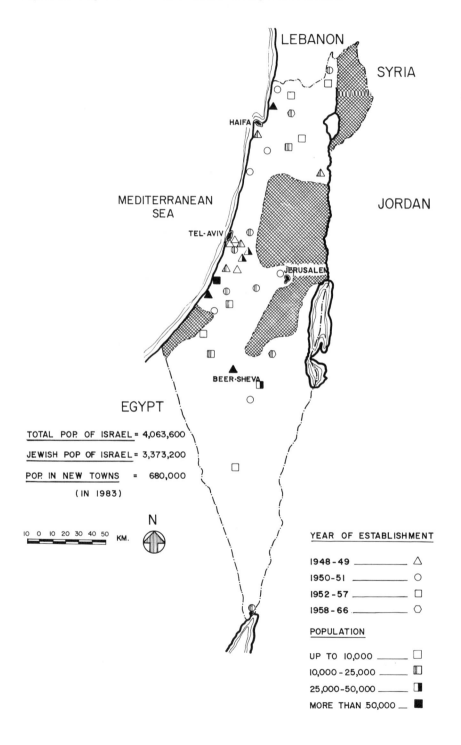

established urban and rural centers. Most of the neighborhoods that today are included in the national Neighborhood Rehabilitation Project were planned and constructed at that time.

As the state became more administratively complex and economically stable, planning gradually lost its primacy, and planners became less directly influential in decisionmaking. The commitment to planning as a major attribute of society has declined. Since the mid-1960s, planning thought has become more technical and less ideological, and planners have played mostly an advisory role to government (Law Yone and Wilkansky, 1984). The consensus over goals has also eroded considerably. In recent years planning, rather than symbolizing consensual goals as it did in the past, is often the target of conflict over goals. Since the 1967 war and more so since the traumatic change of government in 1977 when power shifted for the first time in Israel's history from Labor to the nationalist Likud party, more and more national land use goals are the subject of controversy: should the West Bank be settled by Israelis, as the Likud party would argue, and if so, which parts of the West Bank? Should these settlements be rural or urban? Should there be a policy of encouraging Jews to move to the Galilee, Israel's northern region (which is largely settled by Israeli Arabs), and if so, should this policy take precedence over the West Bank? These controversies and others have figured prominently in the past elections and are expected to be emphasized even more starkly in the elections to come.

The discussion so far applies to initiatory planning more than to regulative planning. After all, the task of creating a new nation and a new society requires the primacy of initiatory planning. Regulative planning has always been overshadowed by the initiative of government agencies, which carry out their own planning and also have the financial resources for implementation. However, regulative planning too has been part of Israel's planning ideology, as described later. Despite the relative weakness of regulative planning (which is not untypical of many other developing as well as some developed countries), it too serves as an expression of societal values.

Land Use Patterns and Planning Goals

Historically land use planning goals may be distinguished as belonging to four periods:

1. 1920s to 1948—dominance of the rural ideology and rural orientation of land use planning; large-scale land assembly through purchase from Arabs during the British Mandatory period
2. 1949 to 1963/4—rural ideology still dominant but compromises with trends of urbanization sought and the New Towns concept born
3. 1965 to 1977—initial recognition of the needs of the existing urban areas; growing awareness of environmental issues; continued goals from periods 1 and 2
4. 1978 to present—greater reliance on the private sector in development; greater em-

phasis on internal urban and neighborhood problems; emergence of public participation; partial weakening of goals from periods 1 and 2

The dominance of the rural emphasis in land use planning has its roots deep
within the Zionist movement. The ideal of the return of the Jewish people to
the land of Israel was conceived as the return especially to agricultural occupations (Cohen, 1970). Most of the attention of prestate land use planning
therefore was directed to rural planning. This was expressed in an aggressive
policy of land assembly through purchase from local Arabs. The land that the
Arabs were willing to sell was mostly rocky, swampy, sandy, or in an inhos-
pitable climate (Granot, 1952). Much of the attention by planners of the time
was therefore directed to land reclamation through drainage, clearance, and
afforestation, as well as to the desirable regional distribution of new settlements.
Considerable attention was also devoted to the microscale land use planning and
layout of agricultural and residential areas within each type of rural settlement.

As may be seen from Table 6.1 there were 248,000 hectares in agricultural
use and approximately 400 rural Jewish settlements by 1949. Considering that
Jewish landownership in Palestine was severely restricted prior to 1948 and
covered only parts of Palestine, this was a significant achievement by prestate
planners. Despite such constraints, the cultivated prestate areas constitute as
much as 40 percent of the area in agricultural use in the 1980s.

The other side of the emphasis on rural planning was the virtual neglect of
urban planning needs. Any attention devoted to the cities was not by the prestate
Jewish institutions but rather by the government of the British Mandate over
Palestine, which made some significant attempts at setting up regulative town
planning, sometimes with the help of well-known British planners. The major
exceptions were the establishment of the first Jewish New Town of Tel Aviv in
1909 planned by Patrick Geddes and the self-planning of new residential communities in urban or suburban areas by various Jewish cooperative associations.
One would expect that this initial obliviousness to urban land use planning would
be reflected in the population trends; however, the interesting fact that emerges
from Table 6.2 is that in 1949 83 percent of the population resided in urban
areas. This percentage is almost as high as in 1981, despite the subsequent
establishment of some 35 new towns. The fact is that Jewish Palestine was
always a highly urbanized society, despite the emphasis on rural land use planning.

The needs of absorbing masses of new immigrants as well as the economic
and security needs of the new state led land use planners in the second period
(subsequent to independence in 1948) to realize that large-scale absorption of
immigrants could not be undertaken in rural areas. Since the rural ideology was
still dominant, the solution found was a compromise. By establishing new towns,
large-scale solutions for housing and employment needs could be supplied while
helping to achieve the population distribution policy much more effectively than
through reliance on small agricultural settlements. These new towns represented
a major planning feat. By 1956 all but two had been established (see table 6.3;

Table 6.1
Agricultural Land Use in Israel

Year	Cultivated Area (thousand hectares)	Jewish Rural Settlements		
		Moshav	Collective Moshav	Kibbutz
1949	248	157	25	211
1953	356	274	27	217
1960	404	346	20	228
1968	413	367	22	235
1972	417	353	33	233
1978	427	355	29	230
1981	410	409	38	259

*All data pertains to Israel within its pre-1967

borders.

Source: Statistical Abstract of Israel, 1950, 1953,

        1969, 1983

figure 6.2). Today several hundred thousand people live in these towns. As Shachar (1971) has shown, the new towns indeed constitute some measure of achievement of the population distribution policy.

On the ideological level these new towns were acceptable to politicians and planners because they were not viewed as fully urban, and semirural notions were incorporated in their planning. Many of the early towns were in fact planned with a hoped-for home gardening economic base (which never materialized). Moreover, their layout was strongly influenced by the garden cities concept (Howard, 1945), despite the fact that often such planning was unfeasible due to the shortage of water and the desert climate. This obliviousness to reality clearly reflects the ideological conflict and the desire for compromise between rural and urban life. In this second period as well, little attention was paid to the planning needs of existing urban areas and to the quality of life of the vast majority of

Table 6.2

Population in Urban and Rural Areas in Israel, 1948–1981 (in thousands)

Year	1949		1961		1972		1981	
	Population	%	Population	%	Population	%	Population	%
Total Population in Israel	1,173.9	100.0	2,179.5	100.0	3,147.7	100.0	3,977.9	100.0
Population in Urban Localities			1,697.9	77.9	2,684.6	85.3	3,458.0	86.9
Cities			1,409.3	64.7	2,168.1	68.9	2,793.1	70.2
Other Urban Localities			288.6	13.2	516.5	16.4	664.3	16.7
Rural Localities			481.6	22.1	463.1	14.7	519.9	13.1
Total Moshav			120.6	5.5	125.1	4.0	144.6	3.6
Collective Moshav			4.0	0.2	5.5	0.2	8.4	0.2
Kibbutz			77.1	3.5	89.7	2.9	113.7	2.9
Temporary Settlements and Bedouin Tribes			29.0	1.3	44.6	1.4	54.5	1.1
JEWISH POPULATION IN URBAN AND RURAL AREAS								
Total Jewish Population	1,013.9	89.1	1,932.4	88.7	2,686.7	85.4	3,320.7	83.5
Urban Localities	768.7	82.6	1,634.5	75.0	2,429.0	77.1	2,999.6	75.4
Rural Localities	142.3	15.3	297.9	13.5	257.4	8.2	320.7	8.1
ARAB POPULATION IN RURAL AND URBAN AREAS								
Total sum of Arab population	160.0	8.9	247.1	11.3	461.0	14.6	657.5	16.5
Urban Localities			63.4	2.9	164.7	5.2	234.5	5.9
Rural Localities			183.7	8.4	205.7	6.5	199.2	5.0

Sources: Israel Statistical Yearbook – 1950, pp. 14–15; 1956, pp. 9–10; 1983, pp. 42–43

Table 6.3

New Towns in Israel

Locality	Yr.of estab.	Location	Population (1000s)		
			Yr.of Estab.	1972	1982
1 Bet Shan	1948	Bet Shan Valley	2.9	11.9	13.5
2 Yahud	1948	Shefela	3.1	8.6	13.0
3 Acre	1948	Western Galilee	0.9	25.5	29.9
4 Lod	1948	Shefela	1.1	29.3	34.4
5 Ramle	1948	Shefela	10.8	29.8	36.6
6 Ashkelon	1948	Judean Plain	5.1	40.1	54.1
7 Beersheba	1948	Negev	8.3	77.4	112.6
8 Azor	1948	Shefela	3.1	4.5	6.6
9 Bet Dagan	1948	Shefela	1.0		
10 Yavne	1949	Judean Plain	1.5	10.1	13.7
11 Tirat Carmel	1949	Carmel	5.2	13.3	15.5
12 Kiryat Shmone	1950	Huleh Valley	1.4	15.1	15.9
13 Shlomi	1950	Western Upper Galilee	2.4		
14 Yoqnean Illit	1950	Carmel		3.8	5.5
15 Rosh Haain	1950	Shefela	5.9	11.6	12.6
16 Or Yehuda	1950	Shefela	1.3	12.3	19.8
17 Bet Shemesh	1950	Hills of Judea	0.2	10.2	13.0
18 Or Aqiva	1951	Coastal Plain	1.2	6.3	8.1
19 Mevaseret Zion	1951	Hills of Judea	1.9	4.7	7.1
20 Kiryat Malachi	1951	Judean Plain	0.6	8.0	12.4
21 Sderot	1951	Judean Plain	0.4	7.5	9.0
22 Yeruham	1951	Negev	0.1	5.4	6.6
23 Eilat	1951	Southern Arava	0.3	14.6	19.6
24 Migdal Haemeg	1952	Yezreel Valley	0.1	8.8	14.1
25 Hazor Hagelilit	1953	Galilee	2.0	5.2	6.5
26 Maalot	1957	Upper Galilee	1.2	3.2	5.2
27 Nazareth Illit	1957	Southern Galilee	4.3	15.0	23.4
28 Ashdod	1955	Southern Coast	4.6	37.6	68.0
29 Kiryat Gat	1954	Lachish region	10.1	18.0	24.9
30 Mizpe Rimon	1954	Negev	4.0		
31 Dimona	1955	Negev	0.3	22.5	27.6
32 Ofaqim	1955	Negev	0.6	9.2	12.7
33 Netivot	1956	Negev	2.9	5.3	8.5
34 Arad	1961	Negev	1.3	5.6	12.9
35 Carmiel	1964	Galilee	0.9	3.8	15.7

Source: Israel Statistical Yearbook 1983.
          Berler, A. (1970) New Towns in Israel, p.xxvi

Israel's population. This period ended in the early 1960s which saw the last two new towns, the most consciously urban among them, being established.

The third period, beginning approximately in 1964, coincided with growing economic prosperity and national security. The borders were relatively secure and settlements were spread out in most areas of the pre–1967 borders. Immigration slowed to a trickle. It seemed as if, for the first time, national land use planning took time to examine the needs of the large urban population, which perhaps was no longer willing to show complete deference to a national policy so strongly biased in favor of rural planning. This period saw the enactment of a new planning act in 1965 that made local plan making mandatory and offered tools for obtaining generous amounts of land for urban public and social services. Significantly, however, it is this same act that also set up one of the world's most stringent agricultural preservation laws, a strong reminder that agriculture is still viewed as a major national value. The amount of cultivated land in fact declined somewhat in the 1970s due to scientific improvements in agriculture (see table 6.1). Rural settlements, especially the *kibbutzim*, began to industrialize part of their economic base.

During this period, the attention of national planning was diverted for the first time to the Tel Aviv metropolitan area (Israel Institute for Urban Research, 1972). By that time the area had grown rapidly to contain over one-third of Israel's total population, seemingly almost unnoticed by national planning. But perhaps the most indicative developments during this third period are those directed at the quality of urban life. Some initial attempts at fostering environmental consciousness led to the establishment in 1974 of the Environmental Protection Service. This period also saw the beginnings of urban renewal, with several abortive and some partially successful attempts based on the use of the bulldozer and relocation but also with some initial steps toward genuine neighborhood revitalization.

Today Israel is at a fourth, still somewhat undefined, period. The political transition of 1977 brought about many changes, including greater involvement of the private sector in planning and development. This approach has figured most prominently in the controversial planning and development of Jewish settlements in the West Bank but has made some inroads in other areas of the country as well, such as the tiny new semirural settlements in the Galilee, many initiated and planned by groups of prospective private settlers.

This trend has seen a major shift away from the prevalent long-term tendency to rely almost exclusively on the central government for most land use planning and development activities. Notably the percentage of public housing of total annual building starts declined gradually from 60 to 70 percent in the 1950s to 35 percent in the 1980s (Table 6.4). Significantly the centerpiece of the Likud government's social and urban policy—the large-scale, ambitious, national Project Renewal—has for the first time in Israel's history given clear government encouragement to local decisionmaking and public participation. But perhaps the most ideologically symbolic issue of land use planning of this period has

Table 6.4
Percentage of Housing Unit Starts by the Public and Private Sectors

Year	Percent Public Sector	Percent Public Sector
1958	70	30
1959	66	34
1960	49	51
1961	68	32
1962	61	39
1963	49	51
1964	54	46
1965	50	50
1966	36	62
1967	50	50
1968	35	65
1969	37	63
1970	47	53
1971	35	65
1972	46	54
1973	67	33
1974	55	45
1975	52	48
1976	35	65
1977	22	78
1978	23	77
1979	39	61
1980	39	61
1981	36	64
1982	39	61

Source: Statistical Abstract of Israel
          1958 - p. 180
          1960 - p. 202
          1963 - p. 398
          1965 - p. 450-451
          1968 - p. 257
          1975 - p. 26
          1982 - p. 463
          1983 - p. 499

been the controversial proposal by the Lands Authority to allow sale to private hands of some of Israel's hard-won and long-cherished land. The country is still immersed in this period. The economic recession of early 1984 and an inflation rate of 400 percent have slowed some private development activity. The state of the national economy undoubtedly will lead to some rethinking about national land use planning goals. The contours of future changes are still quite hazy.

LEGAL AND INSTITUTIONAL FRAMEWORK FOR REGULATIVE LAND USE PLANNING

National Land Policy

An estimated 92 percent of Israel's total land area is publicly owned or controlled and is administered by the Israel Lands Authority. This land has three major sources: land assembled through purchase by the Jewish National Fund, mostly in prestate times; large tracts of state land, including most of the southern Negev desert and much of the Galilee, which in the past belonged to the British Mandate government by virtue of its being the sovereign over Palestine and which subsequently became the property of the state of Israel; and some land that belonged to Arabs who left the country during the war in 1948 for enemy territories and is legally held under a special government custodianship.

If so much of the land is public, one may ask if there is need for a regulative land use planning system. After all, there seem to be few private landowners to regulate. In order to understand the answer, a few more facts about the other 8 percent are in order.

The small percentage of private land does not fully reflect its role in development. The 8 percent is concentrated mostly in the large urban areas, in Arab villages and towns (where most land is private), and in several formerly rural towns and settlements, some of which have grown into medium-sized cities dating back to the early twentieth century before the cooperative mode in agricultural settlement became dominant. Thus in many of the older urban areas, private land plays an important role. But even when there is a relatively large proportion of private land, such as in Haifa, one usually still finds considerable tracts of public land.

Furthermore, the policy of the Lands Authority has been to dispense of its land by means of long-term leases, usually for the biblical jubilee period of 49 years (when, says the Bible, all land is to revert back to its original owners). The majority of Israel's housing units and many of its industries are based on such leaseholds. Because of weak or nonexistent controls over resale, especially in the urban areas, such long-term leaseholds have tended to function in the marketplace virtually as freehold property. This tendency has been reinforced by the Lands Authority's policy in recent years to charge the leasing fee in advance and to calculate it almost at market prices, as if the property were private (Borukhov, 1980). Nevertheless, the Lands Authority does extend some control over change in use of the property.

The regulative planning system thus has reason to be in business. Since the 1965 law, planning controls apply to government-initiated development, of both central government and local government (unlike the traditional jurisdiction of

U.S. zoning, for example). That is not to say that such control is easy to achieve. The powerful spending ministries or the Lands Authority itself naturally have a much more dynamic pace than the slow-moving, reactive regulative planning system. However, infringements of planning law by public authorities, which had been rampant in the past, have diminished significantly in recent years through both intra-agency and external public pressure.

Interestingly Israel has developed virtually no municipal land policy. The powers of local government in Israel are weak. Municipal landholdings have never been large. Due to strict financial and legal-administrative control by the central government over most financial decisions by local government (any land purchase, for example, requiring the approval of the district commissioner), local governments have not adopted any land assembly policies. Yet there is one important exception: the 1965 Planning and Building Law empowers local authorities to exact up to 40 percent of all unsubdivided land for public purposes. They tend to use this tool. However, due to high density and an average family size that is by no means small compared to Western countries—4.0 persons in 1982 (Statistical Abstract of Israel, 1982)—there is a need for many public services. Little surplus land therefore is accumulated, and, in fact, more land is often necessary for public services in areas of higher density (Alterman and Frenkel, 1983). That is sometimes obtained through agreement or compulsory purchase. The Lands Authority too usually agrees to dedicate an equivalent percentage of land to public use.

A discussion of land policy would not be complete without reference to the perpetual problem of betterment, more recently called the plus value (Alterman, 1982). Here one finds—perhaps somewhat surprisingly, given the national orientation of most land policy in Israel—a major power allotted to local authorities: the obligation to levy 50 percent of all betterment value due to plan-derived increments in land values. It may be noted for comparison that in Britain the development land tax is levied nationally. This important financial tool was until 1981 either dormant or misused due to major ambiguities in the previous legislation (Alterman, 1979). Changes in the law in 1981 institutionalized the betterment levy as a major aspect of land policy and the planning process (Alterman, 1982).

Given the small amount of private land in Israel, a betterment levy that applies only to such land can be partially useful at best. Through a special arrangement in the law, however, the levy applies to long-term leaseholds on public land as well. Yet a number of recent regulations have set up a growing list of exemptions that apply to all housing of average or modest size and to declared neighborhood revitalization areas. Thus the levy is often much less effective as a financial tool in most development towns (New Towns) and other publicly initiated housing areas.

Planning Institutions and Their Power

Regulative land use planning was introduced into Palestine by the British Mandatory government. One of the earliest measures enacted by the civil administration, which took over from the Turks in 1920, was the Town Planning Ordinance of 1921. This ordinance, based on British legislation, particularly the Housing, Town Planning etc. Act of 1909, introduced planning principles that have remained the basis for planning legislation to this day.

The Town Planning Ordinance of 1921 was replaced by the Town Planning Ordinance of 1936, which remained in force for 29 years and was the basis for the present town planning law in Israel. After a long and arduous process, the current Planning and Building Law was adopted in 1965.

The new law introduced some major changes. They included extending the planning hierarchy up to the national level, subjecting all government agencies' actions to local planning control, and increasing the authorized exactions to 40 percent. On the whole, however, much of the 1936 ordinance was carried over in the new law, especially with regard to local planning. Whereas planning statutes in the United Kingdom have been repeatedly overhauled, Israel has been saddled with an intricate law of the 1930s with a somewhat negative approach.

The current statutory planning system in Israel operates under the Planning and Building Law of 1965 (State of Israel, 1965). It set up a three-tier structure of planning institutions: the National Planning Council, the District Planning Commissions, and the Local Planning Commissions (see Figure 6.3).

In the National Planning Council, the law institutionalized a set of informal powers that central ministries exercised previously in association with the Planning Bureau of the Ministry of the Interior (Gouldman, 1966, 47). The council is a public body made up of representatives of central government ministries, local authorities, professionals, and public representatives. Its duties are threefold: to initiate and approve national plans and intervene in district plan preparation if necessary, to review district plans, and to hear certain appeals from local and district authorities.

In the second tier are the six District Planning Commissions. These are dominated by representatives of government ministries but also include a few members of local authorities and one or two professionals. On the regional level, the District Planning Commissions have duties similar to those of the council on the national level. In effect, the District Planning Commissions are the central decisionmaking bodies about most day-to-day local planning and permit-granting problems, and they tend to intervene heavily in local planning decisions. These range from final approval of nonconforming uses to hearing appeals on refusals by Local Planning Commissions to grant building permits. One of the problems that plagues the system is the tendency of these commissions to spend most of their time on small-scale administrative decisions rather than on planning policy. They have also been criticized for not fulfilling the coordinative function that their multiministry structure clearly implies (Alexander, Alterman, and Law Yone, 1983, 132, 133).

In the third tier of planning bodies are the Local Commissions. There are over 100 Local Planning Commissions in the country. Where a local planning area includes only one local authority, the Local Council constitutes the Local Plan-

Figure 6.3 Israeli Planning Institutions and Their Powers

National Planning Board
• Initiates and approves national plans
• Approves district plans
• Hears certain types of appeals

District Planning Commissions (6)
• Initiate and approve district plans
• Approve all local plans; sometimes initiate these
• Approve most types of local building permits and hear appeals on rejection
• Hear all objections to local plans

Local Planning Commissions (about 110)
• Prepare local outline and detailed schemes and approve initially
• Give initial approval on privately initiated detailed schemes
• Grant permits that conform and give initial approval on permits with variations
• Appropriate land for public uses
• Levy betterment tax

Alexander, Alterman, Law Yone, 1983, p. 126.

ning Commission. In the case of cities, the council designates a subcommittee for planning. Where a local planning area includes more than one jurisdiction, the commission is composed of a designated number of local government members and central government representatives.

The duties and powers of the Local Planning Commission are many, but most are conditional on the approval of the District Commission. The Local Commission is mandated to prepare the local outline scheme and may initiate detailed schemes. It decides whether to accept privately initiated detailed schemes and approve subdivisions that do not deviate from the approved plan. It grants permits for buildings that conform to standards and do not deviate from approved plans and may permit nonconforming uses and minor variances after District Commission approval. The Local Commission may expropriate land for public purposes, and it is empowered to levy the betterment levy.

The relationship between Local and District Commissions can be understood only against the background of the relationship between central government and local government. The structure created by the British Mandate over Palestine (which understandably desired to assume as much control as possible) for the most part has been maintained by the state of Israel (Naor et al., 1978). Even some of the municipal legislation, such as the Municipalities Ordinance from British Mandate times, has not been amended for the most part. Today Israel's local government is dependent for most of its budget on the Ministry of the Interior, though larger cities tend to be somewhat more self-supporting than smaller towns. Many of its decisions require approval by central government, and this also applies to the planning system.

Since various central government agencies also act as developers, especially for housing and roads, the local planning commission is paradoxically expected to regulate central government activities or struggle with large developers although it is in effect weak and financially dependent.

The courts also play a role. But they are not like U.S. courts, which tend to serve as appeal bodies not only for procedural issues but for planning decisions as well. Their role is more similar to that of the courts in the British and European systems, with judicial involvement limited to procedural matters. Thus, in the past, the High Court of Justice declined the role of an appeal body in planning matters, which it tends to leave in the exclusive domain of the planning institutions. Recently, however, some relaxation of this approach is apparent, and the court has become somewhat more influential on substantive planning matters as well.

APPROACH TO PLANNING

Hierarchy of Plans

The Planning and Building Law of 1965 sets out a hierarchy of plans (see Figure 6.4) and prescribes the content of each. Two types of plans are mandated; the others are optional. All plans are intended to guide decisions on building permits. District plans were to be prepared by the District Planning Commissions and submitted to the National Council within five years of the law's enactment. None was approved by that date, but four were approved by 1984 and the last two are under preparation. Local outline plans were to be prepared by the Local Planning Commissions for areas still lacking them and were to be presented to the District Commissions for their approval not later than 1969, but most were not. Even today some municipalities, including Tel Aviv, do not have an outline plan.

Supreme in the hierarchy of plans is the national outline plan (or rather plans), which may apply to the country as a whole or to parts of it. It is mostly a land use physical plan and may include designations for industrial areas, major arteries, recreation and afforestation areas, and archaeological sites. The interesting important exception is the national plan for population distribution, which is a policies plan and has been consistently prepared and updated since independence. National plans require approval by the government and then take precedence

Figure 6.4 Hierarchy of Statutory Plans Pertaining to a Given Local Area

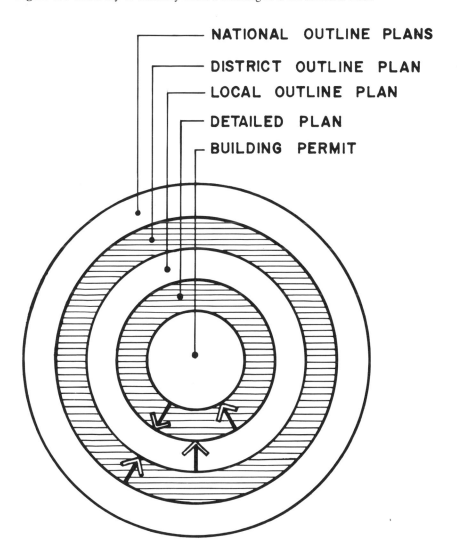

NATIONAL OUTLINE PLANS

DISTRICT OUTLINE PLAN

LOCAL OUTLINE PLAN

DETAILED PLAN

BUILDING PERMIT

over all other plans. Although no single unified national plan exists, many sectoral plans have been approved—for example, in population distribution and settlement policy, transportation, power plants, seashores, parks, and tourism. These plans have full legal status. National outline plans may also include anything subject to a district plan. Thus a nesting structure emerges (see Figure 6.2).

Unlike the national outline plan, the district outline scheme is intended to cover the entire district and to achieve some explicit nonphysical goals: "to set the necessary details for the implementation of the national scheme in the district, and among other things, adequate conditions for the district in terms of security and employment." The district scheme "may include anything subject to a local outline scheme," ranging from industrial areas to coastal zone preservation and down to conditions for granting variances.

A typical set of traditional, physically biased goals for land use planning is to be found in the prescriptions for the local outline plan (Alterman, 1981). They are: control over land development; provision of suitable conditions from the point of view of health, sanitation, cleanliness, safety, security, transportation and comfort; prevention of nuisances; and preservation of historic, archaeological and natural sites. The local plan includes the usual elements of a land use plan, such as densities, building lines and setbacks, public land, utility easements, and so on. The local outline plan is prepared by the Local Commission and is approved by the District Planning Commission.

The final level of plans is the detailed scheme, which presumably is to be prepared closer to the time of anticipated development when specific information about the site and project design is known. In practice, detailed schemes and outline plans are often interchangeable, depending on the degree of detail in the latter, as expressed by the reversed arrow in Figure 6.2. This leads to the frequent undesirable phenomenon of the tail wagging the dog (Alterman, 1980). The detailed scheme may specify land uses and subdivisions, designate roads and public areas, and indicate the location of buildings, their clearance and reconstruction or preservation, their bulk, height, shape, and appearance, and may include details of urban design such as street planting and furniture. They can cover areas of any size, even as small as spot zones. Anyone with an interest in a given area of land can prepare a detailed scheme, but it must be approved by the Local and District Commissions.

Last in the hierarchy is the building permit. Although it is not a plan per se, it is the focal decision in the system that the hierarchy of plans is expected to guide. Furthermore, the request for a variance—a permit that exceeds permitted bounds—is one of the major motivations for preparing an amendment to a detailed plan or, all too often, even an amendment to an outline plan. Thus the directive function of plans is often eroded away through bottom-up decisions (Alterman, 1980).

The building permit serves two functions, functions that in the United Kingdom and the United States are separated: it marries planning control with building control. In addition to concretizing planning decisions, the building permit serves as a compulsory check on structural soundness and construction specifications and as an opportunity for assessing whether various regulations have been met (fire, civic defense) and levies been paid. An evaluation study of the Israeli planning system (Alexander, Alterman, and Law Yone, 1983) has seen this marriage of planning and building controls as one of the reasons for the prevalent problems of compliance with planning control and has in fact recommended a divorce.

Implementation Tools

The Israeli planning system does not lack the tools for implementation and enforcement. The principal tools for implementing land use plans are the all-embracing regulatory powers that the law confers on the planning authorities. No development or change in use may take place without a building permit. Generally for a permit to be granted, the proposal must accord with the area's detailed plan, which in turn must be consistent with the relevant outline plan. If the detailed plan does not follow the specifications in the outline plan, it must be approved as an amendment to the latter. However, the Local Planning Commission is empowered to grant minor variations in height, bulk, or setback requirements within legally set limits. Once approved, an Israeli statutory plan becomes an implementation tool itself in that it becomes a legally binding document. Furthermore, unlike British development plans, Israeli plans require full compliance with them of all permit-granting decisions (except minor variances).

Another important implementation tool is the power to appropriate land for public purposes. These powers are more extensive than in most Western countries and enable the local government to expropriate up to 40 percent of privately owned land in the course of implementing detailed plans or a local outline plan. This is without being liable for any compensation or even having to grant any building rights in lieu of the land that was taken. In addition, the central government has virtually open-ended powers in eminent domain.

Besides the powers of subdivision control, which are commonplace in many countries, public planners in Israel have the authority to undertake reparcelations, if necessary, without the landowner's consent. This power is an important positive (rather than negative, or regulatory) implementation tool and has been used to open up areas where development was inhibited by fragmented ownership.

Finally, the planning system in Israel on the local level has the rare quality of being (at least potentially) self-sustaining from the fiscal point of view. Planning activities can be funded by the Betterment Levy under which landowners are required to pay the municipality 50 percent of the added value of their land that is the result of planning decisions. The levy has not yet been fully implemented.

The local and district commissions have extensive legal tools for enforcement. They can administratively stop construction until a legal order is obtained. They can also demand, and the courts would usually agree, that the structure be torn down or that the offender be fined double the value of the illegal structure, sanctions that entail an enormous amount of money and are extremely onerous.

Problems of Implementation and Compliance

Tools for implementation and enforcement are apparently not enough. The Israeli land use planning system has several problems of implementation that are quite similar to problems encountered in other countries with similar governmental and demographic characteristics, such as some Mediterranean countries.

The first problem is the style and function of land use plans. These are often prepared in the traditional static blueprint style, thus generating numerous spot amendments. Such amendments often make the outline plan superfluous, as has been empirically documented (Alterman, 1980; Alexander, Alterman, and Law Yone, 1983: 134–37).

A second problem relates to the administration of planning decisions. The approval route for plans and building permits is long and arduous. It allows for some avenues for defensive public objections, which although quite basic and traditional are sometimes blamed for lengthening approval time unnecessarily. This blame is probably misplaced; however, the approval time is indeed often unjustifiably long and is often perceived as contributing to the high cost of real estate. This complaint may not be more severe than in some West European countries.

A third problem is that of compliance of private and public bodies with building controls. On that count Israel differs from other Western countries, exhibiting some of the trends prevalent among developing countries. (This similarity is not surprising considering that the majority of Israel's population originated in Arab countries.) However, the degree of noncompliance is probably not as severe as in developing countries and in recent years has been going down significantly due to stricter enforcement. Still, probably as many as one-quarter to one-third of all building starts are still illegal or not fully legal even today. In the recent past this rate would have been much higher and would have included not only small-scale but also large-scale private and public development. Today the phenomenon of gross and almost routine infringement by public bodies has been reduced considerably. One could guess (in the absence of empirical research on this sensitive issue) that most infringements today are by small-scale owner-occupants who undertake construction of an additional room for a growing family or close off a balcony to serve as additional floor space in a crowded apartment.

Alexander, Alterman, and Law Yone (1983) have suggested that rather than stricter control, as the trend has been in the past two decades, the Israeli planning system is in need of deregulation. The suggestion is that small-scale development by owner-occupants be placed outside the sphere of planning control. This proposal is not widely accepted in Israel yet.

Finally there is the problem of enforcement. The manpower allotted for inspection is much less than needed in a society where one cannot as yet rely on social norms to ensure self-compliance with planning and building regulations. Such social norms have been slow to institutionalize, despite ample and severe legal sanctions, including stiff fines and demolition orders.

A major challenge facing Israel's regulative planning system is undoubtedly the challenge of improving implementation. In a planning system with sufficient powers of implementation and in a society that has always viewed planning as an important means to the achievement of societal goals, one would expect that this challenge could be met. It is perhaps paradoxical that a planning-oriented society, such as Israel has always been, would have such a lethargic and little-esteemed regulative planning system. This ostensible paradox may be indicative of the different functions that regulative planning and initiatory development planning play in society.

MAJOR CHALLENGES AND FUTURE THRUSTS

Four major challenges are prominent at present or need to be addressed. Since these challenges are pressing and pertinent, future thrusts in land use policies can be expected to focus on these issues. The following major planning challenges in Israel today are to be considered: metropolitan areas, the development of Galilee and the Negev, neighborhood rehabilitation, and planning for the occupied territories.

Metropolitan Areas

The older and larger cities face severe problems if only because they affect more people and because solving them may require more resources. The solution of their problems is a major planning challenge.

The population dispersal policy and the constraints on the availability of public resources have meant that in practice these cities, particularly those on the coastal plain and in metropolitan areas, have received less than their relative share of public investment. The growth of the Tel Aviv metropolitan region and, to a lesser extent, the Haifa region has, however, continued unabated particularly as a result of industrial and commercial development generated by private sector and worker-owned enterprises. Although government policies have helped to check the physical growth of Tel Aviv, it remains the economic capital of the country. Today the Tel Aviv metropolitan region accounts for more than a third of the population of the country, about 1.5 million. The Haifa metropolitan population is about 400,000, as is the population of the Jerusalem area.

After the 1967 war the old and the new parts of Jerusalem were reunited and the city began to flourish after many years of stagnation. Major public investments were funneled to the city, but their allocations were inadequately coordinated. The development processes included the transfer of many governmental institutions from Tel Aviv to Jerusalem, consistent with the city's role as the political capital of Israel. Concomitantly there has been considerable public investment in housing to absorb the rapidly increasing population as part of the government's policy of increasing the Israeli presence in the united city. The central government's controversial policy of constructing large, new neighborhoods at the city's periphery is ideologically motivated, to the consternation of the energetic mayor, Teddy Kollek, who would like to see greater consolidation of the city.

A common problem in the larger cities has been the inadequacy of the basic infrastructure, particularly transportation facilities and sewerage systems (originally constructed for much smaller populations with a low car ownership rate), to meet the needs of the rapidly growing and increasingly motorized population. These cities were laid out with narrow thoroughfares and limited sewerage. The government has been loathe to make the necessary investments to improve the urban infrastructure even in times of relative prosperity because it was always seen as taking population away from the development regions. There was concern lest the larger metropolitan areas on the coastal plain be made too attractive and act as magnets attracting population away from the development towns in the peripheral regions.

The allocation of land for the solution of these problems in the larger cities was complicated by Israel's land policies. Whereas only 8 percent of the land in Israel is privately owned, this private land tends to be concentrated either in the traditional Arab villages or in or adjoining the older, larger cities. In an inflationary economy that experienced continual growth for a long period and more recently has been subject to considerable turbulence, landownership is attractive not only because it protects the value of money but also because it is likely to bring speculative gains. Land speculation and the proliferation of private ownership of relatively small parcels make for difficulties in the redevelopment of the older centers of the metropolitan areas and the renewal of the urban infrastructure. On the other hand, strict controls to ensure the preservation of agricultural land at the periphery of the older cities prevent the development of large commercial centers in the metropolitan fringes.

Setting metropolitan policies for controlling environmental pollution, improving transportation systems, and providing accessible parks and beaches for outdoor recreation requires not only a comprehensive multisector approach but also treatment at the appropriate geographical scale. Solutions to these problems require a perspective that geographically overlaps the historic boundaries of the cities. Thus Tel Aviv, with a population of 350,000, holds about a quarter of the total population in its intensively urbanized metropolitan area.

Metropolitan institutions, which would work in concert with existing local governments, have been proposed for the Tel Aviv and Haifa metropolitan regions. A two-tier level of government was proposed for the Tel Aviv region, the upper level to be composed of representatives of all towns in the region presided over by the mayor of Tel Aviv. This proposal has proved politically unfeasible for the time being but no doubt will reemerge at a more politically propitious time. Some metropolitan planning has been introduced in the Tel

Aviv region. There is a metropolitan plan for a joint highway system and flood drainage system entitled *Netivei Ayalon*, which is built along the Ayalon stream. There are also separate metropolitan special purpose districts for the disposal of solid waste and sewage. In the Haifa metropolitan area there are similar special districts, and there has been a proposal for a multipurpose metropolitan special district that can deal with all metropolitan-wide issues. The establishment of metropolitan bodies with a great deal of discretionary power is not easy in Israel because it would mean that the national government ministries would have to share power with relatively strong and broadly representative regional bodies. National ministries, jealous of their power, can be expected to have reservations about the establishment of powerful metropolitan institutions.

The present challenge is how to solve problems whose solutions require a metropolitan perspective in the absence of metropolitan institutions to initiate action and to carry it through.

Development of the Galilee and the Negev

Since the establishment of the state of Israel in 1948, the development of Galilee and the Negev has been a central challenge to successive Israeli governments. Population distribution from the dense coastal plain, where the major metropolitan centers of Tel Aviv and Haifa are located, has been the most important feature of Israel's development policy.

The policy of population distribution is intended to serve several purposes. It helps to preserve the rich agricultural land that adjoins the metropolitan centers on the coast; it enables the exploitation of the natural resources on Israel's periphery; it counters pressure for growth in the larger and older urban centers by diverting the population to newer urban centers on the periphery, this being consistent with the antiurban bias of Zionist ideology; it ensures that peripheral areas that could be in danger of being lopped off the country in future boundary disputes with Israel's neighbors are part of Israel.

Located in the northernmost section of Israel, Galilee is a typical hill region, which, like most other hill regions, has a lower average income than that of the rest of the country. It has the largest concentration of Arab villages in the country. One of the challenges of plans for the development of Galilee is to achieve greater balance between Arab and Jewish populations. It is hoped that there will be a major development thrust on the basis of this balance.

Galilee is a composite quilt of human settlement endeavor: Arab towns such as Nazareth and Shfaram; Jewish towns such as Safed and Carmiel; mixed Jewish-Arab towns such as Acre. The towns are small to medium sized with a hinterland of rural villages: Jewish *kibbutzim* (collective settlements); Moshavim *shitufim* (partially collective and partially cooperative settlements); Jewish small-holder settlements; Christian Arab villages; Moslem Arab villages; Druse villages; Circassian villages. Not a prosperous part of the country, Galilee's wealth is in its human variety and variety of types of settlements.

The challenge is how to achieve greater development for Galilee and raise the income of its population while respecting the rich human and historic fabric. Galilee's major historical interest is in its serving as the cradle for the Jewish and Christian religions. One of the immediate challenges is to create institutions that can enable a satisfactory dialogue among the various parts of the population and can provide the basis for a concerted development effort.

The natural environment of Galilee is particularly sensitive and must be treated with respect in development plans. The natural environment is dominated by Mediterranean pine forests. It is the location of most of Israel's water resources, including the Jordan River and the Sea of Galilee. The Sea of Galilee serves as a reservoir for Israel's national water carrier, which pumps much of the Galilee's water to the center and the south, where most of the population and economic activities are located. Thus one of the challenges for planning in Galilee is to enable development without curtailing the accumulation of the water resources and without adversely affecting the quality.

The Negev, with its broad expanses of sparsely populated desert, presents another type of challenge. In the Negev are located Israel's mineral deposits of phosphates, bromides, and potash. Here several development towns were established between 1948 and 1961. In the Negev is Beersheva, the largest development town, with a present-day population of 120,000 and the site of a university and a major medical complex. Beersheva, together with the other Negev towns of Dimona, Arad, and Yeruham, are the sites of Israel's extractive and chemical industries. In spite of the desert characteristics, the Negev is also the site of a large number of agricultural villages located in the northwest Negev on the fertile loess soil of the Lachish region (watered by the national water carrier) and in the Arava valley between the Dead Sea and the Gulf of Eilat.

The Negev contains 50,000 Bedouin Arabs who are at present in a state of transition from their previous nomadic existence to village or urban living in several new planned communities. The Jewish population of 250,000 live in the development towns, on *moshavim* and *kibbutzim*. The Lachish region with its 40 settlements and regional town of Kiryat Gat is a successful, internationally recognized model of rural regional planning.

The challenge of the Negev is in its relative open spaces in an otherwise crowded country. Most of the desert land cannot be cultivated, thus leaving large areas for potential urban and industrial development. Recognizing this, the Israeli government has provided material incentives for prospective immigrants to the Negev in order to achieve more rapid growth and development. After the final Israeli withdrawal from Sinai in 1982 in the wake of the peace agreement with Egypt, however, the Negev has come under intensive development pressure. Much of the southern Negev has been devoted to military enclosures for airfields and training areas, thus effectively preventing civilian settlements in large parts of the region. But much of the Negev may still come under development, and the challenge is to find the desirable balance between military and civilian needs.

One of the problems associated with the allocation of so much of the Negev to military purposes is that it has removed from civilian use large land reserves for future development. Thus alternative civilian options for development have been closed. In a country with very limited land resources, this is of major significance.

Another aspect of the development of the large military areas in the Negev is the inevitable conflict that has developed with regulatory planning bodies. In a country like Israel that has had to face frequent wars with its neighbors, it is difficult to counter proposals justified on the basis of security needs even where these conflict with what is considered good planning practice.

The civilian assets of the Negev are many. The mineral deposits of phosphates, bromides, and potash are very large and enable profitable production for hundreds of years into the future. Thus the continuing profitability of the extraction and chemical industry is ensured. Tourist development along the Dead Sea and the Gulf of Eilat on the Red Sea has been successful, but it is limited because of the need to maintain a fragile ecological balance in the sensitive desert environment. Due to limited water resources at present, only the Lachish and Besor regions of the northern Negev and the Arava Valley of the south enable intensive agricultural production. A large underground lake has, however, been discovered more than 2,000 meters under the Zin desert. Once it becomes commercially profitable to pump out this water, large additional areas of the Negev can be irrigated. Perhaps the greatest challenge is to attract higher-income earning industries, such as science-based industries, to the Negev. At present the Negev is dominated by labor-intensive, resource-based industries and tourism. This has implications for the socioeconomic composition of the population, which at present is primarily made up of immigrants or first-generation Israelis with relatively low levels of education and consequently low levels of income. By working to diversify the economic base in the direction of science-based industries, a more highly educated population could be attracted to the Negev, and income levels would rise. This would add important positive elements to the population of the Negev.

Neighborhood Rehabilitation

The rehabilitation of neighborhoods in social and physical distress is a central feature of Israel's urban policy. In 1977 the Israeli government instituted Project Renewal, the rehabilitation of 80 such neighborhoods, which in some cases encompass the entire population of small development towns. So far the program serves a total population of 600,000. The government has identified 160 neighborhoods throughout the country that require rehabilitation, and this has become a major challenge for urban policy in Israel.

The state of Israel is relatively young, with much of the population living in neighborhoods constructed during the last 35 years. Thus the need for their rehabilitation may not be obvious. However, the need for rehabilitation had its origins in the conditions under which the state of Israel was established, the rapid flow of immigration in the initial years, and the limited resources available at that time. During the first ten years after the establishment of the state, Israel, with a total Jewish population of approximately 750,000, absorbed more than that number of immigrants; 680,000 of these immigrants arrived between 1948 and 1951. The immigrants were virtually all penniless refugees, about half of whom were survivors of the Nazi Holocaust in Europe and the other half were from Arab countries. With the arrival of these masses of newcomers, especially those from the developing countries, illiteracy, poverty, unemployment, and accompanying social problems increased significantly.

The initial housing conditions after the establishment of the state were poor. About half of the housing built between 1948 and 1972 was constructed by government. The standards of construction—building materials, dwelling size, infrastructure—were low in the first years. In addition, such immigrant neighborhoods suffered because of the low quality of social services or the lack of them.

The rapid increase in the standard of living of the better-off portion of the population in Israel tended to draw attention to the gap between the haves and the have-nots, creating political pressure for aid for the have-nots. This situation was aggravated by the tendency for the more capable and conscientious portions of the population in deprived neighborhoods to leave. This negative selection undermined the situation more, causing even greater contrast between these neighborhoods and better-off ones.

The poorer neighborhoods suffered further due to the normative preferences of the authorities in Israel. The early Zionist leadership aspired to the creation of a modern society based largely on agriculture, with little emphasis on the city. The result was that the per capita allocation of national resources favored the rural sector, with older towns and cities being allowed to grow without planning and little public investment. Distressed neighborhoods developed at the center and at the periphery of these towns. The authorities also preferred to allocate their resources to new development rather than to the conservation and the rehabilitation of the old. The pioneering spirit was dominant and was expressed in new construction at the expense of the neglect of older structures.

For all of these reasons, many distressed neighborhoods have developed in the country. In most of them, however, the dynamic processes of deterioration do not lead to a desperate situation in spite of the out-migration of the higher-status population. Most of the residents belong to stable families. Most of the housing units are structurally sound and have basic facilities, although housing density is high and the structures poorly maintained.

Project Renewal has developed some explicit principles for neighborhood rehabilitation based on the experience and professional perceptions of planners and practitioners. Emphasis is placed on the integration of physical and social rehabilitation. It is recognized that in the case of both social dysfunction and physical deterioration in the neighborhoods, it is necessary to tackle both aspects in an integrated manner. Lessons have been learned about the failure of efforts elsewhere that focused on physical rehabilitation. In order to carry out integrated rehabilitation, a high level of coordination has been required among the government bodies involved. Thus a steering committee has been set up for each neighborhood headed by the mayor of the town and composed of neighborhood residents and representatives of relevant municipal departments and the various national ministries.

Unlike traditional social programs where funds are allocated sectorally (for example, for education, housing, and health) and then distributed to towns and individuals, the allocation of resources in the rehabilitation program is on a comprehensive neighborhood basis, dealing with all problem areas simultaneously. Focusing on the neighborhood also means focusing on the residents in their existing place of residence—that is, rehabilitation without relocation—so as to enable residents to continue living in the physical and social environment to which they have become accustomed. Resident participation in the planning and implementation process is a central principle of Project Renewal. It is a major innovation for Israel, contrasting with the usual centralized decisionmaking. Such participation can help to overcome the psychological state of dependence on government so characteristic of such neighborhoods in Israel. Residents are involved in different stages of the rehabilitation process in various ways. They participate in the local steering committee and its subcommittees, usually on the basis of parity with the representatives of central and local government, and are also encouraged to participate in self-help housing programs. Voluntary work by residents is also encouraged.

A unique feature of the program is that it is intended to meet both the aspirations of residents from higher socioeconomic groups in the neighborhoods, as well as the needs of the particularly disadvantaged households. By retaining these elements, the image of the neighborhood is enhanced, and a neighborhood leadership cadre can be developed.

In conclusion, Project Renewal has introduced several innovations to the planning system. At the central government level, there is increased coordination among the various ministries concerning their activities at the local level; at the local level, there is greater coordination among the activities of various municipal departments; and at the neighborhood level, there is greater involvement of residents in planning and implementation processes than has previously been the case in Israel.

At a time of economic crisis in Israel, the challenge is the continuation of the present program in each of the neighborhoods where it has been initiated in order to complete the rehabilitation process. A second and related challenge is the need to begin phasing out the program in some of the rehabilitated neighborhoods, while avoiding their retrogression. The final challenge is the extension of the program to other neighborhoods for which it is appropriate despite budget cutbacks so that the goals of the program may be achieved.

Planning for Israel's Occupied Territories

Planning for the West Bank, Gaza, and the Golan Heights is a complex challenge for land use planners in Israel. These territories have been occupied by Israel since the Six Day War in 1967. Israel's status in most of these territories is that of an occupying authority under international law pending the eventual dispensation of these territories according to international agreement.

The future of the territories is a controversial political issue in Israel. It is one of the keys to possible peaceful relations between Israel and neighboring Arab states. At the same time the territories are considered by Israelis as important to Israel's security since Israel's major centers of population, such as Tel Aviv and Jerusalem, would be vulnerable if the territories are turned over to the control of states hostile to Israel. Whereas Israel's interest in the Golan Heights and the Gaza strip derives purely from security concerns, Israel's interest in Judea and Samaria, which comprise the West Bank, stems not only from security considerations but also because of a strong historical attachment by many Israelis who emphasize that Judea and Samaria were the location of the biblical state of Israel. The planning challenge thus has several partially contradictory dimensions: how to enable Jewish settlement in occupied territories that will not be an obstacle to the final disposition of the territories pending a peace agreement; how to enable settlement in the territories that will strengthen Israel's actual and perceived security; how to enable settlement in the territories that will allow sections of the population to settle in areas to which they have strong historical attachment; how to enable settlement in the territories that will not harm and preferably enhance the relations between Jews and Arabs in Israel and the occupied territories.

There are inherent conflicts between these objectives. Relations with the Arab population in the territories would be enhanced by preventing any Jewish settlements in the occupied territories. Similarly, the best way of ensuring that Jewish settlement in the occupied territories will not be an obstacle to their eventual disposition in a peace agreement between Israel and the Arab states would be by preventing Jewish settlement there altogether. On the other hand, Israel's security needs, according to the security doctrine that has prevailed since the establishment of the state, have dictated the establishment of Israeli settlements in various parts of the occupied territories. The attachment of parts of Israel's population to the West Bank has created strong pressure for settlement there.

The Labor government, which was in power for 29 years until 1977, favored a plan based on security considerations, called the Alon plan (named after its proponent, then the deputy prime minister). This plan called for agricultural settlements of small *kibbutzim* and *moshavim* along the sparsely populated Jordan Rift Valley so that the area would remain under Israeli control in any future settlement. This would ensure a presence, backed up by the army, that could assist in preventing a major military buildup on the West Bank that could threaten Israel. Thus the Labor government established 15 agricultural settlements in the Jordan Rift Valley (Ben-Zadok, forthcoming). The total population involved then was quite small.

The major settlement activity by the Labor government in the occupied territories was in the Jerusalem area. Its aim was to unify the city and to broaden the narrow wedge connecting the Jerusalem metropolitan area to the coastal plain, thus contributing to the security of the city and preventing its isolation. The eastern part of the city was formally annexed. Considerable resources have been devoted to expanding Jewish settlement in the eastern section of the city and beyond in areas previously governed by Jordan. Jerusalem's population has more than doubled and reached 350,000 by 1980. The Labor government also established agricultural settlements on the Golan Heights, which prior to 1967 had been used primarily for military purposes by Syria, threatening Jewish settlements in Galilee below. Today the Golan Heights has 32 settlements including Katsrin, a small town of 1,500 inhabitants (Rubenstein, 1983). The policy regarding the Gaza strip has been different. Although the Gaza strip had frequently been used as a base for attacks on Israel, the Labor government avoided establishing settlements there because of the high density of Arab population living in a relatively small area. Instead a series of agricultural settlements have been established for security purposes in the area immediately adjoining the Gaza strip.

When the nationalist Likud government came to power in 1977, a change occurred in Israel's settlement policies for the West Bank. The Labor government had restricted settlement of the West Bank to strategically important and, except the Jerusalem area, sparsely populated areas. The Likud government, claiming historical rights as well as security needs, supported Jewish settlements in all of the West Bank. This policy does not enjoy consensual support in Israel, whereas the previous elective settlement policy for security reasons was supported by the majority of the population. In 1977 there were 3,000 Jewish inhabitants in 15 settlements in the Jordan Rift. By the end of 1982 there were 105 Jewish settlements with 25,000 residents on the West Bank. In 1984 there were about 800,000 Arabs in 450 settlements on the West Bank, of whom 22,000 are living in the Jordan Rift Valley. The Likud government also established a small number of settlements in the Gaza strip and has added a few settlements on the Golan Heights.

One of the results of the Likud's West Bank policy has been that the conflicts between settlement objectives have been sharpened. The emphasis on security and defense needs has been at the expense of the potential for a future peace agreement with neighboring states. The emphasis on settlement on the basis of historical claims in areas with relatively large Arab populations has been at the expense of good relations between Jews and Arabs, in both the occupied territories and within Israel's 1967 borders. The emphasis on maximizing the dispersion of Jewish settlements throughout the West Bank has led to a large number of small settlements at the expense of their social and economic viability.

Israeli settlement of the West Bank will probably continue for the various reasons cited, but has to meet several challenges. The first challenge is to be able to meet all possible political eventualities. The overall plan for Israeli settlement should take into consideration various scenarios. One extreme scenario might be a change in the present Arab policy, leading to the recognition of the right of existence of the state of Israel and the acceptance of a certain number of Jewish settlements on the West Bank. At the other extreme would be a scenario focusing on the continuing opposition of the Arab states to the recognition of the right of the state of Israel to exist. Whereas it may be impossible to gear settlement policy simultaneously to both extreme scenarios, the challenge is to design a policy that takes into consideration a range of scenarios in the middle ground.

A second challenge is to reduce the grounds for conflict among the Arab and Jewish populations of the West Bank. This might be achieved by planning Jewish settlements in conjunction with Arab settlements in the region so that the welfare of all the residents, Arab and Jewish, can be enhanced. The third challenge relates to the viability of the West Bank settlements. Social and economic problems eventually will create a need for greater consolidation of the settlement effort so that individual settlements have larger populations. This will increase choices and opportunities for their residents, and the settlements can take greater advantage of localization economies. A possible pointer to future policy that could go some way to meeting all three of these challenges is that, whereas many small settlements are dispersed throughout the West Bank, most of the larger settlements that account for the substantial part of the new Jewish population are in areas quite close to the 1967 borders. These settlements are essentially part of the metropolitan regions of Tel Aviv and Jerusalem in which these residents are employed.

In conclusion, the planning for the West Bank and the other occupied territories presents a challenge with several components for Israeli planning: contingency planning in the face of great political uncertainty, planning so as to achieve improved relations between Jews and Arabs, and planning so as to take into consideration the relationship with the metropolitan development of Tel Aviv and Jerusalem.

SUMMARY AND CONCLUSION

Land in Israel is a scarce resource. As a result, land use planning is particularly important. Whereas initiatory planning has been a central guiding force throughout Israel's history, regulative planning has been less effective. This does not stem from lack of powers; on the contrary, Israel exhibits an orderly regulative system linking any given site plan with local, district, and national policies and potentially enabling tight controls. Rather, the problem has been with the conservative and passive stance of the regulative planning establishment, which has been unwilling to innovate.

Israel today faces several planning challenges. In order to deal effectively with them, a better balance has to be struck between the initiatory system and the regulative system. Israel's planning in its early years had an impressive capacity for vision and capability of focusing on the central objectives. The planning challenges of the 1980s require the introduction of vision into land use planning thought once again.

BIBLIOGRAPHY

Alexander, E., R. Alterman and H. Law Yone. 1983. *Evaluating Plan Implementation: The National Planning System in Israel.* Oxford: Pergamon.

Alterman, R. 1979. Land Betterment Taxation Policy and Planning Implementation: Evaluation of the Israeli Experience. *Urban Law and Policy* 2(2):201–40.

Alterman, R. 1980. Decision-making in Urban Plan Implementation: Does the Dog Wag the Tail or the Tail Wag the Dog? *Urban Law and Policy* 3(1):41–58.

Alterman, R. 1981. The Planning and Building Law and the Local Plan: Rigid Regulations or a Flexible Framework? *Mishpatim (Law Journal of the Faculty of Law, Hebrew University)* 11(2):197–200.

Alterman, R. 1982. *Land Value Recapture: Design and Evaluation of Alternative Policies,* Vancouver: University of British Columbia, Occasional Paper No. 25, Center for Human Settlements.

Alterman, R., and A. Frenkel. 1982. Exactions of Land for Public Services as a Tool of Plan Implementation, *Karka* (Land) 23:20–27.

Akzin, B., and Y. Dror. 1966. *Israel: High-Pressure Planning.* Ithaca: Syracuse University Press.

Ben-Zadok, E. Forthcoming. Incompatible Planning Goals: Evaluating Israel's New Community Development in the West Bank. *Journal of the American Planners Association.*

Berler, A. 1970. *New Towns in Israel.* Jerusalem: Israel Universities Press.

Borukhov, E. 1980. Land Policy in Israel. *Habitat International* 4(4/5/6):505–15.

Carmon, N., and M. Hill. 1984. Project Renewal: An Israeli Experiment in Neighborhood Rehabilitation. *Habitat International* 8(2):117–132.

Central Bureau of Statistics. 1950, 1953, 1958, 1960, 1963, 1965, 1968, 1969, 1975, 1982, 1983. *Statistical Abstract of Israel.* Jerusalem.

Cohen, E. 1970. *The City in Zionist Ideology.* Jerusalem: Urban Studies Series: Hebrew University.

Gouldman, M. 1966. *Legal Aspects of Town Planning in Israel.* Jerusalem: Institute for Legislative Research and Comparative Law.

Granot, A. 1952. *The Land System of Palestine.* London: Eyre and Spottiswoode.

Hill, M. 1980. Planning in Turbulence: The Israeli Experience. *Contact* 12(1):55–76.

Howard, E. 1945. *Garden Cities for Tomorrow.* London: Faber and Faber.

Israel. 1965. Planning and Building Law. *Laws of the State of Israel, 1965.* Jerusalem: Government Printer.

Israel Institute for Urban Research. 1972. *Municipal Reform in the Dan Urban Region.* Tel Aviv: The Institute.

Law Yone, H., and R. Wilkansky. 1984. From Consensus to Fragmentation: The Dynamics of Paradigm Change in Israel. *Socio-economic Planning Sciences.*

Naor, G. et al. 1978. *Local Government in Israel.* Publication No. 24. Rehovot: Center for Rural and Urban Settlement Studies.

Rubenstein, M. 1983. *Challenges and Answers in the New Settlement Process on the Golan Heights.* Ph.D. dissertation, Hebrew University.

Shachar, A. 1971. Israeli Development Towns: Evaluation of National Urbanization Policy. *Journal of the American Institute of Planners.* 37:362–372.

PART III

AFRICA

7

Sudan

IAN HAYWOOD and ADIL MUSTAFA AHMAD

HISTORICAL DEVELOPMENT

Sudan, like many other developing countries, is one of those accidents of history where the creation of countries owed more to the interests of the European powers than a consideration of tribal affinities or topographic features. The resultant boundaries have created the largest country in Africa, with an area of some 2.5 million square kilometers, embracing about 20 million people belonging to nearly six hundred different tribes speaking 26 major languages (Figure 7.1). The topography ranges from desert regions in the north, with less than 40 millimeters annual rainfall, to woodland savanna in the south, with nearly 1,000 millimeters of rain, all linked by the Blue and White Niles flowing north to form the River Nile at Khartoum.

Sudan up to 1881

The history of northern Sudan has always been interwoven with the affairs of Egypt through the movement of peoples up and down the Nile. In ancient times Sudan was a province of Egypt. For nearly one thousand years, however, Egypt was ruled by Sudan, until the establishment of a separate Christian kingdom in Sudan in the fourth century A.D. The influx of Arabs into northern Sudan led to the spread of Islam and the displacement of Christianity by a negroid Muslim sultanate in the early sixteenth century. Subsequent internal dissent and fighting among rival tribal groups led to the breakdown of the sultanate. As such, there was little resistance to the invasion and conquest of the country by the Turco-Egyptian forces in 1821.

Figure 7.1 Map Showing Location of Sudan in Africa

The Mahdiya, 1881–1898

In 1881 a nationalistic uprising began in Sudan, led by a religious leader
known as the Mahdi. The Mahdi and his forces ended the occupation of Sudan
by overwhelming Khartoum in 1885 and killing the British governor-general,
General Gordon. In 1882 Britain had invaded Egypt and assumed responsibility for the affairs of both Egypt and Sudan. By the 1890s the European scram-
ble for Africa had begun in earnest. Britain recognized that if it was to maintain
its interests in Egypt, controlling Sudan and the Nile waters was essential. In
1896 the British government decided to reconquer Sudan and dispatched an
expeditionary force, which defeated the forces of the Mahdi in 1898 and reclaimed Sudan for Britain and Egypt. In 1899 the Condominium Agreement
was signed by Britain and Egypt. This agreement served as the constitution of
the Sudan and established the boundaries of the country and the basis under
which Britain and Egypt would administer the country (Holt, 1961).

Beginnings of Development

Sudan had been conquered to protect Britain's strategic interests in Egypt, but it was not intended that Sudan should become a burden on Britain. Therefore economic development would have to take place not only to cover the costs of administering the country but also to provide some economic benefits to Britain.

The first step in developing the country was to establish Khartoum as the administrative center of the country linked to a series of regional administrative centers in twelve new provinces. The next major step in development was to expand the railway and telegraph system to link the new administrative centers to Khartoum and Cairo and to provide the basis for further development. In 1899 the railway was extended from Atbara to Khartoum, and in 1906 a new link was provided across the desert from Atbara to the port at Suakin. In 1909 a new port was developed north of Suakin and officially named Port Sudan. The railway was extended westward to Kordofan in 1911 to assist in the exploitation of gum arabic, and in 1912 it was extended to El Obeid. A new line was laid in 1924 to the east to reach Kassala and eventually provide a second route to Port Sudan. By 1915 automobiles were a common sight in Sudan, providing access in the dry season to areas not connected to the railway system. Communications with the south were improved by clearing a passage through the Sudd swamp on the White Nile and developing river transport (Figure 7.2).

As early as 1840, during Turco-Egyptian rule, experiments had been conducted in the east at Kassala and Tokar in the growing of cotton under rain-fed conditions. It was shown that both cotton and wheat crops were feasible in Sudan. In 1906 a modest scheme of pumps had been created to grow long staple cotton and wheat on the banks of the Nile at Zeidab just south of Atbara. This was followed by a second scheme in 1911 at Tayiba north of Wad Medani and a further scheme at Barakat in 1915 near Wad Medani. The success of these earlier schemes had led to the undertaking of survey work in the area around Wad Medani to locate a site for a much larger scheme. This survey work indicated that the peninsula of land formed by the Blue and White Niles south of Khartoum, known as the Gezira, would provide an ideal location for growing cotton.

As a result of these investigations, construction of a dam at Sennar, across the Blue Nile, to irrigate an area of some 1.2 million hectares of land, was begun in 1913. World War I delayed completion of the dam and the inauguration of the project until 1926. Despite this the general development of agriculture had been so successful that before the end of the war, the national budget was in surplus. Initially only some 120,000 hectares of land were developed for production in the Gezira. The demands of the British cotton industry, the need for development in Sudan to be self-financing, and the obvious importance of cotton to the national economy led, however, to the general expansion of areas under cotton cultivation. New projects were developed in the Gash delta and Tokar in the east, in the Northern Province, and, on a smaller scale, in the Nuba mountains, Upper Nile, and Dongola provinces.

Figure 7.2 Map of Sudan and Its Regions

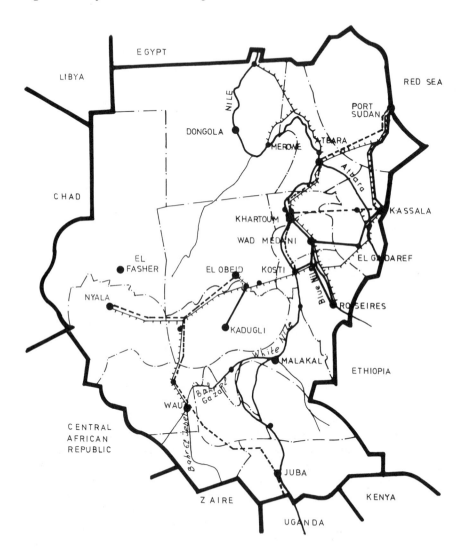

A series of agreements made with Egypt had the effect of increasing the amount of water available to Sudan for irrigation from the Nile. As a result, the original Gezira area was increased in 1929, 1931, and 1950 to bring the total area under cultivation up to 420,000 hectares (Gaitskell, 1959).

Development of the Administrative System

The expansion of agriculture was accompanied by the development of the administrative system. Until 1922 a system of direct rule had operated under governors and district commissioners. At this time efforts were made to revive and integrate the old tribal system into the formal administration of the country by means of the Sheikhs Ordinance of 1922. This gave limited legal powers to some of the tribal sheikhs and chiefs to administer justice, carry out some general administrative functions, and collect taxes. These powers were further strengthened in 1927 with a new Powers of the Sheikhs Ordinance. In 1928 new administrative boundaries were established in an effort to create more practical geographical and economic units. In 1937 the Local Government (Rural Areas) Ordinance was passed, creating representative local authorities in rural areas, and in 1939 similar legislation extended the system to the urban areas and Khartoum. It was an attempt to model local government in Sudan on the British example and to give local authorities a degree of independence, with their own specific functions to perform backed by their own staff and independent sources of revenue (Howell, 1974).

Southern Region

As part of its policy to restrict the infiltration of Arabs into southern Sudan and the spread of Islam, the British government adopted a policy of separate development for the south of Sudan in the 1920s. The government declared large parts of southern Sudan closed areas, which enabled it to control both the movement of people into the areas and trading activities.

As a result, little economic development took place in the south. It was limited mainly to small rubber plantations established in 1921, cotton in 1923, and coffee in 1925. The restrictions on traders and trade had an adverse effect on further development. In 1930 these policies were formally brought together in the Memorandum on Southern Policy issued by the civil secretary in Khartoum. Behind the memorandum was the development of the official view that southern Sudan might eventually be cut off from the north and linked into some other central African grouping.

During the late 1930s and early 1940s, the southern policy came under ever-increasing criticism from the northern Sudanese. The British administration recognized that the only justification for their policy would be if they could demonstrate a reasonable level of economic development in the south. As a result, a ten-year development plan for the south was prepared in the early 1940s, but

World War II intervened before much progress could be made in implementing the proposals. After the war, it was apparent that the southern policy was becoming an increasingly sensitive issue. The north was clearly moving toward independence and did not accept the southern policy; East Africa generally was cool toward any proposal to embrace an increasingly backward country; and world opinion was moving more strongly against colonialism and toward greater concern for the rights of colonized peoples.

The result was that the government was forced to reverse its existing policy in 1946 and accept that, despite ethnic and cultural differences, the future development of the south was inextricably linked with the north (Beshir, 1970).

Independence

On 1 January 1956 Sudan became independent after a three-year transitional period of national rule. The new parliamentary democracy was based on a two-tier system with a House of Representatives and a Senate and an elected prime minister responsible to a five-man Supreme Commission. An armed uprising had, however, already begun in the south in 1955, largely as a result of the southern peoples' exclusion from the constitutional discussions. By 1958 the failure of the new government in addressing the problems of the economy and national unity led to a take-over by the army and the establishment of a military government. In October 1964 this military government was ousted and replaced with a new civilian administration, which itself was overthrown by a military coup in May 1969.

The current political system dates from this revolution and consists of a military oligarchy that ensures its power base through the imposition of a one-party system on the country. Supreme power lies with the president who rules by directive; the People's Assembly serves as a nominal debating chamber and has no effective political power.

Development of Settlements and Land Uses

Sudan at Independence in 1956

At the time of independence, the 1955-56 national census established the total population of Sudan as 10,262,536 people, with an estimated annual rate of increase around 2.8 percent. The country was still rural, with 853,872 people, or 8.3 percent of the population, living in centers that were considered to perform an urban function. Of this urban population 245,736 lived in greater Khartoum. El Obeid, Port Sudan, and Wad Medani formed the next rank of urban centers, each with a population of about 50,000. Kassala, Atbara, El Fasher, and Kosti had populations in the 20,000 to 40,000 range, 11 towns had populations of 10,000 to 20,000, and 16 towns had populations in the range 5,000 to 10,000.

Apart from the railway network, which had been developed during the colonial period, the infrastructure of the country had not yet developed. The railway and the telephone were still the main means of communication because there were no paved roads outside the urban areas and travel in the rainy season was impossible in most parts of the country.

Khartoum served as the administrative center of the country and, with its specially created industrial areas, was the main focus for industrial development. Port Sudan, as the only port, served as a second industrial center with its port-related activities. Apart from intensive horticulture along the banks of the Blue and White Niles and the main Nile and some rain-fed agriculture, the only substantial economic activity in the country was provided by the Gezira irrigated project with an area of some 420,000 hectares. The Gezira project, which had begun in 1926, had established Sudan as a major producer of long staple cotton and provided the main source of revenue for the country.

Sudan in the 1970s

In 1973 the government undertook a second national census. The results, however, have never been officially published, due partly to doubts about their reliability and also because of the political sensitivity concerning the division of the population between northern and southern Sudan. Information that has been released, however, gave the 1973 population of Sudan as 14.171 million with an average annual rate of increase of 1.8 percent. Informal revisions of these figures give a more likely total population of some 17 million with an annual growth rate of 2.3 percent for the period 1960-70 and 2.6 percent for 1970-77 (Satterthwaite, 1979).

The process of urbanization had continued; the number of settlements classified as having an urban function had increased to 111, with a population of 2,605,896, or 17.4 percent of the national total. Within this process of urbanization there had been a change in the pattern of settlement sizes. In 1956 some 40 percent of the urban dwellers lived in towns of fewer than 20,000 people, and some 13 percent lived in Khartoum, the only center with a population of more than 100,000. By 1973 the proportion living in small towns of under 20,000 people had dropped to less than 30 percent, but those living in cities over 100,000 people had risen to 40 percent. Khartoum had increased in size to 784,294 people and still accounted for approximately 30 percent of all the urban population in Sudan. Average annual rates of urban growth were estimated to be 6.25 percent, but there were substantial regional variations ranging from a high of 7.7 percent for Wad Medani and a low of 2.8 percent for El Obeid. These differences largely reflect the poor communications in the country and the reliance on traditional forms of agriculture, the main economic activity of the peripheral regions. There was a concentration of investment in the central region.

By 1973 the hierarchy of settlements had changed. Port Sudan had developed into the second largest city with a population of 132,632, and Wad Medani had more than doubled in size to 106,715 people. El Obeid had grown more slowly to reach a population of 90,078 and had been overtaken by Kassala, which had increased to 99,652. A further seven towns had populations in excess of 50,000 people, and eight towns were in the 20,000 to 40,000 range (Arifi, 1971).

Economic Planning

Shortly after independence the Sudan produced its first economic development plan, "The Ten Year Plan of Economic and Social Development 1961/62–1970/71." By the late 1960s, it was clear, however, that the country was failing in the achievement of the objectives of the plan, due largely to the lack of capital investment. When the civilian administration was replaced by a military government in 1969, the country turned to the communist block for assistance in revising its planning objectives, which took the form of a new five-year plan (1970–75). This plan was, again, quickly seen not to be achieving its objectives. Because of what it considered to be political interference in the affairs of the country, Sudan broke its close ties with the communist block and produced a new five-year plan in 1972 as an interim program of action designed to supplement the five-year plan.

During the period of the five-year plan, a process of evaluation was set up to assess the economic performance of the country as a basis for future planning. The outcome of this exercise was an 18-year perspective plan, 1977/78–1994/95, that formed the framework for a six-year plan of economic and social development, 1977/78–1982/83.

Although all of these plans varied in both detail and performance, they were based on the common objective of achieving self-sustained growth by transforming the traditional agricultural sector into modern mechanized agriculture and using the increased output to reduce imports and stimulate industrial investment. A concern for social equity and the balanced distribution of investment over the different regions of the country were other planning objectives.

One factor that contributed to the poor economic performance of the country was the civil war in southern Sudan, which began shortly before independence and did not end until 1972.[1] During that period all development stopped in the southern region, and there was much destruction of buildings and infrastructure. The administration, it was estimated, had a loss of £s5 million a year.[2] One million people were forced to flee from their homes, and estimates of the numbers killed are as high as 500,000 people (O'Ballance, 1977). The effects of the war were not confined to the southern region and spread throughout the country in the form of economic stagnation and political instability. It was, as well, a constant drain on the nation's meager resources.

Reform of Local Government

Efforts to create some form of national planning were matched by reforms aimed at modernizing the system of local government during the 1970s. The intention was to create an element of decentralization while ensuring continued support for the one-party system. In 1971 the government introduced the Peoples' Local Government Act, which was aimed at breaking the role of tribal leaders

in local administration and replacing them with people more sympathetic politically to the views of the central government. The country was divided into ten
provinces, each with a four-tier system of local administration. At the lowest
level were village and neighborhood councils, with rural and town councils at
the middle level, and a higher tier of regional and city councils. The whole local
government system was responsible to the People's Province Executive Council
under the chairmanship of the provincial commissioner, who was a nominee of
the president with the status of minister. Membership to the councils was by
election, although provision was made for up to 33 percent of the members to
be nominated. To stand for election, one had to be a member of the Sudan
Socialist Union as the only permitted political party. Election to the higher
councils was from members who sat at the lower levels.

Under the 1971 act, it had been intended that all government services would
be channeled through the provincial executive councils, who in turn would
devolve certain powers to the lower-level councils. In practice, the shortage of
manpower at the local level and the reluctance of central ministries to relinquish
power meant that little real devolution took place. The highly centralized system
was maintained with the provincial councils having little power.

In an effort to reduce the power of the central ministries and achieve a genuine
measure of devolution, the Regional Government Act was passed in 1980 dividing Sudan into seven regions. The new regional authorities were to be between
the provincial and central government levels. Each region has a Peoples' Regional
Assembly of elected and nominated members responsible to a regional governor,
again nominated by the president and given the status of minister. The central
government ministries were reorganized and regional offices of the central ministries created, each headed by a regional minister responsible for his department's affairs within his region. Included in this devolution is the development
and control of land use and town planning, which is now a regional government
function (Figure 7.3).

Development of Rural Land Uses

During the colonial era, rural land use policies had concentrated mainly on
the development of irrigated agricultural schemes along the banks of the Blue
and White Nile and the main Nile. A series of water agreements with Egypt
established an overall water use policy aimed at ensuring adequate supplies of
water for both countries. Irrigated schemes therefore were based on either the
use of stored water from newly constructed dams or the limited pumping of
water direct from the rivers. The first of the new dams had been constructed at
Sennar on the Blue Nile, about 250 kilometers southeast of Khartoum. Completed
in 1926, this provided the water for the development of the Gezira scheme. The
second dam was at Jebel Aulia on the White Nile about 40 kilometers south of
Khartoum. The purpose of this dam was to hold back water during the flood
season to enable water to be drawn from the river throughout the year in both
Sudan and Egypt. It was completed in 1937 and led to the development of

Figure 7.3 Regionalization and the Structure of Decentralized Government

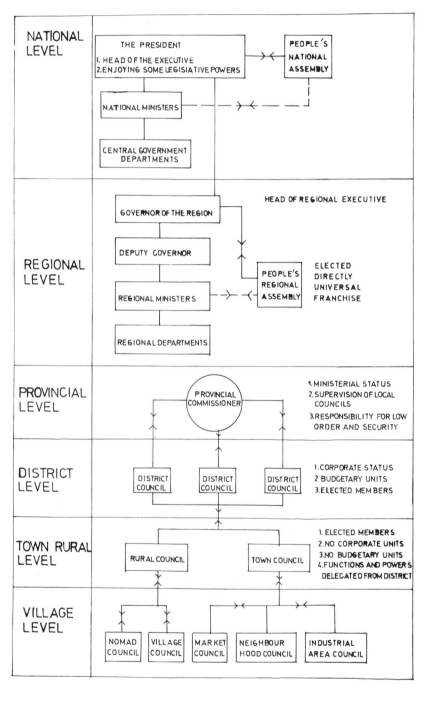

extensive pumped projects along the banks of the White Nile, south of the dam, with more limited projects to the north[3] (Figure 7.4).

The initial development of the Gezira project had demonstrated the feasibility of growing cotton in large-scale irrigated projects. In 1957 proposals were developed for the extension of the project by a further 350,000 hectares, irrigated from a new dam on the Blue Nile. In 1959 a new Nile Waters Agreement between Egypt and Sudan paved the way for the construction of the Aswan High Dam in Egypt. The lake that would be created by this new dam necessitated the evacuation of the 50,000 people forming the population of the Nubian town of Wadi Halfa in northern Sudan just south of the border with Egypt. The government decided to build a new town and irrigated agricultural project in the southeast, between Gedaref and Kassala, to resettle the displaced population. A new dam was completed in 1964 at Khashm El Girba on the River Atbara designed to irrigate some 180,000 hectares of land divided into 30,000 tenancies, growing mainly cotton, groundnuts, and sugar on state plantations. In 1966 the new dam at Roseiris on the Blue Nile, about 450 kilometers from Khartoum, was completed to serve the Managil extension of the Gezira project. This increased the total area of Gezira to about 850,000 hectares, which provided a livelihood for some 100,000 tenants and an estimated 200,000 seasonal workers.

The resolution of the civil war in 1972 brought a measure of political stability to Sudan. This not only released resources for development but also created a more favorable climate for the attraction of investment by international financial and aid organizations. The six-year plan had set out the general objectives for development, and a new impetus developed with the emphasis on the modernization of the traditional agricultural sector, limited industrial development, and the improvement of communications.

The success of growing cotton on a large scale led to a proposal for a new irrigated project at Rahad in the southeast of the country between Gedaref and Wad Medani. This project was completed in 1980 and brought more than 500,000 hectares of land under cultivation by means of a new irrigation system fed by a dam on the Rahad River and water pumped from the Blue Nile. Approximately 16,000 families living in the area were resettled as tenant farmers, growing cotton as the main crop with some subsidiary cash crops. In addition to the tenant farmers, seasonal employment is provided for 90,000 more workers.

A further boost to the production of sugar in Sudan was generated by the development of the Kenana sugar plantation, approximately 315 kilometers south of Khartoum near Kosti. The plantation, begun in 1975 and completed in 1981, covers an area of some 50,000 hectares, irrigated by pumps from the White Nile, to grow sugar cane. The project is largely self-sufficient and includes 81 villages for agricultural workers. Each village houses a population of about 100 people. A main town with a population of some 8,000 people provides accommodation for administrators and managers. Kenana provides employment for about 15,000 people, including seasonal workers.

In a joint effort to increase the amount of water available for irrigation in both

Figure 7.4 Map Showing Sudan's Agricultural and Mineral Resources

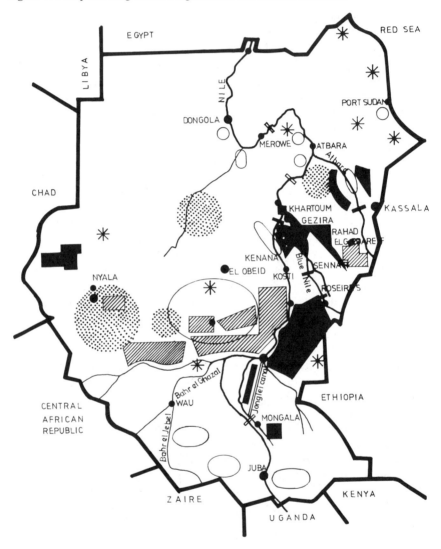

Egypt and Sudan, the two countries began work in 1977 on building the Jonglei canal as a bypass system to the Sudd swamps on the White Nile in southern Sudan. Since the 1890s, various proposals had been discussed aimed at increasing the flow of water and reducing losses by evaporation. The project is scheduled for completion in the mid-1980s. The canal will be 360 kilometers long, with an estimated saving of some 5 billion cubic meters of water a year. In addition to saving water, the new canal, which forms the principal link between the north and south, will provide a more direct river route between Kosti and Juba, saving approximately 300 kilometers on a journey of 1,435 kilometers. It is also envisaged that the new canal will enable a further 1.5 million hectares of land to be irrigated and will serve to assist in settling the nomadic population in the region, estimated at some 350,000 people.

Urban Land Uses

During the British colonial period, a simple form of gridiron urban planning was developed to accommodate expansion resulting from the new economic and administrative growth. The surveyors' grid plan was applied to generate standard street layouts that provided plots of land for housing, administrative areas, *souks*, industrial areas, religious buildings, and open space. Land uses were rigorously zoned, with housing areas divided into first-class areas for the expatriate administrators, second-class areas for the native administrators, and third-class areas for laborers. Industry was generally restricted to industrial areas on the perimeter of the towns, although some small workshops were permitted in the *souk* areas.

The same general design and space standards were applied throughout the country. In some instances, towns, or parts of their centers, were replanned on these gridiron lines. In others, such as Khartoum, complete new extensions were planned to these new standards and contrasted strongly with the traditional organic urban forms that had developed. Limited provision was made for the development of urban services. The administrative and first-class housing areas generally were supplied with water to the site, but other areas and the lesser classes of housing had to make do with standpipes. In the town centers and first-class areas, closed culverts were provided for storm water drainage, but in other areas these were left open. Sanitary systems were restricted to pit latrines or bucket systems depending on subsoil conditions.

With the exception of Port Sudan and Khashm El Girba, the only new planned urban settlements have been in connection with the provision of housing for agricultural developments. In these instances, a generally more innovative approach to land use development has been applied. In existing settlements, the needs of urban renewal or expansion generally have been met through the application of the old colonial design and space standards.

Infrastructure Development

In the 1970s, there was a greater effort directed at improvement of the infrastructure. With the exception of the Jebel Aulia dam, all the new dams have been designed to provide hydroelectric power. Recent improvements have increased the generating capacity at both Sennar and Roseiris dams. It is estimated, however, that of the potential 2,000 megawatts of hydroelectric power, only some 10 percent has been utilized, and there is no national grid system (Suliman, 1975). Until recently there were no tarmac paved roads outside the main urban centers. During the 1970s work began on the development of an all-weather tarmac road connecting Khartoum to Port Sudan via Wad Medani, Gedaref, and Kassala over a distance of some 1,195 kilometers. It was completed in 1980. Apart from this road there are only a few hundred kilometers of tarmac paved roads in the country. There are a further 5,000 kilometers of improved gravel surfaced roads, but over much of the country major connections still consist of unimproved dirt track roads. The general road building policy has been either to develop links off the new Khartoum to Port Sudan road or provide links to railheads.

The railway, a narrow gauge system with a network of 4,758 kilometers, is playing a declining role in Sudan's transport system. The decline is generally attributable to poor management, lack of capital investment, and the poor condition of both the track and rolling stock. The railway still provides the only land connection to Egypt and is an important link with the docks at Port Sudan. During the late 1970s, an improvement program was undertaken in Port Sudan to increase the number of ship berths and the port's handling capacity and to provide some roll-on, roll-off facilities. Preliminary studies were also set to develop a new complex approximately 40 kilometers south of Port Sudan.

USE OF LAND IN SUDAN

Sudan is the largest African country with a surface area of some 250 million hectares. The 1983 census puts the population of the Sudan at about 20 million, with an annual growth rate of some 2.6 percent. Approximately 25 percent of the population lives in urban centers, which are growing at about 7.1 percent per annum. With an overall density of 12.5 hectares per person, Sudan is still a sparsely populated country and also one of the poorest in both Africa and the Arab world, with a GNP per capita figure of $410 in 1980. During the period 1960–80 the GNP declined at an annual average rate of 0.2 percent (World Bank, 1982).

Of Sudan's total surface area, it is estimated that about 15 percent is already developed or unsuitable for cultivation. Of the remaining area, approximately 34 percent is considered suitable for cash and food crops; 36 percent could support forestry; 5 percent is water, which could contribute to the development of freshwater fisheries; and the remaining 10 percent is suitable for meadowland and pasture. In addition to this agricultural potential, attention has concentrated more recently on the mineral potential of the country, particularly since the discovery of oil in Bentiu in the southern region. Other known mineral deposits, only some of which are being exploited, include gold, gypsum, and iron ore in the Red Sea Hills; chromite and iron ore in the Ingessana Hills to the southeast; iron ore in Kordofan; and copper in Darfur to the west.

With an agricultural land potential of more than 100 million hectares, approximately 31 million hectares of land are actually in some form of agricultural production. Only 3.2 million hectares are directly cultivated, comprising 2.6 million hectares under rain-fed crops and 0.6 million hectare in irrigated schemes (World Markets, 1979).

The general pattern of urbanization in Sudan reflects both the prosperity and the magnetism of the central region and Khartoum. As the primate city, Khartoum stands at the center of the administrative and communications networks and is a focus for service employment and industrial investment. The Gezira, just to the south of Khartoum, is the largest agricultural development in Sudan and provides an economic stimulus to the development of both Wad Medani, as the regional center, and Khartoum as the capital. Although some efforts have been made to decentralize industrial development, it is estimated that Khartoum accounts for 73% of all manufacturing investment and around 66 percent of the total manufacturing output (Hassan, 1976).

Because of its huge area, sparse population, poor infrastructure, and acute economic problems, planning is seen primarily as an economic exercise designed to improve the economic performance of the country. Land use planning is seen as an essentially ancillary function of an engineering nature. At present it is restricted to the preparation of zoning and subdivision plans intended to accommodate predetermined forms of development for agricultural schemes, urban expansion, or renewal. As such it is essentially reactive, with hardly any acceptance as a forward integrative function forming an essential part of the development process.

A secondary factor contributing to the neglect of land use planning is that in general there is no land shortage in Sudan as most settlements are surrounded by endless desert or scrub. Also the colonial administration set up quite rigid standards for housing layout and subdivision proposals that are still followed today. In most settlement development, land use planning is seen, therefore, as a surveying exercise setting out more plots in the desert to accommodate expansion. Where planning has tried to raise larger issues concerning the integration of land uses, the allocation of land, use of resources, and priorities, it has run into political difficulties that result from the administration's desire to obtain the maximum revenue from site disposal without consideration of wider issues.

At present there is no general acceptance of land use planning as an essential part of development. The only planning that takes place is concerned with limited upgrading or improvement projects and site disposal for new development, with little regard paid to the broader aspects of integrated land use planning or forward planning.

INSTITUTIONAL AND LANDOWNERSHIP FRAMEWORK

Land Registration

Proper land registration in Sudan began in 1904 when a special office was set up for the purpose and linked to the Department of Agriculture (which was then renamed the Department of Agriculture and Land). In 1909 this office, the Khartoum Land Registration Office, was moved to the Judiciary. Gradually it gained more independence in running its affairs, and in 1914 its first director was appointed. Over a dozen laws, provincial and local, were in operation regarding matters of ownership, tenure, use, restriction of use, arbitration, confiscation, residence in land adjacent to towns, preemption, and others. In 1925 these laws were reexamined, updated, and formulated into the Land Settlement and Registration Ordinance (Minnalla, 1983). One section of the ordinance put under state ownership all waste, forest, and unoccupied land in the country, including land cultivable at irregular intervals. This meant in practice all (99.9 percent) of the country's territory.

A new law was passed modifying some parts of the ordinance in 1970. It increased the state's control over land by declaring that all land is considered as registered to the government until its ownership is established otherwise.

Today, following the policy of decentralization, a new structure is being set up. The Land Registration office was moved in 1983 to operate under the Ministry of Interior Affairs. The new administrative structure is shown in Figure 7.3. The organization of the land administration has still not crystallized, the responsibility being shared between the Ministry of Construction and Public Works and the Commission of the National Capital at present.

Ownership and Tenure Patterns

Agricultural Land

Tenure and use of agricultural land fall into a variety of patterns (government, private, and communal, for example) arising from local environmental conditions such as the availability of land, the system of irrigation (flooding, pumps, rain), and sociocultural conditions. Large-scale projects, such as the Gezira, are run by the government; there, land is plentiful, flood irrigation is available, and intensive cultivation is possible. In this case, land is rented to tenant farmers. This system of rent places a minimum risk on the tenant, whose sole contribution then becomes his effort. But the fact that he is not totally secure, since his tenancy can be withdrawn on the recommendation of the field inspector, is a barrier to any long-term planning by the farmer. This is thought to account in part for the poor housing conditions prevalent in the area.

Where land is in short supply as, for example, along the northern stretches of the Nile, the main problem is its fragmentation among numerous owners. Here private ownership is the rule, and cultivation is small scale and year round.

Privately run seasonal farming exists in the large rain-fed areas in the eastern plains. In this case, land is mostly leased, although private ownership exists to a limited extent.

In the south, where there is subsistence farming together with pasture land and marshes, tenure rights are tribal. Communal use of rainland and pastures for grazing and firewood is common, and tribes are given the exclusive right to exploit their territory. Conflicts have arisen in a few cases when the zones of the different groups overlapped or when those who have traditionally exploited the natural vegetation, for example, came into confrontation with others who had obtained the right to cultivate the land.

Urban Land

Freehold ownership covers only a minor part of urban areas. In the three-town capital, the highest proportion of private ownership is in Omdurman, with a few pockets in Khartoum North and Khartoum. The ownership and occupancy of these plots were established long before proper land registration was introduced. The Law of Eminent Domain, however, gives the authorities full power to intervene and a free hand to carry out acquisition or alterations for the public good. Compensation is usually paid to the adversely affected owners, and nominal charges are collected from those who are favorably affected (for example, in eliminating access lanes and hence increasing plot areas).

Urban land is, however, mostly state owned and leasehold. The duration of the lease is 40 years in third-class areas, starting with an initial period of 20 years and renewable for two further periods of 10 years each. In second-class areas, the duration of the lease is 70 years, starting with a period of 30 years, to be followed by two others of 20 years each. First-class areas enjoy the maximum lease of 80 years with a period of 50 years granted initially and a subsequent extension of 30 years. Fourth-class areas and land at the periphery of large towns settled temporarily by squatters remain state owned until they are planned (or replanned) as third-class areas. They are then provided with suitable infrastructure and their inhabitants granted legal leases. This system of granting land only on a leasehold basis is particularly effective in regaining unearned increments in land value, retaining state control over its use, and ensuring flexibility in adapting to continually changing needs.

Islamic trust or *waqf* land makes up only a small percentage of urban and agricultural land. It can be private or public. Public *waqf* land is affiliated to institutions such as mosques, schools, and cemeteries. In the case of agricultural land, the beneficiary cultivates the plot and pays the trust a certain percentage of the returns, usually a third or a half. In the case of urban property, the beneficiary's contribution is his effort in return for a share of the revenue. Private *waqf*, on the other hand, is offered by the creator or testator of the trust to nominated beneficiaries who may or may not be members of his family. They are thereby authorized to utilize the plot according to the terms specified by the deed of the trust. In the case of any violation or mismanagement, the trust authorities retain the right to take over its administration, in which case the beneficiaries are compensated by being paid 25 to 30 percent of the returns.

Despite this apparently effective system, land titles around old settlements are far from settled. Natives' claims to ownership of land continue and the evidence produced to prove its descent from ancestors are not always easy to dismiss. There was a rush to buy land in suburban Khartoum from the natives in the mid and late 1970s, and speculation reached a peak until the commissioner's strict intervention. Development projects have been held up by these disputes at times.

Classification of Urban Land

Urban land is classified as first, second, third, and fourth (or unplanned). The classification is based on plot size, the minimum standard of building materials, the minimum infrastructure provided, and the building regulations and bylaws that control development. Buildings in first-class areas are required to be built of permanent materials, burned bricks being the minimum acceptable; in second-class areas, semipermanent materials, mud brick walls with a red brick facing, are the minimum acceptable. Both areas must have piped water, electricity supply and sewerage connections to the plot boundary, paved roads for all access and main roads, covered rainwater drains, street lighting, and refuse collection with a house-to-house service by refuse vehicles. First-class areas have, in addition, paved footpaths, trees, and larger plots. Generally, however, sewage disposal in all first- and second-class areas has been through septic tanks and soakaway wells within each plot. The minimum standard for materials in third-class areas is traditional mud construction. The area should be supplied with piped water and with electricity. The minimum provision is unsurfaced access roads, open rain ditches, an asphalted road with covered rainwater drains to the town center, refuse collection services in containers conveniently located within the residential area, and human waste disposal on site by water privies and pit latrines. Services to unplanned and squatter areas are restricted to the most basic: communal water taps and unsurfaced access roads with open drainage ditches. Until recently these services could be achieved only through self-help. These areas are built of perishable materials—mud, thatch and, cardboard (hence the reference to them as "carton" neighborhoods)—until they are replanned and upgraded to third-class areas.

Although this classification, based primarily on income level, is practical in that it provides the various social groups with the facilities they can afford, in reality it tends to emphasize the differences separating these groups. First- and third-class neighborhoods often stare at each other uncomfortably across the street. Corner shops that used to cater to the daily needs of the latter undergo drastic modification when they begin to serve instead the affluent newcomers and fill overnight with luxury and consumer goods.

Acquisition of Urban Land

To acquire a plot of land at the basic price, the Sudanese citizen competes in a closed auction for the site and service projects offered by the government. Priority is determined through a points system that takes into account income, size of family (and other dependents), length of service for civil servants, and similar matters. Special groups, such as couples who cannot have children, are considered separately. The conditions also include certain restrictions as precautions against misuse; examples are the specification of a minimum level of development (one habitable room, the boundary wall, and services) within a year of acquiring the plot and the prohibition of the sale of the property until a specified period of time has elapsed after the completion of construction. These conditions are stated but rarely acted on since the government itself rarely provides the service part on time.

This system has constantly undergone minor amendments. On the whole, it is fair in that it avails a citizen of the services he can afford, maintains a degree of homogeneity within a neighborhood, and sets priorities according to needs. It does, however, tend to classify people, and it also does not take enough account of a person's ability to develop the plot. The ordinary citizen's ability to build usually declines with age as earning capacity diminishes and commitments and expenditure grow. Hence the younger applicants, who can earn more and save more, are handicapped. Recently the government has begun to exploit urban land as a source of revenue. It has introduced a practice in land disposal that is hardly sensitive to the needs of the majority: selling land in open auctions. This proved a crucial factor in the abrupt rise of land prices beyond the reach of ordinary citizens and the accumulation of land in the hands of a wealthy few.

APPROACHES TO LAND USE PLANNING

Development of Planning Laws

Attempts to control and organize the physical development of settlements began in 1927 with the formation of the Khartoum Town Planning Committee. The committee dealt solely with the three-town capital. To guide the development of other regions, municipal regulations were later issued (in 1938) to be enforced by the legal secretary in consultation with the provincial governors. But town planning proper, embracing all the relevant aspects, took its first steps only in 1946. Following the growth of urban centers and the desire for a more comprehensive approach to deal with the issues arising from it, the Central Town Planning Board (CTPB) was established in that year. It was entrusted with the control and organization of the development of settlements at the national level. It thus took over the responsibilities of the committee for the capital, plus those of the municipalities for other regions, and attempted to coordinate all town planning activities. It took over a decade, however, to establish the role of town planning as a separate discipline in proper perspective (Mazari, 1969).

In 1950, with the issue of replanning and urban renewal coming more to the fore, the Town Replanning Ordinance was passed. This ordinance, amended in 1956, 1961, and 1965, gives the state the legal authority to intervene in both freehold and leasehold areas. In addition it has authority to carry out replanning projects whenever it is in the public interest to do so and to regain possession of fourth-class and informal settlements without compensation. All new building in an area can be stopped whenever the area is declared as one subject to replanning to facilitate implementation of the proposals and reduce expenses and compensation. The ordinance provides for a fair measure of public participation and the introduction of a scientific approach to planning. The general plans drafted by the Province Authority Council are to be based on a socioeconomic-physical survey. Interested and affected citizens are allowed to express views on the plan to the CTPB. After approval is given by the CTPB and the minister, the replanning is carried out by a commission, which maintains continuous contact with the citizens, assessing their claims and comments, and estimating the cost of the project and the resultant compensation. Those dissatisfied can still appeal to the judge of the High Court.

After independence in 1956, the minister of local government took over planning responsibilities and more acts and amendments were passed to guide the planning process more effectively. Particularly important were the Town and Village Planning Act of 1956 (amended 1961 and 1965) and the Town and Village Regulations 1957 (amended 1961 and 1965). Under the Town and Village Planning Act, a 10-member CTPB was constituted, and the minister of local government was discharged of his functions in all matters in connection with this board. Through this act, the government gained the power to fix and, from time to time, vary the boundaries of any town or village, classify previously unclassified land, reclassify already classified land, issue regulations to govern land use, and acquire unclassified land on classification. The act also dealt with the loss or enhancement of value of land due to the exercise of its powers and specified the payment to be made (to the individuals or to the state) in each case. It also stated the channels for appeal for dissatisfied individuals. With respect to undeveloped land, the government could either acquire such land or require its owners to pay the amount due to increases in its value.

The laws passed during the 1950s are still in force today, although the CTPB ceased to function in 1977. In 1970 there were serious attempts to formulate a new planning law. But after the project started to take shape and the first drafts were prepared, it was frozen since it was then decided to embark on decentralization.

The Town and Village Planning Act has been criticized on several counts, in essence that it is an unsatisfactory derivative of the British Planning Act of 1947 (Mazari, 1969). Criticism has focused on issues such as the vague reference to an urban center as "the town or village whose name appears in the attached list'' (''a settlement with a population of over 20,000'' was later adopted); the failure to identify the three levels—national, regional, local—at which planning occurs; the absence of any control over building heights in different areas; the absence of laws concerning the conservation of areas of historic interest or natural value (for example, natural parks and woods); and the failure to address the problems of the settlement, or development generally, of nomads.

Urban and Regional Planning after Independence

After independence, the government took positive steps to create a team of well-trained Sudanese town planners and to seek the help and guidance of foreign consultants. Regional planning was also embarked on, for example in Gezira by a United Nations team and the Khashm El Girba scheme where a large part of the population of Wadi Halfa was resettled.

No comprehensive regional land use planning yet exists. The subject has been dealt with in an uncoordinated way in the various socioeconomic plans, without properly linking its aims to those of these plans. Rural areas suffer almost total neglect, and the whole process has been hampered by excessive centralization.

Successive socioeconomic development plans have stated the development of land in all regions according to each region's potential as an objective. Several large projects are in operation at present. Even so, official figures claim that the 31 million hectares or so now under cultivation represent only a small fraction of the potentially cultivable land. It is also estimated that a total of 85 million hectares could be used for cultivation and a further 25 million hectares for intensive grazing (World Markets, 1979).

Urban Plans

Most urban development in Sudan has followed the practice established during colonial times. This consists of simple land use zoning applied over a rigid gridiron layout based on nationally adopted standards for street widths and plot sizes. Apart from some piecemeal requirements, there is no systematic process for controlling development through the application of detailed land use requirements, density standards, parking standards, or aesthetic criteria.

The six-year plan of 1977–83 recognized the deficiencies of the overall planning system and laid emphasis on the need to develop regional planning as a basis for comprehensive national planning and the reduction of migration from rural to urban areas. It similarly recognized the importance of town planning for both satisfying housing needs and providing socioeconomic activities and services on a scientific basis. Particular emphasis was given to the need for preparing plans for towns with populations over 20,000. The following 12 towns were designated to have plans prepared: Port Sudan, Atbara, Ed Damer, Kassala, Gedaref, Hassa-Heissa, Ed Damazin, Dueim, El Obeid, Kadugli, Nyala, and El Fasher.

Khartoum was omitted from this list because it had already been the subject of two master planning exercises. In 1959 Doxiadis Associates of Greece had been invited to prepare master plans for both Port Sudan and Khartoum. The resultant plans represented both general strategies for development and detailed local proposals, including the generation and application of planning standards. In 1977 the Mefit Consulting Group of Italy produced a new master plan for Khartoum, including an overall subregional context for the development of the communications network. The proposals again included a series of detailed studies concerning local layouts and planning standards. Neither of these plans was ever formally approved as a basis for the future development of Khartoum, although various aspects of their proposals have been used in specific local instances. In 1983 BCEOM (Bureau Central d'Etudes pour les Equipments D'Outre Mer) from France prepared a transportation study for Khartoum under the aegis of a French government aid program. This plan uses the basic Mefit proposals as inputs for its future land use projections (in the absence of other more reliable material) and makes recommendations for upgrading the highway network and more closer integrating land uses and transportation.

During the period of the six-year plan only limited progress has been made in tackling the planning problems of the thirteen designated towns. In 1979 DHV Consulting Engineers from the Netherlands prepared an urban development plan for Kassala and the adjacent area under a Netherlands aid program. The plan was concerned essentially with the development of an appropriate housing strategy to accommodate the settlement of local nomads and refugees from Ethiopia and Eritrea. In 1983, also under the French government aid program, BCEOM was commissioned to prepare a subregional plan for Port Sudan and its hinterland. This plan includes proposals for a new port some 50 kilometers south of Port Sudan, which has already been the subject of much discussion. Mefit was also commissioned to prepare an urban structure plan for Juba in 1975. More recently it has been commissioned to prepare a series of local plans for six towns in Darfur and Kordofan.

The lack of skilled manpower and a developed planning system means that forward urban planning has been dependent on foreign consultants generally financed through aid programs. Irrespective of the merits of the resultant plans, they face considerable difficulties in their implementation due to the lack of appropriate implementation machinery. The preliminary steps toward establishing a comprehensive human settlements policy, however, have been taken. The Committee for Physical Planning and Housing was formed in 1980 as the result of an initiative of the National Council for Research. In that year it submitted its proposals for a strategy for dealing with these issues, which are still under discussion and are being modified. The council's preliminary report also discussed the 1976 Habitat recommendations and adopted their general spirit and structure. It also discusses the six-year socioeconomic development plan (1977/78–1982/83), focusing on the physical planning and housing sector and the problems facing the implementation of the plan. It identifies new planning and housing targets and suggests in great detail possible fields of research. The second report was being completed at the time of writing this chapter.

Planning under the Decentralized System

With the adoption of the multinuclear (or decentralization) rule in 1979, a new structure was set up, which allows the different regions almost full voice in handling the issues of land use and of human settlements in general. The new structure is intended to operate at six levels: national, regional, provincial, district, town or rural, and village or neighborhood level (Figure 7.3). For the national capital, the policymaker is the Ministry of Housing and Public Works, and the implementing body is the commission. Six deputies are responsible to the Commission of the National Capital for administrative affairs, engineering affairs, health, education, agriculture, and finance (Figure 7.5). The Town Planning Administration now has a comprehensive structure consisting of three departments: the Land and Survey Department whose responsibilities include informal settlements, surveying, and land; the Social Survey Department; and the Housing and Town Planning Department, which deals with rural, urban, popular, and cooperative housing and services (Figure 7.6).

Regional governments eventually will have the appropriate policymaking and implementing bodies responsible for health, education, housing, and similar areas at the regional level. These bodies will deal with, among other matters, the survey of land, preparation and implementation of physical planning, housing and land disposal programs, waste and sewage disposal services, and the construction of roads and bridges. The Regional Ministry of Housing and Public Services for the Northern Province, for example, has land, survey, and physical planning departments and operates in cooperation with bodies like the Water and Electricity Corporation, the municipal engineer's office, the Ministry of Transport, and the Rural Development and Water Corporation. The hierarchy includes the regional minister of housing and public works, the director of housing, and the Regional Planning Board, an advisory body (Figure 7.7). At present decisionmaking occurs at three levels: at the regional level by the Physical Planning Regional Office, at the town level by the People's Councils, and at the local level by the local planning boards. The neighborhood level still has not been included, but the channels for public participation are considerably extended. On the Regional Planning Board are represented the municipal engineer's office, the departments of land and survey, public works, environment, health, and the Electricity and Water Corporation. Figure 7.7 shows the structure of the Northern Region. Some slight variations occur in the structure for other regions to reflect local conditions and the flexibility inherent in the system.

Building Regulations and Bylaws

The progress in the attempts to revitalize the planning process is sharply contrasted by the retarded state of building regulations and bylaws that are meant

Figure 7.5 Structure of the Commission: The National Capital

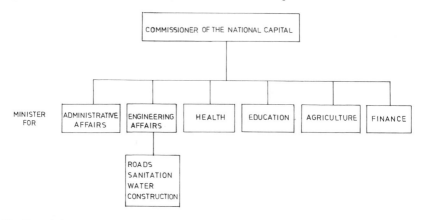

The Commission

Figure 7.6 Physical Planning Administration for the National Capital

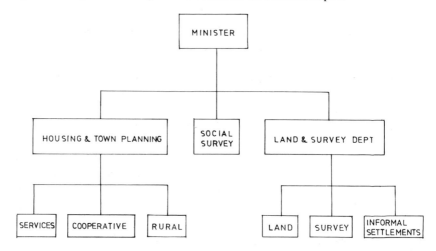

The Commission

to guide development. Vague, obsolete, and highly ineffective, they are confined to issues such as the minimum distances between the building and the boundary wall (thus practically eliminating the option of row and terrace housing layouts), minimum ceiling heights in habitable rooms (fixed at 3 meters), and location of soakaway wells. They do not specify building heights in the different urban zones or dictate the provision of parking lots, especially in business areas. So much subjectivity—and corruption—exists in applying these laws that what is readily granted one applicant can be adamantly denied his neighbor. Shops can

Figure 7.7 Structure of Physical Planning Administration in the Northern Region

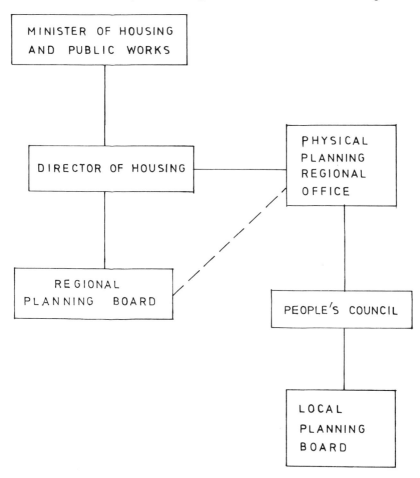

The Ministry of Housing and Public Works

spread at random all over the neighborhood; four-story walk-up apartment blocks with inadequate accommodation can crop up in the yard of an existing villa overlooking neighbors; introducing offices in residential areas creates parking problems and overloads the sewage disposal system. This state of affairs has recently reached alarming stages; 1982 will be remembered as the year in which architect-designed houses started to collapse because of the corruption and incompetence of architects and builders. It may be noted that these regulations do not apply to rural areas, where people have followed common sense in organizing their built environment.[4]

FUTURE THRUSTS

Administrative Changes

Future changes in land use planning in Sudan are likely to come about through the increased demands of the reorganized local government system. There is a general recognition that the move toward decentralization and regionalization offers the possibility of reducing the hegemony of the center and creating a more balanced pattern of regional development. The general emphasis on economic development continues, with modernization of the agricultural sector seen as the key to future industrial development. The new devolution of administrative functions, however, will also offer the potential for developing a more responsive and responsible approach to land use planning based on a wider interpretation of economic development. It is too early to assess the full implications of the new regional structures, but, like many other proposals in Sudan, they are theoretically full of promise but will realize their potential only if adequate capital and manpower are available and the perennial problems of motivation and corruption are tackled.

New Powers and Skills

To complement the reorganization of local government, consistent efforts are being made to improve legislative powers and expand technical competence. New planning legislation is in draft form and is expected to be approved soon, resolving the division of responsibilities for land use planning between the center and the various levels of administration in the regions. Professional knowledge and competence are being advanced in three main ways: foreign consultants increasingly are obliged to offer training to Sudanese counterparts; the local research base is being expanded in such institutions as the University of Khartoum and the National Research Council; and new training initiatives are being launched, including the establishment of the first indigenous physical planning program to train planners.

New Emphasis on Urban Planning

Sudan has a dispersed pattern of small-sized urban centers. Even Khartoum as the primate city has a population of fewer than 2 million people. Only an estimated 25 percent of the population live in urban centers. Coupled with the fact that there is in general no land shortage and the old colonial planning standards have provided a convenient means of developing subdivision projects, the larger problems of urban planning have been ignored. As a result, land use planning has not been carried out in an integrated manner, and there is no system of forward land use planning in general operation, with only a very rudimentary system operating for the control of development. However, the increasing rate of urbanization, now standing at 7.1 percent per annum, has focused greater attention on the problems of urban areas. In the last few years, a start has been made on the preparation of urban plans, largely through the assistance of foreign aid programs, and is likely to receive further impetus as regional government develops and the administrative and commercial functions of the new regional centers expand.

While Khartoum has been the subject of two major planning exercises in the past, there has been little progress in the implementation of the plans due to the inadequate administrative structure and the lack of financing. In attempting to come to grips with the problems of growth and change in Khartoum, a major step forward is the creation of the new administrative system in the form of the Khartoum Capital Commission with a series of commissioners with ministerial status (Figure 7.3). It is expected that this new arrangement, with key administrators at a higher political level, will also help resolve the problems of financing urban management.

Steps toward Regional Cooperation

With its particular features of huge natural resources and close ties with the Arab world, Sudan in the future increasingly will approach its problems of development at the level of the Arab region as its own policies of arabicization progress.

The rapid rates of urban growth experienced by many Arab countries over the last few decades have led to efforts to create a pan-Arab approach to common problems concerning the revival and reassertion of Arab-Muslim traditions in settlement planning. New institutions have been created in the different Arab countries to promote research and the exchange of relevant experience with regard to problems of development and renewal. Regular meetings have taken place already between the ministers of construction from the different countries as part of this process. At the same time, it is anticipated that the oil-exporting Arab states will continue to be an important source of financing for the development of Sudan.

MAJOR CHALLENGES

Distortion of Land Use Policies

Sudan has developed a comprehensive system to control the ownership and use of land, which provides a flexible and adaptive approach to the needs of development through maintaining overall government control. This power, how-ever, can be used both positively, to provide for the needs of society, and negatively, to meet the demands of patronage or particular interest groups.

Over the last decade or so, the declining economic performance of Sudan has emphasized the potential of its land as a financial asset. This has led the government to adopt development policies based on the vision of bringing together the industrialized countries' know-how and Arab capital to exploit Sudan's natural resources. As a consequence, both the rural and urban areas of the country have seen the development of prestigious large-scale projects, designed primarily to ensure lucrative returns to the investors. In many instances, these consist of turnkey projects, often the result of initiatives reflecting the personal interests of officials without regard to any assessment of the project's merit by local experts.

While economic growth is clearly essential for the development of the country, the dangers of following such policies are twofold. First, distortion in the equitable distribution of land will transfer substantial costs to society at large, which may outweigh any possible benefits. Second, if Sudan enters the oil era and other forces come into play, it may continue this trend and adopt the Arab consumption model of increasingly buying neat packages from the industrialized countries of marginal relevance to the real needs of the country.

Planning as a Closed System

A more specific criticism of the land use planning system in Sudan is that in the past it has operated as a closed system. Decisions were made behind closed doors and handed down for implementation without the reasons being made explicit and without any process of consultation with other levels of government, involved agencies, or the public. As a result, many land use planning decisions, in addition to the large-scale projects, were not responsive to local needs except as defined by the administration. Since there was no common agreement on their objectives, land use changes were often received with at best apathy and at worst hostility. Examples of local decisions that have not been exposed to discussion or a consideration of needs include the demolition of squatter housing; relocation of *souks*; moving of transport terminals; closing of petrol stations; development of public open spaces; expropriation of high-quality agricultural land for development; and development of prime riverside sites for commercial development in Khartoum and similar major changes of land use.

Larger-scale proposals that do not appear to reconcile the demands of development with local considerations include many rural development projects (Thimm, 1979). Considerable concern is being expressed over the failure of the government to consider the environmental impact of the Jonglei canal and the possible risks of increased desertification, the destruction of flora and fauna, and changes in the local nomads' economy and life. Agroindustry schemes have been implemented without regard to tribal land rights, migration patterns, or the local economy. Farmers are transformed into wage laborers with minimal services and without the right to keep cattle, which they have traditionally used as a form of economic security (Sorbö, 1977). The layout of irrigation canals and the lack of bridges may mean that tenants live up to 5 kilometers from their holdings;

the need for a hierarchy of settlements to provide a range of services and employment is ignored (Agraa et al., 1980).

If development is to proceed and benefit the population at large, clearly there must be a wider discussion of land use planning decisions, including the involvement of local experts, so that problems are faced and possible deficiencies remedied to ensure that the maximum benefits are obtained from the development. Inevitably in a developing country, the function of participating in the decision-making process is limited by periphery-center tensions and the conflict generated by the dualism of traditional and modern societies living alongside each other. Although legal and administrative provisions exist for greater participation in the decisionmaking process, their activation will be a product of the slow maturing of government. Land use planning has an important role to play in contributing to this process of maturation by ensuring that planning is not merely an instrument of government but a means of ensuring support for the concept of government through the equitable distribution of benefits.

Planning as a Reactive System

The fragile economy of Sudan and the failure of successive long-term economic plans have resulted in land use planning developing as part of a reactive system responding to particular needs as they arise. The situation has been exacerbated by the lack of a skilled cadre of technicians and the fact that, where professional staff are available, political nepotism and expediency often result in their either not being consulted or their advice being ignored.

The resultant reactive nature of the land use planning system means that instead of formulating coherent long-term strategies, which could be achieved through a series of detailed tactical plans, development decisions are often brought about by external factors, including the availability of finance, without there being any clear consideration of the longer-term conceptual framework. Sudan has many examples of development projects that have failed because they have not been integrated into the necessary longer-term plans. Some projects have failed because there were no proposals for the provision of infrastructure. Others, such as food processing plants, have failed because they did not take into account the conservative nature of rural societies and the need to integrate such projects into longer-term plans for social and economic change.

The preoccupation with long-term planning can be seen as an influence from the developed countries where political stability and consistent economic growth are permanent features of their societies. In Sudan, land use planning can contribute to the longer-term process of effecting the transition to political and economic stability. But in the short term there is a need to develop philosophies and techniques of land use planning capable of operating on a reactive basis with particular emphasis on aspects of wealth generation.

Priorities for the Future

Sudan is typical of many other developing countries where land use planning has been essentially concerned with the development of the natural resources to provide a basis for economic growth. What planning has been undertaken is largely reactive, concerned with the provision of land and buildings to meet the specific needs of predetermined uses.

The problem of the underdevelopment of resources has been compounded by the lack of appropriate administrative structures and skilled cadres capable of managing the forces of change. Coupled with the lack of capital for investment, the problems of development come down to trying to expand the resource base to match population growth and maintain at least some form of status quo. The emphasis therefore tends to fall on economic development as an end in itself with less importance attached to the concepts of integrated physical planning as an essential component of social and economic development.

Sudan is a sparsely populated country of considerable agricultural and mineral potential. The topographic and climatic conditions, together with the legacy of colonial development, have, however, left it with wide regional differences in the level of development and a poorly structured hierarchy of settlements linked by a rudimentary infrastructure. The land use priorities for the future must lie in the development of regional strategies, concerned with the provision of local infrastructure and the exploitation of the mineral and agricultural resources, at a scale that will bring direct benefits to the rural populace without abrupt social and economic changes.

The development of such strategies will need to be accompanied by the development of a settlement strategy. This will have to consider controlling growth at the level of the primate city and promoting growth at the lower levels of the settlement hierarchy to provide a wider range of social and economic opportunities throughout the country.

In the short term, land use planning will need to develop wealth-generating reactive systems capable of responding quickly to immediate needs. In the longer term, comprehensive land use strategies will require revision of the planning system to develop a proper forward planning function with effective mechanisms for both promoting and controlling development. Such a strategy will need to consider the role the private sector can play in the development process and how cost recovery and taxation systems can be established to recover the costs of development and maintain a development momentum.

CONCLUDING REMARKS

The basic settlement pattern and land use policies in Sudan were established largely during the colonial era. Part of this heritage consisted of a comprehensive system of legislation to control the disposal and use of land. The political and economic problems of Sudan have meant that only minor amendments have been made to the land use planning system, and over the last decade or so there has been a shift of priorities and a distortion in the application of land use policies to meet particular political demands.

There are now signs of the development of a more radical approach to aid the problems of land use planning in Sudan: new administrative structures, new legislation, and efforts to solve the manpower problem. The hope for the future is that the new regionalization, coupled with the other initiatives, will provide an effective basis for the application of comprehensive land use planning. The hope is also that they will contribute to better economic performance and in the long run the wider distribution of benefits to ensure equitable social development and political stability.

NOTES

1. The recent resurgence of armed conflict in the southern region would appear to indicate that the peace agreement of 1972 brought only temporary relief and that the fundamental political differences between the north and the south have not been resolved.

2. In the 1960s £s5 million would be equivalent to $15 million to $20 million.

3. The Nile Waters Agreement of 1959 specified that the shares of the Sudan and Egypt would be 18.5 billion cubic meters and 55.5 billion cubic meters, respectively. This takes into account that the average annual yield of the Nile is estimated at 84 billion cubic meters, of which 10 billion are lost annually at the Aswan High Dam Reservoir.

4. As this chapter was being finished, a committee was formed as a result of an initiative by the Engineers and Architects Trades Union to review and update the building regulations and bylaws.

BIBLIOGRAPHY

Agraa, Omer M. A., et al. 1980. Human Settlements in Gezira. In Bhooshan, B. S., ed. *Towards Alternative Settlement Strategies.* New Delhi, India: Heritage Publishers.

Agraa, O. M. and A. M. Ahmad. 1980. *Human Settlements in Arab Countries.* Khartoum: Khartoum University Press.

Ahmad, A. M. 1979. Community Facilities in Gezira. *Sudan Notes and Records* 60(60):86–93.

Ahmad, A. M. 1983. Problems of Human Settlements in Arab Countries. Paper presented at Symposium on Human Settlements and Contemporary Housing Needs in the Arab World, Baghdad, 29–31 May. (In Arabic)

Arifi, Salih A. El. 1971. Urbanization and Distribution of Economic Development in the Sudan. *African Urban Notes* VI (2) African Studies Center, Michigan State University.

Beshir, Mohammed Omer. 1970. *The Southern Sudan—Background to Conflict.* Khartoum: Khartoum University Press.

El Tom, M. E. 1984. Illegal Building and Haphazard Housing in Khartoum Region. Unpublished report. (In Arabic) Ministry of Construction and Public Works.

Gaitskell, A. 1959. *Gezira, A Story of Development in the Sudan.* London: Faber and Faber.

Hassan, Ali Mohammed El, ed. 1976. *An Introduction to the Sudan Economy*. Khartoum: Khartoum University Press.

Holt, P. M. 1961. *A Modern History of the Sudan*. London: Wiedenfeld and Nicolson.

Howell, John, ed. 1974. *Local Government and Politics in the Sudan*. Khartoum: Khartoum University Press.

Land Reform. 1962. Extract from U.K. publication Third report on progress in land reform (ST/SOA/49).

Laws of the Sudan. n.d. 7, *Title XX: Land*. London: Haycock Press Ltd.

Mazari, S. A. 1965. Urbanization in the Sudan (Arabic). Engineering Magazine 4, August, 7.

Mazari, S. A. 1969. Thoughts on the Future of Planning and Housing. Unpublished paper. (In Arabic)

Minnalla, M. A. 1983. Land Registration in the Sudan. *Al Ayyam*, Khartoum 5 July. (In Arabic)

O'Ballance, Edgar. 1977. *The Secret War in the Sudan 1955–1972*. London: Faber and Faber.

Physical Planning and Housing Committee. 1980. *The National Plan for Research in the Physical Planning and Housing Sector*. Khartoum: National Council for Research. (In Arabic)

Presidency of the Republic. 1983. *Law of the National Capital*. (In Arabic)

Raji, M. M. 1984. Popular Housing: Problems and Solutions. *Al Sahafa*, Khartoum, 10 January. (In Arabic)

Satterthwaite, D., ed. 1979. *Three Years After Habitat*. London: International Institute for Environment and Development.

Sorbö, Gunnar M. 1977. *How to Survive Development: The Story of New Halfa*. Monograph Series No. 6. Khartoum: Development Studies and Research Center, University of Khartoum.

Suliman, Ali Ahmed. 1975. *Issues in the Economic Development of the Sudan*. Khartoum: Khartoum University Press.

Thimm, Heinz-Ulrich. 1979. *Development Projects in the Sudan: An Analysis of Their Reports with Implications for Research and Training in Arid Land Management*. Tokyo: United Nations University.

World Bank. 1982. *World Development Report 1982*. New York: Oxford University Press.

World Markets. 1979. *Sudan the Country and Its Markets*. Paris: Group J. A.

8

Zimbabwe

G. C. Underwood

HISTORICAL DEVELOPMENT AND CURRENT STATUS OF LAND USE PLANNING

Zimbabwe, a landlocked country in southern Africa, was for ninety years exposed to a colonial system of administration, first under the British government and subsequently under a minority government of white settlers. After independence in April 1980, efforts were made to correct the spatial imbalances of this period, but the land use pattern of the country still reflects its economic and political background.

Past and Current Land Use Patterns

When the early colonists entered the country toward the end of the nineteenth century, they found an entirely rural country. Despite impressive stone ruins at a few places, such as Great Zimbabwe, the indigenous people were pastoralists and did not build towns. The colonial settlers established the basic pattern of urban centers, since towns were built along the pioneer routes and on sites where important primary resources were available, such as minerals and fertile agricultural land. The construction of the railway line connecting South Africa, Mozambique, and Zambia in the early 1900s consolidated this pattern of urban development. Apart from a few mining towns that subsequently developed, the rail line firmly influenced the growth of towns and cities.

The hinterland of these towns consisted generally of good agricultural land developed on a commercial basis by the white settlers. Beyond this hinterland, off the main watershed, was marginal agricultural land that was left for the indigenous African population to cultivate at a subsistence level. The colonial administration institutionalized this pattern of development by enacting legislation that divided the country along racial lines. The Land Apportionment Act and Land Tenure Act, among others, classified the country into different areas for different racial groups, principally marginal land for an African subsistence economy and better agricultural land for a settler commercial economy. This has resulted in a highly dualistic socioeconomic system: a modern sector consisting of commerce, industry, mining, and commercial agriculture and a peasant sector. Although the modern sector is relatively well developed and diversified, the peasant sector is generally underdeveloped, largely subsistence in character, with poor physical and social infrastructure. These two sectors are clearly related to the land use pattern of the country, as can be seen from Figure 8.1. The commercial area represents the modern sector and contains the main towns and cities, lines of communication, mines, and large farms. The communal lands represent the peasant sector and are characterized by overcrowding, poor land husbandry, poor physical infrastructure, and no large towns.

After independence the discriminatory legislation was repealed, but the effects of the colonial administration are still visible in the land use pattern of the country. There are now no legal barriers restricting the acquisition of land or movement of people on racial grounds. Nevertheless, the essential characteristics of the commercial area as the modern sector and the communal lands as the peasant sector remain.

Table 8.1 contains statistics on the basic land use pattern in the country and shows the high population densities in the communal lands, as compared with the commercial farming area, and illustrates the disproportionate land occupation pattern. It is significant to note (Table 8.2) that the commercial farms provide 75 percent of the country's agricultural output, while the communal lands produce only 25 percent.

A sizable proportion of the total land area is allocated for national parks, wildlife, and forest areas. The national parks and wildlife areas comprise land allocated for large wild animal reserves or scenic land, which is preserved and protected from development. The forest areas enjoy a measure of protection, but the timber is exploited commercially.

An examination of population trends indicates that Zimbabwe has a high average growth rate of 3.3 percent perannum, and yet its rate of urbanization has been moderately low, with the result that currently only 23 percent of the population lives in urban centers (Table 8.3). The conclusion that Zimbabwe is underurbanized is reinforced by an examination of the hierarchy of urban centers. If the ranked-size law is applied to Zimbabwean towns, abnormalities can be seen at the top and bottom of the hierarchy since there is a large gap between the two main towns and the remainder, and there are relatively few towns at the bottom of the hierarchy (Table 8.4). This is illustrated in Figure 8.2. It is also evident that the middle-order towns are smaller than might be expected. These characteristics can be explained by past influx control measures that restricted

Figure 8.1 Land Classification Map of Zimbabwe

Table 8.1
Zimbabwe: Land Classification and Population Densities

Land Category	1982 Population No.	%	Land Area Square Kilometers	%	Population Density
Communal Land	4,276,900	56.7	169,556	43.4	25.2
Commercial Farm Land (1)	1,571,349	20.8	167,442	42.8	9.4
Main Towns (2)	1,673,057	22.2	1,921	0.5	870.9
National Land (3)	24,765	0.3	51,840	13.3	0.5
Total	7,546,071	100	390,759	100	19.3

Source: Central Statistical Office

Notes: (1) Includes several small towns.

(2) Figures are for the fifteen main towns.

(3) Includes Forest Land, Parks and Wildlife Land.

Table 8.2
Zimbabwe: Agricultural Output

	Communal Farms	%	Commercial Farms	%	Total
Gross Output	264,600,000	25	775,600,000	75	1,040,200,000
Number of Cattle	3,240,000	57	2,400,000	43	5,640,000
Number Other Livestock	1,181,000	80	299,000	20	1,480,000

Source: Central Statistical Office

Table 8.3
Zimbabwe: Rates of Total and Urban Population Increases

Census	Total Population	Average Annual Growth Rate %	Urban Population (1)	Average Urban Growth Rate per Annum %	Urban Population as % of National Total
1962	4,100,000	–	734,478	–	17.9
1969	5,130,000	3.25	898,890	2.98	17.5
1982	7,539,000	3.35	1,732,600	6.62	22.9

Source: Central Statistical Office

Note: (1) Urban population figures are for the 19 main towns.

189

Table 8.4
Zimbabwe: Population of the Main Towns, 1982

Town	Population	Rank
Harare & Chitungwiza	828,600	1
Bulawayo	413,800	2
Gweru	78,900	3
Mutare	69,600	4
Kwekwe	47,600	5
Kadoma	44,600	6
Hwange	39,200	7
Masvingo	30,600	8
Zvishavane	26,800	9
Chinoyi	24,300	10
Redcliff	22,000	11
Marondera	20,300	12
Chegutu	19,600	13
Bindura	18,200	14
Shurungwi	13,400	15

Source: Central Statistical Office

the movement of people from the communal lands. However, at independence these restrictions were removed. It is significant to note that the rate of urban growth increased dramatically from 6.7 percent in 1981 to 13.6 percent in 1982, indicating that Zimbabwe is on the brink of an extremely rapid phase of urban growth.[1] This has far-reaching implications for land use planning.

The land use pattern of Zimbabwean towns has several features directly attributable to the land tenure laws of the colonial period; these are illustrated in Figure 8.3. There is a clear segregation between the former African residential areas (now referred to as high-density residential areas) and other housing areas

Figure 8.2 Population of Main Urban Centers according to Rank, 1969–1982

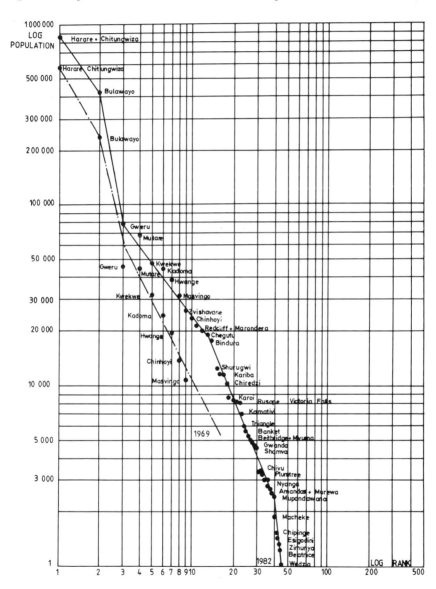

Figure 8.3 Schematic Map of Harare

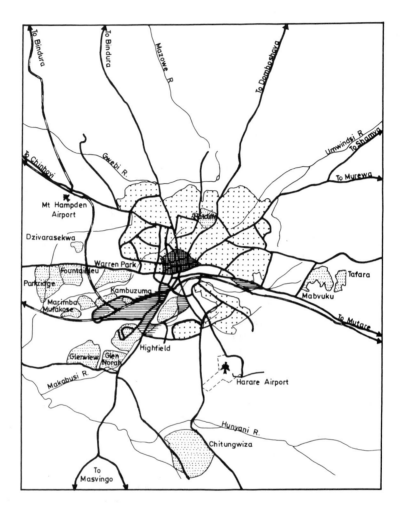

LEGEND

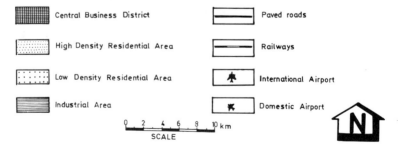

Central Business District   Paved roads

High Density Residential Area   Railways

Low Density Residential Area   International Airport

Industrial Area   Domestic Airport

0 2 4 6 8 10 km
SCALE

of towns. This segregation is often marked by large tracts of undeveloped land between these housing areas and adjacent development. In many cases the high-density areas are on the periphery or even some distance from the town and are sometimes distant from employment opportunities and major shopping centers, with obvious implications for transportation patterns. The most striking example is the case of Chitungwiza, located 23 kilometers south of the capital city, Harare, and 18 kilometers from the nearest major industrial area. With an official population of 172,000 but actually a population probably in excess of this, this dormitory town has no civic center, very little industry, and inadequate community and shopping facilities.[2]

Apart from these features, Zimbabwean towns are not unlike many other modern towns throughout the world with a central business district (CBD), several residential areas of varying status, and an industrial zone usually located on one side of town. Intermingled within this urban fabric are open spaces and community facilities. Modern infrastructure in the form of electrical, water, and sewerage reticulation is available. Due to an abundance of land, the densities of development, both in the CBD and surrounding residential areas, are low. Effective development control laws have resulted in a well-defined urban edge, beyond which is commercial farmland. In a number of cases, however, small-holding areas have been permitted outside the municipal or town boundary, creating a mixed land use pattern.

Evolution of Land Use Planning

At the turn of the century, urbanization in Zimbabwe was limited, and town planning was not considered important. According to Hosford and Whittle (1979) the first effective town planning was exercised by sanitary boards with powers to make bylaws and to levy an annual rate from landowners. Gridiron layouts were surveyed for many of the early settlements, and physical planning, such as it was, was achieved mainly through bylaws and public health ordinances. It was not until after World War I, in the face of growing urban development, that the need for formalized town planning became apparent. Regional and rural planning, however, received scant attention and was not considered a problem since the country was basically underpopulated. Nevertheless, land tenure laws, such as the Land Apportionment Act of 1930 and subsequent legislation on land tenure, played a significant role in determining regional land use patterns.

The first Town and Country Planning Act of 1933 was promulgated with the prime purpose of regulating periurban sprawl and required the five municipalities to prepare town planning schemes to control and direct development within their areas. A second Town and Country Planning Act was promulgated in 1945, which widened the application of town planning schemes to include certain periurban and rural scenic areas. The emphasis, however, was still on town planning and, despite some discussion about regional planning (of a metropolitan character), this was not incorporated in the act.

During this time a number of distinct planning goals and policies emerged, many of which persisted until independence. It is significant to note that these policies (with one important exception) were all directed at the commercial areas. The communal lands experienced virtually no land use planning save for a few irrigation schemes, agricultural programs, and small business centers.

Urban Development Policy

After World War II, there was a development boom in Zimbabwe, and premature residential development was permitted on and beyond the peripheries of the main urban centers. At this time land use planning emphasized the control of land subdivision rather than the development of land. It was not until the mid-1950s that it became mandatory to seek planning permission for development. By 1960 the development boom came to an end, and consequently the concern of town planners shifted to that of building up the existing towns and cities and preventing sprawl and uncoordinated development. In pursuance of this policy, subdivision of land for residential purposes on the periphery of towns was generally restricted.

Rural Subdivision Policy

The aim of the rural subdivision policy was to ensure that farms in the commercial areas were retained as economic units. New subdivisions for agricultural purposes were permitted only if viable entities would result from both the new plots and the remaining extent. Where uneconomic entities existed, the policy was to try to create economic properties through consolidation.

Limited subdivision was, however, permitted in rural areas to meet the specific needs of commerce, the service industry, tourism, and homes for vacation purposes. The last were normally permitted only in areas of scenic beauty, where the minimum size of plot depended on various factors, including the nature of the terrain and the source of water.

Low-Income Housing

For many years, the policy was to site low-income housing close to industry to ensure that the low-paid workers did not have a long journey to and from work. In the early 1970s, however, for political reasons, the policy shifted to siting low-income housing in or close to the communal lands. The expressed reason was a hope that there would be a spin-off benefit to the communal lands. But the real reason was a realization that urban migration of Africans was a permanent and increasing trend. By developing low-income housing areas on the outskirts, it was hoped that the towns would maintain their European character.

Industrial Decentralization

Since the 1950s a number of select committees have attempted to formulate and implement a policy of industrial decentralization. Very little has resulted from their efforts. In general, the decentralization policy was aimed at encouraging development in the smaller centers without jeopardizing the growth of the two main cities, Harare and Bulawayo. Few positive measures, however, were provided to support this policy, and it has remained largely unimplemented.

Communal Lands

Land use planning policies for the communal lands prior to independence were conspicuously absent. The communal lands were left to regulate themselves, and the land use pattern that emerged was determined largely by the arable land. In the mid-1970s, however, some attempt was made to encourage new development linked with agricultural projects. Consequently growth points, or small towns, were developed in conjunction with irrigation projects with the aim of providing a marketing outlet for agricultural produce and some form of urban development.

A New Approach

The Town and Country Planning Act of 1945 served Zimbabwe for 30 years, but over time it became outmoded. By 1970 the country faced grave problems caused by a growing rural population and inevitable urban migration, and the need for planning on a regional level became evident. The 1945 act was virtually silent on regional planning, and despite a reference to country planning in the title, its main thrust was the urban context. In the urban areas effective land use planning within the defined boundary was possible, but beyond the boundary planning authorities had little control. This resulted in the emergence of shanty housing and low quality roadside shop buildings at the urban fringes. The act had not concerned itself at all with what were formerly known as African townships or with the communal lands.

The new approach, enshrined in the Regional, Town and Country Planning Act of 1976, was basically a two-tier system of land use planning, with regional and master plans for the upper tier and local plans for the lower tier. The former cover major land use policies over a wide area; the latter are detailed land use plans for a specific area, which may be either urban or rural.

Current Extent and Acceptance of Land Use Planning

Land use planning is currently accepted by politicians and the public as an important part of the process of development. There is a tendency among laymen, however, to think that with the preparation of a plan, development will follow suit automatically. These expectations have prompted physical planners to concern themselves more with implementation than in the past, an inevitably time-consuming process. Partly as a consequence of this and partly due to government policy, which emphasizes rural development, little progress has been made in the preparation of urban statutory master and local plans. This, combined with the fact that some master plans have been in the course of preparation for three or four years, has generated criticism of the statutory planning process.[3] Many towns are now experiencing problems in the administration of their outdated town planning schemes, and the need for urban planning is becoming more apparent.

Land use planning has become particularly significant in the communal lands because, since independence, planning and development efforts have focused on these areas. Local authorities have been closely involved with this work and have begun to appreciate the purpose and value of planning.

Currently the four main cities have a municipal town planning department, and the government Department of Physical Planning operates from five provincial offices under the supervision of a head office in Harare. Several other government departments employ land use planners, and there are about 60 professionals in the country. This number is inadequate for the work required and is the major factor that inhibits the development of a more effective land use planning system in Zimbabwe. Nevertheless, planning is and will continue to be important. This is clear from the government's economic policy statement, "Growth with Equity," which was produced shortly after independence, and the Transitional National Development Plan produced in 1983 (Government of Zimbabwe, 1981, 1983). Both documents explain the national development strategy as one of "growth with equity and transformation." In order to "promote equitable growth . . . and redress the gross imbalances between the modern and rural peasant sectors," the national plan emphasizes rural development and land settlement. Development of the industrial and housing sectors is also seen as an important element. It is clear from these statements that land use planning has a central role to play, now and in the future.

INSTITUTIONAL AND LANDOWNERSHIP FRAMEWORK

Legal Basis for Land Use Planning

Land use planning in Zimbabwe derives its legal basis from the Regional, Town and Country Planning Act of 1976. In terms of this act, the responsibility for directing the land use planning process lies with the minister of local government and town planning, who delegates most of the responsibility to the Department of Physical Planning. The act provides wide-ranging powers, which include the planning of regions, districts, and local areas, preservation of buildings, acquisition of land, and development control. The principal mechanisms for exercising these powers are through statutory master and local plans.

From its promulgation until independence in 1980, this act was applied only to the towns, cities, and farms in the commercial areas. The result was that there was virtually no land use planning and very little development control in the communal lands. In 1982 it was decided that the act should be applied across the entire country, and amending legislation was passed.[4]

Despite the all-embracing provisions of the Regional, Town and Country Planning Act, which imply that all land use planning activities are undertaken within the framework of that act, in practice this is not always so. Many planning activities are non-statutory, and there are other acts of parliament that either complement or impinge on the Regional, Town and Country Planning Act. In fact most land use plans currently are not prepared as master or local plans since most planning efforts are directed at growth points and district centers and at low-income housing estates. The former are located in the communal lands, which is effectively rural state land. The plans are prepared in terms of section 44 of the planning act, which provides authority for the preparation of layouts on state land and does not include an obligation to follow the complex procedures for the preparation of master and local plans. Low-income housing layouts are normally prepared in terms of section 160 of the Urban Councils Act, which gives a local authority power to develop residential, commercial, or industrial development on its own land. Before a local authority can proceed with this development, it must obtain the minister's consent.

Of particular significance in the field of rural planning is the Agricultural and Rural Development Authority Act, which provides for the establishment of the Agricultural and Rural Development Authority (ARDA), whose function is to plan, coordinate, implement, promote, and assist agricultural and rural development. ARDA operates some 14 estates throughout Zimbabwe, which are essentially irrigation projects but include efforts to establish a commercial, industrial, and residential component as part of a growth point. This act is administered by the minister of lands resettlement and rural development, and since it refers to the planning of rural development, there is some duplication of the Regional, Town and Country Planning Act.

A major land use planning exercise currently being undertaken by the Ministry of Lands Resettlement and Rural Development is the resettlement program whereby the government purchases commercial farms and resettles them with peasant farmers on a planned basis. The mandate for this program is derived from a number of policy statements made in the House of Assembly and synthesized in the government's economic policy statement, "Growth with Equity." One of the objectives stated is to seek "an acceptable and fair distribution of land ownership and use," which will be achieved through a program of land reform and "resettling a significant number of peasant farmers from overcrowded Communal Lands."[5]

Decisionmaking Structure in the Administration of Land Use Planning

The planning system is administered by both central government agencies and local authorities, and work is undertaken at the national, provincial, and local levels.

At the national level, the most influential ministry is that of Finance, Economic Planning and Development, which controls the national budget and therefore influences capital and operating budgets for ministries and local authorities. There is a move to strengthen this ministry's regional planning capacity, but at this stage its significance lies with financial control, not land use control. Land use control is the function of the Ministry of Local Government and Town Planning, which through its Department of Physical Planning administers the Regional, Town and Country Planning Act. Control is exercised principally by means of master plans, which require the minister's approval. In addition, all low-income housing schemes require the minister's approval in terms of the Urban Councils Act, and all land use plans for state land are prepared by ministry officials. It is clear, therefore, that the minister of local government and town planning can exercise tight control over the land use planning process.

The ministry is represented at the provincial level by a provincial planning officer and a provincial administrator. The provincial planning officer is responsible for giving planning advice to all local authorities in the province and prepares most land use plans for all except the large municipalities since most local authorities lack their own planning staff. The provincial administrator is responsible for general administration and coordination of development in the province and concentrates on the communal lands, since it is here that there is greatest need for development. Recent efforts by these officials in some provinces have produced interesting results in the field of provincial coordination. A committee comprising provincial representatives of government and the chairmen of local authorities has been formed to coordinate development in the province. Various subcommittees have been established to prepare detailed plans for specific projects. This provincial development committee has no legal basis but is emerging as a powerful and useful tool in the development process since it is an important forum in which to gain acceptance and cooperation for the implementation of plans.

There are basically three types of local authority in Zimbabwe: urban councils, rural councils, and district councils, each with varying degrees of responsibility for land use planning. Urban councils are elected authorities responsible for the administration of urban areas, which may be either towns or municipalities, depending on size.

In terms of the Regional, Town and Country Planning Act, municipal and town councils are responsible for all town planning matters, including the preparation of master and local plans, the control of development, and the subdivision and consolidation of land. They may approve their own local plans provided these conform to the provisions of a master plan. They also may prepare schemes for low-income housing and commercial and industrial development on their own land in terms of the Urban Councils Act but are required to submit these to the minister for approval.

A rural council consisting of elected members is responsible for the administration of rural districts in the commercial area. In some cases a town or village is included within the rural council boundary, and the council may appoint a committee to administer this center. Land use planning powers of rural councils are limited to the control of development, while the preparation of master and local plans, and the approval of the subdivision and consolidation of land, is undertaken by the provincial planning officer on behalf of the minister.

The third and newest type of local authority is the district council consisting of elected members responsible for the administration of districts in the communal lands. These councils have been established only since independence, prior to which the communal lands were administered by district commissioners. District councils lack experience, and consequently government efforts have been directed at strengthening their administrative and planning capacity. They have the same land use planning powers as rural councils—that is, development control powers but not plan preparation or approval powers.

There is one major exception to this organizational structure, and that is in the case of resettlement schemes. The Ministry of Lands, Resettlement and Rural Development has the responsibility for preparing and approving plans for resettlement schemes and does not need to refer these to the minister of local government and town planning for approval. These schemes are undertaken on state land, which was formerly commercial farmland within the jurisdiction of a rural council. Once the state acquires the land, the rural council is no longer expected to administer the area. This is done by the government resettlement officer. The result is that at this stage, resettlement schemes have no local authority structure.

Extent of Public Participation in Decisionmaking

The Regional, Town and Country Planning Act lays down specific obligatory requirements for public participation. In formulating and before finally determining the contents of a master or local plan, the local authority shall "take such steps as will, in its opinion, ensure that there is adequate consultation in connection with the matters proposed to be included in the plan."[6] These steps are left to the local authority's discretion, but once the draft plan has been prepared, there is a legal requirement to place a copy on public exhibition for two months and to publicize it in the local newspapers. Members of the public then have an opportunity to scrutinize the proposals and to submit formal objections or representations, which are sent direct to the minister with copies to the local authority.

In the case of a master plan, the local authority is required to comment on these objections when it submits the draft plan to the minister for approval. The minister may set up a local inquiry to investigate these objections or may refer them to the administrative court for determination. In the case of a local plan, the local authority must refer all objections to the administrative court. The administrative court is the civil court in Zimbabwe and deals with all land use planning matters. The decision of the court in these cases is final. In determining planning appeal cases, which may include a host of other matters in addition to objections to master and local plans, the administrative court tries to obtain a balanced view of the problem and therefore does not follow the formal legal procedures of the criminal court. Accordingly, a member of the public may, if he or she wishes, represent his or her own case. It is apparent that public participation is very much a passive requirement and centers more on providing opportunities to object to the proposals than requiring that the public participate in the plan preparation process.

Where a layout has been prepared in terms of section 160 of the Urban Councils Act, the requirements for public participation are limited. If there is no approved statutory plan, the layout has to be placed on public exhibition before it is submitted to the minister. A procedure is laid down for the submission of objections. The minister will determine these objections and does not refer them to the administrative court. Where there is an approved statutory plan, there is no obligation to exhibit the layout. Thus most low-income housing estates have been prepared with little public participation.

In the case of layouts prepared for state land, in terms of section 44 of the planning act, there is no requirement for public participation apart from consultation with the local authority concerned. The communal lands are regarded as state land, and all land use plans for growth points and district centers are prepared in terms of section 44. In practice, however, the Department of Physical Planning insists on close consultation with the community before any plans are approved, with the result that in these cases the community generally participates actively in plan preparation.

Landownership Patterns

The landownership pattern can be divided into three basic categories: communal land, commercial areas, and national land. The state owns the communal and national lands, and private individuals or companies own most of the commercial areas.

Because communal land cannot be bought or sold, the concept of landownership has a somewhat ambiguous meaning since land is communally owned. Individuals are allocated rights to land by headmen and the district council. This poses a problem in raising loans for development since there are no title deeds that can be used as security for the loan. In a few cases legislation has been enacted declaring centers as "gazetted townships." This basically excises these areas from communal land, and here individuals may obtain title to their properties. Outside these gazetted areas, commercial and industrial enterprises are operated on a lease with annual payments made to the district council. Not surprisingly many businessmen are anxious to obtain freehold title at all business centers, but this is being resisted by government, which sees it running counter to socialist principles.

The second major land category is the commercial area, a large proportion of which is owned by individuals, containing the towns, cities, and commercial farms. All properties in this area (except state land) have title deeds registered with the surveyor general and may be bought, sold, or bequeathed. Precise cadastral survey of all boundaries is required by law, and a sophisticated land survey and registration system has developed.

A general picture of Bulawayo can be obtained from Table 8.5 and Figure 8.4. Table 8.6 describes landownership in Bulawayo as an example of land-ownership patterns in urban areas. It is significant that a large proportion of land is owned by the municipality itself. This is typical of most Zimbabwean towns since at the time of their development, large areas of commonage were reserved for future expansion. Zimbabwe is therefore more fortunate than many other developing countries because the towns have adequate land for expansion in the forseeable future without the need for expensive acquisition.

The state owns some land in the commercial areas, which is allocated for specific purposes, such as an army barracks or research institute, or may merely be kept in trust for some future use. An increasing amount of state land is now being acquired as part of the resettlement program, in which the state takes possession of the land and allocates it to new settlers under permit. These permits are issued subject to a condition that settlers relinquish all traditional rights in the communal lands. This is an attempt to alleviate pressures in the communal lands but could prove problematic if a permit is terminated, as it theoretically could be.

Both the policy statement "Growth with Equity" and the "Transitional National Development Plan" make reference to the inequalities of landownership in the country, and declared policy is to achieve an acceptable and fair distribution of landownership and use. "Growth with Equity" states that the government will "entrust certain rights in the use of land to private individuals or groups of individuals for as long as such trusteeship best serves the national interest."[7]

Freehold title is not permitted in the national lands since they are allocated for wild animal reserves and parks, but in some cases limited lease agreements are allowed.

Land Acquisition

Various pieces of legislation empower the state, local authorities, or statutory bodies to acquire land. The Land Acquisition Act lays down the procedures to be followed. With regard to land use planning, the most important act is the Regional, Town and Country Planning Act, which gives local authorities wide powers for acquisition either by agreement or by compulsory purchase (expropriation). A local authority, for example, may acquire land "for the implementation of any proposal including development, redevelopment or improvement, contained in an operative master plan or local plan."[8] The acquisition of this land may be by purchase, exchange, donation, expropriation, or the imposition of a condition in a subdivision permit requiring the allocation of a portion of land to the local authority. In the cases where a historic building is subject to a building preservation order and the owner willfully neglects to maintain the building, a local authority is empowered to acquire the building on favorable

Table 8.5

Land Use and Population Statistics, Bulawayo

Land Use	Area (ha.)	No. of Dwellings or (Properties) (1)	Existing Dwellings per Hectare	Vacant or Planned Stands	Existing Population No.	Existing Population % (2)
Residential						
Small holdings	977	424	0.4	358	1,594	0.4
Low density (3)	3,470	2,789	0.8	2,867	9,909	2.5
Medium density (3)	1,519	11,580	7.6	569	42,355	10.8
High density (3)	3,619	48,829	13.5	23,551	292,974	74.7
Flats	438	5,288	12.7	3,476	8,764	2.2
Domestic Workers (4)	–	18,277	–	–	36,710	9.4
Total	10,023	87,187	8.7	30,821	392,306	100.0
Industry	1,432	(805)	–	200	–	–
C.B.D. (5)	18	(1,032)	–	–	–	–
Developed Open Space	1,400	–	–	–	–	–
Public Facilities	1,000	–	–	–	–	–

Source: City of Bulawayo, 1981 "Master Plan".

Notes:
(1) Figures in parenthesis refer to properties.
(2) Population figures do not include "floating" residents and are slightly less than the 1982 census figures.
(3) Low density refers to plots greater than 4000m². Medium density refers to plots between 500m² and 4000m². High density refers to plots less than 500m².
(4) Domestic workers live on their employer's properties.
(5) The Central Business District includes both commercial and office development.

202

Figure 8.4 Schematic Map of Bulawayo

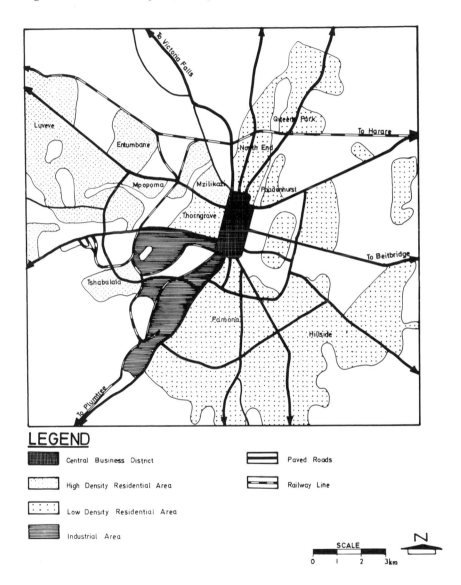

LEGEND

▓ Central Business District

▫ High Density Residential Area

∴ Low Density Residential Area

▬ Industrial Area

▭ Paved Roads

▭ Railway Line

SCALE
0   1   2   3km

N

Table 8.6

Landownership Pattern, Bulawayo

Owner	Approximate Area (hectares)	%
Municipality	24,100	57.1
Private	17,100	40.5
National Railways	800	1.9
State	200	0.5
Total	42,200	100.0

Source: Bulawayo Master Plan, 1981

terms. In cases where land is reserved in a statutory plan for public purposes, an owner may insist that his land be acquired. There is provision in the act for appeal to the administrative court and claims for compensation.

The state has equally wide powers of land acquisition but in the case of the resettlement program has not resorted to expropriation. Currently land is acquired on a willing seller, willing buyer basis, but certain areas of the country have been informally designated for resettlement, prompting farmers to offer their land to government.

MAJOR CHALLENGES

Zimbabwe is still a newly independent country trying to establish a new social order. This inevitably produces problems that affect many aspects of society, including land use planning.

National and Regional Issues

A weakness of land use planning in Zimbabwe is that there are no spatial plans at the national or regional level. As a result, there is little control over major issues such as rural urban population movement or the relationship of resettlement schemes to the commercial agricultural sector. The translation of national sectoral policies to physical action is left to individual government departments and provincial offices. No spatial guidelines are provided. Moreover, the regional plans referred to in the planning act are impractical because they do not provide control over major investment decisions. It is important, therefore, to integrate national economic planning with national spatial planning. If this can be achieved, it may be possible to formulate an effective urbanization policy that recognizes the vital role that towns and cities will play in providing housing and employment, and it could reconcile the conflicting issues of land resettlement while maintaining high yields from commercial agriculture.

A second issue is to rationalize the planning process within the government. Numerous ministries have planning functions and pursue particular policies that may sometimes conflict or overlap with the interests of another ministry. In the field of rural planning, for example, the functions of the Ministry of Lands Resettlement and Rural Development clearly overlap those of the Ministry of Local Government and Town Planning. This can be counterproductive and in view of limited professional staff is a waste of resources, indicating the need for a more rational system of planning at the national level.

Rural Issues

A high priority has been placed on rural development, particularly of the communal lands, because it is here that many pressing issues and problems are to be found, among them overpopulation, resource degradation, and a lack of employment opportunities, social facilities, and infrastructure.

Growth Points and District Centers

Prior to independence facilities in the communal lands were generally located randomly, with no reference to a district plan. Consequently development was widely dispersed, and it was sometimes necessary for an individual to walk in three different directions to visit a school, shop, and clinic. In a few places, however, development was concentrated in selected centers with good economic potential, called "growth points."[9] Although some are successful to a degree, even those growth points that have benefited from large-scale infrastructural investment have not developed any self-sustaining growth or significantly affected rural-urban migration patterns.

Since independence greater efforts have been made to develop the communal lands, including the stimulation of small urban centers. There is a clear need for such centers to provide a range of services and increase employment opportunities. Unfortunately, there are relatively few sites with sufficient economic potential to develop into growth points. It was therefore decided to develop a district center in each district, which would be the administrative headquarters of the area where, it was hoped, development would be encouraged. To facilitate this funds were provided by central government for the installation of infrastructure, and this has aroused a great deal of interest on the part of local businessmen.[10] There is, however, an urgent need to evaluate the program as several problems are beginning to emerge. In most cases the economic base of the district center is relatively weak, and as a result cost recovery is a problem.

It is also clear that in some centers the provision of infrastructure was not a priority, and the community would have preferred the funds to be channeled into other projects. Evaluation is therefore necessary to identify strengths and weaknesses in the program and to help policymakers strike a balance between economic growth and equity in the provision of services.

Implementation of District Center Plans

The preparation of plans for these growth points and district centers was a major undertaking, considering the limited manpower available, but the first phase of planning is now complete. Traditionally the role of land use planners in Zimbabwe was confined to plan preparation, development control, monitoring, and review, but now that these district centers are entering the implementation stage, this role is being seriously questioned. Planners were in the forefront during the plan preparation stage, and it is natural that the district councils turn to the planners for advice on how best to translate the plans into reality. The challenge facing planners is how to promote development with the limited resources that are available. Initially it was hoped that commercial firms would be attracted and that foreign aid would be forthcoming for local projects, but experience has shown that the most realistic approach is to rely on local resources and to develop local markets and small-scale businesses within the district.

Development Control

Without adequate development control, land use plans are meaningless. Unfortunately the public and the district councils in the communal lands are not experienced in dealing with development control. With the emphasis on promoting development, this aspect has been neglected. It is now becoming an important issue; already spontaneous building is encroaching onto road reserves and invalidating use zones. The local authorities are responsible for controlling development, but without sufficient training they find this difficult. Training is a pressing need and must be faced now before uncontrolled development destroys much of the work already done.

Provincial and District Coordination

The pressures of rural development have created problems of coordination. This has stimulated the processes of district and provincial planning in several provinces. These problems have arisen because of the highly sectoral structure of decisionmaking in which one ministry often does not coordinate with another and in which planning and investment decisions are sometimes taken at head office level without a complete understanding of the circumstances. The answer is to develop a planning system that will allow for greater coordination and local decisionmaking without impairing operational efficiency. One of the ways this is being done is by encouraging local authorities to prepare district plans and to coordinate these at the provincial level. While conceptually sound, this procedure has placed a severe burden on the provincial planners as district councils have relied on them to prepare their district plans, and other government ministries depend on them to do most of the work in compiling the provincial plan. With the current staff levels, this is proving difficult, and the planners in those provinces that have tried this process have found it necessary to neglect other aspects of their work. Since staff levels are unlikely to improve in the near future, it is important to streamline the process and, where possible, involve other organizations more closely. District councils, for example, should be trained so that they can prepare their own district plans and call in government professionals only to evaluate and advise on large-scale or complex projects. A more formal structure is necessary to involve uncooperative development agencies in the coordination process, and a simplified procedure for project preparation and approval needs to be developed. Of prime importance is the need to develop a system at the national level to approve these plans and tie the allocation of finance to provincial and district priorities because as the process has evolved from the outlying provinces, there is no machinery at the national level to deal adequately with integrated plans of this nature.

Resettlement

The need for land resettlement has arisen because a relatively small number of commercial farmers occupy large areas of farmland, while communal lands are overpopulated and overgrazed. Some of these problems in the communal lands are due to poor land husbandry, but it is difficult for peasant farmers to achieve good yields with the poor soils, low rainfall, and land pressures in these areas. In order to alleviate these problems and satisfy growing aspirations for land, the government has embarked on a resettlement program whereby commercial farms are bought, and families from the communal lands are resettled on a planned basis.

Although this program will go a long way toward meeting these aspirations, it will not provide a lasting solution to the problems posed by a rapidly growing population and a finite land supply. In recognition of this, the National Transitional Development Plan calls for measures to improve productivity in the communal lands and to increase nonagricultural employment. Currently, however, the resettlement program is a major exercise that affects the land use system of the country.

Urban Issues

For many years land use planning efforts were concentrated in the urban areas, and so it was often assumed that Zimbabwe did not have an urban problem. Indeed, compared to many other Third World countries, Zimbabwe has relatively few problems in the urban areas, but in the face of mounting rural-urban migration (Table 8.7) these problems inevitably will increase.

Low-Income Housing

The provision of low-income housing is likely to remain an issue for a long time. There is currently a backlog in housing provision and in the face of

Table 8.7
Zimbabwe: Recent Urban Population Estimates

Year	Urban Population	% Increase Per Annum
1978	1,348,000	–
1979	1,385,000	2.7
1980	1,428,000	3.1
1981	1,524,000	6.7
1982	1,732,000	13.6

Source: Central Statistical Office

mounting demand and limited resources, planners and architects are beginning to scrutinize their methods more closely.[11] An obvious deficiency in low-income housing strategies is poor locational planning. The basic principle of locating homes close to workplaces has often been ignored (due to past political pressures), and the result is significant transport problems, including unnecessarily high transport costs and long traveling times for individuals.

Recently considerable attention has focused on the question of standards, including planning standards, house design, and engineering standards. Compared with many other developing countries, Zimbabwe has high engineering standards, and it has been suggested that these should be lowered. This has been resisted on the ground that a lowering of standards will be shortsighted, create future maintenance problems, and be inappropriate in a country with a history of high standards. House type is also a very live issue. The official minimum standard is a four-room core house,the cost of which may be beyond the reach of many urban dwellers.[12]

Many designs for low-income housing estates are for a comparatively low density and consequently are less cost-effective than they could be. This is due to a variety of reasons, including difficult topography, which is largely unavoidable. There are, however, other factors that a planner can control to some degree, such as high space standards for schools and parks, excessive circulation space, and weak design, which results in pockets of residual unused land. Recognizing these issues has been an important lesson for land use planners and has prompted them to design more cost-effective layouts. Prior to independence the majority of low-income residential plots had an area of 200 square meters, which was considered the minimum acceptable size to accommodate a housing unit and at the same time derive maximum economies on infrastructure. Since independence the minimum stand size has been increased to 300 square meters because it was felt that the former standard was too small to accommodate a completed house and provide sufficient space for vegetable gardens. Although this size increases development costs, it has presented a challenge to planners to economize through other means such as effective and innovative design.

Many low-income housing estates are extremely monotonous and barren. This is due partly to the cutting down of surrounding trees for firewood but is also due to monotonous design. In an attempt to obtain the most economical sewer arrangement, many residential plots are designed in long, regular rows. Planners now need to generate a more human, community-oriented design without compromising on infrastructure costs.

Urban Squatters

With an annual population increase in urban areas of between 7 and 13 percent over the last few years, it has not been possible to provide sufficient housing. As a result there has been an increase in unauthorized urban squatting. This has occurred mainly in Harare but is by no means confined to the capital; cases are occurring nationwide. The two largest settlements in Harare are interesting because two distinctly different strategies have emerged to cope with them. The first settlement, known as Chirambahuyo, was situated adjacent to Chitungwiza and by January 1980 contained an estimated population of 50,000. The strategy developed here was to provide communal toilets and water supply points at central locations and to allocate formal housing to the residents gradually. As people left their temporary shelter, it was demolished to prevent reoccupation. By 1982 the settlement had virtually disappeared.

The other example is Epworth located on the Harare municipal boundary. Epworth has been in existence for many years, originally as a mission farm containing several villages. Gradually increasing numbers of people settled on the farm so that there are now 30,000 people living in self-built houses with no formal infrastructure or community services. Unlike Chirambahuyo, the government has decided to upgrade Epworth in situ and is preparing a conventional upgrading program for the area.[13]

Considering the national housing situation, the option of upgrading is preferable because it harnesses the community's capacity for self-help and enhances rather than destroys existing shelter. There is, however, a great deal of concern that unauthorized settlements are occurring in the least suitable areas, such as rocky or wet terrain, some distance from existing infrastructure. There is also concern that a precedent will be set,and the practice of squatting will be encouraged. It is important to demonstrate that upgrading is a viable strategy but at the same time to direct new urban migrants to suitable residential locations and assist them in building appropriate structures.

Urban Transportation

The issue of urban transportation is beginning to emerge as a problem. A high proportion of total daily traffic flow in the larger cities is accounted for by peak hour volumes, which last for only short durations. These give rise to traffic bottlenecks, particularly in cities such as Bulawayo where there are only a few routes connecting the high-density housing areas to the city center. Most low-income people rely on public transport, which in Zimbabwe is the conventional bus. There are problems with this system, including inadequate bus access into the city center, poorly located termini, and conflict among buses, pedestrians, and cars. Another problem is that bus companies are finding it difficult to maintain economically viable operations, so cost-efficient routing is increasingly necessary.

Small Towns

At the opposite end of the urban spectrum is the problem of the failing economic base of existing small towns. Due to a variety of reasons, a number of towns with good infrastructure, good locations, and economically buoyant hinterlands are suffering from static or declining development. This can be attributed to the international and national economic climate, but it is of concern to planners, and studies are underway to identify appropriate strategies to alleviate the problem. One such strategy may be industrial decentralization, but this will need to be carefully considered against the need to ensure that the existing cities are kept economically healthy. Certainly in a situation of sluggish economic growth nationwide, an active decentralization policy may be ill advised since this inevitably involves manipulating market forces by providing disincentives in the main cities.

APPROACHES TO LAND USE PLANNING

Theoretically land use planning in Zimbabwe should be undertaken at both the regional and local levels, but in practice it is most effective at the local and city level.

Regional Planning

Although the planning act makes provision for the formulation of regional plans, no statutory regional plans have been prepared.[14] Two studies were undertaken as an experiment in regional planning, but neither has emerged as an effective land use planning mechanism. The first study centered on the communal lands in the southeast of the country and proved useful in identifying problems and initiating the development of district and service centers (Agricultural and Rural Development Authority, 1981). However, it has several major weaknesses, which include unrealistic targets and lack of resources for implementation. The second was a more comprehensive study of the ecologically sensitive northwestern portion of the country (Department of Physical Planning, 1980). Although useful as a study, this exercise did not materially affect the land use planning process, principally because there were few pressures for development in the region and no resources with which to influence development. Regional planning has not developed in Zimbabwe largely due to a severe shortage of qualified planners and an inability to develop sufficient measures to provide regional planners with the authority to implement their proposals.

Provincial and District Plans

A significant emerging trend is the tendency to prepare provincial and district plans. These are nonstatutory plans relating to specific administrative areas and are attempts to coordinate public sector financial allocations and sectoral programs. It is an ambitious concept that at present relies on goodwill and the strength of the coordinating committee chairman. The experiment has gained support at provincial and district levels but lacks formal recognition at the national level; consequently there are problems in implementing the proposals. However, efforts are being made to improve the process, and a directive from cabinet formalizing the approach is expected shortly.[15]

In the preparation of a district plan, the local authority identifies problems and opportunities within its district and translates these into specific projects, subject to feasibility and economic investigations. The plan covers a five-year span and includes an annual program that assists the local authority in making bids to the central government for finance. At the provincial level, the various district plans are integrated and conflicts eliminated. It is hoped that in due course these plans will be accepted by the Ministry of Finance, Economic Planning and Development as the basis for its annual financial allocations.

Growth Point and District Center Plans

Shortly after independence, the Department of Physical Planning mounted a nationwide campaign to identify growth points, district centers, and service centers in the communal lands. In conformity with the government's policy "Growth with Equity," it was decided to identify centers that had some economic growth potential or were central points in the district. A hierarchy of centers was designated with the aim of stimulating development in these places. A growth point is a center that has significant primary economic potential, such as a major irrigation scheme; a district center is a settlement chosen by the district council as its administrative headquarters and generally is the largest commercial center in the district; and a service center is an existing business concentration chosen for its central location, access, and water supply. The planning approach is to accept existing development as far as possible and prepare a layout for plot subdivisions, road reservations, and sites for government and community facilities. A basic zoning system is applied for commercial, industrial, and residential uses, but compatible mixed uses are permitted. Simple development control regulations are applied, and appropriate measures are taken for the provision of water and waste disposal. The layout is discussed widely with the district council and local inhabitants, which often means that the proposed projects have to be marked or staked out on the ground as an aid in decisionmaking.

Once completed, the layout is approved in terms of section 44 of the Regional, Town and Country Planning Act and therefore does not have to conform to the requirements laid down for master and local plans. These layouts are sufficient to direct and control development for the time being, but it is clear that more sophisticated plans will become necessary for those centers that develop successfully.

Resettlement Plans

Resettlement plans are another example of land use planning that do not follow the procedures for statutory master plans. The Ministry of Lands, Resettlement and Rural Development identifies land on offer and prepares a resettlement plan comprised of a project report and set of air-photo mosaics that are used as a basis for making a decision on whether to proceed. The report contains a description of the natural environment, physical infrastructure required, intended agricultural program, staff inputs, and an economic analysis. The photo mosaics identify physical detail, depict proposed development, and in their final form provide a permanent record of land allocation. The project report is submitted for approval to an interministry committee on resettlement, which provides authority for ARDA to open a development expenditure account and authorizes acquisition of the land.

Four basic models are used in the design of resettlement schemes (Ministry of Lands, Resettlement and Rural Development, 1983). To date the majority of schemes follow model A, which consists of settlement in nucleated villages with individual arable holdings and communal grazing within village boundaries. Approximately 38 of these schemes are in the course of implementation involving 1,395,200 hectares of land and a target of 24,300 settler families. Model B schemes comprise group settlement with cooperative organization and management. To date 31 of these cooperatives have been approved, and 10 more are planned. They are generally small schemes involving 50 to 200 members and are located on scattered farms throughout the country. So far only one model C scheme has been implemented, and this comprises an individual settlement with a central estate farm where processing is carried out. Settlers have a commitment to grow and process a cash crop, such as coffee, in conjunction with the central estate. Model D is a cattle ranching scheme designed for regions where ranching is the only viable option.

Despite rapid progress, the resettlement program has come under some criticism from those who consider it uneconomic. But in a newly independent country where land is a central issue, resettlement has become a political necessity. To improve its chances for success, the resettlement program needs to develop and follow a well coordinated national plan sensitive to political realities and at the same time conscious of the need to preserve the economic viability of the commercial farming sector.

Master and Local Plans

It is clear that a great deal of land use planning in Zimbabwe is currently nonstatutory. Turning now to statutory plans, Zimbabwe has a two-tier system. This consists of master plans, which cover strategic issues such as policy, broad land use, and communication networks, and local plans, which are detailed proposals for specific areas within the framework of the master plan. Prior to the formulation of a master or local plan, a study of the planning area is required that includes an examination of the principal physical, social, economic, and environmental characteristics of the area. These characteristics are analyzed to identify problems, constraints, opportunities, and trends. The completed study must be presented in the form of a comprehensive report together with the plan. The master plan consists of a written statement illustrated by maps and diagrams. It must include reference to the relevant provisions of a regional or national plan, clearly state the aims of the master plan, and indicate the policy choices selected to achieve these aims.

There are three types of local plan: a local subject plan, which covers a particular subject; a local development plan covering a wide range of issues; and a local priority plan covering matters identified in the master plan as requiring urgent treatment. Each type of local plan comprises a written statement accompanied by maps and diagrams. The written statement must refer to the relevant provisions of the master plan and include a statement of goals and objectives. The proposals may vary considerably and include provisions for land use zoning, development control, transportation, historical preservation, and urban renewal. An explanation is required as to how the proposals will achieve the stated goals, the constraints likely to inhibit implementation, the resources available for implementation, and the phasing of development.

A clear procedure is laid down in the act for consultation, public exhibition, and submission to the minister. The public is given an opportunity to lodge objections, which are determined in a civil court. The minister of local government and town planning is required to approve all master plans, but specified local authorities are empowered to approve their own local plans provided these conform to the general provisions of an approved master plan.

That, in brief, is the approach to statutory planning in Zimbabwe. It is significant to note, however, that many local authorities still rely heavily on town planning schemes prepared under the 1945 planning act. This is because few master and local plans have been prepared to supersede these schemes. In fact, only one master plan and 12 local plans have been approved since the promulgation of the 1976 act, and several master plans have been in preparation for

years without being completed. This has prompted some criticism of the legislation, and it has been suggested that sweeping changes are necessary. The
problem has arisen, however, not because of deficiencies in the law but because
there are not enough planners to cope simultaneously with the needs of the rural
and urban areas. Consequently statutory planning has been neglected. Nevertheless, decisionmakers are becoming increasingly aware of the need for relevant
master plans. In Harare, for instance, an authority has recently been established
to prepare a master plan for the city and its environs.

Subdivision and Development Permits

Aside from the preparation of statutory and nonstatutory plans, land use planners in Zimbabwe are also processing applications for the subdivision and consolidation of land and for development permits. Procedures for processing these
applications are laid down in the 1976 planning act. Permits are required whether
or not the proposed development is covered by a master or local plan. In the
absence of such a plan, the local authority uses its own discretion. In practice,
most of the procedural issues are dealt with by administrative officers, and only
complex or unusual cases require the attention of a professional town planner.

FUTURE THRUSTS

There are a number of discernible trends in the land use planning field and
several that are not yet apparent but are predictable.

Regional Development

Although there will clearly be greater efforts at regional planning, this is
unlikely to be in terms of the Regional, Town and Country Planning Act. It is
more likely to fall under the Ministry of Finance, Economic Planning and Development, principally because that ministry is able to influence regional decisions through its financial allocations. It is also likely that the section in the
planning act referring to regional planning will be modified to reflect a more
realistic approach. The form that this approach might take is still not clear, but
there have been suggestions that it should consist of regional reports supported
by a five-year capital program, with maps to illustrate the report and locate the
capital projects (United Nations, 1981).

Provincial and district plans inevitably will become more important and widespread. It has been announced recently that provincial governors will be appointed
in each province, and one of their prime functions will be to promote and
coordinate development efforts. The governor will be a political appointee responsible for chairing provincial coordination meetings. Because of the senior
level of the appointment, it is likely that great emphasis will be placed on
provincial plans and the implementation of development. This will emphasize

the planners' role as a catalyst for development and will give greater political support to provincial coordination efforts. Care must be taken, however, to ensure that this new system does not result in a bottleneck, which could be the case if no one is prepared to make a decision without reference to the governor.

Other changes in the local government system can be expected with the amalgamation of rural councils and district councils into one type of rural authority. This will make it easier to plan and coordinate development within the district but may produce problems in the administration of two distinct land use systems with different needs and priorities.

Rural Development

It can be expected that more land will be acquired for resettlement and that an increasing number of these projects will be on a cooperative basis. The ultimate extent of these resettlement programs is not clear at this stage, but it is predictable that certain areas of the country will be resettled and others will continue under their present pattern of large-scale commercial agriculture. This has particular significance for adjacent towns that previously may have catered to a commercial agricultural hinterland and in the future may need to cater to an agricultural hinterland with different characteristics and needs.

A clearly discernible trend is that some growth points and district centers are developing while others are not, despite efforts to stimulate development and provide infrastructure. This is inevitable given the diverse range of physical and economic conditions in the communal lands. It is to be expected that these developing centers will need constant attention during their formative stages. Experience from other developing countries has shown that these centers are not attractive locations for industrial decentralization and often do not develop into economically self-sustaining towns. It is anticipated, therefore, that few growth points and district centers will develop beyond the first phase and that they will do little to stem the flow of migrants to the main towns.

Development control is becoming an important issue in all district centers, and more attention needs to be given to this aspect. In those centers where growth is occurring, it will be necessary to develop a more sophisticated system of guidance and control than is currently applied.

Urban Development

Zimbabwe is on the brink of an extremely rapid phase of urban growth. An examination of employment trends, however, indicates that the growth of formal urban employment may well fall short of that needed to keep up with this rapid rural-urban migration.[16] The consequence is that urban migrants may have to be absorbed into the informal sector or simply be unemployed, resulting in lower than average incomes and a large group of urban poor. Urban planning, and in particular housing strategies, must take cognizance of these trends. Faced with limited funds, spiraling construction costs, and rapidly increasing housing needs, it may become necessary to modify some of the standards currently used in the field of low-income housing. It is also clear that the phenomenon of urban squatters is likely to increase as more people migrate to the towns and are unable to find formal accommodation. Therefore squatter upgrading and site and service schemes are likely to become more prominent.

Zimbabwean towns currently are developed at a comparatively low density, but as they continue to grow, municipal and government land will become scarce. The purchase of private land for expansion will increase development costs, encouraging greater densities and infilling within the existing urban structure. With this expansion, greater attention will need to be given to urban land use planning and a greater share of national investment made to urban infrastructure than is currently the case.

It is clear that more emphasis will have to be placed on urban problems in the future. This is likely to bring about a revival of statutory master and local plans. It is hoped that the lessons that have been learned in rural development will be applied to the urban areas. Planners will be able to promote development through catalytic action and not merely confine their attention to statutory plans.

NOTES

1. See Table 8.4. These figures are released by the Central Statistics Office, and although they may contain some distortions, the trend is clear.

2. The population statistics for Chitungwiza are derived from the 1982 census, but there may have been some underenumeration because some people are reluctant to be identified and others do not permanently live in one place.

3. The Marondera master plan was started in 1977 and by 1983 had still not been submitted to the minister for approval. In contrast the Bulawayo master plan was completed in only 11 months.

4. Although the planning act was applied across the country, it was recognized that difficult circumstances existed in the communal lands, and a special development order was passed that provided relief from certain development control requirements in these areas.

5. Government of the Republic of Zimbabwe 1981, *Growth with Equity*, p. 4.

6. Government of Zimbabwe, *Regional, Town and Country Planning Act, 1976*, section 15.

7. Government of the Republic of Zimbabwe 1981, *Growth with Equity*, p. 4.

8. Government of Zimbabwe, Regional, Town and Country Planning Act, 1976, section 46.

9. These growth points such as Sanyati and Mushumbi Pools were originally developed by ARDA.

10. In the 1982-83 financial year the government provided $8 million for the installation of infrastructure in growth points and district centers.

11. The national housing backlog at the end of 1983 was estimated to be approximately 100,000 units.

12. At 1983 prices the four-roomed core cost $4,700, which is beyond the affordable

level of many low-income workers whose minimum wage level may be as low as $65 or $110 per month. These are the minimum wages for domestic and industrial employees.

13. It is planned to provide security of tenure and basic infrastructure and to encourage households to improve their homes by making small loans available.

14. The Regional, Town and Country Planning Act provides for regional planning councils whose functions are to prepare a regional plan and advise local authorities on the operation of the plan, but the act does not provide effective powers to implement the plan.

15. In a press conference on 4 January 1984 the prime minister announced the appointment of a minister whose functions would include provincial development and coordination. He also stated that a bill was being drafted that would restructure the system of provincial administration.

16. The growth of formal employment over the last few years has been on the order of 3 to 4 percent per annum, and yet the population increase in urban areas is reaching 13 percent per annum.

BIBLIOGRAPHY

Agricultural and Rural Development Authority. 1981. *A.R.D.A. 1 Project Report No. 1.* Harare: Government Press.
City of Bulawayo. 1981. *City of Bulawayo Master Plan.* Bulawayo: City Council.
Department of Physical Planning. 1979. *Memorandum on the Department of Physical Planning in the Ministry of Local Government and Housing.* Salisbury: Government Press.
Department of Physical Planning. 1980. *Interim Sebungwe Regional Concept Plan.* Harare: Government Press.
Government of Rhodesia. 1974. *Policy on Decentralization.* Salisbury: Government Press.
Government of the Republic of Zimbabwe. 1981. *Growth with Equity: An Economic Policy Statement.* Harare: Government Press.
Government of Zimbabwe. 1976. *Regional, Town and Country Planning Act, 1976.* Harare: Government Press.
Hosford, P. J. and A. G. Whittle. 1979. Background and Functions of the Department of Physical Planning. *Zimbabwe Rhodesia Science News* 13(11): 252-55.
Ministry of Lands, Resettlement and Rural Development. 1983. *Intensive Resettlement Policies and Procedures.* Harare: Government Press.
Republic of Zimbabwe. 1982. *Transitional National Development Plan 1982/83-1984/85.* Vol. 1. Harare: Government Press.
Republic of Zimbabwe. 1983. *Transitional National Development Plan 1982/83-1984/85.* Vol. 2. Harare: Government Press.
United Nations. 1981. *A Spatial Planning System for Zimbabwe: A Feasibility Study Commissioned by UNCHS for the Government of Zimbabwe.* Washington, D.C.: United Nations.

9

Ghana

EARL M. BROWN, JR.

The Republic of Ghana, known as the Gold Coast during the colonial period, achieved independence from England in 1957. Located in West Africa, Ghana, bordered by the Ivory Coast, Upper Volta (now named Bourkina Fasso), and Togo, had a population of approximately 11 million in 1980. Historically Ghana has been known as the leading exporter of cocoa, timber, and some precious metals.

Accra, the capital city, had an estimated population of 946,000 in 1980. Kumasi, the second largest city, had an approximate population of 393,000 in 1980. The third largest urban area of Sekondi-Takoradi accounted for approximately another 231,000 people. Tamale is the fourth largest city, with a population of approximately 150,000.

The pattern of development in Ghana is similar to that found in many other West African countries in that the major growth poles are found in one part of the country—in the case of Ghana in the southern one-third. This one-third includes the important centers of Accra, Kumasi, and Sekondi-Takoradi. These southern centers are well integrated through a system of railways and roads, which contains much of the export production which forms the basis of Ghana's economy.

The northern region is considerably less well developed, despite the fact that several areas along the northern border have high population densities. Yet the northern region produces much of the country's foodstuffs, including yams, maize, millet, beans, groundnuts, sorghum, and tomatoes. The development of the northern region has been a stated objective of governments since independence in 1957 (see Figure 9.1).

Figure 9.1 Map of Ghana

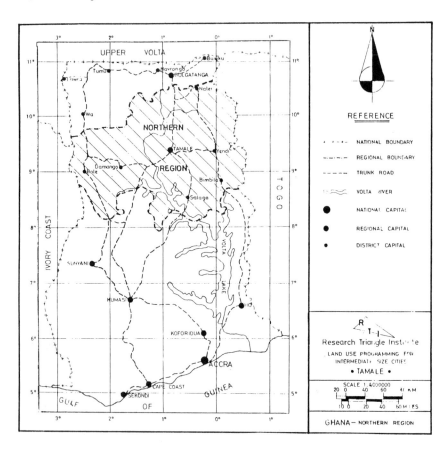

INSTITUTIONAL FRAMEWORK

Development of an Organizational Framework Consistent with Decentralization of Government Activities

The decentralization of Ghana government functions is a formal policy intended to maximize local involvement in the development and implementation of public service programs. Although the process of decentralization is still unfolding, the framework has been established. It creates four levels of government activity: national, regional, district, and local centers. The essence of decentralization in Ghana is to allocate governing responsibility more effectively so that local government handles local issues, while higher levels of government address regional and national issues.

There are three compelling reasons for the present decentralization effort. First, there are important regional differences within Ghana that demand specialized attention. Although the government of Ghana has a moral goal of a unified and equal society, there are considerable regional, cultural, physical, and economic differences. The existence of these variations requires a flexible government policy that can produce locally tailored development strategies.

In addition to a flexible policy that addresses local differences, decentralization, second, also provides opportunity for local participation in the governing process. It is efficient simply because highly centralized government expends large amounts of human and fiscal resources to administering local activities. Indeed, the more local the problem, the more resources must be expended simply to transmit information and provide administrative personnel between central and local government.

Third, decentralization allows the government to focus significant resources on growth centers, such as Tamale, in pursuit of the national goal of diffusing urban growth throughout the country. Under decentralization, the personnel and financial resources required for concentrated regional development efforts in Tamale can be accommodated. Also, decentralization creates an added push for local planning since local government assumed the responsibility for resolving local problems. Tamale is the first site for concentrated regional development under the 1975-80 five-year development plan. The development of a decentralized government structure throughout the country will improve the ability of local governments in other regions to undertake similar land use programming and development efforts.

Although decentralization should increase the chances of effective land use programming, several problems were created by the decentralization. Since these problems relate directly to the effectiveness of planning at local levels of government, it was necessary for such problems to be resolved as a first step in decentralization.

One problem concerns the lack of skilled personnel required to undertake the planning and administration of local government. The Ghana government recognized this problem and initiated a national program of management and skill training of regional and district officers. The national program—the Economic and Rural Development Management project (ERDM)—jointly sponsored by the U.S. Agency for International Development and the government of Ghana (1977-82), was designed to increase the use of appropriate management techniques throughout the national system of local government.

Another problem was one of coordination, both vertical and horizontal. The vertical component relates to coordination and planning activities among the levels of government—national, regional, district, and local. The horizontal component relates to the coordination activities of different line departments within each level of government. Although there are a number of approaches to dealing with this problem at the district level, the best approach can be determined only in collaboration with district officials. These approaches range from instituting formal sign-off procedures on projects among departments to informal exchanges of information about what departments are doing. One of the most effective approaches to fostering coordination among members of various departments was to create working groups that draw members from each of the operating departments. The key was for members to develop strong identification with the working group so that loyalty and ownership in decisions can be encouraged. The degree of affiliation and loyalty to the working group will determine how effective members of the group will be as advocates of coordination within their home departments.

Serious consideration of decentralized development in Ghana began in the late 1960s. In 1967 a commission was appointed to examine the structure of the public service in Ghana. Its *Report of the Commission on the Structure and Remuneration of the Public Services in Ghana* criticized the then strongly centralized government structure. Central and local government civil servants belonged to two separate service classifications with wide gaps in pay and skill levels. The report recommended an integrated civil service in which national and local level officials would be equal in all respects.

Today decentralization in Ghana is a clearly articulated policy manifested in the national economic development guidelines, the regional and spatial development guidelines, and the new local government structure. Guidelines for the national five-year development plan (1975-80), published in January 1975, call for equitable income distribution and the elimination of extremes in the distribution of income and wealth. This was one of the six key goals and objectives of the plan and is preceded only by economic growth and the promotion of full employment.

An important component of the equity goal is the regional planning and rural development program outlined in the guidelines. The government viewed development of the regional and rural areas as a crucial indicator of overall developmental success. As such, the government noted that the more conventional sectoral approach to development will be augmented in the new plan period by a strong emphasis on regional planning and the development of rural areas.

Perhaps the most dramatic component of the government's decentralization policy is the new local government structure. Basically the new program calls for the integration of the civil service and the decentralization of formerly national level functions and authority to the regional and district levels so that the responsible officials will be closer to the problems and programs. A recent government report stated:

The introduction of the new structure of local administration . . . would abolish the distinction between local and central government and create at the local level one monolithic structure to which will be assigned the totality of government activity at the local level. [This will] take the decisionmaking function in respect to matters of a purely local significance away from Accra closer to the areas where the decisions are implemented. (Siita, 1982, 72)

The new system will consist of four tiers of government: regional councils; district councils; municipal, urban, and local councils; and town and village development committees.

HISTORICAL DEVELOPMENT

Historically development projects were conceptualized and developed at the national level of government with regional and local government units operating as implementers rather than planners of local projects. Neither local decision-makers nor community participants had a role in the planning and design of projects, which thus generally resulted in a lack of local support. National and regional administrative bureaucracies were distant from local problems and issues, and inconsistent conceptualization of community priorities resulted. Thus national and regional planned projects rarely gained significant local support.

The recognition of the development gap conceptualization issue has prompted national governments to begin to initiate development policies that shift local development responsibility to local levels of government. In Ghana the recognition of this gap was manifested through the findings of several major studies that focused on methods to encourage local government to become more efficient and responsible for managing local development projects. Consistent with this recognition was the need to increase staff and institutional capacity and increase local government financial management efficiency. The result has been the recognition of the role of local government and citizens in the development process. Government policy, which has evolved since Ghana's independence, reflects the more significant role of local government in the development process. Present public policy places the responsibility for planning, financing, and implementing local development projects with the district council. The shift from a central vertical approach to a decentralized horizontal approach to local development is being pursued by governments in developing countries and by international donor organizations as a means to encourage more substantial economic and human resource development.

Administrative Structure

The administration of local government in Ghana has undergone a number of significant changes from the colonial period until the present. After 1966 a more conscious effort was made to develop a system directed at enabling the local unit of government to undertake locally initiated development projects. The system that operated prior to independence until 1966 is considered the old local government structure.

During the years 1878 to 1936, the structure that existed for the administration of local government services was considered to be direct administration, which operated through a three-tiered structure composed of the central government, municipal and urban councils, and districts, composed of towns and villages.

The larger towns like Accra and Kumasi were developed as municipal and urban councils, and the rural areas were grouped in districts administered by expatriate district commissioners. These district commissioners, who administered the districts within the native authority jurisdictions and, in conjunction with the central government's civil servants, performed all the local government services. The administrative structure responsible for the administration of the local areas was the native authority, which in some instances created the statutory sanitary boards that provided local services in the smaller mining towns.

In the new system, all councils are granted corporate status, which in effect permits the enactment of bylaws, tax levies, fines, and contractual arrangements. Economic viability is a major aspect of the new local government system. District councils are encouraged to improve the effectiveness and efficiency of revenue collection and at the same time are encouraged to explore new revenue-generating opportunities. The new local government system provides, through the Ministry of Local Government, a local government inspectorate unit.

Pursuant to Articles 156 to 161 of the 1969 constitution, the Local Administration Act of 1971 (Act 359) was passed and amended in 1974. It created the four-tiered structure of local government for the country. The main characteristic of the new system was decentralization by creating decentralized ministry structures and at the same time creating district institutions vested with broad powers. Authority is now delegated by the ministry to an official or officials in a local department or region. The new system sought to move the decisionmaking function, in respect to matters of purely local significance, from the capital and place such responsibility close to the areas where decisions are implemented. It is expected that by reason of their local presence, the new district councils will be able to identify the problems of the areas they administer and seek solutions more readily. This will ensure the expeditious execution of projects and services required to bring relief to the population. In place of the previous multiplicity of local councils, most of them small, weak, and fiscally unviable, there are now units of local administration for every administrative district. These units are larger than the previous councils in population and size in an effort to increase their economic base and stability.

Native Authorities

The earliest ordinance in Ghana dealing with the judicial and administrative powers of chiefs was the Gold Coast Native Jurisdiction Ordinance of 1883, which empowered head chiefs and councillors to make bylaws and provided for the establishment of native tribunals composed of head chiefs and subchiefs. Chiefs were also appointed conservators of the peace with wide powers in law-and-order matters. This ordinance of 1883 remained on the statute book until 1936, although its operation was curtailed by the application of the Native Administrative Ordinance of 1927, which established and recognized state councils and provincial councils and generally consolidated earlier legislation on local government administration.

Under the native authority system, no technical officer (specialist) existed. The district commissioner (colonial official) acted as the agent for various ministries or departments. The district commissioners tended to be generalist-type administrators rather than specialists such as health officers or education officers. In most districts, however, technical officers did exist in certain services, such as police service, road maintenance, and engineering.

In 1936, an amending ordinance repealed the ordinance of 1883. Some paramount chiefs used these powers to establish a treasury often referred to as "stool treasuries." In 1939, the Native Administrations Treasuries Ordinance was passed, providing that a state council might, if required in writing by the provincial commissioner, establish a treasury for the state. This was an ordinance of critical importance since it marked a modest beginning of local government in the Gold Coast colony with powers to levy and collect revenue.

When the 1944 legislation was passed, the Native Authority (Colony) Ordinance, the edifice of local government administration through the traditional authority, was completed. The main purpose of this ordinance was to define the relationship of the colonial government to the native authorities and define, as the long title of the ordinance makes clear, "their due place in the administration of the colony." This ordinance represented the establishment of "a unified system in which the central colonial government and the Native Administration are both parts of the one government organizational and administrative structure" (Siita and Brown, 1980, 58).

Regional Councils

The regional councils created by the 1971 act were established to act as the link between the central government and the district councils in order to have a more efficient integrated national planning program. The regional minister, the chief political officer within the region, serves as the chairman of the regional council, while district council representatives serve as members. In addition to key regional staff, traditional leaders (chiefs) within the region serve on regional councils. The regional council has responsibility for the review and approval of district budgets within the broad policy guidelines of the national government, the allocation of central government funds to district councils, and the coordination of functions of the district councils to ensure a fair and equitable distribution of projects throughout the region.

The regional council is primarily responsible for the execution of national development projects within the region. The central government has the responsibility for the administration of the regional council and provides the financing. The key committee of the regional council is the Regional Planning Committee, which is responsible for providing the financial and economic support to regional and district projects. In essence, the regional council serves as the coordinating agency at the regional level for all national and district projects. The regional councils are to supervise the operation and functions of the district councils; act as agents of the central government in national programs and development projects with the region; and act as executing and management agencies for projects and services that by reason of size or complexity of regional character fall outside the competence of the district councils. Since the regional councils do not raise or collect any revenue, the expense of their operations is taken from the general revenue fund.

District Councils

The district council has the primary responsibility for the collection of district revenue rates and fees. Formerly the district council's staff costs and administrative expenses were paid from local revenues; however, the New Local Government Act of 1971 specifies that local government staff salaries are now the responsibility of the central government. This important development relieved the local government of the financial responsibility for administrative costs, thus making more funds available to support locally initiated development and maintenance projects. The district council is responsible for levying all rates and fees and for collecting and administering such revenues. The development of Ghana's local government administration is aimed at having experienced managers and administrators functioning at the basic level of government, the district council. The principal administrative officer is the district chief executive (DCE), an officer classified in the higher administrative grades under the local government system. The DCE is responsible for supervision and coordination of the activities of key district officers; however, the district officers retain for technical guidance, transfer, training, and staff promotion their administrative relationship to the parent department. The purpose of this structural change in local government administration is to encourage greater coordination and efficiency of management.

This organizational approach to local government administration appears workable in theory. District councils are responsible for the efficient administration and development within the district. The key decentralized agencies that are to operate as divisions of the district council are the following:

—Ministry of Agriculture

—Ghana Education Service

—Department of Social Welfare and Community Development

—Ministry of Health

—Controller and Accountant General's Department

—Town and Country Planning Department

—Department of Parks and Gardens

—Sports Council

—Public Works Department

—Department of Game and Welfare

Municipal, Urban, and Local Councils

The new local government legislation allows the district council to create municipal, urban, and local or area councils. These councils constitute another level of the local government system and are subordinate to the district council. Municipal, urban, and area councils have been created for single communities or towns of a cosmopolitan, communal, or industrial character such as Accra metropolitan area, Kumasi, and Sekondi-Takoradi. These types of councils have primary responsibility for refuse collection, incineration and sanitation, and public health. The local councils are generally located in areas identified with traditional authorities. Such councils usually are engaged in identifying and sponsoring projects at the local level that affect citizens of a number of villages and require an effective coordination of resources. In essence, the municipal and urban local council acts as a special interest group for a specific designated area.

Village-Town Committees

To satisfy and respond to the community interests, the district council under the new local government legislation is empowered, in consultation with the traditional authorities, to establish local village development committees. These committees are thought to be responsive to the particular needs of the community within the district. They are responsible for initiating local projects such as self-help programs, ensuring that basic rates and fees are collected and paid to the council, and organizing and supervising general health and sanitation projects within the local areas. They also initiate community dialogue and decisions at the local community level. The results of such decisions are often the recommendation of programs and projects to the district council.

These committees have the chief of each village or town as their chairman. The village-town committee function is to act as lobbyists and pressure groups for their localities and as the vehicle for communication and dialogue with the district council and the local public. The committee does not have the power to raise taxes, but it does assist in the district council's revenue-collection activities.

MAJOR ISSUES

Urban Planning

Plan preparation and implementation in Ghana involves several key government ministries and departments at the national, regional, and local levels; thus national and local offices of three ministries, the Ministry of Local Government, the Ministry of Finance and Economic Planning, and the Ministry of Works and Housing, are of immediate concern. Other government entities, such as the Ministry of Labor and Youth, Ministry of Social Welfare, the Ghana Highway Authority, and Ghana Water and Sewerage Corporation, have an important function in the development process.

The planning process from the initial stages of problem identification and data collection to the final stage of ministry approval involves numerous government agencies at the national, regional, and local levels of government. Siita notes that "despite the great detail in the comprehensive plan and the full regulatory authority vested in the planning committee, actual development of a vast majority of urban areas bears little resemblance to what their physical plans prescribe" (Siita, 1982, 2). The legal authority for the preparation and enforcement of plans is found in the Town and Country Ordinance of 1945.[1] This ordinance makes provision for the establishment of planning committees to develop plans in areas designated by the minister of government responsible for the Department of Town and Country Planning and who are authorized to prepare plans and to develop land use control techniques.[2] The ministry retains the right of final approval of all plans, which becomes the official plan by which all subsequent development must comply. The development of the comprehensive plan corresponding to regulatory authority is significant; however, the practical fact is that development in the urban centers continues to be uncontrolled and haphazard growth. Siita (1982) concluded that the concept of comprehensive planning with its police powers is an ineffective approach to controlling development. He furthermore stated that the existing system is "an inappropriate model which is inappropriately implemented" (Siita, 1982, 2). In theory the planning committee has the responsibility for the development of plans, but in practice the regional and district town and country planning offices develop plans. The Town Planning Committee approves and ensures that the plan is consistent with local goals and priorities. The difficulty in implementing the model is directly related to the basic issue of land tenure, the development application process, and the general lack of financial resources to construct the necessary roads, water, health, and sanitation facilities.

Land Tenure

Land is an important resource in Ghana. In a sense no parcel of land is without an owner, although proper ownership may not be a single individual, government, or private corporation. Several traditional systems of land tenure exist within different regions of Ghana in which patterns of landownership, land utilization, and inheritance differ from one group to another.

There are four basic categories of landownership in Ghana:[3]

1. Private lands: This category includes private individuals and families as owners.
2. Stool/skin land: Stool lands are controlled by any person for the benefit of members of a traditional group, clan, company, or community.[4]
3. Stool/skin lands vested in the state: These are lands that have been vested in the state by executive instrument in what could be called the public good.[5]
4. State or government land: These are lands that have been acquired by the state.[6]

Historically, land registration has been of concern since the colonial period. Since 1883 regulatory mechanisms have existed in Ghana (Mensah-Brown, 1978). Until 1962 the land registration Land Registry Ordinance of 1895 was the governing legislation for what was considered to be the Gold Coast colony. This early registration legislation simply provided for the registration of land with its particular description, often using inaccurate drawings and maps. This initial ordinance did not have provision for the adjudication (Mensah-Brown, 1978) of land disputes, and it failed to take into account the then common practice of oral transfer of land.

The economic importance of land had not been recognized during the colonial period since the northern territories were not considered to be economically viable by land developers of the period. In 1931, at the time some economic viability for land in the north was beginning to appear, the Land and Native Rights Ordinance, 1931, was enacted by the colonial administration.[7] The net effect of this ordinance was the vestment of the administration and management of all land in the northern territories of the governor "for benefit of the indigenous people." No title to occupy or use such land could be granted without the consent of the governor.

After independence, the new government found that the problems relative to land registration and tenure had been inherited from the colonial period. In 1962 the government enacted a series of laws aimed at correcting these problems. The Land Registry Act of 1962, in conjunction with other legislation, was intended to provide judicial and administrative control by the states of land truncation. More recently the government (during the period of Hilla Limann) passed legislation to return the land of the former northern territories—the upper and northern regions—to the control of the traditional authorities, the chief and elders. The state, however, maintains the right and ability to purchase stool land for purposes in the public interest.

The registration procedures for land is cumbersome, time-consuming, and expensive. Two to three years is common to wait for government action on land registration applications. During the period 1921-39 mapping of the larger towns in the Gold Coast colony occurred. This added a higher level of accuracy to the mapping and registration process. During the period of World War II, aerial surveys were conducted, which were a significant asset to mapmakers and surveyors. When independence was achieved, the need for accurate land mapping and registration became an important concern, particularly since the northern part of Ghana was beginning to realize its agricultural potential. This fact, combined with urbanization pressures, demonstrated the need for an efficient land tenure and registration system. Although numerous pieces of legislation had been enacted to rectify the inadequacies of the land tenure and registration system, the practical aspects of the problem continue to exist.

During the Tamale Land Use Programming Project, when efforts were being made to assist the Western Dagomba District Council (WDDC) to establish district development priorities, the question of landownership continued to be a major consideration. However, the delay in processing the land registration application combined with the delay in the plan approval process led many families to develop residential structures without proper authority.

Development Process

Urban physical development plans are developed for both statutory and advisory planning areas, although development control can legally be enforced only in statutory planning areas. The 1945 planning ordinance did not apply to advisory planning areas. The physical development plan consisted of a land use plan illustrating the general distribution of residential, commercial, industrial, recreational and educational areas, transportation networks, and all other categories of public and private land uses.

In 1969 national government policy required that all district and regional capitals submit a 15-year physical development plan. By 1980, of the nine regional capitals only Tamale, capital of the northern region, had submitted a physical development plan. The Tamale plan had been submitted in 1976 after half of the planning period had elapsed. The time period taken to prepare a physical development plan can be attributed to the centralized nature of the plan approval process and the time required to collect and analyze needed data. Siita (1982, 27) notes that "the process of preparation and approval of plans . . . become tangential to the actual development of the town for which they were prepared." All plans must be approved by the appropriate minister, an authority granted by the 1945 ordinance but not delegated. If a plan required changes or revisions, it was returned to the appropriate district or regional office for such changes. With the sporadic telephone and mail communications, such delays significantly lengthen the approval process.

Associated with the cumbersome nature of plan approval is the inadequate system of tracking plans already presented for approval. Siita noted that physical development plans for four urban areas in the northern region of Ghana—Damongo, Savelugu, Salaga, and Gambaga—submitted for an approval in 1975 had not been approved by 1980. In fact, the plans could not be located in the system. Such delays in the plan approval process combined with increased urbanization pressures have resulted in unauthorized, uncontrolled commercial and residential development. Planners frequently find themselves in a situation of not being able to discourage development in a statutory planning area for which the official plan had not been approved.

The frequent delays experienced in the plan approval process were only one aspect of the planning development process. Once a plan was approved, the responsibility for implementation moved to a different agency of government: the local district council and the Land Commission. When development applications are submitted to the local Town and Country Planning Office, an assessment and recommendation is made to the Town Planning Committee by the Department of Town and Country Planning (DTCP). Once the development application has been approved, the Land Commission is responsible for providing legal title (leasehold arrangement) to the land. Notification of development application approval is sent to the district building inspector's office, which is responsible for monitoring the stages of development. A development fee is collected at the time of the application, which is designed to be used by the district to finance infrastructure development. The crucial problem observed in Tamale was the lack of coordination among district departments responsible for district development. For example, once the official plan became a reality, town planning had no further responsibility in the process. If the need arose for plan revision, the DTCP would act, but no formal role existed in the plan implementation process. No institutional framework existed that stimulated coordination between the planning and implementing agencies of government.

District Council Finances and Coordination

The New Local Government Act of 1971 places responsibility for district development with the district council. The district council therefore was required to establish development goals and priorities in addition to collecting revenues and allocating resources for implementation of its programs. The Western Dagomba District Council (WDDC) has been exploring ways to control development in the district and at the same time provide for desired growth and development.

The council has experienced a number of problems associated with development. One primary problem was the inability of the WDDC to collect enough revenue to carry out its total program of development. Some development projects were undertaken, including new school construction or rehabilitation, road graveling or regraveling, underground water-hold tanks, septic tanks, latrines, and health stations throughout the district. The council has been able to undertake some development projects with financial assistance from the national government, but many of the projects were financed by the district's own resources; however, the council sought to develop a more comprehensive development program.

Although the WDDC has been able to undertake some development projects, it has not been able to plan and implement projects in concert with other decentralized departments. Although the national policy on decentralization has established the theoretical framework for local government operation, the practical reality was that the institutional framework had not been developed at the district level to facilitate the implementation of the Local Government Act (Siita and Brown, 1980).

There was a lack of coordination and cooperation among and between the departments and agencies responsible for planning and implementing of projects within the district. The institutional structure or framework necessary to stimulate coordination of both human and fiscal resources had not been developed.

Institutional Development Activities

The findings of the survey of district and regional officers revealed that WDDC district officers did not view the district chief executive as having any significant influence on their activities since their performance evaluations, departmental budgets, and staff promotions were the responsibility of the regional office, not the district council. It was observed that although a policy on decentralization existed, in many instances district officers did not work together or know the functions of other departments or agencies. Plans, programs, and budgets outlining departmental development programs for the year were not presented to the district council for informational or planning decisions on a regular basis. The lack of such coordination resulted in the construction of public facilities without adequate utilities and other infrastructure. In other instances, the development activity undertaken by one department of government created additional problems for another agency. To illustrate the point, during a presentation by the district irrigation development authority engineer, the sites of recently constructed dams and dugouts throughout the district were presented. The presentation included those facilities already constructed, those under construction, and those in the planning stages. The Ministry of Health representative, the medical doctor responsible for primary health care programs, observed that there were increased instances of guinea worm in approximately the same location of the new water facilities. Further investigation by the health officer revealed that significant evidence indicated that the higher instances of this disease among women and children were associated with the same dams and dugouts. The district officers were asked to discuss the reasons for and cause of this situation. The results of these discussions were a recommendation that an additional design feature, a walkway, be added to permit people to obtain water without walking waist deep into it.

In a subsequent session of the district officer workshops, the district highway superintendent presented the development program for road and street repair and construction in Tamale. It was observed that widening a number of streets required the removal of utility poles (both electricity and telephone), a water main, and the removal of approximately two dozen nim trees.[8] Each of these services was managed by different departments of government. After questioning and debate, it was learned that no coordination between the Ghana Highway Authority and other departments had been observed. There had been some discussion between the Ghana Highway Authority and the Ghana Water and Sewerage Corporation, although no noticeable coordination of construction schedules or other activities could be identified.[9]

The Tamale Land Use Programming (TLUP) project team shared these observations with the district officers and discussed ways in which such situations could be avoided in the future. The conclusion reached after discussion and debate in the WDDC was a recognition of the need for a forum in which the plans, programs, budgets, and other locally available resources could be coordinated for the best benefit of the district. The goal of creating a framework for coordinated planning, in order to use scarce resources more efficiently and increase the implementability of district plans, required the development of a two-step training program. The first phase was designed to improve the understanding and acceptance of coordinated planning, the second focused on teaching modern management and budgeting procedures to district officials.

The training process was intended to overcome two basic structural problems in the district organizational system: the relative newness of the district council as an organizational unit with relatively broad decisionmaking powers, and the traditional centralization or vertical orientation of functional agencies. The reorganization of the governmental structure was a result of the New Local Government Act of 1971, which placed the principal responsibility for district development with the district council. Although a large civil service existed and there had been a tradition of locally elected councils, local units had never before had the broad responsibilities outlined in the new structure and therefore had little experience in coordinating development plans with several agencies.

Similarly, the functional agencies responsible for services and development project implementation were accustomed to relying on their central ministry office for project identification and budget matters. Few district-level officers were accustomed to the dynamism required for local control of programs, and even fewer were accustomed to coordinating program phases with other agencies or governmental units.

To overcome these problems the TLUP project team established a series of workshops involving district councillors and district officers to provide a forum in which planning, programming, and implementation activities within the district could be discussed.[10] The WDDC workshops had the following purposes:

—To provide an opportunity for officers of district agencies to present plans, programs, budgets, and implementation schedules to the district council and other officers

—To stimulate individual and group communications in order to begin to build the foundation of a structure to carry out district-level development projects

—To explore and understand the goals, responsibilities, and functions of each government agency operating within the district and to develop a forum in which coordinated developmental action can occur

—To allow district officers to discuss agency priorities for development and highlight problems and resource constraints of those agencies

—To develop an adequate source of social, economic, and physical information on the district.

The target groups of the training activity were the Western Dagomba district councillors, district officers, and town planning officials. Although the workshops were well attended by district officers and town planning officers, the participation of the elected district councillors was significantly lower. During the period the training sessions were scheduled, political campaigns were being conducted throughout the country in which many local elected officials were actively involved. Second, the training sessions were scheduled during the peak farming season; thus, the participation of the elected officials, most of them farmers, was below project expectations.

APPROACH TO PLANNING

In the context of the previous section on Major Issues—urban planning in Ghana, development processes, and institutional development activities—approach to planning will be discussed by means of a case study. The experience gained in the introduction of a basically new approach in this one case will be extended to the rest of the country.

Although the vast majority of technical assistance offered by international organizations had been directed toward the central city or major metropolitan regions, there have been some significant efforts by the U.S. Agency for International Development (USAID) and other international organizations to direct some technical assistance and attention to intermediate-sized cities. The experience of such projects is that the urban pressures associated with the provision of municipal services, social well-being, physical infrastructure, and institutional development have greatly exceeded the availability of locally available physical and human resources.

Intermediate-sized cities in less developed nations, which merit considerable attention of government planners and policymakers, do exist and require greater attention for interregional and intraregional planning and development, local institutional development, and effective coordination of existing resources. One study concluded:

The traditional concerns and skills of regional planning are inadequate to deal with the internal land use questions of the cities themselves. These problems—adequate open space, coordinated utility provision, resolving competition among uses, land speculation, traffic/vehicular relief, desirable densities and so on—must be met at the scale of the city itself. They cannot be afterthoughts or subsidiary concerns within the regional planning framework. For many of these cities are now on their way to becoming the metropolises of tomorrow. (Rivkin, 1976, 18).

Tamale was the only regional center out of nine cited in the five-year development plan for national attention. It was thus selected as the pilot center because of its size as the fourth largest and fastest growing city in the country and its strategic central place function in the upper regions of Ghana. The regions, called the breadbasket of Ghana, are undergoing what rightfully is termed an agricultural revolution in new production of rice and other crops.

The concept of land use programming was developed in the USAID's Office of Urban Development, Division of Technical Support. The initial thrust of this concept was to determine the land use control technique for programming and the control of land that affected intermediate-sized cities. A study by Rivkin/ Carson, Inc. (now Rivkin Associates) focused on a range of practical approaches that may be suitable applications for planning and programming in intermediate-sized cities in developing nations. The purpose of this state-of-the-art study was to identify and determine the crucial issues that affect the growth and development of such intermediate-sized cities.

Selection of Tamale as a Land Use Programming Site

The initial design of the land use programming project was drawn broadly and flexibly to permit each demonstration project to account adequately for local conditions in the host countries. However, several broad criteria were considered necessary for the successful implementation of the project. In terms of the alternative sites in Africa these criteria comprised the following:

—Intermediate size: Cities with populations between 50,000 and 200,000

—Location: Cities located at sufficient distance from the primary cities to act as growth centers in formerly less developed areas

—Urban growth: Cities that exhibited recent rapid urban growth and might be experiencing related urban problems

—Agricultural role: The role of the city as a major center of agricultural development, as a market center for the collection, distribution, processing and servicing of an expanding agricultural hinterland

—Decentralization: The extent to which decentralization is a policy goal of the government and the extent to which administrative and political mechanisms exist to effect such decentralization

—National commitment: The degree of national commitment to effective planning and development of centers outside the major city or cities, including fostering of local planning and implementation capacity.

—Interest: The extent to which interest is shown at both the national and local levels in the major objectives of the project

—Demonstration: The degree to which the project site might be expected to act as a demonstration city for others within the country or similar cities elsewhere

The survey team was invited to Ghana to examine the city of Tamale as a potential demonstration site. The team found receptive officials at all levels of government and a national and local development setting that closely fits the site selection criteria. The government was in the initial stages of a new local government restructuring and an economic development program, both emphasizing decentralization.

The new local development structure contained provisions for a district development council composed of representatives from the functional agencies at the local level and for a secretariat to coordinate the council's planning and development activities. The council had been established in Tamale, and plans were underway for staffing the Office of the Coordinator.

This combination of factors led to the choice of Tamale as the Africa region demonstration site of the USAID land use programming project.

Project Objectives

The TLUP demonstration project was designed to test a model (or more precisely a framework) for physical planning in intermediate-sized cities undergoing rapid growth in less developed countries. The framework describes a process for developing planning activities, informational needs on which planning decisions can be made, and tools or techniques for applying planning decisions. The framework from which specific land use planning strategies can be developed includes the establishment of general goals and operational objectives for land use, an assessment of physical needs, the development of generalized land use and transportation guides, and the development of functional plans that identify specific development packages.

Contextual considerations are particularly important in applying the framework. For example, the institutional setting of a particular municipal government, the degree of autonomy in relation to other levels of government, and the specific positive and negative techniques it can use to influence physical growth will affect the goals and objectives, information needs, and the specific package of tools chosen to implement planning decisions.

The application of the framework to the Tamale setting is focused on two principal areas. First, the adaptability of the framework to the planning structure in Ghana involves a system in which portions of the framework were already in place, an institutional framework in which planning decisions were not necessarily integrated into the budget process, and the degree to which trained staff were already in place. Second, the framework will be evaluated according to its ability to meet the programmatic needs of the Western Dagomba district.

Although the model or framework described activities that are connected by a logical process, the model's application depended largely on the institutional and structural conditions in a particular setting. The redefinition and subsequent development of the Tamale project reflects the latter set of considerations.

Tamale Demonstration Development Project Implementation
Phase Strategy

Early in the TLUP project, district and regional officials recognized that resources were not readily available at the local level of government to initiate a significant development demonstration of planning, coordination, and implementation unless local revenue collection could be improved to the extent that locally initiated development projects could be locally financed; effective linkage could be made between the planning implementation activity in which locally available human and financial resources would be more effectively coordinated; and local government units involved in the developmental process would develop an effective institution to coordinate the district's development effort. It was felt that opportunity should exist to establish planning and implementation linkages so that priorities and plans could be executed to a logical conclusion. Consistent with the experiential training nature of the demonstration project, the project team believed that the decisionmaking and coordination required to implement a demonstration project would be the best training experience.

Also, the district chief executive and district officers recognized that although a national policy on decentralization existed, the practical implementation strategy of such policy did not. The planning-implementation model developed in Tamale during the implementation phase of the project would be the first in the country and, therefore, has great potential for its use in the remaining 62 districts of the country. This was a source of significant pride. The Ministry of Local Government and the Department of Town and Country Planning had expressed interest and support in the project and the applicability of the lessons learned.

The TLUP project had assisted the Western Dagomba District Council in strengthening its development role and capacity to undertake district development projects in the fourth largest city in Ghana. The local, regional, and national levels of government wished to execute an implementation phase and had requested assistance from USAID in conjunction with the government of Ghana to support a development demonstration project, Tamale Demonstration Development Project (TDDP), which would firmly establish the principles and institutions developed during the Land Use Programming Project.

Tamale Demonstration Development Project

The purpose and goal of the TDDP was to develop and demonstrate practical approaches for improving the basic living conditions of the urban poor in the intermediate-sized city of Tamale and to develop a capacity at the district level of government to extend integrated services and improvements to low-income and unserviced neighborhoods, maximizing locally available resources. The approaches developed in Tamale are anticipated to become the basis for a model of local government organization for the remaining districts in Ghana.

The demonstration implementation phase of the project consisted of two complementary activities: (1) development through training, action, and the capacity at the district level to integrate basic services and program delivery into low-income neighborhoods and (2) extension of basic residential roads and infrastructure into two areas as a catalyst for organizing self-help supported community improvements.

Implementation Program Components

From the outset of the project, local officials had stressed two important considerations. First, they believed that one of the major outputs of the project should be physical development that could be seen by average citizens of the district. Second, district government officials wanted to demonstrate that district development projects could and would be implemented as a means to encourage greater levels of citizen involvement and encourage higher levels of revenue generation by demonstrating the government's intention and ability to implement projects.

The financial support for each of the program components of the TDDP was provided through three funding mechanisms: USAID/Washington (Integrated Improvement Program for the Urban Poor, IIPUP), USAID Mission to Ghana (Accelerated Impact Project,AIP), and government of Ghana (TDDP). The IIPUP funding required a series of interrelated activities designed to identify the urban poor, their basic needs and problems, and the underlying causes of their poverty; design and integrate service delivery programs, (employment schemes, health and family planning activities); implement some of these programs on a pilot and demonstration basis; and evaluate the results through a systematic evaluation program.

The IIPUP grant supported the services of the U.S. technician and the project administration. The Ghana government staff seconded to the project were paid and maintained by the government. The project staff during the implementation phase consisted of two technical coordinators, one assistance community development officer, short-term U.S. and Ghanian consultants, and support personnel (two drivers and one secretary).

One of the major activities of the IIPUP project was to support the development of the Technical Coordinating Committee (TCC), which was composed of key district officers and representatives from the local communities involved in studies, pilot or demonstration programs. The TCC was established by the Western Dagomba District Council with the specific responsibility for implementing the TDDP. The TCC was chaired by the district chief executive and consisted of representatives from regional and district departments of government who were directly involved in the development process. Additionally, each community in which development activity would occur selected a community representative to the committee. The TCC was created by district council resolution and given the responsibility for implementing the special demonstration development project.

The agreement between the government of Ghana and USAID stated that the IIPUP project activities were the following:

—Designation of study area to be targeted for improvements

—Survey of conditions of poverty, community dynamics, and resources in the existing target communities

—Analysis of survey results to identify priority problems and develop practical approaches

—Design of pilot and demonstration projects to stimulate further activity

—Implementation of pilot and demonstration projects, including the pilot implementation demonstration project in Ward M Extension and Gumah Residential Area

—Assistance to the district council in packaging projects identified through the IIPUP process in an effort to attract additional financial resources to Tamale

—Development of short-term training in Ghana, the United States, and other countries as appropriate

—Development of workshops on a countrywide basis in Ghana to demonstrate and promote the IIPUP approach to district development

The IIPUP project was designed to provide administrative and organizational support, direction, and training for the district staff while implementing the development demonstration project. The IIPUP and AIP were designed and viewed as companion project activities.

It was recognized that the planning process was not sufficiently connected to the implementation process in the existing system. The components of the TDDP were: TLUP project (planning and priority) setting phase; the IIPUP; the AIP; and the TDDP (government of Ghana) implementation phase. Collectively, the implementation phase of the project became known as the TDDP.

Special Demonstration Project

The special demonstration project concept was included to provide an opportunity to provide support for various development activities outside the primary scope of the project. Special projects would be designed to encourage stronger economic development and opportunity and/or provide support for service delivery activities. The special demonstration project sought to focus on the technical and administrative transferability of these concepts while strengthening coordination among various district departments.

Implementation Demonstration Project Consistent with USAID Mission Goals

The USAID Mission had developed and supported the Economic Rural Development Management (ERDM) project, which provided management training on a national level and also in local government units aimed at improving management capabilities on a national basis. There had been considerable mutual supportiveness between the ERDM and the TLUP project. For example, the ERDM project provided training workshops and assisted in the development of the WDDC district resource development handbook for the TLUP. In return, the revenue and district organizational studies completed by the TLUP project became part of the ERDM instructional training materials. The U.S. Mission had perceived the proposed demonstration development project as being consistent with several important priorities, which had been set forth in the Country Development Strategy Statement (CDSS). These priorities were: (1) increased programs for the poor, (2) extended programs for regional development, (3) improved market towns in support of rural development, and (4) encouragement of greater control over development programs at the district level.

Another strategy noted in the CDSS stressed the strengthening of market towns, including assistance with housing and infrastructure (USAID, 1982). This aspect of the proposed project was consistent with USAID priorities and with the mission's stated intent

to build on successful programs whenever feasible and to make maximum use of relevant centrally funded projects. Thus, the significant objectives established for USAID activities were met by these proposed projects. The project was initiated and managed at the local level thus utilizing local institutions appropriately backstopped by regional and national organizations. Participation of residents residing in the two demonstration communities is assured by their participation on the Technical Coordinating Committee, in addition, to the self-help participation of these citizens who provided the labor required to complete the project. (USAID, 1982, 23)

Thus, the USAID mission concluded,

The project is a pilot demonstration which, if successful, could influence the future patterns of growth in Tamale . . . and other District centers elsewhere in Ghana. The project uses an approach that can be reduced to absolute basics—that is, extension of unsurfaced access roads by bulldozers and graders and still achieve the ultimate objective of controlling settlement patterns to facilitate future community improvements. This should ensure replicability if the demonstration is a success, as anticipated. (USAID, 1982, 23)

Government of Ghana Priorities

The dominant priority of the government of Ghana was to reverse the economic condition of the country. In May 1979 during the TLUP project, the initial discussion involving representatives of the WDDC and USAID were held to discuss the potential for an implementation demonstration activity as follow-up to the planning activity. Between the time of that discussion and the actual signing of the project agreement for the implementation phase in August 1981, Ghana experienced two changes in government. As a result, there were changes in the personnel responsible for local government matters at the national level. A number of these earlier program and policy ideas had been endorsed and retained by the present government of Lt. Jerry Rawlings. The national government had identified the development of market towns and the decentralization of government authority by concentration of more administrative and development responsibility at the regional and district levels of government as priorities. Moreover, the TLUP project, from which the TDDP stemmed, was viewed as a demonstration strategy manifested in the New Local Government Act (1971). The WDDC had taken these responsibilities seriously and had begun to make considerable progress in Tamale toward becoming a development authority. Consistent with this decentralization philosophy, the WDDC had placed high priority on the control of spontaneous and unauthorized development and the expansion of basic infrastructure to meet community needs. It was the WDDC enthusiasm for and receptivity to the land use programming project that in large measure contributed to the initiatives and support by the district for the TDDP.

FUTURE THRUSTS

The lessons learned from the Ghana case study will be used as a model for other districts throughout the country. Present public policy has delegated to local government the authority to plan, implement, and finance local development projects. On a broader scale, the assessment of operation, efficiency, and effectiveness of service delivery and planning systems, often referred to as implementation analysis, is being done in developing countries worldwide. The key aspect of implementation analysis is to determine to whom, how effective, and what the barriers are to effective service delivery. Local government development experience in Costa Rica, Philippines, Indonesia, Tunisia, and Ghana (Brown and Cook, 1984) focus on improving management and financial capacity. The experience gained in these countries—including a focus on participatory approach (Indonesia), improving financial management including tax records systems (Philippines), improving municipal information systems (Costa Rica), and linking planning and implementation (Ghana)—suggests a significant increase of resources directed toward improving local management. The implication of this emphasis by governments in developing countries is increased responsibility and authority being assumed by local governments.

The future thrust for governments of developing nations and international donor organizations requires financial and technical assistance designed to increase the capacity and efficiency of local government to plan, design, administer, manage, and finance local development projects. Support of such approaches, if designed to encourage and promote effective citizen participation, will result in sustained grass-roots development.

CONCLUSIONS AND LESSONS LEARNED

At the outset, the demonstration nature of the planning and priority-setting activity (TLUP project) and subsequently the implementation phase (TDDP) was an effort to link planning and implementation activity at the local government level and to document the techniques and activities developed. Although many external factors influenced project outcome, when institutional and staff capacity were developed to the degree that ownership by local decisionmakers and beneficiaries has occurred, obstacles at the local level are usually resolved.

Influences on Project Planning and Implementation

At the outset the TLUP project and the subsequent TDDP sought to identify those factors that influenced the local government development process by engaging in a planning and implementation process and observing that process. There were positive and negative influences on the project that were largely outside the control of the project staff. Influences within the scope of the project that were negative at the outset of the planning activity became, as a result of the institutional and capacity building activity, more positive as the project progressed. This does not suggest that there were no negative influences affecting the project at its conclusion; rather, those negative influences had been reduced to a point that the project was not affected.

Positive Influence

Institutional and Capacity Building

The development of the work group from the district officers' workshops to the development and formulation of the TCC represented a significant positive influence on the project activity. Consensus and organizational building activity involving elected officials, civil servants, community leaders, and residents significantly contributed to the reduction of suspicion, mistrust, lack of information, and a general unwillingness to work together. Community residents tended to believe that development activity could be done quickly and that the lack of development activity demonstrated the unwillingness of government officials to implement the development program. On the other hand, government officials viewed citizens as being unreasonable and unwilling to contribute either money or labor to self-help efforts aimed at improving the general conditions. Once involved in a dialogue, each group recognized the seriousness and concern each had for development. More important, perhaps, was the recognition that exogenous factors often have great influence on development activity. As participants worked through communications and organizational problems and began to assume some ownership in the process and the outcome, a community developed. The project team served as the catalyst-facilitator, secretariat, and technical advisers to community leaders who had the power, some financial resources, labor, and talent to improve their own environment. Group and personal commitment by committee members was the most significant factor that enabled the district to identify additional financial resources required in the project agreement and to meet the additional unanticipated cost of transporting building materials.

The institutional-capacity building activity included providing continuous formal and informal project information and briefing at all levels of government.

This activity was indeed more time-consuming and a less quantifiable entity, which is generally less desirable when evaluated in terms of costs and benefits.

The institutional-capacity building activity, however, was the most significant positive influence during this project, which allowed the project to achieve an 80 percent completion as reported by the technical coordinator in April 1984. This achievement occurred in spite of severe changing economic conditions, costs, and availability of materials and supplies in Ghana during the project.

Planning and Implementation Linkage

At the beginning of the process, no formal linkage existed between the planning and implementation activities. It was during the initial phase of the implementation activity when the planning base map and other land use principles came into sharp contrast to the reality in one of the demonstration sites. This sharp contrast combined with the time required for land use plan development process had heightened the magnitude of the rapid development being experienced. Community residents, on the other hand, who recognized that most of their structures were unauthorized and did not conform to two planning regulations, were unwilling to accept any demolition or relocation until a series of dialogues was initiated. Although community residents recognized the need for proper planning, the truth was that the demand for housing, combined with the rapidly declining availability and increased cost of building materials, was the most overriding consideration. After long and tedious debate and dialogue, the community residents of Ward M Extension were willing to compromise and allow some demolition in return for upgrading and improvement of the roads and services available in their community.

Resource Allocation

The implementation activity could not have occurred without the availability of financial resources. The timing of the project did not permit an allocation from the national level of government for inclusion of the TDDP project in the national development plan. The Department of Town and Country Planning and the WDDC had to identify potential resources already allocated or new sources of Ghana government assistance. The local government officials were able to identify sufficient financial resources to meet the government of Ghana commitment to the project. Often foreign donor-assisted projects fail to achieve stated goals and objectives because financial resources are not allocated by the host government. Although locally generated revenues were limited, the Tamale District Organization was able to identify sufficient resources from different departments of government because of its commitment and the high priority of this project.

Positive and Negative Influence: Communications

Communications had both a positive and a negative influence on the project. Positively, interpersonal, intergroup communications at the local workshop and committee level or briefings at the regional or national level of government contributed to the project goals and objectives. Once a dialogue was initiated, communications continued to flow with positive effect. Because of the developmental nature of TCC and its more formal relationship to other agencies, communication among district departments concerned with the project was tenuous. As general procedure, all important information relative to the project was distributed to all committee members. The District Chief Executive's office began to assume the role of coordinator for all district development activity. At the national level, communications between the Department of Town and Country Planning and other ministries and departments tended to be less frequent and more formal, with the exception of the Ministry of Finance and Economic Planning. Negatively, electronic and postal communications seriously affected the project. Organizations and activities not located in Tamale, which required the coordination of schedules, timetables, and so on, resulted in an inordinate amount of project staff travel on matters that might have been handled by telephone or mail.

Lessons of the Project

Planning and Implementation Linkage

It became clear at the outset of the TLUP project that planning techniques and capacity existed within the Western Dagomba district through the Department of Town and Country Planning. A 15-year physical plan had been developed for the town. The problem was that planning activity had been divorced and isolated from other activities within the development process such as citizen involvement in the decision-making process, agencies responsible for providing infrastructure, utilities, and other community services. Planners had been unaware of the needs of other functional agencies with responsibility in the development process, and few channels for communications and dialogue existed among them. Therefore the coordinative role that planning normally performs in bringing together the resources required for implementation of a plan had never been realized. Furthermore, initially due to the lack of a national policy and subsequent to the policy addressing the lack of structure to implement the policy, no organizational structure had been developed at the local level of government that created a demand or constituency for coordinated planning and implementation. As a result, the rate of implementation of district plans was low. The project's approach was to develop the capacity and institution at the district level aimed at overcoming this obstacle since the causes were behavioral and institutional. This approach required that key individuals and agencies with responsibility in the development process begin to establish acceptable working relationships. During the course of the evolution of the coordinating institution from the district officers' workshops to the creation of the TCC, participants began to understand the interrelatedness of the agencies' programs and activities.

Through this continuous process of exchange of information and defining of duties and responsibilities, it became possible to discuss and pursue the creation of a permanent organization of coordinated development activities, thus establishing the planning implementation linkage. This process forced the participants to identify the economic, institutional, social, and political constraints that affect planning and development activity. The creation of the TCC and the participation of diverse agencies in the implementation of the demonstration project attest to the acceptance of this approach.

A corollary of this observation was that planning is most effective when linked to the acquisition of resources for implementation. The consensus building, problem identification/solving workshops were a valuable exercise in themselves. Planning, however, took on real meaning when linked to a funded project, the TDDP. The project staff observed that interest and participation in planning activity significantly increased as participants saw the real planning process and the meaning it would have for their respective agencies rather than abstract activities and decisions.

Provision of Basic Infrastructure as a Key Technique for Guiding Urban Growth

Ghana law provides a number of techniques for the management of urban growth. In addition to city master plans and zoning, the law prescribes a process that in theory allows the local government to allocate and demarcate plots through the Lands Commission, to issue permits for land development activities (performed by the Town and Country Planning Department), and to inspect buildings during construction to ensure minimum building standards. This process should permit a local government to develop land use patterns that conform to its development plan.

The district council recognized that these procedures were largely negative controls, however, and in some cases conflicted with traditional systems and were easily circumvented. Their view was supported by the uncontrolled development on the urban fringe (as in Ward M Extension) and the level of land owned or obtained through methods outside of the prescribed method. Government leaders attributed the difficulty in managing Tamale's growth not only to the difficulty in applying the prescribed land development procedures but more directly to the council's inability to provide basic infrastructure to areas planned for growth, thereby failing to attract development in patterns consistent with development plans.

Tamale and other secondary cities will be able to accommodate the inevitable (but not always undesired) growth in a planned manner in which residential, commercial, and industrial developments are mutually reinforcing and adequately supported by physical and human services only if resources are available to place infrastructure as a means to guide desired urban growth. The lack of infrastructure will not prevent in-migration to cities; rather it will increase the development of spontaneous, unplanned neighborhoods to which the subsequent provision of infrastructure and services is more costly. This more positive approach appeared to be more consistent with traditional values and at the same time encourage cooperation among agencies and communities rather than conflict.

Efficient Use of Scarce Resources Through Coordinated Activities

As the workshops increased the interest in improving linkages between planning and implementation activities, they also increased the awareness that coordination and communication among agencies are important in avoiding duplication of efforts or overly dispersed development efforts. The analysis of existing district programs provided an opportunity for district officials to evaluate those activities that were an inefficient use of scarce resources. Combined with this realization was the district need to improve its efficiency in generation and collection of local revenues. The recognition that significant levels of district revenue were being lost due to a lack of efficient financial management and incentives reinforced the need for greater government creativity and efficiency.

Mobilization of Local Resources for Development Projects

Early on the project team identified the lack of apparent resources as a constraint to the district council's implementation of development projects. The request to USAID for assistance in funding the demonstration project was made in recognition that the council could not undertake such a project without external assistance. At the same time the project staff recognized that a thorough examination would identify currently underutilized local resources. The revenue campaigns demonstrated the extent to which improved administration could increase the collection of the basic rate. The revenue study further identified many areas in which improved management and new initiatives could significantly increase district revenue flow. Finally, the identification of self-help projects demonstrated how scarce rural development funds can be stretched by beneficiary participation.

Through the activities it became apparent that the council could mobilize a number of resources at its disposal in order to augment its ability to carry out its own development activities and to leverage external resources. The effective use of these resources depends on both the degree to which institutional flexibility permits innovative approaches and on the dynamism of the local administration.

Importance of Local Citizen Participation

Citizen involvement in the planning and decisionmaking process through the neighborhood survey, the workshops, and the TCC represented a new dimension in planning for Tamale. Historically the role of citizen involvement in the planning development process has been more passive by having citizen meetings in which plans and decisions already made were presented for approval. The involvement of the citizens, which was a more time-consuming process, forced planners to realize that the planning process was better able to define its work because selected alternatives represented the preferences of the ultimate beneficiaries. The product of this process was more realistic and consistent with community perceptions. Conversely, the involvement of the beneficiaries in the decisionmaking process caused the beneficiaries to expect more from the process and thus become stronger advocates of the process. This enlarged constituency increased the commitment of local government decisionmakers and technical staff to implement planned activities. Perhaps the most significant result of citizen involvement was the realization that the lack of serious dialogue heightens suspicions and increases tensions between citizens and decisionmakers and thus was a disincentive to effective development. This project demonstrated that once citizens understood the nature and scope of the problems being confronted, their involvement became an integral part of the process. Problems encountered during the implementation activity were more easily resolved because of the commitment assumed by the citizens in the success of the project.

The focus of much of the development activity in less developed countries is at the local level of government. Greater responsibility for planning, financial management, and implementation is being directed toward such units of government. Efficient management of such resources will require capable human resources, efficient and flexible institutional organizations, and a direct means of positive participation and commitment by the beneficiaries. It is felt that the documentation of the activities of the Tamale Integrated Improvement Project for the Urban Poor in a small way contributes to the knowledge and understanding of the dynamics of planning and implementation at the local government level.

Programming of land use is essential to accomplishing local and regional development goals and to avoiding the chaos that so often accompanies rapid urban growth. Many formerly small and quiet cities have been growing so rapidly in recent years that local institutions are severely strained in trying to guide and accommodate this growth for the best interest of the community. This rapid urbanization which has also a significant role in the development of their rural hinterlands is both a serious problem and a great opportunity for development (Rivkin, 1976, foreword by A. Miner and E. Chetwynd, Jr.)

NOTES

1. Department of Town and Country Planning, "Town and Country Planning Ordinance of 1945," with subsequent amendments, Number 13, p. 2, "to make provision for an orderly development of land towns and other areas, whether urban or rural to preserve and improve the amenities thereof and for other matters connected therewith."

2. Ibid., p. 3.

3. Fred Owusu, "Land Tenure in Ghana" (Ministry of Works and Housing, Government of Ghana, March 1975).

4. Ibid., as defined by Section 31 of the Administration of Wards, Autumn, 1962, Act 13, lands in the upper and northern regions of Ghana since colonial British rule have been vested in the government; however, during the government of President Hilla Limann, northern lands were returned to the traditional authorities.

5. Ibid. Authority is granted by both the Administration of Land Act, 1962, Act 123, and the Public Conveyancing Act, 1965, Act 302, dated 29 September 1965, p. 2.

6. State-owned land is administered by the Land Commission, which was established by an act of parliament, Land Commission Act, Act 362, 1971. The Land Commission consists of a chairman and not fewer than five members. Subsequent regulation (1972) created regional Subcommittees that manage state lands. Money accruing from the management of such lands and paid into the stool lands account of the stool concerned. In the case of urban lands, fees paid to the Land Commission are to be paid to the district council to assist in financing infrastructure.

7. Several legislative acts were enacted that were related to land matters: Administration of Lands Act, Act 123, 1962; Concession Act, Act 124, 1962; and Survey Act, Act 127, 1962, p. 17.

8. Nim trees are large trees planted primarily during the colonial period. They are considered to be important to the aesthetic and ecological well-being of Northern Ghana.

9. The following are responsible for the provision of electricity, telecommunication, and water: the Ghana Electricity Corporation, Ghana Post and Telecommunications, and Ghana Water and Sewerage Corporation. These corporations are quasi-public corporations. The Department of Parks and Gardens is responsible for trees within the Tamale town limits unless otherwise specified.

10. The list of agencies participating were: Agriculture Development Bank, Ministry of Agriculture, National Archives, Arts Council, Cooperative Bank, Ministry of Education, Ghana Electricity Corporation, Fire Service Department, Parks and Gardens Department, Ministry of Health, Ghana Highway Authority, Irrigation Development Authority, Department of Labor, National Council on Women and Development, National Family Planning Council, National Investment Bank, Meteorological Services, Public Works Department, Ministry of Social Welfare and Community Development, Survey Department, Town and Country Planning Department, Ghana Water and Sewerage Corporation, Western Dagomba District Council, and Architecture Engineering Services Corporation.

BIBLIOGRAPHY

Ackoff, R. L., and M. W. Sasieni. 1968. *Fundamentals of Operations Research*. New York: John Wiley.

Brown, E. M., and T. Cook. 1984. Concept Paper. Implementation Analysis in Developing Countries. Research Triangle Park, North Carolina: Research Triangle Institute.

Brown, E. M., and L. Nkrumah. 1983. Updating the Nominal Poll and Other Registries in the Western Dagomba District Council (WDDC). Report for IIPUP Project. Tamale, Ghana, May. Unpublished.

Brown, E., H. Siita, and E. Dorsu. 1981. An Appraisal: The Western Dagomba District Council Revenue Study. Tamale, Ghana: Western Dagomba District Council, April.

Esch, G. D. 1981. Developing Local Government in Ghana: The ERDM Project. Ghana. Paper presented to the 10th International Federation of Training and Development Conference, Dublin, Ireland, August.

McCullough, J. S. and E. Dorsu. 1982. West Dagomba District Revenue Improvement Project Report. Prepared for WDDC, Tamale, Ghana, November.

Mensah-Brown, A. K. 1978. Land Ownership and Registration in Ghana. Kumasi, Ghana: Land Administration Center, University of Science and Technology.

Pfeiffer, J. W., and J. E. Jones. 1970. *A Handbook of Structured Experiences for Human Relations Training*. Vol. 2. Iowa City: University Associates Press.

Rivkin, Malcolm. 1976. *Land Use and the Intermediate-Size City in Developing Countries*. New York: Praeger.

Siita, H. 1982. Urban Land Use Control Techniques in Ghana: A Study of Problems and Analysis of Experience from Other Countries. Master's thesis, Cornell University.

Siita, H., and E. Brown. 1980. Study of District/Regional Organizational Structure in the Western Dagomba District Council. Tamale, Ghana: Tamale Land Use Program Project, Western Dagomba District Council, November.

Siita, H., and J. S. McCullough. 1981. 1980 Household Survey Results Report. Tamale, Ghana: Tamale Land Use Planning Project, Western Dagomba District Council. Unpublished.

USAID. Mission to Ghana, 1982. CDSS Statement. Accra, Ghana.

10

Tunisia

MALCOLM RIVKIN and GOLDIE RIVKIN

To understand how Tunisia approaches planning and development, it is helpful to have some salient facts about the country and its governance. Tunisia is relatively small in population (6 million) compared with some other urbanizing nations such as Thailand, Korea, and Brazil, which have as many people in their primate cities as in all of Tunisia. Ethnically and linguistically, Tunisia is relatively homogeneous: Arabic-speaking Muslims of predominantly Berber stock. From an internal political standpoint, one major party (Destour) has dominated since independence in 1956. One major political figure, Habib Bourguiba, has led the nation and imbued its evolution with his personality and ideas.

Tunisia is an internally coherent and, despite some opposition on economic matters, unified nation. It is also relatively prosperous. The World Bank classified Tunisia as a middle-income country, with a GNP in 1978 of $950 per capita. It is a rapidly urbanizing country, with a primate center. In 1980, 52 percent of Tunisia's population lived in urban areas, compared with 36 percent in 1960. Tunis in 1980 had a population of over 1 million, about 17 percent of the country's total and 31 percent of the urban portion.

Despite the dominance of Tunis, the country has an emerging network of secondary cities, several of which have viable economies and are significant contributors to Tunisia's economic growth. In 1978, 20 cities in Tunisia had populations over 20,000. Of these, Sousse-Monastir, Bizerte, Sfax, and Gabes, all along the coast, and Kairouan in the interior are the most important and the

This chapter was originally published, in slightly different form, by the U.S. Agency for International Development.

largest. All are over 50,000 in population. Unemployment and underemployment are problems in the cities, especially the many smaller centers that are growing in population due to migration from their rural hinterlands.

Although Tunisia has a mixed economy, central government plays a significant role in the economic system and dominates the internal administrative structure. All the factors of context—from the centralized structure, to its relatively prosperous economy, and the personal interest of its leader—come together to explain Tunisia's approach to planning and development.

PHYSICAL-ECONOMIC DESCRIPTION

Tunisia's geographic regions are shown in Figure 10.1. The following excerpts from various country studies provide a capsule description of the country's physical, social, and economic circumstances.

Tunisia has an area of approximately 164,000 square kilometers and a coastline of about 1,600 kilometers indented by the gulfs of Tunis, Al Hammamat, and Gabes. It has six major and nearly a dozen minor seaports. . . . The Atlas mountain system, which begins in southwestern Morocco, terminates in northeastern Tunisia. Most of northern Tunisia is mountainous, but elevations average less than 300 meters and rarely exceed 1,000 meters. . . . Tunisia can be divided into three major geographic regions, determined in part by topography and quality of the soils and in particular by the incidence of rainfall, which decreases progressively from north to south. (Nelson, 1979, 62.)

The majority of the population is ethnically homogeneous, the people being of Arab-Berber stock, practicing the Sunni Muslim religion, and speaking Arabic. After independence in 1956, most of the French community left Tunisia; but minority groups of French, Italian and Maltese background remain and French is still an important second language.

The main agricultural products are wheat, olive oil, wine, esparto grass and fruits. Phosphates, iron ore, lead and zinc are mined, and petroleum was discovered in 1964. Tunisia's industrial base, though still limited, continues to expand. The chemical and paper industries are developing, and Tunisia has the first steel mill in northwest Africa. One of the most important sources of foreign exchange earnings is tourism. Despite the country's economic growth, unemployment remains high, and the country is actively seeking foreign investment.

Most industrial and tourism growth has been along the coast. Combined with productive olive- and fruit-producing agricultural land in the littoral, this results in a relatively prosperous coastal region and a relatively poor interior. Despite the dominance of Tunis, this relative prosperity is not confined to the northeast of the coast but extends along the primary road and rail transportation well down the length of the Mediterranean shoreline, including several secondary cities. Major development efforts during the 1960s and 1970s focused on building up the infrastructure to support economic growth and urban settlement in this region, which has the country's major exploitable resources.

Figure 10.1 Geographical Regions and Subregions of Tunisia

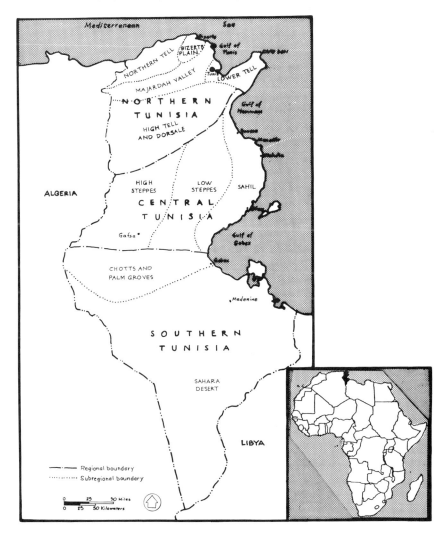

The following paragraph from the 1979 U.S. Agency for International Development (USAID) Shelter Sector Report on Tunisia, together with Table 10.1 and Figure 10.1, describes the present pattern of urban settlement:

Today's settlement patterns in Tunisia feature a heavy concentration of large urban clusters along the coast. The Tunisian economy's most significant industries are to be found in the cities, as in the case in Tunis, Bizerte, Sfax, Gabes and Sousse. To a large extent,

Table 10.1

Tunisia: Summary of Population Information for the *Gouvernorats* and the 20 Largest Cities

Gouvernorat	Population 1975	Percentage Urban 1960	Percentage Urban 1975	City	Population 1975	Projected Population 1986
District of Tunis	925,000	92	94	1. Tunis*	925,000	1,310,000
Sfax	474,879	58	56	2. Sfax	174,900	247,300
Sousse	254,601	67	71	3. Sousse	80,500	113,800
Mednine	292,970	14	23	4. Jerba	74,600	105,500
Bizerte	343,708	47	53	5. Bizerte	68,300	96,600
Kairouan	338,477	21	22	6. Kairouan	56,400	79,700
Gafsa	237,844	53	57	7. Gafsa	45,300	65,600
Bizerte	See above			8. Menzel Bourguiba	43,900	63,600
Gabes	255,717	35	37	9. Gabes	43,100	62,400
Beja	238,770	23	28	10. Beja	41,000	59,400
Sousse	See above			11. M'Saken	33,200	49,000
Monastir	223,150	72	77	12. Monastir	33,100	38,900
Nabeul	368,114	45	48	13. Nabeul	32,300	47,700
Le Kef	233,515	21	23	14. Le Kef	30,700	45,300
Mahdia	218,217	26	35	15. Mahdia	27,200	40,100
Monastir	See above			16. Mornine	26,000	38,500
Kasserine	238,499	16	21	17. Kasserine	25,100	37,000
Sousse	See above			18. Kalaa Kebira	23,200	34,300
Sfax	See above			19. Sakiet Ezzit	22,300	32,900
Jendouba	288,989	12	15	20. Jendouba	20,900	30,800

*The metropolitan area had a population of 257,000 in 1975.

Source: USAID, "Tunisia Shelter Sector Assessment", 1979, p. 12.

inland areas derive their income primarily from farming. With the exception of a few large industrial operations such as the Kasserine paper mill, the Thala cement plant and the Gafsa mines, the majority of the population is dependent on agricultural activities. It is precisely this region that supplied migratory flows to the cities which, in a matter of a few years, aggravated the population concentration problems on the coast and exacerbated further the economic imbalance between the various regions of Tunisia. (USAID, 1979, 8)

Table 10.1 lists the 20 major population centers identified in the 1975 census and their respective sizes in 1986 as projected by the National Statistics Institute. Population statistics are supplied for *gouvernorats* (provinces), as well as for cities, and the percentages of *gouvernorat* population classified as urban are reported. Figure 10.2 shows the location and relative size of the principal communities (USAID, 1979, 8).

One infrastructure effort is worthy of special mention because of its direct effect on the growth of secondary cities and the spread of economic activity away from Tunis: the construction of international airports at Monastir and on the island of Jerba. The airports, combined with the marketing activities of Tunisia's tourist industry, have permitted direct flights between Europe and Tunisia without going through Tunis. Large numbers of hotels and recreational attractions have been constructed in the Sousse-Monastir area and on Jerba, and both prosper from package tours on an almost year-round basis because of favorable climate. Their growth as the third and fourth major urban areas was directly expedited by the physical investments, which are now available to support other diverse economic activities as well.

The Ministry of Planning has classified areas of the country according to five levels of relative prosperity. Generally the gradation moves from the coast (the highest level) to the western and southern borders (the lowest). Urban areas, regardless of location, are more prosperous than rural. The principal coastal cities of Sousse-Monastir and Sfax are in the same prosperity category as Tunis, providing some indication of the extent to which economic development has already been diffused beyond the primate center.

The degree of urban deconcentration now occurring may be noted in figures from the World Bank's *1980 World Development Report*. These indicate that Tunis's share of national urban population fell from 40 percent in 1960 to 31 percent in 1980. The primate center continues to grow, but some other centers are expanding in economic activity and population as well.

CURRENT STATUS OF LAND USE PLANNING

Tunisia has a clear and long-standing policy commitment to physical planning and implementation of the plans for its cities. To some degree that commitment stems from President Bourguiba's personal dedication to shelter for his people,

Figure 10.2 Location and Size Rank of Tunisia's 20 Largest Cities

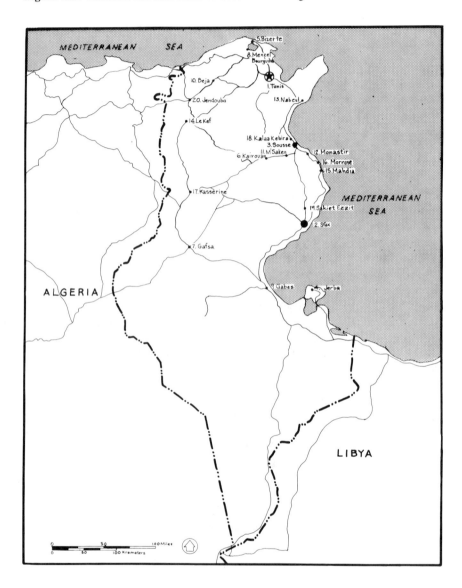

Office of Housing, U.S. Agency for International Development, *Tunisia Shelter Sector Assessment*, Washington, January, 1979, p. 13.

which has been reflected in his nation's development priorities. As one cabinet minister has said:

If Tunisia today affords the spectacle of a vast construction yard, with urban facilities and cities being built everywhere, it is because Bourguiba has understood from the very beginning that a man badly housed is incapable of producing serious work. He has set, from the dawn of independence, ambitious objectives for government in this domain. Efforts to produce decent shelter have become a major Tunisian preoccupation. (Saya, 1980, 5)

In many developing countries with strong leadership, the leader's personal concerns are translated into program priorities. In that sense, Tunisia's preoccupation with the physical aspects of human settlement sets it apart from some other countries whose principal figures have had other compelling interests. Interestingly enough, Bourguiba has frequently cited Ataturk's Turkish revolution of 50 years ago as an example for Tunisia to emulate—a national revival that was the first in the twentieth century to utilize city building and decentralized urban development as major tools of economic and social policy (Rivkin, 1965).

INSTITUTIONAL AND LANDOWNERSHIP FRAMEWORK

There is no economic sector where the state does not intervene either directly or indirectly. One of the goals of the government is to reduce income disparities and make a more equitable division of the economic pie. It thus acts as a lawmaker, planner, investor, manager, and owner. As the source of regulatory legislation and as the author of comprehensive planning for development, the state is supreme. Its role as investor, manager, and owner varies widely among industries, ranging from sole owner to a partnership arrangement with private foreign or domestic owners. For enterprises that are wholly private and deemed to be important to the development of the economy, the state offers direct investment services through public lending institutions (Nelson, 1979, 122).

Tunisia has created a planning and development structure of powerful central government agencies coupled with limited municipal responsibilities designed to organize and regulate development at the municipal level. Objectives are to expand these municipal capabilities in planning, project execution, and finance. Technical assistance and training by both national government and international agencies to permit municipal government to function more effectively are priority matters.

Tunisia is a unitary state. All authority flows from the central (national) government. Lower governmental units have no inherent or residual authority of their own. Constitutional provisions covering subnational government are limited to the statement that "municipal and regional Councils conduct the local affairs, under the conditions foreseen by law." Subsequent legislation has established a well-organized system of regional and local administration that stresses the interdependence of government and party (Nelson, 1979, 181).

Central Government

Within this centralized system, the Ministry of Interior has sole responsibility for local governance and finance. Other national ministries and related parastatal corporations direct the planning and regulation of urban growth, along with the design and execution of primary urban infrastructure: roads, water supply and systems, sewage distribution and treatment, and electric power. By and large these agencies also maintain the systems.

In addition, three parastatal agencies assemble and develop urban land for housing, allied commercial and community services, and industries. Each of these is embarked on a process of regional decentralization. The three (Agence foncière d'habitation, Agence foncière d'industrie, and Société nationale d'immobilière de Tunisie) are discussed at length here because of their critical roles in city development.

Tunisia is divided into 19 *gouvernorats* supervised by the Ministry of Interior, whose chief executive officer (governor) is appointed by the president. Governors are also regional directors of the party and members of the party's national central committee, symbolizing the linkage between political and administrative affairs. Budgets of the *gouvernorats* are funded and approved by the Ministry of Interior (MOI). Governors exercise primary supervision over municipal affairs in their respective provinces.

In terms of urban development, the principal national institutions are as follows:

Physical Planning

The Bureau of Planning (Aménagement du territoire) of the Ministry of Equipment is responsible for all urban land use planning. In addition the ministry supervises land use regulations (zoning) and building permit issuance, provides research in urban matters, and constructs government buildings and roads throughout the country.

Water Supply and Distribution

SONEDE (Société nationale d'exploitation et de distribution des eaux) is a parastatal under the Ministry of Agriculture. It constructs, operates, and maintains all water systems in Tunisia.

Sewerage

ONAS (Office national d'assainissemement) is responsible for design, construction, operation, and maintenance of all sewerage and drainage networks in municipalities. It reports to the Ministry of Equipment.

Electric Power

STEG (Société tunisienne d'electricité et de gaz), under the Ministry of Industry, is the national electric power agency.

Housing, Services, and Urban Land

Two institutions, now associated with the new Ministry of Housing, have special functions in this field. The Société nationale immobiliere de Tunisie (SNIT) is the principal builder of publicly assisted shelter. In 1980 SNIT was directly responsible for building 22,000 units, or about half the national housing production. The Agence fonciére d'habitation (AFH) has a broader shelter and land development role, extending to the middle- and upper-income groups. AFH works with SNIT, but unlike SNIT, its responsibilities are to assemble and develop sites only, leaving actual construction to be undertaken by private or public purchasers of the finished sites.

Industry

The Agence fonciére d'industrie (AFI) is the principal assembler and developer of industrial land. It is responsible to the Ministry of National Economy.

Other Public Services

Solid waste collection and disposal, as well as local (municipal) public finance and technical assistance in administrative fields, are supervised and funded by the Ministry of Interior. Its Direction des collectives publiques locales (DCPL) will expand activities as the government emphasizes local municipal administrative and fiscal responsibility.

Agence fonciére industrielle (AFI)

AFI, the Industrial Land Agency, was created in 1973 with the express mission of assembling and developing land for industrial parks throughout the country. Since then AFI has completed work on approximately 1,000 hectares of land, partly in Tunis and partly in the secondary cities. The sites are strategically located to take advantage of existing transportation systems and proximity to commercial areas and concentrations of population.

AFI began with 2 million dinars of capital from the state (about $3.4 million) and borrows the remainder of its funds. It recently negotiated a seven-year $20 million loan at commercial rates (20 percent interest). Permitted neither to take a profit nor to subsidize projects, AFI must recover all costs incurred in performing its development mission.

As a parastatal agency, AFI can pay its employees wages above the normal government scale and thus has assembled a skilled managerial and technical staff.

Agence fonciére d'habitation (AFH)

AFH, the Housing Lands Agency, is also a land assembly and development agency, created in 1973 at the same time as AFI, with a similar initial capitalization of 2 million dinars. Its role is to produce sites for housing at all income levels that can afford to repay the cost of land services. Thus its focus is mainly on production for middle-income levels although 60 percent of its output is to be social housing, roughly equivalent to the scale of SNIT's public housing program.

SNIT is a major customer, although it handles most of its own land assembly and development. Unlike SNIT, AFH does not build shelter, nor does it continue to maintain projects once they are completed. AFH prepares the land, supervises the installation of services, and then transfers the land to private and public home builders.

Like AFI, AFH is a parastatal with skilled technical staff that it can pay at higher wages than normal government scale. Because it is not empowered to borrow for development financing, as AFI is, AFH must finance its development activities through cash payments for advance sales of its programmed output.

One of AFH's greatest strengths is its commitment to design and develop communities. Each project provides for a range of income levels and housing types from apartment blocks, to private builder subdivisions, and individual lots on which owners build their own units. Depending on its scale and proximity to existing residential areas, each project also has space for commercial services and a complement of community facilities from dispensaries to schools and mosques, along with land for parks and recreation space.

AFH is a powerful organization with a broad mandate. Thus far it has exercised that mandate primarily in and around metropolitan Tunis, although it has begun to decentralize and to expand its activities in secondary cities.

Under the forthcoming five-year plan, AFH will be expected to operate more extensively out of Tunis and to shift its emphasis toward greater accommodation of lower-income households.

Société Nationale Immobiliere de Tunisie (SNIT)

The mission of SNIT, the Housing Development Agency, is the most extensive of all the parastatal agencies concerned with urban development. It is a housing agency but one that builds and manages shelter as well as assembles sites. SNIT is responsible for providing housing to a wide range of income groups but primarily those who cannot afford conventional shelter in the private market. Although the bulk of its production is urban, it also provides housing for rural residents outside the urban perimeters.

SNIT is the largest single home builder in Tunisia and has a truly prodigious output. During the past few years, it has been producing 18,000 to 20,000 units annually, close to 50 percent of the country's total housing construction. Although more of SNIT's output has been in the Tunis area than any other location in the country, SNIT has worked extensively in the secondary cities. In terms of decisionmaking and operations, SNIT is perhaps the most decentralized of the land agencies.

Between 1972 and 1979 SNIT built 90,000 units, of which about 27,000, or 30 percent, were in Tunis. More than 9,000 units were produced in Sfax and 5,400 in Sousse (6 percent of the national production). SNIT's role in Tunisia's decentralization program is thus quite major given the relative sizes of the two secondary cities in comparison with the capital. Through the next five-year plan period, SNIT is slated to continue as a principal instrument of the country's effort to strengthen secondary centers.

Beginning in 1969, the agency's land assembly operations were among the country's first such undertakings. From its inception, SNIT was charged with the full task of site acquisition, development, financing, and construction of shelter. Two years later, when SNIT's output was only 3,000 to 4,000 units, the government created the AFH to assemble land for housing and other institutions to finance shelter. SNIT continues to be a prime purchaser of AFH sites and to work closely with the finance institutions, but its program for building moderate- to low-income housing has expanded to such an extent that it now buys and develops the land for most of its own projects.

International Assistance and Urban Development

For almost two decades Tunisia's commitment to urban development has attracted international assistance agencies' support, particularly from the World Bank and USAID. The nature of this support has broadened along with the country's own efforts to expand benefits of urbanization from Tunis to the secondary cities. Present activities concentrate primarily on shelter for the urban poor, but technical assistance and institution-building projects are included also, with the objective of enabling both municipalities and central government to implement investments more effectively outside Tunis.

Tunisia has enjoyed a favored position in the activities of the World Bank, USAID, and some bilateral European assistance programs. Projects in physical planning, housing, and other aspects of urban development have been undertaken for many years. During the 1960s and 1970s, for example, numerous Peace Corps volunteers in Tunisia contributed to planning for Tunis, Kairouan, and other cities. The World Bank's technical support and investments have helped make tourism the country's principal source of foreign exchange and have supported the growth of Sousse-Monastir as a major secondary center. Both the bank and USAID have undertaken major programs in housing, first in Tunis and now in secondary cities as well. As primate center, Tunis has been a testing ground for international agency shelter assistance and for the central government's own efforts in this field as well. Now as concern for reducing economic and social disparities deepens, both the central government and international agencies are attempting to apply some of the lessons learned in Tunis to communities elsewhere.

Role of Municipal Government

In Tunisia, central government performs many functions that would be considered municipal or private in other countries, such as provision of utilities and assembly and development of land. But it cannot do everything, and the greater the number of secondary centers with development programs, the greater the need for on-site municipal performance so that the central government capabilities will not be stretched too thin.

Despite concentration of power and funds in central government agencies and governors, elected municipal (commune) councils have important responsibilities for land development and for the financing and construction of certain public facilities.

Tunisia has 158 communes, or municipalities, each administered by the communal council ... that is elected by the local population. "The council's powers are narrowly defined, and its actions are subject to the supervision of the governor and, ultimately, the Minister of the Interior. The council selects a president from among its members. An exception is the commune of Tunis, where the president of the Republic chooses the council president from among its elected members. The council president represents both the locality and the central government." (Nelson, 1979. 181-82)

Within this limited framework, the municipality has the right to own and develop land, as well as to levy property taxes and certain other assessments to supplement revenues from the state. Revenue sharing dispensed by the central government comprises a large proportion of municipal funds.

Under a 1976 law, communities with development plans have authority to issue subdivision and building permits both inside municipal boundaries and within a 5 kilometer perimeter outside.

By far the most significant municipal responsibility is the planning and construction of certain public facilities. The municipalities can ask parastatals and other central agencies to build and maintain some facilities and economic investments, such as housing, sewage treatment, primary roads, and industries. For other types of facilities, especially those that affect the quality of community life such as markets, local streets, street lighting, parks, most sports and recreation facilities, local sewerage lines, and day care centers, initiation and financing are up to the communities themselves.

Moreover, with the numerous agencies involved in one form of physical development or another, coordination of investments, if there is any, must be led by the municipality, the only institution in a position to monitor directly what is taking place.

The Bureau of Planning of the Ministry of Equipment is the ultimate authority for all urban plans in Tunisia, as well as for approval of zoning and building permits. In a country with 158 communes, such a high degree of centralization can easily lead to bottlenecks at the top, as well as insensitivity to local conditions in elaboration of urban plans. Although some such problems exist, the ministry has managed to work out partnership arrangements with municipalities, backed by presidential decrees, that permit a much more flexible situation in practice, fairly well tuned to local circumstances and responsive to requirements of specific development projects.

Land Acquisition, Site Development, and Site Disposition

Land Acquisition

AFI and the other parastatals are empowered to acquire land. Although they can negotiate directly with landowners, they normally invoke their right to preempt desired sites and surrounding area. Site selections are approved initially by the municipality and passed up through central government channels to the Ministry of Justice and the MOE. Once AFI receives approval, it can effectively freeze land prices by exercising first refusal on any offer of sale.

At this point, AFI begins negotiations with landowners. It can pay up to 700 millimes (about U.S. $1) per square meter, the maximum price for land anywhere in the country. Apparently most owners come to terms during this negotiation period, since most sites are in agricultural use and the only potential buyer at a higher price is AFI. The negotiation process may take several months, however, because AFI and the other parastatals are reluctant to exercise expropriation. Although expropriation procedures can be pursued through the courts, AFI has done so only twice.

Site Development

AFI begins detailed site planning once the land is identified. The process includes coordination with other parastatals (for example, water and power) and the MOE, which will provide trunk utilities and access if required. AFI lays out plots or parcels, builds roads and sidewalks, and installs electricity, street lighting, and potable water according to set standards. It installs telephone and telex as well.

Of particular interest is AFI's growing commitment to installing community facilities and services as part of its larger projects. A so-called town center approach has been tried in Tunis and is now part of every project larger than 30 hectares. It includes construction of certain core facilities that are sold to industrial purchasers as part of the price of the finished site: cafeteria, dispensary, convenience shops, meeting rooms, police station, gas station, and a central maintenance facility.

As for other worker-oriented services such as day care centers and mosques, AFI officials' basic approach is to try to locate sites near existing concentrations of workers' housing. Alternatively they coordinate their own site development with projects of SNIT and AFH so that residential units for the potential labor force are easily accessible to the industrial areas. They prefer that services such as day care be located in residential settings.

The effects of this policy can be observed in southern Tunis, where new industrial development (apparently not very much constrained by environmental considerations or rigid ideas about separation of land uses) is within easy walking distance of new residential areas accommodating a wide range of income levels. Indeed Tunisia has been more dedicated to coordination of industrial and residential siting than most other developing countries and is probably on a par with Singapore with respect to the importance of this policy principle.

AFI officials are, however, ready to admit that the policy does not always have the expected results, citing some cases in Tunis where nearby residents commute elsewhere and job holders in the plants come primarily from other sections of the city. AFI and related agencies nevertheless try to link workplace with community.

Site Disposition

AFI normally builds for specific industrial clients or proceeds on the basis of a market assessment that identifies a reasonable demand for finished land in the near future. The disposition package rarely includes finished structures, although AFI will provide buildings, if necessary, to attract foreign investment. Because of its cost recovery mandate and its limited capitalization, the agency does not feel it is able to maintain a land bank.

Deals are negotiated with specific customers and in accordance with a basic formula. Total costs, including land acquisition and site development, are roughly the same throughout the country (about U.S. $10 per square meter). Finished prices are set, however, at three levels depending on location. For the most preferred areas (such as Tunis, Sfax, and Sousse) the price is set about U.S. $40 per square meter. For the least well off, in Beja and Jendouba, for example, the price is set below cost at roughly U.S. $7 per square meter. For locations in between, where there is some viable economic activity, the price is about U.S. $10 per square meter. Thus, there is a cross-subsidy for the least developed centers by projects in the most dynamic urban areas, a practice in keeping with national policy to discourage continued concentration of industry in the major cities and distribute it elsewhere.

AFI follows through with a client to the final stage, municipal approval of building permits. It coordinates with other parastatals and ministerial agencies to ensure that all services are in place, and it works with municipal authorities to obtain the necessary permits.

Once the plants are completed and ownership transferred, the finished properties go on the local tax rolls of the respective communities. The revenues become a major resource for the financially pressed towns. AFI officials say that the new owners of the building sites are not reluctant to pay these taxes because once the services and facilities are installed, people realize the need for taxes to maintain them.

In setting the selling price for finished lots, AFI serves its secondary objective of controlling speculation in industrial land. When the agency began in 1973, raw land sold by the private sector for industry in Tunis and Sfax cost about 12 dinars per square meter (about U.S. $5), a price so high as to deter development. AFI then assembled and finished certain government-owned sites at a total cost of 2.5 dinars per square meter. The agency then marketed these at 6.5 dinars per square meter, slightly above half the price of unfinished private lots. New plants moved to the government sites, and private owners dropped their prices. Now there is a general equilibrium. Private finished industrial lots are running about 31.4 dinars per square meter versus the 28.5 of AFI in Tunis. AFI intervention has clearly worked.

Although speculation has been dampened, the three major cities continue to attract the bulk of industrial growth. Even the considerable differential between site prices in the next tier and the major cities (a factor of four) is not sufficient to move a significant portion of new industrial growth to the less developed areas. This is an issue that AFI will be confronting under the next five-year plan.

In the summer of 1981, the Tunisian government announced creation of a "super" regional planning and coordinating body to guide decentralized investment during the planning period. Composition of this body and its leadership have not yet been announced, but officials at AFI stress that skilled apolitical professional direction is called for along with the power to force coordination if the plan objectives are to be achieved.

Site Acquisition and Disposition of AFH

Site Acquisition

AFH acquires land by a method slightly different from AFI's yet with similar results. Decisions are made in consultation with provincial governors and local mayors, and sufficient land is identified to meet an estimated two-year production schedule. Once the site is chosen, AFH asks for a preemption decree covering both the desired land and a significant surrounding perimeter (one means of blocking speculation). A special commission then establishes a price reflective of market conditions. The amount is put in escrow pending negotiations with the owners.

If the owners challenge the asking price, they have redress from the commission on the amount of compensation but not on the transfer of ownership. AFH has what can be termed a quick-take power, which provides immediate expropriation and permits the project to proceed. Meanwhile, three independent appraisers assess the land for proceedings in a court of law, which will award a final sum. The quick-take power reflects the urgency of AFH's mission, and the agency tries to get development underway within the two-year period.

In the case of smaller, less favored communities the build-out time tends to be longer, and AFH, whether by design or accident of market, must move into the position of land banker. AFH may hold a fairly large parcel but develop in the short run only those sections for which there are buyers.

Site Disposition

AFH has an interesting approach to land sales. Even before development, it establishes prices for the various sites, from large-scale subdivisions and apartment land to plots for individual family-owned homes. The land is then sold prior to development, all the private buyers paying the full stipulated price in advance. (SNIT is empowered to make installment payments.) This permits AFH to utilize the funds for actual project development, especially important because the agency has no access to loans.

Housing demand has been so high that prospective developers are willing to make such prepayments. This system is, of course, self-limiting for in effect it narrows the range of available buyers to those who have sufficient capital resources. The payments are provisional; if development costs prove higher than the original estimates, additional charges are levied on the buyers before they can gain access to the land they have purchased.

If demand for subdivisions or apartment sites is sufficiently intense that there is more than one prospective buyer, AFH draws lots to select the successful bidder rather than permit the land to be bid up beyond the established selling price. When demand exceeds supply for individual house lots, AFH asks the municipality to choose the purchasers. Such choice is based on chronological order of signing up. All of the finished housing sites (including those earmarked for SNIT) are priced at cost plus 10 percent, which covers AFH's operations.

On commercial sites, the agency can make a profit. These are sold at auction above a minimum price. Sites for public facilities such as hospitals and schools are transferred to the responsible ministries at cost. Meanwhile the municipality receives at no cost parks, parking areas, and finished streets. As with AFI, all privately owned land then goes on the municipal tax rolls.

Despite professed efforts to complete projects in two years, AFH has been subject to delays, which have distressed buyers who put up the entire purchase price in advance. Now the agency is trying to hold project development to eighteen months and is encouraging builders to use that period to prepare construction drawings for implementation immediately after transfer of finished plots.

Countering speculation is one of AFH's most important tasks since inflation in residential land was one of the factors that brought it about. Here it claims considerable success and contends that its pricing program has caused private landowners to cut back on their expectations or risk being left with unmarketable sites.

MAJOR CHALLENGES

Technical Competence

Public agency officials and technical staff by and large demonstrate a high level of skill. The staff of central government ministries and parastatal organizations tend to be well trained and are quite able to perform. Many in leadership positions dealing with urban development have strong, well-considered ideas. This characterization extends to the embryonic regional offices of parastatal agencies and to the municipal personnel of the larger cities. Serious problems exist, however, and are recognized regarding the lack of trained personnel in the smaller urban centers, which the government is targeting for attention in the forthcoming sixth five-year plan.

The issue, as articulated by the Ministry of Interior, is that municipal staffs lack the ability to conceive, plan, and execute projects. Municipal needs are too often presented as lists of unrealistic requirements. Too many of these projects can be neither funded nor effectively executed.

Thus the need for training and for technical assistance in the smaller municipalities has been noted, and considerable efforts will be made by both the central government and international agencies to fill the gap during the 1982-87 plan period.

Issues of Urbanization

For some time, issues of urbanization, including those of secondary city development, have been recognized as appropriate objects of public policy.

Government is disturbed about deficiencies in the municipal capacity to plan, finance, and coordinate. Interviews with heavily worked central agency officials suggest that the central institutions want local authorities to play these roles but find them lacking. Some secondary cities such as Sousse and Sfax have capable administrations, fairly effective tax collections, and sufficient funds to hire professional planning and management staff. Most others do not. The difficulty of this situation is illustrated by the fact that the national government had to forgive all outstanding municipal indebtedness in 1975.

A 1979 report from the Ministry of Interior states that cities had too little technical skill to design fundable projects and were not utilizing even the financial resources that were available to them. One Interior official reported that the collection rate for local taxes is less than 50 percent of the amount levied. He contrasted this general situation with Tunis where taxes are paid willingly because the municipality provides services: In the smaller communities, however, this is a vicious circle, according to a Department of Interior official. The services are meager, property owners don't come through with taxes because of this, and the city can't improve services because it lacks the funds.

For Tunisia's sixth five-year plan to succeed, local government skills and financial capacity must be upgraded. Thus central government officials have initiated efforts to improve the fundamental situation of personnel, skills, and planning.

Land Issues

In the Tunisian system, land is considered a critical link between planning and implementation, and instrumentalities have been established to ensure that the availability, cost, acquisition, assembly, and development of urban land present no bottleneck to urban expansion.

Tunisia has serious concerns about regional and urban imbalance. The scale of development to meet social needs, particularly jobs and shelter for the urban poor, has fallen short of the need. In this sense, Tunisia continues to be a developing country. Coordination of urban development presents serious issues the farther away from Tunis and the decisionmaking center that it must occur.

Despite these problems, Tunisia does have a framework for efforts to improve secondary cities. The basic issues of secondary city growth, still to be addressed in many countries, have been joined in Tunisia. During the forthcoming sixth five-year plan period, the system will be called on to perform at a greater scale and a higher level of efficiency. A major objective of that plan will be to achieve a marked reduction of existing regional economic disparities. Whether this can be done within the fiscal and human resources available is a key question.

Where communities are not growing, failures by municipal authorities to meet their responsibilities do not ripple through the structure of government to cause undue disturbance. Under a policy mandate that calls for municipal improvements to reduce disparities in the quality of life and that demands economic development in secondary centers, failure of municipal government to perform has serious implications.

Regionalization and Shelter for Low-Income Groups

AFH's considerable success has been in the major cities, principally Tunis. The agency now has two regional offices (in Sousse and Sfax), which can negotiate land sales but have limited development authority. Further decentralization is expected. The agency has been criticized for concentrating on serving higher-income groups, to a great degree a result of its limited capitalization. It purports to be seeking ways of accommodating lower-income groups and exploring schemes for cross-subsidies by higher income purchasers.

AFH is expected to play an important role in the decentralized development program, but like AFI, it is struggling to figure out how this can be accomplished in view of the restrictions in its charter, minimal experience in the outlying centers, and constant problem of finding a paying market for its output in smaller cities.

Problems Facing SNIT

Despite clear success in housing production, SNIT faces certain qualitative problems as it expands its activities in secondary centers. Without affecting the basic shelter mission, these problems have a serious impact on the adequacy of living conditions for occupants of SNIT dwellings.

Site Costs and Location

Although SNIT operates within local development plans and tries to locate projects near industry and other employment centers, the agency functions under a fundamental cost constraint. It has to select and build on relatively inexpensive land. It has to pick land whose purchase and development costs ultimately can be repaid by project beneficiaries, even though some measure of government subsidy may be involved in rental or purchase of units. The search for cheap land, especially in the smaller urban areas, has sometimes led to sites that are far from employment and services, resulting in the isolated development so characteristic of the developing world.

Coordination

Despite efforts at regional decentralization, the farther SNIT operates from Tunis, the more likely it is that the agency will encounter difficulties in coordination with other parastatal or government bodies responsible for critical project elements. Of particular concern are the community facilities essential to livability. SNIT builds the units and convenience shops to serve its development. It only reserves the sites (as does AFH) for schools, playgrounds, dispensaries, police stations, and other facilities. Other agencies have to obtain the budget and manpower to build them. SNIT cannot force their construction to mesh with the opening of the project nor can it handle the building and operations itself. The proper mesh does not always occur, and project residents can be left without important facilities for extended periods. This situation was highlighted in a recent consultant report on USAID-assisted SNIT projects in Sfax and Mahdia that have been completed and occupied but still lack even primary schools.

SNIT's management recognizes the problem, but it is one over which they have limited control. This coordination issue is one Tunisia must resolve as it attempts to apply the housing production techniques so successful in thriving economic centers in places where conditions are less favorable.

APPROACHES

Physical Planning as a Precursor to Development

In secondary cities, there are planning instruments for dealing primarily with land use, utilities siting, and zoning but not for such related subjects as fostering economic growth and private sector investment, project cost estimating and capital budgeting, public finance, upgrading and its community development work, or project scheduling and staging. To the extent that these matters are considered, they are the province of others, and the degree to which the elaboration and coordination of project development fits with physical plans varies from community to community. But the planning instruments themselves are sufficiently flexible to provide guidance for project development, and they are adaptable to changing circumstances.

All capital expenditures of central and parastatal agencies are coordinated within the framework of successive five-year plans by the Ministry of Planning. A report by the World Bank characterized this system in the following way:

The division of responsibilities has often led to some confusion in the design and implementation of urban development schemes. The Government has very cautiously embarked on a process of decentralization to delegate more initiative to local authorities. Important steps in this direction have been taken or are under consideration . . . first, the creation in 1972 of the Tunis District, and second, the creation in 1976 of five "economic regions," each comprising three to four *gouvernorats* grouped according to their socioeconomic characteristics. Also the [Dirección des collectivités publiques locales] is in the process of designing special training programs for local and municipal staff to improve the planning and execution capacities of *gouvernorats* and communes, respectively. The delegation of responsibilities and allocation of resources to the above "regions" is still very limited but is expected to grow. (World Bank, 1979, 2)

The Central Projects Unit (CPU) of the Direction des collectivités publiques locales (DCPL) in the ministries of Interior and Finance will take on a greater direct role in municipal management and technical assistance.

Through CPU the municipalities have been asked to prepare five-year plans. These are not land use plans but rather lists of needed public works similar in form to a five-year capital budget. Where physical development plans exist, the projects presumably will be derived from them. The cities are to set priorities, provide project specifications, and estimate funding requirements. "The work has to start with the cities themselves," says a CPU official, "because the national government cannot know as well as they what are their needs."

Once a preliminary plan has been prepared, CPU staff will review the materials and then provide technical assistance to formulate feasible programs. Technical assistance will come principally from the staff of the relevant sectoral agencies. Other support may be forthcoming through World Bank and USAID technical aid to CPU. Advisers will help define reasonable projects and translate the priorities of the sixth national development plan in terms of projects to foster decentralized urban growth. With CPU's approval, the plans will then become the final development programs for the respective municipalities.

Simultaneously, CPU will try to improve municipal management through training activities, including special seminars, sending personnel overseas for education, and structuring university and vocational school programs to develop better administrators. They will also try to help communities become more efficient in the collection of local taxes.

There is also a commitment to increase allocations of central government resources for municipal capital projects. The Caisse de prethet de soutien des collectivités locales (CPSCL), an urban loan fund allied with the DCPL and in existence for several years, has had quite limited resources. Its funding capacity will be expanded through a special loan fund created in 1979.

Subsidized loans to municipalities will be allocated on the basis of need and project planning rather than through the revenue-sharing formula. Two specific loan programs have now been established. One, for critical infrastructure, such as water, sewers, and parks, carries terms of 2 percent interest. The second program charges 4 percent and can be used for economically productive projects such as markets and commercial centers. Even these nominal and subsidized rates of interest may be difficult for some communities to accept, CPU officials point out, because of the Muslim stricture against usury. But they must be considered part of the inevitable learning process if modernization of these communities is to occur.

Thus, central government is fully aware that only a multidimensional effort will succeed in removing the obstacles to more equitable economic and social development inherent in the nature of municipal government today. That effort will involve intervention to improve project preparation and management, substantial technical assistance and training, and expansion of financial resources available for community development.

Development Plans

Development plans currently exist for all of the major and many of the smaller cities. They are prepared directly by the technical staff of the ministry or under contract with private consultants. These plans function as *guidance* documents, providing a general framework for decisions on land use and infrastructure location. They are not rigid, all-encompassing master plans that define with precision the uses and development densities of all urban land over an indefinite future. Many plans have short-term (10-year) perspectives. They can be revised during their lifetimes and scheduled for reexamination at the end of the planning period.

Where these guide plans exist, local municipal administrations are expected to fill in the details of area and project development through a more or less continual planning process. When major parastatal agencies such as AFH and AFI are scheduled to prepare and implement a project in a given city, they utilize the adopted development plan as a guide to initial site investigation but are empowered to work with the municipality, the governor, and the ministry if particular locations prove infeasible and plan provisions must be shifted. Discussions with parastatal agency officials and the planning staff in Sousse, a major secondary city with an overall development plan, indicate that this generalized system of land use guidance works quite well.

Development of Urban Land

More than most other developing countries, Tunisia has perceived that availability of urban land in appropriate locations and at reasonable cost is a critical element in urban development and a legitimate subject for national policy. Tunisia has established a basic approach to ensure land availability and dampen speculation. Parastatal organizations charged with preparing land for economic activity, housing, and community facilities implement the approach. In operation for about a decade, these agencies differ somewhat in their primary missions and methods of finance, but the three principal organizations (AFI, AFH, and SNIT) share the following characteristics:

Entry into a community at the community's request and/or in response to national development objectives endorsed in advance by the community

Site selection in accordance with the community's development plan but modification of that plan if detailed feasibility analysis proves first-choice sites impracticable

Land acquisition through direct purchase preemption or expropriation

Site planning, parcel assembly, and development on their own account and through coordination with other central agencies and municipal authorities

Disposition of finished sites on a cost recovery basis at prices that set the pattern for area land sales and thus tend to block speculation.

Each agency has tested its methods on projects in the greater Tunis region but has expanded operations in the secondary cities and smaller communities. All are being regionalized to some extent, with field offices in various parts of the country. All will be relied on heavily to meet objectives of decentralizing development during the sixth five-year period.

It is important to underscore the role of these agencies. They create new development areas. They operate on undeveloped land in and outside existing urbanized areas, and, with the exception of AFI's upgrading of an existing industrial park in Tunis, none is being deployed to redevelop existing urban areas at all.

U.S. Peace Corps

Some of the early assistance, during the 1960s and 1970s, came from the Peace Corps, which sent numerous professional architects and planners to Tunisia. Many were located in Tunis, but others were in secondary cities such as Kairouan. Although it is difficult to trace cause and effect, one might surmise that some of the land use orientation, the flexibility, and the guidance character of Tunisia's municipal plans can be attributed to the influence of these volunteers.

In these qualities, Tunisia's planning instruments differ considerably from other developing countries where more detailed and rigid European planning approaches have been utilized.

USAID Office of Housing

USAID became involved in 1966 through its housing guaranty program and has subsequently disbursed almost $35 million in shelter loans in addition to technical assistance. USAID's activities have reflected the changing focus of the agency and have helped to accelerate changing priorities of the government of Tunisia itself. The first project was a middle-income housing development in Tunis. The second, also in Tunis, supported a new residential area with a mix of middle- and low-income families. During the 1970s Tunisia continued to emphasize relatively high-cost new housing, heavily subsidizing the segment of lower-income households who could obtain occupancy.

Meanwhile the U.S. Congress redefined USAID's mission, charging the agency to concentrate on affordable solutions for the urban poor. This included upgrading existing settlements, expandable core housing, and sites and services projects. Despite Tunisia's reluctance to try this approach at first, the economics of limited resources became evident. USAID's next housing guaranty loan to Tunisia (HG-003) for $20 million was an incentive to move in new directions, not only in Tunis but elsewhere in the country. Part of the funds went for additional units in the Tunis satellite town of Ibn Khaldoun. Another portion helped launch a major upgrading project in the Mellassine neighborhood of Tunis. These projects are partially completed. Much of the assistance, however, went to begin a program of core housing (1,400 units) in both Tunis and secondary cities. Sousse, Sfax, and Monastir were among those to receive 100 to 200 core units each, in projects developed and built by SNIT.

When the HG-003 loan was initiated, Tunisia was not yet prepared to accept the minimal shelter approach of sites and services. It is willing to do so now, however. A future HG loan proposed for $50 million will be devoted to sites and services, core housing, upgrading, and community facilities. All of the funds will be used for projects in secondary cities. Neither Sousse nor Sfax, the largest and most prosperous of the secondary cities, nor Tunis will receive projects under the proposed new loan. There are seven target cities ranging from 2,000 to 45,000 in population. None of them has had upgrading projects previously. Thus, AID now will be supporting urban projects that meet the new national plan objectives of wider secondary center development.

An implementation agreement for the new loan has not yet been signed by the government of Tunisia, but the program itself is fairly well established within SNIT and other agencies that will be responsible. Some technical assistance funded through USAID's Integrated Improvement Program for the Urban Poor (IIPUP) has begun, and the government is using its own staff of preproject planning in the expectation that the program will proceed.

It is in technical assistance that the new activity may have some of its greatest benefits. The central government is concerned that the smaller municipalities lack the information and the staff to carry their own weight in project development. The technical assistance from both the central government and USAID will be directed toward filling that gap. Already the IIPUP-funded program has led to field investigations by Tunisian consultants to obtain basic data in several of the candidate cities. Existing statistics have been verified. Extensive questionnaire surveys of resident economic, social, and shelter characteristics have been undertaken. Detailed physical and demographic portraits of neighborhoods have been drawn for the first time, and priorities for specific improvement projects have been established.

Once loans under the new program begin to flow, technical assistance funded through IIPUP and other sources will focus on training and advising municipal staff on matters of relating to public works, including planning, coordination, and execution, and to improving social service and education in upgrading areas. The full range of activities anticipated is summarized in Figure 10.3.

Another important feature is USAID's support, jointly with the World Bank, of a central government agency with explicit responsibilities for financing municipal projects and upgrading municipal administration in cities outside Tunis. This institution building will be critical if Tunisia is to have any hope of achieving its decentralized development objectives. During the 1980s, both USAID and the World Bank will channel their efforts through the Central Project Unit of the Ministry of Interior's Direction des collectivités publiques locales (DCPL).

The DCPL has taken on a new look in recent years. Currently the Ministry of the Interior is considering a reform of the organizational structure of the DCPL designed to ensure a more efficient approach to municipal improvements. The World Bank project, now underway, offers the first major opportunity to develop the staff and organization necessary for channeling international assistance funds to municipal projects, in addition to improving DCPL's ability to deal with the subject matter. The DCPL's Caisse de prets et de soutien des collectivités locales (CPSCL) has also been revitalized so that the national government will have a better financial conduit through which to assist the urban development process.

The CPSCL is under the supervision of the ministries of Interior and Finance. The CPSCL's main purpose is to lend to public entities such as municipalities and *gouvernorats* for financing public facilities, infrastructure works, and municipal housing development.

Initial familiarity with the World Bank project operation will strengthen the DCPL/Caisse staff, which should be ready to expand its focus to the interior of the country by the time the HG project begins implementation. The results of this break-in period should lead to a major new effort to cope with the problems of municipal government as it confronts urban development during the sixth plan period (USAID, 1979a, 42-3).

Figure 10.3 Project Technical Assistance Matrix

Title	Size	Duration	Recipient	Supplier	Funded Via	Purpose
Home improvement and construction loan Mgmt. plus savings mobilization	TDY consultancies	Five months or more	CNEL management	RHUDO/Tunis via DS/H contracts	HG fees and/or HG proceeds	start-up advisory services on forms, guarantees, loan mgmt. and savings mobilization for the irregularly employed
Advisory T.A. for passive solar heating and composter toilets	Up to 10 PCVs or private advisors	starting FY80 for 2 years	municipal tech. services of selected small towns, via DCPL/ SNIT/Private Developers	Peace Corps or privately contracted advisors	"Action" and GOT Interior and Equipment Ministries	Training on installation, inspection and maintenance of solar heaters and composter toilets. Training of municipal counterparts and possibly work crews.
	Up to 10 PCVs or private advisors	starting FY81 for 2 years				
IIPUP support small town technical staff	At least $200,000	up to 48 months	technical staff of small towns as selected by the DCPL	Host Country Contracts	IIPUP grant for FY80 and associated GOT contribution	strengthen the mgmt capacity of municipal cadres to carry out upgrading
IIPUP socio-economic activities for local upgrading beneficiaries			upgrading communities and residents	HC Contracts/ US Contracts/ local support		provide integrated socio-economic services to upgrading areas

Source: USAID, "Project Paper 664-HG-004", 1979, p. 28.

TDY — Temporary Duty

PCV — Peace Corps Volunteer

HG — Housing Guarantee

HC — Host Country

World Bank

The bank has also played a role in urban institution building for Tunisia. Its first urban project in 1973 helped establish the regional governmental and planning agency of the district of Tunis and modernized the capital's transportation system:

In the first years of its existence the Tunis District was able to complete its original work program established in consultation with the Bank . . . to (i) carry out sectoral analyses resulting in the identification of deficiencies and leading to the design of priority action programs, (ii) develop a strategic regional development plan, (iii) establish more realistic and operational programming and budgeting mechanisms, and (iv) initiate a number of important changes in investment programs. (World Bank, 1979, 6)

The bank's second project is for shelter and services primarily for the urban poor and is to be concentrated in Tunis and Sfax.[1] Total project cost is estimated at $45 million, of which the bank loan is $19 million. Additional funds for the upgrading project will be lent by the Dutch government.

In Tunis the emphasis is on upgrading low-income areas, one of which adjoins the USAID-assisted upgrading project, and on solid waste collection and disposal. The program in Sfax is multidimensional. It includes 1,900 sites and services plots with allied workshops and community facilities, construction of schools, loans and extension services to improve small business, and improvements in traffic flow and management.

The World Bank also will provide consultant and advisory services to both Sfax (as a case with replicable consequences) and to the Central Project Unit. The objective is to improve overall management and programming of projects at both the central support level and within the municipalities.

FUTURE THRUSTS

Decentralization of Decisionmaking

Although central government control and execution of major development responsibilities is a basic feature of Tunisia, the state has embarked on a two-pronged decentralization effort. One thrust is increasing regionalization of parastatal agencies that create the physical facilities to support human settlement and economic growth. The second is an increasing reliance on elected municipal administrations to participate in the planning and financing of urban infrastructure and services. Both attempts to bring governmental decisionmaking closer to the people are taking place gradually, almost as if authorities are trying to find the appropriate formula to establish just enough localism while a preeminence of strong centralism is maintained.

The state is performing a balancing act. On the one hand, it recognizes that national objectives to reduce urban and regional disparities can be achieved only with greater local involvement and more expeditious on-site coordination of decisionmaking. On the other, it has no intention of relinquishing centralized planning, budgeting, and control. This process is in its very early stages, and its evolution should be of considerable interest to other developing countries with a similar commitment to decentralization and similar objectives of more equitable distribution of economic growth.

Creation of New Industrial Jobs

This is an objective that AFI approaches with some concern. Under the forthcoming plan, a target has been set for 22,000 new industrial jobs per year. In land development terms, this works out to a requirement of 220 hectares of finished sites annually, almost double the level of past production. At least a major proportion of these sites would be targeted for the less-favored cities where AFI has hitherto had difficult experiences. Marketability is a key factor because of AFI's cost recovery mandate. The agency does not believe it can hold finished sites for an extended period, and marketability in the outlying, smaller centers is a serious problem. AFI officials cite the example of Beja where the municipality requested industrial development. AFI's assessment proved negative, and the agency replied that it would not act even to acquire the land until the city could provide a list of specific company prospects.

Structural Adjustments under the Sixth Five-Year Plan

Tunisia's sixth five-year plan is still under preparation, so many specific features will not be known for some time. Currently, however, it is clear that the plan will involve some fundamental policy and structural changes.

Regional Rural-Urban Focus

The effort to reduce economic and social disparities will be regional in character and will involve concerted attempts to develop rural as well as urban areas outside the most favored coastal region. Thus, although municipalities in general will be singled out for support, specific secondary centers will not be designated for special treatment, at least at the policy level. In this respect Tunisia's program differs, for example, from the growth pole approach being pursued by Korea in its new five-year plan. There, fourteen centers are designated for special attention. In Tunisia, all cities in the less favored regions will be considered poles of development for their respective hinterlands. The objective is to formulate regional strategies that will foster this evolution.

The regions will consist of contiguous *gouvernorats* with similar development charactcristics. Strategies will be evolved at the regional level and within each *gouvernorat*. Special programs will be set for rural areas within the *gouvernorats*, as well as for the cities. Governors will have special loan funds for rural area development, along with the urban assistance of the Caisse de prets.

Presumably this aspect of the plan will be coordinated by the new super regional commission, involving the staffs of various ministries and a professional, rather than a political, director. The precise powers of this commission—whether it will have decisionmaking authority or will be strictly a coordinating body with only advisory powers and whether it will deal with land planning issues or will be limited to economic and social planning—are not yet known.

Carrot and Stick

The government clearly intends to offer a battery of fiscal incentives to both urban and rural areas in support of the decentralization policy. Some of these, such as the industrial incentive law and the municipal loan funds, have been cited already. In addition, planning ministry officials have indicated that denial of location permits will be exercised if needed to block additional concentration of major industry in Tunis. Commensurate with these strictures, the plan will direct industrial development activities of API away from Tunis entirely and into other regions. Similar locational pressures (although not perhaps as extreme) will be put on AFH, SNIT, and the other major parastatals.

An Analytic Component

Analysis on a continuing basis and at a highly professional level will guide formulation of investments under the plan. The policy is to launch carefully thought out programs at every level to minimize the risk of failure. Thus, every *gouvernorat* has, or is to have, a *cellule* of researchers and planners to guide project formulation and funding at rural and urban levels. The supercommission, regardless of its ultimate decisionmaking power, will be staffed with trained professionals in a number of fields who will prepare overall regional development plans and link these with the national plan itself.

Concluding Note

Thus, Tunisia is about to embark on a well-considered national effort to reduce the dominance of Tunis and the coastal region and to build up economic growth in less favored urban and rural areas. Physical planning and the rapid mobilization of urban land will be important components of this effort. Tunisia has already achieved notable success in translating both national and urban plans into action. Certainly the relevant range of issues has now been recognized, and the structure for this new level of comprehensive action is in place. Politically the strategy is probably most appropriate for this stage of Tunisia's history.

Although the objectives and approaches are clear, an observer is still unable to assess the extent to which central government expects success during the period covered by the sixth plan. Unanswered questions remain: how many of the outlying centers can attract viable economic activity? Is a countrywide area development strategy more productive than one that limits targets to the most promising secondary cities and rural regions? Can investment actually occur at the scale intended and be coordinated? Are there enough people and funds to do this job?

NOTES

This chapter on Tunisia is one of five case studies included in *Approaches to Planning for Secondary Cities in Developing Countries*, prepared in 1981-82 by Goldie W. Rivkin and Malcolm D. Rivkin as a report for the Office of Urban Development, U.S. Agency for International Development. Contents of the full manuscript will be published separately in the near future.

1. *Second Urban Project Appraisal Report*. This direct intervention is in addition to the indirect urbanization effects of the World Bank's tourism project.

BIBLIOGRAPHY

Bureau d'études A.E.U.D. 1980. Mission: Visite et Inspection des Chantiers. January.

Nelson, Harold D. 1979, *Tunisia, A Country Study*. Washington, D.C.: American University, Foreign Areas Studies Division.

Rivkin, M. D. 1965. *Area Development for National Growth, the Turkish Precedent*. New York: Praeger.

Saya, Mohamed. Interview. 1980. In *Panorama Immobilier*, September-October.

USAID. 1979a. *National Low Cost Shelter Programs*, Project Paper 664-HG-004. Washington, D.C.: USAID.

USAID. 1979b. *Tunisia Shelter Sector Assessment*. Washington, D.C.: USAID.

World Bank. 1979. *Appraisal Report for the Second Tunisia Urban Project*. Washington, D.C.: World Bank.

PART IV

EUROPE

11

France

CLAUDE HENRI CHALINE

HISTORICAL DEVELOPMENT AND CURRENT STATUS OF LAND USE PLANNING

France is the largest country in Western Europe, but it is also the one with the lowest density by far, with only 100 people per square kilometer (165 per square kilometer of agricultural land). The census of 1982 gave a total of 54,260,000 inhabitants for 550,000 square kilometers. Strong regional contrasts, however, have taken shape since the Industrial Revolution, due to the continuous migrations from rural to urban and industrial areas. These contrasts have been reinforced during the decades following World War II when many immigrant workers from overseas concentrated in the main urbanized areas. Recent trends of counter-urbanization have not been significant enough to modify the overall picture. On the one hand, there are regions of high densities, where strong pressures are at work on scarce land resources, as in the Paris region and the lower Seine Valley; the Rhone corridor and the southeast coastal Mediterranean area, mainly from Marseilles to the Riviera; and the north and northeast industrial and mining belt. On the other hand, there exist large tracts of sparsely populated rural or mountainous areas, such as the Central Massif, which covers one-seventh of the French territory (Figure 11.1).

The land use pattern in France has been directly influenced by the progressive shift of the population toward the urban areas. The percentage of people living in towns was 53 percent in 1946, 56 percent in 1954, and about 75 percent in 1985. If the largest cities were the exclusive beneficiaries of the rural to town migrations up to the 1960s, the latest census indicates a dual trend: (1) the larger cities are no longer growing and they show an overspill process from their center

Figure 11.1 Areas with High Competition for Land Use

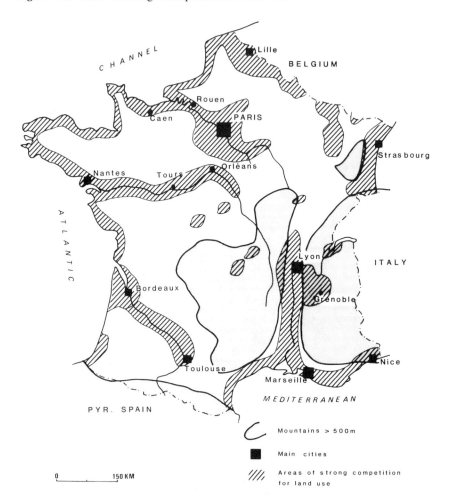

to their periphery; and (2) the highest national rates of growth are found in the small and medium-sized towns.

The traditional imbalance between Paris and the provinces is no longer as apparent. Three decades of planned decentralization monitored by a state agency, DATAR (Délégation à l'aménagement du territoîre et à l'action régionale) have succeeded in controlling the growth of the Paris metropolitan area, while new areas of development have been encouraged in the large provincial metropolises, such as Lyon, Bordeaux, and Toulouse, or have spontaneously developed in medium-sized towns located within a radius of 100 to 250 kilometers from Paris such as Tours, Orleans, Bourges, Caen, and Reims.

Table 11.1
France's Principal Land Uses, 1948 and 1980

	1948 (%)	1980 (%)
Agriculture	60.0	58.8
Forest	20.6	26.6
Uncultivated	11.0	4.4
Urban and developed areas	8.4	10.2
Total	100.0	100.0

Simultaneously, the French tradition of living in apartments has been superseded by an overwhelming preference for detached single-family houses. This has thereby brought about a rapid rate of transfer of agricultural land into various urban or suburban uses and the making of a new so-called *péri-urbain* landscape.

Table 11.1 gives the main categories of national land use. The principal source of the data is *The Abstract of Agricultural Statistics*, whose main purpose is not the measurement of urbanized areas. In fact, in those metropolitan areas where rural and urban uses are widely intermingled, it is impossible to determine accurately the share of each component.

It is estimated that only 5 percent of the French land is effectively urban, rather low by Western European standards. In fact this figure disguises the duality of the French case. On a total of 550,000 square kilometers, 58 *départements* totaling 300,000 square kilometers contain 70 percent of the population. In these *départements* there is strong competition between conflicting land uses. Suburban growth and new industrial and transportation infrastructures absorbed about 178,000 hectares every year during the 1960s and the 1970s. Now with declining activities, the average yearly transfer of rural land is approximately 101,000 hectares. Land scarcity and speculation risks, however, are still strong in coastal areas, in the centers of the large cities, and in the suburbs of most metropolitan and medium-sized towns.

Land use regulation was attempted as early as the interwar period, but efficiency in this field was reached only in the 1960s. This was when land use ceased to be considered as an unrestricted right and instead was seen as a limited resource whose benefits were to be shared in the achievement of private and collective goals.

INSTITUTIONAL AND LANDOWNERSHIP FRAMEWORK

France has centralized institutions, and any land regulation covers the totality of its territory. Private ownership rights is one of the pillars of French society, in particular since the *Code Civil* edict of Napoleon I. As early as 1807, however, the state promulgated a law that encouraged building uniformity at street level. But the first comprehensive town planning legislation was passed by parliament only in 1909. At that time 13,600 cities were expected to plan their development through a *Plan d'amenagement, d'embellissement et d'extension* (plan for management, beautification, and growth). In fact, implementation results of this legislation by 1938 were relatively insignificant. Furthermore, when the city plans were published, they were not legally binding. Following World War II, priority was given to reconstruction when the sole requirement was a construction permit for any new building. Town planning was not made compulsory until 1958 when the *Plan d'urbanisme directeur* (master plan), which included zoning regulations, was made compulsory for any city above 10,000 inhabitants. More than 300 city plans were drawn in the following decade, but this period has been characterized by the ease in which planning regulations could be avoided (for example, in the matter of density and height).

Decisionmaking in matters of land use planning may be considered at three levels: national, regional, and local.

Until quite recently, the national level has been the main source of regulations, controls and implementation of land use planning. This has been undertaken mainly through a ministry of housing and planning, whose name has changed several times, and through its services or Directions départementales de l'équipement (DDE) in each of the ninety-six French *départements*. The real landmark in city and land planning is the law introduced by the Minister E. Pisani in 1967, the *Loi d'orientation foncière* (LOF), which brings to bear severe control restriction on the rights of private ownership. This planning act reflects a hierarchical concept and provides for two levels of planning: at a regional level the Schema directeur d'aménagement et d'urbanisme (SDAU) and at the local level the Plan d'occupation des sols (POS).

The SDAU is intended to indicate strategic land use zoning, road proposals, and large infrastructures, and the POS provides for detailed guidelines for development applications at the local level, consistent with the broad intentions of the SDAU. Some important differences, however, emerge between the master plan (SDAU) and the local plan (POS). First, SDAU is not a statutory document with legal force; in other words, there is no right of appeal by third parties against SDAU. On the other hand, POS is legally binding. An SDAU and a POS must be prepared by any commune that has more than 10,000 inhabitants.[1] In a few large towns an SDAU has been prepared for a single commune (Marseilles is one), but, more often an SDAU has been prepared for a larger area usually covering several communes situated around a city; for example, the

SDAU of the Paris region includes the city of Paris and more than a thousand communes with a total population of 10 million inhabitants.

By contrast a POS is prepared for a single commune, although it is possible for only part of a commune to be covered by a single POS or a group of communes to be covered by one POS. There is no obligation to inform the public of the SDAU, and public participation may not take place at all. Any involvement of the public in an SDAU takes the form of viewing graphically displayed documents. Exhibitions are also the usual form of public participation in a POS; however, the local plans are legally subject to a public inquiry. This procedure, however, is not to be confused with the legal procedures for a public hearing used in the United States. It must be noted that a POS is elaborated by a joint committee including local councillors and representatives of various associations, which can be considered another form of public participation.

A POS essentially contains land zoning regulations for every plot of land included in the designated area. For each zone, building standards, uses, and plot ratios, or *coefficient d' occupation des sols* (COS) are indicated; also included are those zones where building construction is restricted or forbidden. A POS is required to be submitted for a full revision every five years.

A law passed in 1982 has considerably modified the role of the local level in land use planning. Power has been transferred from the national and state to the commune, which now has complete jurisdiction over its development plan and its implementation. But France is divided into more than 36,000 communes; of this total 85 percent have fewer than 500 inhabitants, corresponding to the density of rural France. On the other hand, 1,495 of the communes are cities of more than 5,000 inhabitants each and contain about 63 percent of the French population. Such an administrative division makes comprehensive land use planning at the metropolitan level difficult. To deal with this problem, various forms of voluntary groupings for planning purposes have been arranged in 28 planning agencies covering most of the large cities and their suburbs.

Since the French Revolution, land has been divided. Currently 87 million plots belong to some 12 million citizens. Large private or institutional owners own a fairly large part of urban and rural land. The state itself owns 4 percent of France, mainly forest and military zones and camps. The communes together own, since the Middle Ages, another 4 percent of the land, consisting primarily of agricultural or forested areas. Most of the large national agencies are also owners of considerably large areas; for example, SNCF (the French state railways) owns 101,000 hectares and the Electricity Board 142,000 hectares. The rapid extension of the urbanized area has induced high increases in land values. For instance, the cost of land currently represents between 20 and 25 percent of the total cost of new building and sometimes more in downtown areas. This recent cost increase of building land has led to specific policies aimed at restraining land speculation, which combine legal and fiscal approaches.

MAJOR CHALLENGES AND APPROACHES TO PLANNING

Land Prices

The escalating land costs of new development have been the main source of social dissatisfaction and a highly debated political issue for two decades. In theory, it is possible to deal with land speculation or land retention through compulsory acquisition by a public agency, the price fixed as necessary by a judge. But this procedure is not widely practiced because of its arbitrary aspect; it is poorly perceived and mistrusted by the citizens. In 1962, the French government tried, with some success, to solve this problem by means of a procedure called ZAD (*zone d'aménagement concerte*), or deferred development zones. ZADs are designated by the *préfet* (state representative) in a *département* at the request of a commune or any state agency undertaking a public development, such as a new town, a new industrial zone, or a new airport. One year before a ZAD is established, land values are frozen. Should an owner wish to sell this land to another private party after designation, the public agency responsible for the ZAD has the right to preempt and buy the land at the asking price. If the asking price is approximately the same as the frozen value, the public agency is not likely to intervene; when the price is considerably above the frozen value, the public agency either may negotiate the agreed price or initiate expropriation proceedings. The ZAD declaration lasts for fourteen years. The ZAD system has two purposes: to make easier public acquisitions at relatively low prices and to dampen speculation where future public development is contemplated.

Between 1962 and 1983, this procedure has been extensively used; more than 4,000 ZADs have been designated, covering a total area of 526 hectares. Most of this land ultimately will be resold to public or private developers or single home owners, except in a few commercial schemes where it will be leased to private developers for 25 years or longer.

There is strong competition for land, especially in downtown areas where maximum prices are usually to be found. Since 1975 a system not very different from ZAD has been in force, the so-called ZIF (*zone d'intervention foncière*). It is also based on the right to preempt, a power given to public agencies for an unlimited period. But a ZIF can be created only for social purposes such as the building of low-cost housing or creating public open spaces. To date the total area covered by ZIFs in inner cities is about 405,000 hectares.

Land Appreciation

Although the ZAD system obviously has contributed to placing a brake on land speculation, the fiscal tools introduced by successive laws have never been successful. For decades the state has tried in vain to tax land appreciation through public development. The last act, passed in 1958, was never implemented for technical reasons. Neither was a law of 1961, which created a special tax (*taxe local d'équipement*) to be paid by all landowners in a zone where development occurs; this tax was intended to contribute to the costs of new services and infrastructures.

Because of these difficulties, profits from appreciation since 1976 are simply included in private incomes and subsequently taxed when a property is resold with a profit. The main drawback of the taxation is that it is completely irrelevant to any land use policy because the rate of tax is the same for all zones in local plans (whether agricultural land or proposed building land).

In downtowns a more discriminatory tax has been applied since 1975, the PLD (*plafond légal de densité*), whose first objective was to limit high density and the construction of high-rise buildings. With the PLD, the state has in fact nationalized the right to build above a fixed floor space ratio (built area to surface area of the lot)—1.5 in Paris and 1.0 in the other large cities. If a new building exceeds this limit, the developer has to pay a special levy independently of the construction permit to the commune. In fact, with the PLD comes the ideological and political problem of the transfer of the right to build from the private owner to the state or to the local authority. To date this debate has not evolved significantly, and France's planning procedures are characterized by a mixture of private enterprise and public intervention.

Land Use Planning

More than 20 percent of French national assets are made up of landed properties. This percentage has been growing steadily since 1945. Land is highly regarded as a profitable investment and as protection against monetary erosion. This prevalent attitude has widened the gap between the potential market value of the land and its current market value, making it difficult to implement any public planning policies. French land use planning is based largely on a variety of zoning codes and specific regulations that theoretically cover the entire territory. The efficiency of these controls may be evaluated in terms of results and with reference to the decisionmaking process.

Since 1967, when master plans and local plans were made compulsory in communes above 10,000 inhabitants, 170 SDAUs have been instituted covering 61,000 square kilometers and with a population of 20 million; 3,660 POSs have also been initiated with an area of 72,000 square kilometers and a population of 23 million. Consequently all of urban France is subjected to strict land use planning with regard to zoning and individual plot development.

Building Conservation

It has been thought necessary to adopt special zoning regulations for urban areas of architectural value, the *secteurs sauvegargés*. Between 1964 and 1984, 60 of these have been designated in towns such as Versailles, Nancy, and Bordeaux. In these areas, usually already covered by a POS, a specific plan, or *plan de sauvegarde et mise en valeur*, is enforced. It strictly limits the right to demolish existing buildings and makes provision for the rehabilitation of the building with private and public funds.

Protection of Natural Areas

Interest in the protection of natural areas gathered momentum during the 1970s. Because most of these areas are not included in an SDAU or a POS, specific actions have to be undertaken. Six national parks were designated between 1963 and 1979 (Figure 11.2); five of them are in mountain areas (Alps, Pyrenees, Cevennes) and one on the Mediterranean island of Port Cros. The parks cover a total area of about 364,000 hectares, or about 0.6 percent of the French territory. Additionally, there are 46 regional parks on some 2,428,000 hectares where regulations concerning new construction or any development are much more flexible and less prohibitive than in the national parks.

Coastal Areas

Special attention has been given to coastal areas. France has more than 5,000 kilometers of coastline on both the Atlantic Ocean and the Mediterranean Sea, and with the growth of tourism and recreational activities, many sections are in danger of development and destruction of the natural landscape. To avoid an urban takeover, as has already occurred on much of the Riviera, a state agency, the Conservatoire du littoral, was established in 1975 to protect the seashore, as well as the inland shores of the major lakes. The Conservatoire du littoral has a double function of protection and management; it has power to acquire land, to expropriate, and to preempt; it may also receive donations. But its actions are severely limited by its modest budget. In 1983 it possessed about 16,200 hectares in 145 locations, but approximately 607,000 hectares of the seashore needed urgent protective action. Recently the Conservatoire du littoral has attempted another course of action: negotiating agreements with local seaside authorities which have accepted its authority to protect part of their territory from further development.

Energy

The relationship between land use and energy conservation, or the use of new energy sources, is a matter of discussion. Public inquiry, similar to that which takes place before the construction of new, large infrastructures, helps to determine the location of nuclear power stations. A dozen nuclear plants have been constructed by the nation in accordance with this procedure. However, in two cases, Brittany and Ardennes, the public inquiries led to strong protests of opponents to nuclear energy. Subsequently these projects were abandoned.

Increasingly, geothermal energy is used, especially around Paris in conjunction with the equipping of large-scale suburban low-cost housing schemes. This is a rational use of this energy, which dictates a high density of more than 180 inhabitants per hectare. Geothermal energy is only one component of a more general recent trend to develop district heating in densely urbanized areas, such

Figure 11.2 France's River Basin Conservation Areas

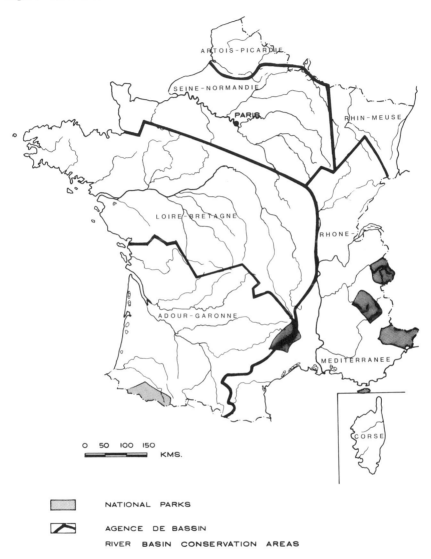

as central Paris. A law passed in 1980 gives any local authority legal power when establishing district heating to compel all nearby homes to be linked to this heat distribution network.

Solar energy, on the contrary, requires low density and individual equipment installation. In a few recent local plans, special regulations have dealt with the

problems of shade, proximity of buildings, and types of separating walls and
vegetation screens.

Decentralization of Decisionmaking

An important recent change has occurred giving more planning powers to the
commune. This is part of the decentralizing process initiated by the 1982 act.
In contrast to the 1967 act, all communes now are encouraged to initiate a POS
or local plan, sometimes in a simplified version for the small communes under
1,000 inhabitants. In the new process, the state, or its representative, loses most
of its power except in maintaining final legal control. Zoning codes and construction permits are the full responsibility of the elected mayor and local council.
The impact of this political reform is yet to be felt. One may question, however,
the capability of the thousands of small communes to deal with the growing
complexity and technicality of land use planning because they have no permanent
planners in their service. One solution in the future might be cooperation between
the communes and a voluntary multicommunal planning agency, particularly for
the location of new infrastructures, such as sewerage plants and airports.

An interesting example of land use planning encompassing several local plans
are the main river basins, which include their catchment areas and downstream
valley. The main planning purpose is to control flooding and to deal with water
pollution. In 1964 six public agencies, Agences de bassin, were created such as
in Seine-Normandy and Loire-Brittany (see Figure 11.2). These agencies are
responsible for the management of water resources; their strategy is carefully
adapted to economic constraints.

Land Reserves

The most recurring issue remains the rational allocation of land for new urban
developments on the periphery of the cities. With the exception of Lyon and
Strasbourg, French cities have no long-range policy of land reserve, as they do
in Sweden. In the previous decade, however, the government gave financial
incentives to local authorities to anticipate their future needs in building land.
To do so, the ZAD procedure is commonly, but not exclusively, used. The right
to preempt is then exercised by any public agency or local authority that buys
agricultural land in advance and then will resell it several years later to public
or private developers. In the Paris metropolitan region, this action is the responsibility of the Agence foncière et technique de la région parisienne. Created
as early as 1962, this agency is considered as a pioneer in this field. For twenty
years, it has devoted its activities to buying in advance open land necessary for
the implementation of the main targets of the regional master plan (SDAU); for
example, it has bought 11,700 hectares for five regional new towns, 2,430
hectares for large infrastructures, and 8,500 hectares of woodlands, which is
part of a discontinuous greenbelt planned for the periphery of the Paris region,
or *zones naturelles d'équilibre*.

It is commonly estimated that to put a brake on land scarcity and speculation, it would be necessary for any local authority to have a permanent land reserve equivalent to about 10 percent of the current demand. In fact, the land reserve provision is far from being systematic, and the rise of land costs is a serious threat to good planning.

In desirable rural areas, the trend toward the construction of individual homes or second homes has been seen as a serious danger to the preservation of the countryside. In an attempt to limit this threat, a law was passed in 1976 based on the principle of the transfer of development rights (*transfert de coefficient d'occupation des sols*). This procedure, which separates the ownership of land from the right to build on it, is still unfamiliar to most of the French people. Encouraging examples, however, can be observed in a few places, especially in winter resorts where it is imperative that large, open, natural areas be left free of any constructions. The transfer of development rights requires a unanimous consent by the community, and zones where building rights are concentrated must be designated in the local plan. This procedure requires participation by the private sector in order to maintain the rights of private owners facing inequitable treatment by planning regulation. It is hoped that this procedure may lead to a balance between private and collective planning goals.

NOTE

1. A commune is the smallest territorial division administered by a mayor assisted by an elected municipal council.

BIBLIOGRAPHY

Attias, Ch., and D. Linotte. 1982. *Le remembrement rural*. Paris: Librairies techniques.
Chaline, Claude, and J. Dubois-Maury. 1983. *Energie et urbanisme*. Paris: Presses universitaires de France.
Documentation française. Paris. Etat de l'Environnement. *Rapport Annuel*. 1983.
Etudes Foncieres, Paris (quarterly).
Givaudan, A. 1975. La question foncière. Paris: Centre de recherche en urbanisme.
Goux, J. F. 1979. La consommation de sol urbain. *Revue d'économie régionale et urbaine* 11: 382-401.
Gravier, J. F. 1984. *L'espace vital*. Paris: Flammarion.
Jégouzo, Y., and Y. Pittard. 1980. *Le droit de l'urbanisme*. Paris: Masson.
Lajugie, J., P. Delfaud, and C. Lacour. 1984. *Espace régional et aménagement du territoire*. Paris: Dalloz.
La Rochefoucauld, B. 1982. *L'abondance foncière*. Paris: Dunod.
Léna, H. 1981. *La commune face à la politique foncière*. Paris: Berger-Levrault.
Lojkine, Jean. 1977. *Le marxisme, l'état et la question urbaine*. Paris: Presses universitaires de France.
Luchaire, Fr. 1983. *Droit de la décentralisation*. Paris: Presses universitaires de France.
Ministère de l'environnement et du cadre de vie. 1980–81. *Plans d'occupation des sols*. 5 vols. Paris.

Ministère de l'urbanisme et du logement. Yearly. *Recueil d'Informations Statistiques sur l'Urbanisme*. Paris.

Ministère de l'urbanisme et du logement. 1980. *Consommation d'espace pour le logement 1976–78*. Paris.

Pisani, Edgard. 1977. *Utopie foncière*. Paris: Gallimard.

Pisani, Edgard. 1983. Rapport pour un réseau d'espaces naturels. Paris: Ministère de l'environnement. Unpublished.

Renard, Vincent. 1980. *Plans d'urbanisme et justice foncière*. Paris: Presses universitaires de France.

Steinberg, Jean. 1981. *Les villes nouvelles d'Ile-de-France*. Paris: Masson.

Wilson, Irene. 1983. The preparation of local plans in France. *Town Planning Review* 54: 155–75.

12

England and Wales

H. W. E. DAVIES

Town and country planning in England and Wales started in a piecemeal fashion in 1909 and reached maturity in 1947 when a universal and comprehensive planning system was created in which every local authority was required to control the use and development of land.[1] That system is still largely intact; nevertheless, many of its aims and methods began to shift in the mid-1970s as the factors that gave rise to the original system changed and new issues started to emerge. This chapter describes that planning system.[2]

POPULATION, EMPLOYMENT, AND LAND USE

England and Wales in 1981 had a population of 49.0 million and an area of 15.1 million hectares, giving a density of 3.24 persons per hectare.[3] By international standards it is densely populated. Only the Netherlands in the European Economic Community (EEC) is more densely populated, with 3.91 persons per hectare in 1971, the comparable figures for the EEC and United States being 1.70 and 0.22, respectively (Best, 1981).

Population density in England and Wales reflects the extent to which it is a highly urbanized country. 77 percent of the population in 1981 lived in the former urban districts and boroughs by which the country was administered until the reorganization of local government in 1974; that figure has remained roughly constant since 1901 (Table 12.1). It is, however, a poor definition. An alternative measure shows that about 96 percent of the population of Great Britain and 97 percent of employment is located in the so-called metropolitan areas, the only nonmetropolitan areas being in the remote, peripheral areas of England and Wales and, especially, Scotland (Hall and Hay, 1980). By that same measure, however,

Table 12.1
Growth of the Urban Population, England and Wales, 1851–1981

	Urban Population ('000)	% of Total Population ('000s)
1851	8,991	50
1901	25,058	77
1951	35,335	81
1971	38,025	78
1981	37,691	77

Definitions: urban population, living in borough and urban district local government areas.

Sources: Hall, et al., 1973 (Table 2.1), and Great Britain, Office of Population and Censuses and Surveys. Census 1981: Preliminary Report for Towns, London, HMSO (2nd edition), 1982.

Table 12.2 shows that population and, to a lesser extent, employment are decentralizing from the core metropolitan areas to the outer ring of suburbs and smaller towns.

The urban population derives its livelihood from manufacturing and, increasingly, from services (Table 12.3). The most striking trend of the past 40 years has been the almost total eclipse of agriculture and mining as sources of employment and the rise of services. Employment in manufacturing, however, took a different path, rising to a peak in 1966 and thereafter losing 1.5 million jobs by 1979 (Fothergill and Gudgin, 1982).

The changes in the structure of employment have considerable implications for the distribution of population and employment, in particular for the unequal growth of the different regions of the country. Table 12.4 shows unemployment ratios for the 11 standard regions of the United Kingdom.[4] The peripheral regions show the highest unemployment; they formerly were the most dependent on mining, iron and steel, and shipbuilding. The central industrial regions originally were more dependent on textiles, engineering, and metal-using industries, as well as mining; their relative rates of unemployment are increasing. The re-

Table 12.2
Distribution of Population and Employment, Great Britain, 1950–1975

	population (%)		employment (%)	
	1950	1975	1950	1975
Core metropolitan areas	53.4	46.6	61.0	58.9
Outer ring metropolitan areas	43.0	50.1	36.1	38.4
Non-metropolitan areas	3.6	3.3	2.9	2.7
Total	100.0	100.0	100.0	100.0

Definitions: core, a local authority area with more

than 20,000 jobs.

outer ring, local authority areas from

which more than half of the commuting

population travels to work daily to a

core area.

non-metropolitan, remainder.

Source: Hall and Hay, 1980 (Tables A.1, A.2)

maining regions were much less dependent on the traditional heavy industries and have consistently had the lowest rates of unemployment. The contrasts in unemployment have persisted since 1945 and were even more pronounced before the war.

If the spatial distribution of employment is analyzed in more detail, however, it can be argued that in the postwar period it has been the urban, rather than the industrial, structure of the regions that has been the main factor characterizing changes in the distribution of manufacturing employment (Fothergill and Gudgin, 1982). The decline in manufacturing has been most marked in London and the main conurbations. Manufacturing has been growing rapidly in the county towns (the older, preindustrial towns) and rural areas in whichever region they are located (Table 12.5). The regions with high unemployment are those with con-

Table 12.3

Structure of Employment, United Kingdom, 1952–1979

	1952 (%)	1979 (%)
Agriculture	3.6	1.3
Mining	4.2	1.5
Manufacturing	39.8	33.2
Construction and Utilities	8.4	7.3
Services	44.0	56.7
Total	100.0	100.0

Source: Fothergill and Gudgin, 1982 (Table 3.1)

urbations (except London as a special case). Growth has occurred only in the regions without a conurbation. Thus industrial restructuring is associated with a spatial redistribution of growth in manufacturing at a local rather than a regional scale.

This picture of a highly urbanized country dependent on manufacturing industry is not reflected in the pattern of land use. England and Wales are still largely agricultural, with cropland, permanent grass, and rough grazing occupying 77 percent of the land in 1971 (Table 12.6). Nevertheless, the pattern is changing, the most significant feature being the increase in the urban area from 4.5 percent in 1901 to 11.0 percent in 1971. The rate of conversion from agricultural into urban land has not been constant, however. At its peak during the 1930s, the average annual rate of conversion was 25,100 hectares; by the 1950s it had fallen to 14,800 hectares and to less than 8,000 hectares in the economic recession of the late 1970s (Best, 1981). Indeed, the most significant feature may have been the changes within the agricultural sector from permanent grass to cropland.

The pattern of land uses within the urban areas varies chiefly according to the size of settlement (Best, 1981). Gross densities are at their highest in London, with 105 persons per hectare, falling to a figure of 20 for isolated dwellings and farmsteads (Table 12.7). The provision of land for housing varies in similar fashion, being least (the highest density) in the larger towns. The provision of other land uses is more variable, as well as being much smaller, than for housing (Table 12.8).

Table 12.4
Regional Unemployment Ratios, United Kingdom, 1951–1981

	1951	1961	1971 (UK = 100)	1981
Peripheral regions				
Northern Ireland	468	468	216	161
Scotland	192	193	163	121
Wales	207	163	127	130
North	169	157	160	134
Central regions				
North West	92	100	111	122
Yorkshire/Humberside	69	63	108	108
West Midlands	31	88	108	120
Core regions				
East Midlands	38	63	84	89
South East	)		(54	71
	) 69	63 (		
East Anglia	)		(84	81
South West	92	88	92	88
United Kingdom unemployment (%)	1.3	1.6	3.7	11.4

Sources: Glasson, 1978 (Table 9.3); Great Britain, Central Statistical Office, Annual Abstract of Statistics, 1983 Edition, London, HMSO, 1983.

Table 12.5

Location of Manufacturing Employment, United Kingdom, 1959–1975

	1959 (%)	1975 (%)	1959-75 (% change)
London	18.8	12.4	-38
Conurbations	33.2	29.3	-16
Free-standing cities	20.0	22.1	+ 5
Industrial towns	19.0	23.4	+16
County towns	7.8	10.6	+29
Rural areas	1.2	2.2	+77
Total	100.0	100.0	- 5

Source: Fothergill and Gudgin, 1982 (Table 4.2)

Table 12.6

Structure of Land Use, England and Wales, 1901–1971

	1901 (%)	1931 (%)	1939 (%)	1951 (%)	1971 (%)
Cropland	32.6	25.8	24.1	36.8	37.7
Permanent grass	41.5	42.3	42.3	29.0	26.4
Rough grazing	9.6	14.3	14.9	14.7	12.5
Total: agriculture	83.7	82.4	81.3	80.5	76.6
Woodland	5.0	5.6	6.2	6.5	7.4
Urban land	4.5	6.7	8.0	8.9	11.0
Other land*	6.8	5.3	4.5	4.1	5.0
Total	100.0	100.0	100.0	100.0	100.0

Note: *includes mineral workings, defense, unutilized
rural areas and land unaccounted for.

Source: Best, 1981 (Table 8)

Table 12.7

Urban Area of England and Wales, 1961

Urban category (population)	population (%)	urban area (%)	density (persons/ hectare)
London	7	2	105
Over 100,000	29	18	52
10-100,000	40	35	36
Under 10,000	18	19	29
Isolated dwellings	6	9	20
Transport land	-	17	-
Total urban area	100	100	31

Source: Best, 1981 (Table 10)

Table 12.8

Land Provision in Urban Areas, England and Wales, 1961

	over 500,000 population	50-100,000 population (ha/000 population)	under 10,000 population
Housing*	7.2	10.7	27.4
Industry	1.2	2.0	1.2
Open Space	2.7	4.8	4.0
Education	0.4	1.4	0.7
Other+	3.5	5.5	1.3
Total	15.0	24.4	34.6
Net Residential Density (pers./ hectare)	139	93	36

Notes: *net residential area

+including transport land

Source: Best, 1981 (Table 13)

301

HISTORICAL DEVELOPMENT: ORIGINS AND AIMS OF PLANNING

The planning system in Great Britain had its origins in the reaction to the consequences of the growth and distribution of population and employment. The first town planning act, in 1909, was the culmination of a long period of concern about the growth of towns during the nineteenth century (Cherry, 1972). One strand of that concern had been the attempt to make towns healthy and safe, moving from policing, street lighting, and water supply to standards for new housing and the closure of slums. The other strand had been the growth of idealism through the industrialists and social reformers who sought to design and build model communities, leading to Ebenezer Howard whose book, *Tomorrow, a Peaceful Path to Reform*, had been published in 1898.[5]

The 1909 town planning act was limited in scope, confined to the preparation of planning schemes for new suburbs, and clumsy in operation. But it was paralleled by other significant events. The first garden city built to Howard's principles was started in 1905. The first university department and the first planning journal were established at Liverpool a few years later. And the Town Planning Institute was formed in 1914, creating the new profession of planning (Cherry, 1974).

It took 30 more years for these beginnings to evolve into the reality of a universal and comprehensive system of town planning. The most important event during the 30 years was the report of the royal commission on the geographical distribution of the industrial population, the so-called Barlow report.[6] The Barlow commission was appointed as a result of serious unemployment in the depressed, peripheral regions and the failure of the first attempts at a regional policy in the 1930s. But the commission achieved a wider synthesis, seeing the two, inter-related sides of the regional problem: the high unemployment, out-migration, and social waste of the depressed regions, and the social, economic, and strategic costs of congestion, urban sprawl, and loss of agricultural land in the rapidly growing region between London and Birmingham. The commission's recommendations were simple and far-reaching: a national planning system embracing industrial location, urban land use, and agriculture.

The Barlow report was swiftly followed by reports on land use in rural areas and on the problem of land values. Together they laid the basis for a national planning system. But although the main principles were accepted by government, the responsibility for planning was divided among three departments. Industrial location and regional policy was given to what later became the Department of Industry; agriculture, to the Ministry of Agriculture, Fisheries and Food; and land use planning to a new Ministry of Town and Country Planning, later renamed, and now the Department of the Environment.

Details of the national system of land use planning were worked out during the war years and the legislation enacted in 1947. Once enacted, the main principles of that planning system have remained intact up to the present day. It is only in the 1980s that serious questions are being posed about its future.

The chief reason for the longevity of the planning system is that it was underpinned by a broad, political consensus about its aims. The one significant exception was the question of land values and ownership, on which the political parties were in conflict with new legislation following every change in government. But land use planning itself was judged to be apolitical (McKay and Cox, 1979).

Later commentators identified three principles that guided the design and operation of the planning system, reinforcing its apolitical character (Ravetz, 1980). Planning was judged to be a science, to be interpreted and applied by the professional planner, validating plans by a planning survey. The concept of survey before plan went back to the turn of the century in the work of Patrick Geddes, but its scientific character received even greater emphasis in the new planning of the 1960s (McLoughlin, 1968). Second, planning was universal and comprehensive, applying to the entire country and every form of development. Third, the planning system was based on an assumption that the physical environment could be treated in isolation, separated from the more contentious issues of social conditions and the economy.

Indeed for many planners, the prime purpose for having a planning system was little more than reconciling the competing claims for the use of land so as to provide a consistent, balanced, and orderly arrangement of land uses. For others, the aim was more ambitious: to provide a good physical environment, an essential prerequisite for the promotion of a healthy and civilized life. And for those with still greater ambition, planning would be part of a broader social program of reform (Foley, 1973).

Each of these ideas could be challenged, and, once challenged, the consensus about the aims and methods of the planning system would begin to fragment. This is what eventually began to happen, but, for more than 30 years after 1947, the ideas remained implicit and the consensus survived.

In practical terms, the aims of the planning system could be seen in its dominant images: low-density residential areas, self-contained and socially balanced, whether in the form of a new town or a neighborhood within an existing, larger town; strict control over the further growth of larger towns, including the redevelopment of the congested inner areas to a lower density; and control over industrial location to prevent a concentration of jobs in towns and to encourage regional balance.

At a higher level of abstraction, these aims could be expressed in two ideas: *containment*—the separation of town and country—and *segregation* of functions within towns into primary land use zones. The countryside could be left largely to look after itself, provided it was adequately protected from urban intrusion, especially in areas under greatest threat because of their attractiveness or their proximity to built-up areas. Regional imbalances were to be narrowed, although the main mechanism of control was in the policy for industrial location rather than in land use planning as such. Finally, underpinning these essentially urban ideas about land use planning was the view that the built environment is subject to a process of continuous development and redevelopment such that what Ravetz called the "clean sweep philosophy of planning" was the correct response (Ravetz, 1980).

INSTITUTIONAL AND LANDOWNERSHIP FRAMEWORK, 1947–1980

Town and Country Planning Act, 1947

The postwar planning system was created by the Town and Country Planning Act (1947). The act did not stand alone; it was supplemented by other legislation for land use planning, notably the New Towns Act (1946) and the National Parks and Access to the Countryside Act (1949). It was complemented by parallel legislation in closely related fields, including the Distribution of Industry Act (1945) and its successors and the stream of Housing Acts. Eventually it was replaced by fresh, amending, and consolidating legislation (Heap, 1982).

The crucial principle is that Parliament gave planning to the local authorities. The local authorities were given three duties. First, they were given power to control all development, whether or not there was an approved plan in being. This was a far-reaching power because development was defined as "the carrying out of building, engineering, mining and other operations in, on, over or under land, or the making of a material change in the use of any buildings or other land."[7] Furthermore, no compensation would be paid if planning permission for development was refused. This remedied a vital weakness in the prewar legislation since, in effect, it meant the nationalization of development rights in land.

Second, every local authority was required to carry out a survey and prepare a development plan for its area, showing a 20-year program for development to be reviewed and rolled forward every five years.

Third, local authorities were given the power to prepare plans and, if necessary, compulsorily acquire land for the comprehensive redevelopment of the so-called blitzed and blighted areas (areas of wartime damage and areas of obsolescent buildings and layout) and the development of new, built-up areas.

Parliament reserved two statutory functions for central government. The first was that of giving formal approval to the development plans of the local authorities, following a public inquiry at which objections to the plan by interested parties would be heard. This was clearly necessary if the minister was to discharge his duty for ensuring "consistency and continuity" in the use and development of land. The other function was to hear appeals by aggrieved applicants against a refusal of planning permission for development. This was more complex because it can be simultaneously a quasi-judicial function, ensuring equitable treatment between local authorities and applicants, and a means for ensuring compliance with national policies.

The reference to national policies raises a further point: there is no formal national policy for land use, simply a mechanism for controlling the use and development of land. Nevertheless, the government does have policies from time to time on particular issues. Examples have included the release of land for residential development, encouraging industrial development, maintaining green-belts, and strict control on the location of out-of-town shopping centers. Government is able to express these policies only in ministerial circulars, press notices, and the like, which have no statutory authority. And it can put these policies into practice only through its power to approve development plans and hear appeals. This has created a major source of tension in the planning system (Great Britain, House of Commons, 1978).

Development Control

The chief distinguishing characteristic of the planning system is its reliance on an administrative means of development control, exercised with a wide degree of discretion. The whole system depends on the granting or refusal of planning permission, with or without conditions, for every development. Each decision is taken on its own merits, having "regard to the provisions of the development plan" and any "other material considerations (Section 29(1), Town and Country Planning Act, 1971)." This is crucial. The decision need not be in accord with a statutory plan; there need not even be such a plan. The other considerations may take precedence whether they are specific to the individual application (such as details about the site and its location) or are covered in some nonstatutory form of plan such as a design guide. Indeed the question of what constitutes a material consideration has been the subject of considerable judicial review (McAuslan, 1980).

To make the system workable, a number of limitations have had to be placed on development control. Changes of use within the categories of land use defined in the Use Classes Order (for instance, from one type of shop to another) do not require planning permission. The General Development Order defines several categories of so-called permitted development, such as minor extensions to buildings or, more significantly, agricultural buildings. The General Development Order also exempts development by government departments and local authorities from requiring planning permission, the permission being deemed to be granted when the public expenditure on the development is authorized.[8]

Nonetheless, there is something in excess of 500,000 applications annually for planning permission, ranging from an outline application for the development of, say, 100 hectares of land for housing, which, if granted, will be followed by a further application on the details of the housing layout, design and materials; to a full application for, say, the conversion of a large house into separate apartments.

Development control is detailed and in theory flexible in its operation. But the basis for making decisions is diffuse and complex, the result of consultations with other government departments and the public; the proposals of development plans; other material considerations; even the training, experience, and skill of the individual planning officer (McLoughlin, 1974). The flexibility which Section 29(1) permits is what makes the planning system effective. Yet development control is a negative power, reacting to the initiatives of others. A recent development has been the growth of so-called planning gain in an attempt to make it more positive by giving more initiative to planners. Planners and developers negotiate, and as a result the grant of planning permission may coincide with a legal agreement by which the developer may, for instance, make a financial contribution to the cost of providing utilities on the site or give land for a school or open space (Cadman and Austin-Crowe, 1983).

Development control is the constant element of the planning system in England and Wales. It has been subjected to procedural review, especially following allegations of delay in the time taken to process applications, the range of consultations to be undertaken, and the question of public participation (Great Britain, House of Commons, 1978). The limits of permitted development have altered from time to time. The legitimacy of particular "other material considerations" has been tested through judicial review. But the basic principles have remained unchanged since 1947.

This constancy is perhaps all the more surprising in view of the changes that have affected other parts of the system: the reform of the development plan system in 1968; the reorganization of local government itself in 1974; and the failure to achieve a consistent land policy covering the questions of compensation and betterment and the public ownership of land for planning purposes.

Development Plans

Development plans in the 1947 act were to be precise documents prepared by each local planning authority for its entire area, using a standard notation on a topographic base map. The development plan would start with the county map (scale, 1:63,360) showing the main settlement pattern, communications and special policies for rural areas such as greenbelts, and areas of outstanding natural beauty or mineral workings. Each large settlement would be covered by an inset plan, the town map (scale, 1:10,560) showing primary use zones (residential, industrial, commercial, and others), the distribution of population, and the average gross residential density within defined areas. Where necessary, further inset plans would be prepared in even greater detail for areas for comprehensive development or redevelopment.

The development plan would be accompanied by a program map, showing the changes of use expected in the first five years after approval and the next 15 years. These two sets of plans and a written statement, which would do little more than contain the basic assumptions about population and employment and a list of the proposals on the maps, would comprise the statutory document. In addition, the local planning authority was required to carry out and publish a report of survey. The whole plan was to be reviewed and rolled forward every five years. At each stage the plan would be open to objection at a public inquiry and would then be approved by the responsible minister of central government.

The system was put into operation and lasted 20 years, by which time the entire country was covered by approved development plans prepared by a fairly standardized methodology (Keeble, 1961). But by 1963 the system needed updating. The time taken to prepare a plan and get it approved was proving very lengthy, chiefly because of the extent to which central government was overwhelmed by the mass of detail to be checked. As a result, the quinquennial reviews were postponed and plans were becoming out of date.

But the reviews increasingly were necessary. Many of the assumptions in the original plans were proving wrong: population was growing faster than anticipated, levels of home and car ownership were rising, and patterns of retailing and leisure were changing. Emphasis in the development process was switching from the public to the private sector, with a consequent rise in the number of planning applications and increasing reliance on development control. But development control was having to work under increasing pressure without the benefit of up-to-date plans, bringing into disrepute the entire planning system.

The answer was for government to appoint a Planning Advisory Group to report on the future development plans (Great Britain, Ministry of Housing and Local Government, 1965). Its main recommendation was to reform the system of development plans by disentangling strategic and local decisions, each of which would have its appropriate form of plan and procedure for approval.

Structure plans would be robust documents, concentrating on strategic issues affecting the entire area and expressing policies in terms that would be flexible, retaining their credibility notwithstanding detailed changes in the underlying assumptions. The plans therefore would be written statements of policy, and their reasoned justification would be illustrated diagrammatically. The form and content of each structure plan would relate to the specific issues for that area rather than follow a standard notation (Great Britain, Ministry of Housing and Local Government, 1970). The structure plan would be approved by the minister, who would have to be satisfied not only on the technical strength of the analysis and proposals and their relationship to national and regional policies but also on the extent to which the public had been involved in preparing the plan. Finally, instead of a public inquiry on quasi-judicial lines at which every objector would have a right to be heard, the minister would appoint a panel of experts to conduct an examination in public at which government departments and interest groups concerned with the key issues would discuss the proposals.

Local plans would carry forward in more specific detail the proposals of the structure plan to provide a framework for development control, to coordinate land use planning, and to bring issues before the public (Fudge et al., 1982). They would have a proposals map on a large-scale, detailed topographic base map, as well as a written statement of policies and their justification. Unlike the old town map, however, the proposals map would not necessarily show a full coverage of primary land use zones nor would it show a program for development. It was much more a guide or exhortation, which planning officials and developers should follow during a comparatively short period rather than a long-term plan for implementation. Furthermore, provided it was in accordance with its parent structure plan, the local plan could simply be adopted by the local authority following public participation and a public inquiry.

The new system of structure and local plans was established in the Town and Country Planning Act (1968). Its measures for public participation were strengthened in the Town and Country Planning Act of 1971 following publication of a report on public participation (Great Britain, Ministry of Housing and Local Government, 1969).[9] The new system would be introduced gradually as it became necessary for a local authority to review its development plans. Until then the old development plan would remain operative.

Fifteen years later, four of the 54 counties of England and Wales still have not had their structure plan approved, and statutory local plans are in force for only a small part of the country (Bruton, 1983). Indeed the current intention is that statutory local plans will be prepared and approved only for those areas where it is essential because of pressures for development or the necessity for conservation. Instead most local authorities rely on a great variety of unofficial policies in the sense that they are nonstatutory, including informal local plans, design briefs and guides, and development control policy notes.

There are several reasons for this slow progress. One has been the propensity of planners to use more sophisticated methods of plan preparation and the requirement for public participation. Structure plans in particular have sought to be more comprehensive than the old development plans with a much more explicit exploration of alternatives and justification for the preferred plan. But perhaps the crucial reason was the reorganization of local government in 1974.

Planning and Local Government

The Planning Advisory Group did its work at a time of intense debate about the form and functions of local government in England and Wales. The old system created in 1888 comprised a patchwork of county boroughs covering the main towns, usually with very tightly drawn boundaries, and administrative counties, which often contained the more recent suburbs. Both were controlled by elected councils, but the distribution of functions was different in the two types of authority. County boroughs were all-purpose authorities, responsible for the entire range of local government services, including town and country planning. Counties were two-tier authorities, the county council being responsible for a fairly large group of functions including town and country planning; the more local services, such as housing, were provided by urban and rural district councils.

The system had many critics. From a planning point of view, the chief criticism was the arbitrary separation of the county borough from its surrounding suburbs and countryside. The other chief criticism was the proliferation of districts thought to be too small for efficient operation.

The emerging orthodoxy was that a more efficient local government system should be created to tackle both of these problems. A royal commission was appointed. It recommended a two-tier system for the three major provincial conurbations of Birmingham, Manchester, and Liverpool following the precedent established for London in 1963. But for the rest of the country, it recommended a system of unitary authorities sufficiently large for the efficient provision of services, with boundaries that would overcome the flaw of the divide between town and country.

Thus the Planning Advisory Group assumed that structure plans, local plans, and development control would be the statutory responsibility of a single local authority; however, the recommendations of the Redcliffe-Maud commission were rejected by the new Conservative government in 1970. Instead a different system was introduced by the Local Government Act of 1972, coming into operation on 1 April 1974 (Alexander, 1982). The idea of two-tier government for the metropolitan areas (increased from three to six by the inclusion of conurbations based on Newcastle, Leeds, and Sheffield) was retained and extended to the rest of the country, with comparatively few substantial changes in county boundaries but a widespread amalgamation of the old, small districts into new, larger districts. In other words, the principle of size and efficiency was generally accepted, but that of the unification of town and country was rejected.

The division of functions between the two tiers in the metropolitan and non-metropolitan (the shire) counties was different. The majority of functions (including the major spending services of education, social services, and housing) went to the district councils in the metropolitan counties and to the county councils in the shire counties. Responsibility for water supply, sewerage, and drainage was taken from local government and given to new, regional water authorities appointed by central government.

Town and country planning, however, was exercised concurrently by both tiers in both types of county, thus adding administrative confusion to the division of town from country. The county councils were responsible for structure planning. The district councils were responsible for most of development control, although there was a gray area of so-called county matters (such as matters of structural importance) for which county councils could be responsible. And counties and districts had to agree on a division of responsibility for local plans. In practice, the majority of local plans have been prepared and adopted by district councils, although they still have to be certified by the county council as being in accord with the structure plan.

This meant that local government planning during the 1970s was seriously hampered by arbitrary boundaries and confusion over powers. Much of the confusion over powers was resolved by the Local Government, Planning and Land Act (1980), which in effect stripped from the county councils virtually all powers for development control other than the right to be consulted.

So by 1980, the formal situation was that the Greater London Council, the six metropolitan county councils, and the 47 shire county councils in England and Wales were responsible for the preparation and review of structure plans; had retained, in agreement with their district councils, responsibility for a few local plans (chiefly the subject plans dealing with matters of specialized control such as for mineral workings or greenbelts); and had responsibility for a very narrow, well-defined range of development control (again, chiefly, mineral workings). All other matters rested with the 402 district councils, though local plans still had to be in accord with the structure plan.[10]

The Land Issue: Acquisition, Compensation, and Betterment

From the Barlow report up to the 1980 act, there has been general political support for the system of land use planning. This has not been the case with the question of land values, which has been a highly contentious political issue with major shifts in policy at every change of government (McKay and Cox, 1979).

The problem has two roots. Land in England and Wales is largely in private ownership, though the pattern of ownership is highly complex and unknown (Massey and Catalano, 1978). The creation of a planning system meant that land values, instead of being determined by the market, would be the result of planning decisions, whether a development plan or the grant of planning permission. Land values would rise or fall depending on whether the future use of land was in accord with planning policy. And it could be argued that a landowner who suffered a fall in the value of land should be entitled to compensation, although equally it could be argued that one who profited from an increase in value should pay part of the increase to the state.

It was this problem that largely undermined effective planning between 1909 and 1947. The Uthwatt committee was appointed to tackle the problem. It rejected nationalization of land as politically impractical and instead recommended in effect the nationalization of all development rights in land while leaving its actual ownership untouched. This solution, with many qualifications, was put into practice in the 1947 act (Cullingworth, 1982).

The assumption underlying the act was that the great majority of development would be in the public sector through the comprehensive development by local authorities of the blitzed and blighted areas, through local authority housing estates, and through new town development corporations. The total forecast increase in population was quite small, the wartime system of building licenses would remain in force, and the role of the private sector would be limited.

The 1947 act attempted a comprehensive solution. No compensation would be paid for a refusal of planning permission. Instead a once-and-for-all payment would be paid as compensation for any loss of development value at the date on which the act came into force. A development charge would be made on any subsequent increase in value, levied on a grant of planning permission for development. The charge was set at 100 percent, in effect leaving the landowner with existing use value. Third, land to be compulsorily acquired for planning purposes would be bought at existing use value.

The system was logical and internally consistent. The problem was that by setting the development charge at 100 percent, landowners were left with no incentive to dispose of their land for development. The incoming Conservative government abolished the development charge in 1953-54 and with a few exceptions restored market value as the basis of compensation for compulsory purchase. It did leave untouched, however, the principle of no compensation for a refusal of planning permission, thus enabling development control to continue, albeit as a negative form of planning.

And that was the problem. An effective planning policy depended not only on the negative power to prevent undesirable development but also on the positive power to ensure desirable development. But that could be prevented by landowners' holding back land from development for whatever reason or by the cost of compulsorily acquiring land at market value. There was, in addition, the question of whether the community should reap all or part of the increase in the value of land generated by the community's own planning scheme. Land policy after 1959 went through two complete reversals, with Labour governments introducing schemes in 1967 and 1975 and Conservative governments abolishing the schemes in 1971 and 1980 before they had time to take effect. The one surviving remnant is the development land tax, unrelated in its present form to land use planning. It owes its survival to the rapid inflation in land values, especially between 1967 and 1973 when there was a threefold increase in real terms (Cullingworth, 1982).

Thus, the only achievement of four decades of argument about land policy is a system of development control that can be exercised without regard to questions of land values but that profoundly affects land values. Land transactions, whether in the private sector or involving acquisition by the public sector, are at full market value subject only to a development land tax imposed for fiscal reasons. This, it can be argued, results in a land use planning system able to operate only through negative controls.

ISSUES AND CHALLENGES, 1947–1980

The planning system created in 1947 continued to operate until 1980 with remarkably few significant changes other than the question of land values. Yet its social, economic, and political context changed dramatically, even setting aside the reorganization of local government.

Roughly the period falls into three phases. Between 1947 and about 1963, the system set up by the initial legislation was being put into operation. Development plans were prepared on the assumption of a fairly low increase in population. Development control was set in motion. Regional policy for the location of industry was initiated. The first new towns and national parks were established. It was a period of traditional land use planning.

By the early 1960s, the context was changing. Assumptions about future growth were rapidly increasing, reaching a peak in 1965 when the population of Britain was forecast to rise from 52 million to 75 million by the end of the century (Hall, 1982). Planning was concerned not only with provision for a much larger population but also for rising standards, including a massive slum clearance program and facing up to road traffic. There was renewed interest in regional physical planning and strong regional economic planning. The new structure plans enshrined the planning style of the period: comprehensive, rational, and objective.

The period came to an end with the collapse of the property boom and, coincidentally, the reorganization of local government in 1974. The new period, however, was marked not only by economic recession but rapidly diminishing expectations about future growth. By 1979, the forecast population of Britain by the end of the century was down to 57.3 million (Hall, 1982). The period came to be dominated by inner-city issues and the problems of countering economic and urban decline. Planners became much more concerned about the problems of implementing their plans at a time when the capacity for intervention by local government was being eroded by cuts in public expenditure, yet private sector investment in industry, commerce, and housing was at a low ebb.

The planning system during these three decades was learning its job and facing a long and varied list of issues and problems it was expected to resolve. They ranged from the siting of a third London airport (still not resolved after 25 years of controversy and inquiry) to devising techniques for the control of advertisements.

Two main themes can be singled out that have dominated planning from 1947 to the present day. One is the regional distribution of population and employment and the question of the relationship between town and countryside. These were the key issues raised by the Barlow report, in a sense the main reasons for which the planning system was created. The theme can be illustrated by a brief review of five areas of policy: regional planning, control over the location of industry, new towns, greenbelts, and national parks.

The second theme is that of local, urban planning, amounting to a major restructuring of the pattern and appearance of towns exercised through the statutory machinery of the 1947 act. It can be illustrated through two issues, the relationships between land use and, respectively, transportation and housing; and four policies: town center redevelopment, slum clearance and redevelopment, suburban expansion, and conservation.

Containment of Urban England

Regional Planning

Physical planning at the regional scale has a fragmented history in England and Wales. Before 1939, many local authorities combined into joint planning boards to prepare advisory regional plans (Cherry, 1974). But with the advent of statutory land use planning, regional physical planning decayed. It came back into favor in the 1960s, partly in response to the real problems of the planning of London, spreading over much of southeast England, partly in the shift toward the rational-objective style of planning. The *South East Study*, prepared in 1964 by officials of the Ministry of Housing and Local Government, paved the way. The idea was quickly extended to the rest of England following the appointment by central government of Economic Planning Councils for each of the standard regions.

The Planning Advisory Group had assumed that regional plans would provide the context for structure and local plans. The new regional strategies did this, showing proposals for capital investment based on forecasts about regional growth and assumptions about the distribution of population and employment. The problem was their uncertain status. The strategies were prepared by, and for, planning councils, which were responsible to a minister. They had no statutory authority. No procedure was laid down for their preparation or for public participation. Nevertheless, while they lasted, the strategies provided a useful coordinating framework, bridging the gaps between national and local planning and between separate departments of central government. Yet the planning councils were abolished in 1980 in the reaction against government intervention, and the strategies, prepared in the optimistic years before 1974, are of little more than historic interest.

The regional strategies were supplemented during the 1960s by a series of subregional studies for a number of conurbations in which planning issues transcended local government boundaries (Cowling and Steeley, 1973). They were the forcing ground for the new, integrated land use–transportation planning, which came to the fore after publication of the Buchanan report, *Traffic in Towns* (Great Britain, Ministry of Transport, 1963). But they were also a main source of research and development in the new techniques of comprehensive planning used extensively in the subsequent preparation of structure plans.

Location of Industry

Regional policy in Britain means control over the location of industry, exercised by the Department of Industry and its predecessors. The main aim of the policy has been to reduce unemployment in the depressed regions by stimulating the creation of new employment in those regions. Positive measures have included a bundle of loans, grants, and other financial assistance to firms setting up in, or moving to, the development areas. Currently they include the regional development grant, which provides a fixed percentage of the capital cost of new investment, and selective financial assistance, which, as its name implies, is discretionary. In addition, the positive measures include the construction of industrial estates and factories for incoming firms and improvements in regional communications. The most effective measure was the regional employment premium, which operated between 1966 and 1976 when it had to be withdrawn under EEC rules (Glasson, 1978).

The negative measures were simple. Planning permission for a new factory or factory extension could be granted only if the Department of Industry issued an industrial development certificate. Certificates were readily granted for factories and extensions in the development areas, but at its toughest operation were refused elsewhere, especially in the Midlands and southeast England.

Although the policy remained in force between 1945 and 1980, its operation altered from time to time. Areas qualifying for assistance varied, reaching a peak between 1966 and 1980 when 40 percent of Britain was covered in a hierarchy, ranging from special development areas such as Merseyside or the south Wales coalfield, where the rates of grant were largest, to the intermediate areas. Policies were at their strongest during the early 1950s and then between 1966 and about 1973. Since 1973, the regional policy has been progressively eroded, with the termination of the regional employment premium in 1976, the relaxation of industrial development certificates, and, after 1980, a considerable reduction in the extent of the assisted areas, which now cover about 25 percent of Britain (Hall, 1982).

Regional policy was effective, adding at its peak about 250,000 jobs in manufacturing industry, or about 10 percent of the 1962 level in the north of England, Wales, Scotland, and Northern Ireland (Fothergill and Gudgin, 1982). Policy was much less effective in the 1970s following the erosion of its instruments and the general economic recession. But there were other reasons. There was a change in emphasis in 1972, giving greater priority to the modernization of industry. There was a growing concern with inner-city issues, irrespective of the region within which they were located. And the policy focused almost exclusively on manufacturing industry apart from a short-lived attempt between 1964 and 1979 to control office development in London.

New Towns

New towns had their origin in the garden city movement. Letchworth and Welwyn had been started in 1907 and 1920 through private initiative. The idea was endorsed in the Barlow report, the aim being to receive the overspill of population and employment from the congested cities or to act as a focus for regional growth in the depressed regions. But in both cases, they were to be self-contained communities, an alternative to the unplanned sprawl that had previously been the method of urban growth.

The New Towns Act (1946) put the idea into practice. Each new town would be designed, built, and managed by a development corporation appointed by government. The corporations would have powers for the compulsory acquisition of land. They would be financed by exchequer advances from government but were intended to become financially viable in the long run (Cullingworth, 1982).

Twenty-three new towns were designated in England and Wales between 1946 and 1970 and five in Scotland. The first batch in England and Wales quickly followed passing of the act. They were to have a target population of between 30,000 and 50,000, designed to be self-contained and balanced communities for living and work, based on neighborhood principles and constructed to what, at the time, were thought to be low densities. The eight London new towns were to receive population and employment from London itself. The other four were to be growth centers in areas of regional decline.

No new towns were designated in England and Wales during the 1950s.[11] Instead, an alternative approach was used, the so-called expanded towns program under the Town Development Act (1952). Local authorities were enabled to enter into a partnership for the overspill of population and employment from a major, congested city to a more distant smaller town. Roughly 70 schemes were started, about 30 from London to places such as Swindon and the rest from the other main conurbations.

Another six new towns were designated in the early 1960s. Four were to receive overspill from Merseyside and the west Midlands, designed on the new principles introduced at Cumbernauld. A fifth new town was intended to stimulate growth in a declining rural area. But the sixth new town of this group was different. Far from being an attempt to prevent the peripheral growth of conurbations, Washington was intended to accommodate the growth of Tyneside as part of a program of regional development.

Finally, five more new towns were designated between 1967 and 1971 and one of the earlier ones extended. All of this last batch had new objectives and were very different from the earlier new towns, their only similarity being their use of the development corporation mechanism and exchequer funding. They were a response to the inflated forecasts of future population growth. The planned population of each was between 200,000 and 500,000. They were located in relation to national communications. Four of the six were to be extensions to existing medium-sized cities, and only one, Milton Keynes, was to be a new settlement. And in all of them, a high proportion of development was to be by the private sector (Osborn and Whittick, 1977).

The new towns program ended in 1971 when national planning policy took a different course with the economic recession, the reduction in forecast population, and the emergence of the inner-city issue. Indeed the new urban development corporations for the Merseyside and London docklands are the inheritors of the new towns as a device for managing urban development.

The new towns were highly significant in their role as seedbeds for successive waves of ideas about new concepts for urban living and the urban environment and in the success of the development corporation as a device for getting things done notwithstanding tight treasury control. The earlier new towns have long since completed their planned growth and have become financially viable. Many of the development corporations have been wound up, their assets handed over initially to a Commission for the New Towns and, after 1978, to the local authorities.

But despite their achievements and the lessons they afford, the contribution of the new towns has been small in comparison with that of the public sector (council housing) and the private sector. All 23 new towns housed only an additional 854,000 by 1980, giving them a total population of 1.8 million, with a further third of a million in the expanded towns (Cullingworth, 1982).

Greenbelts

New towns represented the positive side of the policy for containing the growth of towns within a regional framework. Greenbelts were the converse. The clearest definition of their role came in 1955 when government encouraged local authorities to propose greenbelts as a means of containing the growth of conurbations, preventing the coalescence of separate towns, and preserving the special character of individual towns (Cullingworth, 1982).

By now most of the English conurbations are surrounded by greenbelts enshrined in development plans, defined with precision on large-scale maps, and subjected to stringent development control to prevent new buildings or changes of use. Nevertheless, there are no additional planning powers in greenbelts; it is simply that existing powers are exercised more rigorously and refusals of planning permission upheld on appeal.

Two important qualifications must be made about greenbelts, however. The first concerns the strength of the policy in practice. To some extent, the greenbelt has become a movable feast, with pressure for its erosion on its inner edge and a propensity to extend its outer limits. Thus in the early 1960s and again in the 1970s during periods of an apparent shortage of land for new housing, government encouraged local authorities to release greenbelt land where its loss would not harm the amenity of the area. And counties around London, such as Hertfordshire and Berkshire, sought to extend their greenbelts when reviewing their structure plans.

The second qualification goes back to the aims of greenbelts. Official policy has focused on their negative function. But planners have also sought a more positive function: for recreation, for their scenic value, or even for the maintenance of tracts of ordinary countryside within which farming and rural pursuits can continue. Nevertheless, it is as a control on the spread of towns that greenbelts have their most "popular appeal, widely used by the general public" (Cherry, 1972, 162).

National Parks

The countryside outside the towns for the most part was unaffected by land use planning except in the sense of its protection from urban development. Nevertheless, stronger measures were necessary if "areas of beautiful and relatively wild country [were to] have their beauty strictly preserved, access amply provided, wildlife and buildings of historic interest protected and farming maintained" (Cherry, 1972, 162). These were the aims set for the 10 national parks created under the National Parks and Access to the Countryside Act (1949). All of the parks are in the west and north of the country, and in all of them agriculture is the predominant land use, admittedly much of it rough grazing.

The national parks cover 9.0 percent of England and Wales (Best, 1981). A further 9.0 percent is covered by areas of outstanding natural beauty, and there are heritage coasts in which the emphasis is on the preservation of beauty rather than access and recreation (Cullingworth, 1982).

Responsibility for the system is shared between central and local government. The National Parks Commission (renamed the Countryside Commission in 1968) advises on the designation of national parks and the rest, but their planning and management is by the local authorities, using the town and country planning legislation for development plans and development control, with grants-in-aid from government.

The whole package covers a large part of rural England and Wales. Together with the greenbelts and the areas of high landscape value and special scientific interest designated in development plans, preservation of the countryside from intrusive urban development forms a main thrust of planning policy. That policy is under continuous threat from three directions. There have been the so-called alien intrusions in national parks: nuclear power, oil refineries, mineral workings, water supply. In each, the conflict has been between national interest (and, in many, local economic interest) and the preservation of amenity with amenity losing out in most cases.

The other two sources of conflict are more insidious because they bring into question the aims of policy. One is the conflict between amenity and recreation. Pressure on the national parks and heritage coasts is intense, risking the destruction of the very features which led to their designation in the first place. The response has been to adopt more positive planning and management within the parks to cater for the increased demand, and to create country parks as 'honey pots' to attract people seeking active recreation.

The third source of conflict is that between the traditional rural activities of farming and forestry and the amenity interest. The assumption in the 1940s was that a prosperous agriculture was the best safeguard of the countryside. It underpinned the philosophy of the national parks and the urban bias in the planning legislation. But the assumption is now seriously challenged as a prosperous agriculture, based on mechanization and intensive farming, is changing the character of the rural landscape (Shoard, 1980).

Local Urban Planning

Land Use and Transportation

Land use and transportation were kept apart by administrative boundaries during the 1940s and 1950s, the responsibility of different departments of central government and, in many cases, local government. Transport planning itself was divided among highways, railways, and bus operators. Nevertheless, there were considerable advances in an understanding of the relationship, notably in the planning of the new towns in which Cumbernauld became the first to be based on the new techniques of transport modeling.

The real transformation came with the publication of *Traffic in Towns* (Great Britain, Ministry of Transport, 1963). The argument was straightforward: towns must have areas of good environment for living and working where the needs of the pedestrian should be paramount and a complementary network of roads for vehicular movement. The report demonstrated that this could be achieved only by a massive investment to provide the necessary road space or by curtailing the use of vehicles. The alternative would be "poor traffic access and a grievously eroded environment."

Integrated land use and transportation studies thereafter became the order of the day, initially in the subregional studies of the 1960s and later in the structure planning of the 1970s. Traffic management became common practice as part of the environmental planning of town centers and conservation areas.

For four years after 1970, land use and transport were brought together in the newly formed Department of Environment, but the experiment was short-lived, and the two are once again in separate departments. There was more progress at the local level (except in London where responsibility remains hopelessly divided to the present day). Passenger transport authorities were set up in the metropolitan areas in 1968 to coordinate rail and bus services. The move was given greater force in 1973 when county councils were required to prepare within the context of their structure plans an annual transport policy and program (TPP) showing proposals for investment in highways and public transport and policies for traffic management and parking. This TPP would then be the basis for the annual grant-in-aid by central government for transportation. It became the link between land use and transport planning at the local level. But financial responsibility remains divided at the center where cuts can fall randomly, making nonsense of the plans.

Town Center Redevelopment

Virtually every town in the country prepared a scheme for the comprehensive redevelopment of its central area between 1948 and 1973. At first, the schemes were for the reconstruction of blitzed cities such as Plymouth and Coventry. The movement gathered strength after the removal of building licenses in 1954. The Victorian leases, under which so many town centers had been built in the nineteenth century, were coming up for renewal. In other cities, it was a matter of extending in depth the old high street by building on the backland of fringe uses or on neighboring sites cleared of slum housing (Cherry, 1972).

The redevelopment process was quite standardized. Land was acquired by the local authority, if necessary compulsorily, using its powers under the planning acts. Designs were prepared for the complete reconstruction of the area with pedestrian precincts and malls, hotels, and offices, the volume of new development being controlled by plot ratios that theoretically permitted an innovative approach to design but in practice usually resulted in tall tower blocks for offices or, occasionally, local authority housing. A new road layout was designed with separate access for servicing and car parking. And the whole development was undertaken in partnership with a developer or property company using finance invested by insurance companies and pension funds (Marriott, 1967). The benefit to the local authority lay in a new road system and car parking, increased rateable value, and the prestige of a modern, successful town center. For the developer, who would lease the land from the local authority, the benefit would be a profitable investment.

The appearance of many town centers had been transformed by the mid-1970s and the continued existence of commercial activity at the heart of towns ensured. But there were problems. Office development in London in the 1960s was so rapid that it appeared to be undercutting the prevailing policy for dispersal from the capital. In 1964, the government banned office development in central London, legislating for office development permits; setting up the Location of Offices Bureau to advise on the relocation of offices out of London; and dispersing some of its own offices. The policy had limited success. New office centers were established in the outer suburbs of London, such as Croydon, and in Reading and Bristol and other places with good communications to London. But, arguably, the steep rise in rentals was as much responsible for the dispersal as government policy. And the policy went into reverse in 1977 with the emergence of the inner-city policy.

A second problem was the competing pressure for out-of-town shopping centers. This was resisted by planning policy during the 1960s on the ground of possible damage to existing town centers. But gradually resistance diminished, and by the late 1970s there was a wide network of hypermarkets, usually in suburban locations and near motorway exits. But the typical hypermarket was much smaller than the North American prototype and more concerned with consumer goods.

The third problem, or issue, was the belated reaction against comprehensive redevelopment and the loss of historic or cherished environments. By the time this issue came to dominate planning thinking, most town centers had already been redeveloped, and the collapse of the property boom after 1973 effectively brought to an end the commercial pressure for major schemes for town center redevelopment (Ambrose and Colenutt, 1975).

Housing and Planning

Housing policy in England and Wales is closely interrelated with planning policy at every level, from central government, where they both are the responsibility of the secretary of state for the environment, to local government, where local authorities have to prepare a housing investment program similar to the transport policy and program. Furthermore, housing is by far the largest user of land in urban areas (see Table 12.8).

Housing policy is a vast subject and cannot be treated here (Short, 1982). But the most important facts can be briefly summarized. The system of housing tenure is quite distinctive and has changed dramatically since 1951, with a rise

Table 12.9

Housing Tenure in England and Wales, 1951 and 1981

	1951	1981
Households:		
Owner occupied	31	58
Rented, public sector	17	31
Rented, private sector	52	11
	100	100

Sources: Great Britain, Housing Policy: a

Consultative Document (Cmnd 6851),

London, HMSO, 1977.

Great Britain, Office of Population

Censuses and Surveys, Census 1981:

National Report, Great Britain, Part 1,

London, HMSO, 1983.

in the proportion of owner-occupied dwellings and those rented in the public sector and a very sharp fall in privately rented housing (Table 12.9).

Over 8 million new houses were built in the United Kingdom between 1952 and 1976, slightly more than half by the public sector and the rest by the private sector (McKay and Cox, 1979). But the two sectors were sharply divided. Public sector houses originally were built for general needs, but increasingly after 1954 they were to meet the special housing needs of the elderly, people living in overcrowded conditions, the homeless, and so on and, after resumption of the slum clearance program, to rehouse the displaced population. The replacement housing itself was divided among the redevelopment of cleared sites, overspill council housing estates on the edge of towns, and the new towns. The council house program was supported by subsidies from central government, which exercised strict control of costs and standards.

Houses for owner occupation were built almost exclusively in the suburbs, small towns, and villages. Their location and appearance were controlled under planning legislation. The motivating force was the system of mortgage finance, which itself incorporated substantial subsidies through tax relief on interest payments. Virtually none of this new house building was on inner-city redevelopment sites, and only a small proportion was in the form of flats or apartments. Conservative policy in recent years has been to encourage tenants to buy their council and new town dwellings.

The collapse of the private rented sector was the result of many factors. The oldest, and worst, dwellings were demolished as slums, and many of the better ones were bought by their tenants and improved or modernized with government grants. The legislation for rent control and security of tenure and the absence of tax relief made this sector an uneconomic proposition for landlords and the absence of subsidy an unpopular one for tenants.

Urban Renewal

The plans of the 1940s had seen that the blitzed and blighted areas had to be cleared and rebuilt on modern principles. Congested and unfit dwellings mingled haphazardly with factories, workshops, and warehouses in an obsolete road layout. The aims were the segregation of housing from industry, the removal of nonconforming uses, and a general reduction in densities. The means of implementing the plans lay with the housing acts as clearance and redevelopment were to be by the public sector. Private sector redevelopment was shown to be unprofitable due to the high cost of site acquisition and preparation and the lack of demand.

The key concepts were the unfit dwelling and the clearance area. Unfit dwellings were defined in terms of physical criteria, including lack of basic amenities such as a bathroom. Clearance areas included unfit dwellings and any other buildings needing to be demolished in order to permit a new housing layout built to modern standards. Redevelopment had to be at a comparatively high density (up to 500 persons per hectare) for many reasons: high land values, opposition to overspill from neighboring counties, the need to conserve agricultural land, and architectural fashion for high-rise buildings. The key factor probably was the need for a much larger slum clearance program and the belief that this could be accomplished cheaply and quickly by using new, industrialized building techniques, which required large, cleared sites for operation. With hindsight, almost every assumption in this catalog proved incorrect; nevertheless the urban renewal of the 1960s was typified by high-rise buildings.

Urban renewal policy started to change direction in the late 1960s. The worst slums had been cleared. The concept of unfitness was under challenge because it took no account of location and environment or indeed of the costs and benefits of clearance. The length of time taken to complete the process of renewal and the social upheaval it generated were other factors. The last straw was the growing public rejection of the new "city of towers," whether the cause was bad design, poor construction, or inadequate maintenance and management (Davies, 1980).

The alternative concept of gradual renewal, or neighborhood revitalization, emerged in the Housing Act of 1974. It provided for a bundle of measures, including general improvement areas, where improvement grants for dwellings were matched by environmental improvements, including landscaping and traffic management; housing action areas, where a higher level of improvement grant, support for housing associations, and additional powers for local authority action were available to enforce policies in areas of housing stress; clearance and redevelopment where necessary but on a much smaller scale; and a general availability of improvement grants for older houses wherever they were located.

The effect of the change can be seen in a few statistics. Between 1945 and 1979, 1.5 million dwellings were demolished in England and Wales, but 3.3 million improvement grants were made (Gibson and Langstaff, 1982). The policy became even more flexible in 1980, with a greater use of repairs grants, as it became clear that the chief problem in the older housing stock was no longer unfitness but disrepair. Notwithstanding good intentions, however, the urban renewal program fluctuated throughout the 1970s as government used it as a means of increasing or cutting public expenditure as part of its macroeconomic policy.

Suburban Development

The majority of new housing construction has been on the edge of towns, whether for owner occupation or council tenancies. In either case, the influence of the planning system has been strong given the initial demand for new housing. The policy has been to promote development on large sites in areas designated for housing, imposing a comprehensive plan on estate design. The plan has covered the layout of roads and pedestrian routes on the principle of segregating fast-moving traffic; the layout and design of houses; the provision of primary schools, local shops, and open spaces, often on neighborhood principles; and the incorporation of existing buildings, trees, and hedgerows in the design. Furthermore, the policy has been systematically to discourage individual houses other than as infill on small sites within villages (Hall et al., 1973). But even here planners have been working with current trends as the private house building industry has come under the control of a small number of volume house builders and the building societies have favored a narrow range of house types on which to lend money.

In effect, planners have sought to educate developers to a particular view of site planning and development, which they have been willing to accept. The instruments of control have been the statutory local plan, informal design briefs for the site indicating the planners' wishes, the grant of outline planning permission with conditions, and the subsequent grant of full permission covering details. A more recent trend has been for the developer also to pay a contribution toward the cost of providing infrastructure or to donate land for public uses. This form of planning gain has become a distinctive feature of development control (Healey, 1983).

The real area of conflict has been on the release of land for residential development, especially during the early 1960s and the 1970s. There were complaints of land shortages in southeast England and the Midlands. A number of studies were carried out, suggesting that the problem was more complex than simple enforcement of greenbelt and other restrictive policies. The current situation is that planners are required to ensure a five-year supply of land through joint studies with developers of land availability (Cullingworth, 1982).

Unlike the problems of urban renewal, the planning and development of the new suburbs has been comparatively little studied until recently. But it must be judged one of the main outcomes of the postwar planning system and, arguably, one that has met the needs of people more satisfactorily than many other achievements of the system.

Conservation and Amenity

It has been said that "amenity is one of the key concepts in British town and country planning; yet nowhere in the legislation is it defined" (Cullingworth, 1982, 122). It permeates every aspect of local planning. There are special regulations for the control of advertisements, the protection of trees, and the preservation of listed buildings of architectural and historic interest. Grants are available for the repair of listed buildings, the restoration of derelict land, and environmental and traffic management.

Much of this is promoted by the conservation lobby, a network of national and local interest groups (Dobby, 1978). The Civic Amenities Act (1967) gave local authorities power to declare conservation areas. The areas range from the medieval center of York to the Georgian terraces of Bath and the Victorian villas of Bristol, from attractive villages to a few twentieth-century council housing estates.

Declaration of a conservation area usually is not much more than an indication that development control over the appearance of new buildings and alterations to old buildings will be much more strictly enforced; however, grants can be available for environmental work in some conservation areas, and in all areas planning permission is uniquely required for the demolition of buildings.

Conservation areas, like greenbelts, are probably the most readily understood and popular instruments of planning policy, at least for the people most directly affected. They are intelligible to a lay public, and their impact is both visible and acceptable.

The other aspect of amenity is more contentious. This is so-called aesthetic control, or the power of local authorities to take into account the detailed siting, design, and construction of new buildings, including the materials to be used, in granting planning permission. It has been a constant source of dispute between, on the one hand, professional planners and planning committees of councillors and, on the other hand, developers and their architects. The matter has never been resolved. The courts have said that aesthetic control is a legitimate "other material consideration" to be taken into account in development control. But the most recent government advice is that it should be used sparingly, confined largely to conservation areas.

APPROACHES TO PLANNING: THEORY AND PRACTICE, 1947–80

Planning theory and practice matured during the period. At first, when techniques and procedures for the new planning system were being worked out, theory and practice were closely in accord and relatively straightforward, a single paradigm found in every local planning authority, new town corporation, and consultancy. By the end of the period, the system had fragmented into a wide range of theories, for the most part divorced from the equally wide variety of methods used in planning practice.

Many would argue that the variety, if not the divorce of theory from practice, was a healthy and legitimate response to the diversity of social and economic conditions, administrative styles, and political contexts under which planners had to work in different areas or at different times (Underwood, 1980). The fragmentation arose from a number of factors, including the growing dominance of the social sciences, displacing the traditional, design-based disciplines; the growth of an ideology of public participation; and the politicization of planning.

Planning in the 1950s was still dominated by professional planners trained in the design discipline, chiefly architecture. It was the urban design tradition applied to the grouping of buildings and allocation of land uses expressed in the form of a master plan. The plan was given greater sophistication by the addition of a fourth dimension, showing the stages by which it would be implemented and a procedure for rolling the plan forward. But it was a comprehensive, urban land use plan, allocating the entire urban space to defined uses and setting a clear edge to that space.

Planning in the 1960s marked the emergence of a new paradigm. It came to be known as procedural planning theory, the rational-comprehensive model of planning, strongly hierarchical in character, and applying systems thinking to the study of towns (Healey et al., 1982). For planning practice, the focus was the preparation of plans, starting with the definition of the problem and the goals to be achieved, followed by the generation and evaluation of alternative strategies, and then, in principle, continuing with implementation and monitoring. In the 1960s, however, the growth of the technique concentrated on the earlier stages, culminating in the plan. The forcing ground for new techniques was the series of subregional studies. And policy emerged in the regional strategies and the structure and local plans in a hierarchical sequence.

The plans were not, as previously, programs for implementation. Instead, in effect they were guidelines for use by planners, developers, and the public. The new structure and local plans, with their flexibility or, more accurately, their ambiguity and uncertainty, were effective tools for this new, more indicative style of planning. Nevertheless, the plans were ambitious: comprehensive in scope, going far beyond the limitations of mere land use planning; rational in the belief that objective proof of the plan's logic would be sufficient to sustain a consensus which would inform all subsequent decisions; the consensus itself achieved through a process of public participation for which the procedures were enshrined in the legislation.

But those were also the weaknesses. The plans were comprehensive in scope but not in executive power other than over the use and development of land. The plans assumed a consensus built on public participation, which ignored the conflicts over the allocation of space and resources implicit in their implementation. Above all, the plans relied on the prospect of planning for growth to an extent that was realized only when the prospect was removed.

So by the 1970s procedural planning theory was losing ground, but no new paradigm was emerging to take its place. Instead there was a plurality of theories, from advocacy planning and neo-Marxian political economy to incrementalism and pragmatism (Healey et al., 1982). Research was concentrating on empirical questions about the operation of the planning system and the implementation of planning policies, which has in turn led to explanations about the relationship between policy and action and the meaning of policy in planning (Healey, 1983).

In practice, too, the contrast can be drawn between the entrepreneurial planning authority, often in an inner-city area, concerned with attracting development at almost any cost, relying on a variety of negotiating devices of which the statutory development plan is almost the least important; and the defensive planning authority in a suburban or rural area, still under pressure from developers and relying on a narrower range of more orthodox measures, chiefly the development plan and development control (Davies, 1983a).

CONCLUSION

The planning system created in 1947 has lasted nearly four decades. It has done so despite a change in the style of development plans and the much more significant reorganization of local government. The problem of land values has proved to be insoluble, and so, after the first few years, the planning system has had to operate within a market system in which land has changed hands, or been acquired by the state, at market value. Nevertheless, the system has survived fairly intact.

Containment and Segregation

Two themes dominated the practice of planning during much of this period, containment and segregation. Each has been the subject of a major evaluation: Peter Hall and colleagues on containment (Hall et al., 1973) and Alison Ravetz on segregation (Ravetz, 1980).

The aims of containment were to prevent the growth of towns by limiting sharply the unplanned sprawl of earlier decades, by reducing the congestion that afflicted the cores of conurbations and large cities; and by protecting the surrounding countryside from urban development. The policy relied on the comprehensive redevelopment of inner areas, the planned dispersal of people and jobs to new towns, and the creation of greenbelts. The countryside was left to look after itself, but containment worked within the context of a policy for regional balance.

The paradox of containment in practice is now fairly clear. The larger towns and conurbations are not growing but are losing people and jobs, to the point at which regional imbalance can be attributed chiefly to the urban, rather than the industrial, structure of regions. The planning system is no longer faced with containing growth but with coping with the consequences of urban decline.

The containment policy illustrates a further paradox: its benefits have not been uniformly distributed. The main beneficiaries have been those who sold their land with planning permission for development and those who found houses in the suburbs, small towns, and new towns. The main people to suffer were those left behind in the inner city by the flight to the suburbs. More recent work suggests that the inner-city problem has much deeper roots than a land use planning policy even when reinforced by an industrial location policy. Similar conditions are to be found in countries with much less restrictive planning (Hall, 1981).

It seems that deconcentration, and limiting the growth of population and employment, would have occurred irrespective of the aims of planning policy. Only in the relatively sharp distinction between town and countryside can containment be said to have made a real difference in the pattern of urban development.

Segregation refers to the policy of strict land use zoning: the creation of primary use zones, the separation of incompatible uses (such as industry and housing or, at the more detailed level, of certain forms of retailing), and the eradication of nonconforming uses. The idea of land use segregation was reinforced by the separation of public and private housing. The policy was achieved through clearance and redevelopment in the public sector and by development control in the private sector. Its aim was the creation of a good environment for working and living for all social classes, but its results were a polarization between the inner city and the affluent suburbs and a highly unequal distribution of the spatial and environmental benefits of planning.

It is arguable that much of this inequality would have occurred at least to the same extent under a market economy. But it can be argued that the tyranny of official standards and cost yardsticks and the inflexible application of zoning principles contributed to the inequalities.

Despite these questions, it can be argued that containment and segregation achieved many of their aims and did have beneficial results. That they were able to do so, however, can be attributed to the fact that for most of the period, planning was concerned essentially with affecting the spatial distribution of new investment stimulated by expectations of economic and demographic growth, against the background of, for planning, a neutral agriculture.

The Inner City and the Countryside

Two new issues began to emerge during the 1970s: the inner city and planning for the countryside. The distinctive point about each was the incapacity of the land use planning system to address the problems.

A series of government reports during the late 1960s and early 1970s had investigated conditions in the inner city, initially in the field of education, then social services, quite belatedly in planning and the environment, and eventually in the local economy (Lawless, 1979). There is still much dispute about the cause of inner-city problems, but the symptoms are highly visible: poor housing, environmental dereliction, vacant land; social malaise, crime and vandalism, unemployment; above all an almost complete lack of new investment by the private sector in housing, commerce, and industry (Great Britain, 1977).

By 1978, the issue reached the statute book in the shape of the Inner Urban Areas Act. Partnership areas were designated in Liverpool, Manchester, Newcastle, Birmingham, and London in which central government would join with local government in seeking to regenerate the worst areas by a combination of social and environmental measures funded through the government's urban program.

The policy continued under the new Conservative government, though with a significant change in emphasis away from social and toward economic programs in closer partnership with the private sector. New ideas were initiated, including an urban development grant modeled on U.S. experience. Urban development corporations were appointed by government for the derelict docklands of London and Merseyside, following the example of the new town corporations. Enterprise zones were designated to which it was hoped that new industrial development would be attracted by a relaxed planning regime (little more than a simplified land use zoning map with no necessity for development control) and a powerful set of financial incentives in the form of exemption from local property and other taxes. Industrial improvement areas would seek to revitalize outworn areas by environmental and highway improvements, grant aid, and land exchanges (Home, 1982).

It is too soon to assess the impact of inner-city policies, at least in part because they are unclear in their basic aims. Are enterprise zones intended to stimulate new investment or simply to attract already committed investment from other areas? Is the aim of inner-city policy for Brixton in London or Toxteth in Liverpool (both areas with a large ethnic minority population and the scene of riots in 1981) to benefit the people living there or to attract new employment to these areas without necessarily affecting the local residents? Can any of these aims be achieved during a period of economic recession, when cuts in the general level of central government resources for these areas far outweigh the special assistance they receive under the urban program? Finally, in this context, to what extent can a system of development plans and negative development control contribute to the policy when their chief problem is an absence of resources for new development?

The other newly emerging issue concerns planning for the countryside. National parks and greenbelts were touched on earlier, but there are other, more intractable issues. One is the question of rural deprivation, exemplified in the withdrawal of public and private services from the more remote areas, leaving a population that lacks not only jobs but also village schools, shops and post offices, and public transport. Agriculture has been shedding labor very rapidly, yet planning policy has tended to resist the location of new factories in rural areas. A new, affluent exurban population has been moving into the more accessible rural areas, in some a transient population seeking holiday homes but in others becoming a long-distance commuting or retirement population. In either case, the social structure of the rural areas is changing, bringing new pressures and conflicts.

The major question concerns the impact of changing agricultural technology, sustained by grants and subsidies, on the rural landscape: uprooting of hedgerows, draining of wetlands, ploughing of permanent grassland, tree planting on moorlands. The changes are dramatic (Bowers and Cheshire, 1983). None of these changes is subject to land use planning control. It could be argued that they represent the inevitable consequence of adaptation to new techniques, albeit at a high cost in subsidy. But many of the changes are deeply resented by the urban population for whom the countryside is a familiar backcloth to be visited at weekends or to be lived in for the attractions it affords. For these, the argument is made that agriculture, no less than housing, commerce, and industry, should be subject to detailed land use planning and development control (Shoard, 1980).

Future of Land Use Planning

Planning in the 1980s has to operate in the context of a changing spatial pattern of development and of the new issues of urban decline and planning for the countryside. Statutory land use planning as constituted can do nothing to halt the pace of agricultural change and not much to halt the process of urban decline, although there still remains a large number of tasks for which it remains a highly effective tool. But the political context within which planning has to operate is changing. There is the reaction against state planning and intervention, not simply a matter of cuts in public expenditure but a shift in ideology. There is the increasing centralization of authority in government, whether in the appointment of urban development corporations to resolve the worst problems of urban decline, or the measures taken to control local government expenditure, or the proposed abolition of the metropolitan tier of local government for London and the big cities.[12]

Furthermore, there is the changing attitude to regulatory land use planning, whether in the concern to reduce delay by making the system of development control more efficient (though not necessarily more effective) or in the use of new concepts such as enterprise zones, which do away with the need for development control. And finally, there is the uncertainty about the scope and status of development plans as such in the recent advice to use local plans only when strictly necessary and in the recent legislation affecting structure plans (Heap, 1982).

Together the contextual changes and the challenge of the new issues must raise questions about the future of land use planning in England and Wales. Development control has been the essential, characteristic feature of the planning system, its certain and effective point of decision. Yet development control has always been ambiguous in its aims. The different interests in development control may have divergent aims. For planners, it is the means of implementing the plan; for developers, to facilitate development; for amenity interests, to enhance the quality of the environment; for community groups, to protect their neighborhood (Davies, 1983b).

These differing interpretations reflect competing ideologies of planning law: the conflict of the public interest, private property, and public participation (McAuslan, 1980). It can be argued that the planning system has survived thus far by being flexible and robust, in which the effective point of decision is taken at a local level about a particular development. It is development control, rather than structure plans or new towns, that is the real strength of land use planning in England and Wales. Its strength lies not in its adherence to a single image or ideology but in its capacity to be a forum within which the social control of environmental change can be mediated. It has proved to be very effective for negative control and, with the added stimulus of planning gain, for promoting development in a partnership between public and private sectors. It has been less effective in deciding major government investments, such as the proposal for a nuclear power station, chiefly because the levels of decisionmaking have been confused with development control having to operate in a policy vacuum. The challenge for the 1980s and beyond will be to amend the rules and procedures for land use planning so that they can cope with the problems of urban decline and agricultural change as effectively as they once did for urban growth and expansion.

NOTES

1. This chapter discusses town and country planning, that is, the system of physical, land use, or environmental planning that has evolved in England and Wales chiefly in order to plan for and control the use and development of land. It also refers briefly to matters of regional economic planning concerned with the distribution of industry. It does not consider other forms, such as national economic or social planning.

2. The planning systems in the rest of the United Kingdom are based on the same principles and have the same aims as in England and Wales. Nevertheless, they differ in a number of significant respects because of the different legal system and local government organization in Scotland and the different constitutional status of Northern Ireland.

3. The statistics in this chapter as far as possible are for England and Wales; however, a number of authors refer to Great Britain or the United Kingdom. Their area and population in 1981 were as follows: Great Britain (comprising England, Wales, and Scotland), area, 22.7 million hectares, population 54.1 million; United Kingdom (Great Britain plus Northern Ireland), area, 24.1 million hectares, population 55.7 million.

4. The United Kingdom has never had an elected system of regional government, although certain powers have been delegated to separate government departments for Wales, Scotland, and Northern Ireland. The standard regions are designed for the administrative and statistical purposes of central government.

5. Retitled as *Garden Cities of Tomorrow* in 1902 and later republished with a preface by F. J. Osborn and introduction by Lewis Mumford (London: Faber, 1946).

6. The Barlow report *The Distribution of the Industrial Population* (Cmd 6153, London: HMSO, 1940), was supplemented by two further reports: the Scott report, *Land Utilisation in Rural Areas* (Cmd 6378, London: HMSO, 1942), and the Uthwatt report, *Compensation and Betterment* (Cmd 6386, London: HMSO, 1942).

7. Section 22(1), Town and Country Planning Act 1971.

8. Town and Country Planning General Development Order 1977 (Statutory Instrument 1977, No. 289); Town and Country Planning Use Classes Order, 1972 (Statutory Instrument 1972, No. 1385) (London: HMSO).

9. The Town and Country Planning Act 1971 is currently the principal act, repealing much of the previous legislation. It has itself been amended, in particular by the Local Government Act 1972 and the Local Government, Planning and Land Act 1980.

10. The government has recently published a white paper, *Streamlining the Cities* (Cmnd 9063, London: HMSO, 1983), proposing the abolition of the Greater London Council and the six metropolitan county councils. The proposals are unclear in detail, but the intention is that all planning matters, including structure plans, will rest with the 32 individual boroughs that make up London, the nine districts in Greater Manchester, and so on.

11. Cumbernauld new town, in Scotland, was designated in 1955. It broke with the planning of the first new towns, rejecting the neighborhood principle, building to a higher density, and making greater provision for the car. It strongly influenced the planning of later new towns in England and Wales and overseas.

12. See note 10.

BASIC READING

The best description of the planning system in Great Britain, with extensive bibliographies, including the legislation and official publications, is in Cullingworth (1982). Cherry (1972, 1974) gives a well-illustrated account of urban development and the evolution of the planning profession. Hall is a key author for a general introduction to planning (1982), an account of the inner-city problem (1980), and, with his colleagues, for what is still the most comprehensive analysis of the policy of containment in practice (1973). Ravetz (1978) and Esher (1981) give contrasting interpretations of postwar planning. Planning law is summarized in Heap (1982) and its ideologies examined in McAuslan (1980). Recent research and current practice is discussed in Healey (1983). The *Planner* is the journal of the Royal Town Planning Institute.

BIBLIOGRAPHY

Alexander, Alan. 1982. *Local Government in Britain Since Reorganisation*. London: George Allen and Unwin.

Ambrose, P., and B. Colenutt. 1975. *The Property Machine*. Harmondsworth: Penguin.

Best, Robin H. 1981. *Land Use and Living Space*. London: Methuen.

Bowers, J. K., and P. Cheshire. 1983. *Agriculture, the Countryside and Landuse*. London: Methuen.

Bruton, M. J. 1983. Local Plans, Local Planning and Development Schemes in England. *Town Planning Review* 54 (January):4-23.

Cadman, D., and L. Austin-Crowe. 1983. *Property Development*. London: E & F N Spon.

Cherry, Gordon E. 1972. *Urban Change and Planning: A History of Urban Development in Britain since 1750*. Henley-on-Thames: G. T. Foulis.

Cherry, Gordon E. 1974. *The Evolution of British Town Planning*. Leighton Buzzard: Leonard Hill Books.

Cowling, T. M., and G. C. Steeley. 1973. *Subregional Planning Studies: An Evaluation*. Oxford: Pergamon.

Cullingworth, J. B. 1982. *Town and Country Planning in Britain*. 8th ed. London: George Allen and Unwin.

Davies, H. W. E. 1980. Neighborhood Revitalization: The British Experience. In Donald B. Rosenthall, ed. *Urban Revitalization*. Beverly Hills, Calif.: Sage Publications.

Davies, H. W. E. 1983a. British Planning Practice. In H. W. E. Davies and P. Healey. *British Planning Practice and Planning Education in the 1970s and 1980s*. Working Paper No. 70. Oxford: Oxford Polytechnic, Department of Town and Country Planning.

Davies, H. W. E. 1983b. Development Control in the 1980s. *Report of Proceedings of the 1982 Town and Country Planning Summer School*. London: Royal Town Planning Institute.

Dobby, A. 1978. *Conservation and Planning*. London: Hutchinson.

Esher, Lionel. 1981. *A Broken Wave: The Rebuilding of England 1940-1980*. London: Allen Lane.

Foley, D. L. 1973. British Town Planning: One Ideology or Three? In A. Faludi, ed. *A Reader in Planning Theory*. Oxford: Pergamon.

Fothergill, Stephen, and Graham Gudgin. 1982. *Unequal Growth: Urban and Regional Employment Change in the U.K.* London: Heinemann Educational Books.

Fudge, C. et al. 1982. *Speed, Economy and Effectiveness in Local Plan Preparation and Operation*. Bristol: School of Advanced Urban Studies.

Gibson, M. S., and M. J. Langstaff. 1982. *An Introduction to Urban Renewal*. London: Hutchinson.

Glasson, John. 1978. *An Introduction to Regional Planning: Concepts, Theory and Practice*. 2d ed. London: Hutchinson.

Great Britain. 1977. *Policy for the Inner Cities*. Cmnd 6845. London: HMSO.

Great Britain. House of Commons. 1978. *Planning Procedures: Eleventh Report from the Expenditure Committee*. Session 1976-77. London: HMSO.

Great Britain. Ministry of Housing and Local Government. 1965. *The Future of Development Plans: A Report by the Planning Advisory Group*. London: HMSO.

Great Britain. Ministry of Housing and Local Government. 1969. *Report of the Committee on Public Participation in Planning: People and Planning*. London: HMSO. [Skeffington report]

Great Britain. Ministry of Housing and Local Government. 1970. *Development Plans Manual*. London: HMSO.

Great Britain. Ministry of Transport. 1963. *Traffic in Towns*. London: HMSO. [Buchanan report]

Hall, Peter. 1982. *Urban and Regional Planning*. 2d ed. Harmondsworth, Middlesex: Penguin Books.

Hall, Peter, et al. 1973. *The Containment of Urban England*. London: George Allen and Unwin.

Hall, Peter, and Dennis Hay. 1980. *Growth Centres in the European Urban System*. London: Heinemann Educational Books.

Hall, Peter, ed. 1981. *The Inner City in Context*. London: Heinemann Educational Books.

Healey, Patsy. 1983. *Local Plans in British Land Use Planning*. Oxford: Pergamon.

Healey, Patsy, et al. 1982. *Planning Theory: prospects for the 1980s*. Oxford: Pergamon.

Heap, Desmond. 1982. *Outline of Planning Law*. 8th ed. London: Sweet and Maxwell.

Home, Robert K. 1982. *Inner City Regeneration*. London: E & F N Spon.

Keeble, Lewis. 1961. *Principles and Practice of Town and Country Planning*. 2d ed. London: Estates Gazette.

Lawless, P. 1979. *Urban Deprivation and Government Initiative*. London: Faber.

McAuslan, Patrick. 1980. *The Ideologies of Planning Law*. Oxford: Pergamon.

McKay, David H., and Cox, Andrew W. 1979. *The Politics of Urban Change*. London: Croom Helm.

McLoughlin, J. Brian. 1968. *Urban and Regional Planning: A Systems Approach*. London: Faber and Faber.

McLoughlin, J. Brian. 1974. *Urban Planning and Control*. London: Faber and Faber.

Marriot, O. 1967. *The Property Boom*. London: Hamish Hamilton.

Massey, Doreen, and Alejandrina Catalano. 1978. *Capital and Land: Land Ownership by Capital in Great Britain*. London: Edward Arnold.

Osborn, F. J., and A. Whittick. 1977. *The New Towns: The Answer to Megalopolis*. 3d ed. Leighton Buzzard: Leonard Hill.

Ravetz, Alison. 1980. *Remaking Cities: Contradictions of the Recent Urban Environment*. London: Croom Helm.

Shoard, Marion. 1980. *The Theft of the Countryside*. London: Temple Smith.

Short, J. R. 1982. *Housing in Britain*. London: Methuen.

Underwood, J. 1980. *Town Planners in Search of a Role*. Occasional Paper No. 6. Bristol: School of Advanced Urban Studies.

13

German Federal Republic

EBERHARD SCHMIDT-ASSMANN

HISTORICAL DEVELOPMENT AND CURRENT STATUS OF LAND USE PLANNING

As early as the Middle Ages, there was a simple form of land use planning. Life in the towns, limited as it was by walls, moats, and gates, would not have been possible without exact planning as to how land was to be used. The results of this sort of planning and regulation can still be seen today in the character of old German towns of Rothenburg ob der Tauber, Celle, and Heidelberg. It can be said that the town planners of the Middle Ages often understood more about the harmonious development of towns and building on a humane scale than do their modern successors in our own times.

There is, however, no continuous historical connection between that era and modern land use planning. Individualism and liberalism, establishing themselves as a consequence of the Enlightenment in Germany at the beginning of the nineteenth century, changed the way land was regulated in a fundamental way. Thereafter a person could do as he liked with the land. *Freedom to build* was a characteristic phrase of the time, and any kind of land use planning offended against the spirit of the age. At that time, Germany was an agrarian country.

With the industrialization of Germany in the second half of the nineteenth century, attitudes changed. The ordering of the land use activities of private individuals increasingly was recognized as a task falling within the public domain. So it is regarded today: land use planning is public planning, carried out by the states and local authorities on the basis of their status, not because they owned any land. The original reason for the change in approach was the rapid increase in population: in 1850, the population was 35 million; in 1870, 41 million; and in 1914, 67 million. Industrialization drew people from the countryside to the larger cities. There the consequences were haphazard growth, poor living conditions, helter-skelter settlement of the surrounding areas, and large traffic problems. Slowly, after 1870, a new form of land use planning developed, devoted, in the first instance, to traffic planning. At the beginning, the basis for such plans was provided by public order law. Soon, however, within the individual states of the German Reich separate building and planning statutes came into being (1874 in Prussia, 1900 in Saxony).

With land use plans of this kind, it was possible to regulate the framework of roads but not that of a city as a whole or even part of a city. It was necessary to take into account other requirements of a residential, industrial, and commercial nature. At crucial points during these developments, it was also recognized that it was not enough for each local community to plan for itself alone; neighboring local communities, large cities, and their surrounding areas had to set up common plans. Thus, in some particularly problematic industrial localities, the local authorities, such as greater Berlin and the Ruhr, combined together in planning associations. These were the beginnings of regional planning in Germany.

The two world wars interrupted developments in this area. From its foundation in 1949, the Federal Republic was faced with two preeminent challenges. The first was the reconstruction of the cities destroyed during the war. This also involved the problem as to how a new style of town building was to be developed. Walter Gropius, who went on a lecture tour through Germany in 1947, promoted the idea of readopting the Bauhaus approach. But the problem of reconstruction was above all a quantitative one. Of the 10.5 million dwellings in West Germany, 2.3 million were in ruins and almost half of them were heavily damaged. The second challenge was the integration of the 10 million refugees who had been driven out of the eastern parts of Germany by the Soviet Union.

The individual states of the Federal Republic passed construction laws. These empowered local authorities in the city centers and in areas close to cities to set up plans and to carry out allocation procedures. Moreover, compulsory acquisition of privately owned building land was permitted, and the state also provided subsidies for public housing projects. Local authorities set up companies with limited liability to carry out land development and housing projects. They also made great efforts to attract new industrial concerns to their areas. The "economic miracle" that soon followed filled the coffers of the state exchequers. During these years (1950-70) land use planning was tailored for growth. The provision of employment enjoyed priority over conservation and environmental protection. An extensive network of infrastructural projects—highways, streets, public buildings, schools, and swimming pools—was undertaken. The use of land initially received little attention.

In 1960, the unified Federal Building Law (Bundesbaugesetz, BBauG) was passed, replacing the laws of the individual states and above all regulating urban building and planning of local authorities. In 1965 a unified federal law for land use planning at the regional and state level (Bundesraumordnungsgesetz, BROG) followed. This law did not include any plans but instead laid down how planning should be organized. Planning became necessary at the regional level with the increasing recognition of the economic interdependence of investments within a given area. Furthermore, the living habits of the population began to change after 1960. People no longer wanted to live in city centers and in areas close to cities, preferring to live in small communities in the country. From this arose problems associated with commuting (in German the term is *shuttling*), which the individual local authorities were unable to solve with their own land use planning.

During the last 20 years a system of land use planning, based on the two laws mentioned above, has spread through the Federal Republic. No one in Germany today argues over the necessity of an ordered system of land use planning. This necessity becomes evident as soon as data illustrating the intensity of land use in the Federal Republic are presented. With a total area of 248,000 square kilometers and a population of 61.5 million, the average density of the population is 248 per square kilometer. The equivalent figure for the United States is 22 per square kilometer. Even when a comparison is made with a heavily populated state in the United States, the state of New York, the point is clear. In the Federal Republic, in an area twice as big as that of New York State's 128,000 square kilometers, there live three and half times as many people. The population density in Germany is highly variable. In rural areas, it can be as low as 80 per square kilometer. In the city of Munich the figure is 4,100 per square kilometer.

INSTITUTIONAL AND LANDOWNERSHIP FRAMEWORK

The Federal State

Anyone wishing to understand the functioning of land use planning in the Federal Republic must first take into account a number of constitutional provisions in the Basic Law (Grundgesetz). Under the Basic Law, the Republic is a federal state consisting of 11 states. The state with the largest population is North Rhein-Westphalia, which comprises 34,000 square kilometers and has a population of 17 million. The state with the greatest area is Bavaria (70,000 square kilometers and a population of 11 million). The smallest state has an area of only 2,571 square kilometers and a population of 1.6 million. Three states (West Berlin, Bremen, and Hamburg) are city-states; the state authority and local authority are a single body.

The federation and the states are mutually independent entities having their own parliaments and constitutions. In each state a parliamentary government is headed by a minister president. The Basic Law does, however, provide for a division of powers, which differs from the U.S. model. Generally, the federation has the most important powers as far as legislation is concerned; in administrative undertakings, its powers are more circumscribed but include foreign relations, military affairs, customs and excise, railways, the post office, highways, labor affairs, and social insurance. The states have only a small number of legislative tasks; on the other hand, they are concerned mainly with administrative tasks. Since land use planning is traditionally an administrative task and also since the parliaments have only latterly taken part in the process, the most important decisions are made by the states.

The federation can, however, set up individual and particular plans in pursuance of its administrative tasks—for example, the building of highways. It also exercises a de facto influence over the local authorities in its provision of money for important projects in the states. There is, however, no overall federal land use planning. In the mid-1970s, an attempt was made by the federal government to set up such a plan to include the priorities for future developments, but in practice this Federal Land Use Program (BROP) failed to get off the ground.

The federation carries out land use planning in abstract terms by laying down laws (the BBauG and BROG and environmental laws) that create a legal system for land use planning and formulate general principles for land development (para. 2, BROG; para. 1, BBauG). In addition, the federation publishes a planning report each year that gives an account of the overall situation and developmental tendencies. The responsible minister is advised by a planning advisory council.

This system is properly in operation only when the activities of the states are added. The states set up the most important plans. The federation makes concrete planning decisions only in single instances and schemes and indirectly by means of its financial influence.

The federation and the states work together in the Conference of Ministers of Planning. This permanent conference can only discuss important questions; it is not empowered to reach binding decisions (see para. 8, BROG). A scholarly institution financed jointly by the federation and the states, the Academy of Land Use Research and Planning in Hanover (Akademie für Raumforschung und Landesplanung), has existed for 30 years.

Local Authorities

The local authorities are the other important actors in land use planning. In organizational terms, they belong to the states, but they are independent bearers of sovereignty with a right to self-government guaranteed by the constitution. There are about 8,500 local authorities. Of these, 7,400 have populations of fewer than 10,000, with 26 percent of the entire population living in these smaller communities. Fourteen percent of the population lives in communities with populations of between 10,000 and 20,000, and a further 26 percent is in communities with populations between 20,000 and 100,000. Seventeen percent of the population lives in cities with over 500,000 inhabitants.

Every square meter within the Federal Republic comes under a local authority. The jurisdiction of a local authority is not only over the center of a place or town and its areas under habitation but also includes all forest and agricultural areas. Moreover, the areas that belong to the federation (for example, military areas) or the state in administrative terms come under a local authority. Local authorities border on each other back to back.

Every state land use plan will affect at least one local authority. Local authorities occupy an important position in land use planning. At the local level, the local authorities are the bearers of planning power. They set up the important outline building plans (para. 2 (I), BBauG). In the land use planning of the states, the local authorities affected must play a part; at the very least, they must be given a hearing. As a basic rule, the land use plans of the states may be only for purposes that extend beyond a given locality (such as regional traffic or regional water supplies). Plans that bear only on the purposes of the local community may not be set up by the states; only the local authorities are empowered to do this.

It is apparent from the institutional framework outlined here that land use planning is lawful only if it respects certain constitutional limits: the independence of the states and the self-government of the local authorities.

Landownership

Another important limit to land use planning is the role played by property rights. The ownership of land in particular enjoys high esteem among the population and constitutes 27 percent of privately held capital. Today somewhere around 50 percent of all households own some form of realty. Even for the lower middle class this constitutes a kind of capital formation. Often the land owned will amount to only a tenth or a fifth of an hectare, but it will be carefully protected as a garden or building plot within a family. People receive state support in the form of policies favoring home ownership and save-and-build societies. In a time of high unemployment in particular, the effect of real estate ownership has been to stabilize, since it preserves the basis of the social status of those affected by the times. Of course, landownership on a large scale also exists; agricultural and forestry lands are owned by large farmers and often by formerly aristocratic families. Large-scale landholdings in areas of high population density are owned by industrial concerns, banks, insurance companies, and individual families. Article 14 of the Basic Law guarantees private property, and this is an important determining factor within the German legal order. However, this guarantee is not without limits. According to the constitution, property "should also serve the public weal." The laws of the state may set limits for the exercise of property rights. These limits on property rights arise out of the laws relating to the rights of neighbors, to building, to nature conservation, to the environment, and to land use planning. The situation in the surrounding environment is also of importance. If the surroundings are important for the protection of nature or historic buildings or for securing supplies of drinking water, the owner of a given piece of land is obliged to take account of this.

The constitutional framework serves as the basis for the relationship between private property and land use planning. In principle, a person's right to build on his or her own land is guaranteed by the constitution; it is not something that has to be purchased from the state. In practice, however, the right to build is heavily qualified because under the law the entire area under the jurisdiction of the local authorities is divided into three kinds of zone:

1. Zones where a building plan exists (para. 30): In such zones land may be built on in any way that does not conflict with the plan.
2. Zones where no building plan exists but where surrounding areas have already been built on (para. 34): In such zones, land may be used in the same way and to the same degree as in neighboring plots.
3. Zones having open land (para. 35): In such zones only specific kinds of houses may be built. Ordinary dwelling houses, business places, and industrial factories as a rule may not be built, although exceptions can be made.

In forests and fields, most kinds of building undertakings are prohibited. Here property rights are heavily limited. Some outside observers find this exceptional. But in Germany this is generally seen and recognized as a legal limit to property rights, and even liberal lawyers do not question this. In a country as densely populated as the Federal Republic, open spaces cannot be developed helter-skelter; they may be built only on the basis of a plan.

Today private property is subject to a planning reservation: land use planners must take notice of the wish of landowners to build on their property, and they must allow for it as far as is possible. If there are public or private requirements that argue against a given building project, then planners may accord these precedence. This is not an unlawful violation of property rights, and, as a general rule, the owner is not entitled to compensation. It is only when land use planning is taken into account that property rights assume substantial significance. Planning prevents conflicts that arise between potential uses of a given piece of land in a particular area, and for this reason it is wrong to see land use planning solely as a limit on property rights. The use of land free of conflicts is made possible only by land use planning (Schmidt-Assman, 1972).

The federation, states, and local authorities also own land, and state property and property belonging to the local authorities is considered as private property, subject to the same provisions of civil law as is the private property of citizens. The former amounts to about 25 percent of the entire area of the Federal Republic. Much forest and agricultural land belongs to the states. The federation owns land set aside for military exercises, military camps, and closed military areas.

In terms of land use planning, land owned by the local authorities is of greater interest. This comprises about half the land held in public hands and often consists of building land and prospective building land. A great many local authorities carry out building land availability policies under which they buy land before they have designated it as building land under a plan. Land can be acquired for particular public uses (such as road building), and in addition local authorities have a right of preemption over many pieces of land within their jurisdictions. In both instances, strict procedures must be followed, and for this reason compulsory purchases and the use of rights of preemption are not resorted to often. In most cases, the authorities try to buy the land privately without the use of compulsory measures, even when this means having to pay more for it. Expropriations must receive just compensation under Article 14(3) of the Basic Law. This must be the fair market value, the decisive criterion being the amount a reasonable buyer would pay. The possible uses of the land in the foreseeable future must also be considered, but this is subject to a number of difficult qualifications (paras. 93, 95, and 142, BBauG).

Often local authorities work in cooperation with private housing development companies. They are often, however, set up by the local authorities, or within them the local authorities' influence is dominant. The largest company building houses, though, belongs to the labor unions, and because it is active within many localities, it has an influence on the planning by local authorities. Some people complain that the land belonging to such concerns receives excessively favorable consideration where land use planning is concerned. Moreover, the houses built by these companies are often monotonous; the overall effect is bureaucratic and lifeless.

Popular opinion, confronted with the land availability policies of local authorities and such powerful development companies, has tended to be skeptical. No one is interested in the communalization or nationalization of property in land. Opinion in Germany holds that liberty is better served if landed property is distributed in as many private hands as possible. It is sufficient for the state and local authorities to have the means of steering the use of land by means of land use planning. It is not necessary for them also to be the owners of the land. The division of the powers of ownership (dominium) from jurisdictional power (imperium) is a kind of separation of powers, designed to secure the freedom of the individual. An important element of this freedom is represented by property in land.

The Courts

The courts play an important role in land use planning. Article 19(4) of the Basic Law contains a wide-reaching guarantee of legal protection against the state. Anyone who believes his or her rights have been violated by a public authority may have recourse to the courts. This right may not be restricted by any law.

The courts that review the actions of the state are mostly the administrative courts. These are completely independent courts, which in organizational terms have nothing to do with administrative organs. There are three levels. First, there are the lower administrative courts where an action begins. Whether the public action complained of has been committed by a local, state, or federation authority is of no consequence. Second, the higher administrative courts in the states are primarily appellate courts of fact and law. Third, the Federal Administrative Court in Berlin is a court of legal revision, being a federal court that decides on the actions of federal and state authorities. The administrative courts see themselves as organs whose job is to enable citizens to exercise their rights. These courts enjoy the esteem of public opinion and are staffed by judges of high educational and professional attainment (only the most highly qualified of the judges seek to become judges in the administrative courts). Often law faculty professors are judges in the higher administrative courts. Close contacts exist between the administrative court judges and the representatives of the law faculties, above all, professors of public law. Administrative law has developed out of this into one of the most important disciplines, constituting a major part of the study of law. German administrative law is systematically subdivided to a rigorous degree; land use planning and the judicial review of land use plans is an important part of this whole.

Since land use plans are set up only by state and local authorities and not by private institutions, they are all official acts. They may become the objects of judicial review as soon as any individual's rights are violated and that individual brings an action in court. Local authorities may also ask for judicial review of state land use plans if their right to self-government has been violated (Article 23(2), Basic Law). As a basic rule, any plan can become the object of judicial proceedings.

The courts test the legality of land use plans by special review. First, they check whether the planning procedure has been properly observed. Since there are a large number of provisions governing the procedure, authorities often make mistakes. Such mistakes lead to the plan's being declared invalid. Along with the procedure, the courts also check whether the contents of the plan comply with the law. For this to be so, the authority will have had to have observed the legal groundwork and to have recognized and tested all the requirements at issue. Finally, no requirement may be neglected disproportionately. A plan may also be unlawful if it is not in accordance with another plan that is on a higher level within the planning system. Although the discretion of planning authorities may not be reviewed in its entirety, important aspects of it are. Planning discretion is a separate category within the ordinary discretion of the administrative authorities. To review planning discretion, the Federal Administrative Court has developed firm criteria. Thus, for example, it is unlawful for a local authority to commit itself to a particular kind of planning at the beginning of the planning procedure vis-à-vis an industrial or housing development firm without taking account of other considerations such as the protection of the environment.

Actions against land use plans are frequent. In fact, today actions are always started against plans for large-scale undertakings such as airports, power stations, or highways. Often the plaintiffs in such cases are in the hundreds or thousands.

When planners are questioned on this connection, they wonder why plans should be subject to review by the courts. Under the constitution, however, nothing can be done about this, nor should it be. The courts have restricted the power of planners. In a country with the rule of law, this is necessary. In the beginning, the courts were sometimes impractical, overtheoretical, and rather rigid. In the intervening years the Federal Administrative Court has helped the courts to find a middle way. The essential core of planning discretion is respected. In other cases, the courts have settled unresolved issues to the benefit of the planning authorities. Planning thus has become stabilized, and planning procedures have become less complex. The reservations of citizens in the face of difficult plans of great complexity have been reduced. It is nevertheless true that the courts have also contributed to the perfectionistic and static load with which planning is weighed down.

MAJOR CHALLENGES

National and Regional Levels

Land use planning at the national and regional levels between 1950 and 1970 has been growth planning (see Akademie (ed.) 1982, 227, 247). The potential for growth was great. Land use planning was designed to achieve the optimal distribution of this potential throughout the nation. One goal was to prevent growth from being too densely concentrated in a few areas. Also, areas dominated by agriculture that suffered from a decline in available agricultural labor or from some other problem were to be assisted in remaining attractive (the anticonurbation strategy). Land use planning aimed at establishing ''living conditions of as equal a value'' as possible throughout all parts of the Federal Republic (the principle of decentralized concentration, para. 2, BROG). Central to this principle was the concept of central places. Local communities and towns were divided into places of differing centrality (small centers, lower centers, middle centers, and upper centers). Particular kinds of service provision were laid down for each type of center, with each designated place seeking to provide its central services accordingly (schools, hospitals, administrative offices, employment provisions). The overall concept concentrated on the small scale. The area for the provision of services by a middle center had to comprise at least 20,000 inhabitants. One hour by public transport was taken as the reasonable maximum for reaching the central services from the surrounding area. Some things were considered standard: the provision of secondary schools leading to the *Abitur* (high school diploma), vocational schools, hospitals, large sports facilities, and a wide variety of shopping possibilities. As long as sufficient growth potential was present, it was possible to provide such generous services in all these centers. However, with the stagnation of population growth (from 1974), fewer employment opportunities, and lower disposable income, the consequent potential for growth was too little to ensure that all localities could expand to this high standard of services provision. Because of this, other principles were devised, designed to thin out the concept of central places. Initially it was recommended that concentration should be at development centers and in development axes (BROP).

In the intervening period it has been recognized that it was wrong to interpret the "equal value" of living conditions as meaning the "equality" of them. The different natural advantages and tasks of each individual area were not correctly recognized. Moreover, in no way do the wishes of the inhabitants of areas always coincide with the ideals of urban living. The advantages of rural living are once again being recognized, not least as a consequence of the ecology movement. There is, accordingly, a willingness to accept some of the drawbacks in the reduced availability of cultural offerings and other services normally provided. Today an attempt is being made within large-scale planning to work according to the concept of regional task setting. Areas of low population density are given priority functions—for example, agriculture or forestry, rest and recreation, water conservation, ecological balancing, or as locations for large-scale projects that affect a wide area (airports, atomic power stations, storage areas). On the other hand there is no willingness to forgo minimum infrastructural standards for all areas. Land use planning requires complex thinking in several dimensions. Not everyone is capable of this, and thus often the results are empty maxims and opaque compromises struck between several concepts.

Local Level

Similar problems are exhibited at the local level, but these are of a more concrete nature. Local land use plans having an integral character are set up by local authorities on their own behalf, but they do require state approval.

Initially local land use plans were aimed at encouraging reconstruction and urban expansion. Since dwelling, industrial, and commercial buildings may not be constructed in unbuilt-up areas, one of the important tasks for the land use plans of local authorities is to make building land out of ordinary land. Building land is always in short supply, and prices are always high, particularly in the cities. Thus, there is always pressure to set up new plans to free more land for building. Even the stagnation in population growth has changed nothing; expectations are higher and each citizen now demands more living space than in the past. In addition, building land is always an object of investment. Whoever owns land but does not wish to build on it will often retain it for speculating on rising prices. Although there is the possibility of compelling such owners to build (para. 39(b), BBauG), the law is hardly ever resorted to. A consequence is that there are many building plots in the cities that may be built on under the law but remain empty even though demand and prices are high. Prices can only fall when more building land is released by plans. Some local authorities try to do this, but the state authorities, when considering plans for approval, check to see whether too much of an area is being subject to indiscriminate development.

There are other reasons why local authorities do not set up enough plans. Often there are complaints that the planning procedure takes too long and the law governing it is very difficult. Judicial review plays some part in the reluctance of a few local authorities to set up any plans at all. The legal and bureaucratic obstacles are large. The present task facing local planning is to improve older areas and to enable a recycling of the older industrial areas. It is not possible to lay down the standards for a new and optimal plan here. The requirements that local planning has to follow are too strict. Accordingly, no planning takes place. Some of the environmental standards—for example, noise protection laws—will have to be lowered. Many people are prepared to tolerate somewhat more noise if this enables them to live closer to where they work.

The revitalization of inner cities is subject to similar considerations. Around 1970, the city centers and the areas surrounding them were no longer attractive residential areas. In terms of social prestige, these areas declined. Today younger and older people *again* prefer to live near the city centers. Here the challenge is to improve the quality of life by improving the old building stock. This improvement will also satisfy higher expectations and facilitate a better social mix in the population. The legal basis for this already exists. The Federal Urban Renewal Act of 1972 (Städtebauförderungsgesetz, StBauFG) was passed to encourage local authorities to pass special improvement plans.

A long learning process was necessary. First, the impulse was to improve large areas. Old houses were torn down, and although the new buildings were more comfortable, they were often ugly concrete blocks void of atmosphere. Now local authorities plan smaller improvement schemes. They seek to preserve old buildings while improving the residential quality. More attention is paid to aesthetics and historic preservation. A number of cities have achieved much in this respect. Attractive residential and commercial areas have arisen out of areas that were once eyesores. Although they retain their older style, the areas are not arrested in time like museums. Often this careful kind of improvement scheme is very expensive due to the slow pace and attention to detail that is necessary. The renovated houses often are so expensive that their former inhabitants can no longer afford them. In the years to come, it remains to be seen how well simpler, less expensive improvement schemes to improve the quality of the living environment can be carried out.

APPROACHES TO LAND USE PLANNING

In Germany, land use planning is solely the planning of state and local authorities; it is public planning. It takes place within the forms of public law and is a subject of constitutional and administrative law. Planning is disciplined by means of public law. The German understanding of planning is that it is not only a creative undertaking by the planners (and architects, geographers, and sociologists) but is equally an undertaking guided by the principles of the legal order. Planning and planning law are closely interconnected. Usually lawyers will also be found working for planning authorities. Often it is they who actually set up the plans after consulting with other specialists.

Plans by private individuals, industrial firms, or building development companies are not land use plans. State and local authorities may not delegate the right to carry out public land use planning. Private individuals may make proposals for the land that belongs to them, but such private proposals and outline plans are binding on no one. Since all building and commercial uses of land require state approval, all decisions relevant to the land remain the responsibility of public administrative authorities.

The various land use plans are closely interconnected. Indeed, one speaks of a land use planning system laid down by federal laws. The most important pillars of the system are the BBauG and BROG. Of additional importance are the laws pertaining to environmental and nature protection, water, and highways because these also contain additional planning provisions.

When one speaks of a system of land use planning, one should not think of a centrally planned economic system. Nor is this planning of the French kind. Central planning is ruled out at the outset in a federal state. Moreover, it would appear that the complex problems of highly industrialized countries cannot be solved by a central planning mechanism. Complexity can be grappled with only on a decentralized basis. The German system of land use planning should not be considered closed.

Two distinctions are necessary for an understanding of the system of land use planning (Schmidt-Assmann, 1982). The first distinction is in the matter of levels. The planning levels roughly represent the general administrative levels in a federal state (federation, state, and local authorities). There are, however, a number of things that diverge from this scheme, such as the regional planning level. The second important distinction is between particular and comprehensive land use plans. The latter often comes to mind when land use planning is the issue. In systematic terms, however, this is not correct. There are numerous particular plans (such as for highway construction or clean air) that are important for the regulation and development of an area. There are, additionally, a few places where particular and comprehensive plans connect with each other.

Particular Land Use Plans

Particular land use plans exist at all administrative levels. They are plans that individual departments set up when they require land to carry out their functions. The federation may also set up such plans, although the constitution severely limits the tasks it may carry out by administrative means (Article 83, Basic Law). Where it is allowed to exercise its own administration (as in railways, postal, and military matters), it may also set up particular land use plans for these tasks. Planning power is part of the general administrative power of administration.

Most particular plans are set up by the states. It is difficult to estimate their number. Some of the plans have a statutory basis; waste disposal plans, environmental protection plans, and state highway construction plans are in this category. In such cases a special planning procedure is prescribed. Many plans are, however, set up without a statutory basis. They may not violate existing laws, but they are not dependent on some form of statutory approval. Where authorities set up particular plans, they must observe the provisions laid down in the comprehensive plans of the state (para. 5(4), BROG). Such plans are not binding on private individuals or for bodies having the right of self-government (such as local authorities).

Comprehensive Plans

Comprehensive plans are the heart of the land use planning system. These plans exist at the state and local authority levels. There are two different types of planning within the states: statewide plans and regional plans.

Comprehensive Statewide Plans

Under paragraph 5 (1) of the BROG, all states are obliged to set up statewide plans for the development of the state. Such plans consist of a text, maps, and explanations. What must be set down in these plans are population developments, the system of central places (upper and middle centers), the division of the state into regions, the larger priority areas (for example, for water conservation, rest, and recreation), the development axes, the locations of large-scale undertakings over a wide area (such as petrochemical industries and atomic power stations). These high-level land use plans have existed in the states of the Federal Republic for about 15 years. At present some are being revised to take account of population changes and environmental protection priorities.

Comprehensive Regional Plans

Of greater importance are the regional plans. This kind of planning takes place at the second level of land use planning within a state. Regional planning developed historically out of a number of particularly difficult metropolitan problems. Today it is no longer limited to these areas but is generally applied. The regions are not typical administrative districts; they were created entirely for planning purpose. Some have a population of 2 million to 3 million; most are considerably smaller. Bavaria, with a population of 10.5 million and an area of 70 square kilometers, is divided into 18 regions. Thus, in the planning system, regional planning closely approaches local planning.

Regional plans are considerably more detailed than the higher-level land use plans of the states. They contain binding provisions on the following points: central places (small and lower centers); the subdivision of land in development axes; priority areas for rest and recreation, environmental protection, water conservation, agricultural and forestry matters; the location of infrastructural plants of regional importance; and the desirable directions of development in the distribution of residential and working places among the local authorities. Such plans appear as a combination of text and maps. The text consists of binding declarations and accompanying explanations. A regional plan resembles a book of 100 pages. The maps also in part contain binding statements. They are usually to a scale of 1:50,000.

In some states, regional plans are drafted by state authorities. In other states, regional planning associations exist that are public law bodies and thus part of the public administrative system. These associations have their own officials who work out drafts. The responsible minister may give general directions. The drafts must then be discussed with the local authorities. The plan is then adopted as an administrative rule, ordinance, or bylaw by the association's assembly, whose members are elected by the local communities. By these means, regional planning is given support.

Land use plans are long-term plans, but they are never static and must instead remain flexible. Because of this, the law specifies that the plans be periodically checked and then continued or modified. In most states at present second-generation regional plans are being set up. Until a new or continued plan is passed, deviations from the old plan are allowed in individual instances. This form of ministerial dispensation is equally an instrument for promoting flexibility.

Comprehensive Local Plans

There are also two types of comprehensive plans at the local level. Their legal basis is provided by the BBauG. They consist of an official map containing the most important statements. Particular symbols must be used for the statements in the maps that are valid throughout the Federal Republic. Thus, the plans of local authorities have a common appearance. In addition, the symbols must be explained in a key so that people are able to understand the plan. Along with the map, the plan may contain further statements in the form of a text. The plan must also contain the reasoning for its actions.

Both types of plans are designed to regulate the use of land. Because land is the most important basis of all local authority activities, both of these kinds of comprehensive plans at the local level are the most important instruments in the hands of the local authorities. In terms of the system of planning, both types are derived from the planning process. In the first type of plan, an initial all-inclusive plan is set up for the whole local community; from this more exact plans of the second type are developed.

The first plan is called an area use plan and resembles the master plan under U.S. law. It should contain a program for the regulation and development of the entire local authority area. It must therefore cover the entire area of the local authority, including open land. The scale of such plans is 1:10,000, in cities 1:20,000. Under paragraph 5 of the BBauG, the plan specifies what is to be indicated: future zoning areas, the most important streets, particularly those that extend beyond the immediate locality, and areas for public services and public buildings. This master plan is an administrative rule, but it is not binding on private individuals in general or on landowners in particular; it is binding only on local authorities, which have to develop the second type of plan out of the master plan and cannot overturn what is contained in the plans program. If the master plan seems to be outdated, the local authorities must change it using a required procedure. A form of self-obligation is involved here. In addition, the public must be informed of decisions that have to be made. Landowners may begin to take account of the plan. On the other hand, a local authority does not have to pay damages when it alters its master plan, and some piece of land falls in value.

The second type of plan, a building plan, looks like a combination of an official map and a zoning regulation. The plan is inclusive; it shows not only the permitted uses of private land but also sets down the areas for streets, public buildings and services, antinoise and clean air zones, and flood areas (para. 9). This plan is an administrative rule that binds all private individuals and landowners in particular. If a landowner applies for building permission, the authority responsible will check to see whether the project is in accordance with the plan. If this is not the case, building permission must be refused. Where smaller deviations from the plan are concerned, there is the possibility of being granted a dispensation. The plan cannot, however, enjoin an existing use from then on. A special consent is also required when the subdivision of a piece of land is proposed. The subdivision may not be approved if the proposed uses would conflict with the plan. In other cases, the landowner has a right to obtain approval. The authority has no discretion otherwise.

Local authorities play an important role in the realization of the plan. Land under their jurisdiction initially must be provided with the necessary infrastructure (waterlines, drainage, roads). As a rule, these land development measures must be undertaken by the local authorities, who are entitled to charge 95 percent of the cost of these measures to the landowners. Where large-scale measures are being undertaken, the local authorities may hand these tasks over to a development company under a contract governed by public law. Often land plots are too small or the wrong shape to be built on in accordance with the plan. In such cases, the local authorities may carry out a consolidation of the land. This is also a public administrative task, which must be carried out under the provisions, and using the procedures, of public law. Finally, the plan is the basis for compulsory purchase measures—for example, the acquisition of land for the erection of a public school.

Land use planning at the local level is a power possessed by local authorities and is a process of administrative rulemaking. The BBauG lays down a particular procedure, which applies equally to the master plan and the zoning regulations. A distinction must be made between an internal and an external procedure.

Under the provisions of internal procedure, the planners must gather precise information, study maps, and make analyses and prognoses. Even at this stage they must inform themselves on public opinion. Many local authorities have planning offices for this work; a few have the work carried out by some other entity or by a private firm of architects. Once the data are collected and a vague idea of goals has been formulated, the various aims and measures must be combined and alternatives must be examined until a balanced draft is arrived at. From a legal point of view, a special kind of discretionary power is involved here; however, land use planning today is no longer based on public order law. There are other grounds for planning besides health, morals, and safety. Planning is no longer solely concerned with safeguarding against substantial dangers; it can also serve general social welfare purposes.

The external procedure is regulated precisely. Local authorities should inform the public of their planning intentions at an early stage and must give other authorities the opportunity to explain their wishes as far as the plan is concerned; the latter must also be given an account of the local authority's goals. That done, the draft plan must be laid before the public for one month. This must be announced in the daily papers. Anyone may send in comments or reservations. The local authorities examine the reservations. The local council—that is, the elected representatives of all the citizens—then passes a resolution on the plan. After this, the state supervisory authority must confirm the plan and may refuse to do so only when a plan contains errors of law (para. 6, BBauG). The discretionary power of the local authority may not be trespassed on. Finally, the approved plan must be published. Anyone at any time must be able to view the plan at the town hall.

In practice, the planning procedure is often fraught with difficulties. The participation of other administrative authorities and the public has become excessive. The procedures take several years and may be blocked by opponents. The perfectionism for which the courts are responsible must be reduced. No one gains if the local authorities no longer plan at all out of anxiety over long drawn-out procedures.

Particular problems of local planning arise where several local authorities are closely connected, above all in metropolitan areas. Here also, as a rule, each local authority sets up its own plan. Some coordination is attained in that local authorities are bound into the system of regional planning (para. 1(4), BBauG). In addition local authorities must come to an agreement with neighboring local authorities about their plans (para. 2, BBauG).

Often, however, these instruments are not enough to ensure sensible planning for a whole metropolitan area. Here there is the possibility of local authorities either joining together in a planning association or being forced together by means of state law. The association, in itself part of the apparatus of public administration, then takes over local planning. The most important organ of the association is its assembly, which consists of the representatives of the participating local authorities. Thus, each local authority continues to play a part in the land use planning process without being able to advance its interests in absolute terms since it may be outvoted in the assembly. Such planning associations exist in many metropolitan areas.

FUTURE THRUSTS

The system of planning is on the whole positive. It is well organized and reasonably effective. Although it is by no means optimal, it has certainly avoided grievous problems. After viewing the problem areas in the Federal Republic, some outside scholars in the field are inclined to ask why so much is spoken in Germany about the defects of planning. One problem is the whole idea of a system of planning under law. I approve of this idea. It guarantees clarity and logical consistency; however, one must recognize that systems are always somewhat rigid. Planning is a flexible process that never allows itself to be fully captured within a system. It is important that stability and flexibility stand in the right relationship. This can be attained by the goodwill of the public, the planners, and the judges.

The most important guiding elements of federalism, the self-government of local authorities, private property rights, and judicial review will not change. The tendency today is away from centralism and toward smaller entities and an emphasis on the legal position of the individual. This tendency is reinforced by the pronounced legal supervision under which land use planning is placed in Germany.

Foreseeable challenges tend to be concentrated in the medium term. Land use planning must take care that the current search for new jobs does not lead to industrial concerns being set up without thought being given to environmental tolerances. In Germany there is no review of environmental tolerance on its own. Environmental requirements are only reviewed once an industrial undertaking receives approval; each factory must obtain building approval. In the future the environmental requirements must be examined carefully at the land use planning stage to create the basis for later approval. Using land use planning, larger districts can be made into protected or improvement areas. Review of environmental tolerance and preventative environmental actions can thus be combined in land use planning.

On the other hand, land use planning cannot be used solely for environmental protection. It is an inclusive system of planning and accordingly must create the land use basis for economic development in the country. This development is no longer determined by heavy industry. New technologies are becoming increasingly important and include industries that create less noise and air pollution problems for the environment. For these, the requirements of places where they are to be established should not be overdrawn. A flourishing economy is not possible without some basic minimum environmental drawbacks. For less important cases, nonbureaucratic measures need to be created. This applies, for example, to the planning of technology parks, which today is still much too cumbersome.

The new communications technologies will also sound new notes. It will be possible to locate workplaces in a decentralized way. In some fields people will be able to work at home from a terminal. Rush-hour traffic to and from the city centers at the beginning and end of the working day may decline. Road building will perhaps need new emphasis and also include better access to recreation areas. The shortening of the work week would also seem to support this trend.

Finally land use planning in the Federal Republic will need to take greater account of international cooperation. Already there are conferences and agreement procedures with Germany's neighbors to the west. Nevertheless, transboundary environmental protection measures need major improvement. Europe is too small for each nation to be able to solve the problems of environmental protection by itself.

BIBLIOGRAPHY

Akademie für Raumforschung und Landesplanung. 1970. *Handwörterbuch der Raumforschung und Raumordnung (Dictionary of Land Use Planning and Research), 2. Auflage 2d ed.* Hannover: Jänecke-Verlag.

Akademie für Raumforschung und Landesplanung (Academy of Land Use Planning and Research). 1982. *Grundriss der Raumordnung (Basic Outline of Land Use Planning).* Hannover: Vincentz-Verlag.

Bielenberg, Walter e.a. 1982. *Raumordnungs-und Landesplanungsrecht des Bundes und der Länder.* Bielefeld: E. Schmidt-Verlag.

Ernst, Werner and Werner Hoppe. 1981. *Das öffentliche Bau- und Bodenrecht, Raumplanungsrecht, 2. Auflage (The Public Building—Law and Law of Land Use Planning. 2d ed.)* Munich: Bech-Verlag.

Evers, Hans-Ulrich. 1972. *Bauleitplanung, Sanierung und Stadtentwicklung (Building Law, Urban Reconstruction and Development).* Munich: Goldmann-Verlag.

Evers, Hans-Ulrich. 1973. *Das Recht der Raumordnung (Land Use Planning Law).* Munich: Goldmann-Verlag.

Schmidt-Assmann, Eberhard. 1972. *Grundfragendes Städtebaurechts (General Principles of Urban Development Law).* Göttingen: Schwartz-Verlag.

Schmidt-Assmann, Eberhard. 1982. Umweltschutz im Recht der Raumplanung (Protection of Environment and the Law of Land Use Planning). *Grundzüge des Umweltrechts (Basic Outline of Environmental Law), S. 117-170.* Berlin: E. Schmidt-Verlag.

Wahl, Rainer. 1978. *Rechtsfragen der Landesplanung und Landesentwicklung (Legal Questions of Land Use Planning), Bd. 1 und 2.* Berlin: Duncker & Humblot-Verlag.

14

German Democratic Republic

DEAN S. RUGG

Analyzing the use of land in the German Democratic Republic (GDR) requires some background on this comparatively new state. As a result of occupation by Soviet military forces after World War II, Germany was divided into two parts; the eastern part eventually gained acceptance as a communist state (East Germany), and the western part became the Federal Republic of Germany (West Germany). Unlike the other states of Eastern Europe, East Germany was relatively well developed economically but had problems to overcome connected with wartime destruction, the status of West Berlin, and the loss of some 3 million refugees. Although East Germany's recovery has not rivaled that of West Germany, its regime can point to considerable progress in its number one goal of industrial growth. Industry contributed to 62 percent of national income in 1980, an increase over the 42 percent of 1949; at the same time, the share of agriculture and forestry declined from 31 percent to 9 percent, although their combined net produce increased (*Statistisches Jahrbuch der DDR*, 1981, 80).

These economic changes have required the transfer of considerable agricultural and forest land into land uses connected with industry and urbanization. Agricultural land in the GDR, however, is actually in short supply; 16.7 million people and 6.3 million hectares of agricultural land translate into only 0.38 hectares per person, the smallest amount in an East European country except for Albania. Thus, a second goal of the communist regime is greater efficiency in agricultural production, a measure that requires a more capital-intensive approach, such as use of fertilizer and machinery (Roubitschik, 1982, 36). The goal of greater efficiency also includes the objective of self-sufficiency in feeding its people (Francisco, 1977, 190). A primary requirement of such goals of efficiency and self-sufficiency is a rational land use policy, including the optimum use of each parcel.

The emphasis in East Germany on industrial growth frequently leads to regional imbalance in production and to damage of the environment in areas of industrial-urban concentration. These problems of regional variation and environmental pressure go against a third goal: a Marxist-Leninist objective of greater regional equity in the quality of life. Long-standing differences between the industrialized south and the agrarian north, however, have made the goal difficult to attain. The same is true of imbalances between urban and rural areas. A primary question to be answered in this chapter, then, is the following: how is the land use policy of East Germany affected by these different goals of industrial growth, economic efficiency of agriculture, and regional balance in living environment?

An evaluation of land use in this communist country presents analytical problems. In 1980, I found that restrictions are placed on fieldwork, especially in cities, and that maps of large scale are classified and therefore impossible to procure. Although the *Statistical Yearbook* contains data on land use groupings, it does not include details on urban areas. Of help is the work of East German geographers who have compiled a number of maps on land use, especially those published in the impressive national atlas (*Atlas DDR*, 1970-84). Tourist plans of major cities are available, but none of these shows land use. Interpreting the changes that have taken place is especially clouded because ideology is sometimes mixed with fact. Nevertheless, it is still possible for an outsider to present a fairly accurate representation of the situation today.

HISTORICAL DEVELOPMENT AND CURRENT STATUS OF LAND USE PLANNING

The Regions

Land use in the GDR today results from a long period of settlement by Germans operating in different political systems. Nonetheless, regional patterns of this land use, especially those associated with agriculture and forests, have remained remarkably stable because they are associated with physical factors of terrain and soil. Thus, the relative size of land use groups exhibits a remarkable degree of continuity with the past. This is not to say that changes associated with collectivization under communism have not been important, but these alterations have affected the patterns of fields rather than overall proportions of uses. In addition, the loss of agricultural and forest land to urban and industrial development has been significant. These changes—collectivization and transfer of land—dominate any discussion of land use in the GDR. Hence, rural and urban land uses are interrelated, but for purposes of clarity they are separated in the analysis here.

The geographic distribution of crops in the GDR is affected more by soils than by climate. In general, climatic conditions do not vary greatly within the country in any season, although slight differences exist from north to south and with elevation. The climate, in comparison to that of northwestern Europe, is less affected by the Atlantic Ocean, and accordingly exhibits continental characteristics, with greater extremes between winter and summer. For example, Berlin has about a month with temperatures below freezing, but Paris is generally frost free except on individual days. In precipitation, East Germany receives adequate amounts for agriculture, although given places and years may be dry.

The terrain and soil conditions that affect land use in the GDR resemble those of the entire north European plain from the Rhine River to the Soviet Union. These physical elements result largely from regional variations in the effects of continental glaciation on the landscape. In the Middle Ages, a dense forest covered the plain, but today much of this woodland is gone. Nonetheless, the presence of trees is a dominant aspect of the landscape, in part because of afforestation of pine trees. The European plain in East Germany varies in width from 320 to 480 kilometers, and although most elevations are less than 90 meters above sea level, the plain is quite diverse in regional characteristics. From north to south, four zones can be recognized (see Figure 14.1).

The first zone extends from the Baltic Sea to the Baltic Ridge, the latter a series of parallel hills some 64 to 112 kilometers south of the coast. In this zone, the more recent unstratified glacial deposits of ground moraine have served as parent material to produce soils of moderate fertility. The generally flat to rolling terrain is broken up by only one major valley, that of the east-west Peene River. The Baltic Ridge itself is composed of terminal moraine—unstratified deposits of drift that accumulated at the edge of glacial advance—and is often forested. These terminal moraines have dammed up water to create a number of lakes, giving the Baltic Ridge region of East Germany the name Mecklenburg Lake Plateau. Historically this entire area north to the Baltic Sea was known as Mecklenburg and was dominated by large estates of the Prussian Junker families.

A second zone, south of the Baltic Ridge and extending to the Elbe River, has sandy uplands alternating with broad glacial valleys that run in an east-west direction across the entire country. The uplands, called Geest, represent outwash that was deposited by meltwater from the glacial lobes to the north. Sand dominates these stratified deposits—coarse grained to the north and fine grained to the south. In places, these sands have been eroded away, exposing old ground and terminal moraines from previous glacial periods as exemplified by the Fläming and lower Lusatian areas. The sands tend to be sterile from podzolization—a process by which the plant minerals are leached to lower levels of the soil—and are often used for pine forest or crops like rye and potatoes, which do well in infertile soils. The ground moraine areas are generally less podzolized and can be cultivated for a greater variety of crops. The margravate or principality of Brandenburg, which with its capital at Berlin became an electorate of the

Figure 14.1 Terrain Regions of the German Democratic Republic

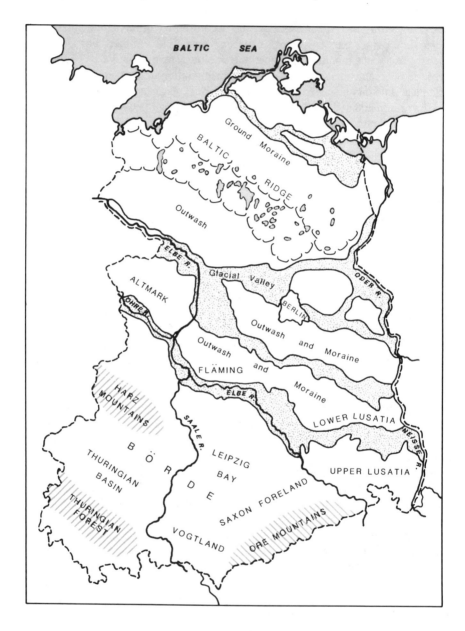

Figure 14.2 Administrative Districts in the German Democratic Republic, 1945 and the
Present

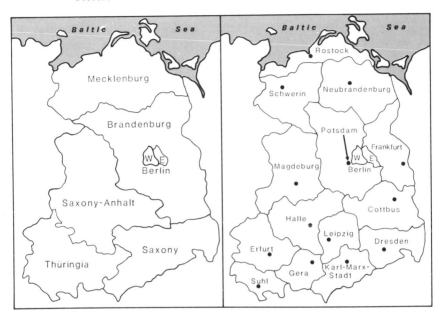

Holy Roman Empire and later the core area of the Empire of Hohenzollern
Prussia, occupied this sandy area (Figure 14.2). For a good reason, then, Brandenburg was referred to derisively as the "sandbox of the Empire."

Within this second zone, the *Urstromtäler*, or ancient glacial valleys of the
north European plain, cut the Geest areas into low islands of sandy terrain. The
broad but shallow valleys represent the locale of great rivers of meltwater that
flowed along the front of the glacial lobes as they advanced and retreated in
Europe over a period of a million years. At the close of this period, north-flowing
rivers reestablished themselves, often following portions of these valleys. In
other places, the valleys are only broad, mushy troughs devoted mainly to pasture
and forest land but also the sites for routeways of canals linking the rivers. The
location of Berlin can be explained in great part as being a site where several
of these valleys focused. Later these valleys were utilized as routeways; for
example, the Oder-Spree canal linked the Oder River with a canal to the Elbe
River. In addition, the site lies where the drier Geest or sandy uplands come
closest to meeting, thus providing both an easier crossing of the damp valleys
in medieval times and abundant well-drained land for later expansion of the city.

A third zone of the north European plain in East Germany lies south of the
Elbe River and extends to the Thuringian Forest and to the forestland of the Ore
Mountains. This area is known as the Börde, a fertile plain bordered by mountains

where fine wind-blown material called loess was deposited at the end of the glacial period. Soils derived from this rich and water-retentive material are regarded as the most fertile in Europe and are often planted in wheat and sugar beets, both demanding in their requirements. In East Germany, the zone extends in a wide arc around the Harz Mountains from Magdeburg to Leipzig and to Erfurt.

To the south and west lie low mountain ranges, which make up a fourth terrain zone of East Germany. Flanking these mountains are forelands, partly forested, that are covered by loess and cultivated in food and feed crops. The mountains, called *Mittelgebirge*, are actually forested uplands ranging from about 760 to 1,220 meters, which represent older mountains worn down by erosion over long periods and then uplifted as blocks along fault lines. The largest of these mountain blocks is the Ore Mountains whose crestlines form the political boundary with Czechoslovakia. West of these mountains is the Thuringian Forest, and farther north, separated by a portion of the Börde, is the Harz Mountain block. All of these mountains have been important for mining activities from the Middle Ages to the present.

Temporal Change

The primary categories of present land use in the GDR are shown in Figures 14.3 and 14.4 and Tables 14.1 and 14.2. Agricultural land, which covers 57.8 percent of the territory, is by far the largest category. Three-fourths of this agricultural land, or 43.8 percent of the total East German area, is arable land, and an additional 11.5 percent is grassland divided almost equally between meadows and pasture; 2.5 percent is classed as gardens, fruit, and grapes. Slightly over a quarter of the land (27.3 percent) is in forests. Economic areas, mostly made up of settlements, cover 10 percent of the GDR. Finally, the remaining small areas of the country (4.9 percent) can be broken down into fallow, waste, mining, and water.

East German land use under socialism shows the most significant changes in the decrease of agricultural land and the increase of settlements, two factors that according to Stams (1982, 38) are directly related. Between 1950 and 1970, agricultural land decreased from 60.7 percent to 58.0 percent and arable land from 46.6 percent to 42.6 percent. The yearly loss from these changes increased from 14,000 hectares before 1960 to 17,000 after (*DDR Handbuch*, 1979, 229). Among the other categories only "other economic uses"—mostly settlements— showed a corresponding increase, from 7.4 to 10.0 percent.

In the 1970s, arable land increased slightly, mostly at the expense of grassland. Settlements, however, ceased to expand and remained rather stable, a development hard to explain in view of the continued economic development. Hoffmann (1982, 54) feels that this may mean the regime now has greater ability to prevent withdrawal of agricultural land for other economic purposes but that it is premature to make this evaluation. Certainly the loss of agricultural land poses

Figure 14.3 Land Use in the German Democratic Republic

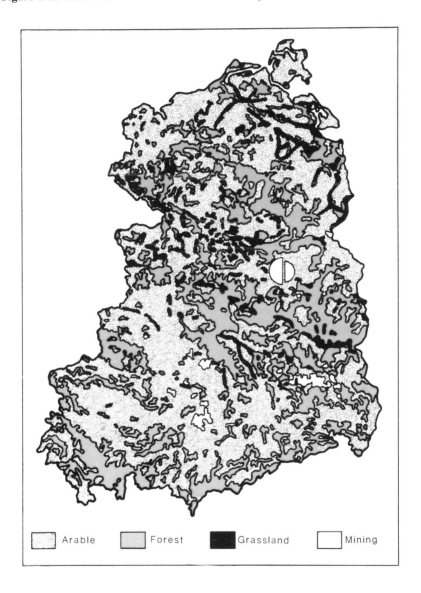

Arable   Forest   Grassland   Mining

Figure 14.4 Location and Relative Sizes of Cities and Towns in the German Democratic Republic

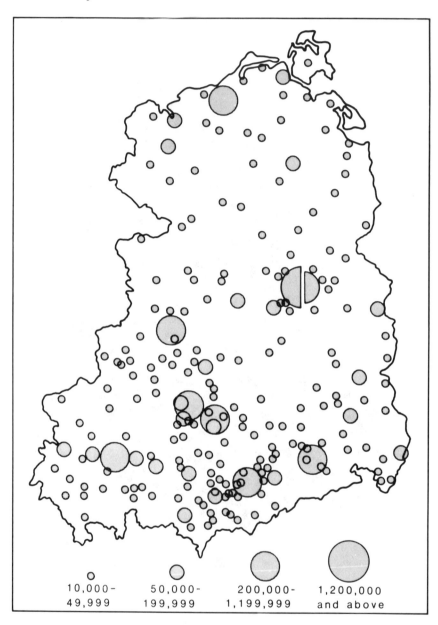

o	◯	⬤	⬤
10,000- 49,999	50,000- 199,999	200,000- 1,199,999	1,200,000 and above

Table 14.1
Land Use Changes in East Germany, 1938–1981: Area (in 1,000 hectares)

Type	1938	1950	1960	1970	1981
Agriculture	6,654.2	6,526.6	6,419.8	6,286.4	6,263.8
Arable	5,093.0	5,017.3	4,847.8	4,618.1	4,741.4
Grassland	1,361.6	1,291.1	1,362.0	1,469.2	1,248.7
Meadows	970.7	861.9	822.9	724.6	599.7
Pasture	390.9	354.3	440.1	661.8	547.5
Other	–	74.9	99.0	82.8	101.5
Gardens	(199.6	157.8	129.0	199.1	273.7
Fruit & Grapes	(	60.4	31.0		1.7
Osier (for baskets)	2.3	1.8	2.5	2.5	
Forests	2,945.8	2,898.6	2,955.2	2,948.0	2.961.6
Fallow	(	104.4	81.7	81.9	70.3
Waste	247.6	(202.2	149.5	146.9	137.7
Mining	(		45.6	75.4	87.1
Water	248.6	220.7	204.4	210.6	227.1
Other (settlements, etc.)	681.5	800.5	968.7	1,079.2	1,083.4
Total	10,780.0	10,754.8	10,827.4	10,830.9	10,832.7

Source: _Statistisches Jahrbuch der DDR_, 1960–61, pp. 442–443 and 1982, p. 168.

359

Table 14.2
Land Use Changes in East Germany, 1938–1981: Percentages

Type	1938	1950	1960	1970	1981
Agriculture	61.8	60.7	59.3	58.0	57.8
Arable	47.3	46.6	44.8	42.6	43.8
Grassland	12.6	12.0	12.6	13.6	11.5
Meadows	9.0	8.0	7.6	6.7	5.5
Pasture	3.6	3.3	4.1	6.1	5.1
Other	–	0.7	0.9	0.8	0.9
Gardens	(1.9	1.5	1.2	(1.8	(2.5
Fruit & Grapes	0.0	0.6	0.7		
Osier (for baskets)	0.0	0.0	0.0	0.0	0.0
Forests	27.3	27.0	27.3	27.2	27.3
Fallow	(	1.0	0.8	0.8	0.7
Waste	2.3	(1.9	1.4	1.4	1.3
Mining	(		0.4	0.7	0.8
Water	2.3	2.0	1.9	1.9	2.1
Other (settlements, etc.)	6.3	7.4	8.9	10.0	10.0
	100.0	100.0	100.0	100.0	100.0

Source: *Statistisches Jahrbuch der DDR*, 1960-61, pp. 442–443 and 1982, p. 168.

a problem in all industrializing countries. In the GDR, however, the shortage of land and the commitment of this society to become self-sufficient in food production make the control of land use urgent.

The tables reveal other significant changes. Most visible is coal mining, which almost doubled between 1960 and 1981 (Figure 14.3 and Tables 14.1 through 14.4). Open-pit excavation of brown coal, a resource in which East Germany leads world production, almost entirely accounts for this increase. The Germans have long used brown coal as a raw material for a variety of chemical products (including synthetic gasoline and coke), but the primary use today is for electric power generation. Mining employs modern technology such as large *Förder-brücken* (conveyor bridges), which strip the overburden from in front of the exposed coal, transport it back over this coal, and deposit it behind (Barthel, 1962). These large operations disrupt the landscape of central East Germany, but remedial, offsetting efforts include the reclamation of land including the development of recreational lakes, such as near Senftenberg.

Open-pit mining is largely confined to three administrative districts (*Bezirke*)— Halle, Leipzig, and Cottbus (see Figures 14.2 and 14.3)—where much of the coal is used for generating power; the pattern of power plant distribution shows a concentration in these three districts (Kohl et al., 1979, 111). Major development occurred in the first two of these districts (both west of the Elbe River) before World War II and has continued during the communist period. Some indication of the effects of this mining on land use along the Geisel River north of Halle is shown in Figure 14.5. In addition to new open pits, those that existed before 1945 were enlarged by 1968, with the result that reclamation has not kept pace with excavation.

With the decline of brown coal reserves in these districts west of the Elbe, recent expansion has occurred in the Cottbus district to the east, from which ultimately 60 percent of the output will come. In 1960, about two-thirds of the total area of open pits (65.14 percent) in the country was in these three districts, with 41.23 percent in Halle and Leipzig. By 1981, the percentage of mining areas in the three districts had risen to three-fourths (75.66 percent), but Cottbus accounted for over one-half (38.58 percent) of the 75.66 percent. The transformation of the landscape in this district since 1950 has been remarkable. The new industrial towns of Lauchhammer and Hoyerswerda, whose respective populations increased from 6,400 and 7,300 in 1946 to 25,000 and 70,700 in 1980, are related to the accelerated changes.

Other changes in land use over time have taken place, but the explanation is not always clear-cut. Fallow and waste land decreased, a trend attributed to attempts to bring marginal land into agricultural use as provided by Article 18 of the Land Improvement Law of 1970 (*DDR Handbuch*, 1979, 231). Similarly grassland as a whole decreased only slightly between 1950 and 1981, but this change masks quite opposite trends of its two components, pasture and meadow. As seen in Tables 14.1 and 14.2, the increase in pasture is more than offset by the decrease in meadow. Although sources are unclear about the reasons for

Table 14.3

Land Use in East Germany, 1960: Percentages That Districts Comprise of Each Type of Land Use

District	Total	Agric.	Arable	Other	Forest	Fallow	Waste	Mining	Water	Settlements
Berlin	.38	.19	.13	.38	.25	.24	.20	.00	1.27	1.87
Cottbus	7.63	5.55	5.12	6.88	11.64	11.51	7.76	23.91	3.23	9.04
Dresden	6.23	6.39	6.17	7.05	5.85	1.83	5.62	4.82	4.11	7.34
Erfurt	6.76	7.47	8.41	4.60	5.59	3.92	6.02	1.97	.39	7.51
Frankfurt	6.65	5.76	6.34	3.99	8.67	4.41	5.35	2.63	10.71	6.02
Gera	3.71	3.32	3.07	4.08	5.00	1.35	3.41	2.85	1.96	3.00
Halle	8.10	9.21	10.48	5.31	5.61	6.85	8.56	19.96	2.45	9.06
K. Marx St.	5.55	5.42	5.12	6.34	6.08	3.92	5.69	2.41	1.37	5.95
Leipzig	4.57	5.62	6.17	3.93	2.26	2.32	3.75	21.27	2.00	4.81
Madgeburg	10.62	11.76	11.94	11.23	9.27	4.53	6.69	5.70	2.89	10.16
Neubrandenburg	10.09	10.49	10.65	9.98	8.38	17.75	13.98	3.51	34.15	6.57
Potsdam	11.59	10.11	9.05	13.38	14.13	13.83	8.36	3.95	14.73	13.70
Rostock	6.53	7.78	7.77	7.81	3.85	12.61	11.44	2.85	5.53	5.52
Schwerin	8.03	8.57	7.74	11.11	6.91	10.16	8.96	3.29	14.87	6.24
Suhl	3.56	2.36	1.84	3.93	6.51	4.77	4.21	.88	.34	3.21
DDR	100.0	100.0	100.0	100.0	100.0	100.0	100.0	100.0	100.0	100.0

Source: Statistisches Jarhbuch der DDR, 1960-61, p. 441.

362

Table 14.4

Land Use in East Germany, 1981: Percentages That Districts Comprise of Each Type of Land Use

District	Total	Agric.	Arable	Grass	Other	Forest	Fallow	Waste	Mining	Water	Settlements
Berlin	0.42	0.18	.16	.03	1.34	.25	.57	.15	.11	1.67	2.06
Cottbus	7.64	5.51	5.41	6.27	3.82	11.48	9.81	5.00	38.58	6.26	7.50
Dresden	6.23	6.41	5.90	7.43	10.57	5.78	1.28	5.58	4.02	4.05	7.46
Erfurt	6.75	7.48	8.13	4.65	9.27	5.45	4.41	5.73	1.84	.66	8.01
Frankfurt	6.59	5.74	6.27	3.92	4.72	8.62	3.56	6.53	1.72	9.78	5.92
Gera	3.69	3.31	3.07	4.09	4.03	4.94	1.71	3.70	1.38	1.94	3.08
Halle	8.12	9.05	10.13	3.97	13.34	5.78	8.82	6.96	18.25	3.92	9.31
K. Marx Stadt	5.58	5.40	4.55	8.17	7.38	6.21	4.12	6.67	1.84	1.59	5.99
Leipzig	4.54	5.44	5.99	2.93	7.38	2.26	2.28	3.63	18.83	1.89	5.21
Madgeburg	10.63	11.77	12.14	11.01	8.79	9.29	3.98	7.25	4.36	2.99	10.63
Neubrand-enburg	10.13	10.67	10.85	11.32	4.43	8.53	20.77	15.37	2.18	31.50	6.23
Potsdam	11.59	10.20	9.61	11.99	12.25	14.21	5.55	9.65	2.52	13.57	13.45
Rostock	6.53	7.83	7.99	8.01	4.25	3.89	14.79	11.89	1.84	5.11	5.69
Schwerin	8.00	8.73	8.29	11.15	5.45	6.85	10.53	7.54	1.84	14.67	5.88
Suhl	3.56	2.28	1.51	5.06	2.98	6.46	7.82	4.35	69	.40	3.58
DDR	100.00	100.00	100.00	100.00	100.00	100.00	100.00	100.00	100.00	100.00	100.00

Source: Statistisches Jahrbuch der DDR, 1982, p. 168.

363

Figure 14.5 Spread of Open-pit Mining of Brown Coal in the Halle District of East Germany, 1945–1968

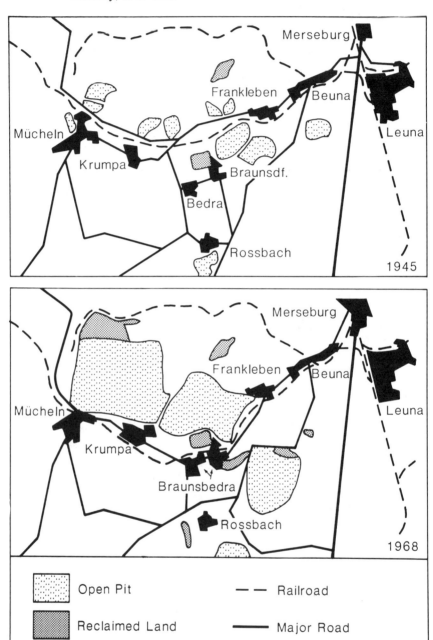

these trends, apparently certain meadowland is being brought into cultivation, while marginal agricultural land is becoming permanent pasture. This trend especially shows up in southern districts—a "migration of grassland to the south" (Hoffmann, 1982, 50).

Trends in garden and fruit-grape production are obscured because they have been grouped together statistically since 1965. Other sources report that specialized areas of fruit and grape production show high degrees of concentration. For example, two-fifths of the fruit production in the GDR comes from the districts of Potsdam, Halle, and Leipzig, with the largest single area of surplus from the Potsdam and Werder city areas, which supply the Berlin market (Kohl et al., 1976, 413). Grapes for wine are climatically restricted in East Germany, being confined largely to the upper portion of the Saale and Elbe River valleys.

Regional Distribution

The Baltic region of Mecklenburg historically was the land of the big Junker estates for a century or more before World War II. Today these estates have been converted to collective or state farms. Many old manor houses of the estates remain, often as administrative centers for the new socialist farms. The primary distinction in land use today is between the areas of ground moraine where grain and root crops (potatoes) are cultivated and the more hilly terminal moraine areas dominated by forest and heath. On the ground moraine, the primary crops of the past—rye and potatoes—continue to be planted on the poorer soils, but the growing of wheat and sugar beets has increased, especially on soils of slight leaching. Poorly drained areas are in meadowland and are used as pasture for livestock. Oats, formerly grown as a feed crop for draft horses before World War II, has declined greatly as the use of machinery has increased. Forestland dominated by scattered stands of pine, oak, and birch is not as extensive as in the central region. In the terminal moraine and lake country of the Baltic Ridge, however, the proportion of land in pine forest increases, as does that of water surface (Figure 14.1 and Table 14.5). In addition, the Baltic Region has the highest percentage of fallow and waste land, composed of dunes along the coast and moor or marsh areas elsewhere.

Land use in the central region of East Germany reflects the changes in glacial landforms (see Figures 14.1 and 14.3). In this area between the Baltic Ridge and the Elbe River, the ground and terminal moraines of the northern region give way to meltwater deposits of sand (outwash plain) and the damp meadows of the broad glacial valleys; however, scattered areas of ground and terminal moraine from earlier glacial periods are exposed in places. Consequently, the pattern of land use is more varied than in the Baltic Region. The sandy soils, whose quality is often quite low because permeability has increased podzolization, generally underlie the monotonous pine forests, which are often the

Table 14.5

Land Use in East Germany, 1981, by Administrative District: Percentages

District	Agric.	Arable	Grass	Other	Forest	Fallow	Waste	Mining	Water	Settle-ments	
Berlin	25.1	16.1	0.9	8.1	16.4	0.9	0.4	0.2	8.3	48.7	= 100.0
Cottbus	41.8	31.0	9.5	1.3	41.1	0.8	0.8	4.0	1.7	9.8	= 100.0
Dresden	59.5	41.5	13.7	4.3	25.4	0.1	1.1	0.5	1.4	12.0	= 100.0
Effurt	64.1	52.7	7.9	3.5	22.1	0.4	1.1	0.2	0.2	11.9	= 100.0
Frankfurt	50.3	41.7	6.8	1.8	35.8	0.3	1.3	0.2	3.1	9.0	= 100.0
Gera	52.0	36.4	12.8	2.8	36.7	0.3	1.3	0.3	1.1	8.3	= 100.0
Halle	64.4	54.6	5.6	4.2	19.5	0.7	1.1	1.8	1.0	11.5	= 100.0
K. Marx Stadt	56.0	35.7	16.9	3.4	30.4	0.5	1.5	0.3	0.6	10.7	= 100.0
Leipzig	69.4	57.8	7.5	4.1	13.6	0.3	1.0	3.3	0.9	11.5	= 100.0
Madgeburg	64.0	50.0	11.9	2.1	23.9	0.3	0.9	0.3	0.6	10.0	= 100.0
Neubrandenburg	60.9	46.9	12.9	1.1	23.0	1.3	1.9	0.2	6.5	6.2	= 100.0
Potsdam	50.9	36.3	11.9	2.7	33.5	0.3	1.0	0.2	2.5	11.6	= 100.0
Rostock	69.4	53.6	14.1	1.7	16.3	1.5	2.3	0.2	1.6	8.7	= 100.0
Schwerin	63.1	45.3	16.1	1.7	23.4	0.9	1.2	0.2	3.8	7.4	= 100.0
Suhl	37.0	18.5	16.4	2.1	49.6	1.4	1.6	0.2	0.2	10.0	= 100.0
DDR	57.8	43.8	11.5	2.5	27.3	0.7	1.3	0.8	2.1	10.0	= 100.0

Source: Statistisches Jahrbuch der DDR, 1982, p. 168.

result of afforestation projects; less permeable soils are in rye and potatoes. The proportions of forest covering the total area reach as high as 33 percent to 41 percent in the districts of Cottbus, Frankfurt/Oder, and Potsdam (see Table 14.5). Ground moraine soils also exhibit crop differentiation: rye and potatoes on the poorer soils and wheat and sugar beets on the better. Glacial valleys are well suited to meadow grazing and hay crops used for cattle or dairy cows; thus the proportion of land in grass is high. The poor quality of this grass, however, necessitates fodder crops, including roots, such as potatoes, and feed grains.

Overall the landscape of the central region forms a mosaic of arable land, pasture, heath, and pine forest (see Figures 14.1 and 14.3). Specialized areas mentioned before—the large city of Berlin, fruit and grape areas, and the brown coal mining of Cottbus *Bezirk*—are located in this region. Tobacco also represents a specialized crop in a small area near the new town of Schwedt on the Oder River. In addition to the expansion of settlements, the primary change with time has been the increase of open-pit mining, which has been at the expense of other uses and has resulted in some expansion of water areas through reclamation.

In contrast to the northern and central regions of East Germany, the southwestern region, which lies between the Elbe River and the *Mittelgebirge*, has larger proportions of arable land (see Figures 14.1 and 14.3 and Table 14.5). The Börde, a term applied to this area, is known for its rich soil derived from loess, soil that is ideal for crops of wheat and sugar beets. The core of this area lies amid the cities of Magdeburg, Leipzig, and Erfurt, with only the upland of the Harz Mountains intruding from the west. The landscape is almost solidly agricultural except for the large cities and activities connected with industry, especially the open-pit mining of brown coal around Halle and south of Leipzig. Sugar beet factories, using coal as a source of energy, are common. Forests, except for some shelter belts to reduce wind erosion, and pasture are limited in this important agricultural area. Winter wheat is rotated with summer barley, which is used for brewing purposes. Although wheat and sugar beets dominate the landscape, fodder crops such as corn and alfalfa are grown for livestock feeding.

A ring of somewhat poorer soils surrounds this core area of arable land; however, the greater precipitation of the ring area favors increased fodder crops like clover and potatoes (Kohl et al., 1976, 421, 440-41).

The final terrain region of East Germany consists of the *Mittelgebirge* ranges of the Thuringian Forest and of the Harz and Ore mountains, where the percentages of forest are high (see Figures 14.1 and 14.3 and Table 14.5). Characteristically pine at lower levels and spruce at higher elevations cover the mountain slopes. Many of the cultivated crops—such as potatoes, oats, and hay—on the available arable land, which is generally below 30 percent, are used for livestock feeding.

INSTITUTIONAL AND LANDOWNERSHIP FRAMEWORK

Role of the State

The institutional framework for land use planning in the GDR is much more difficult to summarize than it is in the Federal Republic of Germany because the GDR has no series of comprehensive laws. Instead, a variety of laws, decrees, and ordinances spell out the planning basis for land use policy. The role of the state in East Germany, however, is fundamental in reaching planning goals. The state owns the means of production, including land and resources, plans and manages the national economy, protects and utilizes the land, and emphasizes the promotion of the collective good for society. The following articles from the GDR Constitution (1968) illustrate this key role of the state in a planned economy, including the management of land use:

9(1) The national economy of the German Democratic Republic is based upon the socialist ownership of the means of production.

(3) The German Democratic Republic bases itself on the principle of the management and planning of the national economy and all other social spheres.

10(1) Socialist property exists in the following forms: as nationally owned property of society as a whole, as joint cooperative property of collectives of working people, and as property of social organizations of citizens.

12(2) The socialist state ensures the use of nationally owned property for the greatest good of society.

15(1) The land of the German Democratic Republic is one of its most valuable natural resources. It must be protected and utilized rationally. Land used for agriculture and forestry may only be removed from such use with the agreement of the responsible organs of the state.

15(2) In the interests of the welfare of citizens, the state and country shall protect nature.

These articles not only emphasize the collective goals of a Marxist-Leninist ideology but also directly affect land use.

It is planning that most directly affects land use. Werner (1972, 19-23) provides the following summary of the planning administration of the GDR in the early 1970s. No overall office has responsibility for regional planning. Indeed there is a separation of offices responsible for economic planning and those for physical planning. Economic planning is conducted by the State Planning Commission (*Staatliche Plankomission*) through its department of territorial planning, which deals with aspects of growth under a centrally planned economy. This department coordinates district (*Bezirk*) and county (*Kreis*) offices; the former generates plans, and the latter carries them out. Physical planning, on the other hand, is coordinated by the Ministry of Building (*Ministerium für Bauwesen*) through regional, city, and village offices. Perhaps the biggest difference from West Germany is that no administrative structure exists for coordinating regional planning between districts except for Berlin (districts of Frankfurt/Oder and Potsdam). Planning within the fourteen districts in the GDR is facilitated because these units were created out of the historic states specifically for economic-planning purposes.

Land use legislation in East Germany first developed from problems faced in the country after World War II (*DDR Handbuch*, 1979, 229-31). The *Aufbau-gesetz* (reconstruction law) of 1950 established the planning basis for rebuilding the destroyed cities, and in the same year a decree outlined sixteen principles of city planning (Werner, 1976, 132-34). By the 1960s, from the loss of agri-cultural land to industry and urbanization and the harm done to land through economic development, the state began to show interest in protecting the land. This attention resulted in a series of acts that affect land use in the country. In 1964, an act for the protection of agricultural land and forestland regulated changes and provided for compensation if necessary. A 1967 act established fees to be paid for different changes in land use. In 1970-71, laws and regulations were passed that controlled the extensive open-pit mining of brown coal, in-cluding the reclamation of the land for agricultural, recreational, or other pur-poses. In 1970, a land improvement law (*Landeskulturgesetz*) incorporated a series of comprehensive measures designed to protect the environment. Other acts that affected land use, either directly or indirectly, followed during the 1970s.

All of these laws served to stabilize land use change in the GDR, especially the loss of agricultural land resulting from the physical expansion of industry and settlement (*DDR Handbuch*, 1979, 230). This stabilization has been viewed as contributing to the national goal of greater self-sufficiency in food and re-sources. In turn, pressure on land has been reduced by the decline of population from 19.1 million in 1947 to 16.7 million in 1982, a change due in great part to extensive migration to the West before 1961 when the wall was constructed in Berlin to restrict this flow.

Two types of plan were traditional in the local planning of prewar Germany: the land use plan (*Flächennutzungsplan*, FNP) and the building plan (*Bebauung-splan*, BBP). The first shows the intended distribution of land uses for a *Gemeinde* (commune), thereby providing a basis for land use policy without legal basis; the second contains the legal mechanisms of planning control for new construc-tion projects, especially on the edges of the built-up area. In West Germany, these two plans are used by local agencies in their planning within a framework set by the Federal Building Laws (*Bundesbaugesetze*) of the 1960s. In East Germany, the status of these two plans has changed as planning increasingly has conformed to laws or principles expressed by the central government. An example is the group of sixteen principles of city planning (*Städtebau*), which dates from 1950 and established general guidelines for urban design in the cities of East Germany. With state control over all local land, the *Flächennutzungsplan* ceased in the 1950s to serve as a tool for local planning as it does in West Germany (Werner, 1972, 88-89). In the 1970s, a new phase of planning began in which *Generalbebauungspläne* (GBP) (general building plans) provided planning guidelines for districts, component counties of districts, and cities (Werner, 1972, 89). These plans have no legal basis, however, and planning continues to be directed by the central government through various laws and decrees.

Effects of Collectivization

The GDR, like the Soviet Union and most other communist countries, has transformed its agricultural system through collectivization, an institutional factor that has been important in land use change. The process involves the creation of state-run farms and the application of large-scale methods of production to agriculture. Marxist-Leninist ideology supports collectivization because of certain advantages in not only transforming peasant societies but also controlling the rural areas and reducing the difference between town and country. In peasant countries like the Soviet Union and Bulgaria, collectivization, through the creation of large mechanized farms, erased the peasant hold on the landscape and permitted a capital-intensive approach to agriculture. This process released peasant labor to work in industrial factories in the cities and produced food surpluses on the farms. In turn, capital could be created by selling the farm surpluses at higher prices in the cities. These advantages were less evident in East Germany, where large farms and estates existed before World War I. Nonetheless, Marxist ideology states that a private agricultural system will not work efficiently alongside a socialized industrial system. Furthermore, control of the parochial countryside is deemed necessary. "It was absolutely necessary, according to the communist program, to transform the village and the agricultural sector in the image of the urban and proletarian sector" (Mosely, 1958, 58).

The collectivization programs were carried out in Eastern Europe in the 1950s and 1960s, sometimes with considerable resistance by peasants. In Poland and Yugoslavia, the programs were not successful, and the strip fields remain as a legacy of the Middle Ages and the three-field system of that period. In East Germany, collectivization progressed rather slowly in the 1950s, and as late as 1959 only 46 percent of the agricultural land had switched to the socialist system. One year later, the percentage soared to 92 percent, indicating that 1960 was a critical year (Francisco, 1977, 187). Apparently the East German leader, Walter Ulbricht, decided to force collectivization on ideological grounds after voluntary efforts had failed (Francisco, 1979, 67-69).

Socialist agriculture is based on two types of large-scale units: the collective (*Landwirtschaftliche Produktionsgenossenschaft*, LPG) and the state farm (*Volkseigenes Gut*, VEG). The collective operates like a cooperative—indeed it is often called a producers' cooperative—in that net profits, after the state's quota has been subtracted, are distributed among the members, partly in cash, partly in land, on the basis of work measured by a so-called labor day. Different types of cooperatives exist. The most socialized type, which dominates in East Germany, involves the farmer's relinquishing all private control over land, livestock, and equipment; however, members of all types receive about half a hectare or so to cultivate crops or keep livestock.

Supplementing the collective is the state farm—the true socialist form—owned by the state and financed by the national budget. Employees receive wages in the same way that industrial workers do, and the net profits revert to the state. State farms usually are located in areas with low population densities and where specialization in one type of crop or livestock is feasible; they also serve as models for management, perform experimental functions in terms of technology, and are sources of supply for high-quality seeds and selected breeding stock.

Collectivization in East Germany has exhibited strengths and weaknesses (Francisco, 1977, 185-88; 1979, 80-81). In certain respects, the system has been successful in terms of increasing crop production while also placing greater emphasis on livestock. Capital intensity has shown improvement through greater use of fertilizer (yields per hectare) and increased machinery (yields per worker). The GDR, along with Czechoslovakia, stands out among socialist countries in the quality of the nation's diet and the quantity of foods available for consumption. The regime also has pioneered in developing new forms of horizontal integration, that is, increasing the degree of specialization in areas. On the other hand, despite rather high capital inputs, agriculture still lags behind that of West Germany in terms of yields of crops per hectare and of livestock per head (Lazarcik, 1981, pt. 2, 609-11). In part, this result is attributed to the same factors that hinder socialized production in the Soviet Union: an inflexible centralized bureaucracy and a lack of incentives. However, Francisco (1979, 77-80) finds, paradoxically, that antipathy to collective farming is lacking in the GDR because the most vigorous opponents of the process fled to the West and the regime has made this type of farming attractive in terms of earnings and hours of work.

Land use in the GDR has been remarkably stable in a historical sense because of the limits set by physical conditions. Thus, startling changes under socialism are not evident. Nonetheless, certain aspects of agricultural land use have changed. A primary planning goal of socialist East Germany has been to become self-sufficient in feeding its people. To do this it needed to be more efficient in production; it also wanted to provide a better diet for its people, and this meant more livestock production. Progress in efficiency and diet has been made, but these are not easily visible in land use statistics. Arable land decreased in area, yet net crop output between 1950 and 1973 increased by 11 percent through use of fertilizers. However, net animal output increased threefold (Francisco, 1977, 188-89). This increase in livestock has necessitated greater production of fodder crops such as corn and alfalfa, an achievement that has come about at the expense of grain, especially oats formerly fed to horses. The emphasis on livestock is also reflected in higher prices paid to producers of slaughtered cattle than to producers of wheat. To maintain its priority of high livestock levels, however, the GDR has had to purchase feed grains from the West at high prices using scarce hard currency.

The socialization of East German agriculture is less apparent in land use changes than it is in modernization through larger fields and technology. Obviously the transformation of fields is not as evident here as in other parts of Eastern Europe because the pre–World War II estates of Germany had large fields. Today these fields are even larger, and the degree of specialization is greater than in the 1930s. Although the proportions of agricultural land use categories may not have changed greatly, the distribution of this land within fields on individual farms has. The enlarged farms also make use of more machinery; for example, the number of tractors has quadrupled, from 36,000 in 1950 to 145,000 in 1980 (*Statistisches Jahrbuch der DDR*, 1981, 26).

In 1981, the socialist sector included about 95 percent of the agricultural land in the country, with the remainder being private plots (*Statistisches Jahrbuch der DDR*, 1982, 168-69). Collective farms accounted for 84 percent of the agricultural land, state farms for 7 percent, and specialized forms of socialized production for the remainder. The most important effect of this socialization of the landscape—and one that indirectly has affected land use—is the continued trend toward concentration, specialization, and integration of farm operations. LPGs and VEGs have been combined and specialized toward crop farming or livestock production. Essentially this policy has gone through three stages (Bajaja, 1980, 280-89).

In the 1960s, LPGs and VEGs combined into cooperative associations (*Kooperationsgemeinschaften*,KOGs) for the joint use and purchase of expensive machinery. Since these larger cooperative units retained their multibranch crop and livestock activities, however, they did not effectively further specialization of production. Then in the 1970s, in an effort to break down the mixture of crop and livestock production and thereby to further specialization, East German farm units were restructured. In some cases, LPGs and VEGs, though retaining their identity, were combined into cooperative crop-growing farms (*Kooperative Abteilungen Pflanzenproduktionen*, KAPs). In addition, some LPGs and VEGs were established as interenterprise organizations for crops or livestock (*Zwischenbetriebliche Einrichtungen*, ZBEs). Furthermore, centers for agrochemical services (*Agrochemische Zentren*, AGZs) were founded to handle fertilizer application for given areas. Finally, county enterprises for rural technology (*Kreisbetriebe für Landtechnik*) now had the responsibility for repair of machinery for given areas, having replaced the earlier machine loan stations (*Maschinenausleihstationen*, MASs) and machine tractor stations (*Maschinen-Traktoren-Stationen*, MTS).

These cooperative arrangements, however, were only a transitional stage toward more stable specialized forms. In the late 1970s, the third stage began; the cooperative associations were dissolved, and the legal entities—specialized crop-farming and livestock-producing LPGs and VEGs—became dominant. These farms grew in size and in doing so seemingly moved away from collective management in the direction of centralized control. Although the larger size brought advantages of economies of scale, some felt that costs of supervision and transportation had increased (Bajaja, 1980, 288-89). Nevertheless, these changes have made GDR agriculture unusual in the world and have affected land use patterns.

Official statistics illustrate these changes in size. The number of LPGs decreased from 19,313 in 1960 to 3,969 in 1981, and the VEGs declined from 669 to 479 (*Statistisches Jahrbuch der DDR*, 1982, 169). Up to the early 1970s, these two enterprises produced both crops and livestock; since then they have been designated separately as specializing in one or the other. The area covered by these reduced numbers of LPGs and VEGs remained nearly the same, which means that their average size increased greatly in the 21 years, the LPGs from 280 hectares to 1,333 hectares and the VEGs from 591 hectares to 909 hectares. The average size of the LPGs specializing in crop production grew more spectacularly, averaging some 4,750 hectares. As the permanent LPGs and VEGs were created, the number of transitional enterprises (KAPs and ZBEs-crop) dropped from 1,210 in 1975 to 36 in 1981.

The effects of these changes on land use influence the landscape, as illustrated by the example of Dedelow, a KAP located in the northeast part of the country (*Atlas der Erdkunde*, 1978, 13). In 1967, the nine different components of Dedelow—LPGs and VEGs—exhibited considerable diversity of crops and animals. By 1970, degrees of concentration and specialization appeared. Areas of grain, root crops, forage, and grass, which formerly existed as part of separate farms, now were combined in larger fields on larger farms. At the same time, the specialization of livestock production created a concentration of dairy cows in one area, cattle in another, and pigs in still another.

The introduction of these changes in specialization on large farms represents forms of horizontal integration. Although the horizontal types dominate the structural changes in East German agriculture, vertical integration is also found, but to a lesser degree. With this method, processing of agricultural raw materials takes place in a factory located right on the farm, for example, the growing and refining of sugar beets at the same place.

MAJOR CHALLENGES TO LAND USE POLICY

Although many challenges exist to land use policy in the GDR, only three major ones are discussed here: loss of agricultural land and forestland to settlements and mining, inadequate recreational land, and problems connected with attaining the ideological goal of regional balance in living environments.

A rational land use policy is based on coordinating the use of land with future needs, an objective inadequately met in the GDR. Because of a shortage of agricultural land, this country emphasizes a policy of self-sufficiency. Yet a predominant land use trend has been the withdrawal of agricultural land and forestland for settlements, especially in the southwest area where the best arable land occurs. In all areas, the need for settlement land is most easily met by developing it on the outskirts of cities and villages where there are no barriers;

within settlements, costs increase because of restricted sites where buildings must be demolished. In addition, using mass construction methods of prefabrication on a large scale presents problems within small urban sites. Finally, pressure for preservation of certain historic buildings exists within cities or even villages, providing an additional stimulus to peripheral construction. Even the collective farms require much land that is most easily found on the village outskirts. The overall result is continued pressure for withdrawal of agricultural land and attempts to intensify production on the existing farms.

Open-pit mining of brown coal, especially in the Cottbus district, also utilizes agricultural land and forestland. This change in use presents a special challenge because of the potential for restoring the old pits that previously have been mined out. Although the East Germans have made considerable progress on conservation of the landscape, certain problems remain. Pounds (1969, 262) points out that only a portion of the land can actually be restored to previous quality, for the soil profile has been disturbed and the water table has been made dangerously high. The results mean a reduced agricultural output and a disturbed environment.

A second challenge facing East German planners after the loss of agricultural land is the problem of providing adequate recreational land. Citizens of the GDR, by not being able to travel easily to foreign countries, place undue pressure on existing facilities. According to Hoffmann (1982, 66-69), land use policy has not kept pace with the demand for sufficient public recreational land. Part of this problem results from private owners or squatters in weekend homes occupying large percentages of the available land on water bodies. Such occupancy apparently began in the early part of this century and has continued in the socialist era because restrictions have not been enforced. For example, in the Frankfurt/Oder district, only 24 kilometers of lakeshore out of a total of 736 kilometers remains for public use. Stream frontages are also alienated from public use. In most cases, the inadequate infrastructure of sewage and other services creates a poor environment.

A third challenge to land use policy, and perhaps the most difficult one to meet, is the Marxist-Leninist goal of attaining regional equality in living environments. The goal does not refer to strict equity in terms of production and services but assumes a rational contribution of each region to national growth with the idea of giving every person in a communist society equal access to opportunities for work, education, health, recreation, and consumer goods. This living environment also includes equity regarding such hazards as water and air pollution.

In the area that is now the GDR, regional differences existed before World War II between the agrarian northern districts and the more heavily industrialized southern ones. Thirty years of planning by the communists have not made the north and south equal, but the north has been transformed by the addition of industry. Table 14.6, using data from Lüdemann and Heinzmann (1978, 123-26), shows how industry now surpasses agriculture in the employment pattern

Table 14.6
Economic Changes in Selected Districts of East Germany

| District | Employment | | | | Index of Industrial Gross Production 1975 (1965 = 100) | Urbanization Increase in Towns over 10,000 (1955 - 1975) |
| | 1939 | | 1975 | | | |
	Industry	Agriculture	Industry	Agriculture		
North						
Bostock	45.4	54.6	69.3	30.7	184	+ 10.5
Schwerin	32.5	67.5	59.7	40.3	213	+ 7.1
Neubrandenburg	33.4	66.6	51.2	48.8	232	+ 11.2
South						
Halle	69.4	30.6	83.7	16.3	180	+ 4.9
Leipzig	80.4	19.6	85.1	14.9	173	+ 1.5
Karl-Marx-Stadt	86.0	14.0	91.2	8.8	180	+ 2.3

Source: Ludemann, Heinz, & Heinzmann, Joachim. On the settlement system of the German Democratic Republic: Development trends and strategies. In Niles Hansen (ed.), Human Settlement Systems. Cambridge, Mass.: Ballinger, 1978, pp. 123-126.

of the three northern districts, a reversal from 1939. These changes obviously have affected the land use patterns in the northern districts (see Table 14.5): settlement, including industry, increased at the expense of grassland and, in some places, arable land. Although the relative changes in the southern districts were not as great, absolute increases in settlement were impressive, mostly at the expense of both arable land and grassland.

The East German government also has attempted to reduce regional differences in the availability of services. This planning employed principles of central place theory in order to locate services in a hierarchical fashion and thereby minimize travel time (Scherf, 1975, 29). The most ubiquitous services typify villages, whereas towns and cities provide increasingly specialized types. Kluge (1979, 102-3) provides a list of the central place functions for the Neubrandenburg district (see Figure 14.2), which illustrates the systematic attempt to establish a consistent hierarchical provision for services in the GDR (Table 14.7). Each higher rank has those services of the lower ones plus its own.

Although East German geographers maintain that citizens now benefit from more equitable accessibility to services such as consumer goods, housing, education, and health, a U.S. geographer has some doubts. Berentsen (1980, 297-98) found, for example, that retail sales per capita varied among districts in 1974. This situation is caused in part by the higher costs of providing goods in the more isolated areas of low population. Services still tend to be most available in the larger cities, where concentration of the population reduced the per capita costs of physical infrastructure and provision of these goods. Consequently, Berentsen feels that efficiency seems to have a higher priority than the ideological goal of greater regional equity.

This social goal of greater regional balance in living environments, however, is not always compatible with the other goals of industrial growth and economic efficiency of agriculture. Although the regime emphasized industrial and urban growth in the agrarian north, this type of policy often was not as economically efficient because of reduced external economies as locating new growth in existing urban areas. In this sense, the goals of equity versus efficiency conflict, and the attempts to meet the latter generally have been more evident. In other words, the big cities have continued to get bigger in an absolute sense. The relative growth of cities and services in many rural areas, however, has been significant, for example, in the northern districts.

APPROACHES TO LAND USE PLANNING

Specific details on local approaches to land use planning in the German Democratic Republic are not easy to obtain. In this section three topics are covered: reorganization of fields for agricultural land use, the changes in land use within villages, and the changes in land use within cities. These microchanges are basic to the planning process in any country because they represent the constant change

Table 14.7
Central Place Hierarchy in Neubrandenburg District

1. Small village:

   General Store providing daily needs
   Services for water, gas, and electricity

2. Medium village:

   Restaurant
   Schools
   Physician and dentist
   Culture and recreation facilities
   Mail service

3. Large village (e.g., Dedelow):

   Drug store
   Movie
   Post office
   Gas station
   Inn

4. Town (e.g., Anklam):

   Department store
   Special schools
   Hospital
   Special cultural and recreational facilities
   Hotel

5. City (e.g., Prenzlau):

   Theater
   Gymnasium
   Regional hospital

6. Regional city (e.g., Neubrandenburg):

   Large department store
   Large hospital and clinic
   Special cultural and recreational facilities
   Hotel

Source: Kluge, Klaus. Die Entwicklung der Siedlungs-
struktur des Bezirkes Neubrandenburg. In
Hans Richter (Ed.), Eintwicklung der
Siedlungsstruktur im Norden der DDR. Gotha:
VEB Hermann Haack, 1975, pp. 102-103.

occurring on the edges of settlements—the interface between rural and urban land.

Reorganization of Fields

Details on the reorganization of fields are lacking for the post-1945 period in the GDR. We do know that large farms dominated in the area of Germany occupied after 1945 by Soviet forces. The largest of these farms were located in Mecklenburg, a core area of the Prussian Junker estate. Under Soviet influence, a land reform program was carried out in which most large farms were broken up and given to peasants, an attempt to gain the support of this group in the early days of communist rule. Some of the larger estates were converted directly to state farms. Only in 1959-60, when collectivization was carried out, did large fields again appear throughout the GDR. In most cases, these fields did not correspond to those of the old estates (for example, as in the village of Stresow in the county of Greifswald), but the old manor houses often served as the headquarters while additional farm buildings were also constructed. The reorganization of the landscape into collective and state farms apparently was based on transportation possibilities to county and district centers of administration. Actual field boundaries seem to have been laid out in part on the basis of properties that were brought into the collectives by the individual farmers.

Village Land Use

The East German rural population lives in villages rather than on dispersed farms as in the United States. This nucleation is connected with the history of settlement in the Middle Ages. Germans moved into this area as colonists from the western part of Germany and laid out villages in regular form (*Strassendörfer* or street villages, *Angerdorfer* or green villages, and so on) as part of planned corporate settlements. The periodic allocations of the strips within the medieval three fields made dispersion of population out of villages very difficult. In addition, factors of defense, water supply, and community activity favored nucleation.

Socialist plans for altering the internal structure of villages often start with the construction of a collective or state farm at the edge of the village and then include changes in other parts of the settlement (Rugg, 1978, 68-72). In East Germany, one of the principles of village planning concerns the development of separate but adjacent areas of residence (*Wohnbereich*) and economic activity (*Wirtschaftsbereich*) (Ogrissek, 1961, 101). Although the principle is theoretical, Schröder (1964, 303) explains that it is actually implemented throughout the northern plain of East Germany. Placing residential and economic areas together follows the ideological principles of reducing differences between town and countryside as the *Wirtschaftsbereich* becomes a "factory in the village," a place where all economic processes related to the collective or state farm are concen-

Figure 14.6 Model of Village Planning: Marxwalde, East Germany

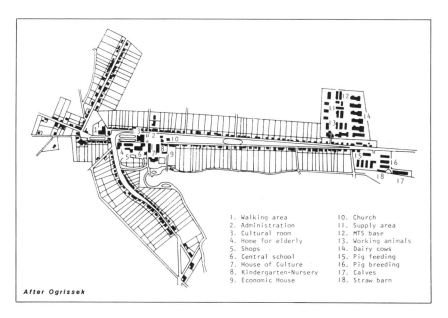

1. Walking area	10. Church
2. Administration	11. Supply area
3. Cultural room	12. MTS base
4. Home for elderly	13. Working animals
5. Shops	14. Dairy cows
6. Central school	15. Pig feeding
7. House of Culture	16. Pig breeding
8. Kindergarten-Nursery	17. Calves
9. Economic House	18. Straw barn

After Ogrissek

trated. The adjacent *Wohnbereich* is usually a village that in many cases has been altered by the addition of apartment buildings and single-family houses for agricultural and even industrial workers. The village also performs certain functions—political, economic, and social—that taken together determine its position in the socialist hierarchy of settlement.

The hierarchy outlined for East Germany, however, is idealistic, and each village may differ according to local circumstances. A concrete example is Marxwalde, formerly called Quilitz, a village about 32 kilometers northwest of Frankfurt/Oder. While visiting this village, I saw that the map by Ogrissek (1961, 109) accurately portrays the socialist model (Figure 14.6). As a German *Angerdorf* (green village), Marxwalde has been adapted to conform remarkably well to the theoretical plan for development of a village with residential and economic areas. The former residence of a nobleman has been turned into an administrative and cultural center. Grouped around the wide portion of the village common are administrative buildings, a school, shops, and a church. The cultural center, an ubiquitous structure in Eastern Europe, serves as a focus of communist party activity in the village. An electronics plant with nearby apartment buildings for workers demonstrates Marxist rural industrialization. At one end of the village is the economic area of the collective farm whose conspicuous buildings are elaborate stables for cows and pigs; other structures are for housing oxen, the breeding of pigs, and storing farm machinery. Stables for calves are located near the meadowland, and sheep and poultry installations are situated farther out. The addition of the collective farm to the village, of course, not only changed land use in the settlement but also took up former agricultural land.

Urban Land Use

The most visible changes in land use under socialism are those connected with urban functions (see Figure 14.4). Tables 14.1 and 14.2 have already been used to show that considerable land was transformed into the settlement category of land use as cities expanded into rural areas. In addition, extensive changes have taken place in internal urban patterns. The communist regime promotes these changes as evidence of the ability of socialism to institute modernization. This raises the question: are socialist cities in East Germany different from Western capitalistic cities? This question is difficult to answer. East German cities do have certain unusual characteristics that are reflected in their land use and are related to the application of sixteen socialist principles of urban planning (*Städtebau*) that were established as early as 1950 by the Council of Ministers (Werner, 1976, 132-34). The major principles are summarized as follows:

—The city should reflect the collective needs of the people.
—All cities should emphasize industrial functions, but the capital city should first of all stress administrative and cultural functions.
—Unregulated growth of cities must be avoided.
—Planning of cities should take into account historical heritage.
—The city core represents the focal point of political, administrative, and cultural life. Here one finds the monumental buildings, which fix the character of the city, and the squares, around which planning is organized. The squares are important as collective meeting places.
—Traffic must serve the city but not interfere with the quality of life.
—Residential neighborhoods are to be made up of economical multifamily housing, which is to be served by a hierarchy of services.
—Cities are to have adequate open space (parks and recreation areas).
—Urban plans must be practical rather than abstract.

These principles of urban planning illustrate the Marxist-Leninist ideology that was diffused into Eastern Europe from the Soviet Union. In great part, this ideology as reflected in cities emphasizes the ability of communism to eliminate the defects of capitalistic cities: unregulated growth including sprawl, congestion based on a central business district (CBD), inequality in housing, and a paucity of green space. The socialist model is interpreted in detail in *The Socialist City*, edited by R. A. French and F. E. Ian Hamilton (1979). However, the application of this model varies within Eastern Europe. My own opinion, based on research over a long period, is that East German and Bulgarian cities most closely mirror those of the Soviet Union. In Soviet cities, especially Moscow, one sees the characteristics mentioned in the principles: political and cultural functions in the central core, industrial districts, a hierarchy of residential neighborhoods, and parks of rest and culture. However, attempts to regulate growth and restrict pollution have not been especially successful. Even conserving the historical heritage has encountered difficulties.

In East Germany the socialist model takes form not only in East Berlin, the capital, but in other cities as well. For example, the historic city of Dresden, which was badly damaged during World War II, was rebuilt to provide a dual image: the historic part, represented by the legacy of the Saxon kings, and the present as seen in socialism; or a former provincial town like Neubrandenburg, which not only added industrial functions, thereby tripling in population, but also created a modern urban center within the medieval walls. East Berlin and Dresden can be used to illustrate East German policy with respect to urban land use; however, statements tend to be general in nature because detailed maps and data of urban land use are not available.

After World War II, Berlin was divided among the Four Powers. Although the Russians attempted to dislodge all Allied occupation rights there, these efforts failed, and the city remained divided: the Allies in the western part and the Soviets in the eastern. This separation was completed in 1961 with the erection of the Berlin Wall. Today East Berlin, a city of 1.2 million, is the capital of the German Democratic Republic, and West Berlin (2 million) is an enclave of the Federal Republic of Germany. In visits to this city over the years, I found that Berlin offers an ideal opportunity to make a comparison between the impacts of two different ideological systems—socialism and capitalism—on the urban landscape. These striking effects are especially noticeable because much of Berlin had to be rebuilt after World War II.

The line dividing Berlin after the war included the central district (*Mitte*) within East Berlin, thereby offering an opportunity to perceive how Marxist planners handle the problems of historical relics in urban design. This combination of old and new forms creates a primary aspect of the landscape today. Although the impression is subjective, the feeling is that here are seen urban forms that reflect two imperial systems—Prussian-German and socialist—existing side by side, each symbolizing the power of a centralized regime.

The core of East Berlin reflects the application of certain socialist planning principles: promotion of administrative and cultural functions in the center; retention of the historical legacy; use of squares, boulevards (*Magistralen*), and monumental buildings to fix the character of the city; development of multifamily residential areas with services; and creation of open space. In addition, the principle of using the core as a national and international meeting point has been developed. Articles published in *Deutsche Architektur*, especially those by Joachim Näther, chief architect of East Berlin in the 1970s, reflect these principles.

Instead of adopting a new format, the older axial layout has been preserved,

Figure 14.7 Model Depicting the Primary Axes in the Socialist Planning of East Berlin

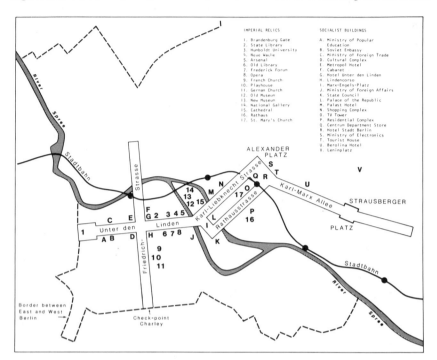

owing in part to the high cost of a complete reconstruction and in part to the desire to preserve elements of the past. The theoretical-ideological conception for the socialist master plan on the city stresses an east-west axis composed of three elements: the old, renowned avenue of Unter den Linden; a new political and cultural center between Karl-Liebknecht-Strasse and Rathausstrasse; and a residential shopping boulevard called Karl-Marx-Allee (formerly Stalin-Allee) (Figure 14.7).

Unter den Linden retains the old imperial image, especially along its eastern portion, with many reconstructed buildings of the imperial era—library, university, theaters, and museums. The west end features a postwar administrative zone with lesser ministries and the prestigious headquarters of two mass organizations—the Free German Trades Union and the Free German Youth—plus the embassies of three socialist countries, including the Soviet Union's massive structure. Crossing Unter den Linden is the subaxis of Friedrichstrasse, a historic commercial street whose function is supplemented now by cultural attractions such as theaters; in addition, two international hotels have been built. A station of the pre-World War II *Stadtbahn* or elevated train affords excellent access to the area.

The political-cultural center between Karl-Liebknecht-Strasse and Rathaus-strasse—a showpiece for socialist planning and the second element of the axis plan—contains two great squares: Marx-Engels-Platz on the west end is laid out on the site of the former imperial palace and is flanked by three massive buildings in modern style—the Ministry of Foreign Affairs, the Council of State, and the Palace of the Republic; Alexanderplatz on the east end is a historic square that has been enlarged as a meeting place for the city with new focal points of the International Berlin Hotel, the Centrum or department store, and a large international travel center. A series of other public, cultural, commercial, and residential structures flank Karl-Liebknecht-Strasse and adjacent Rathausstrasse. The chief architectural dominant is the television tower, but nearby remain three symbols of historic Berlin: the *Rathaus* (city hall), the *Marienkirche* (Marien Church), and the Alexanderplatz station of the *Stadtbahn*.

The third element of the axis is Karl-Marx-Allee, lined by blocks of apartment buildings in ornate Stalin-baroque architecture with ground floors typically containing stores and tourist offices. During the Stalin period, this rebuilt street was the solitary expression of postwar recovery planning in a socialist city that was slow to reconstruct, in vivid contrast to West Berlin. Like a movie set, the buildings along this street stood as a facade for the empty, debris-cleared lots behind it. Since 1965, however, other buildings have been built to fill the gaps.

Flanking this east-west axis with its political-cultural functions are compact residential areas of high-rise apartment buildings, the largest of which are located to the south of Unter den Linden along Leipzigerstrasse. This section of old Berlin has probably witnessed a greater change from the pre-1945 pattern than any other district. Leipzigerstrasse, formerly a leading shopping street in greater Berlin, today has only local neighborhood services available in ground-floor enterprises of the apartment buildings.

A walk along the total length of this axis from the Bradenburg Gate to Strausberger Platz enables one to capture something of the spirit of urbanism in a socialist country. The German imperial image of the past blends rather naturally with the international image of socialism. In fact, the intermixture of both periods of design portrays a Marxist-Leninist version of compatibility between past and present. The German heritage of the past can be preserved without compromising either modernization or the representation of a socialist image. The massive Hohenzollern and socialist buildings built up and down a wide boulevard reflect the power of the state; at least this is the feeling that is conveyed. An observer also sees changes in socialist architecture and planning, from the heavy Stalin-baroque of the 1950s along Karl-Marx-Allee to the more modern style buildings like the Palace of the Republic or the apartment buildings of Leipzigerstrasse. Another impression indicates that function might not follow form under socialism. In some cases, the imperial function of the past has not changed, (such as in the theater, opera, university, and museums from the Hohenzollern period); in other cases, a new function has been superimposed, as in the conversion of the former Reichsbank to the headquarters of the *Sozialistische Einheitspartei*

Deutschlands (SED)—the Communist party of East Germany—or the *Zeughaus* (arsenal) to a museum for German history emphasizing socialism.

A final impression in the landscape of central East Berlin comes from the low density of buildings and enterprises, giving a spread-out aspect that may be related to the attempts at grandeur in a socialist capital. Of course, government control of this land permits these low densities. Many functions, however, are spatially concentrated; for example, Heineberg (1979, 314-15) reveals that the entire insurance system of the GDR is localized on three sites in the eastern city center. Legal and medical services are also concentrated, as are tourist facilities.

In this political-cultural center of the socialist city, retail trade plays a reduced role by Western standards. Although exact figures are lacking for East Germany, Hamilton (French and Hamilton, 1979, 215) reports that in 1960 only 5 percent of urban employment was in retail trade in Eastern Europe, a figure that should be approximate for East Germany; in the United States, this figure is 19 percent. There are no large CBDs in communist cities similar to those of the United States. In part, this results from the attempt to decentralize retail sales to the neighborhood centers; however, communist regimes have not given priority to the production of consumer goods, a measure that reduces the need for large retail establishments and service facilities. Perhaps the biggest single difference in land use between the U.S. capitalistic city and the socialist city is the near absence in the latter of uses relating to the automobile: showrooms, garages and service stations, parts stores, parking lots, used car establishments, and all drive-in facilities such as fast foods and banks.

I found the choice of retail facilities in East German cities limited as compared to the United States. For example, the core of East Berlin has only one large department store—the Centrum on Alexanderplatz—and it, understandably, is always crowded. Crowded, too, are the restaurants, since too few exist to accommodate the public. Finding a private table is rare; patrons usually share an available table. On the other hand, bookstores flourish in number. Because the state owns and runs all large sales outlets, the uniformity in storefronts is a monotonous and peculiar aspect of the socialist landscape. The density of shops (17) along a showpiece block in East Berlin's Karl-Marx-Allee contrasts with the density of shops (42) in a block along Kurfürstendamm in West Berlin (Schöller, 1974, 428). In parts of East Berlin where private shops still exist, however, the density and choice of service are more like that of West Berlin.

A special aspect of urban land use in communist countries, including East Germany, is the importance of public space over private space. The emphasis on public space reflects the Marxist focus on collective benefits for society. Therefore Western visitors to East Germany remark on the significant role of public facilities: parks, museums, exhibition halls, educational and health institutions, squares and wide boulevards, concert halls, extensive transportation systems, recreation of all kinds, and kiosks selling a variety of daily needs. In East German cities, these percentages of public uses remain unknown because land use figures and maps are not available. Yet the proportions appear to be higher than in the United States.

On the other hand, in the GDR as in most other communist countries, the government limits private space. Most people (after a long wait) live in small apartments, which are often without many of the conveniences Westerners have come to expect. The outstanding example of the scarcity of private space is the automobile. In a way, the emphasis on public space serves as a form of compensation for the lag in consumer goods, including autos.

Two examples of public space in the GDR deserve mention here. One, the enormous Palace of the Republic on Marx-Engels Square in East Berlin, a structure that houses the legislative body of the country, actually acts as a gathering point for the public in the use of its cultural facilities—theater, reading and club rooms, and restaurant. The second example, Pragerstrasse in Dresden, is somewhat different. This wide pedestrian mall with fountains, international hotels, a film theater, and shops serves as a meeting point of the city and reflects new socialist urban design. It connects the old part of the city with the main railway station to create an impressive use of open space.

The single most striking change in urban land use in East European cities, including those of East Germany, is the explosion of standardized housing projects. The panorama from a high point in any large city shows the preponderance of large blocks of apartment houses rising 4 to 12 stories. These residential areas represent the housing constructed for factory workers, thereby illustrating the emphasis placed on industry in a communist society. Because East Germany was, and is, the most industrialized and urbanized country in Eastern Europe, the postwar changes do not always stand out in comparison with an agrarian country like Bulgaria. Nonetheless, the changes in the northern part of East Germany, not an industrialized area before World War II, are easily discernible. For example, Neubrandenburg, now much larger and more industrialized than in the prewar period, has new, large apartment projects in the outer portions of the city near recently built factories.

The Soviet approach to residential planning uses the concept of the microdistrict, a neighborhood unit of apartment buildings with services that generally has 6,000 to 12,000 inhabitants. The district concept also applies to East German cities, where basic planning allots each family 9 to 12 square meters of floor space. The district contains an assortment of daily services such as a food store, hairdresser and barber shops, a day care center, and an elementary school. A second-level service area results when several districts are grouped together to include special shops, a movie theater, a library, a public health establishment, and recreation facilities. Thus, a hierarchy of services exists in the city just as it does in the countryside. Although such large apartment projects occur in other parts of the world, the socialist ones characteristic of East Germany have centralized design standards and a unified set of services. According to Marxist ideology, all East German citizens, whether working in town or country, should

Figure 14.8 Transformation of a Portion of Dresden, East Germany, after World War
II

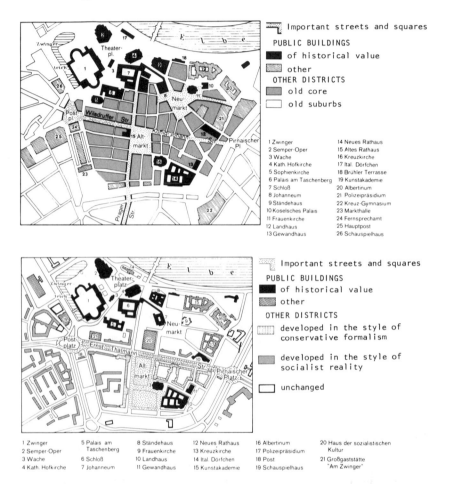

have equal access to services of shops, health, education, and others. The realization of such a goal lags behind theory, however.

Design changes with time have affected residential land use. Dresden provides an example of several historic planning changes (Richter, 1974) (Figure 14.8). The first phase (1945-56) involved the complete transformation of the street pattern when 26 prewar blocks were converted to eight large housing blocks in the form of a series of massive apartment buildings enclosed around courtyards.

The phase is called conservative formalism because it represents an imitation of the Soviet style. To the west of this area in downtown Dresden is a different style of housing block: free-standing apartment buildings aligned in rows. These structures represent the second phase (1956-62), which reflects a plainer style of architecture called socialist realism. Finally, a third phase (1962-present), which emphasizes mass production methods featuring prefabrication, completes the planning and design changes. In Dresden, as throughout the rest of Eastern Europe, this last phase emphasizes the use of high, narrow buildings in large clusters—in East Germany called *Wohnscheiben*, or housing "walls" of concrete—that meet a rational means of accommodating large numbers of people in a short time and yet represent the ultimate in standardization—a true "classless" image. Housing plans in the GDR call for construction of 3 million apartments between 1976 and 1990 using the new mass methods of construction (Richter, 1974, 187).

THE FUTURE

The answer to the question asked at the beginning of this chapter—how is the land use policy of the GDR affected by the goals of industrial growth, economic efficiency in agriculture, and regional balance in living environment?—seems to be that the three goals are difficult to realize simultaneously. A focus on industrial growth means that more and more arable land is taken up for factories, residences, mining, and similar uses, thereby affecting the goal of agricultural self-sufficiency in a country where land is in short supply. At the same time, the goal of regional balance is not always compatible with the other two goals because an emphasis on growth in underdeveloped areas is often costly and less efficient because it requires new infrastructure such as roads. A growth policy also has a strong impact on the environment, whether it is pollution or the provision of recreation facilities in a country where foreign travel is restricted. Thus the regime has difficulty balancing the goal of growth with those of self-sufficiency and regional equality. Equity as an ideological aim of Marxism is now thought of in terms of accessibility to services and less on strict possession of such services.

Apparently the problem of loss of agricultural and forest land to industry and settlement will get worse. Hoffmann (1982, 54, 63), in his evaluation of East German land use, believes that pressure on agricultural land for industrial-settlement use increased in the late 1970s and will continue to rise in the 1980s. This pressure will be especially evident on the periphery of settlements where open land is available and industry can outbid agriculture for its use. Rural land will also be used for open-pit coal mining, especially in the Cottbus district as Soviet supplies of oil decline, a situation that will force East Germany to be more self-sufficient in energy. Some of the pressure for housing on urban peripheries could be relieved by renewal of housing in the older portion of cities, but such projects seem to be low in priority.

The potential for land use policy in the GDR has not been realized. Despite the power to institute such a policy, the demands of industrial production and growth have prevailed over a rational policy of conserving agricultural land and promoting regional development; reclamation of mining land has not reached expectations; and a significant heritage of historical buildings remains unrenewed. In addition, ideological goals of socialist grandeur in cities represent investment that could have been better spent. Although not discounting certain advantages with respect to central planning, a socialist society like that of East Germany encounters considerable difficulty in developing a comprehensive land use policy. Not surprising, then, were the demands made in 1981 for reform of this policy.

ACKNOWLEDGMENT

I am very grateful to Helen Ruth Aspaas for the preparation of the maps in this chapter.

BIBLIOGRAPHY

Atlas der Erdkunde. 1978. Gotha: VEB Hermann Haack.
Atlas Deutsche Demokratische Republik. 1970-84. Gotha: VEB Hermann Haack.
Bajaja, Vladislav. 1980. Concentration and Specialization in Czechoslovak and East German Farming. In R. A. Francisco et al., eds. *Agricultural Policies in the USSR and Eastern Europe*, 263-93. Boulder, Colo.: Westview Press.
Barthel, Hellmuth. 1962. *Braunkohlenbergbau und Landschaftdynamik*. Gotha: VEB Hermann Haack, Ergäzungsheft No. 270 of Petermanns Geographische Mitteilungen, Annex No. 10.
Berentsen, William H. 1980. Spatial Pattern of Retail Sales per Capita in the German Democratic Republic and East Berlin. *Die Erde* 111:293-300.
Bundesministerium fur innerdeutsche Beziehungen. 1979. *DDR Handbuch*. Cologne: Verlag Wissenschaft und Politik.
The Constitution of the German Democratic Republic, 1968, 1974.
Francisco, Ronald A. 1977. The Future of East German Agriculture: The Feasibility of the 1976-80 Plan. In Roy Laird, Joseph Hajda, and Betty Laird, eds. *The Future of Agriculture in the Soviet Union and Eastern Europe*, 185-203. Boulder, Colo.: Westview Press.
Francisco, Ronald A. 1979. Agricultural Collectivization in the German Democratic Republic. In Ronald A. Francisco et al., eds. *The Political Economy of Collectivized Agriculture*, 63-85. New York: Pergamon Press.
French, R. A., and F. E. Ian Hamilton, eds. 1979. *The Socialist City*. New York: Wiley.
Heineberg, Heinz. 1979. Service Centers in East and West Berlin. In R. A. French and F. E. Ian Hamilton, eds. *The Socialist City*. New York: Wiley.
Hoffmann, Manfred, 1982. Der Wandel der Flächennutzung in der DDR. In Ekkehard Büchhofer, ed. *Flächennutzungsveränderungen in Mitteleuropa*, 41-76. Marburg/Lahn: Marburger Geographische Schriften, Heft 88.
Kluge, Klaus. 1975. Die Entwicklung der Siedlungsstruktur des Bezirkes Neubrandenburg. In Hans Richter, ed. *Enwicklung der Siedlungsstruktur im Norden der DDR*. Gotha: VEB Hermann Haack.

Kohl, H., et al. 1976. *Ökonomische Geographie der Deutschen Demokratischen Republik*. Gotha: VEB Hermann Haack.

Kohl, H., et al. 1979. *Geographie der DDR*. Gotha: VEB Hermann Haack.

Lazarcik, Gregor. 1981. Comparative Growth, Structure, and Levels of Agricultural Output, Inputs, and Productivity in Eastern Europe, 1965-1979. In U. S. Congress, Joint Economic Committee, *East European Economic Assessment*, pt. 2, 587-634. Washington, D.C.: Government Printing Office.

Lüdemann, Heinz, and Joachim Heinzmann. 1978. On the Settlement System of the German Democratic Republic: Development Trends and Strategies. In Niles Hansen, ed. *Human Settlement Systems*. Cambridge, Mass.: Ballinger.

Mosely, Philip E. 1958. Collectivization of Agriculture in Soviet Strategy. In Irwin T. Sanders, ed. *Collectivization of Agriculture in Eastern Europe*, 49-66. Lexington, Ky.: University of Kentucky Press.

Ogrissek, Rudi. 1961. *Dorf und Flur in der Deutschen Demokratischen Republik*. Leipzig: VEB Verlag Enzyklopädie.

Pounds, Norman J. G. 1969. *Eastern Europe*. Chicago: Aldine.

Richter, Dieter. 1974. Die Sozialistische Grossstadt: 25 Jahre Städtebau in der DDR. *Geographische Rundschau* 26:183-91.

Roubitschek, Walter. 1982. Socioeconomic Effects of Agricultural Development and Rural transformation in the GDR. In György Enyedi and Ivan Volgyes, eds. *The Effect of Modern Agriculture on Rural Development*, 35-44. New York: Pergamon Press.

Rugg, Dean S. 1978. *The Geography of Eastern Europe*. Lincoln, Nebr.: Cliffs Notes.

Scherf, K. 1975. Zu den Wechselbeziehungen zwischen der Siedlungsstruktur und anderen territorialen Teilstrukturen der gesellschaftlichen Reproduktion in der DDR. In Hans Richter, ed. *Entwicklung der Siedlungsstruktur im Norden der DDR*, 21-36. Gotha: VEB Hermann Haack.

Schöller, Peter. 1974. Paradigma Berlin. *Geographische Rundschau* 26:425-34.

Schröder, Karl Heinz. 1964. Der Wandel der Agrarlandschaft in ostelbischen Tiefland seit 1945. *Geographische Zeitschrift*, 52:289-316.

Stams, Werner. 1982. Hauptarten der Flächennutzung in der DDR (Erläuterungsbeitrag Karte 34 der Atlas DDR), *Geographische Berichte*, Heft 1, 102:33-8.

Statistisches Jahrbuch der DDR (Staatsverlag der DDR). Various years.

Werner, F. 1972. *Zur Raumordnung in der DDR*. Berlin: Kiepert KG.

Werner, F. 1976. *Stadtplannung Berlin: Theorie und Realität*. Berlin: Kiepert KG.

15

Hungary

GYÖRGY ENYEDI

HISTORICAL DEVELOPMENT AND CURRENT STATUS OF LAND UTILIZATION

Hungary is a small country, even by European standards: 93,030 square kilometers. Hungary's territory approximately equals that of the states of Indiana or Kentucky in the United States. The country's population density is 112 people per square kilometer, higher than the European average. Thus, the 10.7 million Hungarians have to organize their social life and economic activity in a limited area, which gives special importance to land use planning. Since Hungary has no important mineral resources, except perhaps its bauxite deposits, its soil cover represents the most important natural riches. Ecological conditions for agriculture are favorable; food export has a long tradition. Since the 1970s, when food products were reevaluated in the world market, the efficient use of agricultural land has received more attention.

Three phases of land use transformation during the last 100 years can be distinguished. The last third of the nineteenth century represented the first phase. This was the era of the Hungarian industrial revolution, the take-off of modern urbanization. Agricultural land was extended remarkably due to important land reclamation and river regulation works.[1] Consequently the urban explosion did not diminish agricultural land. Even the main zones of industrialization were located outside the Great Hungarian Plain, the most important grain-producing area in Austria-Hungary at that time.

Spontaneous urban sprawl represented the most visible land use problem, mostly from the point of view of the functioning of cities. Land use planning began within urban areas. The first master plans in the modern sense of zoning and general physical planning started in Hungarian cities in the 1860s.

The period between World Wars I and II was the second phase. As a result of World War I, the Austro-Hungarian monarchy was subdivided. Austria and Hungary were separated and became two small states. According to the provisions of the Paris Peace Treaty (1920), Hungary's territory was reduced to one-third of its size during the Austro-Hungarian monarchy (Jászi, 1929). Recovery from the collapse was very slow. In this period of economic stagnation, land use patterns did not change significantly. In the 1930s, war preparations stimulated economic growth. Planning of optimal land use for maximizing food output was also introduced (Beke, 1941).

The third phase started in 1945. The most important events of this period from the point of view of land transformation were rapid industrial growth, widespread urbanization, the collectivization of agriculture, radical shifts in landownership, and the introduction of a planned economy (Enyedi, 1976a).

There were marked changes in land use patterns and land management as well. First, the size of the agricultural area has diminished remarkably. Since 1945, 500,000 hectares have been used for afforestation, and 370,000 hectares have been lost to production (Hoffer, 1982). There are growing land use conflicts in the urban fringes (Daróczi, 1982). There is a general public fear that further declines in the amount of cultivated area will hamper agricultural production and food export.

Second, land use planning became general at various geographical levels. At the national scale, land use plans formulate the desirable long-term direction in land transformation for an optimal use of land resources. Land protection has been one of the key elements of long-term land use planning. At the regional level, medium- or short-run resource utilization has been the main focus; at the local (settlement) level, land use planning has been dominated by physical planning. Local physical planning also follows centrally elaborated guidelines. The changes in guidelines reflect the discussions among urbanists concerning the vision of a modern socialist city.

Table 15.1 shows the main land use changes during the last 100 years. The reasons for changes are summarized in the following paragraphs.

1. Cultivated areas were expanding until World War II. Built-up areas enlarged but slightly; arable land grew substantially, mostly in the form of pastures and meadows.

2. Arable land has diminished continuously since World War II, mostly during the 1950s and the 1970s. Arable land covered 60.3 percent of the country's territory in 1938; its proportion dropped to 50.3 percent by 1982. Mass media usually dramatize this fact and blame the wasteful use of industrial or urban expansion for it. It can be assumed that the disappearance of the earlier rural overpopulation has been the basic reason for the changes, although many examples for nonefficient use could be quoted too. In the early twentieth century, under demographic pressure, arable land expanded onto steep slopes and poor

Table 15.1

Land Use Pattern in Hungary, 1895–1980

Land Use Form	1895[+]	1938	1947	1958	1977	1982
	in percent of total national area					
Arable land	55.5	60.3	60.2	57.8	52.8	50.3
Meadows	8.7	7.0	6.9	5.4	3.9	13.8
Pastures	13.8	10.4	10.2	10.1	10.1	13.8
Orchards and gardens	1.0	1.3	1.4	1.9	3.4	4.6
Vineyards	1.9	2.2	2.3	2.1	2.1	2.0
Forests	12.9	11.9	12.1	13.7	16.9	17.5
Built-up and non-used	6.2	6.9	6.9	9.0	10.8	11.8
Total	100.0	100.0	100.0	100.0	100.0	100.0

+Calculated on the present territory of the country.

Source: Bernát-Enyedi, 1961, p. 19; Bernát 1981,

p. 189. Magyar Statisztikai Zsebkönyv/

Hungarian Statistical Pocketbook/ 1982,

Budapest, Központi Statisztikai Hivatal/

Central Statistical Office/ p. 139.

soils as well. Afforestation of these lands was later justified by the low efficiency of farming, soil erosion, and the difficulties in mechanizing agricultural works.

3. The expansion of forests and woodland was useful for both lumbering and the preservation of watersheds. The proportion of forests is still relatively low in Hungary.

4. Pastures and meadows play an ever diminishing role in land utilization. They usually occupy poor, sandy, or alkaline soils. The low standard of meadows and grazing lands contributes to the high costs of beef and cattle raising in the country.

5. The area of vineyards was practically stagnant during the last 100 years. The geographical location of vineyards has changed remarkably. The decline of

traditional vineyards, located on the southern slopes of the Hungarian highlands, was counterbalanced by the growth of large-scale, mechanized vineyards on the plains, mostly between the Danube and the Tisza rivers. Wine production is a risky business in Hungary, which lies at the northern limit of the European wine zone. Market situations have been unstable since cheap Italian and Spanish wines inundated the world market.

6. Urban-industrial development led logically to the expansion of built-up areas. Nevertheless, the pattern of Hungarian land use still clearly shows the great importance of agriculture. In Europe, Hungary ranks second to Denmark with regard to the proportion of cultivated area. Population density is only 1.6 persons per hectare in agricultural areas. Agriculture is a successful sector of the national economy. Its importance is shown by the fact that in 1981, one-quarter of the total value of exports (and one-third of exports in hard currency) was made up of agricultural products.

LANDOWNERSHIP

Landownership in socialist countries is characterized by collective ownership. In certain socialist countries, including the Soviet Union and Bulgaria, the land was nationalized after the revolution or after the consolidation of the socialist system. All land is owned by the state, which entrusts the right of utilization to the users.

In Hungary, nationalizations were restricted to mineral resources and water surfaces. There have been several radical changes in landownership since 1945. As a consequence, collective ownership became dominant in Hungary in the early 1960s. Cooperative (and not state) ownership is the main form of collective ownership.

First, changes were introduced by the Land Reform Act of 1945. According to the act, all the land owned by landowners exceeding 140 hectares and all the land belonging to war criminals were distributed among landless peasants and small farmers.[2] Land reform was executed within a few months. Altogether 643,342 persons were given land; 34.6 percent of all the arable land was divided among them. Part of the confiscated land was nationalized, and state farms were organized on these lands (Orbán, 1972). In 1949, state-owned areas extended to the cities as a consequence of the nationalization of industrial plants, banks, and block houses.

The next fundamental change was caused by the collectivization of agriculture. The first wave of collectivization started as early as 1949; the process was completed in 1962 (Donáth, 1977). Since then, the landownership structure has changed but slightly (Table 15.2).

State ownership is composed mostly of state forests, followed by state farms (12 percent of the cultivated area). City land is in collective ownership and is administered by the city council, but it is owned formally by the state.

Table 15.2
Landownership in Hungary, 1982

Ownership Form	Territory in 1000 hectares	Percent of the total
State	2,933	31.5
Co-operative	5,684	61.1
Private	686	7.4
Total	9,303	100.0

Source: A Magyar Népköztársaság földterülete 1982.V.

31-én, 1982.   (The Land of the Hungarian

People's Republic on 31 May 1982).   Budapest:

OFTH (National Service of Geodesy and

Cartography).

Cooperative ownership is characteristic of most of the agricultural land. Of 5.6 million hectares of cooperative land, 3 million hectares are in the common ownership of cooperative farms.[3] This indivisible land is collectively owned by the members of cooperatives; 2.4 million hectares represents members' property, the bulk of which is collectively cultivated. And 326,000 hectares of cooperative land is privately cultivated by member families; these are the so-called household plots (Lázár, 1976).

Finally, the 686,000 hectares of private land also has different forms. Individual owner-operated farms cover a mere 136,000 hectares; the other private land belongs to the auxiliary farms of the nonagricultural population, family home gardens, and so forth. Private landownership is strictly limited: 3 hectares in the case of farming, 6,000 square meters in the case of home or second home gardens.

In 1978 a government decree forbid the selling of state land to individuals. Since then there have been subdivisions of state lands, in which pieces of land have been offered for long-term use, either in the form of rent (in the case of cultivation), or for an acquisition fee (in the case of construction). This fee is rather high, close to the market price of private land.

LAND ZONES

The administrative areas of Hungarian settlements are divided into inner and outer areas, and some have garden zones too. Distinctions are made according to specific functions.

The inner area is designated for settlement construction. It is managed by the local council, which fixes its boundaries and decides on its use. Modifications are made as the realization of the master plan advances.

The boundaries of Hungarian cities are usually overextended. More than half of the inner areas' territory is under cultivation. The inner areas cover 6.9 percent of the national area. It is interesting to note that 58 percent of inner areas is in private ownership. Since in Hungary the majority of new dwelling construction is private, in the form of condominiums, family homes, or cooperative homes, a relatively important real estate market has developed within the inner area.[4]

The outer area is the land between the inner zone and the administrative border of the settlement. Over 90 percent of the outer area is agricultural land and forests; certain industrial, mining, and recreational activities are also located there. Only 2 percent of outer areas' land is privately owned.

The garden zone, which covers 2 percent of the country's territory, is a special land use form. Traditionally, garden zones were orchards and vineyards planted separately from the main farming areas. The garden zone is typically in the hilly countryside, where, usually, meadows were located in valley bottoms, arable land on flat areas or gentle slopes, and orchards and vineyards (mostly for family use) on the steep slopes. More than three-quarters of the garden zone is privately owned; over 1 million auxiliary farms are cultivated intensively in this zone.

APPROACH TO LAND USE PLANNING

Land use planning is part of regional planning. Regional planning obtained its comprehensive legal framework from a government decree in 1971. According to this decree, regional planning has two main aims: to improve the efficiency in the use of local resources and to stimulate the equalization of the standard of living and the living conditions of the people of different regions.

There are two types of regional plans: development plans and physical plans. Both cover the whole national territory. Physical plans have a long-term character; they are prepared for the whole country, for large landscape units, for special regions, for functional urban regions, and for settlements. Long-term physical plans contain: the settlement system of the given territory, including settlement functions and hierarchy; an infrastructural network of the area and the location of institutions for different types of services; location in terms of potential sites for different units of production and an efficient land use pattern of the planned area; and measures for environmental protection (Köszegfalvy, 1982).

The first national physical plan to a scale of 1:100,000 was prepared during the late 1970s. More precisely, it was a series of plans with different time horizons, the years 2000 and 2025, using alternatives for future urban development, and showing territorial population distribution. The long-term physical plan concentrates on the built-up areas. Since Hungary's population probably will continue to decline during the planning period, the plan forecasts but a modest expansion of the built-up areas, 120,000 to 160,000 hectares up to the beginning of the next century (Baráth, 1981).

The long-term physical plan reflects concern for limiting the built-up area and for protecting the agricultural land.

MAJOR CHALLENGES AND INSTITUTIONAL FRAMEWORK

The growing concern over land protection is justified by the fact that agricultural land has decreased by 21,000 hectares a year during the last 40 years. The need for land protection was recognized in the Land Protection Act of 1961, but this act did not have much of an effect.

The basic problem has been the lack of real value for agricultural land. Since there is no land market for agricultural land, one cannot express the monetary value of agricultural land. Consequently land does not form part of the fixed assets of large-scale farms. For a long time, nonagricultural users obtained agricultural land free of charge from the state. Also the Land Protection Act required only that investors apply for permission to convert agricultural land into industrial or urban uses. Permission usually was always given since industrial or urban activities were estimated to be more important or more efficient than agricultural use. After 1968, with the introduction of the New Economic Mechanism (the economic reform), the government attempted to draw land into the economic scheme. Calculated land prices and land rents were introduced for state enterprises too. The low cost of acquiring and using land has not encouraged investors or users to economize on land.

In the 1970s more significant steps were taken to achieve more efficient land protection. In 1975, the Hungarian Socialist Workers' party stated in a program declaration that in the advanced socialist society, "Land in the Hungarian People's Republic—irrespective of the form of ownership—represents national wealth" (*A Magyar Szocialista Munkáspárt XI. Kongresszusa*, the 11th Congress of the Hungarian Socialist Workers' Party). Calculated land value provides 17.4 percent of the national wealth. The Land Protection Act has been amended several times, but the first comprehensive enacting clauses appeared only in 1977. The great number of modifications, however, has led to confusion in land legislation. In 1981, there were 230 legal provisions concerning land and real estate. Preparations are underway to elaborate a new, comprehensive Land Code (Egri, 1983).

The main legal measures that make the conversion of agricultural land into a nonagricultural use controlled and economically sensible can be summarized as follows. Since farmers sometimes are more interested in selling the land than retaining it for agricultural use and due to strict restrictions concerning the market in land as a means of production, legislation plays an important role in land protection in Hungary.

Both the expansion of settlement inner areas and land conversion from agricultural to other uses are subject to permission. Permissions are issued by the town and county land offices. For agricultural land above 10 hectares in size, the consent of the Ministry of Agriculture and Food Economy is required. This obligation also relates to areas designated for building in master plans. Thus, at present, land offices have the main controlling power over urban expansion.

Many Hungarian cities have overextended boundaries. Consequently there are large agricultural areas within the inner areas. Legal measures were taken to revise the inner area boundaries of all Hungarian settlements. Lands that are cultivated by large-scale farms and on which construction is not expected within five years will be transferred from inner to outer areas.

When land is converted from agricultural to other uses, an indemnity usually is levied irrespective of the compensation paid for the acquisition of the land. The size of the indemnity depends on the soil quality, among other things.

In Hungary, land within each agricultural land use is grouped into eight quality classes, the best land being first class. According to the regulations of 1977, indemnity was to be paid only for the conversion of lands in classes 1 to 5. Tax rates were moderately graduated depending on the quality of land. The rate of indemnity, for example, on first-class arable land was double that of the fifth class. Regulations, valid from 1982, however, stipulate that an indemnity shall be paid for the conversion of land in all eight quality classes. Tax rates have been significantly increased as follows: in class 5, tax rates increased 3 ¼ times, in class 4, 3 to 6 times, in class 3, 3 ⅚ times, in class 2, 4 times, and in the first class, 4 ⅛ times (Daróczi, 1984).

An indemnity is not levied if the interested party recultivates land to a value equivalent to the sum otherwise charged or if the investment concerned serves soil protection or irrigation. Where conversion takes place without permission, the usual indemnity is tripled.

Until 1982, such indemnities were paid into the development fund of county councils. County councils usually spent this money for nonagricultural purposes. Currently only half of the receipts from such indemnities are paid into the county council development fund. The other half goes into a newly created Land Protection Fund, which may also have other financial resources. It would be preferable if all indemnities, as well as all taxes and fees related to land use, went into this fund. The fund is used for land reclamation and recultivation.

FUTURE THRUSTS

The effects of the 1982 measures cannot yet be evaluated, but the first results are promising: the area of land withdrawn from agriculture decreased by 21 percent, and the land withdrawn from arable land actually decreased by 81 percent in one year. One cannot forecast how this process will continue. Lasting results probably will be achieved if the actors in land transformation (farmers and urban users) are financially interested in maintaining cultivation and in protecting agricultural land. Legal measures can be effective only if they are based on reasonable land values (Nagy, 1982). A new evaluation system for agricultural land is already in preparation. Production capacity is the principle of this evaluation, but there is no similar basis for the evaluation of urban land, a serious shortcoming of land use planning.

NOTES

1. Before flood control works were introduced, there were 3 million hectares of land that were inundated regularly by overflowing rivers. This huge area was used for temporary grazing only. Land reclamation was stimulated by the growing population and by the expansion of the European wheat market. Under the river regulations, 4,000 kilometers of levees were constructed along the Danube and the Tisza rivers. In addition, the main settlements along the Tisza were surrounded by circular dams. The fertile cultivation zone produced by flood control amounts to 20 percent of the country's present arable land and to about 30 percent of the territory of the Great Hungarian Plain (Somogyi, 1965).

2. Landownership in prewar Hungary was characterized by the great importance of the big landed estates (latifundia); 1,250 landowners owned more than 30 percent of the total land. On the other hand, 1.3 million small farmers (each with less than 4 hectares of land) owned only 12 percent of the land. Moreover, 1.5 million agricultural workers had no land at all (Held, 1980).

3. The terms *collective farm* and *cooperative farm* and the official name of *agricultural producers' cooperative* alternate in the literature. In 1982, 68.1 percent of agricultural land was owned by 1,302 cooperative farms. The average land size of a cooperative farm was 4,085 hectares. The Soviet *kolkhoz* are the equivalent; nevertheless, there are important differences. Hungarian cooperative farms are self-managing economic units, and they own their land and other fixed assets. Consequently, they can buy or sell land and fixed assets. Their members receive an income on a profit-sharing basis according to the work performed on common fields.

4. Government housing represents 20 to 25 percent of the new dwelling units built in a year.

BIBLIOGRAPHY

A Magyar Szocialista Munkáspárt XI. Kongresszusa (The 11th Congress of the Hungarian Socialist Workers' Party). 1975. Budapest: Kossuth.

Baráth, Etele. 1981. Az országos területrendezési tervkoncepció *(Concept for the national physical plan). Városépítés* 17, 2:5-18.

Beke, László. 1941. *Mezõgazdaságunk irányitásának alapjai (Basis for Planning Our Agriculture).* Budapest: Pátria.

Berényi, István. 1980. A területhasznositás átalakulásának főbb irányai az Alföldön (Main directions in land use transformation of the Great Hungarian Plain). *Alföldi Tanulmányok* 4:63-84.

Bernát, Tivadar, ed. 1981. *Magyarország gazdasági földrajza (Economic Geography of Hungary)*. Budapest: Közgazdasági.

Bernát, Tivadar, and György Enyedi. 1961. *A magyar mezögazdaság termelési körzetei (Production Regions of Hungarian Agriculture)*. Budapest: Mezögazdasági Kiadó.

Daróczi, Eta. 1982. Suburban Land Economy. In *Development of Rural Areas*, Proceedings of the 4th Hungarian-Polish Seminar, ed. by J. Kostrowicki and W. Stola. Warszawa: PWN.

Daróczi, Eta. 1984. The Protection of Agricultural Land on the Urban Fringe. In *Environmental Management*, ed. P. Compton and M. Pécsi. Budapest: Akadémiai.

Donáth, Ferenc. 1977. *Reform és forradalom (Reform and Revolution)*. Budapest: Akadémiai.

Egri, István. 1983. A földkódex néhány gyakorlati kérdése *(Some practical problems of the land code)*. *Állam és Igazgatás* 33, 1:23–32.

Enyedi, György. 1960. La cartographie de l'utilisation du sol en Hongrie. In *Etudes sur les sciences géographiques Hongroises*, 65-70. Budapest: Akadémiai.

Enyedi, György, 1967. A brief characterization of agricultural land utilization in Hungary. In *Land Utilization in Eastern Europe*, 74–88. Budapest: Adakémiai.

Enyedi, György, 1976a. *Hungary. An Economic Geography*. Boulder, Colo.: Westview.

Enyedi, György, ed. 1976b. *Rural transformation in Hungary*. Budapest: Adakémiai.

Enyedi, György. 1977. Transformation of the Hungarian Village. *New Hungarian Quarterly* 67:69-86.

Held, Joseph ed. 1980. *The Modernization of Agriculture: Rural Transformation in Hungary, 1848-1975*. East European monographs. Boulder, Colo.: Westview.

Hoffer, István. 1982. A nemzeti kincs megörzése *(Preserving the national wealth)*. *Figyelö*, 3 February.

Jászi, Oszkár. 1929. *The Dissolution of the Hapsburg Monarchy*. Chicago: University of Chicago Press.

Kosöszegfalvy, György. 1982. *Regionális tervezés (Regional Planning)*. Budapest: Müszaki.

Lázár, István. 1976. The Collective Farm and the Private Plot. *New Hungarian Quarterly* 66 (Autumn):65-78.

Nagy, László. 1982. A földtulajdon és a földhasználat szabályozásáról *de lege ferenda* (On the regulation of landownership and land use *de lege ferenda*). *Állam és Igazgatás* 32, 8:686-95.

Orbán, Sándor. 1972. *Két agrárforradalom Magyarországon (Two Agrarian Revolutions in Hungary)*. Budapest: Akadémiai.

Somogyi, Sándor. 1965. Geographical Effects of Flood Control and River Regulations in Hungary. In *Hungarian Geographical and Cartographical Studies*, 37-57. Budapest: Hungarian Geographical Society.

16

Sweden

IGOR DERGALIN

With an area of 450,000 square kilometers, Sweden is the fourth largest country in Europe. Half of its land surface is covered with forest. Less than 10 percent is farmland. A long mountain chain in the northwest has peaks as high as 2,000 meters. Nearly 100,000 lakes are spread over the country. Most of them are connected in a lacework of waterways, and many large rivers flow down the mountains, through the forests, to the sea. There are thousands of islands along the jagged coast.

In spite of the fact that the Arctic Circle slices through Sweden's northernmost province, Lapland, the country is not an Arctic one. Thanks to the Gulf Stream in the Atlantic, Sweden has a rather mild climate considering its location. Nevertheless, the distance between the northern tip of the country and the southern edge is nearly 1,600 kilometers, and this means that its natural features and climate are quite varied. Stockholm, the capital, is situated at almost the same latitude as southern Greenland but has an average temperature of about 18°C in July. The average winter temperature is slightly below the freezing point, and snowfall is moderate (Figure 16.1).

Sweden has a population of 8.3 million, with 90 percent living in the southern half of the country. The country has a low birth rate like most of the highly industrialized countries. Average length of life is high—about 74 years for men and 79 for women. Although Sweden is a large country, almost the area of France, it has a small population—8.3 million—which results in an average of fewer than 20 inhabitants per square kilometer. The population is very unevenly distributed, as shown in Figure 16.2 (Swedish Institute, 1983).

Figure 16.1 Map of Sweden

Figure 16.2 Two Schematic Maps of Sweden

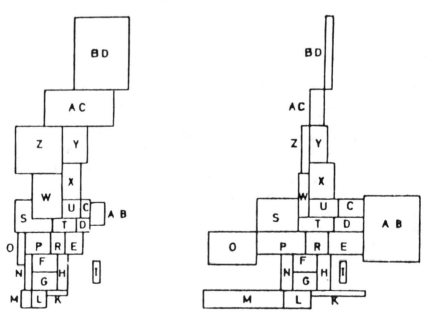

HISTORICAL DEVELOPMENT AND CURRENT STATUS OF
LAND USE PLANNING

The residential patterns have changed radically over the past century. In 1900, about 30 percent of the population lived in cities. Thirty years later, the majority still lived in rural areas. In 1960 the urban proportion was 70 percent and around the year 2000 it is estimated that 90 percent of the population will be living in urban settlements. At the same time, the standard of living has risen steeply.

In the early 1930s, the newly formed Social Democratic government introduced an economic program in which housing construction was to be used as a small but important tool in an effort to fight unemployment. The contribution was to support certain household groups, in particular those having low incomes. In this respect, important progress was made in raising the standard of urban housing but was cut short by World War II. After the termination of hostilities, town planning and town building made rapid progress in the whole of Europe. Sweden, though not damaged by war, developed a remarkable activity in building and rebuilding its cities.

Several efforts have been made to assist development. For instance, as a result of a revision of the housing law, the municipalities were now required to assist with housing loans and subsidies and also required to take on part of the responsibility of constructing and administering housing.

Such responsibilities were followed by corresponding rights. Consequently the municipalities were given stronger control over land use and planning in their territory. In order to obtain control over implementation as well, the municipalities followed an active land policy. The municipality of Stockholm, for example, owns almost all the land that has been used for housing construction since the 1920s, and furthermore it owns very large land areas for recreation.

When a comprehensive regional policy was introduced in the 1960s, rapidly diminishing employment in agriculture and forestry was the basic reason for regional imbalance. In 1960, about 15 percent of those gainfully employed worked in these sectors. This figure had fallen to 8 percent in 1970 and at present is about 5 percent. In some sparsely populated counties of the north, agriculture and forestry accounted for between 20 percent and 30 percent of total employment in 1960, which meant that the industrial sector was very small.

As a result, during the 1960s the northern part of Sweden—seven counties with a total population of 1.7 million inhabitants—showed a net outflow of more than 10,000 inhabitants each year to the growing industrial regions farther south. This loss of population was one of the major arguments for the location support policy introduced in 1965. Basically this policy is still the central instrument of Swedish regional policy.

The 1970s saw a regional population stability. Although the differences between regions with regard to population density (Figure 16.3), unemployment and the rate of participation in the work force now are less marked than before, they are still fairly large. The conclusion to be drawn from the fact that regional

Figure 16.3 Generalized Land Use Density

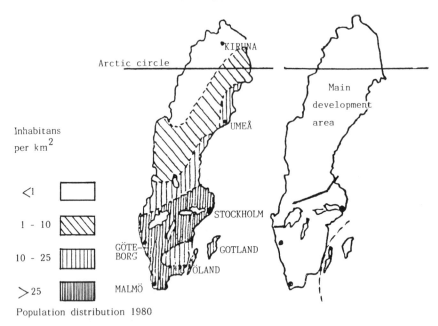

differences remain is that the solution to the long-term problems of the northern counties must continue to be the major goal of regional policy. This option would be changed according to current forecasts on industrial changes in the years to come. During recent years the recession in the world economy has affected the traditionally strong sectors of Swedish industry: mining, steel, shipbuilding, and pulp and paper. This has led to considerable unemployment even in regions that previously had no such problems. It is common in Sweden for a town to be heavily dependent on a single firm and, owing to the great distances involved, it is often difficult for the town's inhabitants to commute to other jobs. The closing down of firms has severe repercussions for the people living in such a region.

In the Regional Policy Act approved by the Swedish parliament in 1982, the relevant aims are summarized as follows: "The aims of regional policy are to create conditions by which a stable population trend can be maintained in the different parts of the country and to give people access to jobs, services and a good environment regardless of where they live in the country."

In order to achieve these objectives, the government and parliament have designed a set of regional policy measures and have specified guidelines as to the priorities among different regions. The national guidelines traditionally used in the implementation of regional policy in Sweden are threefold: (1) population frames, (2) a regional structure plan, and (3) designation of regional development areas (assisted areas). The main significance of the 1982 act with regard to county planning is that it decentralized the system and made it less formal.

In 1972 the parliament (Riksdag) adopted the National Physical Plan for the management of Sweden's land and water resources. The guidelines suggest how trade-offs can be treated among conflicting interests that lay claim to the same geographic area; for example, a plant that is likely to consume natural resources on a large scale or cause a potential pollution threat might compete with a tract proposed for leisure-time dwellings, a fishery, a reindeer breeding preserve, or outdoor recreational areas.

The national plan identified on maps (see Figure 16.4) those places that will be preserved intact, the feasible sites of future power station and heavy industry, and which mountain areas and rivers are to be left untouched.

INSTITUTIONAL AND LANDOWNERSHIP FRAMEWORK

The parliament has also passed legislation on planning and building to be adopted by the municipalities. Various bodies can influence local community planning by providing general advice, regulations, and recommendations. One example of this is the Swedish building code. Control methods can be of a positive character, such as grants, or negative, such as controls and coercive measures.

Physical planning and building development in Sweden is regulated primarily by two instruments: the Building Act and the Building Ordinance. In addition there are a number of regulations concerning building and recommendations concerning physical planning that are issued by the National Board of Physical Planning and Building. Changes in conditions, higher standards, and new materials can rapidly result in new regulations.

The legislative framework for physical planning stipulated in Swedish law, however, provides detailed legislation on such issues as purposes for which land can be used, who is allowed to use the land, how land should be managed, and who can acquire land for different purposes.

Although most of the rights in Sweden are stipulated by law, there is an important exception, the right of common access (*Allenmansrätt*). This right is not fully laid down in written law but in consuetudinary law. The right of common access means that everyone has the right to move freely around in nonurban areas, the right of way over another person's land or water irrespective of whether the area is privately owned. Anyone may pick wildflowers, berries, or mushrooms, swim, or go by boat and camp (but only for one night) providing no damage is caused and the landowner's "private life" is not infringed.

Of direct importance in this chapter is legislation concerning when and where building development and urban land use changes may take place. This is to be found in the Building and Planning Act where the local authorities—that is, the municipality—are invested with the sole responsibility for drawing up both synoptic plans and detailed development plans and to specify the purpose for which

Figure 16.4 National Physical Planning Proposals Concerning Vacation Cottage Development and Camping

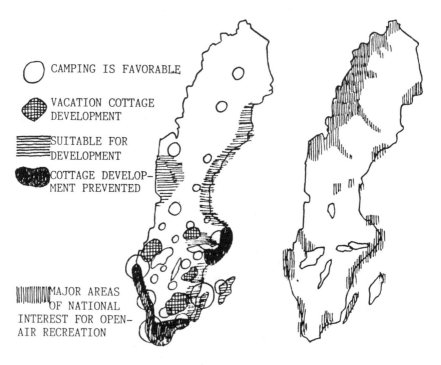

CAMPING IS FAVORABLE

VACATION COTTAGE DEVELOPMENT

SUITABLE FOR DEVELOPMENT

COTTAGE DEVELOPMENT PREVENTED

MAJOR AREAS OF NATIONAL INTEREST FOR OPEN-AIR RECREATION

Ministry of Housing and Planning, Stockholm

land and buildings are to be used. This in practice means that the local authority can veto the right of landowners to develop land without any obligation on the authority to pay compensation.

Historic outline of Laws and Decrees Affecting Land Use and Building

1400. During the fifteenth century municipal inspectors ensured that buildings did not project onto the street.

1700. Around 1720 building regulations enforced by a building burgomaster were in use in towns in Sweden. The post of town architect is mentioned from 1660 onward.

1874. The first building laws common to all Swedish towns were introduced. These regulations covered primarily matters of hygiene and fire safety. In cities and towns, the heights of buildings, rights of development, widths of streets, sizes of open places, and parks were regulated; however, no indication was given as to how the buildings within each city block should be used. A block could contain factories as well as housing. These regulations were a decisive factor in the formation of a town's urban pattern and of its housing conditions. Building permission requirements were introduced in the same year.

1907. Parliament passed a law governing town planning and the division of building lots. Compared with the 1874 laws, this new law gave townships the right, and in some cases an obligation, to buy land so that their building plans could be carried out. The law also contained an effective prohibition against the erection of any new building contrary to the town plan. It also obliged property owners to pay some of the costs for the realization of the infrastructure of the new formal town plan.

1931. Town planning regulations were introduced that allowed the limit of the use of land to that which could be judged in each particular instance to be compatible with the public interest. The shaping of all building could now be regulated in detail. The town plan and its planning process became an accepted legal institution.

1947. The Building Act gave the municipal authorities greater power over property owners. The basic principle that it is the municipality solely that shall decide when and in which form building construction shall occur was established. Two planning instruments were introduced: the outline plan and the regional plan.

1959. Common building regulations were introduced for the whole country governing the shapes of buildings themselves. This building ordinance resulted in a simplification of regulations and their application by transferring the right of decision from the government to the county administrations and the local authorities.

1978. In November the government ordered the head of the Department of Housing to appoint a special adviser to work out a proposal for a new building act.

In September 1979, a report containing the proposal for a new planning and building act, known as the PBL (*Plan- och Bygglag*), was submitted to the minister of housing. It was sent to a large number of organizations, including all the municipal councils, for their comments. Comments concerning the proposal had to be submitted to the Department of Housing before June 1980. The proposal would mean that the building acts from 1947, the building regulations from 1959, and the law concerning unlawful buildings from 1976 will be abolished and be replaced by the PBL, a special law governing municipal roads, and another special law regulating the granting of permission for certain forms of industry. This new act is expected to come into force in January, 1987. The proposal suggests the following reforms:

—The PBL involves a decentralization of decisionmaking from the state to the

Figure 16.5 Building Permission Avenues

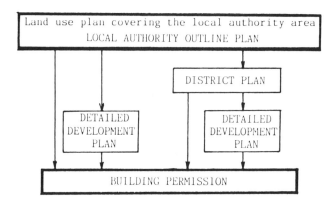

local municipalities. The state's approval and ratification of plans would no longer be required except in special circumstances.

—Matters of national interest have been collected into a special chapter. In this way the parliamentary guidelines given in connection with the national physical plan will have a clear legal status.

—County administration boards can order that a municipal plan be submitted for state approval. This can occur only on certain special grounds stated in the new law. These apply mainly when the local plans appear to be in conflict with national or intermunicipal interests.

—The boundary between public interest and the interests of the individual will be more clearly defined. Among other things the individual is given building permission rights for any measures taken within the framework of an approved land use chart (Figure 16.5).

—The system of plans is modernized. The outline type of plans in use today are usually without any form of legal support. These plans, such as municipal outline plans and land use plans, will be adjusted in the PBL. Development rights stated in the detailed town plans will be given a time-limited validity. These detailed town plans will have a so-called execution period of five to 15 years. In this way the difficulties with eternal development rights, and their consequence, eternal prohibition of new buildings, which often occur today, will be avoided.

—The extent of the compulsory permissions system—the obligation to seek building permission—can be varied by municipal council decisions. The new law gives a normal list of measures for which building permission should be sought. Municipal authorities can both increase and decrease the number of these measures in a number of different fields.

—The responsibility of care for areas of great natural beauty is also decentralized. The rules for the protection of shores and beaches, previously part of the laws for the care of areas of great natural beauty, now become part of the PBL. Municipal authorities can, through special land decrees, pass regulations that protect local wildlife and satisfy the needs for local open-air activities.

—The influence of local citizen groups is increased. Rules introduced in the PBL aim at guaranteeing the local population an influence over the design of local physical plans. All inhabitants in a municipality are given the right of appeal should the municipal authorities not respect these rules. Tenants and tenant flat owners are considered as being part-owners.

—Questions concerning the carrying through of plans are given special importance in the PBL. Special rules are given for the cooperation of property owners in development matters.

—Municipal planning decisions shall influence land use decisions based on other laws. This applies, for example, on public roads and highways, large quarries, mines, large power lines, and hydraulic engineering projects. With regard to building, it is expected that the new act will also deal with such matters as groundwater, underground services, the properties of new building materials, and durability. It is also expected that the new act will involve amendments concerning the regulations covering testing and inspection and introduce more stringent regulations concerning the do-it-yourself supervision of building works.

Other important controls of land use and development are:

Expropriation Act. A local authority can implement the compulsory purchase of land needed for urban development. Compensation should correspond to the market value 10 years previously.

Right of preemption. The right, introduced in 1968, means that a local authority can take the place of another buyer and purchase land and buildings.

Local authority site stipulation. The regulation, introduced in 1974, means that government loans for new building, or the modernization of existing buildings, are provided only if the local authority leases or sells the sites. A current exception concerns individually erected one-family dwellings.

Development agreements. The agreements enable a local authority to make detailed decisions concerning, for example, who is to pay for certain communal facilities, the size of dwellings, and whether they are to be owner-occupied or let.

Joint Installation Act. This is needed when the implementation of a plan requires landowners to take joint responsibility for roads, underground services, and so on. Special regulations apply concerning, among other things, the division of costs and responsibility. The Joint Installation Act and the Private Road Act are examples of such regulations.

The Environment Protection Act regulates various impacts on the natural environment.

The Water Act regulates, among other things, construction in water areas.

The Nature Conservancy Act incorporates regulations concerning the protection and care of the natural environment.

The Mineral Deposits Act involves the principle of applying for permits and concerns mineral deposits, as well as oil, natural gas, coal, uranium, and peat.

Decisionmaking Structure

Sweden is divided into 24 counties (*län*) and just over 280 local authorities-municipalities. There are also 23 county councils responsible for particular services common to local authorities. The smallest local authorities have a population of approximately 3,000. The average population per municipality is around 15,000. Stockholm, the capital, is the largest municipality with about 700,000 inhabitants. Greater Stockholm has, however, 1.4 million inhabitants and includes 25 municipalities.

Matters concerning community development and the utilization of natural resources are dealt with by several ministries and national boards.

The Ministry of Housing and Physical Planning contains the National Housing Board, responsible for government housing loans; the National Land Survey of Sweden, which deals with land surveying; the National Board of Physical Planning and Building, which deals with building regulations, advice, and guidance on physical planning; and the Swedish Council for Building Research and the Swedish Institute for Building Research, which deals with planning and building research.

The Ministry of Agriculture oversees the National Environment Protection Board, which deals with the application of the Nature Conservancy Act and the Environment Protection Act.

The Ministry of Industry is responsible for certain regional policy measures and has under it, among others, the State power board, responsible for the production and distribution of electrical power.

The Ministry of Education and Cultural Affairs contains the Central Office of National Antiquities, which among other things is responsible for the preservation of historical monuments.

The Ministry of Public Administration houses the county administration (*Länsstyrelsen*), with responsibility for interpreting central government administration in the counties (Figure 16.6). The county administration is divided into two departments: a taxation department and a planning department. The planning department is responsible for community planning. In most counties the department has a general office and eight special units. Planning and building matters are mainly dealt with by the physical planning unit. The planning unit provides advice and comments during the drawing up of different types of development plans by local authorities in the county area. It ratifies detailed development plans, participates in some aspects of strategic planning, and su-

Figure 16.6 Public Administration System

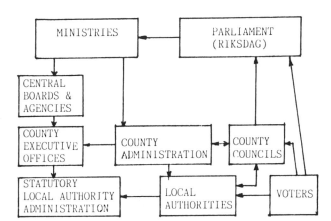

pervises building activity. The main task of the county administration is, however, the coordination of central government, local authority, and county council activities within the county and ensuring that these are in accordance with national policy guidelines regarding population and employment.

Finally the local authorities-municipalities are responsible for social services and all education below the university level. The municipalities are also responsible for local planning, not only for construction and building work but also for land utilization in a broader sense. They are also assigned the task of synoptic physical planning covering the whole jurisdictional area of the municipality.

Landownership Patterns

Swedish real estate stock amounted to about 2,550,000 assessment units (approximately the same as owner units), with an assessed value of 1,200 billions skr and with an estimated fair market value of 2,000 billions skr, in 1984. The stock consists of single- and two-family houses (about 45 percent of the total value), residential and commercial estates (20 percent) industrial estates (15 percent), agricultural holdings (15 percent) and estates for other purposes (5 percent).

Although the single-family house sector is dominated by owner-occupiers, the residential and commercial estates have different owner categories. The housing stock can be divided into four main groups on the basis of owner category:

1. Private owners of single- and two-family houses. These account for about 40 percent of all dwellings.
2. Private owners who let the dwellings; approximately 20 percent of all dwellings.
3. Associations that lease flats to members (tenant-owner associations). Members make a small cash deposit. These associations are non-profitmaking. Members can, however, sell their flats (their shares) at a profit. This category of housing represents approximately 15 percent of the total.
4. The public-owned sector consists largely of corporations owned by local authorities— that is, public housing corporations. These corporations let the dwellings and are non-profit making. The public sector owns about 25 percent of the total housing stock and approximately half of all rented dwellings.

For many decades, Sweden's housing policy has concentrated on promoting non-profit-making housing corporations. This category's share of the housing market has therefore increased markedly. In the context of new construction, the public sector was responsible for 40 percent of all dwellings completed between 1960 and 1975. Private, single-family houses had 30 percent of the market. In recent years, however, radical changes have taken place in the distribution of ownership of new dwellings. The number of privately owned single-family houses has increased, and since the end of the 1970s it is the leading group. (See Figures 16.7 and 16.8.)

MAJOR CHALLENGES

Industrialization in Sweden came late and was dispersed among many small communities. For this reason, Swedish towns are relatively small and rather new. In the 1930s, the greater part of the population was still living in rural areas, and even in 1982 there were only 17 towns with more than 50,000 inhabitants each. Greater urbanized areas can be found mainly around Stockholm, Gothenburg, and Malmö. Although Sweden does not have a powerful tradition of urban living and culture, several Swedish towns can compete in urban ambience with most of the beautiful towns of continental Europe.

After World War II, Sweden's urbanization was proceeding rapidly. Housing shortages were the main problem and the driving political force. The most important force behind postwar urban development came from rapid economic growth, which provided investment and purchasing power. This force, particularly after 1950, influenced the entire urbanization process. Industry, commerce, public services, and administration not ony expanded but changed in structure. They became concentrated in large units and were located in large cities and regional centers. Naturally people had to follow them.

Urbanization has been more perceptible in a zone defined to the east by greater Stockholm and to the west by the Gothenburg and Malmö regions. The rest of the country has not been affected to the same degree. Consequently the shortage of housing and overcrowding concerned primarily Stockholm, Gothenburg, Malmö, and some other cities within this zone.

Figure 16.7 Number of Dwellers per Type of Accommodation

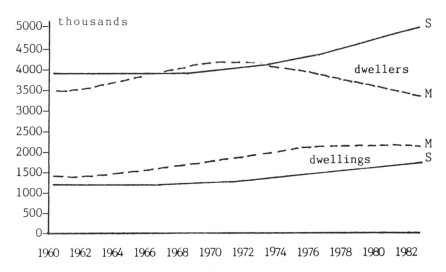

Figure 16.8 Persons per Dwelling

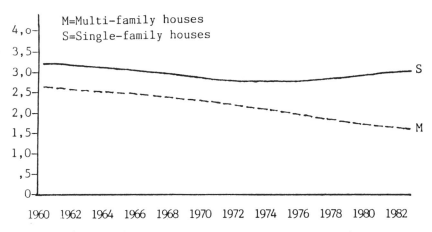

Statistika centralbyrån (SCB), 1982, Stockholm.

The flight to the cities and the move from the older, usually central districts to newer ones on the periphery created a great need for new housing. There was another reason for the intense postwar housing production. When Sweden began to implement its official housing policy, approximately 70 percent of all dwellings consisted of no more than one or two rooms. These conditions were also an important force driving the decisionmakers and were used effectively by those who recommended the decisions. These were the experts from different technical and economic disciplines and representatives of powerful interests including the representatives of purely financial interests. It was easy to convince people who had lived under crowded conditions to move. Whenever people were able to afford it, they raised the standard of their living space. For example, between 1950 and 1970 the municipality of Stockholm built 100,000 new dwellings. The population, however, was the same size in 1970 as it had been 20 years earlier. All housing production was absorbed by the rise in space standards. The most dramatic changes have taken place in Stockholm's inner city (Figure 16.9). The number of inhabitants there today is only half of what it was 30 years ago, in spite of the substantial increase in the volume of buildings; 80 percent of the people who lived in the inner city of Stockholm in 1960 have moved to the outer parts of the region. In other words, Stockholm went through the development process by clearing the inner city of old dwellings to make way for rebuilding the downtown area as a central business district, while new suburban communities popped up on virgin land surrounding the old suburbs. This is a well-known pattern in many cities of the industrialized world. During the 1960s housing production became an important activity for the whole country.

Production has been stimulated continuously by state loans at a low rate of interest and a long amortization period. Conditions for loans have also favored cooperative and municipal building companies; 90 percent of all housing construction has been financed with the aid of state loans. As conditions for these advantageous loans, however, the state and municipalities imposed detailed demands for standards—mainly physical ones, as well as general guidelines.

Where quality is concerned, the objectives have concerned primarily floor space. Two persons per room at the most was the first goal. Today there is an average of two rooms per person. The goals have also been applied to equipment. Dwellings have been provided with increasingly better kitchen equipment and hygienic facilities of specified standards. In the 1960s requirements were also introduced in connection with the surroundings, such as play areas for children, open space for recreation and activities, a pedestrian network, and parking lots.

Where quantity is concerned the goals have been determined by the desire to build as much as possible, as soon as possible, and to concentrate production in districts where the shortage was most severe. Financial resource and availability of labor and of land suitable for development have, among other difficulties, been limited. In spite of that, in the mid–1960s, the Swedish parliament passed a resolution stating that 1 million new dwellings should be constructed in the next 10 years in order to eliminate the housing shortage, an impressive goal for a country with 8 million inhabitants. This target has been reached.

Until the mid-1970s, the national government continued to cooperate in housing development by contributing additional loans for new housing programs. Their goals were to eliminate overcrowding, increase dwelling areas, and upgrade

Figure 16.9 Inhabitants in Stockholm County 1750–1978, within Development Growth
Rings

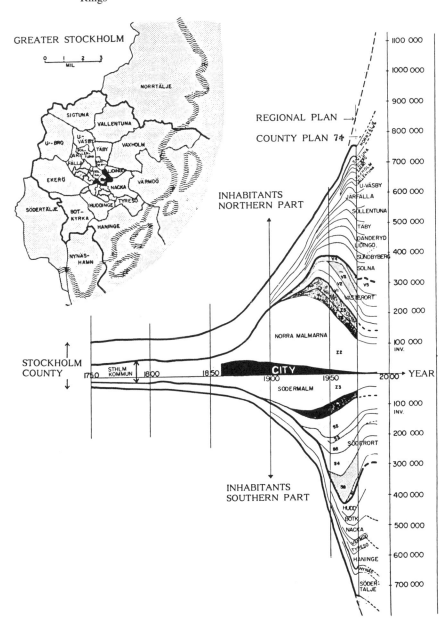

Stockholm Municipal Investigation Bureau

interior amenities. Through an intense housing production program, the government has declared that it has overcome the housing shortage.

Sweden has had a rapid and strong urbanization. Today 80 percent of the population live in urban areas, the majority in spacious, modern houses constructed during the past 40 years. The housing shortage has been eliminated.

Does this mean that Sweden has solved all problems concerning the built environment? Certainly not. But it might have reached the ceiling of urban expansion. Criticism of contemporary Swedish architecture and town planning has been frequently expressed by the press and the people during the last decade. Town planning is now, among other things, criticized as a concept and an activity limiting the freedom of action of individuals, mainly in relation to new housing development.

There are, for example, still over 100,000 dwellings in older houses, mainly in inner-city areas, in need of renewal and modernization. Moreover, the majority of dwellings built in the 1930s and 1940s had only one or two rooms plus a small kitchen and bathroom. These dwellings are usually situated in semicentral tracts around the core of several Swedish towns, which had expanded during the prewar decade. This category comprises about 500,000 flats.

A considerable number of the 1 million dwellings from the 1960s require improvement. They were built quickly during a hectic period of urban development. In many cases there are some technical shortcomings. Above all there are deficiencies in the environment itself. These include a lack of working opportunities, a lack of certain facilities and public communications, a uniformity in building appearance, and, to a large extent, a separation of uses and activities.

Although the average living space in Sweden probably is the most spacious in Europe, there are still a number of families who live in very crowded conditions. These people are at the low end of the socioeconomic scale.

In most Swedish towns, what is now needed is renewal, completion, refurbishment, and a general improvement of the urban milieu independently of the age of the built-up area. Larger new housing development is not needed. On the other hand, there are demands for office buildings and even new industrial plants, mainly to replace older ones.

Sweden has taken part in the urban renewal campaign initiated by the Council of Europe in 1979. The main task of European interest has been in older, inner-city areas and in nineteenth-century urban development. The problem in Sweden is somewhat different.

Having accomplished its urbanization, Sweden is now facing new requirements caused by higher fuel prices and scarcer resources, which severely restrict urban and suburban mobility and indoor comfort. By necessity a greater percentage of the future population in Sweden may have to live in urban settings as patterns become denser and community services more concentrated. The revitalization of the existing urban fabric to accommodate densification will occur predominantly through the adaptive reuse of existing structures and incremental infill operations on a rather small scale.

APPROACHES TO LAND USE PLANNING

The decisionmaking process in Swedish land use and urban planning is based in principle on active participation of all interested parties. Planning work is pursued openly and is closely watched by the press, the public and interest groups.

In spite of this fact, planning was almost solely of a technical and functional character during the 1950s and the 1960s. Public interest in matters of urban development was rather insignificant. It is surprising that the essential feature of urban development during those decades, the most rapid period of urbanization in the country, was that there was nearly no opposition, at least not in any organized way. Criticism and opposition began in the early 1970s and continues. Tenant organizations, local environmental protection movements, and growing demands for preservation of the architectural heritage are flourishing in most Swedish towns.

The scope and vehemence of the repeated criticism of the built environment is a symptom of a growing understanding of a greater importance given to urban life and is less a symptom of an urban crisis. People's participation in decisionmaking and even in shaping the environment is now a reality, though a more substantial contribution is to be desired. The Tenant's Association has become the negotiating organization and is responsible for agreements with property owners on rents and modernization of dwellings. The tenants can, for example, refuse to agree to renovation that goes above a certain minimum standard, and they can take initiatives to compel reconditioning in cooperation between various property owners. This is an important step toward a real user influence in the administration of residential buildings.

The pressure from radicals and reactionaries, who were united in the 1960s in protest against the establishment in all of Western Europe, has vitalized Swedish municipal democracy and established organizations. It has forced clearer explanations of programs and planning proposals so that they can be better understood by laymen and users.

Today planning takes place in several stages, the most important of which is the programming stage. It is here where the wishes of the various parties are surveyed and presented. Viewpoints on alternative policies and proposals are obtained by circulating them for consideration and through discussions and interviews. Various municipal and state authorities also express their opinions. In addition, organizations representing tenants and property owners, local organizations, commerce and industry, trade unions, and many others express their views. Particularly sensitive groups, such as the handicapped and children, are given special attention.

At this stage exhibitions and information meetings are organized at every major planning subject. The problem of this stage is getting out the information in an understandable way to everybody.

After the program has been approved by the municipal council, the planning and designing stage follows, also divided into several parts. Before municipal decisions are taken, the proposals are examined by landowners in the area, which means that they still have a privileged position in Swedish planning legislation. Other groups also examine the proposals and comment to the authorities. After the municipality has made its decision, the proposal must be ratified by the county administration on behalf of the state in order to become legally binding. Actually the county administration's chief concern is only to verify that the planning process has followed the correct procedure.

Since the early 1980s the planning process has been reorganized, so organizations and the public take part in joint consultations on planning matters of major importance; however, these changes in organization are in the view of many people still inadequate compared with the impact of attitudes that, for example, the environmental movements have had. The following requests have been met to varying extents by the different municipalities:

—Reduced private motoring in cities and the improvement of public transport

—Improvement of the pedestrian environment

—Demands for a greener townscape

—Greater consideration for nature

—Reconditioning rather than rebuilding

—More day care centers and better local services

The environmental movement has not been alone in the contribution to new attitudes, but its importance has been considerable. Other action groups have also played a part. Clearly by the 1980s public participation in planning had become a subject of increasing importance. One of the bodies in Sweden that has sponsored considerable research into problems associated with public participation in planning is the Swedish Council of Building Research.

FUTURE THRUSTS

Conservation of natural resources, long-term protection of the environment, and architectural heritage are now accepted preconditions of future development. The 1980s will probably be not only a decade of awakening and edification but also a decade in which concern over the environment will conflict with economic considerations.

The fabric of connections that exists between energy flows and the physical structure of dense settlements is so complicated that simplified conclusions should be approached with great caution. If planning is to contribute to solving energy problems, then planning will become, in terms of knowledge, organization, and political implications, even more difficult and complex. It must be admitted that the social problem can hardly be approached in depth. The decisive factor for success will depend on the ability of public corporations—politicians, experts, and administration—to master bundles of connected problems under conditions of high uncertainty. This is a very difficult task.

The quality of life and the spirit of a society is linked to a high degree to the quality of its towns. An urban environment that fails to offer a positive human experience may foster hostile behavior, anxiety, and social disruption. Of course, urban environments are not only form; they also contain the equipment to meet the necessary functional requirements.

The in-depth study of nature, sociocultural structure, and tradition tied to the place of its origin is imperative. There can be no universal and uniform solutions. Instead care and respect for the existing environment and consciousness of the limits of our resources will be the characteristics of planning philosophy for the coming decade in Sweden.

BIBLIOGRAPHY

Aström, K. 1967. *City Planning in Sweden*. Stockholm: Swedish Institute.

Federation of County Councils. 1981. *The County Councils and Their Functions*. Stockholm.

Heinemann, H. E., ed. 1975. *New Towns and Old*. Stockholm: Swedish Institute.

Ministry for Foreign Affairs, Ministry of Agriculture, and Ministry of Physical Planning and Local Government. 1972. *Management of Land and Water Resources*. Stockholm: P. A. Norstedt & Söner.

National Board of Physical Planning and Building. 1979. *Physical Planning in Sweden*. Stockholm.

National Board of Physical Planning and Building. 1983. *Planning and Building in Sweden*. Stockholm.

Ödmann, E. and G. B. Dahlberg. 1970. *Urbanization in Sweden*. Stockholm: Allmänna Förlaget.

Plan International. 1976. *Habitat 76*. Stockholm: Föreningen för Samhällsplanering.

Swedish Institute. 1983. *Swedish Regional Policy*. Stockholm: Swedish Institute. Classification: FS 72 d Odg.

17

Union of Soviet Socialist Republics

DENIS J. B. SHAW

THE SOVIET LAND RESOURCE

Having by far the largest territory of any other country in the world (22.5 million square kilometers), equivalent to 15 percent of the earth's land surface, the Soviet Union is particularly well endowed both with respect to space and with respect to most types of natural resources. Its relatively northerly situation (the greater part of Soviet territory lies north of the 50th parallel) coupled with its position astride the great Eurasian land mass, however, gives it a generally harsh, continental climate. Most Soviet territory therefore is unsuitable for dense human settlement or for agricultural activity. The lands to the north and the east are dominated by tundra and boreal forest associated with poor, infertile soils and frequently with swampy conditions. The boreal forest occupies about one-third of Soviet territory, including the greater part of Siberia. Southward, and particularly in Central Asia, semiarid or arid conditions predominate, producing semi-desert or desert environments and alkaline soils. In these regions, human settlement is restricted to the riverine oases or to the better lands along the piedmont fringe to the east. Most of the Soviet population thus dwells in the mixed-forest, forest-steppe, and steppe vegetation zones, which occupy the southern two-thirds of European USSR, and southern part of west Siberia, and northern Kazakhstan. It is in these areas, together with the oases lands of Central Asia, where cities, industry, and agricultural activity are concentrated. Their limited extent is indicated by the fact that only 10 percent of Soviet territory is used for arable farming.

The Soviet Union's characteristic agricultural problems have long prompted its political leaders to interest themselves in measures of land improvement.

Through irrigation schemes in the arid lands and drainage and associated measures particularly in the northern regions (approximately 10 percent of Soviet territory is subject to swamp conditions), some progress has been made in the extension of the arable area. Other programs, such as the planting of shelter belts and the breeding of hardier crop strains, have also made a small contribution to this aim. It is unlikely, however, that land improvement measures will have a significant impact on Soviet agricultural performance in the near future. As a reflection of this fact, official concern has recently been voiced at the not inconsiderable losses of arable land to urbanization, industrial and mining pollution, water management schemes, and other activities.

The presence of important energy and other types of resources in regions remote from major population centers means that the Soviet authorities cannot afford to ignore the environmentally less favored regions. The costs of economic activity in such areas, however, are frequently high. One factor contributing to these is permafrost, which is endemic throughout much of the north and east. Approximately 45 percent of Soviet territory is affected by permafrost conditions. Such conditions are associated with high construction costs. Mountainous terrain also impedes economic activity in parts of eastern Siberia and the far east and along much of the USSR's southern fringe. Only 15 percent of the USSR's territory, however, is classified as high mountain.

The Soviet Union's rapid economic development since 1917 has inevitably had widespread environmental and landscape effects; however, in spite of the highly centralized nature of the Soviet economy and despite the agricultural problems, it is only recently that anything like a coordinated policy on land use and land allocation has been attempted. As will become clear in this chapter, such attempts have not as yet been rewarded with complete success.

Tables 17.1 through 17.3 indicate the current situation with regard to Soviet land uses. This information is supplemented by Figures 17.1 through 17.3, which illustrate the major natural vegetation and soil zones and also the distribution of the main types of land use. The USSR has yet to evolve a complete land inventory, although the composition of a state land cadastre has been official policy since the end of the 1960s.

SOVIET LAND LAW

Soviet jurists regard the basic source of Soviet land law as Lenin's decree "On Land,"[1] which was adopted by the Second All-Russian Congress of Soviets on 8 November 1917.[2] This decree confiscated the estates of the nobility and the church and placed them under the jurisdiction of the local soviets of peasants' deputies; specifically excluded from confiscation were the lands of ordinary peasants and cossacks.[3] In an annex, the decree nationalized all minerals, coal, oil, and forests and water bodies of national significance and declared openly for the socialization of land. According to Hazard (1961, 121), however, state ownership of land was not fully established until the decree of 19 February 1918,

Table 17.1

Land Resources of the USSR

Category	Area	(millions of hectares)
Land Mass	2231	
All agricultural land	601	
of which: arable land		218
perennial plantations		4.5
hayfields		47
Pasture	327	
Forest	770	
Shrubs		37.4
Marshes		115.5
Under water		90.8
Buildings, roads, etc.		17.4
Sands, ravines, glaciers and other areas	249	

Source: Victor Kovda, "Land resources and the prospect for their use", Society and the Environment: a Soviet View, Progress, Moscow, 1977, p. 118.

which finally defined socialist land tenure in accordance with socialist principles.[4] Only on 20 August 1918 was urban land nationalized.[5] Finally, on 14 February 1919 the principle that all land now constituted a single state fund, irrespective of who was using it, was enunciated, with the consequence that land now came under the direct control of the competent government department.[6]

The ambivalences in Soviet land policy in the uncertain years of the 1920s have been traced by Sawicki (1977, 40–50). During the years of the New Economic Policy (1921–28), the Soviet government committed itself to a strategy

Table 17.2
Natural Zones and Composition of the Soil Area of the USSR

Zones	Subzones	Total Area (millions of hectares)
Polar tundra	Arctic soils	60
	Tundra soils	120
	Total area	180
Taiga	Gleyey podzolic soils	240
	Podzolic soils	255
	Turfy podzolic soils	260
	Total area	755
Forest-steppe and steppe	Grey forest soils	64
	Podzolized, leached & typical chernozem	89
	Ordinary and southern chernozem	100
	Dark chestnut and chestnut soils	68
	Total area	321
Semi-desert and desert	Light chestnut and brown desert steppe soils	130
	Grey-brown desert soils	140
	Grey soils (serozem)	33
	Total area	303
Mountain territories	Mountain tundra	165
	Mountain meadow	27
	Mountain podzolic, permafrost-taiga & grey-forest soils	400
	Other	60
	Total area	652
Total area		2211

Source: N.N. Rozov, "Pedological description of land resources", Natural Resources of the Soviet Union: Their Use and Renewal, W.H. Freeman and Co., San Francisco, 1971, Table 2, pp. 108-9.

Table 17.3

General Land Fund in the USSR and Distribution of Land among Landholders, 1 November 1970

	Total Area	Agricultural Land (except reindeer pasture)	Arable	of which: Hayland	Pasture
Collective farm land	357.1	209.3	109.7	15.5	80.7
of which: collective land	352.1	204.5	105.7	15.3	80.7
personal plots of collective farmers	4.7	4.5	3.8	0.2	----
collective farm land in personal use of other workers	0.33	0.30	0.25	0.01	----
State farm and ancillary land	687.5	333.1	111.3	24.3	193.7
Land in personal use of workers (other than plots on collective farms)	3.6	3.4	2.5	0.4	----
Total land of agricultural enterprises	1048.5	545.8	223.5	40.2	274.4
State reserve land and land under forestry organizations	1119.5	41.5	0.4	5.7	35.1
Other land users	59.5	19.5	0.5	1.1	17.5
Total land	2227.5	606.8	224.4	47.0	327.0

Source: Bol'shaya Sovetskaya Entsiklopediya, Third Edition, "Sovetskaya Entsiklopediya", Moscow, 1972, vol. 9, p. 463.

Figure 17.1 Natural Vegetation Zones of the USSR

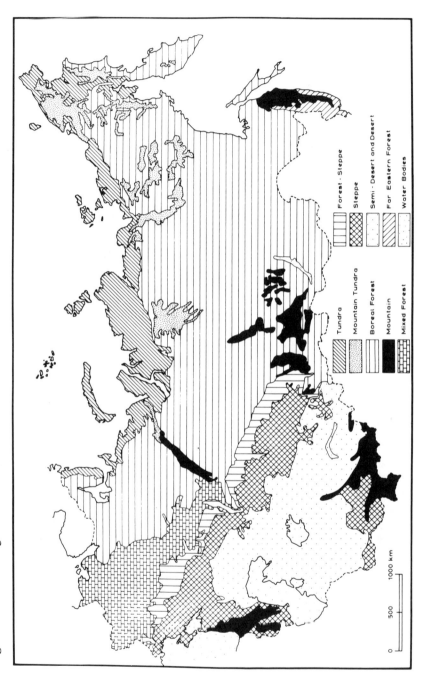

Tundra

Mountain Tundra

Boreal Forest

Mountain

Mixed Forest

Forest - Steppe

Steppe

Semi - Desert and Desert

Far Eastern Forest

Water Bodies

0   500   1000 km

Figure 17.2 Distribution of Land in the USSR under Agricultural Use

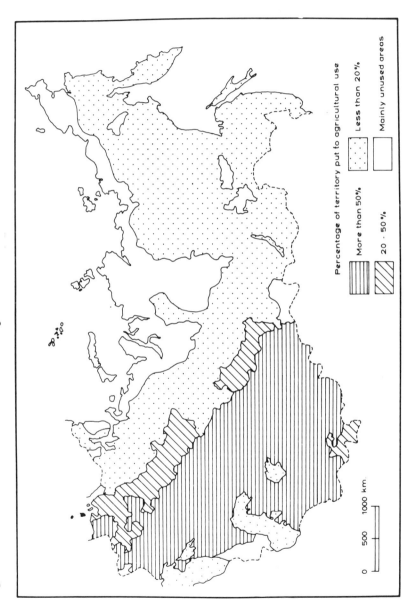

Figure 17.3 Distribution of Forested Land in the USSR

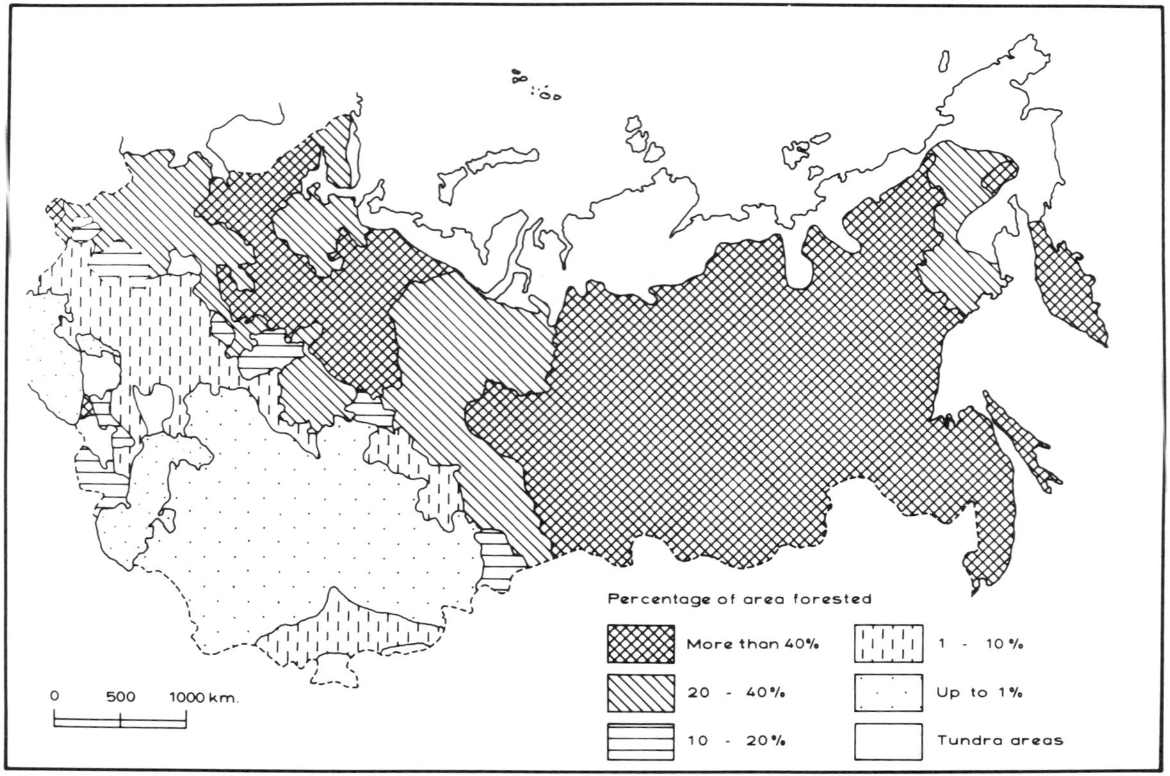

Percentage of area forested

More than 40%

20 - 40%

10 - 20%

1 - 10%

Up to 1%

Tundra areas

0   500   1000 km.

designed to promote economic recovery from the ravages of revolution and war. The problem at this period was the extent to which rural land tenure was to move toward individual or communal forms and, if the latter, the extent to which state control over agriculture was to be enforced. Some of these ambivalences were reflected in the land codes adopted in these years, notably those for the Russian Federation (1922), Ukraine (1922), Georgia (1924), and Belorussia (1926). However, by the end of that decade, a considerable portion of the legislation concerning agricultural land tenure became outdated as the government launched its policy of compulsory collectivization. By the end of the 1930s, the overwhelming majority of rural households belonged to collective farms, as did almost the whole of the cultivated area. A model charter for collective farms governing their organization and land use was issued in 1935.

In the 1950s the Soviet government began to turn its attention toward the need for the codification of law in the light of the profound economic and social changes that had occurred in the USSR since the 1920s, and also in reaction to the lawlessness of the Stalin era (Hazard, et al., 1977, 7–8). Regarding legislation on land, not until the 1960s was any attempt made at codification, and by then the need was urgent in view of growing environmental problems and the developing body of law directed at environmental protection. On 13 December 1968 the Supreme Soviet ratified the Fundamentals of Land Legislation of the USSR and Union Republics.[7] The Fundamentals, which came into effect on 1 July 1969, codified and renewed all land legislation and formed the basis for all future legal enactments on land. Since the Fundamentals underpin present-day Soviet land law, they are worth analyzing in some detail.

Central to the provisions of the Fundamentals is the principle that all land in the USSR is state property, and nothing can be permitted to interfere with the rights of landownership vested exclusively in the state (Article 3). Land cannot be alienated from the state; only the use of land can be permitted to various organizations and to individuals (Articles 3, 7). All land in the USSR constitutes a "single state land fund," and land is divided into a number of categories according to the economic purpose or use it serves (Article 4). The categories are: (i) lands of agricultural designation, allocated to the use of collective farms, state farms, and other land users for agricultural purposes; (ii) lands of populated places (cities, settlements of urban type, and villages); (iii) lands of industry, transport, health resorts, preserves, and other nonagricultural designation; (iv) lands of the state forest fund; (v) lands of the state water fund; and (vi) lands of the state reserve. Legislation provides for the allocation of land to each category and for the transfer of land between categories. Matters concerning the use of minerals, forests, and water are the subjects of further special all-union and republican legislation (Article 2).

Other provisions of the Fundamentals concern such issues as the nature, rights, and duties of land tenure and measures for the transfer of land between users. In addition, there are detailed sections on each category of land listed and sections dealing with the development of a state land cadastre, land surveying, the resolution of disputes about land, and the liability of those who break the laws on land.

The outline legislation contained within the Fundamentals was further developed in the redrafted or newly drafted land codes for each of the union republics, which were approved in 1970–71. In addition, the Fundamentals formed the basis for those provisions of the new 1977 Soviet Constitution that relate to land.

INSTITUTIONAL FRAMEWORK AND APPROACHES TO LAND USE PLANNING

According to the Fundamentals of Land Legislation, the purposes of Soviet land law include "the regulation of land relations in the interests of securing rational land use and of raising its efficiency" (Article 1). Despite the principle of the single state land fund, however, and the fact that the Soviet economy is highly centralized, there is no single body of legislation in the USSR that deals with the entire area of land use planning. Rather Soviet jurists recognize a separate legal regime relating to each land category specified by the Fundamentals (Syrodoyev, 1975, 30), together with laws relating to general planning supervision and control over land use.

With respect to the latter, current land legislation specifies that general state supervision over land is exercised by the various organs of the state within their particular territories and districts—from the supreme soviets of the USSR and union republics, down through the regional, city, and district soviets to that of the individual village. Depending on their status in the hierarchy, the soviets are obliged to see that the laws relating to land allocation and land use are observed, that the principle of state ownership of land is not infringed, and that the regulations concerning conservation are upheld.[8] In addition to the authority exercised by the soviets, a coordinating and supervisory role over the whole area of land use and conservation was given in 1970 to the USSR Ministry of Agriculture and to its subsidiary organizations.[9] This role was to be exercised even over organizations with no agricultural significance, although the ministry's authority in the case of urban land would appear to be at most an indirect one.

There is no doubt that the local soviets' competence with respect to land use planning has been best and longest exercised in the area of urban planning. The history of urban planning in the USSR goes back to the prewar era when various laws stipulated that cities and urban settlements were to have development plans.[10] The 1935 General Plan for the Reconstruction of Moscow was regarded as a model for the urban plans of the period. It was only in the 1950s with the adoption of Khrushchev's housing program that a coordinated urban planning system began to emerge. Laws of 1959 and 1971 defined the responsibilities of the soviets with respect to urban planning. Since the early 1960s, the major bodies responsible for urban planning at national level have been the State Construction Committee (*Gosstroy* USSR) and the State Committee for Civil Construction and Architecture (*Gosgrazhdanstroy*).

A concern with urban planning led to a concern with the planning of city regions, systems of settlements, and planning at the village level. In all these cases, leading roles are also played by *Gosstroy* and *Gosgrazhdanstroy*. Early experience in physical regional planning, including the planning of city regions, goes back to the prewar period.[11] However, only since about 1960 has regional physical planning been tackled in a systematic way and at various scales. Attempts to plan the settlement system at the scale of the USSR as a whole as well as that of the union republics and major economic regions date from the late 1960s. It was in the late 1950s that rural settlement planning began to emerge, and a series of laws and regulations relating to it were issued at the end of the 1960s.[12]

Gosstroy's physical planning system is regarded as the major instrument for the physical control of development, construction, land utilization, and similar matters. In a country in which the activity of the state is central to economic life, it is inevitable that the term *land use planning* should not be exhausted merely by reference to physical planning. Indeed *Gosstroy*'s sphere of competence is by no means well defined, and in many areas its concern is restricted to the broadest scale of oversight while detailed decisions concerning land use are made by other official bodies. For example, in agricultural areas, the Ministry of Agriculture and its local organs play a primary role and make numerous decisions concerning rural land use. It is mainly in the villages themselves where development has been controlled by *Gosstroy* and even then not always effectively. In forested areas, the USSR State Forestry Committee has had the primary supervisory function since 1962, and on the lands of the state water fund and the state reserve there are several supervisory organizations, including the Ministry of Land Reclamation and Water Resources, the Ministry of Public Health, and the Ministry of Agriculture. In these regions, development control by the local soviets and by *Gosstroy* is often of limited importance, although their activities grow where urban pressures are apparent or where major new developments, such as those associated with recreation, are undertaken.

Urban Land Use Planning

It is in urban areas that the Soviet system of physical planning may be said to operate with the greatest degree of success. The outstanding characteristic of Soviet urban planning is its normative nature. *Gosstroy* and *Gosgrazhdanstroy* at the national level lay down a series of guidelines and norms to which urban plans and development decisions are expected to conform. Such norms include many instructions relating to land use, including zoning principles, normative densities and structures for residential development, norms for open space, the distribution of services, and the spacing of industrial developments. In terms of zoning, for example, urban territory usually is divided into zones of settlement, industrial zones, communal servicing zones, zones for external transport, and buffer zones. Details can vary according to local circumstances, but the approval of *Gosstroy*, either nationally or through its regional organs, is necessary for all urban plans, and by this means its norms supposedly are enforced. Moreover, the detailed participation of national or republican organs of *Gosstroy* in the compilation of urban plans is a common practice, which provides an additional check that plans conform to the standards laid down.

Gosstroy's representative at the local level is the chief city architect, supported in the largest cities by an organization known as the Administration of Architecture-Planning (Glav Apu). The chief city architect is an appointee of the *Gosstroy* system and a member of the executive committee of the city soviet. It falls to him and his administration to participate in the composition of the city's general plan and other plans and to see that these plans are fulfilled. He has wide powers of inspection, legal sanction, and direction. In smaller towns and cities, planning powers are generally exercised by a department known as the Department of Construction and Architecture.

The basic document that guides urban planning in the USSR is known as the general plan. According to instructions issued by *Gosstroy* on 23 March 1966, "The construction and reconstruction of cities must proceed on the basis of general plans"; "The urban general plan is the fundamental urban planning document, within which, on the basis of national-economic plans and of social and scientific-technical progress, the prospects for the city's future development and the comprehensive solution of all its functional elements are defined"; "A general plan approved according to established procedures is binding on all organisations undertaking construction within the city."[13] The general plan thus has a legal basis, being approved by a specified level of government (all-union, republican, or regional) depending on the size and status of the city being planned and agreed to by numerous other official organizations. Most general plans have a life span of 25 to 30 years and are subject to regular review and revision.[14]

General plans have a basic territorial function, defining the structure of the city and outlining the overall functional zones. As long-term plans, however, they are necessarily limited in planning detail. This detail is provided by those plans that are drawn up at the next stage, when development is about to begin: first-stage projects for building layout, projects of detailed planning, projects for urban industrial or communal servicing zones, and building plans and work drawings. It is at these stages when the actual selection of sites for building is done and when the architect-planners ensure that the general plans' provisions are observed.

Article 30 of the Fundamentals of Land Legislation defines urban land as consisting of: (i) building land, (ii) land for general use, (iii) agricultural and associated land, (iv) land occupied by urban forests, and (v) land used by railway, water, air and pipeline transport, by the mining industry and others. The first two categories are the subject of detailed regulation by the general plans and other development plans. However, according to the same article of the Fundamentals, all land within the urban boundary is urban land and therefore (Article 31) falls under the jurisdiction of the city soviet. All urban land is thus, by implication, subject to urban planning. Categories iii and iv of urban land contain land that fulfills some present urban function or may be developed or called on to serve such a function in the future. For such undeveloped land, a decree of the RSFSR Council of Ministers of 1948 stipulates the need for a special plan, called an urban land management program.[15] Although this type of plan is frequently referred to in the legal literature, the planning literature has little to say about it and, where they exist as separate entities, such plans may be presumed to fulfill many of the same functions as the general plan.[16]

Article 34 of the Fundamentals of Land Legislation defines a special regime for that land situated outside the urban boundary that serves as a resource for future urban expansion, as a place where functions necessary to the normal functioning and environmental protection of cities can be located, and as an area where forests and open spaces can be preserved to provide recreational attractions and to protect environmental quality. This land is known as the suburban and green zone, and special plans are drawn up to regulate development in such areas.

Land within cities is therefore allocated to users within the context of a regime of urban planning. The law on land tenure allows for socialist organizations, cooperatives, and individual citizens to apply for the use of plots of land according to a set procedure and for city soviet executive committees to grant plots in accordance with established norms. In such cases, title deeds are also issued; however, it is only the right to use land, not the ownership of land, that is being vested, and there are various procedures whereby the state may repossess or reallocate such plots.

According to evidence collected by numerous Soviet and Western scholars, urban land use planning often appears to fall short of theoretical standards (Bater, 1980; Pallot and Shaw, 1981; Shaw, 1983). Investigations have revealed that urban land frequently is left undeveloped for long periods or, when developed, is at a density below approved norms. Land that may be more costly to build on than usual is frequently bypassed by construction agencies. In many cities, there is an alarming tendency for urbanization to spill over into the greenbelt. Zoning principles may also be transgressed, and land that is designated in the general plan for open space or residential development is often used for other purposes. Industrial concerns that are administered by powerful all-union or union-republican ministries pose a particular problem for urban planners, and the competence of the city soviets over their land in many cases is limited.

One important reason for such problems lies in the weakness of the urban planning machinery under *Gosstroy* relative to the big industrial ministries. It is the latter, after all, that are responsible for the key areas in the Soviet economy and in most instances exercise decisive political, financial, and economic muscle. By comparison the city soviets, on which the physical planning system relies so heavily, are usually relatively weak. Added to this problem is the fact that urban planning has tended to be a rather rigid and mechanical exercise, often based on unrealistic norms, and city plans have failed to keep pace with changing needs. It is therefore easy to ignore them in practice. Recently considerable efforts have been devoted to devising a flexible and comprehensive system of urban planning that will be a more effective instrument for the control of urban development (Shaw, 1983). It is too early to say whether such measures will be successful; however, the so-called economic levers favored by many Soviet and Western analysts—such as charging rent for land—have not as yet attracted much support in high places.

Regional Physical Planning and Settlement Planning

In the same way that Soviet legislation stipulates that urban development must proceed on the basis of general plans, it also demands that the development of such features as major industrial complexes, individual large industrial, hydro-electric or agricultural schemes, industrial estates, resorts, lines of communication, and settlements associated with such developments be undertaken on the basis of schemes and projects of regional planning. "The purpose of regional planning," states *Gosstroy*'s instructions issued in July 1972, "is the rational ordering of the territorial-economic organisation of the planned region, the formation of its architectural-planning structure and its functional zonation, with the aim of fostering optimal conditions for the development of production, urban development and the conservation and enhancement of the natural environment, together with the efficient and comprehensive utilisation of natural, economic and labour resources."[17] Schemes of regional planning embrace fairly large areas: a territory, region, autonomous republic, or one of the smaller union republics. They form the basis for projects of regional planning, usually embracing smaller areas with common problems or geographical characteristics. Schemes and projects are composed for 10-year periods with long-term prognoses for 25- or 30-year periods.

Schemes and projects of regional planning therefore entail the application of the central concerns of the urban general plan to a broader regional scale. As with the general plan, land use is a central issue. Regional and district soviets, together with their construction and architecture departments, play a major role in the composition and implementation of such plans. In the case of agricultural regions, an important role is also played by the local agricultural authorities. Since projects of regional planning may contain material relevant to agricultural or forestry land uses, the participation of the agricultural and forestry authorities in the planning process is regarded as a significant part of the procedure.

Since the end of the 1950s, the USSR has pursued a policy of planning the evolution of the rural settlement system (Kovalev, 1972; Pallot, 1977). This has taken the form of attempting to reduce the number of small villages and hamlets and to increase the size and orderlines of the larger settlements. According to a joint resolution of the Communist party Central Committee and the USSR Council of Ministers issued on 12 September 1968 and entitled "On the Regulation of Rural Construction," the aim is to endow such settlements with modern housing,

services and cultural activities and efficient production facilities that will encourage the intensification of agriculture and provide employment to the population at agriculturally slack periods of the year.[18] The resolution laid particular
responsibility on the *Gosstroy* system for composing village and rural district
plans that would further this aim and ordered the appointment of two new officials
to the staff of the rural district soviets: the district architect and the district
engineering-inspector of the state architecture and building inspectorate (both
Gosstroy officials). An innovation of the 1968 Fundamentals of Land Legislation
was the designation of the land of rural settlements as a separate category from
agricultural land. The implication was that rural settlement land was now subject
to a new planning regime, analogous to urban planning. The responsibilities of
both the village soviets and especially of the district architects in village planning
were thus enhanced. However, in view of the fact that it is often difficult to
draw a distinction within agricultural villages between the interests of the village
as such and the interests of the collective and state farms of which they form a
part, representatives of the Ministry of Agriculture and of its local organs, as
well as the farms themselves, play an important role in planning decisions.

   A development of the late 1960s and the 1970s has been the beginnings of a
policy to plan the settlement system on a national scale. In 1971 a long-term
plan to guide the location of industrial development, known as the General
Scheme for the Distribution of Production, was officially approved with an
operational life to 1980. A second General Scheme was then developed, operative
from 1976 to 1990, and each branch of the economy was ordered to compose
its own long-term locational-development plan. Based on the second General
Scheme, organizations within the *Gosstroy* system were then commissioned to
work out a General Scheme for the Distribution of Settlement, with a similar
life span from 1976 to 1990. The General Scheme for Settlement is designed to
forecast general developments in the distribution of population and systems of
settlement over this 15-year period, although its legal and operational significance
is not clear. The scheme defines a significant number of so-called grouped systems
of populated places, which are systems of cities, towns, and rural settlements
recognized as being functionally interconnected. The aim is to increase this
interconnectedness and interdependence and thereby reduce the still-marked distinctions between town and country. The resulting settlement system is sometimes
referred to as the Unified Settlement System. As the basis for this General Scheme
for Settlement, a series of more detailed settlement plans has been worked out
for the union republics and major economic regions.

   Many of the problems of urban planning noted earlier also characterize regional
physical planning.[19] As with urban plans, regional plans frequently have been
notable for their rigidity and their tendency to be overridden by new economic
developments. Also this area of planning has enjoyed a lower degree of priority
than has urban planning, and many regional developments have occurred in the
absence of operational plans. A standard complaint of the Soviet press, for
example, has been the fact that the new energy-based industrial complexes of

Siberia (the so-called territorial production complexes) have been permitted to develop without effective regional plans. The result has been a serious lack of coordination between the ministries and other agencies responsible for such development. In rural areas, planning frequently has lagged behind demand, and rural development programs have suffered accordingly. Nevertheless, in recent years it has become increasingly clear that many problems in the Soviet economy cannot be solved without a more effective system of regional planning. Efforts have therefore recently concentrated on the tasks of coordinating physical planning more effectively with economic planning and of strengthening the powers of the regional planning agencies.[20]

Planning and Management of Nonsettlement Land

Land use planning in the USSR is by no means the monopoly of *Gosstroy*'s physical planning system. Indeed the *Gosstroy* system developed out of the attempt to meet the needs of cities, and its regional and rural roles are a comparatively late development. In nonurban territories, numerous other state agencies play primary roles in planning and managing land use and making land allocation decisions. In the case of all these territories, the law allocates general supervisory functions to the local soviets, although it is not always clear how important this function is in practice.

Agricultural Land

About half of the USSR's land fund is designated as agricultural land. According to Article 21 of the Fundamentals of Land Legislation, agricultural land is land allotted to or intended for agricultural purposes. Much of it consists of land that is ancillary to agricultural enterprises rather than land directly used for agriculture as such; however, Soviet legislation is firm on the principle of the primary importance of agriculture on this land. Agricultural land, states Article 21 of the Fundamentals, "is used in accordance with agricultural development plans for the satisfaction of the growing needs of the national economy for agricultural production." The chief users of this land are the collective and state farms whose tenure is governed by the various legislative acts dating back to the 1930s. In addition, agricultural land can be used by research, educational, and other agricultural organizations for scientific or instructional purposes, by nonagricultural organizations for subsidiary farming, and by individual citizens for personal farming or gardening providing that no hired labor is used. In certain circumstances, land plots can be granted to enterprises or other organizations for collective fruit and vegetable gardening by their employees.

Legislation specifies both the rights and obligations of the users of agricultural land. Article 23 of the Fundamentals, for example, specifies various land conservation and land improvement measures that agricultural land users are obliged to undertake. The use of land within the farms is controlled by legal documents such as collective farm statutes and land management projects in the case of state farms. Legislation allows for some farmland to be used by state and collective farmers as personal plots, and land also can be granted for the same purpose to other village residents. Indeed recent legislation has been particularly encouraging for the private sector of agriculture, a marked departure from earlier policy (Hazard, 1982, 104–5).

Because of the USSR's agricultural problems and in view of the serious losses of agricultural land to urbanization and other uses, its laws accord special protection to such land. Article 16 of the Fundamentals states that the taking of land from agricultural enterprises may occur only in circumstances of particular need, and Article 10 stipulates that the construction of industrial plants, housing, and other facilities should occur primarily on nonagricultural land or on agricultural land of the lowest quality. Article 16 also states that the most valuable land, such as irrigated and drained land and orchards and vineyards, can be used only for nonagricultural purposes in exceptional circumstances and only by resolution of a union republic Council of Ministers. Republican legislation repeats these instructions.[21]

Forest Land

Article 43 of the Fundamentals of Land Legislation deals with the state forests. The forest fund is extensive, covering over one-third of the land area. It is defined as land either covered by forest or designed for forestry needs, and its conservation and use are governed by both all-union legislation (enshrined in the 1977 Forest Code) and also in the legislation of the union republics. All-union legislation divides forestland into three groups. The first group includes forests in greenbelts around cities, forests in preserves, and protective forests such as those alongside railways and rivers. This land is accorded special protection; in the RSFSR, for example, the withdrawal of plots from such forestry use requires the approval of the RSFSR Council of Ministers.[22] In such forests industrial felling is forbidden; only felling in connection with forestry maintenance is permitted. Second-group forests are those forests located in areas such as the southeastern and central portions of the European USSR where forest resources are limited. In these areas, industrial felling is allowed on a limited scale. Forests of the third group are situated in areas rich in timber such as Siberia and the Far East, where the timber processing industry is mainly to be found.

Forestland is under the protection of the USSR State Forestry Committee and also of forestry ministries or organizations at the republican level. Locally forestry enterprises carry out tasks associated with the care and maintenance of forests and lease tracts of forest to timber procurement agencies, game farms, and other enterprises or organizations. Forestry enterprises are responsible for seeing that conservation laws are carried out on all the land under their jurisdiction. It is interesting to note that the importance of agriculture is stressed in the law even with respect to forestland. According to Article 43 of the Fundamentals of Land Legislation, for example, forestry enterprises and other bodies are to grant agricultural land from the state forests in their use to agricultural bodies and also to citizens for temporary agricultural use, providing that such use is not at variance with forestry interests. The law is designed to preserve the forest area as a whole. However, Article 10 of the Fundamentals states that construction affecting the state forests should take place primarily on forestland that is not actually tree covered or on land where the timber is of little value.

Water Resources Land

State water resources-land is a new category of land recognized in the Fundamentals. Its designation is a response to the increasing problems of water conservation and to the growing need for water management. This land includes inland water bodies (rivers, lakes, reservoirs, canals, landlocked seas, territorial waters), glaciers, and hydroengineering and other water conservation installations. It also embraces land strips along the shores of reservoirs and canals, protective zones, and land generally needed for water management. The land in this category is subject to a special regime of law, as codified in the Water Code (1970).

Although the designation of this land as a special category is clearly an attempt to come to grips with the problems of water conservation, however, the Soviets have yet to evolve the institutional structure and the policies to cope with the many complexities of conservation in this area. The Ministry of Land Reclamation and Water Resources, for example, now commands a network of river basin inspectorates with various powers of inspection and sanction, but their powers and resources are limited in practice, and in any case the Ministry's major responsibilities are in irrigation, drainage, and other matters (Gustafson, 1981, 112–15). There is also a network of public health inspectors under the Ministry of Public Health, but it is doubtful whether their remit is clearly defined in many cases. Other ministries, such as those for fisheries, agriculture, and river navigation, as well as the many industrial and other enterprises coming under yet other branch ministries, also operate on this land. The conservation and associated responsibilities of each user are not fully defined or, if defined, are too frequently unenforced. Gustafson has analyzed the lack of cooperation between the irrigation and drainage boards, operating under the Ministry of Land Reclamation, and the collective and state farms under the Ministry of Agriculture as just one example of the many problems of water management (Gustafson, 1981, 123–33).

Reserve Land

Land that has not been allocated on a permanent or long-term basis to a particular user and does not fall under any other category of land is designated by the Fundamentals as state reserve land. Most of this land is in remote areas of the far north, Siberia, the far east, and Kazakhstan. From time to time this land is allocated to particular users on a long-term basis and then ceases to be reserve land. The Ministry of Agriculture assumes responsibility for compiling inventories of this land and for conservation measures.

In an era of continuing industrial development, it is frequently necessary to allocate land from the state forests, the state reserve, and even from agricultural land for other purposes. For this reason the Fundamentals specify a particular category of land, situated outside the land of towns or rural settlements, which is devoted to these other purposes. In previous legislation this was known as land of special designation, but the Fundamentals term it the "land of industry, transport, health resorts, preserves and other non-agricultural land" (Article 38). Particular legislation of the USSR and union republics specifies the legal regimes pertaining to each of these categories of land, stipulating that the land so allocated does not exceed the necessary minimum, that other land users are protected, and that land temporarily unused must be allocated wherever possible to agricultural agencies. The responsibility for supervising the correct use of land in this category falls to the particular branch ministries involved (the trades unions in the case of health resort land) and also to the local soviets.

Where land has to be transferred between categories or between users within a single land category, the local or republican soviets (at various levels in the hierarchy depending on the size and type of land in question) are responsible for approving transfers and issuing the necessary documents. Enterprises and other organizations seeking land plots must file an application to the local soviet concerned, together with the necessary plans. However, whereas in the case of settlement land, it is the chief city architect or the district architect (appointed by the *Gosstroy* system) who has to approve such transfers, in that of all other land the responsible official is the chief land management engineer. The latter is an appointee of the Ministry of Agriculture, and this underlines both the responsibility of this ministry for land as a whole and also the way in which the competence of the physical planning system under *Gosstroy* is largely restricted to settlement land. The chief land management engineer is concerned with all rural land, but in the case of certain types of land, other interested parties are also consulted—most notably, the forestry organizations in the case of forestland. Legislation provides for compensation for losses sustained where land is withdrawn from a particular user (although no payment is made for the land itself, being state property). The Fundamentals of Land Legislation also provide for compensation to be paid to collective and state farms for losses of agricultural production arising from land withdrawals. It is unclear how such compensation arrangements work in practice.

MAJOR CHALLENGES

Although the USSR clearly has a comprehensive body of land law, the enforcement of that law faces many of the same difficulties as law enforcement in other areas of Soviet life. Despite the complex procedures and safeguards involved in transferring plots of land and the penalties for illegal land occupation, there is evidence of flexibility in the way the law is applied. Considerable alarm, for example, is expressed at the continuing losses of even the most valuable land to industry and urbanization processes, and the decline in the arable area per head of the population (from 1.06 to 0.86 hectare in the last 20 years) cannot be put down to population growth alone.[23] An important factor here is the power of the industrial ministries and associated organizations compared with those bodies most intimately concerned with planning land use—the Ministry of Agriculture and the local soviets. In Siberia and elsewhere, the ministries are frequently accused of adopting a branch approach to regional and urban development, implying that they fail to take into account both the need for coordination with other branch ministries and the elementary requirements of good spatial planning and conservation. No doubt the ministries are encouraged in this attitude by the inadequacy of physical planning in many parts of the country, especially outside urban areas. Random industrial development in the suburban zones of large cities, for example, has been attributed to the lack of land inventories and the consequent ignorance of the authorities as to the best sites for industrial and other uses.[24] Gustafson (1981, 101–10) has charted the long history of land losses induced by the influential Ministry of Power and the hydroelectric interests. Currently a more conservationist attitude prevails, but the Soviet authorities have yet to evolve the machinery to ensure that land is not treated as a limitless resource or one that can be used or built on at will.

A further problem for Soviet land use planning, and one that is common to the industrial world at large, arises from the complex demands that a modern society makes on land. Legal, administrative, and planning arrangements that arose to tackle the fairly uncomplicated requirements of society just undergoing industrialization do not necessarily work well once cities and industry dominate. Simple systems whereby cities are planned by city soviets, agricultural land is managed by agricultural authorities, and forest-land by forestry bodies run up against all kinds of problems. Recreational pressures on forests, for example, have been a source of concern for some time in certain areas. After a long period of suspicion of such developments, the forestry authorities are beginning to see recreation as a phenomenon that has to be coped with and managed.[25] Whether they are the best authorities for dealing with such problems is another matter. Similar things are beginning to happen in the case of water recreation. By many rivers, lakes, and reservoirs recreational developments have occurred in almost random manner, and there are many sorry tales of the difficulties that the authorities have had in coping (Shaw, 1980, 207). Lines of responsibility, of course, are often intertwined. The Fundamentals of Land Legislation made a special effort to deal with certain of these issues by recognizing a category of health resort land, which is accorded particular protection within which sanatoria, tourist camps, and other recreational facilities can be situated. Such land can cater to only a small part of the recreational pressure, but at least it is an attempt to tackle some of the problems. Even so the administrative arrangements are not always straightforward, and there is evidence of the usual bureaucratic tangles among the trades unions, local soviets, and other organizations.[26]

On the periphery of large cities, complex problems arise in the attempt to interweave the demands of the urban area with the surrounding rural milieu. Despite the special planning regime designated for such areas, involving the recognition of forest parks and the marking out of other areas for specific urban needs, there still appears to be plenty of scope for unplanned development. Even in Leningrad's case, for example, the greenbelt has been relatively neglected in spite of the fact that the plans have existed on paper for many years.[27]

A final example of the way land use planning fails to come to terms with modern needs is in the case of preserves, reserves, and national parks. Since the early Soviet period, nature reserves and preserves have been recognized as areas having scientific or geological interest and requiring special protection. The Fundamentals of Land Legislation make provision for them; however, there are many complaints in the press that preserves are not being sufficiently well protected and are subject to abuse. For years the status and purpose of natural, or national, parks has been debated, but many issues of policy pertaining to them remain unsettled.[28]

FUTURE THRUSTS

Over the years the USSR has evolved a sophisticated body of land legislation and a complex system of land use planning. The central features of the Soviet system are the state ownership of all land and the central planning of its use. Central planning does not, however, entail the easy solution of all land use problems. The state must devolve its planning tasks to numerous agencies and enterprises, and controlling their activities is not easy. Attaining the necessary degree of coordination among the different parts of the planning system remains a task for the future, and many legal, administrative, and planning problems are apparent. Moreover, the system is in need of constant evolution as modern society makes new and more complex demands on its land resources.

Continuing experimentation and development in land use planning are to be expected in the future. For example, the continual loss of valuable agricultural land to industrial and other purposes can be expected to be a source of concern. Stricter legislation to protect agricultural land is likely, especially if agricultural problems endure, as seems probable. Stricter attention to the processes of land allocation should be eased by the completion of a land cadastre. There may also be greater interest in the further use of economic levers, such as compensation payments for land occupation. On the other hand, without the direct and decisive intervention of the highest party authorities, the competition for land between industry and agriculture is unlikely to benefit the agricultural interests. Indeed, in the entire field of conservation, it is difficult to escape the conclusion that economic growth and industrial development invariably are first priorities. The only exceptions appear to occur when other vital areas such as public health are threatened. With certain exceptions, land conservation will hardly provide decisive solutions to the problems of agriculture, and therefore it cannot be expected to be a major priority. However, the more spectacular losses of land to hydro-electric power schemes, water engineering projects and major industrial developments, which regularly occurred in the past, probably will be tempered by the new conservationist attitude.

It is in the field of agriculture that some of the most interesting experiments have occurred in recent years with a direct bearing on land use. During the latter part of the Brezhnev era, renewed encouragement was given to the small, private sector of agriculture, and even city dwellers, rural professionals, and other nonfarmers were urged to take up small-scale gardening. This tendency was strengthened during the brief Andropov period with the cautious moves toward autonomous work teams on certain farms (implying a move away from the traditional system of centralized planning). The present leadership, however, is expected to adopt a more conservative attitude toward reform generally.

On the whole, cautious experimentation rather than radical reform of the current system of land use planning seems the most likely situation in the near future. This means a continuing reliance on administrative methods of control, with continuing attempts to streamline and coordinate planning systems. The move toward more comprehensive planning methods in cities and other regions undoubtedly will continue, but their success probably will be limited, as in the past, by bureaucratic difficulties. At the same time, interest in the use of economic levers—for example, implementing charges for the use of various types of resources such as land and laying greater emphasis on enterprise and other types of profitability—undoubtedly will be encouraged by the need for economic efficiency. Political and ideological factors, however, have always induced a cautious attitude toward such policies in the USSR since they inevitably have radical implications that would be unwelcome to many influential elements. In this situation, state control over and central planning of land use will remain pivotal features of Soviet policy on land. But the emergence of a truly coordinated land use policy seems as elusive as ever.

NOTES

1. *Sobraniye uzakoneniy i rasporyazheniy rabochego i krest'yanskogo pravitel'stva*, Moscow, 1917, no. 1, st. 3.

2. *Normativnyye akty o zemle*, (Moscow: 'Yuridicheskaya literatura', 1978), 3.

3. Ibid., 25.

4. *Sobraniye uzakoneniy*, 1918, no. 25, st. 346.

5. Ibid., 1918, no. 62, st. 674.

6. Ibid., 1919, no. 4, st. 43.

7. *Vedomosti Verkhovnogo Soveta SSSR*, 1968, no. 51, st. 485.

8. *Normativnyye akty*, 27–42. Fundamentals, Articles 5, 6, 10, 16, 17, 20; *Zemel'nyy kodeks RSFSR* (Moscow: Yuridicheskaya literatura, 1974), articles 6, 7, 8, 12, 13, 18, 33, 34, 36, 40, 41; Polozheniye o gosudarstvennom Kontrole za is-pol'zovaniyem zemel', *Sobraniye postanovleniy SSSR*, 1970, no. 9, st. 21, article 1.

9. Ibid., articles 1-9.

10. Eg. Yu. P. Kuzyakin, Poryadok ustanovleniya gorodskikh granits i rol' gorodskish sovetov v ikh opredelenii, *Vestnik MGU. Seriya Pravo*, no. 1 (1977):50-56.

11. Ye. N. Pertsik, *Rayonnaya planirovka* (Moscow: Mysl', 1973), 11.

12. *Normativnyye akty*, 45, 46, 47, 310, 315, 317, 346, 354, 357, 359.

13. Instruktsiya po sodtavleniyu proektov planirovki i zastroyki gorodov, SN 345-66, *Normativnyye akty*, 329-336, articles 1.1, 2.1, 2.2.

14. *Spravochnik proyektirovshchika: gradostroitel'stvo* (Moscow: Stroyizdat, 1978), 322-25.

15. Postanovleniye Soveta Ministrov ot 3 Fevralya 1948g. *Normativnyee akty*, 323-29.

16. Syrodoyev, N. *Soviet Land Legislation*. Moscow: Progress, 1975:82; V. B. Yerofeyev, *Osnovy zemel'nogo prava* (Moscow: 'Yuridicheskaya literatura,' 1971), 124–25; V. B. Yerofeyev, *Pravovoy rezhim zemel' gorodov* (Moscow: 'Yuridicheskaya literatura,' 1976) 55. An urban land inventory appears to be part of the function of the RSFSR Ministry of Communal Economy, and this program may be part of this work.

17. Instruktsiya po sostavleniyu skhem i proyektov rayonnoy planirovki, Article 1.2. *Normativnyye akty*, 95.

18. *Sobraniye postanovleniy i rasporyazheniy pravitel'stva SSSR*, 1968, no. 18, st. 121.

19. Shaw, D. J. B. 1983. The Soviet Urban General Plan and recent advances in Soviet urban planning. *Urban Studies* 20:393-403; I. V. Mezentsev, 'Problemy kachestva proyektnykh resheniy,' *Stroitel'stvo i arkhitektura*, no. 4 (1977):3-4; A. P. Cherebyachko and I. A. Fomin, 'Pervoocherednyye zadachi sovershenstovovaniya praktiki rayonnoy planirovki,' *Stroitel'stvo i arkhitektura*, no. 2 (1980):5-6; Pallot, J. and D. J. A. Shaw, 1981. *Planning in the Soviet Union*. London: Croom Helm, Chapter 10.

20. Shaw, 1983: 396, 399–400; V. I. Nudel'man, B. V. Palyshin, and G. I. Fil'varov, ''Regional'naya skhema rasseleniya na territorii USSR,'' *Stroitel'stvo i arkhitektura*, no. 2 (1980):8-10.

21. See, for example, *Zemel'nyy kodeks RSFSR*, Articles 13, 35, 43. But see Syrodoyev, 1975: 51.

22. *Zemel'nyy kodeks RSFSR*, article 13. See also Syrodoyev, 1975: 51.

23. *Current Digest of the Soviet Press*, Vol. xxxiv, No. 23,3.

24. V. I. Marchukov and L. A. Golub, ''Razmeshcheniye proizbodstvennykh kompleksov v prigorodnoy zone krupneyshego goroda,' *Promyshlennoye stroitel'stvo*, no. 1 (1975):19-21; Denis J. B. Shaw, ''Problems of Land Use Planning in the USSR,'' *Soviet Geography* 22 (May 1981):293-305.

25. *Rekreatsionnoye lesopol'zovaniye v SSSR*, (Moscow: 'Nauka,' 1983).

26. Ibid., 207, 209; Denis J. B. Shaw, ''Recreation and the Soviet City,'' in R. A. French and F. E. I. Hamilton, eds., *The Socialist City: Spatial Structure and Urban Policy* (New York: Wiley, 1979), 140.

27. Shaw, 1981: ''Problems''; Yu. B. Khromov, ''Dlya tekh, kto otdykhayet,'' *Stroitel'stvo i arkhitektura Leningrada*, no. 10 (1979):28-31.

28. *Arkhitekturno-planirovochnaya organizatsiya natsional'nykh parkov* (Moscow, 1976); N. F. Reymers and F. P. Shtil'mark, *Osobo okhramyayemyye priordnyye territorii* (Moscow: 'Nauka,' 1978).

BIBLIOGRAPHY

Bater, James H. 1977. Soviet Town Planning: Theory and Practice in the 1970s. *Progress in Human Geography* 1, 2:177-207.

Bater, James H. 1980. *The Soviet City*. London: Edward Arnold.

Gustafson, Thane. 1981. *Reform in Soviet Politics: Lessons of Recent Policies on Land and Water*. Cambridge: University Press.

Hazard, John N. 1961. *The Soviet System of Government*. 3d ed. Chicago: University of Chicago Press.

Hazard, John N. 1982. Legal Trends. In Archie Brown and Michael Kaser, eds. *Soviet Policy for the 1980s*, 104-5. London: Macmillan.

Hazard, John N., William E. Butler, and Peter B. Maggs. 1977. *The Soviet Legal System*. 3d ed. Dobbs Ferry, N.Y.: Oceana Publications.

Kovalev, S. A. 1972. The transformation of rural settlement. *Geoforum* 9:33-45.

Pallot, Judith. 1977. Rural Settlement Planning in the USSR. *Soviet Studies* 31, 2:214-30.

Pallot, Judith, and Denis J. B. Shaw. 1981. *Planning in the Soviet Union*. London: Croom Helm.

Sawicki, Stanislaw J. 1977. *Soviet Land and Housing Law*. New York: Praeger.

Shaw, Denis, J. B. 1980. Achievements and problems in Soviet recreational planning. In J. Brine, M. Perrie, and S. Sutton, eds. *Home, School and Leisure in the Soviet Union*, 207. London: Allen and Unwin.

Shaw, Denis J. B. 1983. The Soviet urban general plan and recent advances in Soviet urban planning. *Urban Studies* 20:393-403.

Syrodoyev, N. 1975. *Soviet Land Legislation*. Moscow: Progress Publishers.

PART V

NORTH AMERICA

18

Canada

WILLIAM T. PERKS

Canada's land mass of 9.2 million square kilometers (9.9 including freshwater) is as variable in its attributes of soil, climate, and ecology as it is enormous in geographic dimensions. The country's resource endowments are as richly varied as they are enormously abundant for its 24.3 million population. Such is the inspiring, if not enviable, image of Canada to be drawn from casual acquaintance with resource maps and economic indicators. A close examination of Canada's land resource and use can produce some problematic images, however. These revolve around adaptive and socially appropriate relationships: between land yield and use, and the prospects of a sustainable prosperity with affordable infrastructure; between competing urban and agricultural claims on land; between property rights, conservation, and a reemerging social concept of land stewardship.

Canada's preoccupations with land use began with a national Commission of Conservation in 1909 and the four provincial planning acts of 1912. Over the 1970s, institutional developments were phenomenal; they include a national land inventory, monitoring and remote sensing system; the national Lands Directorate; the widespread adoption of environmental assessment practices; a federal ministry of urban affairs (now abolished) and native people land claims negotiations. Between 1960 and 1980, countless federal and provincial enactments and novel administrative structures were introduced to deal with land planning. Countless policy measures and inquiries touched on such issues as urbanization, regional development, agricultural, forestry, acid rain, petroleum and minerals, recreation, and freshwater use and diversion.

Today the significant truths about Canada's land mass–variety–abundance image are that there are several relative scarcities and highly localized competitions for land allocation. Not all of the lands suitable for the highest economic or social purposes are in great abundance. Canada's prime agricultural soils are scarce, and much farmland is not free from want of irrigation or a lengthy growing season. Because of land suitability and climatological factors, 94 percent of Canadians live within a 300 kilometer belt along the country's southern border (Figure 18.1). In the past few years, a flagging economy and high indebtedness of governments in Canada have tended to inspire reaction to regulation in general. In some instances, there have been budget cuts or the withdrawal of mandates and personnel in departments dealing with land use and management.

HISTORIC DEVELOPMENT

Early Land Settlement

Before the arrival of Europeans, the native peoples occupied the lands of Canada without a concept of property and ownership. Land yielded their sole means of survival through hunting and gathering. Today the surviving native communities aspire to preserve their traditional culture, albeit mediated by the modernizing industrial society. Most of Canada's Indians are now located on reserves, tracts of land dedicated by the government for their exclusive occupation and use (Table 18.1).

Land use patterns under European regimes assumed two principal forms: the narrow long lot, a river-fronted seigneurial property division during the French regime; and the one-mile-apart concession road system of the British (from 1770 on). In eastern Canada, the latter system produced farm units between 40 and 100 acres (16 and 40 hectares). When the great plains were opened for settlement beginning in the 1870s, land was subdivided on the section system (one mile by one mile), and farmlands were allotted in quarter units. Few soundly productive farms in the prairies today measure less than a section (640 acres/259 hectares), while for cattle farming, upwards of tens of sections assembled into a single ownership are not uncommon.

The initial phase of planned land use in Canada proceeded directly from national policies for settlement and strategic interests; that is, interests first of expansionary French and British empire economies and later (post–1870), the will of a newly created, sovereign Canada to secure from threatened U.S. intrusions its southern boundary west of the Great Lakes all the way to the Pacific Ocean. Private land companies were formed and given land grants. Large tracts were allotted to the established religious institutions. In the preconfederation period, for example, Ontario was extensively settled in this manner. In 1881, in return for building a railway from central Canada to Vancouver, the Canadian Pacific Railway (CPR) was granted 10 million hectares flanking its rail line. These were in the form of alternate sections 24 miles (38.6 kilometers) deep. The CPR became the single most influential agent in determining settlement locations and the physical form of towns in western Canada. And because of its rights-of-way, yards, and downtown and suburban property holdings, the CPR has continuously been a strategic actor in shaping the layout and general character of major cities.

Figure 18.1 Population Distribution and Urban Locations

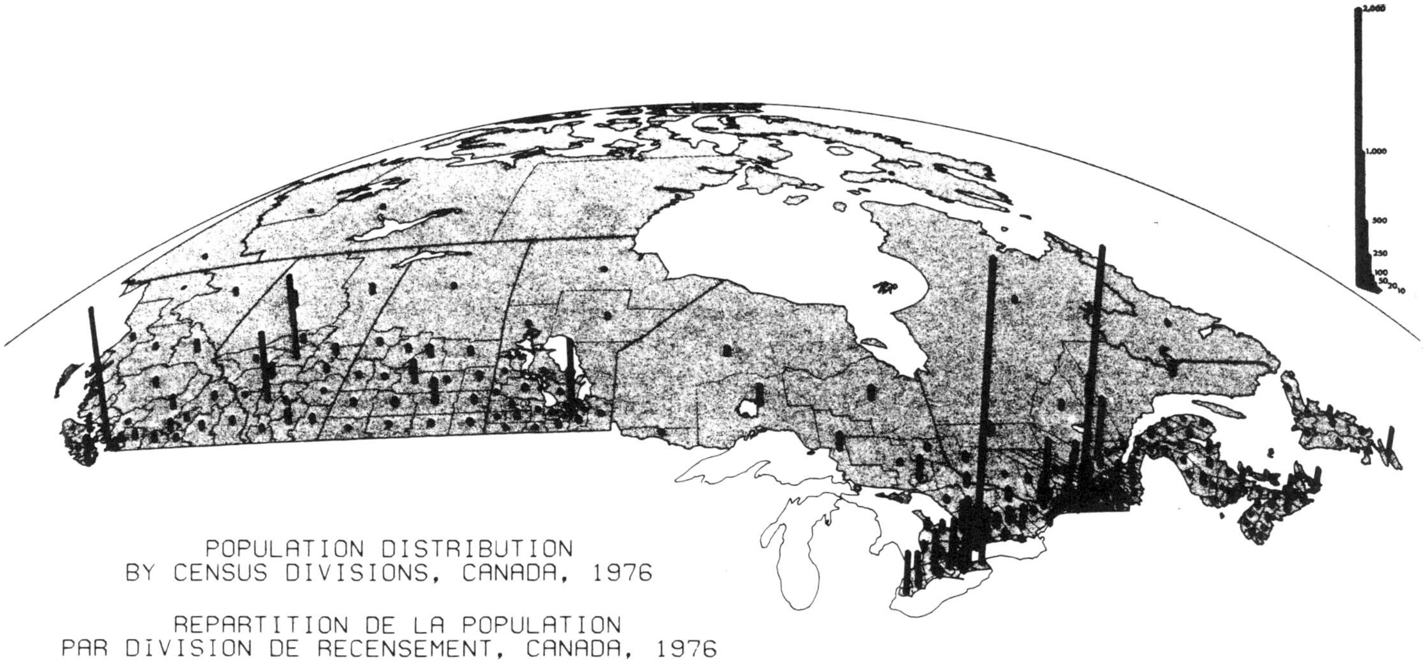
2,000
1,000
500
250
100
50
20
10
POPULATION DISTRIBUTION
BY CENSUS DIVISIONS, CANADA, 1976
REPARTITION DE LA POPULATION
PAR DIVISION DE RECENSEMENT, CANADA, 1976

1976 census of Canada

Table 18.1

Indian Lands and Population, Canada

Province or Territory	Reserves		Indian(1)
	No.	km^2	Population
Prince Edward Island	4	8	
Nova Scotia	39	114	11,093 [2]
New Brunswick	23	168	
Quebec	34	779	30,175
Ontario	163	6,703	66,057
Manitoba	96	2,145	43,349
Saskatchewan	134	6,322	44,986
Alberta	91	6,566	35,162
British Columbia	1,625	3,390	54,318
Yukon	6	5	3,217
Northwest Territories	1	135	7,541
TOTALS:	2,216	26,335	295,898

(1) Includes Indian populations living off
Reserves; 1976 Partial Census of Canada

(2) Includes Atlantic Provinces and
Newfoundland

Source: Corpus Almanac of Canada. (1979); Canada
Year Book 1980-81.

Urban Settlement

Settlement patterns in Canada have been largely determined by physiography and climate (Figures 18.2 through 18.4). Major cities arose where first agricultural settlements and then transportation and trading centers were established. Beginning in the mid-nineteenth century and again at an accelerated pace in the mid-twentieth century, urbanization grew upon and around the earliest centers. Exceptions to this evolutionary pattern were the implanted resource towns having their origins in a series of decisions to extract and process minerals and wood products in the remote regions.[1]

Towns and cities account for less than 1 percent of the land area of Canada. They are clustered as illustrated in Figure 18.5. The size distribution of Canadian cities results from settlement, transportation, and economic development policies that date to the beginning of confederation.[2] The present land use regime within Canadian cities is the product of two eras of development: one prior to 1945, characterized essentially by free market forces little inhibited by planning control; the second, from 1950 forward, characterized by institutionalized planning and land use regulation. In the second era, although national housing policies were well diversified in the range of options of private ownership, rental, and social housing, the stronger of incentives was home ownership. Consequently, low-density, single-family housing land uses dominate the post-1950 urban landscape. Some 55 percent of the land in cities is now in residential use. Roads and parking account for 15 percent and 7 percent, respectively. Lands for recreation, open space, and public institutions amount to 8 percent.

Outline of Present Land Uses and Capabilities

The following commentaries provide the broad national outlines of land allocations. (See also Table 18.2 and Figure 18.6.)[3] Urbanized lands account for under half a percent of the country's land. "Less than 7 percent of our land is used for agriculture, about 2 percent by commercial forest industries and only 0.17 percent for actual mining and energy production" (Welch, 1980, 26).

Agriculture

—Lands having "any agricultural capability whatsoever" amount to 122 million hectares (McCaig and Manning, 1982, 5). By including marginal lands, the total of potential agricultural land amounts to 136 million hectares, or 14 percent of the country.

—Only 46 million hectares, or 5 percent of Canada's land, are suitable for field crops; 71 percent of these are located in the prairies.

—4.4 million hectares, or only 0.5 percent of Canada's land, are uniquely suited for crops like fruits and vegetables.

Figure 18.2 Principal Physiographic Regions of Canada

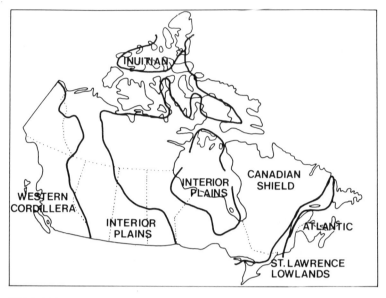

Welch (1980, 6)

Figure 18.3 Climate Regions of Canada

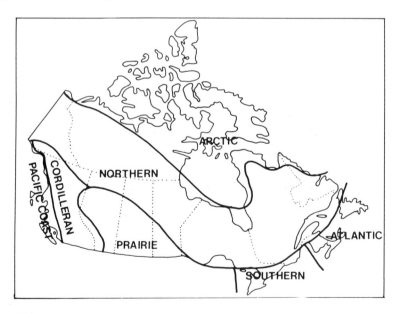

Welch (1980, 10)

452

Figure 18.4 Zones of Soil Limitations for Agriculture in Canada

PREDOMINANTLY FROZEN GROUND

UNFROZEN, BUT WITH BEDROCK AT OR NEAR THE SURFACE

PRINCIPAL ZONES WITH SOIL POTENTIAL FOR AGRICULTURE

Welch (1980, 12)

Figure 18.5 Isodemographic Map of Canada

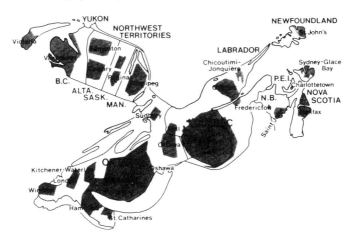

Welch (1980, 25)

453

Table 18.2
Land Use Data, Canada

	Subtotal: km²	%	Total: km²	%
Canada: total including land and freshwater, not territorial waters			9,976,140	100
land	9,220,974	92.43		
freshwater	755,165	7.57		
Land with Agricultural Capability, Classes 1 to 4			713,650	7.15
LAND USES				
Agriculture: total including woodlots			671,682	6.73
improved	437,074	4.38		
unimproved	234,608	2.35		
Forestry: private forest land tenure			199,000	1.99
average annual logged area	5,500	0.06		
Parkland, reserves & wildlife protection areas: total			964,668	9.67
national parks	129,941	1.30		
provincial parks	202,618	2.03		
park reserves	64,243	0.64		
other wildlife protection areas	567,866	5.69		
Mineral & Energy Development & Production: total			1,069,000	10.72
area disturbed by mining	1,285	0.01		
hydro-electric head-ponds (reservoirs)	16,200	0.16		
pipelines & electrical transmission	4,800	0.05		
claims, grants, leases, exploration permits	1,046,715	10.49		
Indian Reserves			29,272	0.29
Urban Areas, including built-up, roads, parks, etc.: total			34,000	0.34
built-up	15,691	0.16		
Transport, including roads within urban areas, and railways and airports			37,525	0.38

Source: Welch, 1980, p. 26.

454

Figure 18.6 Land Use by Region

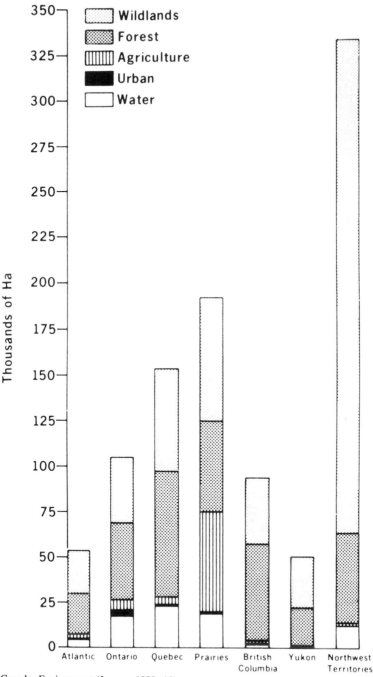

Canada. Environment (January 1980, 19)

Parklands and Wildlife

—Parklands and wildlife protection areas account for nearly 10 percent of the land mass—some 56 million hectares.

—Roughly five times the amount of land allocated to Indian reserves has been set aside for national parks.

—The number of parks held by various governments number 1,880 (1976 figure) and amount to 33 million hectares.

—National parks account for 13 million hectares; half are located in the Yukon and Northwest Territories.

Forestry

—Forests account for 37 percent (3.4 million square kilometers) of the land; only 2 million square kilometers are considered productive.

—Three-quarters of forestlands are provincially owned; 16 percent federal; and 7 percent private.

—Some 50 to 60 million hectares are harvested annually.

Minerals, Energy, and Transportation

—Lands actually in use or assigned for minerals and energy developments amount to about 10 percent (1.07 million square kilometers of which hydroelectric reservoirs take 0.2 percent (16,200 square kilometers).

—Petroleum and gas pipeline easements and electrical transmission rights-of-way account for nearly 5,000 square kilometers.

—Railways occupy 5,000 square kilometers, airports 6,000 square kilometers, and streets and highways another 26,000 square kilometers.

—All transportation land uses amount to 0.38 percent of Canadian lands, about twice the amount occupied by "houses, factories, offices and other buildings combined" (Welch, 1980, 27).

Urban Settlement

—Fifty-five percent of the population has been concentrated along the 1,200 kilometer Quebec-Windsor axis.

—Three cities (Vancouver, Toronto, and Montreal) accommodate a third of the population.

—The single greatest pressure on land scarcity has been urbanization; for example, the 72 cities of population over 25,000 converted 87,712 hectares of farmland to urban uses in five years alone (1966–71).

—Land consumption has occurred at a rate of 44 hectares per 1,000 population added to cities and towns.

INSTITUTIONAL FRAMEWORK AND EVOLUTION OF AND APPROACHES TO PLANNING

Key Historical Influences

Canada is a federal state composed of ten provinces, two territories, and a federal government. Table 18.3 shows the distribution of land and population by jurisdiction. In respect to private property, the fundamental jurisdiction having the power to determine land uses is the province. This derives from section 92 of the British North America Act of 1867, now incorporated in the Constitution Act, 1981.[4] Section 92 enumerates the matters in which the legislature of each province "may exclusively make laws." The more relevant matters are municipal institutions, local works and undertakings, property and civil rights, and, under the 1981 amendments, exploration, development, conservation, and management of nonrenewable and forestry resources. The municipalities are creatures of the province; they may undertake land use planning only as provided by provincial legislation.[5]

It was the federal government that first promoted the conservation of resources and introduced planning to Canadian society. This occurred through the Commission of Conservation, established in 1909 by act of Parliament. The commission brought to Canada as expert adviser Thomas Adams, a town planner.[6] Adams and commission colleagues spent nine years doing surveys of rural and urban life and environments, proselytizing, writing reports, drawing up urban plans, drafting model planning legislation, and eventually forming a Canadian planners' association.[7] Several provinces were moved to adopt planning legislation, and a number of municipalities began the preparation of master plans. These beginnings waned as the depression and then the war years (1939–45) arrived, to be revived only in the 1950s.

The federal government has been an instrumental factor in shaping land use patterns and in developing Canada's planning institutions as well. Such occurred mainly by the exercise of regulatory powers and constitutional functions. A primary example is that of transportation. Three other influences are defense, the regulation of lending institutions under the Bank Act, and the federal spending power itself. Spending refers not only to investments in right of the federal government's lands and infrastructure and buildings but to grants-in-aid and shared-cost programs with the provinces.[8]

The most significant of federal institutions has been the Canada Mortgage and Housing Corporation (CMHC).[9] The CMHC was established as a result of recommendations of the Post-War Reconstruction Committee's *Report on Housing and Community Planning* (1944), which offered a comprehensive review of housing needs and planning. It recommended programs in land assembly and slum clearance and university programs for community planning.[10] Thus, provisions were made in the National Housing Act (NHA) to fund research and to assist in the training of professionals and education of the public on the "problems

Table 18.3
Land and Population, Canada and the Provinces

Province or Territory	Land km^2	Freshwater km^2	Total km^2	Population
Newfoundland	370,485	34,032	404,517	557,725
Prince Edward Island	5,657	-	5,657	118,229
Nova Scotia	52,841	2,650	55,491	828,571
New Brunswick	72,092	1,344	73,436	677,249
Quebec	1,356,971	183,889	1,540,680	5,234,445
Ontario	891,194	177,388	1,068,582	8,264,465
Manitoba	548,495	101,592	650,087	1,021,506
Saskatchewan	570,269	81,631	651,900	921,323
Alberta	644,389	16,796	661,185	1,838,037
British Columbia	930,528	18,068	984,596	2,466,608
Yukon Territory	478,034	4,481	482,515	21,836
Northwest Territories	3,246,390	133,294	3,379,684	42,609
Canada	9,167,165	775,165	9,922,330	343,181

Sources: Canada. Statistics. 1981; Canada Year Book 1980-81; 1981 Census of Canada.

of housing and the planning of communities'' (Carver, 1976, 104–5). These and other provisions of the NHA were also instrumental in the birth and development of institutionalized planning across the country. As the policies of the CMHC took effect, municipal planning organization so evolved. Mortgage funds would not be allocated unless appropriate plans were in place and minimum standards of subdivision were employed. Funding for sewage treatment came available on condition that municipalities prepare master plans. Urban renewal schemes under CMHC funding were introduced, thus inducing further development of planning institutions.[11] To illustrate how planning evolved, in 1950 there were 50 persons enrolled in the Canadian planning profession; in 1967 there were 650; in 1983 about 3,500.[12]

Evolution of Planning Legislation

Canada's first planning statutes were passed in 1912–13 in the provinces of Nova Scotia, New Brunswick, Ontario, and Alberta.[13] By 1916, Manitoba and Saskatchewan had also proclaimed planning acts. All of these were derivative of the British Housing and Town Planning Act of 1909. None of them had application to all municipalities in their jurisdiction, nor was planning made mandatory. Whereas the earliest statutes adopted the British development control technique, in the 1920s and 1930s U.S.-style zoning came into practice. It was only in 1925 that workable planning legislation was introduced, first in British Columbia. Only in 1946 did Ontario adopt an act that urged official plans at the municipal level.

With the arrival of the environmental movement and activism in urban affairs in the 1970s, the provinces embarked on redraftings of their legislation. By 1981, all jurisdictions had in place new acts that more fully elaborated procedural matters (for example, plan preparation and content, appeals and public hearings) and generally required municipal authorities to adopt plans of a specified nature. In addition to zoning, Canada also adopted U.S. practices of the nonpolitical appointed planning commission and special-purpose boards. The National Capital Commission, for example, is a federal agency engaged in land use planning, beautification, and development assistance in the national capital region.[14]

Legislation today provides that a local policy plan be prepared, in some jurisdictions called an official plan, in others the general plan or the municipal plan. These set out a broad framework for the location and phasing of urban developments, together with statements on social and quality of life objectives, fiscal management of new infrastructures, and policies or guidelines concerning building development conditions in the various land use districts. Zoning or land use classification plans and bylaws are then drawn up.

On the matter of what local municipal plans may or may not cover or entail, Fitzpatrick (1982, 10) states:

there are different views on what a municipal plan should be. In Ontario a plan means ''a program and policy designed to secure the health, safety, convenience and welfare of the inhabitants of the area, and consisting of the texts and maps describing such program and policy. . . . '' In fact, the broad definition has been interpreted by some municipalities as enabling the preparation of what are much more than physical plans: this has sometimes led to meaningless policies.

In the latter half of the 1970s, six provinces conducted public reviews and redrafted their planning legislation. As the acts were rewritten, three major changes occurred: centralization, or a greater attention to provincial interests in local land use plans and tighter central authority for plan approvals; a requirement that the municipalities plan and regulate by bylaw replaced permissive or enabling statutes; and enlarged recognition of public input to planning by formalized, sometimes multiple, hearings.

Land Use Law, Regulation, and Property Rights

Land use law in Canada evolved from the common law of nuisance and restrictive covenants, to public health statutes allowing cities to regulate the location of selected types of activity, (for example, factories, tanneries) and then to laws granting urban municipalities authority to designate land uses in the suburbs, and, eventually, comprehensive plans with zoning and building controls. The progress was neither rapid nor easily won. It took 20 years from the passage of the 1921 Ontario enactment before municipalities began passing zoning bylaws (Fitzpatrick, 1982), while everywhere the regulation of land and building activity was steadily resisted by the property industry.

With respect to land use regulation, in a few jurisdictions, development control of one form or another has been and is still employed. Zoning bylaws are more widely favored for the certainty they offer property owners and for relative ease of administration. The superior courts have upheld certain important principles inherent in public planning and regulation, and they have enunciated the boundary conditions of private enjoyment of land. For example, the most recent Supreme Court of Canada judgment (*Hartel Holdings* v. *Calgary*, 1984-05-03) upholds the right of a municipality to freeze privately owned land in an agricultural classification for an indeterminate period leading to its acquisition for a public park. The court denied both the owner's claim to be compensated on the basis of an expected value in residential use and the owner's claim to be paid now. In an earlier case, the Supreme Court upheld the right of a public authority (National Capital Commission) to plan and expropriate lands for a 4,000 acre (1,620 hectare) greenbelt even though the authority could not specify precisely what public needs would be served or precisely what public land uses were intended for each of the several parcels. In a built-up area, down-zoning may be introduced without consideration for owners' expectations under the higher zoning existing before the change. And it is accepted that a municipality may share in the betterment value of land, produced in part by public policy and plans, by exacting from owners wishing to subdivide their land dedications of parcels or cash payments for community land needs, such as schools, parks, or roadways. On the other hand, representative actions that would argue a general or even special public interest in a specific property or land use matter are generally impossible to advance. This has been particularly evident in attempts to preserve from destruction buildings or sites of significant historical or architectural merit.

Quebec Planning Act

The Development and Urban Planning Act in Quebec (LAU) was decreed in 1979).[15] The LAU gives effect to a coordinative regional planning system.[16] It establishes a middle-tier authority, the Regional Municipal Council, from which a local municipality must obtain consent to its land use plans and bylaws. The LAU codifies procedures, rules, powers, technical prescriptions, and the distribution of regulatory authority, among the province, regional municipalities, and local authority. The LAU is possibly the most comprehensively structured statute of its type in Canada. It is divided into four sections: rules, administration, penalties, and transitional and final dispositions (269 articles grouped into 11 chapters). The first three deal with the content of a regional development scheme (DS);[17] the content of local municipal plans and how they are to be processed; public participation; and interim control during a plan-making phase.

Each regional municipality must undertake the preparation of a DS. A local municipality may then undertake the preparation of an urban plan in conformity with the DS. The act specifies a mandatory set of elements for incorporation in the DS and a set of optional elements. The DS produces an integrated organization of land use and infrastructure layout over several municipalities, specifying broad zones allowed for urbanization and major uses such as open spaces, industry, major roadways, and regional-based facilities, and it identifies zones in which land uses shall be constrained for reasons of public security or for cultural, aesthetic, or ecological preservation. The DS must outline the costs anticipated for intermunicipal infrastructure and facilities.

Regulatory instruments and rules for plan adoption are set out in chapter 4: zoning, subdivision, building bylaws, and permits for development. Chapter 5 deals with citizen advisory committees. Chapter 6 covers government intervention: the rules of notice, hearing, and resolution of conflict by which a provincial agency may modify any provision in a plan; and it reserves for the province the right to accomplish its will by decree. The government may, also by decree, create special zones for historical, cultural, scientific, aesthetic, recreational, or ecological preservation; the protection and/or rehabilitation of waters and shorelines, gravel pits, and similar areas; and the resolution of a development problem for which, in the government's opinion, intervention is justified.

In the Quebec act, a zoning bylaw allows the municipality to specify "the architecture, the exterior symmetry and appearance of buildings, the manner of grouping [them]"; regulate or prohibit the removal of humus materials from land; prevent the destruction of trees; force any owner to embellish property with "lawn, shrubs or trees"; and restrain the destruction of buildings. As in

all other provinces, the act provides for the final approval of plans at the provincial
level and for appeals. Quebec employs a Provincial Planning Commission of
five members.[18] They are empowered to receive and register plans but may only
render opinion on the soundness of plans or proposed zonings. Ultimately legal
appeals proceed through the Cities and Towns Act and the Courts.

Alberta Planning Act

Alberta "has long had progressive planning legislation" (Fitzpatrick, 1982,
18), which includes the first regional planning body (established in 1950). In
1975 a new framework was introduced for public debate, and in 1977 a new act
was passed. As in the other provinces, several departments other than municipal
affairs also exercise land planning functions; they include Energy and Natural
Resources, Environment, Transportation, Culture and Recreation, and Parks and
Wildlife. And a number of special purpose agencies undertake planning; the
Special Areas Board, for example, administers over 7 million hectares of public
lands in agricultural use.

The 1977 Alberta Planning Act prescribes four types of plan: the regional
plan and three statutory plans: general municipal plan (GMP), area structure plan
(ASP), and area redevelopment plan (ARP). The key instruments of regulation
are the land use bylaw, development permits, and subdivision controls. Other
special regulatory devices are replotting schemes; innovative areas for which a
municipality may waive bylaws in order to encourage low-cost innovative housing construction; special areas that give the province "planning control over land
use changes in the vicinity of facilities or developments having national, provincial, or regional significance" (Murchie, Stuart, and Taylor, 1978, 28); and
the reserve land dedication, by which the municipality obtains sites for public
parks, environmental reserve, and schools.

Regional planning commissions (RPC) are created by the provincial cabinet;
they generally administer the act in their territories. Regional areas encompass
rural settlements and are centered on a city or town. RPCs are empowered to
designate lands for agricultural use and to prepare municipal plans. A regional
plan must be adopted by two-thirds majority vote of the RPC members, and all
statutory plans, bylaws, and other regulations drawn up by a municipality must
be in conformity with it. The regional planning process provides for public
hearings, appeals, ultimate approval, and so on, shown in Figure 18.7. A similar
process applies to the preparation of GMPs (Figure 18.8).

The GMP is expected to derive from broad policies enunciated in the regional
plan. A city, town, or village having a population of 1,000 or more and counties
or municipal districts with populations of 10,000 or more are required to adopt,
by bylaw, a GMP. Its content is but broadly prescribed: proposed land uses,
proposals for future development and the manner of development; areas suitable
for the ASP or an ARP designated or described. The purposes of a GMP are
confined to orderly and economic development and land use and the physical
environment.

Figure 18.7 Alberta Regional Planning Process

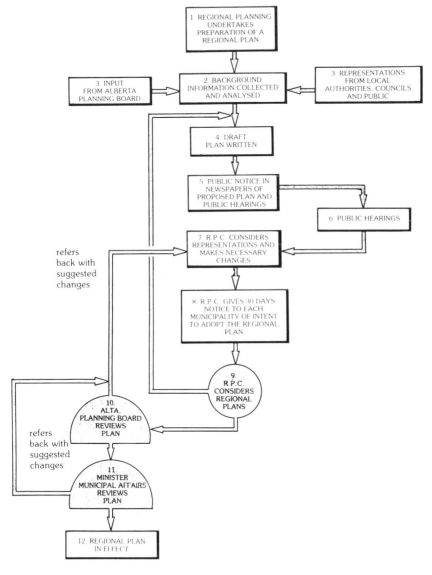

Murchie et. al (1978, 17)

Figure 18.8 Alberta Municipal Planning Process

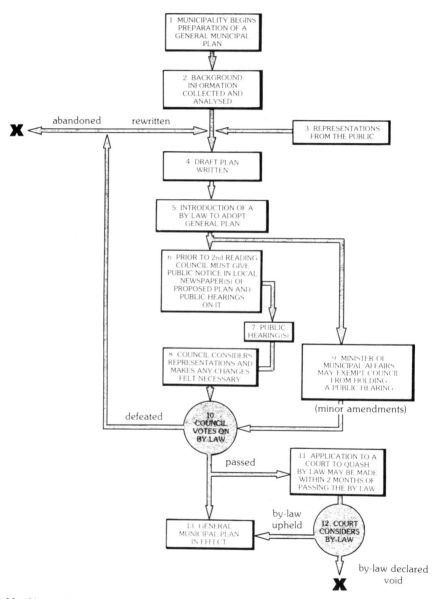

Murchie et. al (1978, 20)

An ASP deals with selected tracts of undeveloped land expected to form a community base. This statutory plan broadly defines land uses, population densities, location of community facilities and transportation routes, and development phasing, all at levels of detail sufficient for fiscal and other public management decisions. In the process of preparing ASPs, municipal officials and property development interests are afforded opportunities to negotiate conditions.

An ARP relates to a built-up sector where market forces or public policy anticipate substantial changes in land use and physical environment. Various objectives may be contemplated: preserving or improving land or buildings, rehabilitating or removing buildings, and improving or relocating public roadways, public utilities or other services.

Zoning and Development Control

Development control (DC) once again came into use in the 1960s and 1970s, primarily as a means to achieve public benefits and positive features in a development project that could not be obtained from an owner under zoning. In effect DC legitimized by statute the several extralegal techniques long employed by municipalities to get around the rigidities of zoning (Makuch, 1983, 228–40), such as the technique of forcing developers to do more in exchange for ready cooperation by the municipality in effecting land exchanges or purchases for roads; by spot zoning (case-by-case passing of bylaws); and by giving density bonuses in return for special site improvements or public spaces.

Makuch (1983) relates that in addition Alberta, Ontario, Manitoba, and Nova Scotia had provisions for development control in their statutes. In Nova Scotia powers to regulate architectural design and appearances were granted, as well as powers to create a comprehensive development district for which permit applications were to be judged by the municipal council. The city of Vancouver charter empowers that council to set up zones "in which there shall be no uniform regulations" and "to impose conditions upon the issuing of the (development) permit." The City of Winnipeg Act (1971) also allows DC areas under a bylaw "in which zoning ceases to operate"; however, a detailed area plan must be drawn up in order to guide DC decisions or, conversely, to circumscribe discretionary power; and the act restricts the conditions to a set of specified concerns: "(a) the use of the land, building or structure; (b) the timing of development; (c) the siting and design, including exterior materials . . . ; (d) traffic control and . . . parking . . . ; (e) landscaping and grading and provision of open space."

Development Control and Zoning in Alberta

Under the old Alberta Planning Act, both zoning and DC were allowed. Zoning prescribes in bylaw the types and minimum standards of uses to be permitted on any land parcel. A DC system grants, without passing a bylaw, discretionary decision powers to municipal officials who review development proposals and then designate allowable uses and building forms on a case-by-case basis, attaching conditions as they believe necessary. Between 1969 and 1977 the city of Calgary operated a DC system. As summarized by Dais (1979, 261):

Development control gave city officials a strong position from which to bargain with developers for sharing the costs of utilities, open space, parking, landscaping and the like [and] control over the size, location and timing of development with an obvious preference for larger developers who had the resources to assemble land.

Proposals for the new Alberta Planning Act, under public review between 1974 and 1977, intended the elimination and ad hoc DC decisions and strengthened public participation. In reality, the new act hybridized zoning and DC. A municipality may now designate direct control districts wherever a council "considers it desirable to exercise *particular* control over the use and development of lands and buildings." The council may regulate these districts "in any manner it considers necessary." A land use bylaw, however, must also be adopted to define all other types of districts and to specify land uses, much as zoning does. The bylaw also establishes "a method of making decisions on applications for development permits," including a description of any discretion given to administrative officers.

Protection of Agricultural Lands

Municipal authorities always had at their disposal the device of zoning for preventing urban expansion onto valuable agricultural lands. But zoning was rarely used; where it was, generally it has not been made to stick. Municipalities more consistently have taken the view that provincial authorities must take responsibility for agricultural lands protection; what municipalities do is only control urbanization. The provinces, with the exception of three, have shied away from contraverting either the territorial expansion plans of urban centers or the speculative property market where it operates on urban peripheries to the disadvantage of agricultural policies. The exceptions are British Columbia's Land Use Commission, Prince Edward Island's Land Development Corporation, and Quebec's 1978 Agricultural Lands Protection Act (ALPA).[19]

Not only is the Quebec act unique in Canada, it is noteworthy for its scope and manner of implementation. ALPA defines by decree a designated agricultural region composed of lands within 615 named municipalities, and it emulates by inversion the French planning procedure known as *perimètres d'urbanisation*; that is, rather than delimit the expansion allowable for each urban center, a protected agricultural zone is delimited by the government ("green areas"), thus leaving the residual areas for urbanization ("white areas"). ALPA operates independently of the Quebec Planning Act; it is administered by a government-appointed commission (CPTAQ) having the powers of an administrative tribunal.[20] These are substantial: the CPTAQ can authorize the use, the subdivision, or the severance of lots; issue soil removal permits; delimit the agricultural zone within a municipality; and order the stopping of actions or building works contrary to the act and the restoration of land to its former state.

In the discharge of its duties, the CPTAQ must

take into particular consideration the biophysical conditions of the soil and environs, the potential agricultural uses of farm lots and the economic consequences flowing from these potentials, the effects of recognizing agricultural soil preservation in the municipality and the region as well as the homogeneity of the community and of agricultural production. (Article 12)

Within five years, the CPTAQ brought into effect a province-wide, valued agricultural land regime. Among the many positive results has been a change in land values. Speculative land prices around Quebec's cities and towns have dropped to levels more closely reflecting agricultural productivity.

Heritage Land Use and Conservation

As in urban planning, the federal government historically has initiated and given leadership in conservation and heritage land use. The Banff National Park was created in 1887. Today 13 million hectares are preserved in national parks alone. In 1953, the Historic Sites and Monuments Act was introduced. Later, federal action created Heritage Canada (established in 1973; $12 million initial endowment) and the Federal Advisory and Coordinating Committee on Heritage Conservation (FACCHC) to ensure that "federal projects and programs respected heritage."

Heritage Legislation and Programs

Under the federal enactment, the responsible minister may "designate the structure as a national historic site and erect a plaque or enter into a cost-sharing agreement (for purchase and maintenance) or acquire the property" (Denhez, 1978, 71). This is the essence of Canada's national program. In addition, Canada adheres to the World Heritage Convention (1972).[21] In the 1960s a nationwide inventory of historic sites and structures was initiated, including domestic housing. Canada then embarked on a modest set of restoration programs for historic sites already in the government's possession, including Louisbourg. Since the late 1950s, the National Capital Commission (NCC) had been acquiring historic properties along the nation's mile of history (Sussex Drive, Ottawa) and elsewhere in the capital region. By 1970, the NCC was offering outstanding examples of restoration and preservation and an aggressive historic land uses policy. Out of these experiences grew research and technical expertise and an awakening interest on the part of the provinces.

The provincial governments have authority to control the use of privately owned heritage properties, but only eight have enacted statutes providing for the enduring protection of sites.[22] In only some instances are the Heritage Act purposes complemented by regulations within the provincial planning act. "The main feature of most of these statutes is that they authorize provincial governments to designate heritage sites, and then to prohibit any alterations or demolition on those sites unless ministerially approved" (Denhez, 1978, 82). Alberta and Quebec statutes are of interest for their enablement to protect entire urban districts. Generally, though, public planning policies and will to act are weak or parsimoniously underwritten. Moreover, only two provinces force themselves to consider cultural properties protection within a land use planning process: Alberta, through the Historical Resources and the Land Surface Conservation and Reclamation Acts, and Ontario, through the Environmental Assessment Act 1975.[23]

Conservation and Ecological Reserves

Canada has subscribed to the International Biological Program (IBP) since its inception in 1965.[24] The process of researching and designating sites for conservation is conducted by means of panels coordinated by the Canadian Council on Ecological Areas (CCEA). Panel members are drawn from the governments, university researchers, nongovernmental agencies, and private citizens. Eight of ten provinces have enacted ecological reserves legislation or made some provision within an existing enactment. British Columbia (BC) provides a singularly outstanding example of commitment; over 100 ecosystem reserves have been designated in law. In other provinces and on federal lands north of latitude 60, surveys, site research, and interest group lobbying continues, but official designations of sites has been slow (Revel 1981).[25]

The object of designating sites is to preserve unique natural ecosystems having demonstrated biological value and to close these to human intrusions. In the lands of the Arctic and sub-Arctic regions, five federal acts have bearing: National Parks, Migratory Birds Convention, Territorial Lands, Fisheries, and Canada Wildlife. The limitations in these are summarized by Revel (1981). In the Parks Act, very general legal terms in the legislation and policy discretion in the office of the minister combine with a historical mandate to serve people with recreation facilities, such that perfectly preserved ecological sites cannot be guaranteed. For the Wildlife Act, considerable flexibility, including an enablement to enter into arrangements with private organizations, is offset by ministerial discretion that can militate against commitments. In the Birds Convention, powers are there to protect, regulate hunting, and designate feeding grounds, yet there are no powers to extend protection to other wildlife resources.

In summary, Canada does not yet have a unitary federal enactment or an adequate institutional force to advance the securing of preservation sites. It remains to be seen if the recently created crown corporation, Wildlife Habitat Canada, will remedy this situation.[26] Among the provinces, except for BC, progress is nominal; strategic planning for ecological reserve sites appears to be nonexistent.

Environmental Impact Assessment

Impact assessment was formally adopted for all federal crown land use planning in the 1970s, and the provinces have generally instituted similar procedures. These developments in the past decade or so arose from three main forces: advancements in the biological sciences linked to special concerns for nature preservation; sharply increased public awareness of and interest in environmental values, including the notion of public lands stewardship;[27] and a rapid development in advanced interdisciplinary education programs for environmental planners and other practitioners.[28]

Federal Environmental Assessment Review Office (FEARO)

The federal government's policy and procedures (cabinet decision of 1973, amended 1977) are designed to "ensure that the environmental effects of federal projects, programs and activities are assessed early in their planning, before any commitments or irrevocable decisions are made" (Canada, Environment, 1979). Reviews are conducted by panels of experts chaired by the executive chairman of the FEARO or a delegate. Public servants from the provinces or territories can be named panel members. To protect their independence and status, the panels report directly to the minister of environment. The process is shown in Figure 18.9. A panel issues guidelines to the project proponent, who then presents an environmental impact statement (EIS). Participating departments of government may introduce additional or complementary information or studies, and the panel may, depending on their judgment of all the documentation before them, request further information or rectifications from the proponent or other sources. Public meetings are conducted informally; "rules of evidence normally followed by commissions of enquiry or other tribunals do not apply."

Environment and Integrative Planning Organization in Government

Earlier discussion has indicated a somewhat broadened scope and mounting complexity in the development of organization for land planning. Organization has not only become complex but multilayered in a functional sense and centralized with respect to decisionmaking. During the 1970s the Departments of Environment, Energy, and Resources began to occupy instrumental positions in public lands planning through regulatory management functions or in mediating between senior and local planning authorities. Gradually attempts were made to integrate policies across the horizontal structure of government departmental programs, particularly where land habitat, resource developments, recreation schemes, and environmental reserves competed for allocations of crown lands.

Environment departments began by monitoring pollution in the air and water.

Figure 18.9 FEARO Process

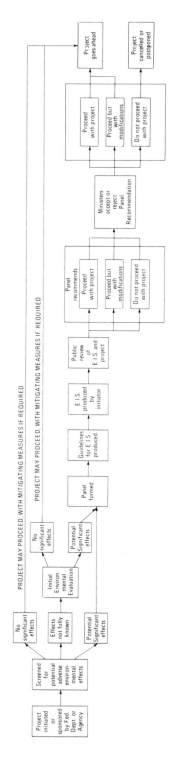

FEARO (1979, 12)

Their mandates were expanded to incorporate the administration of a burgeoning repertoire of environmental regulations, foremost among which were impact studies and public hearings related to development projects on crown lands (for example, of oil and gas, recreation parks and nature reserves, nuclear and hydroelectric power, and coal and forestry). Environment mandates in most provinces have diversified to the extent of embracing all lands, public and private. They now straddle the spheres of traditional land use planning and responsibility (urban and regional), and environment departments increasingly provide coordinative functions among all provincial departments, sometimes with ultimate decision authority. Such, for example, is the role of Environment Canada in the stewardship of federal crown lands.

Alberta Environment (AE) incorporates a wide set of responsibilities. The organization comprises three service branches—Environmental Protection (EP), Water Resources Management (WRM), and Environmental Evaluation (EE)—all touching on land use issues and planning. The WRM unit prepares river basin plans (including diversion schemes); performs benefit-cost analyses and water management projects; provides assistance to municipalities for water projects; and administers various water enactments. Under the EE branch, the Land Surface Conservation and Reclamation Act is administered; restricted development and transportation and utility corridors (surrounding major urban centers) are managed; public participation programs and the environmental impact assessment (EIA) system is operated; and the Alberta Remote Sensing program is managed. The protection service deals with all legislation and programs related to air and water quality, including municipal systems for waste disposal, soil and groundwater protection, and the funding of research. These varied roles of AE involve land use decisions for the main part focused on crown lands and secondarily on agricultural lands and resource extraction projects where reclamation or conservation components are to be implemented. Increasingly the planning of land use in urban contexts requires close coordination and the satisfaction of provincial environmental standards.

The Alberta system is no less complex for the fact that the province's Public Lands Act is administered not by Environment but by Alberta Energy and Resources (AER). To achieve integration among all resource and land-relevant departments, the Resource Integration Committee (RIC) was established.[29] Essentially the system operates from a base of planning teams generally consisting of a representative from each division of AER and participants from other agencies of government directly involved in the planning area (Figure 18.10). Public involvement is provided through an advisory committee headed by an associate minister on which sit representatives from six major provincial interest groups concerned with public lands and resource uses. The guiding principles of Alberta's integrated resource planning are described as flexible plans regularly refined as new information and circumstances warrant, a team approach that combines expertise and builds interdepartmental commitment, a comprehensive approach, and public involvement.

Figure 18.10 Alberta Integrated Resource Planning

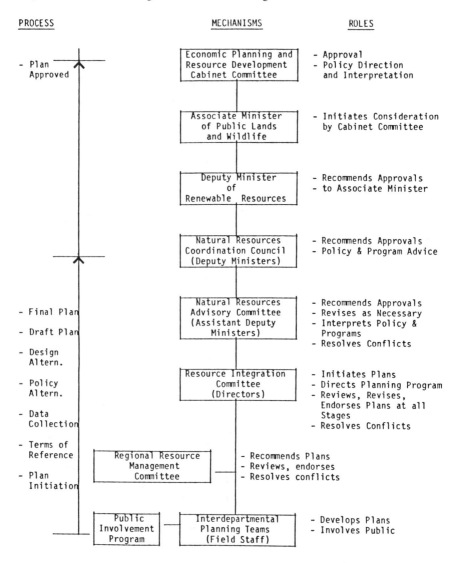

PROCESS   MECHANISMS   ROLES

- Plan
  Approved

                    Economic Planning and   - Approval
                    Resource Development   - Policy Direction
                    Cabinet Committee   and Interpretation

                    Associate Minister   - Initiates Consideration
                    of Public Lands   by Cabinet Committee
                    and Wildlife

                    Deputy Minister   - Recommends Approvals
                    of   - to Associate Minister
                    Renewable Resources

                    Natural Resources   - Recommends Approvals
                    Coordination Council   - Policy & Program Advice
                    (Deputy Ministers)

- Final Plan   Natural Resources   - Recommends Approvals
                    Advisory Committee   - Revises as Necessary
- Draft Plan   (Assistant Deputy   - Interprets Policy &
                    Ministers)   Programs
- Design   - Resolves Conflicts
  Altern.

- Policy   Resource Integration   - Initiates Plans
  Altern.   Committee   - Directs Planning Program
                    (Directors)   - Reviews, Revises,
- Data   Endorses Plans at all
  Collection   Stages
                                                  - Resolves Conflicts
- Terms of
  Reference   Regional Resource   - Recommends Plans
               Management   - Reviews, endorses
- Plan   Committee   - Resolves conflicts
  Initiation

          Public   Interdepartmental   - Develops Plans
          Involvement   Planning Teams   - Involves Public
          Program   (Field Staff)

Alberta (1983)

Table 18.4
Land Tenure in Canada

Item	km^2	Percent
Federal Crown lands (1)	3,868,241	38.8
National parks	130,168	1.3
Indian reserves	26,335	0.3
Privately owned land or land in process of alienation from the Crown	962,292	9.7
Provincial or territorial area other than provincial parks and forests (2)	3,104,212	31.1
Provincial parks	244,513	2.4
Provincial forests	1,640,378	16.4
	9,976,139	100.0

(1) Other than National Parks and Indian Reserves; includes 281 km^2 federal forest reserves

(2) Includes freshwater area

Source: Canada Year Book 1980-81

Crown Lands and Native People Land Claims

Land use planning applies in the main to privately owned lands. Two other major land regimes exist in Canada: crown lands and native people lands.

Crown Lands: Institutional Arrangements and Use Planning

Crown lands comprise upwards of 90 percent of the surface of Canada (Table 18.4). They are held either in right of the provinces or in right of the federal government. Practically the whole of federal crown lands are in the two territories located north of latitude 60, inhabited by some 40,000 native and nonnative peoples. Within the provincial jurisdictions, impressive proportions of crown lands also pertain; for example, in British Columbia 94 percent (770,828 square kilometers), in Ontario 88 percent (784,250 square kilometers); in New Brunswick and Nova Scotia, respectively, 45 and 25 percent.[30] Generally until the 1960s, land use planning and management were rudimentary. During the 1960s and 1970s multiple land use and management practices were introduced, in turn spurred by nationwide land capability studies. And crown lands were seen increasingly as performing a vital role in sustaining sensitive ecological regimes, frequently covering vast geographic zones (such as the Arctic tundra, covering 2,199,000 square kilometers)

The more pertinent commonalities of administration and planning *among all jurisdictions* are these:

Administration for Crown lands is distributed amongst several departments in each jurisdiction but usually one department has a dominant role;

Advice on land management is provided by inter- or intra-departmental committees;

Public input in decision-making is directly or indirectly obtained in the land management process;

The use of Crown land in accordance with land policies, directives, environmental impact reviews, and any regional plans is a primary concern;

Most [crown land] inventories are in, or are in the process of conversion to, automated or computerized formats which undergo periodic updates.

(Canada, Environment, 1980, 6, 7)

In at least four provinces, crown land planning decisions are highly centralized. In British Columbia the cabinet directs the Environment and Land Use Committee (ELUC) and the Cabinet Committee on Economic Development, both of which play the key roles in land planning and development decisions. Manitoba operates a six-member ministerial committee, which closely supervises the two major agencies, the Interdepartmental Planning Board (IPB) and the Crown Land Classification Committee (CLCC).[31] Ontario centralizes all essential matters with a single minister (Natural Resources). Centralization is of only modest proportion on Prince Edward Island. The PEI Land Development Corporation divides responsibility with Highways and Public Works, while the corporation membership includes appointed citizens.

The federal system allows departments, crown corporations, and other agencies to assume responsibility for their own lands: downtown office properties, defense installations, ports and harbors, forestry lands, and so forth. Autonomy notwithstanding, all land use plans are subject to cabinet policies, notably the Federal Land Management (FLM) Principle, the Federal Policy on Land Use (FPLU), and the Federal Environmental Assessment and Review Process Office. The FLM Principle was enunciated in 1973: "Federal lands should be managed so as to combine the efficient provision of government services with the achievement of wider social, economic and environmental objectives."[32] The Interdepartmental Committee on Land (ICL), chaired by Environment Canada, coordinates the implementation of the FPLU and serves as a bureau for federal and provincial discussions on land use questions.

The primary data base on federal lands is a computerized central real property inventory (CRPI), maintained and updated monthly by the Public Works Department. Legal, location, area, and use information for every federal landholding are recorded. Complementary data on biophysical and socioeconomic characteristics are compiled by Environment Canada.

Native People Lands and Claims

The British North American Act (1867) made the federal government responsible for Indians and Inuit.[33] For land use planning, therefore, provincial enactments do not apply. In turn, the Indian Act is silent on land use matters; Indian communities have been left relatively free to determine land uses on reserves, and only occasional planning services are provided by federal public servants.

The subject of native land claims is now prominently before the Canadian public. Claims have been pressed continuously since the 1920s, only to be alternately suppressed and ignored until a decade or so ago. The resolution of these claims will be extremely consequential for both native peoples' cultural survival and the future economic exploitation by nonnatives of a substantial portion of Canada's land base. Two examples illustrate the point. Some 13,500 Inuit of the central and eastern Arctic regions proposed in 1977 that a new territory be created to encompass all lands north of the treeline, and claims were made for extensive land and wildlife rights and monetary compensation (Canada, Indian and Northern Affairs, 1981, appendix). A second claim, successfully negotiated by the James Bay Cree and Inuit, "provided for ownership of land; exclusive hunting, fishing and trapping rights; substantial participatory roles in the management of local and regional governments, financial compensation, control over education and social and economic benefits."[34]

The 1970s witnessed renewed and concerted attempts by the native people to win their claims: "The various demands for natural resources, vast amounts of which have been discovered in some of the areas being claimed, have pressed Native people" (Canada, Indian Affairs and Northern Development, 1981, 8). Meanwhile, a Supreme Court decision in 1973 had prepared the way for negotiated settlements rather than judicial process.[35]

Native people claims divide into two categories. The first is termed specific and deals with "actions and omissions of government as they relate to obligations under treaty" (Canada, Indian and Northern Affairs, 1982, 3). The administration of lands is a recurrent theme; grievances include the taking or damaging of reserve lands by federal agents and fraudulent actions in acquiring or disposing of reserve lands. The second category is comprehensive: "claims based on the concept of 'aboriginal title.'" These "relate to the traditional use and occupancy and the special relationships that Native people have had with the land since time immemorial" (Canada, Indian and Northern Affairs, 1981, 7). Consequently the settlement of claims "could include a variety of terms such as protection of hunting, fishing and trapping, land title, money, as well as other rights and benefits (Canada, Indian and Northern Affairs, 1981, 11) such as participation in social decisionmaking and in economic development.

Several inquiries and environmental hearings in the decade 1970–80 served to elucidate the crucial importance of a land base in sustaining Indian and Inuit communities. (See, for example, Brody, 1981; Drury, 1980; Berger, 1977; and Canada, 1966). The crisis of survival and their social and economic development prospects were vividly shown to the Canadian public as inextricably tied to land title. The granting of Indian and Inuit land claims would alter the accustomed manner and style of land and resource use and management practiced by non-natives. The MacKenzie Valley Pipeline inquiry in 1977 concluded emphatically that the pipeline should not be built until land claims had been settled and not before agreements had been reached on how native people would share in economic benefits and technology transfers. In his inquiry into self-government for the Northwest Territories, Drury (1980) also recognized the necessity for native people to have control over land and resources development.

Comprehensive claims respecting twenty-two native communities are either in process or settled. Lands so far affected amount to 111,000 square kilometers.[36] The governing policy for claim settlements embraces the following land-related provisions (Drury, 1980, 23–4):

Lands selected for claim will be for continuing use by native people.

Nonnatives who have acquired rights in lands subject to claim are deserving of equitable consideration in any settlement, while "other rights of basic access" must be considered (for present holders of exploration rights, resource production leases, and so forth).

"Protection must be ensured against unlimited expropriation powers in the case of lands granted in settlement."

"Settlements may provide for prescribed preferential rights to wildlife on Crown lands," and natives can be given meaningful involvement in government planning and policies for wildlife areas, including setting of harvest quotas.

Subsurface rights may be considered "in certain cases," either as incentive for native participation or as a "protective measure" against potential resource developments close to native communities.

These policy elements are well reflected in the comprehensive agreement concluded in March 1984 with the Committee for Original Peoples' Entitlement, the negotiating agent for 2,500 Inuvialuit living in six communities in the western Arctic. Surface and subsurface title to 11,000 square kilometers surrounding the communities was received, along with title to a 2,000 square kilometer area in Cape Bathurst, to be held free of any industrial development, and another 7,800 square kilometers, excluding mineral, gas, and oil rights. Various Inuvialuit rights and autonomies were also established, such as a right of access to subsurface resources; the right to negotiate participation agreements in development; and the right to obtain wildlife compensation when development projects go ahead and rents for the use of surface lands. A number of Inuvialuit corporations

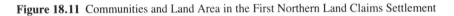

Figure 18.11 Communities and Land Area in the First Northern Land Claims Settlement

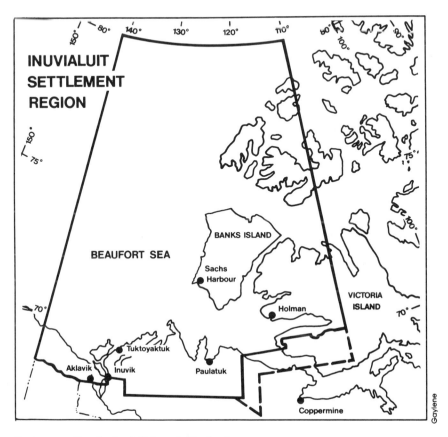

Environment Canada; *Land*, Volume 5, Number 2.

will be created to receive and manage benefits flowing from the settlement; examples are for investment, development, and land management. Two subgroups composed of Inuvialuit and government officials in equal numbers now assume responsibility for land use planning in the designated region (Figure 18.11).

Land Use Classification, Inventory, and Monitoring

Canada Land Inventory

When the federal government launched an agricultural rehabilitation program in the late 1950s, there was no uniform method for rating the quality of land units for one or other types of farm activity or for other conceivable uses.[37] If development projects brought forward from the various regions were to be properly judged and compared, a system of describing land capability would be necessary.[38] The Canada Land Inventory (CLI) was initiated in 1963 as a federal-provincial program. The salient features of the CLI are as follows:

A reconnaissance type of inventory covering . . . about 26% of Canada.

Mapping was initially completed at the 1:50 000 scale. . . . The classification system rates land from Class 1, the highest potential, to Class 7, negligible capability. The classes are further defined by sub-classes which relate to physical limitations, such as wetness and steepness of slope for agriculture. . . .

The data tabulation documents list area and class information by province, census division, electoral district, and watershed.

(Rump, 1983, 2–8)[39]

Land units were color coded and mapped according to soil properties and an appropriate potential activity within their geographic context. Letter codes indicate such limiting or opportunity factors as rocky formations or unique vegetation. Agriculture and forestry capabilities were codified for production of common field crops and commercial timber, respectively. Outdoor recreation classifications focused on unique topographic and aesthetic features. Capability ratings for wildlife recognized the habitat needs of waterfowl, ungulates, and sport fish. Table 18.5 summarizes the percentage of first-class land capabilities in the CLI inventory.

As Rees (1979) and others have discussed, the CLI was an outstanding program in its scientific ambition and geographic scope. As Rump (1983, 7) states:

[The] information has contributed to the formulation of a national land use policy, the increase in public awareness of the land resource, the establishment of land use monitoring and ecological land classification programs, and land use research programs focussing on such issues as agricultural land loss. . . . The CLI has been applied in zoning to protect high capability lands, national park planning, identifying areas with forest management potential, environmental impact assessments, regional planning studies locating sites suitable for cottage development, and industrial park site selection.

Northern Land Use Information Program

A second phase of inventory began in 1971, inspired by the need for environmental impact studies as oil and gas and mineral exploration and production expanded into Canada's north.[40] Information-gathering techniques range from satellite remote sensing to community meetings (Figure 18.12). The program covers 3.9 million square kilometers of land in the Yukon and Northwest Territories; maps are at 1:250,000 scale.

"The NLUIP provides . . . comprehensive appreciation of the environmental

Table 18.5
Canada Land Inventory: High Capability Lands and Percentage of Inventory

	Class 1 (%)	Class 1-3 (%)
Agriculture	0.50	4.83
Recreation (total)	0.05	2.38
Recreation (shoreline length)	0.28	14.90
Wildlife - ungulates	2.20	42.20
Wildlife - waterfowl	1.00	7.78
Forestry*	0.09	14.90

*Forestry data available for 53% of the CLI area only.

Source: Rump, 1983, p. 5.

and socio-economic character of the north on a regional scale. . . . There are four major uses of NLUIP outputs: the administration of land use regulations, regional planning, project planning and evaluation, and public information and education.'' (Rump, 1983, 13)

Canada Land Use Monitoring Program (CLUMP)

Initiated in 1978, CLUMP monitors "amount, location, and type of *land use change* on national and regional scales" (Rump, 1983, 15). A five-year periodicity is employed for urban regions and ten years in rural areas, thus allowing correlations with census demographic, agricultural, and other data. Basic features of the system are: "(a) it is hierarchical to accommodate different interpretation scales; (b) coding permits easy computer manipulation; (c) it is flexible, but comprehensive to meet a variety of user needs; and (d) the separation of productive activities from site uses is possible" (Gierman, cited by Rump, n.d.) CLUMP records two pure systems, one for land cover and the other for land activity. (Figure 18.13).

The program divides into urban-centered regions (the rural-urban fringes) and prime resource lands (including scarce lands). Projects in the latter program currently include fruitlands and wetlands. Remote sensing data are relied on heavily. For the urban project, 79 cities each with 25,000 population and over are being studied. Data compilation relies on series air photography from 1966; data analysis "relies on standard selections, on-line interactive graphics, and map plots" (Rump, 1983, 17).

Figure 18.12 Northern Land Use Information Program: Sectors and Data Acquisition
Methods

Sector	(1)	(2)	(3)	(4)	(5)
Ecological Overview	*	*	*	*	
Coastal Classification	*	*	*	*	
Wildlife Information	*	*	*	*	
Fish Resources	*	*	*	*	
Hunting and Trapping	*			*	*
Historical & Archaelogical	*		*	*	*
Resource Development Activities	*		*	*	
Areas, Routes & Interest Points	*			*	*
Community Information	*			*	*
Other (sea-ice, transportation facilities, bibliography)	*		*	*	

(1) Literature Review   (4) Consultation with Experts

(2) Remote Sensing   (5) Community Meetings

(3) Field Survey

Source: Rump (1983), P. 10; adapted from Moore (1982)

SELECTED ISSUES AND CHALLENGES [41]

A National Perspective: Interjurisdictional and Substantive

In 1975 Environment Canada began a study of federal departmental land use
policies and a review of issues seen from a national perspective (Manning, 1980;
Canada, Environment, 1980). Concurrently, a series of reports on provincial
and territorial land use programs were compiled under Environment Canada
sponsorship.

Figure 18.13 CLUMP: Cover and Activity Classifications: Illustrative Examples

<u>LAND COVER CLASSIFICATION SYSTEM</u>

```
01000 WOODY VEGETATION
      01100 Mature Trees
            01110 Regular Spaced (Planted)
                  01111 Fruit and Nut Trees
                  01112 Other Deciduous Trees
                  01113 Coniferous Trees
            01120 Irregular Spaced
   •
   •
   •
   •

04000 CONSTRUCTED COVER
      04100 Structures
            04110 Buildings
            04120 Other Structures
                  04121 Solid or Enclosing Structures (Other than
                        Buildings)
                  04122 Open Structures
                  04123 Other
      04200 Surfaces
            04210 Hard Surfaces
            04220 Unconsolidated Surfaces

05000 WATER
      05100 Permanent and Solid
            05110 Snow
            05120 Ice
      05200 Liquid
            05210 Streams, Rivers, and Canals
                  05211 Streams and Rivers
                  05212 Canals
```

<u>LAND ACTIVITY CLASSIFICATION SYSTEM</u>

```
01000 AGRICULTURAL ACTIVITIES
      01100 Productive-Land Agricultural Activities
            01110 Growing Annual Tillage Crops
                  01111 Growing Grain
                  01112 Growing Vegetables
                  01113 Growing Rootcrops and Tubers
                  01114 Growing Seed Crops
                  01115 Growing Leaf Crops
                  01116 Growing Flowers and Bulbs
                  01119 Other
            01120 Growing Forage Crops and Grazing
                  01121 Growing Forage Crops
                  01122 Grazing
   •
   •
   •

07000 TRANSPORTATION & COMMUNICATION ACTIVITIES
      07100 Transporting Activities
            07110 Transporting by Roads
                  07111 Transporting by Expressways (Limited Access)
                  07112 Provincial Highways
                  07113 Lower Order Rural Roads
                  07114 Urban Roads and Streets
                  07115 Other Roads
                  07116 Associated Building and Maintaining
                  07117 Bus Terminals
                  07118 Parking
                  07119 Other
```

Canada. Environment (March 1981)

Habitats, river basins, and the ecological regimes of Canada's land mass seldom respect jurisdictional boundaries. To this horizontal complexity is added the vertical layering of jurisdictions: federal government and native lands located within the provinces and territories, provincial crown lands and interests present in urban municipalities and regional planning districts. For constitutional reasons, the conflicts of interest and the sometimes differing ideological perspectives on land use inherent in this pattern remain irreconcilable by means other than enlightened leadership and cooperative administrative mechanisms. It should also be noted that international jurisdictional issues also present some challenge to Canadian land management; examples include the Garrison Dam (North Dakota, United States) water diversions into western Canada; acid rain produced in both Canada and the United States and the despoliation of forestry and agricultural lands; pollution of the Great Lakes; and dumping of U.S. toxic wastes on Canadian lands.

The joint Canada-Alberta-Saskatchewan task force on the Peace-Athabaska delta illustrates the direction in which interjurisdictional cooperation is moving. Its origin lies in a unilateral decision by British Columbia to build a hydroelectric dam near the headwaters of the Peace River in disregard for predictable downstream impacts in two neighboring provinces. Beginning in 1966, the reservoir was gradually filled over a four-year period. This process drastically lowered water levels and produced crucial changes in the delta's annual flood and ponding regimes some 600 kilometers away. Wildlife habitats were destroyed, and the livelihood of 5,000 Indian people was almost destroyed. The provincial-federal task force undertook remedial work in the 1970s to restore water and habitat conditions, and scientific monitoring and impact assessments are continuing. The delta episode marked a turning point in interjurisdictional land management arrangements.

Turning to substantive use issues, Manning (1980) provides a categorization of these. His method is to view an issue as occurring within user sectors and/ or between user sectors:

Within individual sectors, the principal issues concern the manner in which land is managed by that user. Between sectors, the principal issues relate to the allocation of land to a particular use, or the relationship of the use of land to adjacent or other affected areas as a consequence of the manner in which the land is being utilized. (Manning, 1980, 4, 5)

Within-sector issues embrace two types of concern (Manning, 1980, 5): for ecosystem stability (maintaining the resource itself or ensuring its inherent qualities are preserved) and for "improvement of the productivity or quality of use." Sector-to-sector issues are also divided as to major concerns: for allocation (the question of competition, to be judged in terms of such criteria as preservation against increasing scarcity, social or economic trade-offs, highest national interest, altruism and so on) and for "compatibility or incompatibility'' (the question of how one land use may threaten or interfere with either the enjoyment of a neighboring human activity or the functioning of adjacent natural habitat and ecosystem). The analytical framework Manning devised is illustrated in Figure 18.14.

Among the ten priority issues Manning identified, the loss of high-productivity agricultural land, competitions for land allocation on the urban fringes, and coastal use and management figure most prominently. Some others he identifies are sound management practices to sustain good productivity, pollution abatement, access to recreation lands, and ensuring security of persons and property by firmer regulation over the use of hazard lands.

In a national perspective, therefore, the largest set of issues arises from competition for significantly valuable land allocations. The one with the lengthiest history is the competition between urban growth requirements and agricultural lands. More recently, two additional competitions have come into prominence: large-scale resource development projects (examples are hydroelectric, strip-mining, and pipelines) versus natural habitat management and expanded demands for recreation sites (urban centered in origin) versus agricultural, forestry, and nature reserve uses.

Agricultural Lands

Self-Sufficiency in Food Production

In 1930, the federal government estimated there were 142 million hectares of potential farmland in Canada. Sixty-one million hectares were then being farmed, and 81 million were reserved for colonization. Reserves were discovered to be either too northerly for profitable agriculture or located on wetlands, difficult slopes, or areas with other problems. It is now estimated that 122 million hectares have agricultural capability; only 4.4 million are suited to raising prime field crops. In addition, the amount of land in production has been decreasing. At the peak in 1951, there were 70 million hectares under production. Between 1961 and 1976 a net loss of 1.4 million hectares occurred. This was composed of 3.9 million lost east of the Manitoba border, mainly top-quality land, and 2.5 million of lesser quality gained in the west. Since 1961 the number of farms has decreased from 73,212 to 58,000 (21 percent). Farms have become bigger but not without penalty. Expanded monoculture and soil degradation, slackened conservation practices, redistribution of surface water, and erosion are the more dramatic consequences. Although 65 percent of Canada's trade surplus in 1980 ($5.3 billion) came from agriculture, food imports have risen dramatically— from $854 million in 1961 to over $2 billion today. Among the imports are products capable of being produced in Canada such as beef, oil seeds, fruits, and vegetables. What has been wanting are strategic planning for both use and preservation of agricultural lands and fiscal policies more conducive to the improved management of farmlands.

Figure 18.14 Analytical Framework for Land Use Issues

Causal Factors	Land-Use Problems/Issues to be Evaluated	Resultant Symptoms (Complaints)	Means to Deal with Issues	Considerations Affecting Means
	Framework			
A within	(A) Issues within sectors			Ownership of the land
1-a exploitation/ protection	1) Management of the Land Resource	1-a ecosystem destruction	sound management solutions	
1-b demand for product	a) to maintain ecosystem stability within each user sector	1-b changing productivity per unit area		Jurisdiction to influence the use of land
	b) to improve productivity or quality of use or product			
B between	(B) Issues among and between sectors			
1-a noxious uses	1) Static (in place):	1-a reduced utility of land for certain use	sound planning solutions	Power to carry out influence
1-b proximity of uses	- Compatibility and/or incompatibility between uses because of (a) relative location or accessibility, (b) nature of use (pollution)?	1-b reduced utility of adjacent land		Political priority Inadequacy of info.
2-a supply/demand	2) Dynamic (changing demand):	2-a loss of product	(In some cases sound management is all that is required to solve problems of compatibility, in others, relocation of one activity may be required	Inadequacy of the market function
2-b accessible land too scarce	- Allocation between uses competing for use of the same land; and (a) actual changes in land use, and (b) potential changes brought about by competition	2-b high pricing of land		Limits of jurisdiction
	Examples			
A	(A) I Management: a) farmers should contour plough to prevent destruction	A 1-a high food prices, wood prices	A enforced management practices on land of certain quality	Owner usually is decision-maker in management of land
1-a mismanagement	b) foresters should use improved sustained yield method	1-b lower yields, higher fertilizer costs		
1-b management technique	(B) I Compatibility: a) wildfowl refuge at end of airport runway	B 1-a,b not enough rec. land, overcrowding	B zoning, creation of preserves, co-ordination of policies, etc.	Government can influence both mgt. & allocation/relative location decisions
B	b) factory waste pollutes beach area			
1-a poor location	2 Allocation: a) change of farmland to urban/industry	2-a high food prices		
1-b poor location	b) pressure on farmers to sell (outpricing farmers)	2-b high housing prices		Government may lack power to effectively enforce
2-a changing demand, inter-dependence accessibility				
2-b growing demand for some uses				

Loss of Prime Agricultural Lands to Urbanization

About half of Canada's prime lands are in Ontario, mainly in the urbanizing southern areas. Within 160 kilometers of the center of Toronto alone are located 37 percent of Canada's class 1 agricultural lands (Canada, Environment, 1980, 19). These lands are six times more productive than the poorest farmlands. Over 5,000 hectares, or 93 percent, of class 1 to 3 lands were taken up by Toronto's expansion in a single five-year period (1971–76). The city of Edmonton (Alberta) expanded at similar cost: 85 percent of urbanization occurred on class 1 to 3 lands. With these patterns common across the country, conversions to urbanization reached crisis proportions in the 1970s. Some indicators of the crisis are these:

"Each year [urban] construction removes about 17,000 hectares of agricultural land from gainful use. Twice this amount . . . becomes idle" (Welch, 1980, 32).

"In southern Ontario and southern British Columbia . . . growth of cities is taking place on land of special value to Canada's vegetable, fruit and wine industries . . . more than 13,000 hectares of farm land were lost to Toronto, St. Catherines, Hamilton and Chilliwack (1966–71)"; (Welch, 1980, 32)

Fifty-seven percent of class 1 lands lie within 80 kilometers of 23 Canadian cities.

In British Columbia before 1973, permanently converted prime lands figured as high as 6,000 hectares annually (Canada, Environment, 1980).

Nearly half of the total value of Canadian agricultural products derived from lands within 80 kilometers of 19 cities.

The dramatic permanent conversions of good agriculture lands in the period 1950 through 1980 were accompanied by equally dramatic losses of a temporary nature, mainly lands acquired by the property industry to expand inventories. Most cities are now enveloped by such holdings. Within the boundary of Calgary, for example, an estimated 11,000 hectares destined for residential construction is held in temporary agriculture or idle use, the equivalent of three times the aggregate area of currently urbanized lands. The quality of these lands ranges between class 1 and 4 (Perks and Bond, 1983).

The Niagara peninsula in Ontario presents a particularly tragic illustration of Canada's ambivalent public policies on agricultural land. This region historically produced over two-thirds of the value of tender fruit and grapes in Canada. At the beginning of the century, Niagara fruitlands comprised 15,200 hectares. Between 1961 and 1971, 23 percent of Niagara district farms (33,230 hectares), representing 16 percent of the fruitlands, were converted to urban use (McCaig and Manning, 1982, 29). Public concern compelled the Ontario government to initiate in 1967 a series of studies and planning arrangements.[42] These culminated in an approved regional plan of zoning only as late as 1980. By 1977, however, lands remaining available for agriculture were only 62 percent of the original district. When the plan finally received approval in 1980, a further 1,600 hectares were allowed by zoning to be converted to urban uses. The fruit belt would now be only half its original size.

Since 1974 Ontario has operated a Food Land Development Branch (Ministry of Agriculture) whose role is "to ensure that agricultural concerns are considered in land use decisions" (Ward, 1976; 77). The branch reviews municipal planning decisions intended to direct urban development to the least valuable agricultural lands. Elsewhere two examples of special instruments bear mentioning: the British Columbia Land Commission (BCLC) and the Prince Edward Island Development Corporation (PEIDC). The PEIDC (established 1969) is empowered to implement comprehensive land management programs by acquiring, selling, and leasing lands and by adjusting farm tenure patterns so as to create larger, stable, and more productive units. The corporation may also take lands for public recreation purposes and financially assist farmers wishing to improve land use and management practices.

The BCLC was formed in 1973 with powers to curtail the conversion of good agricultural lands to urban uses. It would establish and administer agricultural zoning for the entire province and conduct studies and make recommendations concerning conservation and recreation land uses. Using the CLI, agricultural land reserve plans were drawn up while the power of zoning was removed from rural municipalities to the province (Rawson, 1976).

Degradation of the Agricultural Land Resource

Foremost among degradation problems is the increased practice of monoculture. A chain of consequences is induced, leading from loss of organic matter and reduced soil stability through to redistribution of surface water and erosion, to discharged phosphors into lakes and streams. More nutrients are being removed from soils than are being replaced. A particular issue for Canada's prairie region is increasing soil salinity; 2 million hectares of cultivated land in Saskatchewan are so affected. In Alberta some 50,000 hectares, or 22 percent, of irrigated lands have reached the state of crisis salinity (Marshall, 1982, 198). In addition, the decline of family farms and their substitution by large corporate owners having only pecuniary interests in the land have compounded problems associated with monoculture.

These are not issues that can be remedied by traditional land use planning mechanisms alone. Remedies lie in a variety of means, including variable taxation of land according to utilization and conservation, fiscal incentives, and the provision of better and readily available agronomist and business services to farmers. The challenge now before Canadian institutions is one of devising concerted national-provincial policies embraced within a strategic plan of stewardship.

Conservation and Heritage Planning

BC Forests and Land Planning

Users of Canadian forestlands have not been particularly good stewards. Upwards of 60 million hectares are harvested annually, yet less than a quarter of these lands have been the subject of restoration programs. Neglect of this kind has been exacerbated in recent years by relaxations in resource management rules and cutting operations standards, either encouraged or allowed by certain governments wishing to acknowledge the financial difficulties of the forest industries.[43] Since three-quarters of forestlands are provincially owned, the principal focus of responsibility for mismanagement and inadequate regulation falls on governments.

Canada's legacy of profligate practices is graphically illustrated in the predicament of British Columbia (BC), the province that accounts for half the national harvest. This harvest is likely to be diminished by one-third within a few years. The BC forests took centuries to grow, cannot be duplicated, and are now running out. Meanwhile substantial forestlands have been and continue to be converted to hydroelectric reservoirs, some to farms, and others to urban development. Equally significant, large amounts of cut-over and wild-fire burned lands are not satisfactorily restocked. At issue is the fact that these conditions are not universally appreciated or acknowledged among BC policymakers and industrialists. Moreover, while research has already produced quick-growing, valuable, and genetically superior species, these are not being raised for the reforestation operation currently underway. Nor are progressive cultivation practices being utilized, mainly because they are labor intensive and unattractive to cost-conscious companies.[44]

BC's integrative land use resources planning system, established over the past two decades, is now effectively in a process of dissolution. This system functioned through a committee of deputy ministers (the Environment and Land Use Committee, ELUC) and eight regional resource management committees structured on local political and citizen leadership. In what appears to be a program aimed at eradication of public intervention, the BC government has since 1982 dismantled the ELUC system and with it removed land use planning functions from the province's regional districts. The government's attitude to the agricultural conservationist ethic of the BC Land Commission has effectively become oppositional. These recent events (albeit in one province only) may only be transitory, but they have raised widespread concern that the twin foundations of conservation and public planning, on which the progressive march of Canadian society has always relied substantially, may be disintegrating.

Heritage Properties and Districts

"In most provinces, heritage enjoys no more protection from provincial works than it does from federal works. Again, the toll on heritage has been considerable" (Denhez, 1978, 85). Even under heritage or environmental impact statutes, it appears that public administrations have neither sufficient political support for cultural properties protection nor appropriate funding to secure protections on anything but a most popular case basis (Figure 18.15). In one jurisdiction at least (Ontario) administrative regulations explicitly exempt from its environmental assessment consideration those projects that deal only with the demolition

Figure 18.15 Heritage Legislation in Canada: Key Questions

Question	Number of Provinces with Response in Legislation Indicated (at July 1978)			
	Yes	No	Nd/Un	Condt'l.
Are clear criteria given for the definition of Heritage Property?	–	10	–	–
Must notice be given of impending demolition of unregistered Heritage Property?	1	8	–	AS
Is Government under any obligation to attempt to protect unregistered Heritage Property?	0	6	2	S
Can demolition of unclassified building be delayed pending study?	6	4	–	–
Can definitive protection against demolition be given to a building (short of expropriation)?	8	1	–	AS
Can governmental decisions on designation be appealed to higher authority by statute?	–	10	–	–
Can Heritage Properties be exempted from building codes?	1	9	–	–
Can illegally altered Heritage Building be restored at owner's expense?	5	4		SBO

AS: Archaeological sites only; S: Sometimes; SBO: Subsidized Buildings only
Source: Denhez (1978), Chart pp. 80-81. Partial and Summary Replication only; Denhez chart provides province-by-province responses.

of a structure (Denhez, 1978, 87). For all the encouragement given in planning and other legal instruments, therefore, heritage preservation is still situated within a wide philosophical gulf between entrenched private property ideology and historicocultural idealisms.

A further issue relates to creating the historic areas or districts, as permitted in a number of provincial enactments. The designation of a district for architectural or historical significance involves the same kinds of problems as are encountered in designating a single building, only more of them. The added complexities are, for example, the necessity to put controls on those properties in the district that do not meet the criteria of significance; wider planning and transportation concerns must be contemplated; and the number of actors in negotiations and decisions rises dramatically. Added to these encumbrances, the heritage movement is underwitten by palpably few education resources.[45] As for the present state of government heritage programs, Denhez (1978, 90-91) has pointed to "four legal obstacles":

(i) no citizen rights to compel government to protect a given heritage asset, (ii) no right to information concerning implementation of laws, (iii) no tax deductions for citizen expenses related to public interest advocacy (which contrasts with deductions allowed for private property interest advocacy and promotion), and (iv) no citizen rights to oppose "blatantly illegal" acts of governments harmful to a heritage interest.

The resolution of these issues, rooted as most are in private rights in property, cannot be expected to lie entirely in legal reforms, fruitful as those would be. Changes in public attitudes and policies must also be sought, particularly at local levels where the largest repertoire of heritage assets is located. In addition, changes to federal tax laws, particularly incentives such as have been introduced in the United States, would significantly increase private sector interest and motivations in historical preservation. Development rights transfer, mixed use zoning, and urban design bonusing are coming into use. Recent experience would suggest, too, that enlarged joint public-private funding of preservation and restoration projects offers a promising avenue to achieving heritage goals.

FUTURE THRUSTS AND DIRECTIONS

Planning in Canada arose in the early 1900s out of twin ideational movements: resources conservation and wise use and urban social reform. For a long time it was missionary in its character and application. Today planning will be seen more as a complex set of public institutional responses, frequently mechanistic, designed to accommodate changing economic and demographic conditions and to regulate land development. This is not to say that new ideational themes, new technologies, or even renewed societal visions will not find a place at one or other locus of Canadian planning practices, only that planning is now solidly institutionalized and therefore bureaucratically established with a life of its own.

Generally the early ideals of planning are today more co-opted than resisted by social values and conventions. And planning activities are now closely governed by political authority in their purpose, scope, and style. Thus, future thrusts in planning are being shaped equally by forces internal to modern institutions and by the settlement and economy trends that so far have escaped the control, attention, or ethical orientation of these institutions.

The more influential of these newly perceived directions are the following:

—A slowing down of the growth of major urban centers with significant dispersal of populations to rural lands and small communities (a U.S. trend as well; see Robinson, 1981)

—An accentuating degradation, wasteful management, and faltering renewal of natural resources, such as agricultural lands and forests

—General economic depression and localized stagnations, leading to constrained or reduced budgets for planning and implementation and producing sectoral attitudes less enthusiastic about regulation and public intervention

—Energy-conscious value shifts combined with diminishing real personal incomes, leading to a popular search for more home-based leisure and recreation opportunities

—The high-technology revolution, with implications for both dispersed industrial location and decentralized information and decision capabilities

—With the recent passage of a 15-year period of crisis management land planning in a climate of economic boom and population surge, public planning institutions are repositioning functions and roles to embrace some of the shelved or forgotten themes of earlier planning, such as urban form and its three-dimensional design, urban-based food production, and heritage conservation.

In short, the trends and institutional changes will induce a mix of adaptations in types and techniques of planning while introducing new opportunities as well as acknowledged issues to be confronted. The land use conflicts and conservation issues arising from population dispersal and the new technologies economy, for example, suggest rather strongly a new emphasis of combined regional economic development strategy and regional resource and land planning. In this domain, because of the largely federally driven economy and the national interest in resource base, provincial and federal policy making will have to converge, and regional planning authorities will need strengthening in meaningful ways. Similarly, the crown lands resource base will become more and more the subject of integrated resource management and planning. My discussion of the Alberta approach illustrates this new thrust. It is conceivable that in the future, provincial and federal roles in this activity will become administratively unified on project bases. The growing Canadian and continental demands for water—and therefore major diversions affecting the interests of multiple jurisdictions—would hasten the movement of integrated resource planning toward this supraprovincial arrangement, as would, also, inevitable national efforts to resolve the mounting food production and agricultural lands degradation crisis.

Leisure, recreation, and mixed use planning are already on the rise, partly in response to energy and income factors. One new form of planning making an appearance in metropolitan centers is theme or character districts delineated over obsolescent waterfront and railway lands; examples are Montreal's canal corridor, Toronto's harbor front, Halifax's waterfront restoration, and Vancouver's False Creek. Quite apart from the substantive nature of these plans, two new aspects of planning are particularly relevant: the remodeling of zoning and land use instruments to fit concepts of layered and intermixed land or building uses and new techniques for long-term, sustained fluid planning in which multiple owners, including large private and public corporations, are partners. In this sense, planners and their institutions will be moving further in the direction of managers, negotiators, and information system designers. The other dimension of recreation planning is large-scale, day trip, and extended stay parks located close to major urban centers. Again, integrated resource planning is of paramount importance here.

As the energy factor of urban living and the persuasion of deregulation take further root (as they seem bound to), urban land use planning will undergo a change of character. Policy planning conceivably will assume more of a place, with guidelines, design frameworks conceived in three-dimensional form, and less rule-bound review and adjudication decision processes replacing reliance on zoning maps and regulations. This new thrust is already evident in central areas redevelopment, and it appears feasible, if not desirable, for the planning and development of new districts where innovative community forms ought to be invited and tested. In parallel, three-dimensional (as opposed to planar land use) planning takes on greater importance to the degree that heritage properties conservation and urban in-filling are demanded. Localized urban stagnation, energy factors, and the growing conservation ethos of Canada's urban populations undoubtedly will thrust upon public planners this return to one of the traditional arts of planning.

Finally, the high-technology factor in relation to planning technique and land use decisionmaking is important. Already integrated resource planning and land data monitoring are well advanced in simulation design and applications of computerized technology. It is foreseeable that communities, within major centers as well as those regionally dispersed, increasingly will seek autonomies of one degree or another in land and resource use decisions closely affecting them. This is already evident among native communities and in certain metropolitan centers. Small computer technologies make it possible to transfer into the hands of any community of interest, however small, information and data banks, decisionmaking models, impact analyses, graphic simulation of land form and spatial environments, and eventually simulated intelligence (models for replicating the logic of successful discoveries and problem solutions). As these technology transfers occur, radical alterations in planner training and the public processes of land use decision will accompany them. Such devolution of technique and knowledge capacity to communities in turn radically alters the balance of responsibility and power and ushers in a new phase of institutional development in planning.

NOTES

I wish to acknowledge the special assistance of Helen Heacock and Patricia Bond in documentary research and bibliographic compilation; Heather McGowan, Anne Johnston, Yasmin Lhada, and John Alley for word processing and production assistance; and Ira M. Robinson for advice and guidance.

1. An inventory and discussion of Canada's new towns planning, many of them in the category of resource towns, is provided in Pressman (1976). See also Stelter and Artibise (1982) and Robinson (1962, 1979) for discussion of resource towns planning and issues.

2. Industrialization concentrated in the central provinces of Ontario and Quebec; staples produced in the prairie regions and transported cheaply to eastern markets and ports. For discussion of Canada's settlement geography, see McCann (1982).

3. See Welch (1980) and Manning (1980).

4. The Constitution Act, 1981, was proclaimed in 1982. In addition to amending and incorporating the 1867 act, the constitution provides anew: a "Canadian Charter of Rights and Freedoms" and "Rights of the Aboriginal Peoples of Canada," procedures for constitutional amendments, measures for dealing with regional disparities, and a further conference (1983) on defining the rights of aboriginal peoples.

5. While municipalities may raise revenues and pay for indebtedness through property taxation and licenses, they cannot tax incomes. Nor do they operate on the basis of formula income tax sharing with either the province or the federal government.

6. Adams had been manager of the first garden city at Letchworth, England, and founder and first president of the British Town Planning Institute. His major work, *Rural Planning and Development*, was published by the commission in 1917.

7. The Town Planning Institute of Canada, predecessor of the Canadian Institute of Planners.

8. The constitutional legality of these grants and funding programs has often been questioned. Scott and Lederman (1972, 40) offer this opinion: "Also, even though the field of activity concerned may be legislatively within exclusive provincial jurisdiction, the Federal Government has conditions to its offer of grants-in-aid, and these conditions give it a certain regulatory influence. The prevailing opinion among constitutional experts has been these federal conditional grants are valid . . . the argument in favour of validity cuts both ways. The provinces likewise enjoy an equally broad spending power. It is our opinion that conditional grants and the guarantee of the loans of private mortgage lenders under the National Housing Act are valid exercises of the Federal Spending Power."

9. Originally the Central Mortgage and Housing Corporation. The CMHC is a crown corporation, an agent of the federal government that enjoys substantial independence and is governed by an appointed board of directors. CMHC reports directly to Parliament (through the minister of public works).

10. See Leonard Marsh, "On Housing and Community Planning" in Oberlander

(1976). Marsh gives a good summary account of the report and assesses its impact on planning affairs.

11. For a more complete discussion of the federal-CMHC role and influence in urban planning and the nuances of its impact, see "A Retrospective Look at Canadian Planning and Development" in Perks and Robinson (1979); also see Oberlander (1976) and Lithwick (1970).

12. Other measures are the ratio of planners to the Canadian population: 3 per million in 1950, 32 in 1967, and 64 in 1977; and the number of university planning education programs: in 1947, one school and one professorial post, five programs in 1963, 10 in 1977, and 16 in 1983 (does not include diploma programs in community or technical colleges). See Perks (1980).

13. See Weisman (1977) for a history of planning legislation; also see Fitzpatrick (1982) and Makuch (1983).

14. The National Capital Commission (established 1958 by act of Parliament) is the successor agency to the Ottawa Improvement Commission (established 1899) and the Federal District Commission (established 1927). The NCC is empowered to "prepare plans for and assist in the development, conservation and improvement of the National Capital Region." Unlike many other capital agencies in a federal state the NCC does not govern or fully control planning and development. The NCC and predecessors have since 1899 provided a model of land use planning, civic design, and conservation works for Canadian municipalities. See Fullerton (1974) for a discussion of planning history and jurisdictional concerns. See National Capital Commission (1982) for a synopsis of land use plans and development and improvement schemes from 1899 to present.

15. Author's translation; *La Loi Sur l'Amenagement et l'Urbanisme*. For the full text, see Quebec (April 1981). Two other publications can be consulted: Quebec (1981), an explanatory document on what is a development scheme and how to go about preparing one; and Quebec (1980) which explains procedures for adopting or modifying plans and regulations.

16. Revised statutes of Quebec, 1964 (Ch. 193) and 1977 (Ch. C-19). The LAU repeals certain articles of the Cities and Towns Act.

17. Author's translation: *Le Schema d'amenagement*.

18. The chairman and vice-chairman of the commission are appointed by the government for terms up to five years; two are appointed after consultation with representative municipal associations. Members serve full time.

19. Author's translation: *Loi sur la Protection du Territoire Agricole*, proclaimed 1978-11-09.

20. *Commission de Protection du Territoire Agricole au Québec*. The commission's decisions may be upset only by the minister of agriculture, fisheries and food or an appeal court.

21. As Denhez remarks, however, "Canadian heritage sites are not owed the same attention Canada legally owes to, say, the Statue of Liberty or Big Ben" (Denhez, 1978, 78).

22. Denhez (1978) lists the Acts: Alberta: Historical Resources; British Columbia: Heritage Conservation; Manitoba: Historic Sites and Objects; New Brunswick: Historic Sites Protection; Newfoundland: Historic Objects, Sites and Records; Prince Edward Island: Recreation Development, and Archaeological Investigation; Quebec: Cultural Property; Saskatchewan: Heritage, and Provincial Parks, Protected Areas, Recreation Sites and Antiquities.

23. See "Issues and Challenges," below, for further critique and mention of issues respecting Heritage land use.

24. The IBP officially ended in 1974. The task of completing the work in Canada was sponsored by the federal government, first through the Associate Committee for Ecological Reserves and subsequently the Advisory Committee on Canadian Ecosystem Conservation.

25. See Revel (1981) for a list and description of proposed northern ecological sites. Some 150 sites have been identified and documented, but so far only one has been designated by the federal government.

26. Announced in February 1984. The corporation's mandate is to encourage natural habitats preservation and help prevent their destruction. Federal government funding is currently $2 million. There is an expectation that private-sector funding will follow.

27. See, for example, Social Science Research Council of Canada (1974) and Perks (1979).

28. Canada's universities were among leading innovators in this field. In 1969, York University established the first interdisciplinary faculty-based program in environmental studies in which the unifying curriculum was planning. A new and similar faculty concept, environmental design, was begun in 1971 at the University of Calgary. The University of Waterloo united various departments under a major environmental studies faculty. Variations and adaptations of these three models appeared subsequently in several other universities, colleges, and teaching and research institutes. See Perks (1980).

29. See Alberta, Energy and National Resources (1983).

30. Figures and other information in this discussion on crown lands are taken, for the most part, from Working Paper No. 27, Lands Directorate, Environment Canada, August 1983.

31. Committee composed of ministers of agriculture, northern affairs and environmental management, municipal affairs, natural resources, highways and transportation, and energy and mines.

32. From the Canada Treasury Board *Administrative Policy Manual*, December 1980, cited in Canada, Environment, (1983, 64).

33. Between 1871 and 1923, a series of treaties were signed between Indian peoples in the prairie provinces, the Northwest Territories, and Ontario. By treaty the government provided reserves for Indian bands, cash payments, and other continuing services and benefits "in return for the relinquishment of the native interest in the land" (Canada. IAND, 1978, 2). In some jurisdictions, however, not all Indians entered into a treaty. In these instances, provincial planning enactments would be expected to apply.

34. The Cree Indians were being displaced and otherwise affected in the enjoyment of lands by the gigantic James Bay hydroelectric project.

35. The Nishga Indians lost their land claim legal battle by a split decision on a technical point, but six judges acknowledged the existence of aboriginal title. For a discussion of how and why the Canadian government and the native people moved to a process of negotiated settlements and away from the legal arena, see Canada, Indian Affairs and Northern Development (1981, 1982).

36. This land figure applies to two claims only, both in the territories north of latitude 60. For all other claims, no land area has yet been decided upon. The number of claims listed in Canada, Indian Affairs and Northern Development (1981), is 17; five have since been added. Personal communication, Sandra Smart, IAND; May 1984.

37. The Agricultural Rehabilitation and Development Act (ARDA, 1959); successor

legislation and departmental arrangement was Department of Regional Economic Expansion; see Webster (1979) for policy and approaches discussion.

38. See, for example, Perks (1964, 1965) for discussion of how regional development planning emerged from the ARDA program.

39. Other sources consulted for this section include Gierman (1981), Pierce and Thie (1981), and Rees (1979).

40. The Departments of Environment and Indian and Northern Affairs administer the program.

41. Limitations of space have dictated the selection presented here and the depth of discussion. Other issues and challenges have been referred to implicitly in preceding sections of this chapter. See also Blumenfeld (1976). He discusses such Canadian planning issues as settlement distribution, urban-rural land competition, land use and transportation, planners, and public and private interest in lands.

42. In 1967, a government study of the Niagara escarpment, followed in 1968 by the appointment of Len Gertler and a study team of planners and geographers; in 1970, the creation of the Niagara Regional Municipality; in 1972, an interministerial task force on the Niagara escarpment; in 1973, the Niagara Escarpment Planning and Development Act and a 17-member permanent commission; in 1977, the Ontario Food Land Guidelines policy.

43. From *Globe and Mail*, 23 March 1984, citing a memorandum issued by the British Columbia deputy minister of forests. A University of British Columbia forestry professor describes the present situation as a "gang rape" of the forests.

44. Ibid.

45. Thus far, there are no opportunities for planning students to gain full training and academic accreditation in preservation heritage planning in Canada. More important, there is no agreement on the nature of the field or the training required. Currently, the faculty of environmental design, University of Calgary, offers an informal program in historic resource management.

BIBLIOGRAPHY

Alberta. 1983. *Planning Act*. Revised Statutes of Alberta 1980, Chapter P-9. Edmonton.

Alberta. Energy and Natural Resources. 1983. *A System for Integrated Resource Planning in Alberta*. Edmonton.

Berger, Thomas R. 1977. *Northern Frontier, Northern Homeland: The Report of the MacKenzie Valley Pipeline Enquiry*. Vol. 1, 2. Toronto: James Lorimer & Co.

Blumenfeld, Hans. 1976. *Canadian Planning Issues*. Ottawa: Canadian Institute of Planners.

Brody, Hugh. 1981. *Maps and Dreams: A Journey into the Lives and Lands of the Beaver Indians of Northwest Canada*. Penguin Books.

Canada. 1966. *Report of the Advisory Commission on the Development of Government in the Northwest Territories*. Vol 1. Ottawa: Queen's Printer.

Canada. Department of Regional Economic Expansion. 1969. *Land Capability for Outdoor Recreation*. Canada Land Report No. 6.

Canada. Environment. 1976. *Land Capability for Agriculture Preliminary Report*. Canada Land Inventory Report No. 10. Lands Directorate, April.

Canada. Environment. 1978. *Objectives, Scope and Organization*. Canada Land Inventory Report No. 1. Lands Directorate.

Canada. Environment. August 1979. *Prince Edward Island Land Development Corporation: Activities and Impact 1970–1977.* Land Use in Canada Series, No. 16.

Canada. Environment. 1980. *The Report of the Interdepartmental Task Force on Land-Use Policy.* Land Use in Canada Series. Lands Directorate.

Canada. Environment. 1982. *Agricultural Land Use Change in Canada: Process and Consequences.* Land Use in Canada Series No. 21. Lands Directorate.

Canada. Environment. 1983. *Environment Update.* Vol. 4, no. 4.

Canada: Indian Affairs and Northern Development. 1978. *Native Claims: Policy, Processes and Perspectives.* Ottawa.

Canada. Indian Affairs and Northern Development. 1981. *In All Fairness: A Native Claims Policy.* Ottawa.

Canada. Indian Affairs and Northern Development. 1982. *Outstanding Business: A Native Claims Policy.* Ottawa.

Canada. Minister of State for Urban Affairs. 1976. *Human Settlement in Canada.* Ottawa.

Canada. Supply and Services. 1979. *Revised Guide to the Federal Environmental Assessment and Review Process.* Ottawa.

Canada. Supply and Services. 1980. *Environmental Assessment Panels: What They Are, What They Do.* Ottawa.

Canada. Supply and Services. 1981. *Canada Year Book 1980–81.* Ottawa.

Carver, Humphrey. 1976. *Passionate Landscape.* Toronto: University of Toronto Press.

Dais, Eugene E. 1979. Development Control in Calgary: The Case of the Fortuitous Hybrid. In William T. Perks, and Ira M. Robinson, eds. *Urban and Regional Planning in a Federal State: The Canadian Experience.* Toronto: McGraw-Hill-Ryerson.

Denhez, Marc. 1978. *Heritage Fights Back.* Toronto: Fitzhenry and Whiteside.

Drury, C. M. 1980. *Constitutional Development in the Northwest Territories.* Report of the Special Representative. Ottawa.

Fitzpatrick, Gerald W. 1982. Planning Legislation and the Developed World: The Canadian Experience, Unpublished Paper. Nicosia: Commonwealth Association of Planners, June.

Fullerton, Douglas H. 1974. *The Capital of Canada: How Should It Be Governed?* Vol. 1. Ottawa: Information Canada.

Gierman, D. M. 1981. *Land Use Classification for Land Use Monitoring.* Working Paper No. 17. Ottawa: Lands Directorate, Environment Canada.

Lithwick, N. H. 1970. *Urban Canada: Problems and Prospects.* Ottawa: Central Mortgage and Housing Corporation.

McCaig, J. D., and E. W. Manning. 1982. *Agriculture Land-Use Change in Canada: Process and Consequences.* Ottawa: Lands Directorate, Environment Canada.

McCann, L D., ed. 1982. *A Geography of Canada: Heartland and Hinterland.* Scarborough: Prentice-Hall Canada.

Makuch, Stanley M. 1983. *Canadian Municipal and Planning Law.* Toronto: Carswell Co.

Manning, E. W. 1980. Issues in Canadian Lands Use. Working Paper No. 9. Ottawa: Lands Directorate, Environment Canada.

Marshall, I. B. 1982. *Mining, Land Use and Environment.* Land Use in Canada Series No. 22. Ottawa: Lands Directorate, Environment Canada.

Murchie, Graham David Stuart and Neil Taylor. 1978. *Planning in Alberta: A Guide and Directory.* Edmonton: Department of Municipal Affairs.

National Capital Commission. 1982. *A Capital in the Making: Reflections of the Past, Visions of the Future*, Ottawa, June.

Nicholson, E. M. 1968. *Handbook to the Conservation Section of the International Biological Programme*. IBP Handbook No. 5. Oxford: Blackwell.

Northern Pipeline Agency. 1980. *Alaskan Highway Gas Pipeline*. British Columbia Public Hearings. 18 vols. Vancouver and Calgary: Northern Pipeline Agency.

Oberlander, H. Peter, ed. 1976. *Canada: An Urban Agenda*. Ottawa. Community Planning Press and ASPO Press.

Perks, William T. 1964. Quebec: What Future for Rural Regions? *Community Planning Review* 14, 1.

Perks, William T. 1965. Towards a Regional Development Policy. *Town Planning Review* 36, 3.

Perks, William T. 1979. Public Lands and Prospects of a Canadian Urbanism. In William T. Perks, and Ira M. Robinson, eds. *Urban and Regional Planning in a Federal State: The Canadian Experience*. Toronto: McGraw-Hill-Ryerson.

Perks, William T. 1980. Planning Education: One Way or Another. *Ekistics* 47, 285 (November–December).

Perks, William T., and Patricia Bond. 1983. *Calgary Residential Land Supply 1982*. Ottawa: Canada Mortgage and Housing Corporation.

Perks, William T., and Ira M. Robinson. 1979. A Retrospective Look at Canadian Planning and Development. In William T. Perks and Ira M. Robinson, eds. *Urban and Regional Planning in a Federal State: The Canadian Experience*. Toronto: McGraw-Hill-Ryerson.

Peterson, E. B. 1975. Development of a Selection Criteria for Ecological Reserves. In *The Legal Aspects of Ecological Reserve Creation and Management in Canada*, ed. R. T. Franson. IUCN Environmental Policy and Law Paper, No. 9. Morges, Switzerland.

Pierce, T. W., and J. Thie. 1981. Land Inventories for Land Use Planning in Canada. In G. Peterson and M. Beatty, eds. *Planning Future Land Uses*. American Society of Agronomy Special Publication No. 42.

Pressman, Norman E. P. ed 1976. New Communities in Canada. University of Waterloo, Special Issue of *Contact*, 8(3), August.

Quebec. 1978. *Loi sur la Protection du Territoire Agricole*. November.

Quebec. 1980. *Procedure d'Adoption et de Modification d'un Plan ou de Reglements de'Urbanisme*. Quebec: Department of Municipal Affairs, December.

Quebec. 1981. *La Loi sur l'Amenagement et l'Urbanisme: Table des matieres et index analytique*. Quebec: Department of Municipal Affairs, April.

Quebec, 1983. *Le Schema d'Amenagement*. Quebec: Department of Municipal Affairs.

Rawson, Mary. 1976. *Ill Fares the Land: Land Use Management at the Urban, Rural, Resources Edges: The British Columbia Land Commission*. Ottawa: Minister of State for Urban Affairs and Mcmillan Company of Canada.

Rees, W. E. 1979. The Canada Land Inventory and Its Impact on Regional Planning. In William T. Perks and Ira M. Robinson, eds. *Urban and Regional Planning in a Federal State: The Canadian Experience*. Toronto: McGraw-Hill-Ryerson.

Reid, Ian. 1977. *Land in Demand: The Niagara Escarpment*. Agincourt, Canada: Book Society of Canada Ltd.

Revel, Richard D. 1981. Conservation in Northern Canada: International Biological Programme Conservation Sites Revisited. *Biological Conservation* 21:263-87.

Robinson, Ira M. 1962. *New Industrial Towns on Canada's Resource Frontier*. Chicago: University of Chicago Press.

Robinson, Ira M. 1979. Planning, Building, and Managing New Towns on the Resource Frontier. In William T. Perks and Ira M. Robinson eds. *Urban and Regional Planning in a Federal State: The Canadian Experience*. Toronto: McGraw-Hill-Ryerson.

Robinson, Ira M. 1981. *Canadian Urban Growth Trends: Implications for a National Settlement Policy*. Human Settlement Issues 5, Center for Human Settlements. Vancouver: University of British Columbia Press.

Rump, Paul C. 1983. Land Inventories in Canada. Unpublished paper, Canadian Association of Geographers, McMaster University, Hamilton, Ontario, nos. 2-3, 1983.

Rump, Paul C. n.d. Land Use Monitoring in Canada, Ottawa. Distributed papers, Lands Directorate, Environment Canada.

Schubert, J. S. 1978. *Computer Processing of Landsat Data for Canada Land Inventory Land Use Mapping*. Canada Land Inventory Report No. 13. Lands Directorate, Environment Canada.

Scott, F. R., and W. R. Lederman. 1972. A Memorandum Concerning Housing, Urban Development and the Constitution of Canada. *Plan Canada*, 12, 1.

Social Science Research Council of Canada. 1974. *Canadian Public Land Use in Perspective*. Symposium. Ottawa.

Stelter, Gilbert A., and Alan F. J. Artibise. 1982. Canadian Resource Towns in Historical Perspective. In Gilbert A. Stelter and Alan F. J. Artibise, eds. *Shaping the Urban Landscape*. Ottawa: Carleton University Press.

Union of British Columbia Indian Chiefs. 1980. *Final Submission on the Northeast British Columbia Land Use and Occupancy Study*. Vancouver.

Ward, E. Neville. 1976. *Land Use Programs in Canada: British Columbia*. Lands Directorate, Environment Canada, July.

Webster, Douglas. 1979. Development Planning: State of the Art and Prescription. In William T. Perks and Ira M. Robinson, eds. *Urban and Regional Planning in a Federal State: The Canadian Experience*. Toronto: McGraw-Hill-Ryerson.

Weinstein, Martin. 1976. *What the Land Provides: An Examination of the Fort George Subsistence Economy*. Montreal: Grand Council of the Crees.

Weisman B. 1977. Provincial Planning Legislation in Canada 1912-1975. Unpublished paper, School of Community and Regional Planning, University of British Columbia.

Welch, David M. 1980. *For Land's Sake!* Ottawa: Lands Directorate, Environment Canada.

19

United States of America

RICHARD H. JACKSON

Land use, planning practices, and land-related issues in the United States reflect the historical development of the country from a preindustrial agrarian society to a mature industrial society moving to the postindustrial age. The practices and issues that affected the United States during most of its history reflected an abundance of land with minimal planning or regulation of land use. The practices of planning by communities largely date from the post–1900 era as the United States changed from a primarily rural to a primarily urban population. Between 1910 and 1920, according to the census definition, the population distribution changed from a majority resident in rural areas to a majority resident in urban areas. The demographic change coincided with the first nationwide concern for planning epitomized in the development of zoning regulations. Increasing urbanization in subsequent decades combined with the development of a strong environmental movement in the post–World War II era to increase concern for planning, has led to the present status of land use, planning, and regulation in the United States.

HISTORICAL DEVELOPMENT OF LAND USE PLANNING

The fundamental factor affecting U.S. land use planning centers around the prevalent view of private property rights, which developed during the settlement period of North America in the fifteenth and sixteenth centuries and represented a major break with the European experience the settlers had left behind. In feudal Europe, landownership was restricted to the ruling classes, because ownership of land was the basis of power, wealth, and position. Typically the European peasant was tied to a manorial system with little or no possibility of being anything other than a tenant farmer. The concept of universal landownership developed in the United States by these European settlers and their descendants was a major change from this pattern (Babcock and Bosselman, 1975). Landownership became nearly universal, and the abundance of land in the United States led to development of the concept of freehold tenure of land. Adoption of the system of township and ranges for surveying land made the land easily describable and hence transferable, introducing the concept of speculation to the private ownership of land in the United States. These two trends of universal ownership of land and ease of transfer of title underlie much of the attitude and resultant regulation that affects land in the United States even in the present. The ownership of land included rights to use that land in a manner determined by the owner. Unlike Europe, where the lord of the manor largely dictated the land use, in the United States the landowner was, and was viewed as, an independent and individualistic yeoman farmer (Smith, 1950).

The emergence and dominance of the idea that individual landownership and private property rights were sacrosanct affected the use of the land resource of the United States historically and to the present. Until the post–World War II era, the overwhelming acceptance of private property rights meant that there were few, if any, land use controls affecting the majority of the land of the country. The rural land was primarily controlled by the economic realities or perceptions that affected the individual property owner's activities. From colonial times, however, there were incipient land use controls related to land use in the colonial settlements. These early planning attempts restricted the location of noxious activities outside the community to protect residents from unhealthy nuisances (Reps, 1965). Location of tanneries, slaughterhouses, and other nuisance activities where they would not affect the community date from the 1600s. Of more importance in the long term was the adoption of a regular grid pattern plan for communities. The most important of these was that adopted by William Penn in establishing Philadelphia in 1783. The plan for Philadelphia consisted of a rectangular grid with streets 50 or 100 feet (about 15 or 30 meters) wide with a central square; this was the basis for most of the settlements beyond the Appalachian Mountains. The regular geometric grid of Philadelphia was applied across the United States with little variation, and this has affected land use in the urban sections of the United States until the present (Jackson, 1981). Although colonial towns never occupied as much as 1 percent of the inhabited area of the United States, they ultimately became the focus of the planning movement that has affected the country since the beginning of the twentieth century.

For the bulk of the land of the United States, the period from the Revolution until recently was primarily affected by the actions of the federal government regarding disposal, reservation, and management of the public land. At the end of the Revolution, the new nation of the United States had fewer than 4 million inhabitants. The 1790 census recorded 3,929,214 people with a population density of 11.7 per square kilometer (U.S. Bureau of the Census, 1981). Following the Revolutionary War, the new federal government acquired the lands formally claimed by the colonies, and actions concerning the disposal of these lands greatly strengthened the traditional view of private landownership with minimal control of land use.

The most important action of the new government was the enactment of the Ordinance of 1785. This ordinance provided the basic surveying system that divided land into townships of 6 miles (9.65 kilometers) square, subdivided into 36 sections of 640 acres (259 hectares). Initially land was sold at auction. Over the next century, the federal government enacted as many as 5,000 specific acts related to land disposal. Although only some 100 of these dealt with broad aspects of the public domain, the net effect of the government actions was to provide cheap or free land for prospective settlers and to facilitate speculation since the easily describable parcels of land simplified identification and exchange of property. As a result of the Ordinance of 1785 and subsequent federal actions, it became as easy to trade in land as in any other commodity (Rohrbough, 1968). The role of the federal government in regulating the land was minimal; it transferred the land into private ownership with no federal regulations to control its subsequent use.

The actions of the federal government regarding the lands of the United States have been divided into three broad time periods: a period of land disposal, a period of land reservation, and a period of land management (Clawson and Held, 1957). For the first century after the new nation's government had acquired title to the land of the original thirteen colonies, the prevalent action was disposal. Over time, increasingly liberal land disposition acts favored transferring the public lands into private ownership, culminating in the Homestead Act of 1862 when it became possible to obtain a 160-acre (64.75 hectare) farm for only a filing fee and five years of residence (Jackson, 1981). As immigration and natural increase led to increasing pressure on the land resource, the settlement frontier advanced into the marginal lands of the western United States, and a period of reservation of land began. The first public land reservation occurred in 1872 when what is now Yellowstone National Park was withdrawn because of its unique characteristics (Poffer, 1951). Subsequently large tracts of land in the western United States were reserved for forestlands, and between 1891 and 1909 over 73 million hectares of lands in the West were reserved as forestlands (Poffer, 1951).

During the early decades of the twentieth century, several attempts were made to withdraw the nonforested marginal lands of the West from the Homestead Program, culminating in passage of the Taylor Grazing Act in 1934. This bill authorized homesteading only on those areas suitable for agriculture and ended the process of federal disposal of lands. Withdrawal of the bulk of the federal domain from transfer to private use signaled a major change in the U.S. land ethic. The traditional public and private view of the land resource began to change from the popular perception of an infinite land base that needed minimal control, regulation, and management to the view that the land resource was not only finite but damageable through human actions. This change in view marked the beginning of the period of management of federal lands. The major federal agencies involved in managing the public land resource included the Bureau of Land Management, the Forest Service, and the National Parks Service, and these and other agencies were increasingly engaged in managing the public land for multiple uses. These uses included grazing, forestry, recreation, wildlife, watershed, mineral, and aesthetic related activities. In terms of the federal land, this dawning planning ethic culminated in the late 1960s and early 1970s with passage of the National Environmental Policy Act (NEPA) of 1969 and subsequent environmental actions relating to land and water resources (Moss, 1977).

The beginning of the planning ethic reflected in the change from public disposal to withdrawal to management of federal lands was reflected in attitudes toward private lands. The majority of land use controls in the United States are oriented to regulating private lands, and these regulations and the planning methodology on which they are based had its origin in the cities of pre-twentieth century America.

Regulation of Urban Land

At the same general time as the withdrawal of public lands from settlement began, another trend in urban land use addressed the organization and beautification of the city. From the time of the early plans of Penn for Philadelphia and Pierre L'Enfant for Washington, D.C., there had been an interest in the morphology of the city. The prime movers during the late nineteenth and early twentieth centuries included Frederick Law Olmstead, who designed the construction of New York City's Central Park after 1857, and Daniel H. Burnham, who collaborated with Olmstead to design the 1893 World's Columbian Exposition in Chicago commemorating the discovery of America. They produced a plan that included a focus of public buildings and public open spaces planned in relationship to one another. The world's fair was the first time that a large-scale area was constructed at one time on the basis of a unified design and a general plan. Although some critics argue that it focused on the city beautiful rather than the real needs of the public of the time, it represented the dawn of comprehensive planning in the United States.

While Olmstead, Burnham, and others were planning for parks and public buildings, the great migration of people to the United States fostered rapid urban growth. With little or no control over such growth and with large numbers of migrants and laborers to house, urban living conditions for America's poor were intolerable. The social reforms that these conditions prompted led to the first effective planning and land use regulations designed to upgrade housing quality in low-income neighborhoods. Land use regulations affecting tenements were upheld by the U.S. Supreme Court in 1877. The court stated, "When therefore, one devotes his property to a use in which the public has an interest, he, in effect, grants to the public an interest to that use and must submit to be controlled by the public for the common good, to the extent of the interest he has thus created'' (So et al., 1979).

Adoption of the concept that the costs to society of crowded unhealthful slums justified imposition of regulations on private land and its use marked the beginning of widespread land use regulation. Recognition that an individual is free to pursue private actions only insofar as they do not harm others justified regulation of density of tenement housing and subsequent land use regulations in the United States. The need to protect the welfare of the public is the predominant justification for existing land use regulation in the United States. The earliest communities in the United States based their regulation of land use on English common law, which prohibited nuisance activities such as bad odors or noise, but because these were limited by the need to deal with them on a case-by-case basis, there emerged in the United States the concept of zoning, which was and is the major method of land use regulation.

Zoning: Tool of Land Use Planning

The extension of nuisance regulation to the concept of use of the police power held by a governing body to regulate all aspects of land use is embodied in zoning regulations. The first U.S. zoning laws were developed in Washington, D.C., Los Angeles, and Boston and regulated land use or size of building (Williams, 1966). The rights of cities to regulate use and size of buildings were upheld in 1909 when the U.S. Supreme Court ruled in the favor of a Boston ordinance affecting height of buildings and their use (Fordham, 1974). In 1909, the city of Los Angeles divided its industrial land into seven districts and retained the balance of the community as residential land, providing the first true zoning of land use. The first comprehensive zoning ordinance was created in New York City and adopted in 1916. The commission that drafted New York's comprehensive zoning ordinance enacted specific requirements for land use districts, area or lot coverage, and height of buildings. By 1922 zoning had spread rapidly, and 20 states had passed enabling acts granting the cities power to zone, 50 cities had adopted similar ordinances, and 100 were in progress of developing zoning ordinances (Haar, 1959).

The rapid adoption of zoning as a means of regulating land use led to its challenge in the famous *Ambler* v. *Euclid* case heard by the U.S. Supreme Court in 1926. The village of Euclid, Ohio, a suburb of Cleveland with fewer than 10,000 people, adopted a zoning ordinance in 1922 that divided the community into six land use districts, three classes of height districts, and four classes of area districts. The Ambler Realty company challenged the constitutionality of zoning on the basis that it violated the Fourteenth Amendment to the Constitution, which protects against properties being taken without due process of law. The Supreme Court ruled that communities have the power to adopt and enforce regulations and laws to further the general welfare of the community as part of the general police power and concluded that zoning was part of that power. With this mandate from the Supreme Court, by the end of 1927, 45 states had adopted legislation enabling community zoning, and by the end of 1930 all states had granted authority to zone to municipalities (Haar, 1959). So-called Euclidian zoning became and remains the basis for both land use planning and regulation of private property in communities. Its adoption at the county level followed a similar pattern as the widespread adoption of the automobile and resultant suburban sprawl after World War II led to the beginning of widespread adoption of zoning at the county level. Although not as ubiquitous as Euclidian zoning at the community level, county zoning is now the rule in essentially all counties where there is a large urban area and related suburban land pressures on agricultural lands.

Planning and Euclidian Zoning

The majority of the enabling acts adopted by state legislatures granting municipalities the power to zone were based on the Standard State Enabling Act published by the U.S. Department of Commerce in 1926. The key elements of the Enabling Act are its grants of power to municipalities for the purposes of promoting health, safety, morals, or the general welfare of the community; and the right to divide the city into districts (zones) and to regulate and restrict the area, use, and density of construction in each district in accordance with a comprehensive plan. The important aspects of the enabling acts were in granting control over height, bulk, and area of buildings constructed. Justification for such controls was the need to minimize problems of congestion of people and traffic, fire hazard, or loss of access to sunlight and to provide urban services to promote the general public welfare. The standard Enabling Act required that zoning regulations be based on a comprehensive plan, and in practice it was assumed that the act of zoning by a city implied that the city had developed a comprehensive plan on which to base the zoning ordinance. In actuality, however, most community planning tended to consist of only a map showing different districts or zones. In order for zoning ordinances to be enforceable, they must meet the following minimum requirements:

1. Zoning ordinances must meet requirements of the nation's constitution and must conform to the state enabling act.
2. Zoning requirements must be uniform within a zone, and there must exist a reasonable basis for classifying a particular zone as different from surrounding areas.
3. Zoning should apply to the entire city, not to restricted parcels of land.
4. Regulations must be reasonable as applied to a specific parcel of land and provide a reasonable use of that property.

Implementation of zoning ordinances was handicapped by interpretation of *reasonable use*, or the question of the most appropriate use of lands. Attempting to answer these questions and reflecting them in the zoning ordinance and the plan on which it is based often created opposition between landowners and the governing body. The idea of regulation of land use inherent in zoning conflicted with the individualistic view of private landownership and was often viewed as unfair or illegal interference with private property rights. Numerous legal challenges to planning and regulation for private land since the *Euclid* v. *Ambler* case have consistently supported the legality of zoning, and it remains the primary tool for implementing planning in the United States (Mandelker, 1982).

As commonly adopted, zoning ordinances emphasized use districts and their separation, generally into business, industrial, and commercial districts. Justification for such action was the separation of noncompatible activities from one another to protect the public. In some instances, zoning has been used to exclude different economic, ethnic, or racial groups from a neighborhood through prevention of multiple-unit housing or minimum floor area or lot size requirements. From the standpoint of the middle-class home owner, such actions are justifiable to protect property values. From the community level, they are justified as necessary to protect the tax base of the community. In consequence, zoning has been the focus of criticism and related efforts to create a more equitable means of planning and controlling land use.

Changes in Zoning, 1930–1980

The most widespread change affecting land use planning and zoning in the past half-century has been the increasing use of comprehensive planning as a basis for zoning regulations. Although implicit in the original zoning ordinances, the existence of a comprehensive plan to guide and regulate the rate of land use development is primarily a function of the post–World War II period. Prior to this time, large cities such as New York, Chicago, and Los Angeles developed comprehensive plans, but most communities adopting zoning ordinances initially did not prepare anything but fragmentary plans (So et. al, 1979). As long as the majority of the population resided in small communities, the broad zones of residential, commercial, and industrial use were adequate. Population growth and increasing urbanization rates led to greater emphasis on the need for planning in the mid-twentieth century. Suburbanization combined with the aging of the central cities fostered plans to revitalize downtown areas, culminating in the federal government's provision of planning assistance in the form of financial grants for the preparation of community renewal plans. Specific federal programs such as section 701 of the Housing Act of 1954 made funds available for preparation of comprehensive plans at the metropolitan, state, and regional scales. The availability of federal money to fund planning was one of the major forces stimulating comprehensive planning. Later federal actions relating to the environment, such as the National Environmental Policy Act of 1969, directly and indirectly affected planning and land use on private lands. This act affects local land use since it required that federal actions causing a significant land use impact must have an environmental impact statement prepared. The regulation and control of private land uses is indirect, but through decisions on timing and location of federal actions, local land use decisions are affected. Other federal controls include the Clean Air and Water Acts, the Coastal Zone Management Act, and the federal flood plain insurance program. These programs require comprehensive planning in order for localities and individuals to qualify for federal funding for land use–related activities (Moss, 1977).

Although the comprehensive plans are advisory in most areas of the United States, their existence is an important aspect of the planning process. The preparation of the comprehensive plan provides an inventory of existing land use, an analysis of potential problems, and a broad guideline or master plan for the direction of land use in the future. In some states, individual municipalities have made the comprehensive plan a mandatory part of the use and regulation of land. Typically such regulations require that no zoning change or land use conflict with the comprehensive plan or its goals. In a few states, most notably Oregon, zoning ordinances must conform to a comprehensive plan (Mandelker, 1982). Although the comprehensive plan is not legally the basis for planning and regulating land use in most states, public involvement in the preparation of such a plan focuses the attention of the local legislative body on the goals and concerns of community members concerning land use.

Development of federal support for land use planning in the post–World War II era has been partially paralleled by a concern for planning and regulation of land at the state level. All states have regulations providing for zoning regulation, and all states have a state agency or agencies, program, or regulations affecting some types of land use activities. Few states have comprehensive land use planning legislation or a state planning agency to handle all aspects of land use. The fragmentation of state control and problems created by large-scale developments whose impact overlaps municipal boundaries has increased interest in statewide planning (Council of State Governments, 1976). Factors prompting states to consider more actively controlling land use include the following (Healy, 1976):

1. When there are problems that cross the boundaries of existing levels of jurisdiction and do not confine themselves neatly to municipal or county entities
2. Where there are problems created from the actions of a local body that may result in a negative impact on the interests of the broader public
3. When there are lands that have limited local controls that do not effectively protect the land resource of the state
4. Problems or conflicts involving implementation of state policies or state funds

The emergence of statewide concern for land and the adoption of comprehensive state regulation is part of what is known as the quiet revolution (Bosselman and Callies, 1971). Fewer than one-fourth of the states have actually adopted comprehensive land use acts, and the extent of state regulation of land use planning varies widely. State requirements range from de facto statewide zoning of Hawaii, to California's regulation of the coastal zone, to Florida's regulation of activities that are statewide in impact affecting critical areas or are of regional impact, to Oregon's requirement for each community and county to have an approved comprehensive plan (Jackson, 1981). In practice in most states, statewide regulation is of secondary importance. Local planning and regulation of land use is the norm in the United States, with zoning or some modification of zoning as the major tool of land use planning.

INSTITUTIONAL AND LANDOWNERSHIP FRAMEWORK

The Planning Process in Practice

In practice, the planning and regulation process for land in the United States is relatively similar from one locality to another. Although the legislative body (city council, county commissioners, or state land Agency) is generally responsible for enacting the laws that affect land use planning and regulation, public and agency personnel, individuals, and groups are involved in the planning process. Typically the community prepares a comprehensive plan through the efforts of either the permanent planning staff or a hired consultant. The preliminary comprehensive plan is the basis for public meetings to obtain information on the various elements of land use, housing, transportation, and city infrastructure. This preliminary plan is then the subject of a public hearing to consider its adoption, and on its adoption by the legislative body it nominally becomes the basis for the zoning ordinance. The preliminary zoning ordinance generally is prepared by the planning staff in conjunction with legal counsel for the city or prepared by a hired consultant or in cases of small communities prepared by the citizen members of the planning commission. The zoning ordinance is discussed in public meetings and when adopted becomes the basis for regulating land use in the city.

Changes in the zoning ordinance generally can be undertaken at any time the legislative body of the community or county or state determines, although in some municipalities and states the time period for considering zoning changes may be restricted to a few periods per year. At the time of the public hearing to consider a change in the zoning ordinance, public participation is requested, and at that point the legislative body will decide on what changes to adopt in either the specific types of requirements for the various zones or in the special extent of existing zones. In most states, the public is invited to have a voice in the public hearing, and generally a citizen planning commission must also hear the issues in a public hearing, but with few exceptions the local governing body elected by the people decides on changes in the zoning ordinance. Once adopted, the zoning ordinance is rarely subject to wholesale changes; rather, the local legislative body makes adjustments to the boundaries of districts or adds or deletes requirements to the respective zones (Moss, 1977).

Individuals whose property has been zoned in a manner they feel unfairly limits its use can appeal to the board of adjustment. The standard state enabling act requires that where a planning commission and zoning ordinance exists, there be a board of adjustment to consider situations not anticipated by the ordinance. The board of adjustment hears appeals relating to variances and special exceptions. Variances are specifically described as a relaxation of specific zoning requirements such as amount of front yard setback or size of lot in a specific zone. The variance does not extend to permitting uses that are not allowed in the zone but rather are designed to ensure that where some physical attribute of the property is in question, not caused by the property owner or appellant, it does not prevent the use of that property for the purpose intended in that zone. Special exceptions are those cases where all other aspects of the zoning ordinances are met, but a special use such as a church, school, or airport is requested. Generally, these uses are not granted if it can be shown that they will negatively affect adjacent landowners. Boards of adjustment may also hear requests for conditional uses, which are specific uses allowable in a zone only if they meet certain conditions or allowable after conditions have been established to prevent their negative impact on the community. As a last resort, people who feel that the zoning ordinance discriminates against them can appeal to the courts to overturn or change the zoning ordinance.

Other Land Use and Planning Regulations

Subdivision regulations form another type of land use control in the United States. Subdivision regulations generally grow out of the zoning ordinance and enable the community to regulate the division of land and size of lots and street widths and other morphological aspects related to subdivision. Technically the subdivision regulations are supplemental to zoning and do not regulate land use, building placement, parking requirements, and so forth found in zoning ordinances (Smith, 1979). In practice, subdivision regulations may include a variety of controls affecting planning, including design characteristics and building materials.

A final form of planning, which is becoming increasingly important, is related to capital improvements in a community. The extent of city investment in new roads, water systems, sewer systems, or fire or police protection effectively controls the development of land in the community. In some cases this is handled as a direct part of the comprehensive planning process; in others the city reacts to demands for additional services and planning requirements are not met. Uses of capital improvements as a planning tool range from Ramapo, New York, where a capital investment budget adopted in 1969 tied approval for new development to the availability of services, to specifying reasonable boundaries beyond which the extension of public services will not occur. The technique of planning through directing or phasing capital improvements of a community is an important alternative tool for planning for orderly development of a community.

Ownership of Land

There are a total of 916,681,517 hectares of land in the United States. Of this land, roughly one-third (304 million hectares) is owned by the federal government (Table 19.1). The remaining two-thirds (approximately 612 million hectares) is in private ownership of some type (*National Agricultural Lands Study*, 1981). This land is primarily rural land, with roughly 5 percent of the total private land (28 million hectares) located in urban areas. The federal land is concentrated in the western United States, where Alaska, Nevada, Utah, Arizona, and Idaho have over two-thirds of their land in federal ownership (Table 19.2). The federal lands are administered primarily by the Bureau of Land Management and the U.S. Forest Service, which administer 189 million (60 percent) and 65 million (24 percent) hectares, respectively. The other large regulatory agencies include the National Parks Service (8 million hectares), the Bureau of Indian Affairs (1.7 million hectares), the Bureau of Reclamation (2.3 million hectares), and the Department of the Army (2.8 million hectares) (U.S. Department of the Interior, 1981). Most of the land in the federally owned sector is unsuitable for agriculture and consists of mountains and desert or heavily forested regions at high latitudes or high altitudes.

The privately owned land is divided into cropland, rangeland, and forestland. Cropland in 1977 comprised 167 million hectares; rangeland, 168 million hectares; forestland, 152 million hectares; and pastureland, 54 million hectares (Figure 19.1). The figures given for land in the various categories reflect the report of the official National Agricultural Land Study of 1981, but there is debate over the exact figures. The amount of land that is agricultural versus that which is urban depends on the definition of urban used. If all land within city limits is classified as urban, it incorporates some land used for agricultural purposes. If, as is more common, the boundaries of Metropolitan Statistical Areas (formerly Standard Metropolitan Statistical Areas) as defined by the census are used, a much greater extent of land is classified as urban than is actually used for urban uses. The Metropolitan Statistical Areas (MSA) are defined as a county with one city of 50,000 or more people or twin cities with 50,000 population. Such definition includes large quantities of agricultural land. The average land use in SMSAs (now MSAs) in 1970 is indicated in Table 19.3. It should be apparent that the majority of the land within the average SMSA is not in urban-related land uses. Only 10 percent of the land is devoted to urban activities, indicating that the actual figure for urban land is much smaller than commonly reported.

The uses of land that are truly urban can be subdivided in numerous ways, but the categories are generally residential, industrial, commercial, roads and highways, public or quasi-public uses, and vacant lands. The categories are self-explanatory except public or quasi-public, which includes community parks, community recreation areas, and quasi-public activities such as churches and schools. Figures on the division of land into these categories are misleading if

Table 19.1
The Land of the United States, 1980

State	Area					
	Land		Inland Water		Total	
	Square km	Hectares	Square km	Hectares	Square km	Hectares
Alabama	131,487	13,148,734	2,429	242,944	133,916	13,391,678
Alaska	1,478,457	147,846,660	52,243	5,224,321	1,530,700	153,070,982
Arizona	293,986	29,398,754	1,274	127,429	295,260	29,526,182
Arkansas	134,882	13,488,285	2,870	286,974	137,752	13,775,259
California	404,814	40,481,691	6,234	623,417	411,049	41,105,108
Colorado	268,311	26,831,271	1,285	128,465	269,596	26,959,736
Connecticut	12,618	1,261,856	381	38,073	12,999	1,299,929
Delaware	5,004	500,391	290	29,008	5,294	529,399
District of Columbia	163	16,317	16	1,554	179	17,871
Florida	140,256	14,025,714	11,683	1,168,356	151,940	15,194,070
Georgia	150,365	15,036,597	2,212	221,187	152,577	15,257,784
Hawaii	16,641	1,664,085	119	11,914	16,760	1,675,999
Idaho	213,447	21,344,840	2,986	298,629	216,433	21,643,469
Illinois	144,121	14,412,144	1,813	181,301	145,934	14,593,445
Indiana	93,064	9,306,445	655	65,527	93,719	9,371,973
Iowa	144,949	14,495,025	803	80,291	145,752	14,575,316
Kansas	211,805	21,180,633	1,292	129,242	213,097	21,309,875
Kentucky	102,743	10,274,334	1,917	191,661	104,659	10,465,995
Louisiana	115,309	11,531,010	8,366	836,575	123,675	12,367,585
Maine	80,277	8,027,755	5,879	587,934	86,156	8,615,688
Maryland	25,478	2,547,799	1,614	161,358	27,091	2,709,157
Massachusetts	20,264	2,026,429	1,191	119,141	21,456	2,145,569
Michigan	147,511	14,751,177	4,074	407,410	151,585	15,158,587
Minnesota	206,029	20,603,059	12,572	1,257,194	218,601	21,860,253
Mississippi	122,333	12,233,423	1,184	118,364	123,517	12,351,786
Missouri	178,568	17,856,865	1,948	194,769	180,515	18,051,635

State	Land		Inland Water		Total	
	Square km	Hectares	Square km	Hectares	Square km	Hectares
Montana	376,555	37,655,725	4,292	429,166	380,847	38,084,890
Nebraska	198,508	19,850,918	1,841	184,150	200,349	20,035,069
Nevada	284,625	28,462,722	1,728	172,754	286,353	28,635,476
New Hampshire	23,292	2,329,201	741	74,074	24,033	2,403,276
New Jersey	19,342	1,934,224	326	82,662	20,168	2,016,845
New Mexico	314,258	31,425,959	668	66,822	314,926	31,492,782
New York	122,706	12,270,719	4,483	448,332	127,190	12,719,051
North Carolina	126,503	12,771,110	9,909	990,940	136,413	13,641,355
North Dakota	179,487	17,948,811	3,634	363,379	183,121	18,312,190
Ohio	106,200	10,620,102	844	84,435	107,045	10,704,536
Oklahoma	177,816	17,781,755	3,370	336,961	181,136	18,118,716
Oregon	249,117	24,911,810	2,303	230,252	251,419	25,142,062
Pennsylvania	116,260	11,626,064	1,088	108,781	117,348	11,734,844
Rhode Island	2,732	273,247	407	40,663	3,139	313,910
South Carolina	78,226	7,822,625	2,354	235,432	80,580	8,058,058
South Dakota	196,716	19,671,690	3,015	301,478	199,730	19,973,167
Tennessee	106,591	10,659,211	2,562	256,153	109,153	10,915,363
Texas	678,624	67,862,822	12,406	1,240,613	691,030	69,103,440
Utah	212,569	21,257,038	7,319	731,939	219,888	21,988,977
Vermont	24,017	2,401,722	883	88,320	24,900	2,490,041
Virginia	102,833	10,283,400	2,753	275,319	105,587	10,558,718
Washington	172,263	17,226,455	4,214	421,396	176,477	17,647,851
West Virginia	62,468	6,246,860	290	29,008	62,758	6,275,868
Wisconsin	140,963	14,096,421	4,473	447,296	145,436	14,543,717
Wyoming	251,202	25,120,306	2,124	212,381	253,325	25,332,687
Total	9,166,755	916,681,517	205,856	20,585,709	9,372,613	937,267,220

Source: U.S. Department of the Interior, Public Land Statistics, 1981, p. 2.

511

Table 19.2

Federal Ownership of Land as a Proportion of State Area

State	Percent Federal	State	Percent Federal
Alabama	3.4	Nebraska	1.4
Alaska	96.4	Nevada	86.5
Arizona	44.0	New Hampshire	12.3
Arkansas	9.5	New Jersey	2.7
California	45.0	New Mexico	33.5
Colorado	36.1	New York	.8
Connecticut	.3	North Carolina	6.2
Delaware	3.0	North Dakota	5.2
District of Columbia	26.1	Ohio	1.3
Florida	9.9	Oklahoma	3.5
Georgia	6.0	Oregon	52.3
Hawaii	10.2	Pennsylvania	2.3
Idaho	63.7	Rhode Island	1.1
Illinois	1.6	South Carolina	6.0
Indiana	2.1	South Dakota	6.7
Iowa	.6	Tennessee	6.7
Kansas	1.3	Texas	1.9
Kentucky	5.3	Utah	66.2
Louisiana	3.7	Vermont	4.6
Maine	.7	Virginia	9.2
Maryland	3.2	Washington	29.5
Massachusetts	1.5	West Virginia	7.0
Michigan	9.3	Wisconsin	5.2
Minnesota	6.6	Wyoming	48.0
Mississippi	5.4		
Missouri	4.7		
Montana	29.6	TOTAL	33.5

Source: United States Department of the Interior,
         1981. Public Land Statistics, 1981.
         Washington: U.S. Government Printing Office.

512

Figure 19.1 America's Land Base, 1977

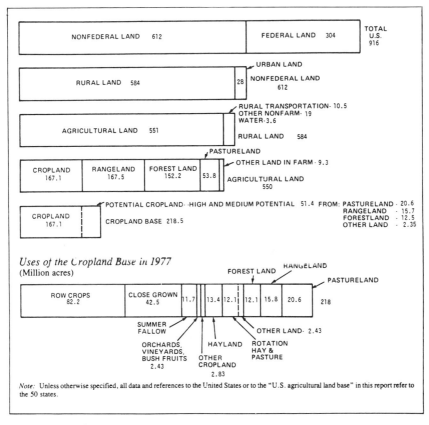

Note: Unless otherwise specified, all data and references to the United States or to the "U.S. agricultural land base" in this report refer to the 50 states.

Source: National Agricultural Lands Study, (Washington: U.S.
           Government Office, 1981) p. 9.

they are calculated for the entire MSA, but it is difficult to obtain reliable information on categories for only the central cities of the MSAs. The data in Table 19.4 provide some insight into the relative importance of the various types of land use in larger U.S. cities. Approximately one-third of the land in larger cities is devoted to residential use, and cities such as Los Angeles or other suburban communities developed around an automobile transport network have even higher percentages. Other land uses vary depending on the age, location, and economic activity of the city. Changes in the categories of land use occur as zoning changes take place at the local level.

Changes in ownership from public to private ownership are relatively infrequent in the United States. The public domain generally is maintained for public use, although at the present time there is some discussion of transferring unneeded and unused federal lands to private ownership. For all intents and purposes, the

Table 19.3
Land Use in Metropolitan Areas, 1970

Use	Hectares
Total	422,496
Urbanized	42,083
Rural	380,409
Cropland	101,173
Pasture and range	80,129
Forest and woodland	135,976
Other	63,132

Source: The Changing Issues for National Growth,

Washington, D.C.: Government Printing

Office, 1976, p. 80.

(Average land use for SMSAs in 48 states.)

Taylor Grazing Act in 1934 ended the transfer of land from public to private ownership. The federal government has recently been exchanging land with states in the West to consolidate state-owned and federally owned public lands into blocks large enough to be effectively managed, but obtaining federal lands for a private individual is nearly impossible at the present time.

CHANGES AND CHALLENGES TO LAND USE PLANNING

The challenges and changes affecting land use planning in the United States are a result of forces that have been changing the demands made on land and planning and regulating land use for the past two centuries. As the United States moved from a rural nation to an urban nation, the increasing concentration of people in small areas resulted in the first programs for land use planning. Continual growth coupled with increased mobility have changed the concerns from strictly zoning to separate types of incompatible land use, to concern for broader issues affecting the land resource of the country. The net effect has been to

Table 19.4
Average Land Use in 22 Cities

Use	Percent of Developed Land
Residential	39.8
Industrial	10.4
Commercial	5.0
Road and Highway	25.4
Other Public	19.3

Source: Urban Land Policies and Land-use Control

Measures, Vol. VI, Northern America. (New

York: United Nations, 1973), p. 136, Table

26.

expand the concern from zoning to environmental and social issues, affecting a gamut of land use issues from housing to agriculture.

At the local level, the changing demographic character of the population of the country as family sizes have decreased, more women have entered the work force, and the costs of land for building have increased while opportunities for leisure activities have increased proportionately have led to changes in zoning from the strict single-use zones. The emergence of zoning categories such as the planned unit development (PUD) provides for greater densities within residential zones through a form of negotiated zoning or performance zoning. The advantage of performance standards is that they free the community from the need to specify a specific site for an activity but allow activities to locate where they will not have a negative impact on the community (Jackson, 1981). Performance zoning allows construction at a greater density in return for which the developer provides more open space through clustering the residential units on part of the property while maintaining a larger area of common, open space and recreational area than is customarily found in the traditional single-family or multifamily development on an individually owned lot. PUDs involve planning for a larger plot of land as a unit, eliminating the conventional lot-by-lot approval requirement. Cluster zoning is a variant of PUDs, which specifically requires maintenance of open space. In the 1950s, single-family detached units accounted for more than 90 percent of new housing starts in the United States. By the 1980s this proportion had decreased to less than 50 percent (So et. al, 1979).

At the same time, the demand for greater density to reduce the cost of single-family homes fostered PUD or cluster zoning, many communities in suburban areas adopted large lot or other restrictive zoning ordinances that effectively excluded the poor from their neighborhoods. The challenges to communities caused by the rapid suburban growth in the form of additional demands for public services prompted some communities to regulate their growth, which culminated in the Supreme Court approval of the Petaluma, California, growth management plan in 1976. Faced with rapid growth from suburban pressure from San Francisco, Petaluma had adopted a growth management program based on limiting the number of building permits to 500 per year. The city was sued by property owners and developers who argued that this was a restriction of constitutional guarantees to freedom of travel. In supporting Petaluma's growth control management program, the Supreme Court ruled that Petaluma had not prevented growth, it had only acted to prevent growth from overwhelming the community's capabilities to provide services for that population.

Closely related to the problems and challenges presented to planners in rapidly growing suburban areas are the problems of the central city areas. As the oldest portion of the urban environment, these areas are faced with population losses. The growth of the suburbs largely reflects migration from the central city, and the population that is unable to move is increasingly composed of the elderly and the poor. Because poverty in the United States is much higher for non-Caucasian ethnic and racial groups, the central cities increasingly are becoming ghettos for the politically powerless and economically impoverished minority groups. This issue poses important challenges for planners as they are faced with the necessity to provide services for a population increasingly incapable of providing a tax base to maintain those services. The nature of the problems presented to planners in the central city of metropolitan regions can be classified as follows (Sternlieb and Hughes, 1976, 1978):

1. Racial and social problems associated with land use growing from the concentration of low-income and ethnic minorities in one section of a metropolitan area
2. Obsolescence of buildings, homes, industries, and commercial activities
3. Fiscal problems associated with declining commercial and industrial activity and decreased property values affecting taxes
4. Housing quality problems associated with obsolescent and deteriorated housing stocks
5. Population loss
6. Transport-related problems associated with the decline of public transportation
7. Loss of jobs as industries leave the old metropolitan areas.

The challenge to the metropolitan regions of the United States, particularly the older ones, created by the concentration of older, obsolete housing, industry, and commercial areas will remain a focus of attention for the foreseeable future. The challenge of renewing the central cities was part of the Housing Act of

1954, which gave such an impetus to planning in the United States, but to date the efforts of the 1954 and subsequent acts have been unable to reverse the general trend of urban decay of older central cities, which constitute such an important challenge to planners. The other end of the housing continuum is related to suburban areas where residents who have fled urban areas practice exclusionary zoning by placing restrictions on multifamily housing to prevent the perceived deterioration of the quality of life that attracted them to the suburbs. This tension between the largely white, middle-class Americans who desire to live in a suburban setting of single-family homes and the largely elderly and poor minorities who desire to have the same quality of life but cannot afford large single-family detached homes represents a major challenge for both local and regional interests. The most famous court ruling relating to exclusionary zoning involves Mount Laurel, New Jersey, a suburban community located just east of Philadelphia. The community had an abundance of vacant land zoned for single-family residential use and was challenged in court because such single-family zoning effectively excluded the poor population who could not afford such expensive housing. The New Jersey Supreme Court ruled in 1975 that Mount Laurel's zoning ordinance was invalid since it failed to provide for a fair share of the housing needs of the broader region. The court ruled that developing communities such as Mount Laurel needed to plan affirmatively and provide reasonable opportunities for a variety and choice of housing, including "low and moderate income housing by way of multi-family dwellings, town houses, mobile homes, small houses on small lots, . . . to meet the needs, desires, and resources of all classes of people who may desire to live within its boundaries" (Rose and Rothman, 1977, 41). In a society in which planning has generally been at the local level, problems presented by population shifts, shifts in the location of industries, and shifts in demand for public services result in an inefficient allocation of resources. The major challenge facing the United States will be to develop some type of regional planning that can effectively deal with the problems presented by the movement of population to the suburbs.

Closely related to these problems of city and suburb are those in nonmetropolitan areas (Platt and Macinko, 1983). Land use issues in these areas are different from those associated with city and suburb because they are occurring in areas often remote from the traditional source of city services. The demand for recreation lands in isolated areas of western states such as Arizona, New Mexico, Utah, Colorado, or Oregon; or the emergence of boom towns related to energy development in the West; or the sudden growth of rural towns that had historically experienced population loss pose new issues for planners. The challenges of growth in rural areas range from loss of agricultural land to remote subdivisions for recreation purposes, to boom towns based on resource extraction that subsequently suffer a bust leaving a relatively small population to repay the larger bonded indebtedness required by providing infrastructure during the boom years, to issues of providing basic services to residents of rural areas, to the need to deal with natural hazards in rural areas. Rural lands traditionally have received relatively little attention from planners in the United States since their problems have not been as pressing as those of the urban regions. From a planning standpoint, it is necessary to develop the techniques that will provide solutions to the unique problems that face such rural regions.

Another major area of challenge for planning in the United States at both the local and national levels centers around the perceived loss of farmland to suburbanization and rural and recreation developments. The Soil Conservation Service estimated in 1977 that 1.2 million hectares of cropland were converted to nonagricultural purposes annually in the years from 1967 to 1975 (U.S. Department of Agriculture, 1977). Other estimates place this figure at only 364,230 hectares per year, but the perception is that a significant portion of cropland is being lost to urban uses, necessitating a planning program to maintain the agricultural base of the country (Platt and Macinko, 1983).

Another issue for U.S. planners is the need to continue progress made in environmentally related land use questions affecting the quality of land, water, and air. The need to improve air and water quality and to prevent further deterioration of the land resource presents the problem of maintaining jobs while providing changes that will be environmentally beneficial.

Another challenge for planners is in the area of resource extraction. Strip-mining of lands to obtain resources results in thousands of hectares of land referred to as "land disturbed by surface mining." Much of the stripped land is associated with coal mining, and the present demand for energy makes planning for wise use of stripped land difficult. This is particularly a challenge at the national level where federal ownership of large tracts of energy and other resource-rich land poses important questions concerning private extraction of these resources. The perceived need to extract the finite resources is at variance with the public policy of maintaining the pristine quality of these lands.

Another area of concern is the need to ensure proper utilization of sensitive lands. Sensitive lands are defined as those that are subject to flooding, seismic activity, high water table, drought, severe erosion, avalanche, or other natural hazards. The Coastal Zone Management Act and the Flood Plain Insurance Act attempt to deal with elements of these concerns, but the continued loss of property from natural hazards indicates that these programs do not adequately plan and regulate land use in these sensitive areas.

The challenges that face planning in the United States generally revolve around the issues of public versus private interests or local versus regional, state, or national interests. The challenge at the national level is to provide a mechanism for planning and regulating those elements of local land use decisions that have an effect beyond the local level and to ensure that every individual has an adequate opportunity to share in the quality of life provided by the abundant land resource of the United States. There have been numerous attempts to create a national land use policy, but at present there is little interest in such a program. When the economy is struggling, programs that provide greater regulation are generally unpopular. At the state level, the need to provide state planning to protect state or regional interests from local actions is perhaps even more pressing. Several states have adopted mandatory statewide planning that mandates comprehensive planning based on concern for both local and statewide concerns. Many of these, most notably Vermont and Florida, have adopted elements of the model land use code published in 1976 by the American Planning Association. In the absence of either nationwide state land use planning programs or a nationwide planning program, the only regional planning direction has resulted from requirements of federal programs such as the National Environmental Policy Act of 1969, the Coastal Zone Management Act of 1972, the area-wide waste water planning provided by section 208 of the Water Quality Amendments of 1972, the river basin studies under the Water Resources Planning Act of 1965, and the quasi-zoning associated with the Clean Air and Water Act of 1970. The challenge for the future is to harmonize the demands of the environmentally concerned segment of society with the broader group that argues for nongovernment intervention.

CHANGING APPROACHES TO LAND USE PLANNING

In response to the challenges and issues facing the use of the U.S. land resource, traditional zoning and planning methods have been augmented. Although zoning is still the basis for most land use regulation, there has been an increasing effort to tie zoning to a comprehensive plan and to ensure that changes made in the zoning ordinance are consistent with both the comprehensive plan and with previous planning decisions (Mandelker, 1982). Modifications of traditional zoning are numerous and include the use of historic preservation zoning to maintain historic areas, transfer of development rights to allow the higher density requirements of one zone to be substituted to another, bonus or incentive zoning in which the provision of standards beyond the level of basic requirements of a zone may result in additional density or other benefits, and other efforts to make the zoning ordinance more responsive to the changing social and environmental issues of the 1980s (Jackson, 1981). In practice, the modifications to traditional Euclidian zoning are designed to deal with specific problems found in a particular area. The transfer of development rights enables a community to preserve open space in a unique or highly valued area such as a floodplain, while allowing developers to place greater density in a highly valued area such as a downtown region. Bonus and incentive zoning has been used to encourage developers to include housing in office buildings in residentially deficient areas of the downtown (Brown, 1982).

To meet problems presented by the loss of agricultural land or to preserve greenbelts around cities, the concept of preferential assessment of land has become an important tool to plan for land use. Under preferential use statutes, land that is maintained in a specified use is taxed at a value based on its use rather than its value. This enables farmers to maintain farms in the face of the pressure of suburbanization. Regulation of such taxation schemes is at the state level and generally requires that at such time as the land is converted to residential or other higher-density uses, at least some back payment of taxes is required. Such preferentially assessed lands must also meet the requirements of value of production or length of use for the specific activity.

The continuing concern for environmental issues related to land use has prompted the renewal of federal regulations concerning clean air and clean water. Efforts to deal with the problem of blighted central city areas continue to receive attention, primarily through programs aimed at either providing incentives for private development or funds to allow for planning or land acquisition to provide for recycling of the urban area, or through federal grants to restore historic buildings or to restructure them for alternative uses. Efforts to deal with the problems of urban sprawl and the migration of population to suburban communities have resulted in more communities adopting programs that manage the growth rate of the community.

In practice, efforts to modify land use regulation during the 1960s and 1970s did not always equal expectations of their advocates. Preferential assessment, while designed to allow farmers to continue their occupations in the face of mounting demand for land or to maintain open space, often provides simply a means for speculators to purchase land far in advance of its actual development and maintain it in quasi-rural uses without fear of higher taxes. The tax penalty required when these lands are converted is only a fraction of the taxes that would be paid if the taxes were based on land value rather than present land use (Jackson, 1981). Incentive zoning, designed to provide more amenities, has been criticized because the amenities installed (such as plazas in large office buildings) are inaccessible or of little use or because the incentive bonus has become almost a right rather than a privilege (Miller, 1982). Transfer of development rights was discussed as a revolutionary new breakthrough in controlling the use of land in the 1960s and 1970s, but purchase of development rights to maintain open space has proved prohibitively expensive. Development rights have been used primarily in the form of scenic easements; examples are the Appalachian Trail and the Sawtooth National Recreational Area of Idaho in which development rights on relatively low-value land were purchased to ensure that it will not be subdivided. Where there is a high demand for land, the cost of purchasing the development rights is generally prohibitive except on a small scale. Development rights transfer is being used in several areas to protect unique resources such as Lake Tahoe in California and Nevada through the concept of land trusts, where the land in question is donated to a trust established to maintain a specific characteristic. Purchase of development rights on farmland has been achieved on Long Island in New York (1,295 hectares purchased by 1978) and in Massachusetts where development rights on eight farms had been purchased by 1980 (Platt and Macinko, 1983). Development rights transfer has also been successfully applied in historic preservation in downtown areas of New York, Chicago, and other major cities. As practiced, a developer who owns a parcel of property that has been designated as a recipient area for development rights transfer can transfer the increased density associated with a parcel on which a historic building is not utilizing all of the zoned building rights (Ervin et al., 1977).

In response to exclusionary zoning by suburban communities that effectively excludes poor or minority group members, some states have moved to require that zoning regulations do not discriminate against any economic or ethnic group. Related to this problem has been the adoption of performance zoning to allow a PUD or cluster zoning to increase the density in certain areas through large-scale planned residential development. Applied primarily to residential land use, such zoning techniques have been successful in upgrading the quality of the planning involved in multiple dwelling unit developments but have not overcome the prevalent attitude of residents of single-family neighborhoods who oppose multifamily units in their neighborhood.

Another policy change affecting planning is related to the attempts of cities to gain reimbursements of costs associated with land development. Traditionally, cities have been able to require dedication of streets, but now cities are requiring dedication of land for park, recreation, or school use if it can be shown that the demand is specific to the development. Cities are also requiring payment in lieu of dedication of land, or are charging impact fees to pay for the cost of providing such facilities. The basis for this policy and procedural change is the growing recognition that the cost of subdividing land should be borne by the developer and those who will use it (Mandelker, 1982). Concern for quality of life has prompted many communities to adopt regulations that slow growth, and although such measures have been effective in Petaluma, California; Boulder, Colorado; and Ramapo, New York, the trend to judge such regulations as exclusionary coupled with a slower rate of family formation and lower birthrate and a slower rate of economic growth in the United States has prompted some of these communities to reevaluate their stand. Most noticeably, the community of Ramapo has removed the point system, which was the basis for their growth regulation plan (Geneslaw and Raymond, 1983).

FUTURE THRUSTS: TRENDS IN PLANNING AND LAND USE

The general trend in land use planning and regulation in the United States seems to be one of increasing public concern for and regulation of private land use. Court response to challenges to increased regulations associated with zoning of floodplains, historic preservation, wetlands, exclusionary regulations, and other uses and regulations indicates a general consensus that the public's interest in land use planning and regulation is of ever greater importance (Mandelker, 1982). As part of this trend, there is an increasing degree of flexibility in traditional Euclidian zoning. Adoption of contract or conditional zoning gives broader latitude of uses within a zone but bases each development on specific conditions or agreements in terms of how the land will be used and the neighbors and the public protected. Adoption of tools such as floating zones allows a community to adopt a zone for a use and not map its location until a specific request is reviewed and approved. To ensure good planning in new developments, there will be increasing use of the process of site plan review in which communities require as part of their zoning ordinance that detailed plans be submitted for applications for development projects. Such site plan reviews are useful because they allow the community to know what the actual physical morphology of the development will be and thus to foresee problems presented to the community by the specific land use. The adoption of increasing flexibility of zoning may well include continued use of both traditional zoning techniques and new techniques such as floating zones, development rights transfer, historic preservation, and zoning of unique areas such as floodplains.

Because there is an increased interest in private land use, a recent trend has been the greater interest of courts in the actions of local planning commissions and governments affecting private lands. An important trend indicated by some land use law specialists is the definition of zoning actions by local governments as quasi-judicial rather than legislative in nature. If widely adopted, this change may radically change the land use planning and regulation process in the United States since it requires findings of fact by the governing body in support of decisions made regarding zoning (Mandelker, 1982). The impact of adoption of this view would be to give the courts a greater interest in land use planning and regulation than at any other time in the past. Such influence may be beneficial since the rights of citizens will be better protected if local governments must act in a quasi-judicial fashion and clearly state any conflicts of interest and provide a clear statement of the reasons for a specific ruling.

The trends affecting the traditional planning process, with its emphasis on the comprehensive plan and the zoning ordinance, will augment, not replace, the conventional planning process in the United States. Planning and regulation of land use will remain at the local level for most of the United States in spite of a seemingly clear-cut need for either state or federal guidelines to ensure some homogeneity in land use planning and regulation in the nation. States that have strong state regulation or guidance for land use planning and regulation are the minority, and since the mid–1970s, there have been no major efforts to institute a national program for land use planning or regulation. The United States will remain a nation whose most important resource, its land, is controlled by a plethora of regulatory agencies whose decisions will continue to be fragmentary and in large part parochial and self-serving.

BIBLIOGRAPHY

Babcock, Richard F., and Fred P. Bosselman. 1975. Land Use Controls: History and Legal Status. In Randall W. Scott, *Management and Control of Growth*, vol. 1, 196–310. Washington, D.C.: Urban Land Institute.

Bosselman, Fred, and David Callies. 1971. *The Quiet Revolution in Land Use Control.* Washington, D.C.: Council on Environmental Control.

Brown, Daniel C. 1982. New Activism in Zoning, Building Design, and Construction. *Building Design and Construction*, September: 42–43.

Clawson, Marion, and Burnell Held, 1957. *The Federal Lands: Their Use and Management.* Baltimore: Johns Hopkins Press.

Council of State Governments. 1976. *State Growth Management.* Lexington, Ky.: Department of Housing and Urban Development.

Ervin, David E. et al. 1977. *Land Use Control.* Cambridge, Mass.; Ballinger.

Fordham, Richard C. 1974. *Measurement of Urban Land Use.* Cambridge: University of Cambridge Press.

Geneslaw, Robert, and George M. Raymond. 1983. Ramapo Dropping Its Famed Point System. *Planning* 49, June: 8–9.

Haar, Charles M. 1959. *Land-Use Planning.* Boston: Little, Brown.

Healy, Robert G. 1976. *Land Use and the States.* Baltimore: Johns Hopkins Press.

Jackson, Richard H. 1981. *Land Use in America.* London: Edward Arnold (Publishers), Ltd.

Mandelker, Daniel. 1982. *Land Use Law.* Charlottesville, Va.: Michie Company.

Miller, Michael. 1982. Crowd Control: Zoning in Mid-Town Manhattan. *Building Design and Construction*, September: 44.

Moss, Elaine, ed. 1977. *Land Use Controls in the United States.* New York: Dial Press.

National Agricultural Lands Study. 1981. Washington, D.C.: Government Printing Office.

Platt, Rutherford H., and George Macinko, eds. 1983. *Beyond the Urban Fringe: Land Use Issues of Non-Metropolitan America.* Minneapolis: University of Minnesota Press.

Poffer, Louise. 1951. *The Closing of the Public Domain.* Palo Alto: Stanford University Press.

Reps, John W. 1965. *The Making of Urban America.* Princeton: Princeton University Press.

Rohrbough, Malcolm J. 1968. *The Land Office Business.* London: Oxford University Press.

Rose, Jerome G., and Robert E. Rothman. 1977. *After Mount Laurel: The New Suburban Zoning.* New Brunswick, N.J.: Center for Urban Policy Research.

Smith, Henry Nash. 1950. *Virgin Land: The American West as Symbol and Myth.* New York: Vintage Books.

Smith, Herbert H. 1979. *The Citizen's Guide to Planning.* Washington, D.C.: American Planning Association.

So, Frank S., et al. 1979. *The Practice of Local Government Planning.* Washington, D.C.: International City Management Association.

Sternlieb, George, and James W. Hughes. 1976. *Housing and Economic Reality: New York City, 1976.* New Brunswick, N.J.: Center for Urban Policy Research.

Sternlieb, George, and James W. Hughes, eds. 1978. *Current Population Trends in the United States.* New Brunswick, N.J.: Center for Urban Policy Research.

U.S. Bureau of the Census. 1981. *Statistical Abstract of the United States: 1981.* 102d ed. Washington, D.C.: Government Printing Office.

U.S. Department of Agriculture. 1977. *Potential Crop Land Study.* Washington, D.C.: Government Printing Office.

U.S. Department of the Interior. 1981. *Public Land Statistics*. Washington, D.C.: Government Printing Office.
Williams, Norman J. 1966. *The Structure of Urban Zoning*. New York: Butterheim Publishing.

PART VI

CENTRAL AND SOUTH AMERICA

20

Mexico

LEO F. POZO-LEDEZMA

After World War II, Mexico developed rapidly; population increased over 3 percent; urbanization over 4.9 percent; and gross domestic product over 6 percent. By most standards, these growth rates should not spell problems. But Mexico, despite its vast resources, has not been able to solve the major problems of poverty, rural land tenure, and demographic, urban, and industrial imbalance. Therefore the high rates of population growth, rural land shortages, and the need for land for future urban and industrial areas pose serious questions about the future of land use and land tenure in Mexico.

ISSUES OF LAND TENURE AND LAND USE

Historically land tenure has defined socioeconomic and political life in Mexico. Certainly Mexico's rural land tenure problems have been similar for all Spanish Latin American countries. Moreover, even their national efforts to solve those problems have been similar, mostly including social conflicts and even revolutions (Landsberger, 1969; Stavenhagen, 1970; Birou, 1971). Mexico's agrarian reform, a product of its revolution, solved the legal aspects of rural land tenure by reinstituting traditional forms and providing lands to the peasantry (Padgett, 1966). Indeed, land distribution for small-scale agriculture, the agrarian reform's main objective, has been met to commendable levels and has been imitated throughout Latin America (Landsberger, 1969; Stavenhagen, 1970; Birou, 1971; McEntire and McEntire, 1975).

Today land for large- and small-scale agriculture is an expensive commodity, as well as a touchy political issue. Large-scale agriculture shows technological advances and increased productivity that seem to justify more attention to it than to small-scale agriculture. In fact, it promises self-sufficiency in some main crops and export crops to afford agricultural goods that must be imported. To what extent are these objectives to be met by undermining the objectives of the agrarian reform? Furthermore, the lack of arable land makes for difficult choices, but they must be made (Yates, 1981).

Urban growth and demographic concentrations are also land issues. In fact most development frameworks in Mexico consider the solution of urban growth problems pivotal for economic development in general. But in view of the trends of urbanization, continued rural-urban migration and the concentration of such growth in three major urban areas requires effective measures beyond plans for decentralization. Without changes in the current trends of urbanization, land issues could become grave matters, especially in the largest metropolitan centers, increasing the possibilities of social and political unrest.

HISTORICAL DEVELOPMENT

Aztec land use did not imply ultimate possession by the individual. But most writings seem to stress that communal landholding patterns suggested communal ownership in perpetuity—especially in the *calpullalli*[1] and *altepetlalli*[2]—land-holding patterns that remained unchanged even long after the Spaniards settled the country. Besides those types of land allocation and uses, other patterns of landholding and uses had already been developed by the time the Spaniards arrived. Therefore in one sense, the Aztecs' disregard for measuring value or riches in terms of landholding may have effectively precluded the development of a land market and the formation of large landholdings with an accompanying exploitation of the landless in latifundia. Yet in another sense, as other research indicates, other types of land allocation and possession were well developed by the time the Spaniards arrived. Lands of local and regional chieftains and nobles, initially inalienable, had become hereditary (implying possession) and were even exploited by serfs and sharecroppers (*mayeques* and *tlalmatecas*) for private usufruct. To that extent, the Spanish seemed to have adopted and improved for their own ends what they saw working among the Aztecs (McBride, 1923, 115–23; Melgar, 1959, 15–38).

Consolidation of Spanish Landholding during the Colonial Period

The history of the conquest of Mexico has been detailed in a vast literature (Melgar, 1959, chap. 3; Diaz, 1981). Certainly it was an ambitious endeavor that resulted in the possession of a vast empire by a very few. The conquest, carried out in the name of the crown and church of Spain, was followed by a colonial rule in which the crown enriched its coffers with bountiful taxes, but the church and others ended possessing the land. This happened because the lust for gold of the *conquistadores* was soon satisfied (to the extent that there was no more gold to exact or rob), and lordship over the land and its people became their prime endeavor. Consequently Cortès, Alvarado, and other principals of the conquest became owners of landholds larger than that of any noble in Spain. The crown, unwilling or unable to limit the claims of those ambitious captains, resorted to profit from their enterprise by consolidating Spanish rule, providing laws and administration, and taxing and regulating their commerce. It was that almost unlimited freedom of action on the land that made it possible for Spaniards to think in terms of landholding in grand scale, the origin of Mexico's historic land problems.

Spanish Villas

After consolidating their conquest, the Spanish founded *villas* (new towns), established outposts where Indian attacks seemed possible, and built roads for travel and commerce. Where appropriate, the new towns were the old Aztec cities somewhat reorganized. But as production and commerce grew, more and more towns, located in appropriate places, were founded and populated. The royal decrees that established the new towns favored the pattern of towns in Castille, where latifundia had also been widely established. The new town usually included space for homes, public buildings, and croplands known as *propios* and *consejiles*, the rentals of which produced the income to support the local government. There was also the *ejido*, or common lands, that were used for grazing, wood, fuel, storage, and other purposes. The distribution of cropland in the *propios* and *consejiles* was by lot. The size of the plots varied according to the land available, location, water resources, and other considerations. Although the *villa* provided for ownership by Spaniards (of plots in the *propios*), in those villas that included Indian settlers, the crown retained landownership. Furthermore, the crown could reclaim lands left unused, or on request it could avail additional lands (usually from the *ejido*), for a rental fee. McBride (1923, 105–11) provides figures that show that rather long tracts of lands were allocated to new towns formed in the states of Texas, Coahuila, New Mexico, and others throughout the eighteenth century. Nonetheless, despite their different sizes and locations, most Spanish new towns remained almost unchanged in their features and functions well into the Republic.

Colonial Urbanization

Demographic aspects were the key for the growth of *pueblos, villas*, and *haciendas* during the colonial period. First, the kinship basis for village life broke down as the Spanish destroyed the old Aztec order and its land tenure system. Also, the Spaniards mixed and transferred large numbers of conquered Indians to less desirable lands. And in some areas, the diseases brought by the Spaniards decimated the Indian population. Such demographic convulsion, especially in the central zone, served the Spaniards' aims to accrue and control their new landholds, keeping only enough Indians to work the land. In time, those landholds, administered as single operations, and due to their particular use or exploitation of Indian labor, gave way to the *hacienda* system. The *hacienda* system, the basis for agricultural production and wealth during the colonial period, survived well into the twentieth century, a Spanish legacy, and root of most rural conflicts in Latin America. (McBride, 1923, chap. 7; Simpson, 1937, chap. 2).

The growth of the *hacienda* system was paralleled by the growth of the Indian villages and their farming at somewhat above the subsistence level. Some Indian villages developed sizable settlements, including merchants, a church, craft, and tradesmen. In a sense these Indian villages satisfied similar needs as did the Spanish towns and other growing settlements: commerce and services for their region. But the classist and racist sentiments of the Spaniards precluded an integration of those settlements. That was cause for a deep gulf between Indian local life in the villages and the more continental aspects of life in colonial urban settlements. The gulf was wider, indeed, when compared to Mexico City or other cities in which administrative, military, and church bureaucracies resided and set the tone of social life.

While most of the Indian population grew into more and more villages, the inflow of Spanish colonists and the *creoles* increased the population of the *villas*, along with the growing stratum of *mestizos*, and even some Indians—whose trades and occupations made them necessary. But what also influenced growth of many of these settlements was the upsurge of mining in New Spain (of silver, copper, iron, lead, mercury, and other minerals). The exploitation of mines required various services (legal, commercial, transportation, trades) that were located in the Spanish towns, therefore making them supporting centers. Although the mining enclaves grew settlements, those were usually minimal encampments for the Indian workers and some accommodations for the foremen and managers, along with the necessary installations. The families of the Spanish, *creoles*, and some of the *mestizo* employees generally lived in the next supporting urban center. The riches generated by these mines produced a new wealthy class who often were the main contributors to urban construction of churches, schools, orphanages, monasteries, etc. (sometimes in competition with the landed rich) and encouraged the local governments to improve parks, plazas, and so forth. Along with their administrative role, this class aided the growth of colonial towns in Mexico to the detriment of (except for taxation) the organization or type of growth of Indian villages during that period. McBride (1923), for example, points out that by 1810, there were 95 *villas* and 4,682 *pueblos*. The pattern of two Mexicos was already clearly visible.

The *Porfiriato* and Changes in Land Tenure

After the War of Independence and the establishment of a Republic, the *Reforma* legislation of the mid-nineteenth century opened Mexico to liberal development policies. The *Porfiriato* (the regime of Porfirio Diáz) took them to their extremes. The opening of the country to roads and railways was seen as a cure to Mexico's underpopulation and poverty, as well as a lure for foreign capital. Foreign banking, mining, industries, and other enterprises invaded Mexico, affecting land prices and land tenure patterns drastically. Since land was no longer viewed only in its agrarian perspective but in an industrial age perspective as well, its potential uses made it more valuable. The increased value of land placed the poor further away from landownership.

While life in the growing cities showed signs of modernization and progress, rural Mexico developed differently. Much of the Indian population remained in the *pueblos*, subsisting on smaller and smaller plots. The bulk of the landless Indians toiled in the *haciendas* and remained in *hacienda* villages. Others survived in the mining towns and in other types of small communities. Although only rough estimates exist about the size of the rural population in *haciendas* as compared to *pueblos*, it is clear that in both cases the peasants had become poorer:

By 1910, the rural inhabitants of Mexico, who held no individual property were probably more numerous than had been at any previous time in the history of the country. Thus, in this important respect and in spite of the marked material development of the country, Mexico was in worse condition than she had ever been during the most stationary periods of the Spanish Domination. (McBride, 1923, 155–56)

Revolution

The end of the nineteenth century, like the end of the eighteenth century, was characterized by rural unrest that affected the political climate: isolated uprisings, revolts, and other challenges to the Diáz regime. Although the fall of Diáz was not due to a single cause, land issues were the unifying cause among rural folk who wanted an end to their exploitation. The urban politicians, however, faced the Diáz machine with an electoral maneuver that rallied other urban groups as well. The motto, "Effective suffrage, no reelection," consolidated them around Francisco I. Madero, who eventually was elected president. Madero's early support for returning lands to the peasant was lost during his indecisive and short-lived administration. The resulting chaos and the rise of contending forces engulfed the country in a full-blown revolution at the end of the first decade of this century.

INSTITUTIONAL AND LANDOWNERSHIP FRAMEWORK

Decree of 6 January 1915

In the face of the pressures for action on the issue of agrarian reform and certainly for political reasons, this watershed decree was issued at the outset of 1915. Whatever its shortcomings—and even its blunders—it tried to correct the historical despoliation of communal lands and its impact on the Indian population.

It decreed that all misapplications of the Law of 26 June 1856 were null and void, thereby allowing for the restitution of communal lands to *pueblos* and other *communidades* (Indian villages with shared landownership). It further decreed that *pueblos*, which for various reasons ended without *ejidos* (village land about a square league, or about 2,500 hectares), had the right to claim and obtain such lands from the government (which would resort to expropriation, if necessary, for those purposes). To ensure the implementation of the decree, the decree established the National Agrarian Commission, with state commissions and other appropriate bodies.

The thrust of the decree was the restoration of communal lands, or *ejidos*, which limited its application to those *pueblos* that could show title or prove that they had *ejidos* previously. Consequently it failed to address the problems of the Indians who lived in villages that had never acquired titles to the communal lands they had lost subsequently, nor did it take note of the condition of those landless suffering *peonage* in the *haciendas* or the large segment surviving in other small *communidades, congregaciones*, and *rancherias*[3] who continued to hope to own a plot of land. The vast landless population in rural Mexico seemed to have gained nothing at all. Even those who were supposed to benefit were undermined by the lack of resources to deal with the governmental bureaucracy that was to implement the decree, by the legal maneuvers used by the landholders, and by the government's lack of specific machinery that would reach local levels to decide on specific claims.

In view of the decree's ineffectiveness, various peasant leaders and politicians sought a more definite resolution. When a constitutional convention was convened, the serious measures passed by the agrarian interests were not opposed. The convention ended with the Constitution of 1917.

Constitution of 1917

The contrast of the Constitution of 1917 with its predecessors has been subject of a vast amount of writing. Its impact on Mexican development has been broad, if not comprehensive. Some of its salient aspects can be summarized as follows: unlike the individualistic (liberal) spirit of the Constitution of 1857 and its subsequent legislation, its spirit is eminently collectivist; its main concern is society, not the individual; its emphasis on social function places social or national interests above those of corporate or vested interests; and it focuses on the masses as a national concern.

With respect to land and related issues, Article 27 is important; with respect to labor (urban and rural), Article 123 is important. Article 27 sought to define the limits of the concept of private property in a comprehensive way, define what persons and legal entities can enjoy the right to property, and establish the bases on which to forge a national solution to the agrarian question. Article 27 establishes that the nation is the only source of titles to lands and water; it reserves the right to impose limitations on private property and its use; it has the right to expropriate (by paying) for the public interest; and it conditions the leasing of water and mineral rights on adequate regulation (the nation retains all ownership). Although all citizens have the right to become property owners, foreigners can own property in Mexico only under very limited conditions. The church and other nonprofit institutions cannot own property or hold mortgages (except in special cases), and commercial stock companies and banks can own property only for their office operations.

With respect to the landless peasants, the Constitution of 1857 established that communal groups (*condueñazgos, rancherias, pueblos*, and others) could own communal lands until appropriate laws to provide them with ownership of individual parcels could be implemented. But in a broader perspective, the agrarian emphasis of Article 27 would help address the following areas: the consolidation of the *ejido* for *pueblos* and other Indian settlements, recovery by the government of lands and water illegally alienated, or needed for public interest, which included policies to solve agrarian issues, and giving the states more powers to deal with the regulation and breakup of large landholds, thereby eliminating latifundia and its undesirable practices, as well as increasing the land market and private landownership. Mexico until recently used Article 27 as the basis for actions dealing with rural and urban lands. That is an important consideration in view of the urban land use problems that have mushroomed in recent decades (McEntire and McEntire, 1975, 247–54; Simpson, 1937, chap. 5).

Agrarian Reform and Its Impact on Land Use

Few revolutionary measures in history have become such solid elements of the ruling ideology as has agrarian reform in Mexico. Although, as Simpson put it a long time ago, it "was conceived in confusion and prosecuted in disorder" it has also seemingly satisfied the peasantry's call for "land and liberty," making them a strong sector within the ruling party (1937, 75). And despite the many criticisms of agrarian reform and its implementation, vast amounts of land have been allotted to previously landless peasants.

At another level, however, the agrarian reform, even with its modifications, will remain mainly a tool for distributing land to the rural landless. The agrarian question in Mexico today has overwhelmed the previously more limited conceptions of its nature, and land distribution should be only one of the many tools of the comprehensive approach to solve agrarian, agricultural, and other land-related issues of Mexican development.

Current Rural Landownership Patterns

The main objective of agrarian reform—to provide land to the rural landless and establish their inalienability—has been successful. Other expected consequences have been the breakup of most of the large estates, the end (at least of the protection) of the exploitative *peonaje*, and the regulation of public lands and water resources with due regard for the needs of the rural peasantry. There has been a vast increase in the number of small landholders (mainly among the *ejidatarios* and not as much among private landholders) and the controlled existence of large landholds, dedicated to special agricultural and cattle raising production, as allowed by the same legislation (although most of the land above a prescribed size is subject to a 25 year lease for such specific purposes).

Today, the support of the official party, *Partido Revolucionario Institucional* (PRI), of agrarian reform is clear. To some extent, all administrations have supported land distribution. President Lázaro Cárdenas (1936–40), of course, had no equal to his commitment to the cause and the amount of land distributed. Yet in 1967, for example, President Gustavo Diaz in Chihuahua presided over the distribution of over 1 million hectares of lands previously in private hands to about 960 future *ejidatarios*, the largest single land distribution in recent times. In the 1970s in Campeche and in other low-density areas, the government provided lots (some with a house on it) to landless peasants from other areas in another effort at colonizing and relieving the demographic pressures on land in the dense areas. Therefore, agrarian reform is still viable as a tool for the allocation of lands. But the availability of arable land is a critical consideration, especially in view of demographic trends and future food requirements, and some reassessment of policies would be justified (McEntire and McEntire, 1975, chap. 10).

Background of National Planning

The issue of national planning in Mexico was not resolved by a debate on whether to plan. The forces of the revolution, reacting to the uses of government for the enrichment of a small sector of the population, ensured that future governments would have the masses and the nation in mind. To that end, representatives of various popular sectors formed part of the structure of the now institutionalized national revolutionary party (PRI) (Padgett, 1966; Johnson, 1971). Although the first years emphasized specific agrarian and labor policies (especially distribution of land), by the early 1930s, issues of national development of all sectors of the economy had become prominent in governmental rhetoric, and some budgetary appropriations were made. In time, however, the complexity of developmental policies required technocracy and a bureaucratization of the process of planning, and this is reflected in the development of plans and planning in Mexico.

After the nationalist and institutionalizing Calles administration (1924–28), the Law on General National Planning was approved in 1930, but implementation was hampered by the effects of the worldwide depression. Under Cardenas (1934–40), the first six-year plan was presented (followed by laws on agricultural loans for farmers and *ejidos*), with an emphasis on social services, infrastructure, and sectoral objectives. Under Manuel Avila (1941–46), the second six-year plan adhered to the objectives of the first, but the impact of World War II limited its implementation. Nonetheless, the country continued its drive toward industrialization. During the Aleman administration (1946–52), the effects of World War II still hampered plan implementation. But new legislation redefined public and private participation in basic industries, thereby anchoring the future national control of economic growth in Mexico. During the Ruiz administration (1952–58), the Program of Investments became a key element in the budgetary allocation of funds for development and established the basis for sophisticated budget planning in the Office of the President. The Lopez administration (1958–64) followed this trend; the president developed an investment program for 1960–64, mainly budget outlays that emphasized sectoral objectives and coordination. Similarly, based on a report of his Interagency Commission for Economic Development Planning, Lopez presented the Plan of Immediate Action to deal with the international recession, as well as to attract investments, including those through the Alliance of Progress.[4] By this time, urban growth, migration, poverty, rural unemployment, and other critical socioeconomic issues had become recognized as prime concerns of national planning. Therefore, Diaz (1964–70), based on another interagency proposal, presented the Plan for Social and Economic Development (for 1966–70), and his Office produced the Public Investments Program for that plan. The programs required public outlays in all sectors, promotion of industry and exports, and creation of employment. In 1966, Diaz signed the Plan for the Industrialization of the Northern Border Zone, which gave place to the twin and other in-bond plant systems and enormous job creation in the U.S.-Mexico border region (Baerresen, 1971; Hansen, 1981b). These policies were followed by the Echeverria administration (1971–76), which promoted new growth strategies and compartmentalized development, but the problems of the cities and the masses increased. In 1974, the president's office and other agencies prepared a set of guidelines for a social and economic development program for 1974–80, the implementation of which was hampered by the international recession of 1969–73. Nonetheless, some of the recommendations for national sectoral programming were implemented later, and some agencies were reorganized to implement the necessary coordination and planning. During the Lopez administration (1976–82), the party-approved Basic Government Plan (1976-82) discussed a comprehensive approach to development. Also Lopez's own Bases for Development of an Agenda for Government proposed a comprehensive system of planning by government agencies, features of which were included in his Global Development Plan, 1980–82.[5]

In sum, until the past decade, the progression of planning as a basis for governmental action was steady but not systematic. It started with an emphasis on budgetary outlays to promote sectoral development. Statistical and econometric units to quantify objectives (as bases for budget proposals) came after World War II, by which time the state-owned industries represented a large portion of public investment. But such plans also promoted private capital growth (domestic and foreign) within controlled parameters, which has helped industrialization on all fronts. And lately national planning has produced trend scenarios for all sectors, which will make development plans more realistic and consistent. From what passed as planning in the 1920s and 1930s, Mexico now has an officially instituted planning system.

MAJOR CHALLENGES TO LAND USE

General Developmental Consideration

Unlike other industrializing nations Mexico has an orderly democratic political life, the military is subordinate to the civilian institutional order, and the bases for its economic system, including the role of the government, have been resolved with the institutionalization of the revolution. Therefore, the question remains: with those roadblocks removed, why is Mexican development still so problematic and imbalanced? Why,under a revolutionary regime, do such vast inequalities in income and productivity remain? In this section the focus will be on issues related to land and urban development.[6]

Past policies and programs were inadequate to promote broad development, especially in their implementation phases. There were less planning and more budgetary sectoral outlays for somewhat imprecise objectives. The main lack was that of appropriate statistical and sectoral economic analyses—as well as public and private mechanisms to evaluate market and economic trends—on which development must be based. By the 1960s, technocracy and comprehensive planning notions were sufficiently established, but the problems of development overwhelmed the capacity to plan and to have plans implemented. The quality of plans, even at state and local levels, is excellent; however, there is a gap between the plans and their realization—the administrative system seems uncooperative in that respect. Implementation is a weak link in the process.[7]

Mexican development needs a realistic and precise conceptualization of its development objectives. Too often policy sounds like political rhetoric. Or, as Azuela observes, even specific laws provide the opportunity to include politico-ideological pronouncements.[8] Steady development relies more on limited program objectives that can be fully implemented than on broad efforts that cannot. The machinery and expertise to plan in comprehensive framework exist and should be used in that fashion.

There also exists the unfounded expectancy (fueled by political rhetoric) that some of the major problems can be solved in the short run, a claim that can often force unrealistic planning. The problems are compounded when one considers that important structural changes are necessary and that such changes take time. The most pressing structural factor that will affect Mexican development is that of decentralization. It is estimated that Mexico City, Guadalajara, and Monterrey together use only 0.2 percent of the land but hold about 26.5 percent of the population, have about 40 percent of the jobs (or 53 percent of the country's payrolls), sell close to 50 percent of all durable goods, and produce about 90 percent of all electrical goods, pharmaceuticals, and others. Obviously Mexico City is the major pole of such centralization. Income per capita in the federal district is over six times that of Zacatecas, and federal expenditures in the federal district are about 12 times more than for Oaxaca and other of the least benefited states.[9] Rectifying or eliminating the results of such centralization will take time, and in the interim, those areas will continue to drain resources and funds at higher rates than other areas. For example, providing water to a citizen in Mexico City costs about eight times more than doing the same in Tampico. Certainly all appropriate options should be considered (Looney and Fredericksen, 1982; Unikel, 1982). Obviously the political aspects of realigning the allocation of resources and services weigh heavier than cost-benefit considerations. These aspects affect developmental planning and can even undermine it.

Another factor delaying development is the lack of effective cooperation between the public and the private sectors, especially at the local level. The government supports and owns most basic industries (electricity, railways, communications, highways, oil, health), but it also provides incentives (loans, tariffs, import restrictions, export incentives) to private sector industries. The operating climate, however, portrays a private sector that, though enjoying government protection, is interested only in exploiting the highly lucrative markets. Except for good construction contracts they were loath to participate in areas such as housing, mass transportation, basic foodstuffs, and other mass services activities. The development of those sectors has been costly to the public treasury, depriving funds for other social sectors and making the state's role in that arena permanent. Such overreliance on the public sector complicates developmental options. Some areas that offer opportunities for private capital (water, sanitation systems, electricity, railways, metro systems, communications, health systems) should be considered. Housing for low-income sectors, for example, will suffer from lack of sufficient resources. Land appropriate for housing also requires better management of a scarce resource which calls for effective measures to control the land market and profits made in it. Developmental programs need the effective participation of all sectors, especially the private sector, lest imbalances continue to delay development.

The institutionalization of public participation would be most functional for development in the long range. With so many interests competing for public funds (for housing, urban development, transportation, health, education), crucial choices need be made without sacrificing the credibility of the political and planning processes. Certainly, the more sustainable choices would be those that involved the people. A broad effort at educating them about the objectives of plans should strengthen implementation. This route should be preferable to continued centralization of decisions, which seems to be under constant threat of being undermined by politically motivated criticism on the one hand and mass apathy on the other.

Urban-Rural Tensions

Urban-rural tensions are the mire on which developmental efforts rest in the Third World. In fact, various theories have been developed about their relationship in development (Gilbert and Gugler, 1982). In Mexico it seems that only the recent problems are forcing approaches to solve that crucial relationship.

Rural Demographic, Land Tenure, and Employment Trends

The Mexican population doubled between 1900 and 1950; it took only two more decades to double again (1950–1970). Current population policies aim to bring the average annual rate of growth (AROG) to about 2 percent, or population of about 100 million for the year 2000. Rural population growth has grown at a lesser rate. While the urban population increased eighteen–fold since 1900, the rural population has only slightly more than doubled in the same period. Current trends indicate that the rural population may stabilize at its current size. Some figures and projections are shown in Table 20.1.

Undoubtedly rural-urban migrants, most of them landless, have been a major component of urban growth. Yet while the landless were about 3.5 million during the revolutionary period, there are about 4.5 million rural landless today (Scott, 1982, 123–36). Therefore migration provided a relief valve to the rural demographic pressure on land. The plight of the landless, however, has been complicated by the shortage of employment in rural Mexico.

Shortage of land is the major factor for unemployment among the rural folk who reach working age. Past subdivisions of *ejidos*, communal lands, and other landholdings resulted in plots so small that they are now insufficient even for subsistence farming. Therefore the landless unemployed are pushed to migrate. Another factor that contributes to migration is the decrease in jobs in the large commercial and export farming and ranching. The end of the *hacienda*, new methods of production and cattle ranching, and increased use of machinery have reduced the need for rural manpower. Also, the middle– and small–sized farms reduced sharecropping and their use of temporary labor, and even the small landholders and *ejidatarios* use temporary labor mainly from their immediate family. To compound the situation, some labor–intensive projects that previously accommodated rural manpower (road, irrigation works, construction) now use more machinery and employ mostly urban workers with some experience or training.

A less than thorough understanding of rural unemployment can cause serious problems in developmental plans. For example, when large industrial development projects were located away from the large metropolitan areas, the prospects of jobs in roads, site preparation, and other work caused an influx of rural unemployed to those sites. When the planned industrial activities got underway, the camps and other planned facilities were overwhelmed by the waves of migrants in search of jobs. Instant urbanization happened, to one extent or other, in Villahermosa, other port complexes, Lazaro Cardenas, *maquila* industrial

Table 20.1

Population by Urban-Rural (thousands), and Average Rate of Growth (AROG), Mexico, 1900–2000

Year	Urban	(%)	AROG	Rural	(%)	AROG	Total	AROG
1900	2,639.8	(19.4)		10,967.5	(80.6)		13,607.3	
1910	3,668.8	(24.2)	3.3	11,491.6	(75.8)	0.5	15,160.4	1.1
1920	4,472.2	(31.2)	1.8	9,861.9	(68.5)	-1.4	14,334.1	-0.5
1930	5,541.1	(33.5)	2.6	11,007.5	(66.5)	1.3	16,552.6	1.7
1940	6,898.4	(35.1)	2.3	12,755.2	(64.9)	1.5	19,653.6	1.8
1950	10,986.9	(42.6)	4.6	14,804.1	(57.4)	1.5	25,791.0	2.7
1960	17,706.1	(50.7)	4.9	17,217.0	(49.3)	1.5	34,923.1	3.1
1970	29,757.7	(58.7)	5.0	20,936.9	(41.3)	1.5	50,694.6	3.4
1980	46,254.4	(66.7)**		23,092.5	(33.3)**		69,346.9	3.3
1990	62,621.6	(72.8)**		23,397.1	(27.2)**		86,018.7*	1.3*
2000	77,432.0	(77.4)**		22,609.4	(22.6)**		100,041.4*	1.0*

Source: México Demográfico, Breviario 1980–81 (CONAPO, April 1982), tables pp. 11, 13, 56, 57 and 103.

*CONAPO's Programmatic projections assume rates of growth of 2.5% for 1982, and 1% for 1982–2000.

**Demographic Indicators of Countries; Estimates and projections as assessed in 1980. (United Nations, October 1982). These percentage figures correspond to the "medium variant" projection and were used to compute the urban and rural population figures for 1980, 1990 and 2000.

areas along the U.S.–Mexico border, and other places.[10] Despite the limited number of jobs available, the migrants remained, some of them engaging in town–like commerce and services and soon developing a sizable settlement with substandard conditions. In border cities migrants who intended to enter the U.S. or work at the in-bond plants have created unparalleled rates of growth in Matamoros, Laredo, Ciudad Juarez and Tijuana.[11] Such migratory trends forced corrective urban planning and costly provision of infrastructure lest the situation became socially and politically explosive.

Lack of industrial employment in rural Mexico resulted from the concentration of industry in Mexico City, Guadalajara, and Monterrey. Their postwar industrial expansion absorbed an estimated 75 percent of the population growth. Such a rate of absorption is impossible today (Scott, 1982, Chap. 2; Schumacher, 1983, Chap. 5). In fact, current efforts to regionalize development include incentives to promote industrial growth in other areas. But the trends show that the three large metropolitan areas will continue to absorb migrants, though at reduced rates.

Rural unemployment is not only a result of industrial centralization and demographic pressure on rural land; it is also a cause for the pressures on urban land. Therefore policies for the creation of rural employment are necessary and justifiably the object of national concern.

Agricultural Productivity and Rural Landownership

The National Institute of Agrarian Reform (INRA) deals with the distribution of land and matters related to *ejidos*. Agricultural policy has always been the purview of the Secretariat of Agriculture and Husbandry (Secretaria de Agricultura y Ganaderia, SAG). On the whole, SAG managed to increase the productivity of the commercial agricultural sector. Today, although Mexico still imports large quantities of foodstuffs (mostly grains), it also exports various products from efficient farms and ranches.

From the point of view of productivity and development the emphasis on the imbalance of landholding is appropriate. Close to 90 percent of all rural landholds (about 42 percent of total area) is held in parcels of 10 hectares or less. On the other hand, about 21 percent of the rural land in parcels of over 100 hectares is held by less than 1 percent of properties or landholds (Table 20.2).

The trends of ownership show that the number of *ejidatarios* grew, seemingly at the expense of private landowners (Table 20.3). But while the numbers of both *ejido* and privately owned parcels under 20 hectares are predominant (about 76 percent and 91 percent, respectively), there are no *ejido* parcels over 100 hectares, and about 2 percent of the private landholds account for over 40 percent of privately held land (Table 20.4).

The vast outlays for large-scale agriculture (electricity, irrigation works, machinery, expertise) cannot be afforded to all rural areas, no sound economic rationale would support it. Similarly, further distribution of land seems less

Table 20.2
Size of Rural Landholdings, Mexico, 1970

Size (hectares)	% of Parcels	% of Area
0 - 1	22.8	1.9
1 - 5	42.8	17.2
5 - 10	22.4	22.9
10 - 20	8.5	17.9
20 - 100	2.9	19.0
100 or more	0.6	21.0
Total	100.0	100.0

Source: Government of Mexico Census Data, 1970.

Table 20.4
Rural Land Distribution by Type of Ownership, Mexico: Percentages

Size (hectares)	Ejidos		Private	
	Parcels	Area	Parcels	Area
0 - 1	13.3	2.1	34.1	1.6
1 - 5	46.1	27.0	34.7	7.6
5 - 10	28.2	40.4	12.1	7.4
10 - 20	8.4	23.7	9.7	12.9
20 -100	1.0	6.8	7.3	30.0
100 or more	-	-	2.1	40.5
Totals	97.0	100.0	100.0	100.0

Source: Government of Mexico Census Data, 1970

Table 20.3
Rural Land by Type of Ownership, Mexico, 1930–1970 ('000s hectares)

Year	Ejidios	(%)	Colonos*	(%)	Private	(%)	Total**	(%)
1930	8,345	(6.3)	6,000	(4.6)	117,250	(89.1)	131,594	(100)
1940	28,923	(22.5)	6,069	(4.7)	93,757	(72.8)	128,749	(100)
1950	39,894	(26.7)	7,554	(5.2)	99,069	(68.1)	145,517	(100)
1960	44,497	(26.3)	8,735	(5.2)	115,852	(68.5)	169,084	(100)
1970	60,553	(43.3)	9,191	(6.6)	70,144	(50.1)	139,868	(100)

Source: Government of Mexico Census Data, 1970.

*Land in public "colonization" areas awarded to mostly landless peasants, at cost, who usually become small farmers.

**Total area for Mexico is 196,500,000 hectares.

Table 20.5
Land Classification, Mexico, 1960

Classification	Hectares (000s)	%
Arable	23,816.9	14.1
Grazing	79,092.2	46.8
Forest and Woodlands	43,678.6	25.8
Unused (productive)	11,142.7	6.6
Agricultural (unproductive)	11,303.7	6.7
Total in Census Units	169,084.2	100.0
Other (unusable)	27,410.0	
Total National Area	196,490.2	

Source: McEntire, Davis, and McEntire, Iras L.,

"Agrarian Reform in Mexico", Toward Modern

Land Policies, Ch. 5. (Padua, Italy:

University of Padua, 1975), p. 233.

justified today. Some who favor it exaggerate the amount of available arable land in Mexico. Others stress the high costs of preparing additional land for distribution. Nonetheless arable land could be increased from the current 23 million to 24 million hectares to an estimated 31 million to 37 million hectares (McEntire and McEntire, 1975, 266) (Table 20.5). Such an increase could help alleviate pressures on the land market for agriculture expansion, help the promotion of agricultural policies, and redress the losses due to soil depletion, erosion, and the increasingly larger losses due to urbanization and industrial growth. But topography (Figure 20.1) and economic conditions conspire against there being large increases in arable land in the near future.

Rural land policies will depend on effective rural land use, increased agricultural productivity, and diversification and generation of employment for the rural masses. Controlling the ownership of land is not enough; assigning it a best use for developmental purposes is necessary and urgent.

Figure 20.1 Map Showing Topography of Mexico

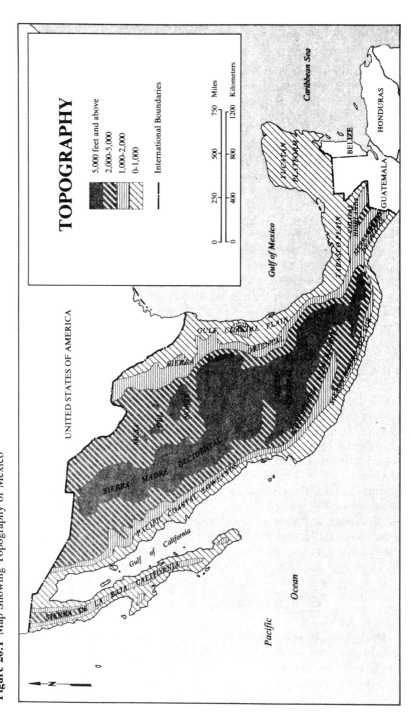

Demographic Trends and Land Requirements

In the past, it was common to consider some developing countries, especially Mexico, as demographic time bombs. Mexico indeed had one of the highest population growth rates, but the trends are less distressing today, and there are indications that they can be dealt with.

Mexico's demography has been subject to difficulties of precision because various methodologies and estimates have been used, with discrepant results. Table 20.6 summarizes population figures for 1980 and estimates for 2000 from different sources.[12] The estimates for 2000 range from 100 million to 131 million. The high projection would mean almost another doubling of Mexico's current population. The low estimates, in view of current trends, probably will not be achieved. A likely figure for 2000 is the UN's medium variant of 113.4 million. Even this figure, however, spells strong demographic pressures on land and urban development in the next two decades.

The corresponding low variant estimate for the urban component is 89.5 million and 26.2 million for the rural component. That means that the present urban population will almost double. Land for urban growth could amount to about 1.3 million hectares.[13] In 2000, the population will be mostly young (under 30) and have an average life expectancy of about 70 years (about six more than in 1980). Besides land for industrial and commercial expansion, adequate land will be needed for housing, highways, streets, urban facilities, parks and recreation areas, airports, services, and other infrastructure. To a large extent, land for these uses will reduce the inventory of agricultural land. Therefore comprehensive land use planning for urban areas is essential.

A crucial problem in urban development planning is the imbalance in Mexico's urban structure. The main aspects of such imbalance have been summarized in the National Urban Development Plan. In 1940 the number of localities with a population of over 2,500 was 686; in 1980, it was 2,152. The population in those localities increased from about 5.9 million to about 46.6 million during the same period, about an eight-fold increase. The problem comes into focus when one observes that there were 224 cities of 15,000 or more, accounting for about 53 percent of the population, but that only three major cities—Mexico City, Guadalajara, and Monterrey—accounted for about 26.5 percent of the population. In 1980, 95,410 settlements of less than 2,500 accounted for about 33 percent of the total population (Table 20.7). The small number of middle-sized cities shows the structural imbalance that requires correction.

By the year 2000 the three largest cities are estimated to hold over 34 percent of the total population (minimum estimate, 40 million), which would engulf disproportionately much of the GNP, industrial production, expenditures and consumption, commerce, and other activities. The costs of providing services would be staggering, increased by the costs of infrastructure to move goods and people. At another level about 33 percent of the total population lives in settlements of fewer than 2,500 and another 15 percent in settlements between 2,500

Table 20.6
Demographic Estimates, Mexico, 1980–2000 (000s)

Type of Estimate	1980 (AROG)*	2000 (AROG)
	United Nations	
Low Variant	69,752 (2.8)	113,443 (2.0)
Medium Variant	69,752 (3.0)	115,659 (2.2)
High Variant	69,752 (2.9)	119,113 (2.4)
	United Nations	
Growth Formula	69,965	131,244
Urban	46,660	102,293
Rural	23,305	29,951
	Alvarado-Fox	
Growth Formula	68,902	128,855
	Mexico, CONAPO	
Historical Projec- tion	69,347 (2.8)	128,356 (3.2)
Programmatic Pro- jection	69,347 (2.7)	100,041 (1.4)
Alternative Pro- jection	69,347 (2.7)	106,570 (2.1)

Sources: Demographic Indicators of Countries:
Estimates and Projections Assessed in 1980
(New York: United Nations, ST/ESA/SER.A/82,
1982), p. 212.

Pattern's of Urban and Rural Population Growth.
(New York: United Nations, ST/ESA/SER.A/68,
1980), Table 48.

Fox, Robert. Urban Population Growth Trends
in Latin America. (Washington, DC: Inter-
American Development Bank, 1975), Table 30.

México Demográfico. (Mexico City: Consejo
Nacional de Población, 1982), p. 13.

*AROG - Average Rate of Growth

Table 20.7

Mexico: Distribution of the Population* by Size of Settlement and by Year**
(1940–1960–1980–2000)

Settlement Population Size	1940 No.	1940 Pop.	1940 %	1960 No.	1960 Pop.	1960 %	1980 No.	1980 Pop.	1980 %	2000 No.	2000 Pop.	2000 %
1,000,000 or more	1	1,560	7.9	1	4,910	14.1	3	18,380	26.5		36,998	34.0
100,000 – 999,999	5	781	4.0	16	4,059	11.6	51	12,103	17.4		26,704	24.5
15,000 – 99,999	49	1,587	8.1	106	3,778	10.9	170	6,119	8.8		8,029	7.4
2,500 – 14,999	631	1,973	10.0	1,089	5,288	15.1	1,928	9,954	14.4		12,419	11.4
Up to 2,500	104,801	13,748	70.0	87,793	16,888	48.3	95,410	22,791	32.9		24,582	22.6
TOTAL	105,488	19,649	100.0	89,005	34,923	100.0	97,562	69,347	100.0		108,732	100.0

Source: Working document, "Projecto Estrategico Ciudades Medias" (Mexico, SEDUE, 1984). Tables 1.1-A, 1.1-B.

*In thousands

**Estimates for 2000 are based on SEDUE projections.

547

and 15,000, most of them lacking amenities. It is impossible to provide adequate services to such a large number of dispersed small settlements within the fiscal limitations expected for the next decade or so. Therefore, those people will suffer inadequate services or drastic inattention. Certainly efficiencies of scale must be realized, for which medium–sized cities must be encouraged and large metropolises discouraged. Current efforts are aimed to those ends, especially in priority population centers.[14]

Urban Land Problems

In Mexico scarcity of arable land precluded the allocation of extra land for future urban growth. The trend was solidified by the agrarian reform laws, which made *ejido* and communal lands strictly agricultural and inalienable. Much of Mexican urbanization, however, shows the gulf between what is established as legal and what is done in practice.

Land has always been big business. And although all interests (industry, housing, agriculture, mining, ranching, and others) vocally support public land policies, in practice their political influence and the profit motive (aided by the ease with which officials can be bribed) help them undermine the objectives of state and local land use plans, adding to the undisciplined development. At another level urban growth and scarcity of land led to the development of high–density urban settlements of substandard quality (*colonias, tujurios, vecindades, barrios*).[15] The growth of illegal settlements in *ejido* and communal lands has been more dramatic and unstoppable. That illegal growth, however, has shown that the role of government agencies and officials, private developers, peasants, and low–income sectors can be counterproductive in terms of land uses and planning.[16]

Land Market

The urban land market is full of irregularities, especially in the fastest growing cities. On the whole old urban land was acquired by industries, developers, and government agencies, exacerbating the costs of land in the process. Since there were no vacant urban lands, the low–income sectors were driven to areas of cheaper land—most often to otherwise undesirable land (such as in hillsides or dried–up lake beds) or to areas of dubious tenure and not planned for housing.

Communal and *ejido* lands have been transferred to urban uses by various illegal though common and profitable processes, distorting the regular land market. At times, the government's role had a counterproductive effect on the prices of land, especially when it legalized illegal settlements, thereby sanctioning the profitable corruption of *ejido* officials, developers, and public officials. The public sector's development projects cause increases in the price of land surrounding or near them. But the minimal debate on how government should intervene in the capture of the windfall profits involved will likely continue, allowing still higher prices for land.

The land market in Mexican cities is unlikely to improve in the face of expected demographic growth, especially in the priority areas where urban development will be promoted and in border cities as well. The lower–income sectors will be the most affected.[17]

The area of Lazaro Cardenas, for example, developed urban settlements for low–income and migrant populations that overwhelmed the planned urban settlements. In the end, the illegal settlements had to be provided with costly services, ironically establishing exactly what planning had aimed to avoid.

Legal Aspects of Urban Land Tenure

Desirable lands changed hands on a large scale in Mexican history, and not all of those changes have been recorded appropriately. Titles and tract surveys are not up to date everywhere. In urban areas the costs of developing modern plat systems have discouraged their implementation. Therefore titles too often are the subject of legal wrangling.

The legality of tenure is much more complex for lands previously in *ejido* or communal tenure. Therefore this issue affects large parts of the urban populations. In Mexico City, for example, from 1940 to 1975, about 47 percent of the new growth took place in *ejido* or communal lands—therefore illegally. By 1977, the low–income settlements, most of them illegal and substandard, covered about 64 percent of metropolitan Mexico City. Current Mexican legislation is inadequate as Azuela shows.[18]

In the same vein, Schteingart, after analyzing the role of the participants in the process of creation of urban land, concedes that the poor fare badly because they have "insufficient power to alter the capitalist logic of developing urban land."[19] It is clear that the role of government is not that of an unwilling or innocent bystander.

Impact of Urban Development on Land Costs

As in all other industrializing nations urban land costs have soared, due mainly to the role of the government. But a clear cause of large increases has been the provision of services, which often prices those lands beyond the low–income sector's ability to pay. Ironically, after helping to legalize newly urbanized areas, the government, when it needed land for public housing, had to buy those same lands at the market price, essentially paying for its own contributions to the price.[20]

The high price of land places low–income sectors in worse circumstances than ever. In 84 cities households earning the minimum income cannot afford the cheapest lot available; and in 25 cities even those households with two to two and a half times the minimum income cannot afford the cheapest lots available.[21] Yet Mexico needs over 80,000 hectares for current housing programs alone, and estimates show that by the year 2000 it will need at least to duplicate its current urban areas. Inevitably scarcity of land will increase prices of urban land to new heights.[22]

Legalization of Land Tenure

Today most *ejido* and communal lands converted to urban uses have been legalized. The various previous illegal means for such land development led to government intervention. The creation of *fideicomisos* (trust funds), which had the right to expropriate lands for public uses, proved inadequate to deal with the amount of *ejido* and communal land being transferred to urban uses. Therefore, in August 1973, the Commission for Regularization of Land Tenure (CORETT) was created. At first it was a weak coordinating commission, dealing with the Institute of Community Development (INDECO) and the National Fund for *Ejido* Development (FONAFE). Article 52 of the new Agrarian Reform Law (1971) reaffirmed the inalienability of communal and *ejido* lands, and CORETT used prescribed processes of expropriation and indemnification to balance the rights of the *ejidatarios* (previous owners of the land) with those of the people who lived on those lands—as new owners or tenants. As part of the overall settlement, the *ejidatario* often received two urbanized lots plus some cash.

CORETT, in the role of a developer, sold the lots—often after providing improvements and services—to those already living on them. But for those new owners, this process usually meant paying a second time since they had already paid for the lots once before. A detailed analysis of the process of *regularizacion* is presented by Legorreta and also in a study on housing by COPEVI.[23] Covarrubias, a key housing official, provides an opinion on the options open to Mexican institutions to deal in this complex arena in the future. He outlines some corrective mechanisms to deal with the windfall profits, rights of squatters, rights of public agencies, legal processes of production of urban land and assignation to low–income sectors, and others.[24]

Housing and Land Requirements

There have been various studies of housing in Mexico, one of the most vexing aspects of its development. COPEVI, for example, focused a broad effort on housing policies and programs during 1975–76.[25] Various federal housing agencies have published reviews of their operations and the housing sector at large. But the first truly comprehensive housing program was the National Housing Program.

National Housing Program

The *Programa Nacional de Vivienda* (PNV) is a detailed document developed within the guidelines established by the General Law of Human Settlements and the PNDU.[26] It is divided into four parts or levels. Its major objectives, as summarized by SAHOP, include the improvement of the housing conditions of the low–income sectors and framing the housing programs within the nation's economic, social, and political possibilities. The areas for priority action are: support for self–help construction; broad promotion of cooperative housing;

promotion of rental housing for low–income sectors; support for rural housing appropriate for each region; and provision of emergency housing to those affected by natural disasters. The normative level provides a summary of housing conditions and estimates of housing demand, emphasizing the period of 1977–82. It provides details on how each major aspect of housing was conceptualized and the programs resulting from such analyses. This section includes objectives by types of production and sources of funding.

The strategic level describes how the PNV will provide programs to meet the needs of housing (at different levels of income, types of housing, size of urban area). It specifies aspects that deal with construction of housing, such as materials and technologies, and how the programs will affect those factors. This level deals with aspects of land for housing at the national and state levels.

The sectoral coresponsibility level describes the participation of federal agencies and housing institutions (trust funds, institutes, banks, programs) in the achievement of the PNV's housing objectives. It takes into consideration the programmed emphasis on priority population centers and the deemphasis in planning and regulation zones. It specifies the types of housing to be produced not only by the different agencies but by the private and the social sectors as well.

The instrumental level deals with legal, regulatory, and other instruments that affect the development and implementation of the PNV. It provides a summary of previous legislation on housing, regulations that affect or allow specific actions at state and local levels, and intergovernmental agreements. It summarizes investments by agencies, production by all institutions involved, costs, other information, and administrative and evaluative considerations.

Urban Housing Land Problems

As the PNV points out land-related problems of cities include inadequate location of housing projects, lack of coordination of housing programs with local development plans (causing overloads on available services and infrastructure and undesirable development), and the inability to capture or benefit from the large windfall profits caused by public programs, thereby making these programs continuous resource drains. The public housing agencies must face increasing land prices, difficulties in obtaining services and permits at local level, lack of land in the market, lack of land reserves, and difficulties in building such reserves or land banks. The land market faces the disorganized demand for land by the competing public agencies and continuous shortages of land, which makes it difficult to prepare land at reasonable costs, especially for low–income housing.

By most standards average land costs in Mexico are high, with choice spaces in Mexico City among the highest in the world. INFONAVIT and other agencies estimate that costs of developed land for housing amount to about 24.5 percent of all costs; housing construction about 59 percent; and financing and other administrative costs amount to about 16.5 percent.[27] Therefore, given the high prices of land, even proposed low–income housing is already beyond the reach of low-income sectors. Covarrubias indicates that households earning a minimum income cannot buy land in 86 cities.

Certainly there are doubts that current housing policies and programs (see Table 20.8), even with increased funding, could manage even to keep up with demographic growth by 2000. Public housing production in Mexico, which began in the 1920s, has not been impressive. From 1925 to 1977, all public housing production amounted to only 600,000 units. There are, however, current efforts to try various innovations in housing finance in Mexico, as well as to introduce new building technologies, industrialized methods, and new materials to the construction sector. Nonetheless, it should take some time to get those innovations to production stage. Consequently the estimates for housing deficits in the future should be considered severe threats to future urban quality and quantity of housing.

The land requirements for the programs proposed in the PNV are vast and costly. Some figures, using low estimates for demographic growth, are shown in Table 20.9.

Urban land required for the year 2000 is over 230,000 hectares. Using Schteingart et al.'s estimates for the current size of metropolitan Mexico City (1,000 square kilometers), demographic growth alone will require land enough for 2.3 times the size of metropolitan Mexico City today.

RECENT APPROACHES TO LAND USE PLANNING AND DEVELOPMENT

Constitutional Amendments

In 1976, along with the General Law of Human Settlements, Congress approved amendments to Articles 27, 73, and 115 of the Constitution. Article 27 clarified the concept of social benefit for use or disposition of public property; stressed the equal distribution of public wealth to benefit national urban and rural development; cleared the way for adoption of legislation or regulation on land use, urban planning, and conservation and regulation of energy; and redefined territorial waters and the economic exclusivity rights to them. Article 73 increased congressional powers to legislate in matters dealing with the federal district and to involve federal, state, and local levels in the use of public resources for development. Article 115 (which deals with political subdivisions) was amended to provide for minority representation in local councils, proportional representation in *municipios* with over 300,000 inhabitants, and increased powers of states and *municipios* to legislate on the use of natural resources for urban development and to participate in the decisions regarding conurbations.[28]

Table 20.8
Urban Housing Trends, Mexico, 1977–1982 and 1982–2000 (units)

Needs Due to:	1977-1982	1982-2000	
		Low Estimate	High Estimate
Demographic Growth*	1,814,398	4,732,142	9,500,500
Replacement**	600,795	2,162,852	2,162,852
Rehabilitation**	363,083	1,307,030	1,307,080
Total Housing needs	2,778,273	8,202,292	12,969,950
New Stock into Market	1,746,358	4,000,000***	4,000,000***
Estimated Deficit	1,031,915	4,200,000	6,900,000

Source: Mexico, Programa Nacional de Vivienda (PNV), Abridged Version, (Mexico City:

SAHOP, 1979–), pp. 4, 10.

*Pre-1980 estimates by the Consejo Nacional de Población. For 1977-82, an annual growth rate of 3.2% would mean 178,571 additional units, for a total deficit of 1,210,386 units.

**Replacement (within 25 years) is for 'non-acceptable stock', and rehabilitation (within 50 years) is for 'acceptable stock'.

***These are conservative estimates. Choice of projections for 2000 result in different estimates. See, ibid., p. 145.

Table 20.9

Urban Land Use Requirements, Mexico, 1977–1982 and 1980–2000

	1977-1982	1980-2000
Demographic increase	11.0 million	30.8 million
Urban land needed	84,000 hectares	234,000 hectares
Land for housing*	10,000 hectares	27,000 hectares

Source: Mexico, Programa Nacional de Vivienda (PNV),

Abridged Version (Mexico City: SAHOP, 1979-),

p. 91.

*Based on 12% of total urban land requirements, Table,

ibid. p. 145, indicates 13,902 hectares for 1977-82.

General Law on Human Settlements, 20 May 1976

The basic objectives of this law (*Ley General de Asentamientos Humanos*) include provisions for the participation and coordination of the federal, state, and local levels in planning and regulation of human settlements; guidelines for human settlements, and guidelines for public decisions on allocations, reserves, and other land uses. These objectives are usually considered to define the National Planning System.

The law specifies that the planning and regulation of human settlements will involve the National Urban Development Plan, State Urban Development Plans, Municipal Urban Development Plans, and the Urban Development Plans for Conurbation Zones, all of which are to be prepared following appropriate guidelines with respect to nature, content, and updating. This law places the new interagency National Commission of Urban and Regional Planning in charge of coordination and plan development and outlines appropriate coordination guidelines for the more instrumental agencies (as well as for the President's Office). Also included are specific planning guidelines for conurbations.

This broad planning process as established by the law involves a two-way flow of coordination and supervision. While the federal level can provide guidelines for state plans, which include guidelines for local (*municipio*) plans, the local level is responsible for following the general guidelines. The process as outlined did not diminish the local level's independence to make decisions about local development. The state, however, must approve those local plans to make them legal planning instruments in the national system. Both the federal and the appropriate state levels participate in planning for federally designated conurbation zones. While the local (*municipio*) level is responsible for complying with the federal planning guidelines (for urban development, housing, industrialization, environment) and having its urban development plans approved by the state, the law provides for federal and state technical and other assistance to develop staff and expertise at local levels to achieve the planning objectives of the law. In practice, though the process has been slow, some local-level authorities feel that their plans, if approved at state level, have a better chance to be funded than others that have not been approved, despite their apparent priority or urgency. Such development was intended by the law, since it requires fulfillment of responsibilities by the next upper planning level. To provide for change, the law prescribes appropriate reviews and updates of the plans and programs involved.[29]

Another aspect to note is the implied effort in the law to decentralize planning responsibilities to state and local levels, something that has been pursued in various ways since then. The impact of this and other efforts on the central bureaucracy was expected to bring decisions on land use and development closer to the citizen. By most accounts, however, such expectations have not been fulfilled to the extent desired. The criticism for the delay is based on the lack of clear long-term regional or state development guidelines designed to end the profusion of (sometimes counterproductive) alternatives being considered and employed at local levels. But as the local levels develop the necessary expertise to plan in the new national framework, it is expected that the decentralization of planning will provide more effective development planning at the local level.

In 1978 the Lopez Portillo administration signed an executive decree establishing the National Urban Development Plan, designed to provide a structure for development options at national, regional, and local levels.

National Urban Development Plan 12 May 1978

The *Programa Nacional de Desarrollo Urbano* (PNDU) has two overall features: it reaffirms national planning as the public tool for development, and it proposes a comprehensive approach (crossing agency-sectoral lines) to study, analyze, and carry out national development schemes. These features involve two levels of action by the public sector: the direct action level (public—mainly federal—projects and financing) and the indirect level (the combination of financial, regulatory, programmatic, legislative, and other measures to promote private sector activities compatible with the PNDU). It is in that framework that the focus on national demography, resource development, and land use aspects becomes important for planning under the PNDU.

The PNDU is structured in four levels: normative, which defines the bases, objectives, and policies pursued by the PNDU; strategic, which outlines specific programs to achieve the stated objectives; sectoral joint responsibility, which determines the program and fiscal responsibilities of all agencies involved at federal, state and local levels; and instrumental, which deals with the legislative and administrative measures to ensure proper implementation of the appropriate programs and actions.

Normative Level

The introductory section provides the rationale for the PNDU and outlines its general framework, as well as its place in the government program structure. The diagnosis zeroes in on the imbalanced distribution of the population. It shows that about 38 percent of the population lives in small settlements of up to 2,500; about 26 percent in the three largest metropolitan areas (Mexico City, Guadalajara, and Monterrey); about 19 percent in small towns of 2,500 to 50,000; and only about 17 percent in cities of 50,000 to 1 million. The small number of medium-sized cities and the large number of small communities imply vast needs for infrastructure, services, and other resources throughout the country. On the other hand, the concentration of population and industrial activities, especially in Mexico City, has led to the concentration of public interest and resources to face urban development problems. A vicious circle developed, leading to the imbalance between the large metropolitan areas and the rest of the country. Such problems are the concern of the PNDU. Therefore, it aims to decentralize or regionalize all growth away from Mexico City, Guadalajara, and Monterrey. Using population estimates for the year 2000, the PNDU outlines the desired changes in urban demographic patterns, as well as the desired shift of population away from the traditionally overpopulated central zone.

Objectives

The objectives of the PNDU include promotion of the distribution of economic activities and population to areas of greater potential, the fostering of comprehensive and balanced urban development, and the fostering of conditions favorable to the provision of land, housing, urban infrastructure, and public facilities and services.

Policies

The PNDU outlines somewhat specific policies aimed to fulfill the objectives. National planning policies are designed to deal with national and regional urban problems by emphasizing distribution of services to all cities, discouraging growth in certain areas and cities, availing all services in a regional developmental scheme, and promoting the integration of development in a national scheme. Policies for urban development of population centers are designed to promote urban planning activities for priority centers. These policies would emphasize promotion (where growth seems compatible with the PNDU and effective federal action is necessary), consolidation (to take corrective action so that growth and

Figure 20.2 Priority Zones and Priority Population Centers

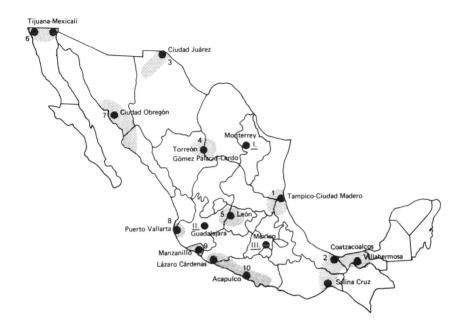

development takes place in a consistent framework), and planning and regulation (to deal with very problematic areas, and establish corrective actions). The policies for rural settlements aim to satisfy the needs of the rural sector. Policies for the human settlements sector focus on solving problems of land banking, urban land, housing, urban infrastructure, facilities and services, environment, urban emergencies, and community participation.

Classification of Priority Zones and Population Centers

Recognizing the limitations of funding, the PNDU established priorities for areas and cities whose growth problems are to be taken into account.

—Priority zones (Mexico City, Guadalajara, and Monterrey), which will require measures to control and regulate further growth; also referred to as planning and regulation zones

—Priority population centers: Ten areas that offer conditions to absorb coordinated economic and demographic growth and for which appropriate urban development policies of promotion and consolidation are recommended (Figure 20.2)[30]

—Cities with regional services: About 13 cities, most of them in the priority population centers, which will offer regional services in areas such as education, health, welfare, food supplies, transportation, and federal technical assistance centers

—Rural systems: Essentially agricultural and *ejido* service centers in about 16 areas where none existed and also in about 19 areas where improvements are needed

Strategic Level

This level outlines the types of programs contemplated in the PNDU.

Concerted action programs are multiagency federal programs aimed at solving problems that affect national urban development. Initially outlined were programs for decentralization of the federal bureaucracy, incentives for the decentralization of industrial sector, regional integration of urban services, interurban transportation networks, rural service centers and management of resources for urban settlements.

Programs to support sectoral priorities are multiagency federal programs that require large investments in infrastructure and facilities in priority areas. Among the main programs are infrastructure for fishing communities, for tourist centers, for energy resources, for priority industrial centers and industrial ports, and facilities for marketing operations.

Joint programs with states and municipalities, based on specific agreements, seek to ensure appropriate state and local actions consistent with their urban development plans and the PNDU. They include programs for urban development of population centers (with policies of promotion, consolidation, planning, or regulation, as appropriate), integration of rural population centers, and new population centers.

The five-year plan for the human settlement sector was put into effect by SAHOP, with the support of other agencies. It seeks to improve the infrastructure of human settlements. Its main programs dealt with planning of human settlements, technical assistance, urban land, water supply and sanitation, industrial parks and cities, urban transportation, housing rehabilitation, core housing, finished housing, cultural facilities and other public services, recreation and sports facilities, and fostering participation in community development.[31]

Joint Sectoral Responsibility

This level concerns the manner in which the federal agencies will coordinate their resources and programs to achieve the goals of the PNDU. It outlines the priorities to be considered and the necessary interagency agreements to carry them out. It mentions funding levels for 1978–82, emphasizing the programs of the human settlements and the transportation and communications sectors (about 790,000 new and rehabilitated housing units, potable water for over 6 million, sewerage for about 3.6 million, 3,800 kilometers of main highways and about

64,000 kilometers of secondary roads, over 250 kilometers of streets, and construction and maintenance of about 52 airports).

Legal and Other Instruments

This level deals with legislation and other instruments that would pave the way for federal, state, and local actions in support of the PNDU. One of the first measures was the executive order that formalized the program for the decentralization of the federal bureaucracy (16 January 78), which also aims to employ the decentralized federal machinery and its sizable budgets as another tool for economic and urban development. Soon after followed the executive decree that formalized the Program for Decentralization of the Industrial Sector (2 February 79), which also involved the major federal agencies. Other tools or instruments involve the Overall Coordination Agreement between the Federal Government and the States and two others specified in the PNDU: Urban Schemes for Federal Action and Common Bases for Planning Population Centers. Included in this level is the creation of an urban development information system, which was implemented by SAHOP and provided various types of publications on the PNDU and related aspects.

National Program for Ecological Development of Human Settlements, 1981

The *Programa Nacional de Desarrollo Ecologico de Los Asentamientos Humanos* (PNDEAH) was the object of much expectation by those involved in planning and development at all levels, especially to settle the qualitative aspects of development in Mexico.[32] In its preface, the PNDEAH recognized that national development problems made it necessary to "define policies and establish appropriate legislation to plan and regulate all aspects of urban life, as well as to plan adequately the managed growth of the cities to bring about improved living conditions to all citizens."[33]

The legal bases for the PNDEAH are Article 27 of the Constitution, the General Law of Human Settlements (especially Article 13), and the executive decree that approved the NUDP (especially Articles 3 and 5). In the planning field it is one of the major national urban development programs. Its application is mandatory, and the implementation of its policies involves interagency as well as federal–state-local agreements.

The objectives of the PNDEAH are to improve and preserve the environment of human settlements. Specific objectives include: rationalizing land use (at intra–urban and interurban levels); regulating the use and consumption of basic natural resources; supporting the provision of basic public services (in rural and suburban areas); developing and preserving sites and areas with natural resources; developing and preserving sites and areas with cultural resources; improving and preserving the landscape of human settlements; and improving housing and urban spaces.

These objectives are to be sought in coordination with and supporting other specific objectives of the PNDU and other development plans and programs. The general policies to guide program implementation include urban ecological and environmental considerations in planning, promotion of urban development in environmentally adequate areas, and coordination with human settlements policies that would help achieve environmental objectives. Consequently the PNDEAH is less a regulatory framework and more a "planning instrument that will aid adequate national planning and use of natural resources, therefore effecting the preservation and generation of environmental quality as well as improving the level of life of the population."[34]

The program is structured in four levels, though two of them are combined into one section of the main text, as they are summarized below.

Normative Level

This section includes comprehensive geographical, cultural, and environmental inventories, accompanied by detailed charts and maps that serve for analyses and programming.

—*Diagnosis.* This section details the following factors:

1. Natural factors analyzed include the climate (rain, humidity, insolation, winds), geological land formations, soil characteristics, vegetation and patterns of agriculture, rural and urban land uses, and resulting complexities of land use.

2. Resource factors analyzed include geological factors of land (seismicity, faults, mineral deposits), hydrological resources (rivers, water tables, recharge and discharge areas), natural and cultural sites that need attention or protection, recreational resources, and others.

3. Environmental factors analyzed include erosion, depletion of water resources, water quality, land use methods and soil exhaustion, solid and other wastes, and environmental pollution and its impact on the Mexican population.

—*Units of Analysis.* This section explains the methodological considerations that led to the division of the country into 940 basic environmental units. Each unit is provided detailed information about the factors mentioned above, as well as recommendations for land uses in that unit. In a larger framework are the areas of environmental analysis (*areas de diagnóstico*), which comprise various environmental units that share economic and productivity characteristics or factors (which involve 13 variables). The resulting comprehensive tables were prepared for planning uses and for other locational documentation as well. These environmental units and areas of environmental analysis are emphasized in planning, especially in areas within the priority zones and in planning and regulation zones.

—*Environmental Classification for Land Use.* With respect to land use and use

of other resources, the analyses led to the recommendation of policies of preservation, use, development (exploitation), and regeneration (improvement). Such
policies have been coordinated with those of the PNDU and therefore use the
development scheme of 10 priority population centers and three planning and
regulation zones. The resulting classifications have been included in appropriate
tables of areas for development, conservation, or improvement. It is expected
that the policy applied reflects the resources available and the area's classification
within PNDU plans.

—*Prognosis.* This section is probably the most directly related to environmental
aspects of developmental planning in Mexico. Besides acknowledging eight
considerations or problem areas, it focuses on the impact of each of them on
future development (short and long term). Its use of demographic estimates of
growth to estimate impacts (or scenarios of impact) of those considerations should
be important for guiding national, state, and local planning, especially for the
population center and the planning and regulation zones. Those considerations
include population, land use, natural resources, cultural resources, water resources (and their use), water pollution, air pollution, and solid waste.

—*Goals and Objectives.* This section restates the general and specific policies
and objectives sought by the PNDEAH in the short, medium, and long term. It
also includes appropriate recommendations for action at all levels.

Strategic and Sectoral Coresponsibility Levels

This section (a combination of two levels) establishes the coordination of the
policies of this program with those of other national development programs.
First it treats the policies of the human settlements sector—mainly housing,
urban infrastructure, land and land reserves, urban development administration,
urban emergencies, and community participation—which are now the purview
of the Secretariat of Urban Development and Ecology (SEDUE), which replaced
SAHOP. It also specifies policy coordination with the Global Development Plan,
the National Plan of Industrial Development (PNDI), the National Agroindustrial
Development Plan (PNDA), the National Plan for Depressed Areas and Marginal
Groups (PNZDGM), the National Tourism Plan (PNT), the National Fishing
Plan (PNP), and the National Employment Plan (PNE).[35]

The PNDEAH focuses its activites on three major program perspectives:

1. Conservation and development of natural and cultural resources: Aimed to preserve
   and improve sites, areas, and resources that have natural or cultural value, not only
   to preserve them but to use them as part of the development schemes
2. Use of natural resources for public services: Aimed at the appropriate exploitation of
   natural resources (water, land, renewable energy) to achieve urban development
   objectives
3. Regeneration: Aimed at reducing and eliminating sources of air, water, and solid waste
   pollution, especially where further urban development is contemplated and where
   dense populations currently suffer dangerous levels of pollution. The specific programs
   established by the PNDEAH, which are to be implemented at all levels, fall in three

categories: programs of the human settlements sector (10 programs), programs of concerted action (four programs), and programs to be accorded with state and local governments (four programs).[36]

The section on program coordination identifies all of the agencies and subagencies involved in the implementation of the above programs. Therefore the matrix tables include appropriate agencies, priority of area in which the program is to be implemented, terms of implementation, and other data for each of the 18 programs and for about 22 subprograms and 28 activities. The main chart in this section explains the relationship of the objectives, policies, and programs. This approach is followed by a summary page that includes appropriate data of the main matrices for each program activity and the locations in which it is expected to be carried out.

Instrumental Level

This level deals with the legal instruments that support or give the necessary authority to the PNDEAH. First, it explains how the PNDU was approved and how the PNDEAH fits within its framework of action (both were authorized by executive decrees). The instruments, including regulatory material and documentation, are presented under several headings:

1. Legal basis: Specific constitutional articles and parts of laws at federal and state levels
2. Administrative regulations: At federal and state levels (including for commissions and other state enterprises)
3. Technical documentation from all sources
4. Others from the appropriate economic, financial, social, and communications agencies

The section on proposed instruments includes proposals for changes or additions to the General Law of Human Settlements (1976), a proposal for a law for environmental planning, and others at federal and state levels. In separate annexes, the PNDEAH provides appropriate maps, charts, and other documentation that clarify the information summarized in the main text or provide more detailed information for use in the development of state and local plans.

National Planning Law, January 1983

The *Ley de Planeación* restates that national planning is the direct responsibility of the executive branch.[37] This law does not affect all the sectoral planning that is required by other laws. Rather, it defines the process of national development planning and specifies how federal agencies and others will be involved in it.

The overseer of the planning system is the Secretariat of Programming and Budget (Secretaria de Programmacion y Presupuesto, SPP), with the participation of federal agencies and state-owned enterprises. Representative organizations of peasant, labor, and other working sectors are also mentioned as participants of the process, as well as others from academia, the private sector, and so on. Public participation provided for in this law took place in the form of *consultas populares* (mass hearings) throughout the country.[38]

The National Development Plan must be published by each administration within six months of taking office. As specified, only this document will be known as the plan. President de la Madrid published the *Plan Nacional de Desarrollo* in mid-1983, and it was given wide circulation.

The National Planning Law evinces that Mexico is involved in national planning. But as the current plan shows, it is much more an overall framework of policies and objectives, with very little quantification and no sectoral targets and allocations or specific indexes of activity associated with state planning in planned economies. Nonetheless, it offers flexibility for adjusting to sudden changes in national and international trends, and it also aims to impose some discipline in program implementation and meeting objectives. For details on housing and urban development, environment, and other aspects related to land and land uses, the relevant documents will continue to be those sectoral plans reviewed in the previous sections.

CONCLUDING REMARKS AND FUTURE THRUSTS

Despite Mexico's tortuous history of policies and practices with respect to land, its efforts have been commendable, especially from the social point of view. Today, however, industrialization presents important priorities. Even in the framework of industrialization, it cannot be claimed that the plight of the landless and homeless has been set aside. To the contrary, their condition is a key consideration in planning. Certainly land use policies that affect the masses could have been more adequate, but the case is that they are improving.

On a broader scale Mexican efforts to regulate land and the environment have been effective. Mexico boasts large tracts of land dedicated to national parks, forests, aquatic preserves, national historic sites and monuments, and ecological protection areas. Ecological considerations for industrial and urban growth reflect the concern for the quality of life in the future, a concern almost unmatched elsewhere in the industrializing world.

The claim that corruption is the other face of socially minded policies cannot be easily explained away. Yet corruption in land-related operations is not a Mexican invention; land deals have been corrupting greedy owners and officials throughout history. The fact that paints those practices in Mexico with sinister colors is that they are so profuse and add to the suffering of the poor. This aspect, however, seems to be less troublesome to Mexicans than to outsiders. Therefore, it is not surprising that calls for national reform do not excite the masses. Consequently the problem may lie more in the people's condescension rather than in officialdom's proclivities for the traditional *mordida* and *negociados*.

The traces of past policies and practices are clear. The *ejido* is a cousin of the *calpullalli* and *altepetlalli*. The *hacienda*, though made obsolete by modern agriculture, has left rural Mexico scarred. And as always, land policies are of national interest and change hard to forge. Therefore, it is recognized that the *ejido*, as a form of land tenure, is one of the most solid institutions of Mexico today. That is essentially the basis on which land policies must rest. The strength of the revolution and the agrarian reform in this area slows the pace of planning and forces compromises in new policies. Consequently, the historical background should not be underestimated in understanding land use aspects in Mexico.

The requirements of industrialization and of large-scale agriculture should not be considered as threats to the *ejido*. By the same token, it is unrealistic to consider the *ejido* as the only solution to Mexico's rural and agricultural problems. What is clear, if worldwide trends are to hold, is that the small and subsistence farming sector will diminish with industrialization and urbanization. In that sense, it is not as important that such a trend be considered a trade of problems of the landless for those of urban homeless. What is more important is that appropriate urban planning today may make the problems of tomorrow more manageable, and perhaps solve them.

Mexican politics most likely will continue voicing rhetorical support for appropriate land use policies, and regulations and plans will be written as well. Political influence in the implementation of policies, however, will continue, especially since the development of an effective independent and impersonal bureaucracy will take time, and the politicized partisan machinery within the bureaucracy is unlikely to fade away. But in the area of land and human settlements, scrutiny by some sectors of the media, in academia, and in some isolated sectors, has affected the working range of political influence. Certainly such hopeful signs need to be nurtured.

Other factors can be pointed out that affect land use policies and practices in Mexico. But on the positive side, development, or the need for it, has forced the convergence of aims and interests of most sectors. Therefore the political sectors are now more attentive to the technical long–term aspects of developmental planning, as are the technocratic sectors of *realpolitik* about policy implementation. Development of plans has provided ample opportunities for *concientizacion* (consciousness raising) of broad sectors to the needs of workable long–term approaches, as is evinced by the aims of the national urban development and housing plans. Indeed, few would claim that current policies and practices in Mexico could not have been improved. But most will agree that the current structure of planning provides adequate grounds to face the future without despairing and to improve the efficiency of the system.

NOTES

Quotations from works in Spanish are the author's translations.

1. The *calpullalli* (from *calpulli*, roughly a clan, extended family, or family group) included lands for homes and crops for all the entitled households of the *calpulli*. Each household used its land with exclusivity but could not dispose of it. The chief of the

calpulli kept a map of the distribution of plots and was in charge of reallotting those lands that were vacated or returned to the *calpullalli*. Similarly, decisions on variances, reallocation to descendants, requests for more land, and others were also decided at this clan or *calpullalli* level, seemingly precluding the rise of tribal or regional frictions because of land issues.

2. The *altepetlalli* were public lands set aside for the *calpulli* for nonagricultural uses (forests for fuel and timber, hunting, storage) and also included agricultural lands worked by the people of the *calpulli*, the production of which served to pay local administrative tributes and other tributes to the king. These commons were an important feature of land tenure since a *calpulli* could grow only with new allotments from *altepetlalli* lands, an important issue in the dense agricultural central zone even then.

3. The *condueñazgo* (shared ownership) involved lands allocated by the Aztecs to a community, which were later redistributed or inherited according to past custom and which managed to survive in such tenure. In some cases, there were clear titles to the *condueñazgo* lands (some of them granted by the Spanish viceroy), and their legal distribution later gave way usually to *ranchos* or private small farmsteads and to *rancherias* (groups of *ranchos*). Where titles did not exist or were unclear, even if the land had been successively distributed, the Indians usually ended dislodged and landless. In most cases, Indians with *condueñazgo* lands formed *congregaciones* or *communidades* (villages) and often included neighbors with lands too small for viable *ranchos* or crops and who therefore were forced to work for others.

4. Mexico's FOVI and FOGA loan–guarantee programs for housing were developed with assistance from the Alliance for Progress.

5. The high profile of President de la Madrid in the announcement of the plan and its aims was well covered in the press; see *El Dia* (Mexico City), 16 April 1980.

6. The revolution is not to be blamed for the vast inequalities; one only wishes it had reduced them more.

7. This is apparently symptomatic. As Eyler N. Simpson put it, "the contrast between the Mexican's ability to formulate the most beautiful *proyectos* for social reform and his lack of enthusiasm for the prosaic business of actually putting these projects into effect." *The Ejido; Mexico's Way Out* (Chapel Hill: University of North Carolina Press, 1937), p. 75.

8. Antonio Azuela de la Cueva, "La Legislación del Suelo Urbano: Auge o Crisis?" Paper presented at the Fourteenth Congress of the Inter–American Society for Planning, Morelia, Mexico, 10–15 October 1982, pp. 9–10 (hereafter cited as Fourteenth SIAP Congress).

9. Regional balance, economic growth, and decentralization are not necessarily directly correlated. See, for example, Scott (1982, 245–55).

10. Daniel Hiernaux Nicolas and Elsa Laurelli, "Políticas de Tierra y Organización en la Microregión de Ciudad Lazaro Cardenas, Michoacan," Fourteenth SIAP Congress.

11. Ciudad Juarez, Tijuana, and Laredo, for example, grew so fast that their efforts to deal with the lack of water, sewerage systems, and other infrastructure were overwhelmed by new growth.

12. If the demographic growth rate does not diminish, estimates for 2000 reach as high as 152 million and a population of about 44 million for Mexico City. See Mexico, Secretaria de Asentamientos Humanos y Obras Públicas (SAHOP), *Programa Nacional de Desarrollo Ecológico de los Asentamientos Humanos*, Desarrollo Urbano Series (Mexico City, 1981), p. 90.

13. A high figure, 4.0 million hectares was estimated by SAHOP; see ibid., p. 91.

14. See "Proyecto Estratégico Ciudades Medias," a project report that sets the basis for just such a comprehensive effort by the Secretaria de Desarrollo Urbano y Ecología (SEDUE).

15. Mexican low–income housing lexicon includes *vecindades* (old buildings subdivided into small tenement units), *tugurios* (slum neighborhoods in old city centers, which have *vecindades*), *jacales* (improvised housing of scrap materials), illegal subdivisions, usually through invasions about the city's outskirts (the invaders are called *parachutists*), and *colonia proletaria* (a large urbanization or illegal subdivision of mostly self–built homes, which usually becomes legalized and is provided services).

16. Francisco Covarrubias Gaitan, "La Problemática de la Tenencia y Uso de la Tierra Urbana," Fourteenth SIAP Congress, p. 3.

17. Jorge Legorreta, "El Acceso a la Tierra Urbana y el Mercado Inmobiliario Popular," Fourteenth SIAP Congress, p. 26. Hiernaux and Laurelli, "Políticas de Tierra," p. 20.

18. Azuela, "La Legislación del Suelo," p. 2.

19. Martha Schteingart, "La Incorporación de la Tierra Rural de Propiedad Social a la Lógica Capitalista del Desarrollo Urbano: el Caso de Mexico," Fourteenth SIAP Congress, p. 16.

20. Ibid.; Legorreta, "El Acceso," pp. 18–26.

21. Covarrubias, "La Problemática," p. 3.

22. Ibid., p. 2. Covarrubias also includes a table that shows urban land requirements for 1978–82, for some federal programs (housing, infrastructure, industrial sites), about 12,105 hectares—about 6,800 hectares of that for housing. In view of overall estimates, the federal participation is certainly small.

23. Legorreta, "El Acceso" pp. 18–26; Centro Operacional de Vivienda y Poblamiento (COPEVI), "Las Políticas Habitacionales del Estado Mexicano," *Investigación Sobre Vivienda* (Mexico City, 1977), 3:127–42.

24. Covarrubias, "La Problemática."

25. See, COPEVI "Las Políticas," and "La Producción de Vivienda en la Zona Metropolitana de la Ciudad de Mexico," vol. 2, same series.

26. Mexico, Secretaria de Asentamientos Humanos y Obras Públicas (SAHOP), *Programa Nacional de Vivienda, Abridged Version*, Desarrollo Urbano Series (Mexico City, 1979).

27. Ibid., p. 14. See also, Demetrios A. Germidis, *The Construction Industry in Mexico*, Technical Paper Series (Paris: OECD, 1972).

28. The *municipio* (akin to a U.S. county) is the lowest level of government; therefore conurbations involve two or more *municipios* in one or more states. The law (May 1976) was amended in 1981 by the addition of Chapter 5, Land for Urban Housing. It provides for *municipio*, state, and federal action to acquire land for low–income housing (including by expropriation).

29. Some of the plans published following those guidelines and other documentation are included in my bibliography; see Leo F. Pozo–Ledezma, *Housing and Urban Development Planning in Mexico; A Bibliography*, HUD–IA–568 (Washington, D.C.: U.S. HUD, 1980).

30. This classification has been used for all planning, with few adjustments.

31. The fiscal crisis and change in administrations affected this plan. In 1983, the

Secretariat of Urban Development and Ecology replaced SAHOP, and some substantial reorganization took place.

32. *Ecología* (ecology) is equivalent to the term *environment*.

33. Mexico, SAHOP, *Programa Nacional de Desarrollo Ecológico de los Asentamientos Humanos*, Desarrollo Urbano Series (Mexico City, 1981), p. xix. This program engulfs the *Programa Nacional de Ecología Urbana* (Mexico City, 1981), same series.

34. Ibid., summary by Sanchez de Carmona, pp. xv-xvii.

35. Ibid., Chap. 6.

36. Ibid., p. 145.

37. Mexico, "Ley de Planeación," *Diario Oficial*, 5 January 1983. This law abrogates the General Planning Law of 12 July 1930.

38. *Consultas Populares* are mass events, held in stadia, conference halls, theaters, and similar places. They are well prepared and have a partisan tone. Although the attendants cannot change the decisions announced, the events provide opportunities to decisionmakers to share information with the masses. The process seems to be functional to the political system.

BIBLIOGRAPHY

Azuela de la Cueva, Antonio. 1982. La Legislacion del Suelo Urbano: Auge o Crisis? Paper presented to the 14th Congress of the Inter–American Planning Society, Morelia, Mexico, 10–15 October.

Baerresen, Donald W. 1971. *The Border Industrialization Program of Mexico*. Lexington, Mass.: D. C. Heath.

Birou, Alain. 1971. *Fuerzas Campesinas y Politicas Agrarias en ⌐ ⌐rica Latina*. Translated Susana Antolinez. Madrid: IEPAL.

Brown, Peter G., and Henry Shue, eds. 1983. *The Border That Joins Mexican Migrants and U.S. Responsibility*. Totowa, N.J.: Rowman and Littlefield.

Centro Operacional de Vivienda y Poblamiento. 1977. La Produccion de Vivienda en la Zona Metropolitana de la Ciudad de Mexico. *Investigacion Sobre Vivienda*, vol. 2. Mexico City: COPEVI.

Centro Operacional de Vivienda y Poblamientou. 1977. Las Politicas Habitacionales del Estado Mexicano. *Investigacion Sobre Vivienda*, vol. 3. Mexico City: COPEVI.

Cornelius, Wayne A., and Felicity M. Trueblood, eds. 1975. *Urbanization and Inequality: The Political Economy of Urban and Rural Development in Latin America*, Latin American Research Series, vol. 5. Beverly Hills: Sage Publications.

Covarrubias G., Francisco. 1982. La Problematica de la Tenencia y Uso de la Tierra Urbana. Paper presented to the 14th Congress of the Inter–American Planning Society, Morelia, Mexico, 10–15 October.

Diaz del Castillo, Bernal. 1981. *Historia Verdadera de la Conquista de la Nueva Espana*. 4th ed. Madrid: Espasa–Calpe.

Dorsey, Robert W. 1980. The Concept of Property; Its Function in Relationship to Social Systems and Housing Therein. *Housing Science and Its Applications* 4:271–82.

Dunkerley, Harold B. et al. 1978. *Urban Land Policy Issues and Opportunities*. 2 vols. Staff Working Paper No. 283. Washington, D.C.: World Bank.

Engineering News-Record. 1982. Construction and Engineering in Mexico. Special Advertising Section, July.

Fox, Robert W. 1975. *Urban Population Growth Trends in Latin America*. Washington, D.C.: Inter–American Development Bank.

Germidis, Dimitrios A. 1972. *The Construction Industry in Mexico*. Technical Papers Series. Paris: Organization for Economic Co–operation and Development.

Gilbert, Alan, and Josef Gugler. 1982. *Cities, Poverty and Development; Urbanization in the Third World*. London: Oxford University Press.

Gilbert, Alan, ed., with J. E. Hardoy and R. Ramirez. 1982. *Urbanization in Contemporary Latin America*. New York: John Wiley.

Hansen, Niles. 1981a. *The Border Economy: Regional Development in the Southwest*. Austin: University of Texas Press.

Hansen, Niles. 1981b. Mexico's Border Industry and the International Division of Labor. *Annals of Regional Science* 14:1–12.

Hiernaux Nicolas, Daniel, and Elsa Laurelli. 1982. Politicas de Tierra y Organizacion Territorial en la Micro–región de Ciudad Lazaro Cardenas, Michoacan. Paper presented at the 14th Congress of the Inter–American Planning Society, Morelia, Mexico, 10–15 October.

Johnson, Kenneth F. 1971. *Mexican Democracy: A Critical View*. Boston: Allyn and Bacon.

Kemper, Robert V., and George M. Foster. 1975. Urbanization in Mexico: The View from Tzintzuntzan. In Wayne A. Cornelius and Felicity Trueblood, eds. *Urbanization and Inequality; The Political Economy of Urban and Rural Development in Latin America*. Latin American Urban Research, vol. 5. Beverly Hills: Sage Publications.

Landsberger, Henry A., ed. 1969. *Latin American Peasant Movements*. Ithaca: Cornell University Press.

Legorreta, Jorge. 1982. El Acceso a la Tierra Urbana y el Mercado Inmobiliario Popular. Paper presented at the 14th Congress of the Inter–American Planning Society, Morelia, Mexico, 10–15 October.

Lindley, Richard B. 1983. *Haciendas and Economic Development*. Austin: University of Texas Press.

Looney, Robert E., and Peter C. Fredericksen. 1982. A Programmed Approach toward a Regional Expenditure Policy for Mexico. *Journal of Developing Areas* 17:1–12.

McBride, George M. 1923. *The Land Systems of Mexico*. Research Series No. 12. New York: American Geographical Society.

McEntire, Davis, and Iras L. McEntire. 1975. Agrarian Reform in Mexico. In *Toward Modern Land Policies*, ed. D. McEntire and D. Agostini. Padua, Italy: University of Padua.

Melgar, A. Antonio. 1959. *La Revolucion, el Latifundismo y la Entrega de Cananea a los Campesinos Mexicanos*. Mexico City.

Mexico. Consejo Nacional de Poblacion. 1982. *Mexico Demografico: Breviario 1980–81*. Mexico City: CONAPO.

Mexico. Secretaria de Asentamientos Humanos y Obras Publicas. [1980]. *Programa Nacional de Desarrollo Ecologico de los Asentamientos Humanos*. Desarrollo Urbano Series, Mexico City: SAHOP.

Mexico. Secretaria de Asentamientos Humanos y Obras Publicas. 1981. *Programa Nacional de Ecologia Urbana*. 2 vols. Desarrollo Urbano Series. Mexico City: SAHOP.

Mexico. 1979. *Disposiciones Legales del Programa de Estimulos para la Desconcetracion Territorial de las Actividades Industriales*. Mexico City.

Nugent, Jeffrey B., and Fayez A. Tarawney. 1983. The Anatomy of Changes in Income Distribution and Poverty among Mexico's Economically Active Population between 1950 and 1970. *Journal of Developing Areas* 17:197–226.

Padgett, L. Vincent. 1966. *The Mexican Political System*. Boston: Houghton Mifflin.

Pozo–Ledezma, Leo F. 1980. *Housing and Urban Development Planning in Mexico: A Bibliography*. HUD–IA–568. Washington, D.C.: U.S. Department of Housing and Urban Development.

Regional and Urban Planning Implementation. 1964. *Urban Development and Housing in Mexico City*. Cambridge, Mass.: RUPI.

Renaud, Bertrand. 1979. *National Urbanization Policies in Developing Countries*. Staff Working Paper No. 347. Washington, D.C.: World Bank.

Rodero G., Pedro. 1958. *El Problema de la Habitacion en Mexico y la Ley del Instituto Nacional de Vivienda*. Mexico City.

Schteingart, Martha. 1982. La Incorporacion de la Tierra Rural de Propiedad Social a la Logica Capitalista del Desarrollo Urbano: el Caso de Mexico. Paper presented at the 14th Congress of the Inter–American Planning Society, Morelia, Mexico, 10–15 October.

Schumacher, August. 1983. Agricultural Development and Rural Employment; a Mexican Dilemma. In Peter Brown and Henry Shue, eds., *The Border That Joins: Mexican Migrants and U.S. Responsibilities*. Totowa, N.J.: Rowman and Littlefield.

Scott, Ian. 1982. *Urban and Spatial Development in Mexico*. Washington, D.C.: World Bank.

Simpson, Eyler N. 1937. *The Ejido: Mexico's Way Out*. Chapel Hill: University of North Carolina Press.

Stavenhagen, Rodolfo, ed. 1970. *Agrarian Problems and Peasant Movements in Latin America*. Garden City, N.Y.: Doubleday.

Stoddard, Ellwyn R., Richard L. Nostrand, and Jonathan P. West. 1983. *Borderlands Sourcebook: A Guide to the Literature on Northern Mexico and the American Southwest*. Norman: University of Oklahoma Press.

Stone, P. A. 1973. *The Structure, Size and Costs of Urban Settlements*. London: Cambridge University Press.

Unikel, Luis. 1982. Regional Development Policies in Mexico. In Alan Gilbert et al. *Urbanization in Contemporary South America*. New York: John Wiley.

United Nations. Centre for Human Settlements. *Land for Housing the Poor*. Proceedings at a Seminar of Experts, Tallberg, Sweden, 14–19 March 1983.

United Nations. Centre for Human Settlements. HS/C/6/3 and HS/C/6/3/Add.1. Report presented at the Sixth Session of the Commission on Human Settlements, Helsinki, 25 April–6 May 1983.

Weil, Thomas E. et al. 1975. *Area Handbook for Mexico*. 2d ed. Washington, D.C.: American University.

World Bank. 1977. *Urban Development in Mexico*. 3 vols. Washington, D.C.: World Bank.

Yates, Paul L. 1981. *Mexico's Agricultural Dilemma*. Tucson: University of Arizona Press.

21

Bolivia

ALBERTO RIVERA

As a result of the national revolution of 1952, Bolivia experienced a profound process of change. Three decades after the revolution, the contemporary characteristics of social conflicts involving rural and urban land are different from those in the past and reveal new problems and challenges.

Planning techniques were first experimented formally in Bolivia from 1960 on as a result of assistance from the UN Economic Commission for Latin America (ECLA) and other international agencies. Bolivia also experienced a variety of legal actions and compulsory land redistribution arrangements that had a profound effect on the livelihood and conditions of the population.

Bolivia is a country that is highly differentiated regionally. The main regions—the highland plateau, valleys, and tropical lowlands—are not only geographically distinct but also have different cultures and socioeconomic conditions. These characteristics make it particularly difficult to deal homogeneously with a phenomenon such as land use.

Tables 21.1 through 21.3 illustrate some geographical characteristics. Table 21.3, which provides a breakdown of land use patterns in Bolivia, shows that cultivated land and urban land show very small coverage: 2.62 percent and 0.01 percent, respectively.

HISTORICAL DEVELOPMENT: INSTITUTIONAL AND LANDOWNERSHIP FRAMEWORK

Patterns of Land Use in the Recent Past

When Bolivia became independent from Spain in 1825, the country maintained an agrarian legacy of a manorial system (*hacienda*) and indigenous communities

Table 21.1
Geographical Regions, Bolivia

Plateau	246,254 square kilometers	22.4%	(La Paz, Oruro, Potosi)
Valleys	168,320 square kilometers	15.3%	(Cochabamba, Chuquisaca, Tarija)
Lowlands	684,007 square	62.3%	(Santa Cruz, Beni Pando)

Table 21.2
Land Area, Bolivia

	Square Kilometers
Plateau	65,446
Salt deposits	11,789
Titicaca Lake (Bolivian section)	3,790
Poopó Lake	2,650
Ridges of mountains	66,305
Mountain ranges	79,000
Lowlands	869,431
Urban area	150
	1,098,561

Table 21.3
Present Use of Land, Bolivia

	Square Kilometers	
1. Pasture land	338,307	30.81%
2. Forest land	564,684	51.40%
3. Cultivated land	28,794	2.62%
4. Damp or flood land	24,201	2.20%
5. Water bodies	14,187	1.29%
6. Uncultivated land	126,101	11.47%
7. Eternal ice and snow	2,148	0.20%
8. Urban centers	150	0.01%
	1,098,561	100.00%

(*comunidades originarias*). The latter were legally recognized as a result of the system of *repartimientos* and *reducciones*, which reshaped the structure of Indian society.

Throughout the nineteenth century, the *hacienda* system underwent considerable expansion at the expense of indigenous, communal land and to the benefit of landlords. The increase in *haciendas* was a result of two processes: subdivision of extensive estates and the forced appropriation of communal land (Peñaloza, 1953, 286–97).

Like other Latin American countries, the *hacienda* expansion in Bolivia generally contributed to a highly structured class society. A small landlord elite, with involvement in silver mining and urban commercial activities, ruled over a great mass of an Indian population considered to be inferior by them.

Perhaps one of the most violent takeovers of communal lands was undertaken during the regime of President Mariano Melgarejo (1866–70), which legally sanctioned the state to undertake the sale and auctioning of communal land:

> In 1866–69 some 356 indigenous communities were taken over by *haciendas* involving an estimated population of 22,000 families or a total of 100,000 persons and an extension of approximately 200,000 hectares, of which, nearly 40,000 were cultivable land. . . . The proceeds of these sales were channeled to cover salaries of the State, ecclesiastical and military bureaucracy. (CIDA, 1970, 1–12)

This is but one example that shows the injustices and extremes of a highly exploitative social order. Quite clearly landed property provided landlords power to exploit indigenous labor under the so–called *colonato* system; peasants were given usufruct plots in exchange for which they had to provide regular labor service and produce. The *colonato* system itself varied from region to region, as well as locally, especially with respect to obligations and the size of usufruct plots. Nevertheless, the salient features were similar:

> The principal role of the *colono* (serf) was to work the agricultural cycle of the *hacienda* lands, generally with his own tools and animals . . . he was in charge of the *hacienda's* livestock and any loss (often the death of an animal) had to be compensated by the peasant . . . who in addition had to provide domestic services in the landlord's house or estate, transport and marketing, as well as the manufacturing of various products and tasks. (CIDA 1970, 1:29)

Labor coercion involved economic, physical, and other punishments. In sum, land use under the manorial system imposed a highly unjust social order and also permanently generated profound social conflicts that lasted until 1952. The countryside was a milieu of numerous rebellions and resistance to exploitation and forceful land appropriation (Condarco, 1965, 50).

During the latter part of the nineteenth century, some governments attempted ostensibly to protect communal land, yet their efforts did not touch the established system of servile labor and *haciendas*. During the first two decades of this

574INTERNATIONAL HANDBOOK ON LAND USE PLANNING

Table 21.4

Public Land Sales to Individuals, Bolivia, 1908–1938 (in thousands of hectares)

Department or Territory	Sales	Consolidations	Inscriptions	Total
El Beni	1,429	606	362	2,397
Gran Chaco	1,327	98	33	1,458
Santa Cruz	841	1,294	501	2,636
T. Oriente	689	94	31	814
Tarija	483	59	514	1,056
Chuquisaca	188	92	726	1,006
Cochabamba	160	31	17	208
La Paz	16	2	582	600
T. Parapeti	3	–	3	6
Total	5,136	2,276	2,769	10,181

Source: Servicio Nacional de Reforma Agraria, 1938.

century, the Liberal regime (1900–20), imbued with positivist and free market ideology, went even further than the Melgarejo laws to promote the individualized appropriation of land, to the detriment of indigenous communities. The legislature passed a law in 1905 (*Ley de Tierras Baldias*) that favored the acquisition of so-called state lands, but the latter actually involved communal indigenous lands. Any foreigner or national was allowed to purchase such lands up to a maximum of 20,000 hectares at ten cents per hectare for livestock of cultivable land or 1 *boliviano* per hectare for tropical rubber lands. This law provided a limit until December 1907 for the legalization of titles; 10 years later, through another law (September 1915), all such sales were suspended (Delgado, 1918, 34). As Table 21.4 shows, over 2,000 landlords benefited from concessions involving 10 million hectares, which were located mainly in the tropical lowlands.

During this same period, legislation provided for the setting aside of land for immigrants, for whom immigration laws and regulations had become more liberal since 1907. At the same time, the first colonization project (1909–12) involving nationals was legally established south of the province of Gran Chaco, Arce y Salinas in the Department of Tarija (Delgado, 1918, 58).

In the aftermath of the Liberal downfall and the emergence of the Conservatives in power (1920 onward), an intense period of passive resistance and rebellions surged in the countryside, especially the highlands. The principal source of conflict during this period centered on the land issue, exacerbated by confrontations between peasant Indians and the army. The conservative regime reaffirmed landlord hegemony and private property for the few, while repressing Indian rebellions and other forms of resistance (including the so-called *huelgas de brazos caidos* or labor boycott within *haciendas*) (CIDA, 1970, 1:53).

The 1930 world depression and the Chaco war between Bolivia and Paraguay (1932–35) precipitated a questioning of and erosion in the traditional system of dominance. The emerging urban middle classes, taking more explicit cognizance of the power structure imbedded in the landlords and of a weakened national economy based on mineral exports, organized mass-based political parties that bypassed the traditional Liberals and Conservatives. For the first time, the need to transform and modernize the state, as well as to introduce planning, was expressed. This was done by the emerging parties that explicitly propounded state policies to limit the political and economic influence of the large mining and international consortia, initiated social legislation, rural education, the legalization of labor and rural unions, and above all, stimulated an open debate on agrarian problems (CERES, 1980, 21). The fragile and scant contribution of the agricultural sector to the national economy was largely due to the unproductive and parasitic manorial system: "69.4% of small property owners controlled only 0.41% of the total private lands, while 8.1% of landlords controlled more than 95%" (Calderon, 1983, 7).

During the post-Chaco war period, some measures were taken on behalf of the Indian population. The nationalist government of Colonel Gualberto Villarroel (1944–46), for example, decreed the abolition of servile obligations in *haciendas*. During this period, the first serious questioning of unproductive latifundia ensued, as well as a debate concerning suffrage rights of the Indian population, and legislation that opened the way toward the revision of private land concessions affecting indigenous communities (CIDA, 1970, 1:59).

The intense process of social mobilization that Villarroel unleashed stimulated a corresponding reaction of the landed and mining elite in defense of private property and the existing social order, causing the government's downfall in 1946. Thus the issue of land and its control was again a major focus of political and social conflict prior to the 1952 Revolution.

Agrarian Reform

One of the major transformations of the 1952 Revolution was agrarian reform, due in large measure to a process of peasant mobilization and organization demanding the right to land. Thus agrarian reform was not the product of an effective process of planning but rather an outcome of popular pressure and a fundamental political act by the Nationalist Revolutionary Movement (MNR) as part of a process to consolidate change in the State.

One of the results of the agrarian reform was the creation of the Ministry of Peasant Affairs, where for the first time a department of land use planning was established, at a time when institutionalized planning was still incipient.

Agrarian reform brought about the following changes:

1. Land redistribution on a massive scale. Most *haciendas* in many regions (highlands, highland plateau and valleys) were totally or partially expropriated without compensation.
2. Abolition of the service system in the countryside
3. Increased peasant political participation, resulting from the recognition of universal suffrage and legitimacy of peasant organizations
4. Increased participation of peasant families in the market, both as producers and consumers
5. A relative improvement in living conditions, health, and education
6. Symbolically, the derogatory term *Indian* was dropped in many contexts of discourse. Instead, *campesino* became general.

The process of land redistribution operated particularly rapidly in regions where peasants were more militantly organized, such as in the Cochabamba valleys and the highland plateau of La Paz. In such areas, peasants took possession of the *hacienda* lands prior to the actual judicial and administrative processes of the agrarian reform decree.

From 1953 on, peasants were entitled to rights of property on their former usufruct plots and in many cases to a larger extension of land as the *haciendas* were formally expropriated either entirely or partially. The process of title distribution was largely consolidated within fourteen years after the agrarian reform decree was signed in 1953.

Agrarian reform comprised three levels of legal authority: the agrarian courts, the National Agrarian Reform Council (Consejo Nacional de Reforma Agraria) and the presidency of Bolivia (CIDA, 1970, 4:35). The decree established three categories of land: individual private property; collective property, to promote cooperative or collective farming; and communal property, consisting of pasture or uncultivable lands.

In many respects agrarian reform formalized a long historical process of individualization of private property in a context of a dependent capitalist economy as peasants themselves accentuated the subdivision of land into small plots and privatized tenure forms. Such a tendency also became pervasive in practice in many peasant communities, which had communal land tenure traditions. Such a situation might have been avoided somewhat with due institutional planning capacity.

The displacement of large landowners from the countryside was based on four legal categories established by the agrarian reform decree: (1) the latifundio or large *hacienda* above 200 hectares, which had a prevailing system of free service obligations and lack of capital investment, were subject to total expropriation;

(2) the agricultural enterprise or property above 80 hectares in size, with a system of salaried labor, technical and mechanical improvements, and capital investment; (3) the livestock raising enterprise with three-quarters of its land as pastures and the presence of large or small animal stock raising; and (4) small property under 30 hectares.

In the case of the *latifundio* type, about 1,160 were expropriated, 70 percent of these in the Departments of La Paz, Cochabamba, and Chuquisaca (Table 21.5). With respect to properties classified as agricultural enterprises, landlords were able to retain legally about 10 percent of the total size of the landed property, subject to indemnification based on the recorded cadastral value and in accordance with negotiations with peasant *sindicatos* (local organizations also legally recognized by the agrarian reform); 2,819 such enterprises or middle-sized properties were legally expropriated and reduced in size (see Table 21.5). The treatment of livestock enterprises was favorable, involving 366 such properties, mainly in the eastern tropical lowlands. In so-called small properties, nonpeasant landowners were able to retain possession of such land.

The Departments of La Paz, Cochabamba, and Chuquisaca were the most affected by the agrarian reform decree because nearly 70 percent of the landed properties were concentrated in these three departments. In many cases, not all landlords were displaced from the countryside, especially in Chuquisaca or the eastern tropical lowlands, where patterns of exploitation remain under a different guise.

Although agrarian reform was intended as a massive and rapid transformation of landed property (Table 21.6), in general terms it affected approximately 42 percent (11 million hectares) of the registered surface in properties (25.6 million hectares).

Urban Reform

With respect to urban land use, Bolivia experimented with some changes as a result of the 1952 revolution, although it was not of the same scope as the agrarian reform. Nor was the intensity of social conflicts comparable to those in the countryside.

The government recognized the significance of the housing problems and the role of speculative capital on urban land. The urban masses played a crucial role during the 1952 insurrection, and soon after the Nationalist Revolutionary Movement assumed power, demands relating to housing, access to urban land, education, and other urban services were put forward. One of the most significant policies that emerged, and stood out in Latin America at the time, was that of urban reform (1955). This measure contained the following arguments:

1. There is an extremely large amount of unoccupied urban land that is claimed as private property, but is prohibitive to the large majority of the urban population due to financial speculation and rising price levels.

Table 21.5

Bolivia: Number of Properties Included in the Judicial Process of Agrarian Reform from 1953 to August 1957, according to Categories and Departments

Departments	Small properties	Middle-size properties	Enterprises	Latifundia	Total	Sub-total excluding small properties	%
La Paz	593	693	59	367	1,712	1,119	26.0
Chuquisaca	508	531	24	118	1,181	673	15.4
Cochabamba	360	856	55	414	1,685	1,325	30.5
Potosi	211	251	16	116	594	383	8.8
Oruro	27	68	20	40	155	128	2.9
Tarija	305	99	19	52	475	170	3.8
Santa Cruz	608	265	108	53	1,034	426	9.8
Beni	52	52	65	--	169	117	2.7
Pando	9	4	--	--	13	4	0.1
Total	2,673	2,819	366	1,160	7,018	4,345	100.0

Source: Servicio Nacional de Reforma Agraria, División de Supervisión y procesamiento de datos. Sección Investigación. Resumido de cuadro anexo IV-19 La Paz, 1970.

Table 21.6
Bolivia: Cumulative Achievement of the Agrarian Reform: Twenty Five Years After

	Hectares
Properties involved	25,816
Titles distributed	565,913
Individuals benefited	404,976
Cultivable surface	4,032,066,107
Pastures	21,683,359,311
Uncultivable land	2,798,974,608
Forest lands	202,033,010
School lands	12,395,089
Sport grounds	1,027,461
Urban areas	19,420,860
Cooperatives	69,407,696
Colonization	21,786,600
Total distributed	28,841,467,447
Reverted to the State	1,042,615,639
Total processed	29,884,083,086

Source: El Diario, August 2, 1978.

2. The extreme profits gained by the few by urban land speculation are based on increased demand from demographic growth and increased land rent rather than on productive investment.
3. In such a context, the housing problem has widened, exacerbating social conflicts and poverty.

As a result, the urban reform decree provided for the expropriation of all extensions above 10,000 square meters (1 hectare). The owner was granted the right to 10 percent of his or her property; the rest was retained by the state in order to undertake public housing programs.

The reform also provided for the expropriation of semiurban land on the urban periphery in order to promote new urban settlements. When making applications, the reform decree required that municipalities or associations do so for at least 50 families. This measure applied to all suburban zones.

The urban reform guaranteed private property within certain limits; "expropriation is necessary when there is priority public need or when property does not fulfill a social function in accordance with the law; in any case indemnization must be just" (Herbas, 1958, 59). Nevertheless, as Calderon points out (1983, 80) "Indemnization was practically nonexistent, due especially to red tape and inflation, thus unfairly affecting property owners."

The right to urban land allocations remained the charge of municipalities, which could transfer expropriated properties by sale to workers and lower middle-class families who did not possess urban housing or land. The reform decree gave priority to associations of individuals, such as unions, federations, civil employees, retired miners, and Chaco war veterans (Herbas, 1958, 61). The reform stressed that after the allocation of an urban land plot, the beneficiary or beneficiaries had a period of two years in which to construct a house; otherwise the land would be regained by municipalities. In 1957 a number of amendments were made to clarify the meaning of an unconstructed property (*propiedad no edificada*) in response to demands and pressure by various civic associations and property owners affected by the reform. These amendments to the reform included a definition of affected properties as those that are above 10,000 square meters that have no evidence of construction, fruit trees, or other improvements (*El Diario*, 18 August 1956). A number of properties remained exempt from this law, such as dairy farms, industrial and sport sites, hospitals, clinics, airports and railways, as well as school and social welfare program sites, even though their extensions were beyond 10,000 square meters.

La Paz, Cochabamba, and Santa Cruz were the cities that were primarily drawn into urban reform: In La Paz some 90 hectares were distributed among the members of 26 labor organizations, which involved about 20,000 persons or 5 percent of the urban population (Calvimontes, 1972, 293). In Santa Cruz, after a prolonged social conflict at the urban and regional levels, including internecine strife within the MNR, there was a process of de facto occupation of urban land and confrontation with property owners, with the result that 39 *barrios* were settled by working class and popular sectors of the city. In the department of Cochabamba, 4 hectares were expropriated in Quillacollo, 2 hectares in Vinto, and, 5 hectares in the neighborhood of La Chimba in the city of Cochabamba (Herbas, 1958, 61).

The urban reform decree enabled the state to exercise a predominant controlling role on urban land in the decade after the 1952 revolution. In many respects, this was a unique opportunity for the state to intervene in and shape the urban land market, with a capacity to plan ahead in response to wider demands of the poorer sectors of urban society.

Urban reform had an effective life span of two years, and not much longer, as pressures by affected groups and interests grew more intense. A morass of legal obstacles and litigation substantially limited the reform's future action in practice eventually. The urban land market in effect became an open and speculative milieu for financial and capitalist interests. Another factor that contributed to the demise of the reform was the growing pressure by popular sectors that had not benefited from it (Rivera, 1983, 32).

The various periods outlined above, such as the appropriation of communal lands during the Melgarejo regime (1866–70) and the Liberal period (1900–20), illustrate forms of political domination in specific historical contexts; the profound changes in rural and urban land tenure and use reveal important responses to popular mobilization. During the authoritarian regimes, the state was able in many respects to exercise a strong and determining role on behalf of a mining and landed elite, appropriating for the latter privileges of use, possession, and property. During the 1950s the new revolutionary context favored a strong state role in the land issue. Today the country faces the effects of demographic pressures in both the rural and the urban areas. There are intense financial and capitalist relations that are more pervasive today than two decades ago.

MAJOR CHALLENGES IN RURAL AREAS

There are two important consequences of land redistribution: peasant migration and agricultural productivity. Contrary to what many suppose, the agrarian reform actually stimulated a process of spatial mobility and migration. Migratory processes are both temporary and permanent, multidirectional and heterogeneous. There is a considerable flow of temporary and permanent migrants, for example, to northern Argentina, as well as Buenos Aires (for rural labor and construction work, respectively). Some estimate that as much as 10 percent of Bolivia's population may be located in Argentina, largely as a result of migration and emigration processes during the last two decades (Albo, 1979, 14).

There is a major flow of rural migration from the highlands and valleys to the tropical lowland frontier in the departments of La Paz, Cochabamba, and particularly Santa Cruz, where regional development (colonization, commercial farming, oil, and an incipient agro-Industry) has been especially marked. There is also a considerable migration flow from the countryside to the cities, mainly La Paz, Cochabamba, and Santa Cruz; in the last, the annual urban population growth rate has been as high as 7.3 percent, far surpassing the national average. A number of recent studies, such as that by CERES (1980), have observed recent migration tendencies with respect to colonization and urban centers.

While rural out-migration is intense, relative to other countries this phenomenon may not be the most striking in Bolivia. What has been shown in various studies is a countertendency of reverse migration flows and the process of tertiarization of the rural economy. This has led to a concomitant growth of urban provincial centers in some areas, as well as the enlargement of villages into larger settlements with urban or semiurban characteristics.

While agrarian reform involved a massive process of land redistribution in the highlands and valleys, the large majority of peasants still face a land shortage. Table 21.7 shows that more than 60 percent of the properties in the highlands and valleys were less than 5 hectares in size each in 1970. The proportion of units larger than 100 hectares is negligible. In the eastern lowlands, on the other hand, the majority of the units were larger than 5 hectares, and more than 35 percent of the properties had an extension of 50 hectares or more.

During the last 30 years, a process of land subdivision in the countryside has been accentuated as a result of inheritance among peasant families that benefited from the agrarian reform. The result is that many families have a fragile, poorer, and smaller land base to sustain themselves. This problem is particularly acute in the Cochabamba valleys, highland plateau, Potosí, and Chuquisaca, leading in some cases to the impoverishment of peasant sectors, processes of migration, or extraagricultural activities to provide the needed cash income for the peasant families to survive.

As a result of the agrarian reform, changes in production and productivity have been substantial, mainly as a consequence of the increased market integration of peasant families as cash crop producers. In some areas, there has been a process of increased crop specialization, while in others, more crop diversification is a prevailing pattern. Both processes have involved an intensification of land use and utilization of chemical inputs with a deteriorating effect on land. At the same time, market specialization has led to a proliferation of rural markets and the growth of focal market towns.

MAJOR CHALLENGES AND APPROACHES IN URBAN AREAS

A factor that has decisively influenced urban growth in the three principal cities of La Paz, Cochabamba, and Santa Cruz has been agrarian reform and the subsequent processes of change in the peasant economy rather than industrial or capital growth. While other processes or urbanization in Latin America, accompanied by a measure of industrial labor demand, did stimulate urban expansion, in the Bolivian case migration from the countryside remained intensely related to spatial mobility and small-scale commercial and self–employment strategies among peasant households. This linked the countryside with the urban sectors, as well as with the expanding agricultural and commercial tropical frontier regions.

In the period 1900–52, urban centers grew at an annual rate of 2.6 percent; in 1950–60 the rate increased to 4.6 percent and in 1960–70 to nearly 10 percent. Thus the urban population actually tripled in the three decades after agrarian reform (Table 21.8).

In contrast to other Latin American countries, Bolivia's urban growth has not been concentrated at one urban pole; rather, three cities (La Paz, Cochabamba and Santa Cruz) have faced urban expansion, sharing among them 70 percent

Table 21.7

Bolivia: Distribution of Agricultural Properties in Highlands, Valleys, and Tropical
Lowlands

Size (hectares)	Highlands and Valleys (%)	Tropical Lowlands (%)
Less than 1	21.75	2.25
1 - 2.99	23.70	7.10
3 - 4.99	15.50	6.90
5 - 9.99	16.70	9.20
10 - 19.99	13.65	14.18
20 - 34.99	3.70	14.40
35 - 49.99	1.80	8.90
50 - 74.99	1.50	22.50
75 - 99.99	0.60	1.70
100 - 199.99	0.58	2.20
200 - 499.99	0.40	2.80
500 - 999.99	0.09	2.50
1,000 - 2,499.99	0.03	2.90
2,500 - 4,999.99	0.00	1.15
5,000 - 9,999.99	0.00	0.70
10,000 and over	0.00	0.62
	100.00	100.00

Source: Servicio Nacional de Reforma Agraria, 1975.

of the country's urban population. Each of these cities reveals rather different
regional developments with contrasting consequences.

The three main cities confront three problems: (1) their respective weak and
incipient productive structures prevent a large-scale absorption of formal, salaried
labor in relation to growth of the urban population; (2) the state and the private

Table 21.8

Urban Growth, Bolivia

Year	Total Population	%	Urban Population	%
1950	2,704,165	100	669,297	24.7
1960	3,330,436	100	1,017,288	30.5
1970	4,101,749	100	1,846,211	45.0
1976	4,647,836	100	1,987,760	42.7
1978	4,857,278	100	2,161,369	44.5

Source: DISOC, 1980.

sector cannot satisfy the growing demand for infrastructure, housing, and collective consumption needs of the urban majority; and (3) there is growing speculation and commoditization of urban land, a process that has long surpassed the capacity for effective control and planning of urban land use.

Each of the three cities has a model of urban growth. Santa Cruz has perhaps been the most effective in developing a regulatory system for planned urban land use and zoning. This may be due especially to a better regional institutional framework and a more clearly defined set of local and regional interests.

In La Paz and Cochabamba, urban processes have resulted more from the work and survival strategies of the urban poor and popular sectors than from planning and institutional leadership. In these cities, the migrants and the urban poor have developed complex settlement and residential patterns. In La Paz and Cochabamba, for example, many of the surrounding hillsides and slopes have been taken over by settlements, many formally illegal. Nevertheless, in the past decade they have experienced an integration into the land market, with resultant price spirals that have contributed to a less intense flow and expansion. At the same time, this situation has contributed to greater densities and overcrowding in other neighborhoods.

Urban land use planning in Bolivia in effect has become a political issue rather than an effective process. In the new neighborhoods of El Alto in La Paz (the rapidly expanding urban periphery of La Paz located in the highland plateau), the municipalities have instituted regulations and paperwork that have compelled the population (mostly urban poor and migrants) to conform to certain controls and planning requisites. In reality, these municipalities have been more effective than others in the urban core or other neighborhoods of La Paz.

A number of plans and regulations have been generated in La Paz during the last decades but with scant effect. In 1976, for example, the country spent $4 million for a development plan for only the city of La Paz. The goals and projections of the study were unreachable because of the astronomical costs involved. In fact, practically all major cities in Bolivia have regulatory plans and models of urban land use, zoning, and expansion. Nevertheless, due to the predominance of a massive small-scale mercantile and family–based economic sector, which reveals the plight of the urban poor, workers, and peasants in the context of incipient industrial or large-scale capitalist expansion, the principal phenomenon is one of self-housing, self-employment, food provisioning, and other strategies. Therefore, there is a varied and intense arena of informal resolution of needs in the face of an ineffective formal planning and institutional outreach. The cities increasingly are surrounded by streams and branches of precarious human settlements, with scant services or infrastructure yet activating a land market and speculative process as their concentration increases.

About 85 percent of constructions in these cities are clandestine or illegal in spite of efforts by municipalities to control and regulate; the latter are only applied in the developed urban core or in housing areas of higher income groups. In most cases, the formal system of decision-making with respect to institutional mechanisms and established procedures supports and legitimizes de facto situations adopted by settlers of new neighborhoods. Santa Cruz stands out among the three cities as one where institutions have demonstrated a capacity for planning land use.

In 1966 a group of UN experts prepared a report on planning in Bolivia, which is still relevant today:

The planning process is pure fiction and does not go beyond periodically producing a document. There does not exist something that can be called a mechanism for planning, since each administrative unit generates its own inertia and self-defensive mechanisms when . . . one needs qualified and experienced technical personnel one does not find them or they have exhausted their capacity for initiative. (UN, 1966, 11)

The report points out that political instability is one of the primary factors that inhibit planning and long-term control of basic development processes.

Within this overall situation, planning of urban land use is still far from being achieved in Bolivian cities in spite of diverse regulatory plans and studies. Except for the brief period of urban reform during the period 1956–58, the cities are increasingly confronting a crisis due to irrational land use. In La Paz and Santa Cruz, there are more clearly defined local economic and political urban elites that so far have managed to utilize the urban structure to their benefit and to the detriment of wider popular demands and necessities. In other cities, where dominant local economic and political elites are weaker, the urban spaces are even more deficient in infrastructure and present a rather uncontrolled sprawl. So far the large mass of lower-income urban sectors has been unable to organize sustained efforts to reshape the distribution and utilization of present urban land arrangements. In many respects, thus, planning is hampered by the presence of a power vacuum and the absence of participatory mechanisms to shape long-term changes in land use and to benefit the broader urban society.

ASSESSMENT

One of the principal problems confronting the countryside in contemporary Bolivia is the increasing shortage of land for the majority of the peasant population located in the highlands and valleys. Agrarian reform formalized a process of subdivision that leaves today's inhabitants facing an even smaller share of the land. The land base in many regions is vulnerable to erosion and the vagaries of high-altitude climatic conditions. A small proportion of the cultivated land is under irrigation. There have been few attempts by the state to improve and ensure productivity under such conditions. Yet the peasant economy in Bolivia, despite its reduced land base, rudimentary technology, and lack of access to technical and financial assistance, continues to produce the bulk of the country's food. Peasants are increasingly integrated into the market as producers as well as consumers. And because their land base in many regions is a particularly acute problem, significant migration flows and spatial mobility are occurring. Within the overall context of development planning, agriculture in the valleys and highlands has received scant attention by the state, in contrast to a far more concerted attempt to stimulate large-scale commercial agriculture and livestock raising in the eastern lowlands of Bolivia.

In the urban context, some of the salient problems in planning urban land use have been highlighted. The cities confront an enormous shortage of housing, transport, and other services, an overall process of increased urban sprawl, and demographic increase in a situation where land use planning, the foresight, and the mechanisms to reshape spatial arrangements and zoning are lacking. As the UN report (1966) stressed, there is no absence of formal planning and rhetoric, but there is no evidence of action on the ground.

Agrarian reform and urban reform were generated largely as a result of far–reaching processes of social mobilization and a crucial juncture whereby the state itself was in the process of transforming society as a result of the 1952 upheaval. For a number of reasons, the state is unable to undertake a sustained effort in development planning. Land use remains a crucial issue.

FUTURE TRENDS

Three main future trends can be discerned:
1. The national economy is being profoundly affected by spiraling inflation. The economy's productivity has fallen sharply, and foreign exchange has dropped in relation to a depressed international market for raw materials. These factors greatly hamper Bolivia's possibilities to meet its external public and private debt obligations. At the same time, Bolivia needs to implement sharply recessionary

policies in order to conform to the International Monetary Fund's conditions for monetary stabilization.

This situation has generated a plunging devaluation of the currency in relation to the U.S. dollar, currency speculation, a black market for dollars, and uncontrolled price rises in all goods and services.

Inflation has also stimulated a heightened pressure by the urban masses on basic consumer goods and food staples. This situation has stimulated more organized demands and greater participatory processes among urban neighborhood organizations in relation to food distribution and other pressing collective needs. Price rises have affected not only basic goods and services but also the urban and surrounding rural land market of the principal urban centers. This arises from the fact that transactions are based on the black market dollar rate, which is often twice the official dollar rate of exchange.

2. Politically the renewal of democratic and constitutional government, established since October 1982, has not brought about transformation or modification in planning and production. There is a certain power vacuum and lack of overall decisionmaking in basic areas of policy; the government, composed of a political coalition of various parties, lacks the capacity to implement a coherent set of policies and programs. It is faced with external and internal pressures from within its ranks, from popular and organized working sectors, and from diverse opposition quarters. This situation contributes to institutional instability and alterations in public administration that make it all the more difficult for the government to develop clear policies toward the broad masses or to consolidate a strong and efficient government with popular support.

In this context, the national planning system faces many obstacles. The democratic process within a generalized economic crisis gives rise to multiple demands and political pressures, not only from opposition forces but also from popular sectors. Thus the government finds itself conceding and negotiating often in a seemingly arbitrary fashion and departing from longer-term priorities or its own programs. In this respect, a significant recent phenomenon has been the rise of regional pressures. The strongest regional movement has developed in the department of Santa Cruz, which has a more clearly defined regional power structure based on a certain degree of economic and ideological leverage in relation to the state. These and other regional movements have been demanding concrete decentralization measures and greater autonomy from the state and national governments.

One of the principal objectives of these regional demands is to achieve political and economic decentralization, thus reinforcing the possibility of exercising democracy and participation in other than the political level. Ultimately these demands imply the establishment of local power structures that are able to modify the utilization of regional resources and factors of production, which until recently have been excessively centralized and bureaucratized. In many respects, these regional movements aim at smoother and more rational planning and a stimulus to economic development unhampered by ineffective national planning. At the same time, these movements in the long run may respond more effectively to regional social demands and establish better planning mechanisms.

Future events will revolve around an alternative to the present, which will present such regional social movements in the formation of the nation-state. Perhaps it may have a greater multiclass structure yet be directed by the interests of a dominant regional elite, challenging in effect a multiparty coalition of divergent interests in a struggle for the control of the state.

3. The future perspectives of urban and rural land use planning in Bolivia will depend on a consolidated and institutionalized democratic process. It has been shown that even if one considers all the deficiencies, there is greater control of land use when there exists a greater degree of popular participation and access to decisionmaking mechanisms in charge of land allocation and planning than during de facto regimes that exclude all channels of participation and give way to favoritism and uncontrolled speculation.

Present urban and rural land needs and the overall direction of population growth and urban expansion require transformations and a set of general policies, especially in relation to the planning of urban growth and a stimulus to agricultural productivity geared toward resolving basic food consumption demands. These general policies are an important element in a context of crisis and overall market speculation in land.

The major question is in identifying which groups will be in a position to lead a process of change in the present situation. One may expect that from the regional social movements and pressures, political elites with a wider social base may emerge with a capacity to face future challenges.

BIBLIOGRAPHY

Albo, Xavier. 1979 ¿Bodas de Plata? o Requiem por una Reforma Agraria. CIPCA. Cuadernos de Investigación No. 17. La Paz.

Anuario de Estadistica Agropecuaria. 1938. Tierras de cultivo y pastoreo inscritas en el Registro Nacional de Tierras Baldías desde el año 1908 al 31 de Diciembre de 1938. Mimeo. La Paz.

Blanes, José. 1983. Bolivia: Agricultura campesina y los mercados de alimentos (experiencias recientes). Documento para CEPAL/FAO. La Paz. June.

Calderon, Fernando. 1983. La Política en las calles. Cochabamba: Ediciones CERES.

Calvimontes, Carlos. 1972. La Reforma de Propiedad del Suelo urbano en la administración de Paz Estenssoro. In Jorge Hardoy y Guillermo Geisse, comp. Políticas de desarrollo urbano y regional en América Latina. Buenos Aires: Sociedad Interamericana de Planificación.

Carranza, Mario. 1972. Estudio de caso en el valle bajo de Cochabamba. Ediciones Servicio Nacional de Reforma Agraria.

Centro de Estudios de la Realidad Economica y Social (CERES). 1980. Factores psicosociales de la migración rural-urbana. Mimeo. CERES. La Paz.

Cochrane, T. Thomas. 1973. El potencial agrícola del uso de la tierra en Bolivia: un mapa de sistemas de tierras. In Misión Botánica en Agricultura Tropical. La Paz: Ediciones Ministerio de Agricultura.

Comite Interamericano de Desarrollo Agricola en Bolivia (CIDA). 1970. *Estructura Agraria en Bolivia. Proyecto de Estructura Agraria en Bolivia. Equipo CIDA. Land Tenure Center.* La Paz. Mimeo.

Condarco, Ramiro. 1965. *Zárate, el "temible" Willka: historia de la rebelión indígena de 1899.* La Paz: Ediciones Talleres Gráficos Bolivianos.

Dandler, Jorge et al. 1982. Economía campesina en los valles y serranías de Cochabamba: procesos de diversificación y trabajo. Cochabamba: Centre de Estudios de la Realidad Económica y Social (CERES). Mimeo.

Delgado, Humberto. 1918. *Legislación de tierras baldías.* La Paz: *Imprenta Artística.*

Flores, Gonzalo. 1982. *Estado, políticas agrarias y luchas campesinas. Revisión de una década en Bolivia.* La Paz: Ediciones CERES/UNRISD.

Geologia Boliviana. 1978. Mapa de cobertura y uso actual de la tierra: Bolivia, memoria explicativa. Programa del satélite tecnológico de recursos naturales ''ERTSBOL.'' Serie de sensores remotos 2. La Paz.

Grober, Isaac. 1967. *Reforma Agraria Boliviana: proceso a un proceso.* Santiago, Chile: DESAL.

Herbas, Carlos. 1958. *Reforma Agraria y Urbana.* Cochabamba: Ediciones Imprenta Universitaria.

Klein, Herbert S. 1968. *Orígenes de la Revolución Nacional Boliviana: la crisis de la generación del Chaco (1920–1943).* La Paz: Ediciones Juventud.

Peñaloza, Luis. 1953, *Historia Económica de Bolivia.* Ediciones Talleres Gráficos Bolivianos. La Paz: Imprenta El Progreso.

Rivera, Alberto. 1983. *Pachamama Expensive: el contexto territorial urbano y la diferenciación social en La Paz.* La Paz: Documentos CERES.

Sociedad Rural de Bolivia. 1942. *Estatutos.* La Paz: Ediciones Sport.

United Nations. 1966. *Informe sobre Bolivia en torno a Planificación. Expertos de Naciones Unidas.* La Paz: IPE.

22

Argentina

HORACIO A. TORRES

HISTORICAL BACKGROUND

The First Settlement to 1930

In the sixteenth century the Spanish settlements in present-day Argentinian territory were grouped in five regions separated by vast areas occupied by a scattered Indian population. The northwest, where the degree of agricultural development allowed moderate territorial densities, was the only exception. Lattes (1974) estimates, quoting other authors, that the total Indian population at the time of the arrival of the Spanish was about 400,000 (Table 22.1); this number decreased in the following century to 300,000. During the sixteenth century, the following cities were founded by the Spanish: Santiago del Estero (1553), Mendoza (1561), San Juan (1562), Córdoba (1573), Santa Fe (1573), Buenos Aires (1536 and 1580), Salta (1582), Tucumán (1585), La Rioja (1591), Jujuy (1593), and San Luis (1596).

The northwest and the center were colonized from Peru, the west from Chile, and the littoral from Paraguay. Buenos Aires was founded twice: the first time in 1536 (the city was destroyed and depopulated five years later) and the second time in 1580. Both foundations were different in origin and characteristics. The first originated in a sea expedition coming directly from Spain. The second originated in the already settled interior territories (Paraguay) and was aimed at securing an outlet to Europa via the Atlantic as an alternative to the Pacific route, which reached the Argentinian northwest from Peru after a long and complicated

Table 22.1

Population Statistics, Argentina, 1550–1980

Years	Total Population+	Growth Rate++
1550	403.0	-3
1650	298.0	3
1778	420.9	12
1800	551.0	11
1809	609.2	14
1825	766.4	14
1839	926.3	19
1857	1,299.6	29
x1869	1,830.2	31
x1895	4,044.9	36
x1914	7,903.7	21
x1947	15,893.8	18
x1960	20,013.8	16
x1970	23,364.4	18
x1980	27,947.4	

+ in thousands
++ mean annual growth rate
x National Censuses

Source: Argentina, 1980.   National Census

itinerary (from Spain to Panama, from there, after crossing over the isthmus, to Peru via the Pacific and finally by land).

The location of Buenos Aires at the mouth of the River Plate estuary made it a convenient outlet for the silver-producing northern regions centered in Potosí (in the Alto Perú, present-day Bolivia), since the transport of goods from Potosí to Lima on the Pacific coast took four months and the trip from Potosí to Buenos Aires only half that time. On the other hand, Buenos Aires had no hinterland, being surrounded by fertile prairies (the Pampas) occupied by hostile nomadic Indians. Its location as an entry to the interior territories was not fully exploited because of commercial restrictions imposed by the Spanish crown on its colonies. Nevertheless, an active illegal commercial interchange developed, exchanging silver for luxury goods and manufactures. The main partners of this interchange were the Portuguese, the French, the Dutch, and finally the English, the last being the principal providers of African slaves.

During this period, Buenos Aires continuously widened its hinterland, where in the meantime the animals left by the first founders produced large herds of wild cattle. The cattle were hunted by expeditions named *vaquerías* rather than bred and provided Buenos Aires staple export: hides and fat.

In the second half of the eighteenth century, the Spanish crown relaxed some of the commercial restrictions affecting its colonies. Buenos Aires was exalted as the capital of a vast political unit, the viceroyalty of the River Plate, which comprised present-day Argentina, Bolivia, Paraguay, Uruguay, and the north of Chile. Various authors point out the differences between the littoral region, centered on Buenos Aires, and the northwest region, which focused on Potosí. The north was traditional, governed by an aristocracy based on land, semifeudal, with a considerable amount of assimilated Indian population; Buenos Aires was more of an open society based on commerce (Cortés Conde and Gallo, 1973; Socolow, 1978).

The obscure origins of Buenos Aires and its limited economic relevance during its first two centuries made it a flat city built with uncalcined bricks, crossed by unpaved streets, and dotted by austere public buildings, which lacked the gilded magnificence of its counterparts in Mexico and Peru. The city, as with all the other Spanish-American cities, was based on a gridiron layout. The main square faced the river bank and was surrounded by a semicircle of 40 original *manzanas* (blocks of about 100 meters by 100 meters). The Cabildo (city hall), the cathedral, and the government house-cum-fort building faced the square, where commerce and main public events took place. The residences of the principal citizens were located near this center.[1]

During the lengthy period of interregional conflicts and civil strife that followed independence, Buenos Aires experienced a rather low growth rate.[2] Only after the 1880s was the eventual solution to many of the political conflicts, which had haunted Argentinian development for so long, achieved. The proclamation creating Buenos Aires the federal capital of the republic was the cornerstone of that solution. On the other hand, the effective occupation of the whole Pampas was possible only after the definitive military campaign against the Indians led by General Roca in 1880. This opened up to economic exploitation one of the richest and largest prairies in the world.

The accelerated growth of Buenos Aires during the last quarter of the nineteenth century was based on the rising position of Argentina as a world exporter of agricultural products—mainly wheat, maize, and beef—and an importer of manufactures (which caused the collapse of many local handicrafts), capital, and people. Government policy was aimed at attracting immigrants, who came mainly from depressed European regions (Italy, Spain, and the Russian Empire). The immigrants, although they were supposed to settle in agricultural regions, ended up mostly in the principal littoral cities (Table 22.2), mainly Buenos Aires, where foreign population during this period was about 50 percent of the total population.

The indisputable predominance achieved by Buenos Aires after the 1880s contrasts with the collapse of the remaining regional economies. A fan-shaped railway network focused on Buenos Aires was completed (40,000 kilometers of tracks were built in less than 60 years). Most of the railway network was financed by foreign capital, mainly British.

Table 22.2

Percentage Growth, Argentina, 1869–1980

Years	% of urban population(+)	% of foreigners	regional percentages (++)						Total
			1	2	3	4	5	6	
1869	29	12	13.2	40.2	10.4	7.4	28.8	----	100.0
1895	37	25	19.8	47.3	7.0	7.3	17.9	0.7	100.0
1914	53	30	25.8	47.8	6.5	5.9	12.6	1.4	100.0
1947	62	15	29.7	42.1	6.4	8.3	11.2	2.3	100.0
1960	72	13	33.7	38.0	6.7	8.1	11.0	2.5	100.0
1970	79	9	35.8	36.7	6.6	7.7	10.2	3.0	100.0
1980	83	7	34.9	35.8	6.7	8.1	10.8	3.7	100.0

(+)   Population living in towns of 2,000 inhabitants and more.

(++)   Regions: 1. Metropolitan Region; 2. The Pampas; 3. Cuyo; 4. Northeast; 5. Northwest; 6. Patagonia

Source: Argentina, 1980. National Census

The amount of hectares of land devoted to agriculture, the bulk of them in the littoral, increased dramatically: 5 million in 1895, 14 million in 1914, 19 million in 1976.[3] The 1914 census shows that urban population exceeded (52.7 percent) rural population for the first time (Table 22.1). Buenos Aires and its surrounding areas had 1.9 million inhabitants, becoming a true metropolitan area with a dense electric tram network (700 kilometers long) and one underground line. Primary production was the predominant component in the national gross product, a situation that lasted until 1958. The expansion of commerce and services in Buenos Aires was such that Scobie (1974) characterized it as a commercial-bureaucratic city.

A more detailed reference to urban development in Buenos Aires will help in understanding the rest of the littoral cities, which share with it, although to a lesser extent, the extraordinary urban growth of the period. As far as the changes in urban structure are concerned, the period can be clearly divided into two parts separated by the turn of the century. Before 1900, central Buenos Aires experienced a high increase in density as newly arrived European immigrants settled in overcrowded slums (*conventillos*). From the turn of the century to World War I, although the arrival of immigrants continued at the same rate and central *conventillos* kept growing, a significant amount of urban growth took place on the periphery at low densities (Figure 22.1 a and b). This process of suburbanization was very much related to the diffusion of the electric tram network and the lowering of the standard transport fare (0.10 peso ticket after 1904).

Scobie (1977) shows that in the first decade of the century, the family income of a qualified blue-collar workman allowed him to buy a small plot on the periphery (within a corridor of about 400 meters on each side of the tram lines), paying for it in monthly installments. It can be hypothesized that those urban workers who moved to the periphery and acquired (with great effort) a piece of land and succeeded in building a modest house on it (with their own hands and family help) were the main basis of the nontraditional urban middle classes in Argentina (Torres, 1975).

Urban industry consisted of two types of establishments: (1) those related to the new exports (such as packing plants), which located in the southern suburbs, continuing the locational trends of the old industry (meat salting tubs and hide drying sheds), and (2) those related to the transformation of imported manufactures (garment workshops), which were centrally located. Also the construction of a new port for Buenos Aires, needed because of the enormous increase in international trade and the difficulties that the shallow waters of the River Plate presented for mooring, separated the city from the river.

The notion that a modern Buenos Aires had to remove its colonial and Hispanic townscape took form as an official policy firmly enforced by Torcuato de Alvear, the energetic first mayor of the recently established (1880) federal capital. The colonial civic center (Plaza de Mayo) was remodeled, and in the process the arcade (Recova) that divided it in two parts was demolished. The Cabildo was modernized beyond recognition, superimposing classical pilasters on its facade

Figure 22.1 Expansion of Buenos Aires, 1870–1972

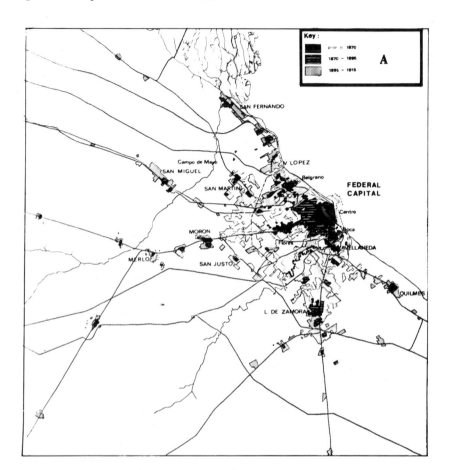

and adding a clock tower on top of it; afterward the tower was demolished, and one of the ends of the building was cut off to give way to the Avenida de Mayo, a boulevard linking Government House and the Congress. For the construction of the Avenida, it was necessary to demolish a row of central city blocks along 1.5 kilometers, and many valuable properties were compulsorily purchased. On both sides of the avenue, the flat-roofed houses were replaced by four- or five-story buildings displaying eclectic styles or an Art Nouveau flavor. Apart from limited government action, almost the total replacement of the colonial past was completed by the private sector. Depending on position in the social pyramid, individuals had residences planned and built either by French architects graduated from the École de Beaux Arts or local contractors of Italian origin. Most of the then-peripheral quarters (*barrios*) were one- or two-story, economically and

Figure 22.1 (continued)

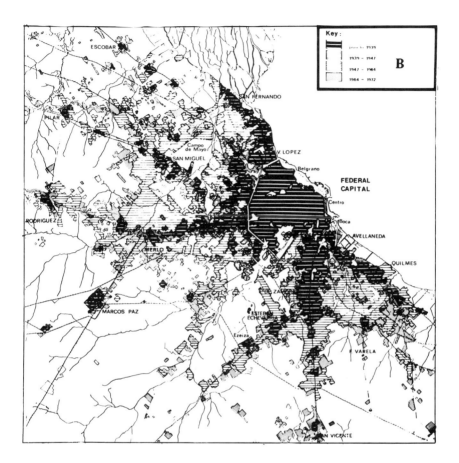

solidly built houses constructed by Italian immigrants, showing in the styling of the facade the Mediterranean background of their builders and owners.

1930s–1960s

The decade of 1930 marks the end of an economy based almost exclusively on agriculture and cattle breeding. The world crisis of 1929–30 and World War II led to considerable reduction in manufactured imports, triggering a process of industrialization in Argentina based on light metal industry and textiles. The new industries were located mainly in the littoral cities—Buenos Aires in particular—reinforcing the existing trend toward spatial concentration. Urban immigrants, who in the previous period came from abroad, now came from the

Table 22.3

Immigrants by Origin, Argentina

(100 = Total Number of Immigrants in each Inter-censal Period)

Origin	1869-1895	1895-1914	1914-1947	1947-1960	1960-1970
Italy	50.7	35.7	25.0	35.8	5.4
Spain	20.2	41.2	26.2	20.4	8.0
Rest of Europe	17.6	11.5	26.2	8.3	5.3
Neighboring Countries	10.5	7.5	17.2	28.9	76.1
Rest of the world	1.0	4.1	5.4	5.6	5.2
	100.0	100.0	100.0	100.0	100.0

Source: Lattes, 1975

depressed regions of the interior provinces and later also from neighboring countries, in particular, Chile, Paraguay, Bolivia, and Uruguay (Table 22.3).

The main factors affecting the urban structuring process of Buenos Aires and, to a certain extent, of other Argentinian towns from the 1940s to the 1960s, can be summarized as follows: (1) urban growth coupled with an intense process of suburbanization (Figure 22.1), (2) a progressive occupation of the suburbs by low-income groups, (3) a sharp increase in the percentage of owner-occupied dwellings relative to rented accommodation, (4) increasing local industry, in particular that of medium and small size, and (5) the development of urban transportation.[4]

The urban immigrants settled in the peripheral areas rather than in the center, as was the case during the previous period. In order to represent this process cartographically, a series of social maps[5] of Buenos Aires corresponding to three census dates (1943, 1947, and 1960) is shown in Figure 22.2.

The 1960 map confirms what was common knowledge among Buenos Aires residents during the period: high-income areas tended to be central and located along the riverside to the north, while low-income areas tended to be peripheral and located in the south, southwest, and west sectors. The 1943 map, however, differs substantially from the 1960 one. In the former, the areas with low social economic scores and poor housing conditions do not display a peripheral pattern as much as is the case in 1960. Although in both cases the poor housing areas tend to be located in the southern sectors, they are clearly more centrally located in the 1943 map.

A measure of the relative distance to the center of the higher- and lower-

Figure 22.2 Evolution of Buenos Aires: Social Maps

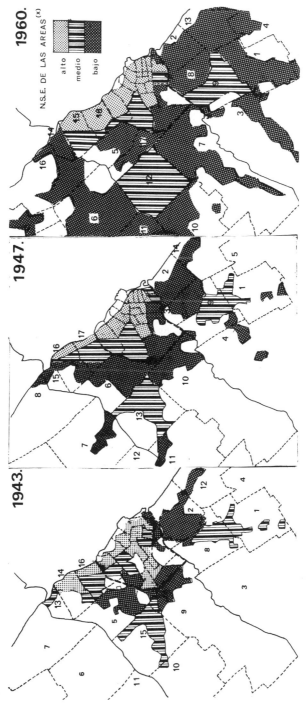

Argentina, 1980. *National Census*, IGM, 1983. Atlas de la Republica Argentina

income areas in different periods can be calculated: the weighted mean distance from the city center for areas with both positive and negative social economic scores in each census. In 1943, this distance is practically the same for both types of areas (9 kilometers), although each occupies a different sector, and they are segregated from one another. From then on, the distance to the center of the higher-income areas remains essentially unchanged, while that of the poor areas increases (12 kilometers in 1947 to 18 kilometers in 1960). This is clearly shown in the maps by the expansion toward the periphery of the shaded zone. The important suburbanization process that took place in Buenos Aires during this period therefore was closely related to and mainly caused by the process of peripheral residential development, which fundamentally affected the lower-income groups.

The suburbanization process was closely linked with the subdivision by developers of large, previously nonurban estates into very small plots, which were sold with a long period of monthly installments. This type of operation was the predominant one in the suburban land market during the years studied.[6] The zones affected by this form of development were normally low-quality areas, some of them affected by floods and lacking basic services, such as paved streets, sewerage, and water supply. Furthermore, these zones had very few, if any, primary schools, practically no secondary schools, and scarce and very distant police stations, post offices, courts of justice, civil registry offices, and similar services. On the other hand, the ever-expanding, privately owned *colectivo* network managed to reach these areas and link them with the suburban railway stations, providing the urban workers the option of commuting at low financial cost but at a high cost in terms of travel time and lack of comfort.[7]

In general terms, the urban policies of the period did not attempt explicit spatial changes (as, for example, a new towns plan or urban renewal schemes) but were rather the result of the application of a general political outlook. Its effects on the spatial structure of Buenos Aires were nonetheless very important, as a study of the city clearly shows.

Other examples of the application of urban policies that affected the spatial structure were the rent law (1943) and the "horizontal property" law (1948), the latter allowing apartments in high-rise buildings to belong to different owners.[8] After the enforcement of this law, many high–rise apartment buildings replaced old, single-family houses in central areas, in the main subcenters, and along the main axis. The horizontal property buildings became from then on the predominant housing form of medium- and medium-high income groups in Buenos Aires. Developers took to the horizontal property business to such an extent that certain zones (mainly in the CBD, along the northern axis) experienced a threefold and fourfold increase in their residential densities. The zones concerned, which eventually included the main subcenters and the central part of the south sector (the traditional location of the turn-of-the-century *conventillos*), improved their socioeconomic status as new apartment buildings replaced poorly maintained old houses and corner shops increased in number and in the variety and quality of goods and services offered. At the same time, there was a substantial increase in the amount of housing loans available to medium- and low-income groups from government banks. These nonindexed loans, in fact, could be considered as a subsidy to housing as progressive inflation made monthly payments very low after a number of years.

There was almost a complete lack of municipal control of suburban development. Developers could subdivide large estates into small plots, to be repaid in monthly installments, without providing proper public services. The predominant type of dwelling built on these plots was the single-family house. The owner and family contributed to construction through their own spare time labor.

Although representing a considerably smaller proportion of the total than the previous type, the development of *villas miseria* (shantytowns) also characterized this period.[9] The peripheral *villas miseria* became a significant number in Buenos Aires in the 1940s, increasing in the following decades, while the *conventillo*— the central slums of the beginning of the century—decreased in number to near extinction (low-quality hotels and lodgings, however, have been increasing in central areas recently). The *villa* dweller is generally from the interior provinces and neighboring countries, is normally a nonskilled worker, and belongs to the lowest income groups. The central trait of a *villa* is its illegal character, occupying public or private vacant plots normally in areas liable to flooding or otherwise unsuitable for commercial or residential development. Some *villas* are centrally located, but most of them are peripheral.

Present Situation

Argentina's demographic, economic, and land use structure are illustrated in Table 22.4 and Figures 22.3-22.6

Region

In the 1970s, the process of industrialization, based on the substitution of imported manufactures by locally made goods, encountered structural limits that did not allow it to go much beyond light industry. Heavy industries did not reach an equivalent stage of development.

In the case of urbanization, Hardoy (1982) points out that as Argentina has exceeded the point where 80 percent of the population is urban, its potential for urban growth has diminished. This is shown by the fact that during the 1970s the greater Buenos Aires area for the first time reduced its share of the total population (from 35.8 percent in 1970 to 34.9 percent in 1980). The larger metropolitan areas that consolidated in previous periods, such as Buenos Aires, Rosario, and La Plata, had lower growth rates than other agglomerations (Table 22.5).

An interesting comparison can be made between the two metropolitan areas that follow Buenos Aires: Córdoba and Rosario. Rosario's greatest growth was registered between 1869 and 1947 (in the same way as Buenos Aires and for

Table 22.4
Male Ratio and Density by Province, Argentina

Provinces and Federal jurisdictions	Population	Male Ratio	Surface (sq.km.)	Density (inhab./sq. km.)
T O T A L	27,947,466	96.9	2,780,091.5	10.1
Federal Capital	2,922,829	83.2	199.5	14,650.8
Buenos Aires	10,865,408	98.2	307,571.0	35.8
Catamarca	207,717	97.7	100,967.0	2.1
Cordoba	2,407,754	96.9	168,766.0	14.3
Corrientes	661,454	98.2	88,199.0	7.5
Chaco	701,392	102.8	99,633.0	7.0
Chubut	263,116	108.0	224,686.0	1.2
Entre Ríos	908,313	98.1	78,781.0	11.5
Formosa	295,887	102.5	72,066.0	4.1
Jujuy	410,008	106.3	53,219.0	7.7
La Pampa	208,260	106.2	143,440.0	1.5
La Rioja	164,217	98.5	89,680.0	1.8
Mendoza	1,196,228	96.3	148,827.0	8.0
Misiones	588,977	102.8	29,801.0	19.8
Neuquén	243,850	107.0	94,078.0	2.6
Río Negro	383,354	104.1	203,013.0	1.9
Salta	662,870	99.0	154,775.0	4.3
San Juan	465,976	95.4	89,651.0	5.2
San Luis	214,416	102.0	76,748.0	2.8
Santa Cruz	114,941	127.6	243,943.0	0.5
Santa Fe	2,465,546	97.0	133,007.0	18.5
Santiago del Estero	594,920	99.2	135,254.0	4.4
Tucumán	972,655	98.0	22,524.0	43.2
National Territory of Tierra del Fuego	27,358	154.3	21,263.0	1.3

Source: Argentina (1980). **National Census.**

Figure 22.3 Age Structure in Argentina

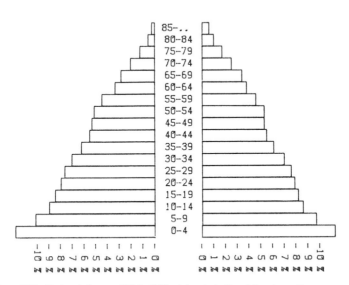

Argentina, 1980. *National Census*, IGM, 1983. Atlas de la Republica Argentina

similar reasons); Córdoba, an important administrative and cultural center during the colonial period, did not register a real metropolitization process before 1947, when important metal industries (aircraft and automobile industries) were established there. In 1980 Córdoba reached a population of 982,000, which is slightly higher than Rosario's (Table 22.5).

In spite of these recent weak trends toward population dispersion, Argentina as a whole still shows an unbalanced population distribution. Its urban network is characterized by a high degree of primacy (a primate city of 10 million inhabitants followed by two cities of 1 million each) (Figure 22.7).

Problems concerning urban structure after the 1960s will be examined using Buenos Aires as a study case.

Intraurban Structure

The fan-shaped zone centered on the CBD, defined here as a central zone, has a radius of about 10 kilometers and includes about one-third of the total metropolitan population of 10 million. The colonial civic center, Plaza de Mayo, still predominates as the government and administrative center. High-rise apartment buildings of good quality are concentrated in the central zone and stretch out along the main axis, in particular toward the north. Since the 1940s, most

Figure 22.4 Domestic Gross National Product Land Use; Agriculture.

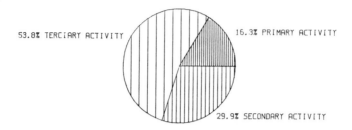

Domestic Gross National Product

53.8% TERCIARY ACTIVITY

16.3% PRIMARY ACTIVITY

29.9% SECONDARY ACTIVITY

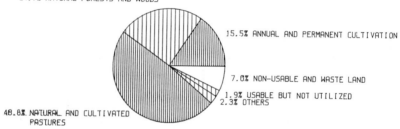

Land Use

24.7% NATURAL FORESTS AND WOODS

15.5% ANNUAL AND PERMANENT CULTIVATION

7.0% NON-USABLE AND WASTE LAND

1.9% USABLE BUT NOT UTILIZED
2.3% OTHERS

48.6% NATURAL AND CULTIVATED
PASTURES

Total hectares under consideration: 210,856,000

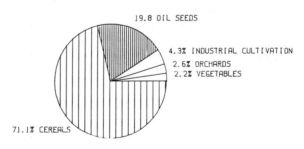

Agriculture

19.8 OIL SEEDS

4.3% INDUSTRIAL CULTIVATION
2.6% ORCHARDS
2.2% VEGETABLES

71.1% CEREALS

Total hectares under consideration: 23,971,379

Argentina, 1980. *National Census*, IGM, 1983. Atlas de la Republica Argentina

Figure 22.5 Educational Level; Cattle Raising; Industry.

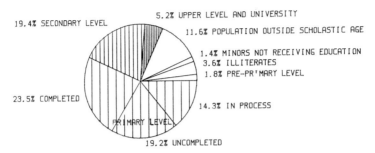

Educational Level

5.2% UPPER LEVEL AND UNIVERSITY

19.4% SECONDARY LEVEL

11.6% POPULATION OUTSIDE SCHOLASTIC AGE

1.4% MINORS NOT RECEIVING EDUCATION
3.6% ILLITERATES
1.8% PRE-PR'MARY LEVEL

23.5% COMPLETED

14.3% IN PROCESS

PRIMARY LEVEL

19.2% UNCOMPLETED

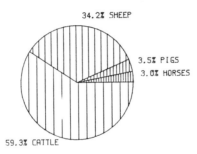

Cattle Raising

34.2% SHEEP

3.5% PIGS
3.0% HORSES

59.3% CATTLE

Total: 102,898,616 heads

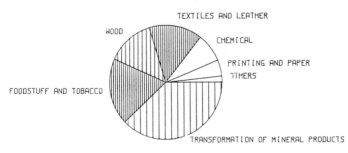

Industry

TEXTILES AND LEATHER

WOOD

CHEMICAL

PRINTING AND PAPER

OTHERS

FOODSTUFF AND TOBACCO

TRANSFORMATION OF MINERAL PRODUCTS

Occupied personnel: 1,558,972

Argentina, 1980. *National Census*, IGM, 1983. Atlas de la Republica Argentina

Figure 22.6 Fishing; Mining; Forestry.

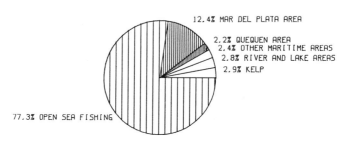

Fishing

12.4% MAR DEL PLATA AREA

2.2% QUEQUEN AREA
2.4% OTHER MARITIME AREAS
2.8% RIVER AND LAKE AREAS
2.9% KELP

77.3% OPEN SEA FISHING

Total: 583,292 tons

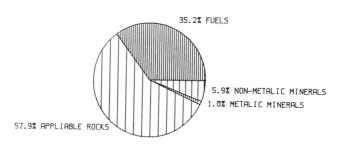

Mining

35.2% FUELS

5.9% NON-METALIC MINERALS
1.0% METALIC MINERALS

57.9% APPLIABLE ROCKS

Total: 101,035,219 tons

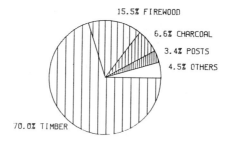

Forestry

15.5% FIREWOOD

6.6% CHARCOAL

3.4% POSTS

4.5% OTHERS

70.0% TIMBER

Total: 4,987,023 tons

Argentina, 1980. *National Census*, IGM, 1983. Atlas de la Republica Argentina

606

Table 22.5

Populations of the Largest Agglomerations, Argentina, 1869–1980 (in thousands)

Agglomerations	1869	1895	1914	1947	1960	1970	1980
1. Greater Buenos Aires	229	782	2,034	4,722	6,807	8,642	9,927
2. Greater Córdoba	29	48	122	370	592	793	982
3. Greater Rosario	25	100	256	516	669	813	955
4. Greater Mendoza	9	29	112	230	331	478	597
5. Greater La Plata	–	45	119	273	404	486	560
6. Greater San Miguel de Tucuman	17	35	112	221	297	366	497
7. Mar del Plata	–	5	25	115	211	302	407
8. Greater San Juan	8	10	36	108	147	223	290
9. Santa Fe	11	25	64	180	209	245	280
10. Salta	12	17	28	67	117	176	260
11. Alto Valle +	–	–	4	29	92	148	255
12. Greater Resistencia	–	1	13	69	108	143	218
13. Corrientes	11	16	29	56	98	137	180

+ Also referred to as Comahue agglomeration. It is formed by various separate but closely neighboring towns (see Vapnarsky, 1981).

Sources: The 1960, 1970 and 1980 figures were taken from the National Censuses, which group the jurisdictions forming "agglomerations".

The previous figures were taken from Randle (1981). They correspond to the urban population of the jurisdictions approximately forming the censal agglomerations.

The figures corresponding to the Alto Valle agglomeration in 1960, 1970 and 1980 were taken from Vapnarsky (1981).

607

Figure 22.7 Argentina's Population Distribution, Provinces, Main Agglomerations, and Regions

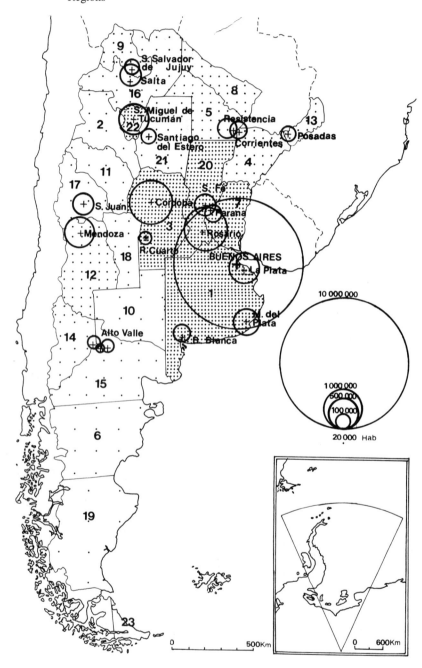

of the low-quality, older housing to the south of the CBD, where the beginning-of-the-century *conventillos* were located, have tended to become—under market forces exclusively—either good-quality high-rise residential flats or office buildings.

A large number of small industries, developed after the 1940s, are interspersed with other land uses, mainly in the outer part of the central zone to the west and northwest. Although they may cause various degrees of nuisance to the residences in close proximity to them, they are, by and large, integrated within the urban structure. Old industries (packing houses, warehouses, and others) located to the south, on the contrary, have caused serious deterioration of the southern zone close to the polluted Riachuelo stream.

Generally the central zone has improved its housing quality and supply of services over time, although it has increased in traffic congestion and pollution (air, noise). Regrettably, many historical sites and buildings have disappeared, replaced by more dense and rentable developments, or have been remodeled extensively.

The vast peripheral zone as a whole can be compared with the central zone. The disorganization, lack of services, and facilities of the vast peripheral zones are in sharp contrast to the more or less well-served central zone. The radial traffic and public transport network follows the main axes (north, northwest, west, and south) that originated in colonial interregional roads. The development of the railway network reinforced the pattern of sectorial differentiation, creating barriers that hinder tangential communications by road. In fact, the road network had to adapt to the existing axial railway network that resulted in a maze of secondary and tertiary roads. There are two high-speed axial highways to the north and the southwest and only one tangential highway (General Paz Avenue), an incomplete semicircle about 10 kilometers from the CBD.

Sectors are differentiated by their socioeconomic level, quality of housing, provision of services, quality of transport, and environmental characteristics. The northern sector rates higher on these characteristics than the southern sector. Commuters depend mainly on suburban railways, the quality of which (frequency of services, speed, comfort) varies greatly among sectors. Only those sectors served by high-speed axial highways have a significant flow of private cars. Peripheral *colectivos* are an important link in commuting. It was, in fact, the development of a dense *colectivo* network that allowed the development of peripheral residential zones (mainly inhabited by low-income groups) located between the main radial axes (intersticial sectors). In the peripheral *colectivos*, commuters travel from scattered low-density residential zones to main suburban railway stations.

As far as the patterns of land and housing ownership are concerned, private ownership predominates over rented accommodation in Buenos Aires. As far as the *villas miseria* are concerned, the number of *villa* dwellers was estimated as falling between 5 percent and 7 percent of the total population of the federal capital in 1970. In greater Buenos Aires, outside the federal capital, the proportion is higher (it may reach 10 percent).

Government policies related to the *villas* changed in different periods. When employment rates were high due to industrial development, the *villas* were not disturbed much. From the 1960s on, official banks opened credit lines specifically directed to *villa* dwellers. Although various residential developments were built in peripheral areas, the number of dwellings involved was insufficient to achieve the stated goal of significantly reducing the *villa* phenomenon.

In 1976, during the time of an authoritarian political regime, a project aimed at the elimination of *villas* was undertaken in the federal capital. The implementation of the project was based on the forced eviction of *villa* dwellers and the subsequent destruction of makeshift dwellings. By 1983, 34,000 families had been evicted from the federal capital out of a total *villa* population of 37,000 families. An unspecified number of them, however, reestablished themselves in other *villas* in the greater Buenos Aires area, outside the federal capital.

LEGAL AND CONSTITUTIONAL BASE OF LAND USE PLANNING

The Argentinian Republic consists of 22 provinces, a federal territory with the federal capital of the Republic, the city of Buenos Aires.[10] The National Constitution of 1853 (which is still in force with various amendments) established a republican, representative, and federal form of government.

The Constitution establishes that the provinces should guarantee the functioning of the municipal system. Municipalities, however, do not enjoy a real juridical autonomy nor do they have legislative powers of their own. Bylaws (including those related to land use planning) are issued by municipalities, but these in fact reflect delegated powers from provincial governments or, in the case of the federal capital, the national government. Municipalities, however, in practice enjoy a wide range of decisionmaking authority by using the powers delegated to them by the provinces or national government. As far as regional planning is concerned, the federal organization of the country makes it impossible to implement plans involving various provinces unless interprovincial agreements are made (Reinhold, 1983).

Private ownership of land is guaranteed by the Argentinian Civil Code of 1868, which states that private ownership of land is inviolable and owners cannot be deprived of it unless a legal sentence is passed and due compensation is paid. Although the prevailing juridical doctrine when the code was brought into force regarded ownership of land as "exclusive, absolute and perpetual," jurisprudence and legal commentators have repeatedly backed less stringent interpretations. It is widely accepted that the right of a private owner is limited when the ownership affects the public interest.[11] The implementation of urban plans implying restrictions of use or compulsory acquisition of privately owned land is based on this interpretation.

In urban planning, restrictions of use concerning land use, height of buildings, and sanitary regulations are much more common than compulsory acquisition. Restrictions on use do not imply compensation; Bercaitz (1983) points out that restrictions should be general, affecting all properties in certain conditions (for example, located along an avenue or within a zone) and not directed to any property in particular, which if it were would be considered a restriction of use and would imply compensation. Bercaitz, along with others, also points out that the right of the state to impose restrictions of use on individuals on behalf of the public interest is the legal basis of planning codes in Argentina. They also state that this is limited by "reasonability criteria." Bercaitz (1983) comments that restricting building on, for instance, 2 meters of a plot 50 meters long can be considered reasonable. If, on the other hand, the restriction affects perhaps half of the plot, this certainly will imply compensation.

Public participation is not required in planning legislation. According to Argentinian law, the individual affected by general restrictions imposed by the administration can only make a claim that has a concrete and individual basis. Hutchinson (1983, 291) maintains that this hinders public participation in urban plans: "in the present situation, the owner of a plot can perhaps fight successfully a compulsory purchase affecting him; on the contrary, the neighbors of a zone can do nothing against an urban plan that hasn't given them enough green spaces."

MAJOR POLICIES ADOPTED AND TYPES OF PLANS, PROGRAMS, OR PROCEDURES USED

Population, Industrial Distribution, and Planning at the Regional and National Level

The unbalanced distribution of population and economic activities at the national level—excessive concentration in the littoral region, particularly in Buenos Aires—has been referred to by planners and authors in different fields. Government action in the form of explicit policies has been implemented only from the 1960s. These policies were set forth by a succession of governments of different and even opposed political views. Although all of them recognized the need for remedying territorial inequalities, the rationale behind their individual policies was presented differently, depending on the institutional and political standing of the particular government. Democratically elected governments based their policies on the need for "more equity" or "efficiency," while military governments based theirs on "national defense" (Rofman, 1981).

In 1959 an interprovincial agreement provided for the creation of the Federal Council of Investments (CFI), aimed at fostering the development of the depressed regions of the interior. The council's policy was to favor the development of capital goods industry rather than consumption goods industry and undertake large public projects, such as interregional roads, bridges, tunnels, and hydroelectrical projects. Tax exemptions were also used to redirect growth to the desired regions.

In 1966, under a military government, a planning and development act (*Ley de Planeamiento y Acción para el Desarrollo*) was put into action, dividing the country into eight planning regions, each with a regional development body (Oficina Regional de Desarrollo). One of these regions is the metropolitan region of Buenos Aires whose regional body produced a metropolitan master plan (*Plan de Ordenamiento Metropolitano*).

During the 1960s and 1970s a series of important infrastructure projects aimed at linking the regions was undertaken. In 1969, a road tunnel under the Paraná River, linking two provincial capitals (Paraná and Santa Fe), was completed. In 1973, a suspension bridge over the same river, farther to the north, linked two other provincial capitals, Resistencia and Corrientes. In 1975 and 1976, two bridges over the Uruguay River, linking the Argentinian province of Entre Ríos with the neighboring Republic of Uruguay, were opened to use. In 1978, an important bridge over the Paraná River, including a road and railway complex linking the provinces of Buenos Aires and Entre Ríos, was opened. All of these infrastructure projects contributed to the integration of the Argentinian meso-potamy (provinces of Corrientes, Entre Ríos, and Misiones), a region almost completely bound by the Paraná and Uruguay rivers.

Also an interregional road (linking the northeast and the northwest through the Chaco region) was put into use. Three international links connecting the western and northern provinces with Chile through the Andes were improved. Concurrently, a series of industrial projects in the interior provinces was undertaken along with some irrigation projects, hydroelectrical dams, and tourist development projects. Although the institutional framework of national and regional planning is far from being established, these projects carried out by different governments and aimed at different goals contributed to the integration of previously isolated or depressed regions. Probably they were a factor to be taken into account in explaining the population trends shown during the last intercensal period (1970–80), when the growth rates of the northwest, the northeast, and the far south (Patagonia) were greater than the national rate.

Planning at the Urban Level

Buenos Aires will be taken as a case study in order to exemplify the characteristics, extent, and problems of urban planning in Argentina.

Building and Planning Codes

Building codes have been the main instrument for the implementation of land use planning since 1944, when the municipality of Buenos Aires issued a code that became the model for many other local authorities all over the country. The 1944 code, in force until 1977, established restrictions of use concerning matters such as height of buildings, restrictions in the occupation of plots, daylighting and ventilation, and zoning.

In 1977, two laws, one national (affecting the city of Buenos Aires, the federal capital) and one provincial (affecting the province of Buenos Aires), were issued by the national and provincial governments, respectively. The former entitled the municipality of the city of Buenos Aires to issue a new planning code, and the latter (Land Use and Territorial Planning Law) requested all provincial municipalities to issue statutory plans, taking into account planning standards established by the provincial government.

1977 Planning Code of the City of Buenos Aires

The bylaws of the city of Buenos Aires were drastically revised in 1977, greatly restricting the allowed building density by lowering the mean FAR (floor-area ratio) for the city from 5 to 2. The previous building code controlled building densities indirectly by maximum height and *gabarits*, street line and back alignments, and daylighting and ventilation regulations. The new code introduces FAR as the main enforcement measure. Its principal aim was to control the spontaneous renewal (as new buildings replaced the old ones) of the dense and compact urban tissue of continuous high-rise buildings, to be replaced by a noncompact fabric.

According to the law, owners are granted a premium in terms of FAR for building high-rise detached towers rather than lower contiguous buildings. They also get a premium for grouping plots rather than using single plots of normal size.[12]

The reasons given for the important changes introduced in the new code were manifold: to impose a limit on the population capacity of the city;[13] to favor the formation through spontaneous renewal of a less dense and less compact urban tissue; to reduce congestion; to improve townscape values by eliminating the frequent occurrence of large, tall, windowless partition walls separating adjacent plots; and to eliminate daylighting wells.[14]

1977 Planning and Land Use Law of the Province of Buenos Aires[15]

This law has generally been viewed by planners as an important step for urban and regional planning in Argentina. The law makes special reference to urban sprawl and includes provisions that attempt to prevent peripheral growth that does not meet basic requirements. The law mentions the "unjustified development" that occurs when large peripheral estates are divided into small plots for economic profit only with little provision for urban facilities. The law is also meant to solve the problem posed by the high percentage of vacant peripheral plots, frequently kept by owners for investment or saving. Low-income owners cannot afford to build a house while they are paying monthly installments on their plot. If they do build, they do so at a very slow pace, leading to the formation of dispersed low–density residential areas, which carry an extremely high cost for the municipality to provide sewerage, water supply, electric power, and paved roads.

The law established that each municipality should submit statutory plans for approval by the provincial government. These plans must deal with land use, occupancy, the road system, and subdivision of blocks, taking into account the planning standards set by the province. The plans must also provide population estimates for the period involved. The law requires the municipalities to classify land as: (1) residential (urban and nonurban), (2) commercial and administrative, (3) recreational, (4) industrial (compatible and noncompatible), (5) open space (public and private), or (6) for future expansion. The statutory plans must also provide a layout of the road system classifying the network in hierarchical levels.

The standards established by the law include: (1) open space: 10 square meters of open space per person, 6 square meters within the city, and 4 square meters in the periphery, (2) maximum densities: 150 persons per hectare in the peripheral zones, 1,000 persons per hectare when urban areas are provided with sewerage and peaks of up to 2,000 persons per hectare in commercial or administrative centers.

The maximum FAR allowed is 2.5 for residential use and 3 for commercial and administrative land use. The proportion of built-up area of a plot must not exceed 60 percent of the total area of the plot. The minimum built-up surface per person ranges from 10 to 15 square meters. FARs can be increased under certain conditions: when the frontage of a plot is greater than 10 meters; when buildings are detached from neighboring buildings; when buildings are set back from the street line; when the proportion of the built-up area of a plot is less than the maximum allowed; and when a plot faces an open public space.

The plans should specify the position of back alignments so that a central core of the block is formed. Inner courts are not allowed as means of illumination and ventilation in high-rise buildings (thus not allowing daylighting wells).

The law gives special consideration to regulations concerning the expansion of urban areas. Precise standards are given as to minimum frontage, back alignments and area of plots, and layout and dimensions of blocks. It is stressed that any development scheme in urban areas should include water supply, sewerage, paved streets, power supply, and public lighting. In peripheral zones where the projected density is greater than 150 persons per hectare, a development scheme should include the mentioned items with the exception of paving, which is compulsory only for the main roads.

A symposium that included planners and jurists held in 1982 (Cassagne et al., 1983), when the Buenos Aires planning law had been in force for four years, showed a clear consensus among planners of the benefits of restraining uncontrolled urban expansion as established by provincial law. The extent to which the province should intervene in local plans, however, was a matter of discussion. Public participation also appears as a controversial point. Because the law makes no provision for such participation, it was concluded that the inclusion of public participation within the framework of the law was a priority.[16]

Buenos Aires City Master Plan and Metropolitan Plan

In 1947, Le Corbusier and two of his Argentinian followers published a master plan for Buenos Aires.[17] It was never put into practice, although it greatly contributed to awakening the interest in urbanism.

In 1948, the municipality of Buenos Aires set up an advisory committee that included outstanding town planners to study a master plan for the city. The plan was published in 1959 (*Municipalidad de la Ciudad de Buenos Aires*, 1959) with a chapter that referred to greater Buenos Aires as a whole, notwithstanding that the municipality has jurisdiction only over the federal capital and does not include the periphery. The latter is in the province of Buenos Aires. The city had outgrown its administrative boundaries, which were established in 1880 when the city of Buenos Aires became the federal capital and enlarged to its present limits in 1886.

The first plan intended to be applied to greater Buenos Aires as a whole had its origin in the Office for the Metropolitan Region (Oficina de la Región Metropolitana). This body published a master plan for the metropolitan region (ORM, 1969) in which careful analysis and diagnosis of the regional problems were made, and a group of detailed proposals related to various aspects of the spatial structuring of the region were set forth. The undesirable consequences of what is termed spontaneous urbanism as opposed to planning are explained, along with the corresponding planning proposals aimed at remedying them.

Many of the conclusions of the study are based on the notion that the semi-circular spatial configuration of the agglomeration has led to excessive urban sprawl and disorganization of the periphery with a lack of adequate surburban subcenters. On the other hand, the excessive concentration and congestion of the main center is also stressed. The plan relates this to the lack of an integrated transport system, which currently has north-south connections with an excessive number of transfers (suburban railway-underground rail-*colectivo*). The proposed solution is based on implementing a preferred north-south axis of urbanization (parallel to the river), discouraging future expansions to the west (Figure 22.8). This preferred axis includes a highway network (three main north-south highways with complementary roads) and an integrated suburban railway and underground network.[18]

As far as the restructuring of suburbia is concerned, the plan proposes the selection of a limited number of existing peripheral subcenters as development poles. In this way, the currently disorganized suburban zone would be structured. Finally, the plan proposes the intensive utilization of the delta of the Paraná River as a regional recreational zone.

The plan clearly relies on the notion that transport developments have an effect on land uses. The fact that the plan was not implemented, notwithstanding the time elapsed since it was first published, showed that the institutional framework behind the plan was not strong enough to secure the support of the successive governments and the coordination between the various administrative jurisdic-

Figure 22.8 Metropolitan Master Plan of Buenos Aires: Proposed Development Scheme

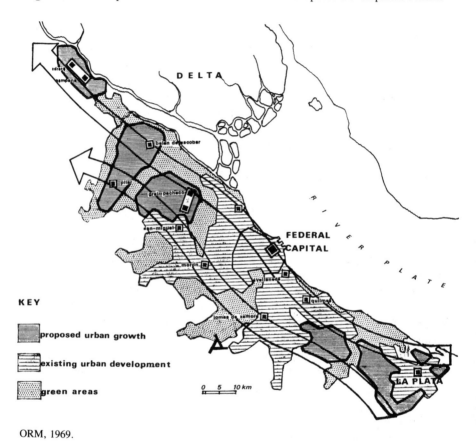

KEY

proposed urban growth

existing urban development

green areas

0   5   10 km

ORM, 1969.

tions involved (national government, provincial government, municipal level). In fact, this important study became one more in the long list of nonimplemented Argentinian urban plans.[19]

1977 Urban Freeways Plan

When the municipality of Buenos Aires developed an elevated freeways plan for the city of Buenos Aires in 1977, which was immediately implemented, it did not take into account previous nonimplemented schemes: the Buenos Aires city master plan, the metropolitan master plan, and the Ministry of Public Works Transport Plan (MOSP, 1972). The city master plan included two freeways that crossed the city from north to south: the riverside freeway, which required few expropriations, and the central freeway, which marked the outer limit of the dense central zone, linking the north and south regional highways. This freeway was planned within an open corridor to be formed from a row of entire city blocks of about 120 meters in width. This scheme implied extensive expropriations. The metropolitan master plan is similar to the previous plan as far as the riverside freeway is concerned but shifts the central freeway to the west, thus affecting less dense zones. In both previous cases, the east-west connection delimits the southern end of dense central zone without crossing it, requiring few expropriations. Both freeway schemes were part of wider transport schemes, which relied heavily on the expansion and interconnection with the public transport system.

The extremely ambitious freeway plan implemented by the municipality in 1977 contradicts the previous schemes in many fundamental ways. First, the plan restricts itself to the federal capital instead of considering the road system of the greater Buenos Aires area as a whole. Second, its implementation was not accompanied by any important development in public transport. Third, it did not follow the layout of previous plans in that the 1977 freeway scheme disrupts the dense historical zone of San Telmo, thus requiring high expropriation costs. Furthermore, expropriations did not affect entire blocks, as in the previous cases, but only a central corridor within the blocks, clearly affecting townscape values in many residential areas.

Planners and planning associations almost unanimously opposed the 1977 freeways plan, stressing the lack of an appropriate justification for its departure from previous plans, the disruption it caused to the urban fabric in central zones, its probable lack of economic feasibility, and, most of all, the lack of consultation with experts and the population before the plan was implemented. This point is clearly stated by O. Suarez (1979, 26), an outstanding Argentinian planner:

Who should make planning decisions and how should they be made? . . . In all countries with planning legislation it is elementary that planning policies should contemplate all urban problems in a balanced way, that a maximum public participation and representativity of all sectors of society involved is secured and that costs and benefits of the proposed solutions are evaluated. None of this has happened in connection with this

Municipal Plan which not only will result in a heavy burden for the future of the city but certainly means a setback as far as the way urban policies are adopted.

MAJOR CHALLENGES

In order to cover Argentina's typical problems in physical planning, various sources were analyzed. The annals of two meetings devoted to urban development and planning were reviewed (the First National Meeting on Urban Law and Planning held in 1982) (Cassagne et al., 1983), and the National Meeting of Planners held in 1977. (MBS, 1978). Diagnoses contained in published metropolitan plans were also reviewed, as well as the preliminary notes of planning codes and laws. Finally, the section on Argentina of Hardoy's work (1968) on urban and regional planning in Latin America, describing the situation in the 1960s, was also consulted.

There is consensus among Argentinian planners of the negative consequences of the unbalanced distribution of population and economic activity over the territory, of uncontrolled urban development—in particular, the formation of disorganized peripheral areas, lack of comprehensive planning legislation, and the existence of legal, jurisdictional, and administrative obstacles that provide difficulties and even obstruct planning at urban, metropolitan, and regional levels.

There is a coincidence in historical and current trends in that occupation of the territory has led to excessive concentration of population and economic activity in some regions to the detriment of other regions whose potential, although important, has not yet been developed. High concentration is also manifested in city size distribution, in which the first city is 10 times larger than the second and where a very high proportion of the total urban population of most provinces is concentrated in the principal city.

There is consequent need to define major planning strategies directed at stopping the flow of population to developed regions and metropolitan areas and to coordinate different types of public action, such as industrial location schemes, with housing and urban development programs.

The negative effects of peripheral urban development with very low densities, due mainly to a high percentage of vacant plots, and lacking basic services is a major challenge. These characteristics are interrelated since the excessive dispersion of peripheral areas makes it impossible for the municipalities to provide services, such as sewerage and water supply. The visual and functional disorganization of such areas, where housing and noxious industries may coexist, is a problem frequently referred to.

There exist in many Argentinian towns large properties that belong to official agencies and that are occupied by railway shunting tracks, warehouses, army barracks, and similar structures. Their location has become inappropriate as urban growth has enclosed them, suggesting to some planners that these land uses should be moved farther out and the land so vacated be used to form a public land stock for urban renewal.

Reserves of public land to develop cultural and recreational facilities are scarce or nonexistent. It has been suggested that projects aimed at mobilizing urban land, affecting both private vacant plots and public land, should be implemented.

Most planners agree that comprehensive planning laws imposing control on urban expansion are needed. On the other hand, the lack of housing programs for the lower-income groups is a major drawback in developing any comprehensive urban project.

Planners also agree that national, provincial, and municipal planning legislation should be coordinated and that general aims and goals should be clearly defined. The jurisdiction of the different state organizations and the procedures to be followed for the approval and application of statutory plans also require clarification. The recent return to constitutional government requires that urgent attention be given to these matters. Also, the development of public participation procedures would be high on the agenda.

One problem frequently referred to but may be very difficult to solve is the multiplicity of jurisdictions in urban agglomerations. Greater Buenos Aires, with its 20 separate municipalities, is a clear example of this problem. This jurisdictional situation has frequently been identified as one of the main causes for the nonimplementation of plans at the metropolitan level. Another case of conflicting jurisdictions is the rapidly growing Camahue agglomeration, located on the border of two provinces, Río Negro and Neuquén (Vapnarsky, 1981). As far as urban information is concerned, only from the 1970 national census onward is the urban agglomeration concept used, in which municipal jurisdictions belonging to the same agglomeration are grouped.

Finally, the lack of continuity in public policies due to decades of political and institutional instability should be mentioned. An experienced Argentinian national planner (Speranza, 1983) points out that during the last few decades, 250 national and 400 urban plans were prepared. Few of these were effectively implemented due to lack of continuity in official efforts, lack of means, or lack of general assent.

NOTES

I express appreciation to the participants of the Seminar on Planning Policies held in the School of Architecture at the University of Belgrano during the second term of 1983, especially Liliana Furlong, coordinator of the study group, and Dardo Arbide, Fernando Diez, Patricia Mariquelarena, and Alvaro Orsatti.

1. Latin American cities inherited one of the most important planning codes ever issued. Philip II of Spain issued the Laws of the Indies (*Leyes de Indias*) in the sixteenth century that included a group of laws related to planning matters, such as detailed requirements on the selection of sites for the foundation of new cities, the standard gridiron layout (a repetition of city blocks, *manzanas*, of about 100 meters by 100 meters), the location of the civic center and its characteristics (its orientation, and its position with

respect to bypassing streets, convenience through the provision of arcades). These laws strongly influenced the subsequent development of Argentinian cities right up to present-day urban expansions, where the regular characteristics of the original plans are normally repeated.

2. For the sake of convenience, this period can be dated from 1810, when a local junta took over the vice-regal authority, and 1869, the date of the first national census.

3. Figures are elaborated by Randle (1981, vol. 2). The following crops were taken into account: wheat, oats, barley, rye, flax, potato, tobacco, peanuts, cotton, tea, and grapevines.

4. A peculiar mode of transport, the *colectivo*, developed in Buenos Aires. *Colectivos* were originally 10-seater and then 20-seater passenger minibuses whose coachwork was made locally and typically were driven by their owners.

5. The computer maps shown are the result of a cluster analysis of a group of census variables related to demographic, occupational and educational aspects, housing condition, and so forth; 1947 and 1960 are national census years. The 1943 figures were taken from a national educational census, which included housing and occupational information. For more detail on the methods used and the conclusions arrived at, see Torres (1978).

6. The proportion of home ownership in the periphery (greater Buenos Aires excluding the federal capital) increased from 43.3 percent to 67.2 percent between 1947 and 1960. This shows the effect of the housing policies applied during the Peronist period (1945–55) when low interest government bank housing loans were available to low-income employees. It also shows the important relative decrease of intraurban transport fares as compared with other prices (a standard suburban railway ticket increased from 1.60 pesos in 1939 to 7.50 in 1959; the cost of living index increased from 2.60 to 78.70 for the same dates). See Torres (1978, 203). The Rent Law of 1943 also has to be taken into account to explain the increases in home ownership during the period under consideration.

7. One important change in the type of management of urban transportation takes place during this period, the rise of the *colectivo*. As a consequence of the economic crisis of 1930, which greatly reduced the number of passengers using taxicabs, groups of taxi drivers who owned their own vehicles formed associations. They followed fixed routes carrying as many passengers as they could accommodate, charging each passenger according to the distance traveled. The resulting fare was higher than the one corresponding to an equivalent run by tram, bus, or underground (all of these means of transport belonging to large companies based on foreign, mainly British, capital), but it was much cheaper than an equivalent run by taxi. On the other hand, *colectivos* were faster than trams and buses, and their popularity increased to the point that by the mid–1930s they had gained a 30 percent share of the total number of trips made by public transport.

Colectivos drew an angry reaction from the large transport companies and from the government; they also were mentioned in the British Parliament when the terms of the treaty between Britain and Argentina, known as the Roca–Runciman Pact, were discussed. In this context, the *colectivos* were viewed as harmful competitors to the large British urban transport companies. In 1936 and 1937 the Argentinian government issued various decrees setting up a corporate body run by the government and the large companies (Corporación de Transportes de la Ciudad de Buenos Aires). This body was to have the monopoly in public transport (trams, buses, underground) in the city of Buenos Aires and was authorized to expropriate with due compensation all *colectivo* lines registered after 1934. *Colectivo* owners reacted violently, hiding their vehicles rather than handing them over to the monopolistic corporate body. The *colectivo* issue became even more entangled when labor and student organizations gave support to the *colectivo* owners' stand in resisting expropriation. This situation made the decrees difficult to enforce, but most of the *colectivos* were expropriated eventually. After 1945, the Perón regime changed the previous official viewpoint regarding foreign-owned public service companies and expropriated all transport companies, including the railways. The urban transport corporate body was dissolved in 1948. From then on the *colectivo* lines began to expand in an astonishing way; whereas *colectivo* trips accounted for about 30 percent of total urban public transport trips in 1938, they accounted for about 80 percent in 1970. By 1970, in fact, a complete reversal of the type of ownership and management of public transport had taken place in Buenos Aires: from the monopoly of the late 1930s, a situation was reached in 1970 in which most daily trips in a metropolitan area of about 8 million inhabitants were catered for by numerous companies, each consisting of many small entrepreneurs.

8. The Rent Law of 1943 froze rents at the level they had when the law was enforced. This discouraged landowners from renting properties. This, in addition to the inflation of the late 1940s and 1950s, affected the housing market. Successive modifications to the law to restrict its application led eventually to its total inapplicability in the late 1960s.

9. The 1947 and 1969 censuses did not specify *villas miseria*. Nevertheless, a rough estimation can be made taking into account all occupants who are not owners, legal tenants, guests, caretakers, and others. According to this it can be estimated that 5 percent of all inhabitants of the greater Buenos Aires, excluding the federal capital, were *villa miseria* dwellers in 1960.

10. The city of Buenos Aires was federalized (nominated as the federal capital of the Republic) in 1880. Its present boundaries were established in 1886 to include the city and the surrounding areas. Although the federal capital today extends beyond its boundaries and an important part of the greater Buenos Aires (nineteen counties are in the Province of Buenos Aires), the 1886 boundaries remain unchanged.

11. The 1949 amendment to the Constitution (revoked in 1955) established the "social function of property." Even without this doctrinal definition attached to the Constitution, most legal commentators agree that private property, as much as every other individual right, should be limited by the laws which rule its exercise. See, among others, Mouchet (1962) and Bercaitz (1983).

12. The modal frontage of plots is 8.65 meters, equivalent to the colonial unit of measurement of 10 *varas*.

13. The old code presumed a population of 7 million within the federal capital under an assumption of maximum occupation. The new code reduced this figure to 4 million (see Suárez, 1983b).

14. In the old code, daylighting standards acted in two ways: regulating the maximum height of buildings, which depended on the width of the front street, and permitting daylighting and ventilation of rooms through daylighting wells, that is, inner courts of variable area dependent on its depth, which were normally inadequate. Elimination of the daylighting wells in 1970 will produce important changes.

15. *Ley de ordenamiento y uso del suelo* (Provincia de Buenos Aires, 1977).

16. This law was put into action between March 1976 and December 1983 within an abnormal institutional framework in which the executive power at the national level was exercised by a military junta, which also exercised legislative power and appointed provincial governors who, in turn, appointed municipal mayors. Therefore, neither national nor provincial parliaments nor municipal councils existed. The return to the con-

Figure 22.9 Comparative View of Buenos Aires' Urban Fabric

Paris   New York   Buenos Aires

stitutional framework in December 1983 implied the need to restructure the law, as Bercaitz (1983) had predicted almost one year before.

17. The plan, originated in Le Corbusier's visit to Buenos Aires in 1929, was completed in Paris in 1938, in collaboration with the Argentinian architects Ferrari, Hardoy, and Kurchan. It was first published in its full version in 1947 (Le Corbusier, 1947). A synthesis is provided in Corbu's complete works (Boesiger and Girsberger, 1960, 314):

"The city of Buenos Aires has grown tremendously during the past few years on the basis of the traditional *manzana* dating from the Spanish colonization. The *manzana* is a group of houses, originally one story high, forming a square with sides of 110 meters, surrounded by streets 7, 9 or 11 meters in width, with all the houses facing inward onto gardens in the interior of the square. . . . Today the *manzana* is overloaded with skyscrapers, which fill it like an egg, with neither a garden nor a court remaining. The city has undergone an amazing expansion (infinitely more than that of Paris). Its molecular structure (the *manzana*) creates an insupportable and completely congested urban fabric. There are no longer arteries, lungs or definite organs whatsoever." (See Figure 22.9.) Author's note: This is a free translation of the original French. In the original, *manzanas* are referred to as *cuadras*; in fact, the city block is known in Buenos Aires as *manzana*, while *cuadra* is the name given to each side of a *manzana*.

18. The layout of the projected network and the ideas behind it were strongly influenced by the French Réseau express régional.

19. Two other projects of metropolitan level should also be mentioned. SIMEB–CONHABIT Program (CONHABIT, 1977) is a metropolitan strategy that in its main aspects follows the metropolitan master plan. It was studied by SIMEB (BA Metropolitan System) under the aegis of CONHABIT (National Program for the Habitat and Territorial Planning). The Ecological Belt (see Kesselman, 1983), a project carried out by agreement between the municipality of the city of Buenos Aires and the Province of Buenos Aires, is aimed at the revitalization of degraded areas (many of them subjected to floods) forming a semicircle at a radius of 30 kilometers around Buenos Aires. Low-lying areas are to be filled in following a sanitation procedure based on the use of garbage collected in the city of Buenos Aires. A parkway and recreational facilities will complete the project.

BIBLIOGRAPHY

Bercaitz, Miguel A. 1983. Régimen Jurídico del Planeamiento Urbano. In J. C. Cassagne et al., eds. *Derecho y Planeamiento Urbano*. Buenos Aires: Editorial Universidad SRL.

Boesiger J. W., and Girsberger, E., eds. 1960. *Le Corbusier 1910–60* Zurich: Editions Girsberger.

Cassagne, Juan C., Juan E. M. Duprat, Alberto E. Mendoca Paz, Augusto L. Reinhold, Edgardo P. Scotti, and Odilia Suárez, eds. 1983. *Derecho y Planeamiento Urbano.* Buenos Aires: Editorial Universidad SRL.

Chiozza, Elena et al. 1982. *Atlas total de La república Argentina.* Buenos Aires: Centro Editor de América Latina.

CONHABIT. 1977. *SIMEB. Sistema Metropolitano Bonaerense.* Buenos Aires: CONHABIT, D.E. 03.

Cortés Conde, Roberto, and Ezequiel Gallo. 1973. *La formación de la Argentina Moderna.* Buenos Aires: Paidós.

Hardoy, J. E., R. Basaldúa, and O. Moreno. 1968. *Política de la tierra urbana y mecanismos para su regulación en América del Sur.* Serie Celeste (Planeamiento Regional y Urbano). Buenos Aires: CEUR, Instituto Torcuato Di Tella, Editorial del Instituto.

Hardoy, Jorge E. 1982. Distribución espacial de la población. In J. E. Hardoy and C. E. Suárez, eds. *La situación ambiental de la Argentina en la década de 1960.* Buenos Aires: CEUR, Cuadernos No. 8.

Hutchinson, Tomás. 1983. Impugnación administrativa y judicial de planes. Denegación y revocación de licencias para construir. In J. L. Cassagne et al., eds. *Derecho y Planeamiento Urbano.* Buenos Aires: Editorial Universidad SRL.

IGM 1983. *Atlas de la República Argentina.* Buenos Aires: Instituto Geográfico Militar.

Kesselman, Julio. 1983. La recuperación de los terrenos degradados. *SCA. Revista de la Sociedad Central de Arquitectos,* No. 125, July.

Lattes, Alfredo E. 1974. El crecimiento de la población y sus componentes demográficos. In E. R. Lattes and A. E. Lattes, eds. *La población de Argentina.* Buenos Aires: CICRED Series.

Le Corbusier. 1947. Plan Director de Buenos Aires. *La Arquitectura de Hoy,* No. 4.

Le Corbusier. 1964. *El urbanismo de los tres establecimientos humanos.* Buenos Aires: Poseidón.

Ministerio de Bienestar Social. 1978. *Políticas de Desarrollo Urbano. Primera Reunión Nacional.* Documento de Desarrollo Urbano No. 15, Series Información y Difusión (C1). Buenos Aires: Secretaría de Estado de Desarrollo Urbano y Vivienda.

Ministerio de Obras y Servicios Publicos. 1972. *Estudio Preliminar del Transporte de la Región Metropolitana de Buenos Aires.* Buenos Aires: MOSP.

Mouchet, Carlos. 1961. Problemas Jurídicos e institucionales del planeamiento de las areas metropolitanas. *La Ley,* 103, 816.

Municipalidad de la Ciudad de Buenos Aires. 1959. *Plan Regulador de la Ciudad de Buenos Aires—Etapa 1959–1960.* Buenos Aires: OPR.

ORM. 1969. *Organización del espacio de la Región Metropolitana de Buenos Aires. Esquema Director año 2000.* Buenos Aires: CONADE.

Provincia de Buenos Aires. 1977. *Ley 8912. Ordenamiento y Uso del Suelo.* La Plata: Secretaría de Urbanismo, October.

Randle, Patricio. 1981. *Atlas del desarrollo territorial de la Argentina.* Vol. 2. Buenos Aires: OIKOS.

Reinhold, Augusto L. 1983. Presupuestos jurídicos del planeamiento. In J. L. Cassagne et al., eds. *Derecho y Planeamiento Urbano.* Buenos Aires: Editorial Universidad SRL.

Rofman, Alejandro B. 1981. *La política económica y el desarrollo nacional*. Bogotá: Universidad Simón Bolívar.

Scobie, James R. 1974. *Buenos Aires: Plaza to Suburb, 1870–1910*. New York: Oxford University Press.

Socolow, Susan M. 1978. La burguesía comerciante de Buenos Aires en el siglo XVIII. *Desarrollo Económico—Revista de Ciencias Sociales*, 18(70): July–September.

Speranza, Vicente. 1983. Premisas y modalidades operativas para el ordenamiento urbano. In J. L. Cassagne et al., eds. *Derecho y Planeamiento Urbano*. Buenos Aires: Editorial Universidad SRL.

Suárez, Odilia. 1979. El problema de las autopistas de Buenos Aires. *Ambiente*, no. 7, October.

Suárez, Odilia. 1983. Elementos para el análisis del planeamiento urbano. In J. L. Cassagne et al., eds. *Derecho y Planeamiento Urbano*. Buenos Aires: Editorial Universidad SRL.

Suárez, Odilia. 1983. Consideraciones urbanísticas en torno al Código de Planeamiento de la Ciudad de Buenos Aires. *SCA. Revista de la Sociedad Central de Arquitectos*, no. 125, June.

Torres, Horacio A. 1975. Evolución de los procesos de estructuración espacial urbana. El caso de Buenos Aires. *Desarrollo Económico—Revista de Ciencias Sociales* 15(58): July–September.

Torres, Horacio A. 1978. El mapa social de Buenos Aires en 1943, 1947 y 1960. Buenos Aires y los modelos urbanos. *Desarrollo Económico—Revista de Ciencias Sociales*, 18(70): July–September.

Vapnarsky, César. 1981. *Crecimiento y redistribución de la población en el norte de la patagonia*. Serie Separatas, No. 1. Buenos Aires: CEUR, March.

PART VII

AUSTRALASIA

23

Australia

RAYMOND BUNKER

Land use planning in Australia owes much of its character to the recent imposition of European culture and populations on a large land mass, most of which is short of water. Australia has a three-level system of government. The commonwealth government was formed by the federation of the states in 1901, and local government operates in each state as developed by state statute. The population is concentrated in large cities, most of them state capitals on the coast, as Figure 23.1 shows.

HISTORICAL DEVELOPMENT AND CURRENT STATUS OF LAND USE PLANNING

Australia was inhabited by roughly 300,000 Aborigines when European settlement began in 1788. The native population lived as hunters and gatherers. This kind of economy supported extraordinarily low densities of population, particularly in the central deserts. In a few generations, European pastoralists had swept across the land and, "an all-pervading homogeneous pattern of land use that had persisted for tens of thousands of years disappeared in less than two hundred" (Plumb, 1980, 15). As far as rural areas go, by "1870 the broad pattern of land use, as it exists today, was generally established," comments the *Atlas of Australian Resources*; "only the tropical monsoon lands of the far north and a large portion of the arid interior remained unused, although their eventual use as grazing land was already predictable" (Plumb, 1980, 15). While that may be largely true, in the last century there had been tremendous advances in the practices and technology of farming this archaean land.

Figure 23.1 Map Showing States and Cities of Australia

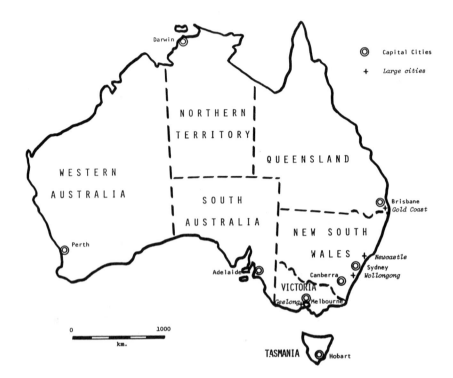

Evolution of Present Land Use Patterns

The early convict colonies around Sydney and in Tasmania grew subsistence crops—mainly wheat and maize—and raised animals for meat. In 1821 the wool trade with Britain commenced, and sheep stocked the extensive interior tablelands and plains as they were explored and settled. The discovery of gold in New South Wales and Victoria in the 1850s slowed the process of extending rural settlement and production, but the gold rushes brought in many immigrants. When the quest for and mining of gold slackened, the expansion of rural pursuits accelerated again.

Cropping then became important. By 1860 a variety of wheat had been developed that was suited to hot, dry conditions, and farming systems became concerned with conserving soil moisture. South Australia began to produce wheat for export to the other Australian colonies and by 1860 to overseas countries.

In the 1860s sugar cane growing started on the wetter tropical coastal lowlands of the north. Cattle were important to early settlers for milk, meat, and draught purposes. But the beef cattle industry did not develop significantly until the present century, with the opening up of new rangelands and export markets.

Toward the end of the nineteenth century, important advances took place in farming practices and export conditions. Wheat breeding experiments on a scientific basis began to produce strains specifically suited to Australian conditions. The use of phosphate as a fertilizer became established. The value of subterranean clover and other sown grasses became apparent, and appropriate cultivation and management techniques developed. Toward the end of the century the first experiments in large-scale irrigated croplands producing fruits, wines, vegetables, wheat, and fat lambs were carried out; however, it was not until many years later that much larger government-assisted irrigation schemes were constructed. Artesian water from the great subterranean basins of eastern Australia provided a basis for the spread of the pastoral industry into the outback. Finally, the introduction of refrigeration and the development of steam shipping services opened world markets to Australian fruits, dairy products, and meats.

The twentieth century saw the application, intensification, and augmentation of these kinds of innovations. In particular there have been massive increases in the areas of sown and fertilized pastures and in grain yields. There has been a significant spread of rural holdings, too, from an area of 340 million hectares in 1900 to 500 million hectares today. Most of that expansion has occurred through the spread of extensive grazing in the hotter areas of the continent.

Ever since the gold rushes, mining has been an important land use in Australia. In addition to gold, the mining of silver, lead, zinc, and copper has led to the growth of important towns in the interior, such as Broken Hill in New South Wales and Mount Isa in Queensland. Coal mining has become more and more important this century. New South Wales, and more recently Queensland with its huge open cast cuts, dominate Australian coal production. Iron ore mining for domestic iron and steel production was concentrated in South Australia initially, but in the last twenty years huge mines for the export trade have been developed in the north of Western Australia. Similarly bauxite mining has developed in the last quarter-century and is concentrated in Western Australia, Queensland, and the Northern Territory. Oil was discovered in the Bass Strait between Victoria and Tasmania in the 1960s, and there are smaller interior deposits in Queensland and South Australia and along the coast of Western Australia. The northwest shelf off Australia has huge quantities of natural gas under development for export and use in Western Australia. Uranium was mined in small quantities after World War II; there are large deposits under development in the Northern Territory and South Australia.

Turning now to the growth of urban land use, the estimate of Australia's population at the end of 1982 was about 15,276,000, 70 percent of it contained in eleven state capitals and major cities. Increasing concentration of growth in the large cities has been a distinctive feature of Australian urbanization. During the nineteenth century the proportion of each colony's population housed in its capital city sank as interior territories were explored, surveyed, opened up, settled, and brought into production. But when that process had gone some way, capital city populations began to increase relative to that of the rest of each colony. So low points were reached by Sydney in 1861-71, Melbourne in 1861, Brisbane and Adelaide in 1871, Perth in 1891, and Hobart in 1901 (Bunker 1977, 386). During this century, domination of the states by their capital cities has continued to increase until recently, and they have been joined by a new federal government capital at Canberra, large manufacturing centers at Newcastle and Wollongong near Sydney and Geelong near Melbourne, and the tourist-recreation center of the Gold Coast near Brisbane. Although there have been some signs of a slackening in the growth rate of some of these large towns in the last decade, their location means that Australia's urban population is represented in seven urban fields: two large, three medium, and two small in size. Newcastle, Sydney, and Wollongong contain about 4 million people on the east coast of New South Wales, with Melbourne and Geelong having about 3 million on the south coast of Victoria. The next size of urban region is about 1 million, with more in Queensland at Brisbane-Gold Coast and less in South Australia at Adelaide and in Western Australia at Perth. Finally, there are two detached cities of a quarter-million at Canberra, the national capital, and Hobart, the state capital of somewhat smaller size in Tasmania. The growth of large cities in this century has some association with the development of the Australian manufacturing industry and its concentration in Sydney, Melbourne, Adelaide, Newcastle, Wollongong, and Geelong.

Characteristics of Present Land Use Patterns

Australia has a land area of 768,284,000 hectares. Climate is the major influence on the way rural land is used, although soils are another major physical factor, and other factors such as demand for products and accessibility to markets are significant. Because of the importance of climate on land use, particularly the availability of water, the *Atlas of Australian Resources* defines six major land use zones in terms of major climate characteristics (Plumb 1980, 18-19). Table 23.1 presents that information.

Three-quarters of the population of Australia lives in the humid zone along the east and south coasts. Almost all the remainder live in the subhumid zone.

The major land using activities of Australia can only be approximated statistically. Almost two-thirds of the continent is used for agricultural and pastoral purposes. As can be seen from Table 23.2, only a small proportion of this is cropped or sown for pasture.

Of the remaining area, about 200 million hectares, or just over a quarter of the total, is not in commercial production and consists of interior desert, sandy mallee country in the south, and rugged, inaccessible country in the north. Almost a third of this area is reserved for aborigines and is used by small numbers of

Table 23.1
Major Land Use Zones of Australia

Land Use Zone	Area (million hectares)	Percent
Humid	45	5.9
Semi-humid	105	13.7
Semi-arid	290	37.4
Monsoon	60	7.8
Arid	270	35.4

Source: Plumb, T. (ed.) 1980. Atlas of Australian
Resources, Third Series, Volume 1. Soils
and Land Use, pp. 18-19.

Table 23.2
Extent of Agricultural and Pastoral Land Use in Australia, 1980–1981

Crops	Million Hectares Sown Pastures & Grasses	Balance*	TOTAL
18.3	25.0	455.7	499.0

*Used for grazing, lying idle, fallow, etc.

Source: Commonwealth Year Book 1980-81, p. 286.

them on occasion for traditional hunting and gathering activities. Another 15 million hectares is forestland used for timber production. National parks and other conservation reserves occupy almost double that area at 27 million hectares. About 9 million hectares is used for transport routes comprising roads, railways, and stock routes and something over a million hectares for urban purposes. Other land uses include open-cut mines, salt evaporators, wasteland, swamps, and ephemeral lakes.

It is difficult to find detailed and recent information on the land uses in Australian cities. One important aspect is the densities of population in urban areas. Table 23.3 shows the overall and gross residential densities in the 11 major urban areas in 1976, the latest date for which such information is available. The boundaries of the built-up areas of the citics are defined using the same criteria; thus the densities are comparable.

The density figures are shown as overall densities, or resident population divided by total contiguous urban area; or gross residential densities—that is, residential population divided by gross residential area. There are indications that, as in the United States, these ruling densities are falling over time. A comparison with similar density figures for 1971 (Harrison, 1975, 16) supports this hypothesis. These falling densities are associated with continued urban sprawl and declining populations of central areas and inner suburbs.

There have been few careful and comprehensive land use surveys of major Australian cities, and the classifications of land use vary. One of the most accurate and detailed is that carried out in Adelaide in 1957 and summarized in Table 23.4. This obviously represents the land use structure of a large city that has grown over 120 years since its foundation in 1836. Table 23.5 shows the land uses in Elizabeth, a new town to the north of Adelaide built largely in the 1960s. Land for roads and parking is more significant than in Adelaide, and there is more open space and recreational land. The high proportion of land taken for industry represents car manufacturing, which forms a large part of the economic base of the town.

One of the distinctive characteristics of Australian cities is the large extent of low–density suburbs. The life-style of much of the Australian population is encompassed within them. Commentators tend to be patronizing or sympathetic about this. One critic writes that "combining many of the features of the country town with a strong sense of identity with their parent city, the Australian suburbs summed up the Australian ethos: the yearning for private ownership taking precedence over either individualism of taste or a great concern for the shared amenities of the community" (Bolton, 1981, 110). One of the most provocative and interesting books on Australian cities of recent years starts by discussing "Australia as a suburb" and concludes "you don't have to be a mindless conformist to choose suburban life. Most of the best poets and painters and inventors and protestors choose it too. It reconciles access to work and city with private, adaptable, self-expressive living space of home" (Stretton, 1975, 21).

Evolution and Present Status of Land Use Planning

In the broad sense, Australian cities, as one commentator puts it, have grown with a multiplicity of plans rather than being without a plan at all (Harrison, 1977, 184). There were three kinds of such plans: the original colonial layout of the central areas dealing with basic street patterns, private and public plans for the subdivision and development of land, and plans for public works or

Table 23.3

Overall and Gross Residential Densities of Australian Major Urban Areas in 1976

Major urban area	Total Urban area (sq. km.)	Overall pop. density (pp.sq.km.)	Resid. Pop. density (pp.sq.km.)
Sydney	1,460	1,894	3,107
Melbourne	1,480	1,676	2,397
Brisbane	810	1,103	1,822
Adelaide	600	1,430	2,092
Perth	670	1,090	n.a.
Newcastle	240	1,046	2,093
Wollongong	180	1,095	2,190
Canberra	225	947	1,578
Hobart	85	1,436	2,442
Geelong	110	962	1,511
Gold Coast	115	1,144	2,192

Source: Division of National Mapping, 1979-1982,

Atlases of Population and Housing, 1976

Census

Volume 1, Perth

Volume 2, Adelaide

Volume 3, Brisbane/Gold Coast

Volume 4, Newcastle/Wollongong

Volume 5, Canberra/Hobart

Volume 6, Sydney

Volume 7, Melbourne/Geelong

Table 23.4

Land Use in Adelaide, 1957

Major Use Type	Area in hectares	Percentage
Industry	877	3.0
Wholesaling and Storage	353	1.2
Business	374	1.3
Public Service Facilities	2,016	6.8
Recreation	1,982	6.7
Education, social & cultural activities	1,272	4.3
Residential	11,263	38.1
Vacant allotments	1,739	5.9
Other vacant land	2,242	7.6
Agricultural land	2,006	6.8
Mineral workings	157	0.5
Rivers	240	0.8
Parking of vehicles	42	0.1
Roads*	5,007	16.9

*This separate item includes all land used for roads.

Source: Neutze, M. Urban Development in Australia, 1977, p. 111.

infrastructure. In the past there was often little coordination of these plans affecting land use. Private investment in the development of land and construction of buildings led the way, and public authorities lagged behind in servicing this growth "without having much influence on when, where and how it has happened" (Harrison, 1977, 184). While matters have improved somewhat since World War II, the speed of development has often outpaced attempts to organize it.

In a narrower sense, local land use controls became established in Australia

Table 23.5

Land Use in Elizabeth, near Adelaide, 1967

Major use type	Area in hectares	Percentage
Residential	788	37.6
Roads and Parking	422	20.2
Schools & churches	157	7.5
Reserves	326	15.6
Shops	36	1.7
Commercial	17	0.8
Industrial	347	16.6

Source: South Australian Housing Trust, Annual Report

1966-1967, p. 18.

in the period 1928 to 1945. Previously some rudimentary powers to control development existed in some states. For example, New South Wales had provisions to prohibit the erection of industrial and commercial buildings in defined areas, and flats could be excluded in a similar manner from low–density residential areas. The 1928 Town Planning and Development Act of Western Australia was the first act to give local government the power to control the use of private land. By 1945 all states but South Australia had legislation that authorized local government to prepare and implement statutory land use plans. South Australia enacted such legislation in 1966.

Much of this flurry of activity was associated with the end of World War II. A Commonwealth Housing Commission was set up to define and satisfy postwar housing needs. The commission was convinced that proper housing provision had to take place within a broader urban planning framework, and its final report in 1944 stated "that planning is of such importance that the Commonwealth Government should not make available financial assistance for housing unless the state concerned satisfies the Commonwealth that it has taken, or is taking, definite steps to erect and implement regional and town planning legislation" (Bunker 1971, 126–27). A rash of such legislation soon followed.

It is important to appreciate the kind of land use planning that this system involves. It is "a function of local government, an extension of the traditional regulatory powers over buildings and sanitation to the layout of subdivisions and eventually to the regulation of the use of land'' (Harrison, 1977, 184). Essentially the initiative lies with the developer, governments cannot force development to take place, and the system has many negative features in that it emphasizes *control* of development. Such control is exercised in the interests of preserving or enhancing residential amenity and land values. Other forms of land use control less onerous than statutory plans are sometimes used. The statutory planning scheme usually consists of an ordinance and a map. The map outlines the broad areas or zones of land that may be used for different purposes and indicates reservations of land for public uses such as highways, recreation, and major open space. Reservations of this kind usually require eventual public acquisition of the land. Typically the ordinance sets out in detail the nature of the uses prohibited, allowed with consent, or permitted as of right (providing certain standards are observed) in the various zones. There is usually some room for discretion in the administration of the scheme.

The intention of this planning system is to provide a guide to the pattern and process of urban development over the next decade or two. Theoretically this will also provide a blueprint for the programming and coordination of public investment necessary to underpin development. The expectations invested in this system have only partly been achieved, and when this has happened, it has been helped by parallel actions such as public landownership and development of residential lots or decisionmaking about public works. The reasons for this somewhat modest performance range from political explanations to technical or organizational failings ''reflecting the insider-outsider dichotomy in the litera- ture'' (Freestone, 1983, 183). They include such factors as a reluctance to impede development on the part of some governments, local or state; chronic inade- quacies of funds for urban development needs; the ability of some public au- thorities to circumvent or alter plans; and the power of state ministers of planning to amend, suspend, or vary the provisions of planning schemes. There is inherent inflexibility in zoning plans that cannot anticipate many of the characteristics of future development and are difficult to adapt and change. Zoning of uses can often be so expansive that it becomes useless for planning and programming purposes or can be too detailed so that it becomes a straitjacket on development and confers scarcity value on land. There are often pressures to rezone land to higher and more profitable uses. Shopping centers are an example of this where poor locations for them have been identified in schemes or a developer wants to minimize costs by avoiding well-sited but expensive areas.

Despite these inherent weaknesses, there are some successes. Land use controls have been valuable in sorting out incompatible activities in the processes of redevelopment. They have been most resolutely applied in the extension of metropolitan areas and the conversion of rural land to urban purposes. They have served to protect the routes of proposed new highways and open spaces pending their later acquisition. But this has most successfully occurred where the public sector has been intimately and powerfully involved in the urban development process. The most obvious example is in the planning and building of the national capital of Canberra. The Australian Capital Territory is largely owned by the commonwealth government. The National Capital Development Commission is responsible for the planning and development of Canberra. It coordinates public works, and private development is required to conform with leasehold conditions and agreements, an arrangement that is more powerful than statutory planning as a means of land use control.

In a country dominated by the larger cities, it is important to appreciate the place of land use planning in their development. In Sydney, the Cumberland County Council, representative of local governments in the region, was set up in 1945 to prepare a plan for the metropolitan area. It produced the Cumberland County plan in 1948, and this plan, with amendments, became law in 1951, "the first statutory metropolitan scheme in the British Commonwealth" (Bunker, 1971, 128-29). Similar plans followed for Melbourne (1955), Perth (1959), and Adelaide in 1967. No statutory plan exists for the Brisbane metropolitan area, but the city of Brisbane, formed in 1925, is a large local authority encompassing much of that area. Its scheme was adopted in 1965. Newcastle and Wollongong, the two industrial cities north and south of Sydney, were covered by plans developed by the Northumberland County Council (1952) and Illawarra Planning Authority (1956). Hobart has had draft schemes of various kinds prepared by the Southern Metropolitan Master Planning Authority, made up of four local authorities in the metropolitan area, the first starting in 1958. In this manner, statutory plans exist for all 11 major urban areas identified earlier in this chapter. In the 1970s and 1980s environmental issues and considerations became prominent and have become an important component of land use planning. In New South Wales, the Environmental Planning and Assessment Act was passed in 1979. Statutory requirements for environmental impact assessment have been established as part of the system of development controls on land use (Fowler, 1982, 43). Similar provisions were incorporated in the Planning Act of 1982 in South Australia. In both states, a Department of Environment and Planning has been formed as part of these changes. Similar moves are taking place in Victoria.

INSTITUTIONAL AND LANDOWNERSHIP FRAMEWORK

Two institutional characteristics of Australian land use planning are of supreme importance. One is the need to relate and associate land use planning to general policies about urban and rural development. This includes policies about housing, transport, job location and accessibility, education, health and welfare services, and the provision of physical infrastructure such as water supply, sewerage, electricity, gas, and telecommunications services. This association has been strongly, if unevenly, pursued over the last decade and has sometimes, if not very appropriately, been described as the process of urban management. The characteristics of this approach include a strong concern for the quality of life in the different parts of the urban system; measures to redistribute resources spatially; concern with levels of service of publicly provided services; issues of access to shelter and to employment in both abstract and physical dimensions; and the influence of decisionmaking processes about the settlement system.

The second institutional feature of general significance to land use planning in Australia is the system of government. Australia is a federation of states that came together as recently as 1901. Local government was created by each of the states. So the states are the source from which the present system of government has sprung. Since federation, the functions and responsibilities of governments have grown vastly. This is particularly the case at the national level, and this has also been accompanied by financial arrangements developing over the years in a way that has meant that the revenue-raising capabilities of the national government have grown much more than those of state and local governments. This means very large flows of money from Canberra to state and local governments, often in the form of reimbursements or taxsharing. The key conclusion from this is that intergovernmental processes and relationships are very important in land use planning, so important that they are responsible for some of its characteristics.

Constitutional and Legal Basis of Land Use Planning

There is little in the Constitution of the commonwealth of Australia of direct reference to matters of land use planning. But there are a number of provisions that have become of considerable relevance. One of the most important of these is section 96, which provides that ''Parliament may grant financial assistance to any state on such terms and conditions as the Parliament thinks fit.'' Given the superior revenue-raising power of the commonwealth government, this power has become a means of influencing land use policy in various ways, for example, in the establishment and operation of government land commissions and trusts by the states.

As a signatory to international agreements, the commonwealth government has argued that it needs to press for their enforcement within Australia. This was one of the arguments presented in stopping the construction of the Gordon-below-Franklin power scheme in Tasmania in 1983. The proposal would have intruded on the wilderness area of southwest Tasmania included in the World Heritage List of the International Convention for the Protection of the World Cultural and National Heritage.

The commonwealth government's responsibility generally for trade and commerce, taxation, and external affairs affects land use planning. It used its constitutional powers of export control and licensing to prevent exports of mineral sands from Fraser Island in Queensland in order to conserve the character of that unique island. Its promotion of strong immigration policies after World War II has been a major factor in the rapid rate of growth of Australian cities and in the contribution that migrants have made to their social, economic, and cultural character. Foreign investment in Australia is controlled, and specific projects, for example, for resort development, are reviewed as a matter of course by the Foreign Investment Review Board. Finally, the way the commonwealth government itself locates and manages its own functions has important land use planning results. This is most spectacularly shown in the development of the national capital at Canberra, but it extends to the manufacture of defense equipment, the location of the large number of commonwealth public servants working in state capital cities, and the location and operation of major airports.

The states are the most significant source of authority and initiative in direct land use planning matters. They controlled, or rationalized, the initial processes of exploration, survey, settlement, sale, and lease of land in the colonial period. This has had much to do with the character of both past and present land use. State governments initiated important projects of their own—towns, ports, forests, irrigation areas, railways. Currently state governments are responsible for education, health, social, and welfare services, as well as for public works such as ports, roads, railways, electricity generation and distribution, water supply, sewerage, and drainage. Their own activities and the urban infrastructure they supply are crucial land use planning matters.

The preparation of local planning schemes and the operation of detailed control for most kinds of development is the responsibility of local government. Each state has its own enabling legislation to this effect, passed by its parliament. Typically since 1945 each state has restructured its planning system two to three times. Table 23.6 shows the principal legislation governing land use planning and land tenure in the states. In recent changes of this kind, there has generally been a move to pass more responsibility and decisionmaking to local governments, for mixed reasons. But state governments usually retain strong supervisory or approval powers over local plans. There are also provisions for major projects or matters of specified concern or significance to be referred to state ministers or instrumentalities. Some central planning departments do develop strong policy imperatives for local governments, but others are fairly permissive.

Local government is at the interface between most planning processes and the community. It also administers and operates the most visible policy instrument regarding land use planning, the control of development. Given the high level of home ownership in Australia (which approaches 70 percent), the historical pride in property, defense of property rights and values, and the domination of suburbia, the processes of land use planning and development control have tended to promote spacious and costly standards of development, considerable uniformity, and predictability of development and resistance to change.

Decisionmaking Structures and Relationships to Land Use Planning

Reflecting the fact that the Constitution says little about the role of the commonwealth government in land use planning, there is no national forum or agency concerned with national land use policies or land resources management. There

Table 23.6

Principal Legislation Concerning Land Use Planning and Land Tenure in Australian States

State	Planning Legislation General	Planning Legislation Special	Land Tenure
N.S.W.	Environmental Planning & Assessment Act, 1979	Coastal Protection Act, 1979	Crown Lands Consolidation Act, 1931 Western Lands Act, 1901 Closer Settlement Act, 1904 Irrigation Act, 1912 Pasture Protection Act, 1934
Victoria	Town & Country Planning Act, 1961 with amendments	Melbourne & Metropolitan Board of Works Act, 1958 Geelong Regional Commission Act, 1977 Crown Land (Reserves) Act, 1978 (coastal protection sections)	Land Act, 1958 Land Conservation Act, 1970 Crown Land (Reserves) Act, 1978
Queensland	Local Government Act, 1936 with amendments State Development & Public Works Organization Act, 1971	City of Brisbane Town Planning Act, 1964 Beach Protection Act, 1968	Land Act, 1962 Irrigation Act, 1922 Irrigation Areas (Land Settlement) Act, 1962 Water Resources Administration Act, 1978
South Australia	Planning Act, 1982	City of Adelaide Development Control Act, 1976 Coast Protection Act, 1972	Crown Lands Act, 1929 Irrigation Act, 1930 Pastoral Act, 1936 Real Property Act, 1886

State	Planning Legislation		Land Tenure
	General	Special	
Western Australia	Town Planning & Development Act, 1928 with amendments	Metropolitan Region Town Planning Scheme Act, 1959	Land Act, 1933 Rights in Water & Irrigation Act, 1914 Closer Settlement Act, 1927 Transfer of Lands Act, 1893
Tasmania	Local Government Act, 1962		Crown Lands Act, 1976
Northern Territory	Planning Act, 1979 Environment Act, 1982		Crown Lands Act, 1931 Agricultural Development Leases Act, 1956

641

have been different proposals about this. The Australian Advisory Committee on the Environment in a report, *Land Use in Australia*, suggested the establishment of a ministerial council of commonwealth and state ministers involved in land use planning and management. It would "formulate a national land use policy which will guide development of land resources and make explicit the goal of environmental quality" (AACE, 1974, 9). The Commission of Inquiry into Land Tenures supported this idea but gave it strategic planning responsibilities including "broad planning postulates such as the optimal population for Australia, the desirable rate of population growth and rate of urbanisation, the scope for achieving decentralisation and methods available for this purpose" (CILT, 1976, 30). Other suggestions have included responsibilities for establishing and maintaining a data bank of land use and an enhanced and improved capability for conducting land use and land system surveys. This mixture of perceptions and purposes, ranging from formulating national development policies to land evaluation, research, technical assistance, and land management, is partly responsible for the present lack of a national focus for land use planning. A recent report, *A Basis for Soil Conservation Policy in Australia*, noted that commonwealth-states ministerial councils are important in national decision-making and the dissemination of information. It suggested that six of these councils were influential in land use planning matters: the Australian Agricultural Council (founded 1934), the Australian Water Resources Council (1963), the Australian Forestry Council (1964), the Australian Environmental Council (1972), the Council of Nature Conservation Ministers (1974) and the Australian Minerals and Energy Council (1977) (Department of EHCD, 1978, 129).

It is appropriate to describe some of the features common to most state planning systems, drawing particularly on those recently restructured in New South Wales and South Australia. Typically a central department of planning, or more recently of environment and planning, is responsible to a minister and advises him as to key state and regional policies about the different uses to which land should be put "based on the wise management of the natural environment and the social and economic needs of the community" (NSW Department of Environment and Planning, 1980). In New South Wales, state environmental planning policies and regional environmental plans result from this process. Within these broad guidelines, local councils prepare plans for their areas with public involvement and consultation. Draft plans are then referred to the central department *and/or* the minister to ensure correctness of procedure and consistency with state and regional policies. If this is so, the draft plan is publicly exhibited and hearings held. The final plan is then submitted to the central department *and/or* the minister for approval. There is provision for an advisory committee to advise the minister on this and other matters. When approved, sometimes with amendments, the plan is published with official state authorization.

Development applications are made to the local council. Typically they are classified as to whether the council is the sole decisionmaking authority; whether consultation with state agencies is required; whether that consultation requires also the concurrence of these agencies; or whether the development is of a kind determined by the state. In South Australia a separate State Planning Commission has responsibility for determining this last kind of development proposal and also makes decisions about development in the large areas of the state where local government does not operate. There are usually reserve powers available to the minister to determine development applications in unusual and unforeseen circumstances.

There is provision for appeal against decisions about development applications. Such appeals can be made to an independent tribunal or court. They can be lodged if the development is approved (for example, by third party citizens), approved with conditions (for example, by the developer), or refused (for example, by the developer). In some cases third party appeals are not allowed, and some decisions cannot be appealed against.

The essential components of the planning system are thus the legislation, which sets up the ground rules, the plans and policies or the substance to be achieved, a central decisionmaking and administrative structure consisting of a department and a minister, local decisionmaking and administrative systems, an appeals mechanism and advisory bodies for consultation and reference.

Public Involvement in Decisionmaking Regarding Land Use

The public is involved in decisionmaking regarding land use in two ways: as part of the formal procedures of preparing plans and controlling development in the statutory planning process and through protests, demonstrations, and representations about land use decisions.

The latter method was more prominent in the 1970s than it is now, although a recent example of this kind of action is the popular opposition to the building of the Gordon-below-Franklin hydroelectric scheme in Tasmania stopped in 1983. Some of the most controversial issues of that earlier era included proposals to construct expressways through the inner parts of the large cities; redevelopment schemes for those areas that often displaced low-income residents; and in defense of open space areas scheduled for redevelopment. Some victories of these forms of protest included the scaling down of the Rocks redevelopment scheme adjacent to the Sydney Harbour Bridge and the inclusion of public housing as well as the purchase of significant inner areas at Woolloomooloo and Glebe in Sydney for rehabilitation rather than redevelopment. A "green ban" by the Builders' Laborers' Federation, prohibiting demolition work on such sites, was a feature of these campaigns.

The more institutionalized form of public involvement in the land use planning process is quite extensive, partly as a result of protests of the 1970s. While these opportunities are significant, it has often proved difficult for interest groups and planners to interact and communicate in an effective manner. There is extensive provision for public participation in the plan-making and development control process. In New South Wales, draft state policies and regional environment plans, together with the studies accompanying them, are publicized or placed on exhibition, with submissions invited and considered. A similar process informs the preparation of local plans. There are usually two opportunities for public comment. One is early in the process and involves publicity about background studies and draft aims and objectives of the plan. The other is after the plan is prepared, when it is placed on exhibition and public hearings are held.

In the development control process, there are comparable opportunities for publicity, comment, and representation. Councils are free to advertise proposals and have to do so for classes and types of development specified in the local plan. Advertisement usually includes notification of persons affected by the proposal, general advertisement in a newspaper, and exhibition at council offices. The form of handling representation varies. In South Australia, it is considered good practice to set a time limit for submissions and to give the proponent of the application time to reply. Council subcommittee meetings dealing with development applications allow brief presentations to be made by proponents and opponents before a decision is taken.

The extent of third party rights of appeal against development approvals varies. In South Australia, provided certain conditions have been met by a third party objector during the course of consideration and decision on an application, then that third party can appeal to the Planning Appeals Tribunal. In New South Wales that right is available only for designated development applications that involve the preparation and exhibition of environmental impact statements.

These provisions for public involvement are criticized as too extensive by some developers and architects. Public participation extends the time needed to process plans and applications even if it enriches it. Costly changes and delays can occur. In another vein, some cynicism about the genuineness of public involvement is evidenced when matters of urgency or importance cause state governments to take arbitrary action. For example, the New South Wales government passed the Botany and Randwick Sites Development Act in 1982 to validate private development proposals for vacant sites in those inner municipalities. "This Bill is about jobs," said the minister for planning and environment in introducing the legislation. "Where does this leave the local community who were led to believe that the Government was committed to seeking community views before making decisions" was the response by the professor of town planning at the University of New South Wales (Westerman, 1982).

Landownership, Tenure, and Acquisition

The processes of European exploration, colonization, and settlement led to the early establishment of lands departments in each of the states. They are concerned with the administration, occupation, and management of crown lands. As a result of this history, there are several different kinds of land tenure. Crown land can be disposed of for public purposes, either by free grant or temporary or permanent reservation. This involves such uses as for traveling stock, water collection and conservation, timber production or conservation, recreational and leisure purposes, or as aboriginal reserves. Then crown land has been disposed of by unconditional purchase of freehold, by public auction, after auction purchase, or special arrangements. Then there are conditional purchases of freehold. Finally there are leasing and licensing arrangements under land acts, closer settlement acts, and mining acts. These last vary in significance from state to state but are particularly important in New South Wales, Queensland, South Australia, Western Australia, and the Northern Territory. These leases are of various kinds; some are perpetual, and others are for grazing and pastoral purposes. Table 23.7 shows the areas of land in each state occupied under the principal land tenure arrangements.

Planning legislation in the states carries provisions for the acquisition or resumption of land to carry out the purposes and functions of legislation if required. Such action is carried out under the normal conventions and procedures governing compulsory acquisition of land for public purposes as laid down in state legislation.

MAJOR CHALLENGES REGARDING LAND USE

Increases in Land Values and Land Development

An ever-present issue is who reaps the reward for increases in land value brought about by changes in use, typically from rural to urban (Neutze, 1978, Chap. 9). One point of view is that these increases are brought about by public sector action such as rezoning and providing infrastructure and should be appropriated by the government. A Commission of Inquiry into Land Tenures reported in 1976 and recommended legislation "to reserve for the community as from a designated base date, the development or new use rights associated with permitted future changes in the nature or intensity of land use" (CILT, 1976, 2). This was not acted on.

Government levies on the increase in value brought about by change from rural to urban use have been tried; for example, a betterment levy was used in New South Wales from 1970 to 1973. Such attempts have not been very successful. Instead government operation in the field of land acquisition, development, subdivision, servicing and production of lots has been used in some states, helped by commonwealth initiatives developed under the Whitlam government of 1972 to 1975. Urban land commissions or trusts operate in some states, although their role varies. In New South Wales, this encompasses the full range of functions, while in South Australia the "Urban Land Trust's development role is restricted to the creation of marketable parcels of broadacre land by plans of land division to meet market demands" (SALT, 1983, 4). A major challenge, then, is the future of this kind of government activity: how much there should be of it, in what locations, and what range of operations it should cover. A related issue is the form of land tenure available to purchasers once a government agency sells a lot to them. The Commission of Inquiry into

Table 23.7
Land Tenure in Australia 1980/81

Area	Private Lands Alienated	In process of alienation	Leased or licensed	Other*	Total area
New South Wales	27,544	1,436	43,958	7,205	80,143
Victoria	13,909	121	2,312	6,418	22,760
Queensland	13,059	20,294	127,476	11,871	172,700
South Australia	7,224	52	55,029	36,132	98,438
Western Australia	16,807	2,151	98,139	135,453	252,550
Tasmania	2,486	90	—4,254—		6,830
Northern Territory	19,682	n.a.	77,196	37,740	134,620
Australian Capital Territory	1	–	66	176	243
AUSTRALIA	100,712	24,144	—643,425—		768,284

*Occupied by Crown, reserved, unoccupied, unreserved.

Source: _Commonwealth Year Book_, 1982, p. 285.

Land Tenure recommended that residential lands should be sold on a freehold basis but that nonresidential land should be leased, "the term of lease related to the anticipated life of the improvements" (CILT, 1976, 105). These principles have generally been followed by state land commissions and trusts.

Land Resources Management

Another major challenge to land use planning in Australia is land degradation, most conspicuously, though not exclusively, in rural and coastal areas. A study of land degradation in 1978 estimated that 51 percent of the total area used for agricultural and pastoral purposes in Australia was in need of some form of soil conservation treatment under existing land use (Department of EHCD, 1978, 135). It advocated

that soil conservation activity in Australia be intensified and extended and better integrated with policies for rural industries and planning for coastal, urban, recreational and mining areas. Structural adjustment and changing circumstances in rural industries make it necessary and possible for soil conservation to be more effectively incorporated in changed farm management practices and methods. Land capability issues are of growing importance in coastal, mining and urban planning and development. Parallel action is required by governments in research, cooperative planning, institutional changes and more effective liaison and coordination. Increased funding is also needed. (Department of EHCD, 1978, 139)

Some action has been taken since this 1978 report. In October 1983 the chairman of the Australian Bicentennial Authority (for 1988) urged a policy of national restoration: "Against the long history of this land, its innate harshness and unforgiving nature, we ought to plan and carry into execution our remedial treatment to restore it to fertility and productivity" (*Melbourne Age*, 20 October 1983).

This issue of rural land conservation continues to surface in many ways. Degradation theoretically could be controlled under systems of conditional leasehold. For example, in South Australia 42-year terminating pastoral leases in the state's arid zone enable some limitation on stocking rates and attention to conservation measures. There have been proposals to convert these terminating leases to perpetual leases to give more security of tenure, "thus giving 241 pastoral leaseholders 60 percent of the state in perpetuity" as one newspaper report rather forcefully wrote (*Weekend Australian*, 21 March 1982).

Aboriginal Land Rights and Interests

Another matter of considerable relevance to rural land use and planning is Aboriginal land rights. In recent years the rather paternalistic system of allocating and managing reserves for Aboriginal populations in all states has come under pressure. The Aboriginal land rights movement has led to important advances in the rights of Aboriginal communities to own and use land; for example, the Pitjantjatjara Land Rights Act of October 1981 granted a large section of the interior of South Australia to the Pitjantjatjara people on a freehold basis. There are special provisions for the control of land by the Aboriginal people, including control of mining activities, access to the land, and for the payment of mining royalties. The conflict of Aboriginal interests with the needs of mining exploration and development is of continuing consequence. One frequent and particular example is the safeguarding of Aboriginal sacred sites, which, to European perceptions, often have a somewhat abstract basis.

Land Use Planning and the Distribution of Welfare

A matter of subtle but salient concern to land use planning is the distribution of welfare that results from it. As far as urban development goes, large Australian cities are conspicuously segregated on a socioeconomic basis. Over the past 10 years, a number of policies have addressed the problems of disadvantaged or underprivileged areas. The most conspicuous of these was the Area Improvement Program of the 1973-76 period initiated by the commonwealth government. But a variety of policies and programs have been developed to redress the patterns of unequal provision of services and amenities in the cities. These include help not only for the rapidly developing outer suburbs with their needs for jobs and adequate physical and social infrastructure but also the inner suburbs, which often contain substantial ethnic groups hard hit by recession, unemployment, and the need to relate to a new cultural context. These inner areas are being invaded by middle-class people seeking the better environments and locations and removing much low-income housing in the process of gentrification. Location-specific policies can be used to influence the distribution of welfare. Either "unavoidable distributional effects should be taken into account when the policy decisions are made or, more strongly, . . . urban policy measures are well suited to pursuing distributional objectives" (Neutze, 1978; 47).

The same argument rages over more narrowly defined land use planning measures. Planning inevitably favors some groups relative to others. In Australia,

planning measures in the 'sixties and 'seventies reinforced the whole structure of financial taxation and rating arrangements that favoured higher income groups, owner occupiers, lower densities and peripheral growth and to freeze in the existing patterns of land use. (Reid, Jones and Wilmoth, 1983, 4).

While few deny these distributional effects or even that they are regressive, there is ambiguity about what to do, if anything. Many planners agree that these are political questions and should be left to politicians. Others argue that planners should analyze the distributional effects of planning decisions because otherwise "distributional effects will determine the decisions through political mechanisms while the policy debate is about technical or resource allocation decisions only" (Neutze, 1978, 54). Still others maintain that land use planning and development should be actively used to promote more equitable urban living (Stimson, 1982; Troy, 1981).

Decentralization

The pattern of settlement has been dominated by the metropolitan areas, for a number of reasons. Most states have developed policies to encourage decentralization or diversion of growth from these large cities. Several "growth centers" were started during the 1972-75 period with commonwealth government initiatives or support. The most successful of these took two different forms. One was the Macarthur growth center forming in effect the southwestern extension of the Sydney conurbation. The other example is the twin city of Albury–Wodonga on the New South Wales and Victorian borders, the name representing the two existing border towns. The growth center lies in the Sydney–Melbourne corridor and is sponsored by two states and the commonwealth governments.

Although incentives to promote decentralization still exist in some states, the recession of the late 1970s and early 1980s has lessened the urgency and thrust of decentralization. But the external effects of individuals, households, and establishments locating in the large metropolitan areas, together with the lack of suitable alternatives, means that decentralization remains a significant issue in national settlement policy.

Urban Consolidation

There have always been spokesmen for more compact and densely developed cities than those represented in the ruling densities of Table 23.3. These arguments have tended to come from a wide range of viewpoints. The case for more compactness, containment, and consolidation has been strengthened by recent trends. These include a shortage of capital for urban infrastructure, changing social and demographic characteristics leading to smaller households, and the difficulties of access to shelter and employment characteristic of recession years.

Some states have developed strong policy thrusts to encourage consolidation. In particular, New South Wales introduced a draft State Environmental Planning Policy in October 1982 to permit medium-density housing up to two stories in height in all residential zones in the state, where flats were then prohibited. The draft policy contained no minimum lot size but had provisions regarding height, density, landscaping, and private open space to ensure that development was not too much at variance with existing conditions. The draft policy was then held in abeyance while local councils in the Sydney area considered if they could accommodate five-year targets for the construction of medium-density or multiunit dwellings in their areas instead. Similar but less preemptory actions have taken place in Melbourne and Adelaide.

Table 23.8

Costs of Building to Different Standards for Representative Dwellings in Sydney, Late 1970's

Dwelling type	Basic cost to build to stds. of lowest value ($)	Added cost to meet modal stds. ($)	Added cost to meet highest std. ($)
Suburban allot.	5,460	3,440	8,830
Allotment plus detached dwell.	29,540	6,240	11,630
Town house	20,880	13,400	30,100
Flat	19,670	5,520	22,400

Source: Department of Environment and Planning, N.S.W.

Residential Development Standards, Technical

Bulletin 15, 1982, p. 10.

This matter continues as a major challenge to land use planning in Australia, although research has demonstrated that under current social and demographic trends, population loss in inner and middle suburbs is likely to continue even with more dwellings and intensification of built form (AIUS, 1982). The issue is directly related to the following one.

Building and Development Standards and the Cost of Housing

The high cost of the Australian's "quarter-acre" block and the dwelling on it is a challenge to land use planning. In recent years with increasing unemployment and high interest rates, home ownership has become more difficult. In this situation attention has been turned to the ruling standards of state and local authorities for size of lot, setback and form of dwelling, open space, and car parking, as well as the requirements for the width and construction of residential streets. These standards have been widely criticized as arbitrary, constraining, and sometimes excessive. Table 23.8 represents an analysis carried out in Sydney to ascertain costs incurred in building to minimum, modal, and maximum development standards. The cost penalties for town house construction at high development standards are particularly striking. A 1976 book posited the choices expressed in that situation in its title, *A Mansion or No House*. The Committee of Inquiry into Housing Costs recommended in 1978 the formulation of "cost-effective minimum development standards within which local and service authorities should be forced to operate" (CIHC, 1978, 1:12). The same committee addressed the difficulties in building multiunit dwellings because of the restricted supply of land available for medium-density development and severe limitations on how much building is allowed on the available sites. It asked for a review of the legislation, ordinances, and regulations relating to multiunit dwelling construction in order "to ensure the supply of this form of housing" (CIHC, 1978, 1:17). Understandably, a major challenge is to provide a wider range of dwelling forms in different localities and to move from controls designed to be obvious and administered efficiently to those oriented more toward the performance of the proposed development in attaining social and environmental objectives.

Administrative Processes, Citizens' Rights, and the Speed of Development

This leads into a related challenge: the balance of citizens' rights, the processes of development application and approval, and the speed and cost of development. In recent years of recession, some state governments have sought to make planning controls less restrictive and have tried to speed up the development application and approval process. It is true, too, that some of these processes are excessively clumsy and doctrinaire. As yet the planning profession has not yet faced this criticism to the degree that British planners have, but there is continuing, and not always creative, tension here.

Liquid Fuel Efficiency

In Australia the energy crisis is not so dramatically represented as in some other countries. The country has a wealth of mineral resources capable of supplying energy, including black coal, brown coal, oil, natural gas, and, controversially, uranium. Despite the fact that Australia produces most of its liquid petroleum needs, the rise in oil prices has had some effect on cities. That effect in terms of land use planning is probably as yet small. As reports have pointed out, initial adjustments have been effectively made in the use of smaller engines in cars, the combination of trip purposes when traveling, and shorter trips (Morgan, 1980). Land use adjustments are still likely to be slow, incremental, and modest. Nevertheless, this latent challenge remains and is part of the urban consolidation debate.

Land Use Planning on the Rural-Urban Fringe

There has been increasing subdivision of farms in rural-urban fringe areas for such activities as rural residential pursuits, hobby farming, rural retreats, part-time farming, horsekeeping, and dog boarding. Many of these are not viable commercial ventures but exist for recreational, part-commercial, or life-style reasons. There are problems of providing adequate water supply, power, sewerage, road, and telecommunication services. There are often conflicts between these activities and the need to safeguard metropolitan water supplies. There are problems posed by the extraction of minerals in quarries and mines in such areas. There are significant recreational demands placed in these fringe areas by metropolitan residents for camping, pleasure driving, walking, cycling, horseracing, car racing, and other activities. Land use planning for these areas has tended to be blunt and arbitrary and has used urban planning techniques for these nonurban zoned areas. Minimum subdivision sizes have been tried to retain the viability of commercial farming and decrease the demand for public network services. The challenge, however, still remains.

Organizational Affiliations of Land Use Planning with Housing and Environmental Policies

A final challenge lies in the organizational affiliations of land use planning at the state level. There has been a trend in recent years to associate environmental management and land use planning. Similarly, housing conditions and access to shelter have become important issues. These moves are reflected in formal and informal organizational structures. The links seem more significant than previous affiliations with local government and transport, although those continue to be important. One interpretation of this trend is a move in state planning from projects to policies, from land use allocation to resource allocation, from providing works to concern with levels of service.

APPROACHES TO LAND USE PLANNING

A distinction should continue to be made between the narrowly defined processes of land use planning and the broader context of urban and rural development policies within which they sit. These levels of planning were well put in a recent report, *Australian Approaches to Environmental Management: the Response of State Planning.*

For most Australians, "planning" means what professional planners do, that is mainly statutory planning: predominantly the preparation and regulation of zoning schemes to control urban development. . . . Although statutory planning is the activity of most planners, it is no longer what most professional planners regard as a sufficient means for attaining the broader, more integrated goals which they are coming to regard as the proper purposes of "planning." . . . Physical planning . . . is still insufficient, unless it is integrated into a broad-scope strategy for managing physical growth or redevelopment together with social and economic planning. (Bowman, 1979, 1-2).

In that report, the association of land use planning with urban and regional development policies is expressed in the structure of discussion. This is concerned with statutory or regulatory planning; operational planning dealing with housing, transport, land development, physical and social infrastructure, recreation, national parks, and the like; and policy planning, whose concerns are regional planning, coordination, urban renewal, growth centers and satellite towns, and the system of planning itself. Land use planning is part of all these kinds of planning but in different ways.

Within the regulatory planning system, the conventional style of planning is a zoning plan of land uses with a supporting ordinance. Such a plan prohibits certain users in a particular zone, allows some others by the consent of the planning authority, and permits others as of right providing certain standards or conditions are met. Standards are also used in determining applications of a consent use nature and form the basis of any conditions that may be placed on development approval.

Outline or strategy plans are often developed as broad statements of planning policy, usually comprising significant documentation and supporting plans rather than vice-versa. The most important of these has been the Sydney Region Outline Plan of 1968. Although never officially adopted by the New South Wales government, like its predecessor, the Cumberland County Plan of 1948, it has acted as a framework for major decisions about the planning, programming, and release of land for urban development on Sydney's fringes.

Action plans are sometimes developed and implemented for comprehensive and concentrated land use development operations. These are almost of a project kind. Examples include action plans for the rehabilitation of the Woolloomooloo area of Sydney for inner-city housing, representing action by commonwealth, state, and local governments.

Some innovative planning approaches have been tried experimentally. Where areas of land for residential development fall into one ownership, planning processes have been devised to plan uses, dwellings, and lots together and in sympathy with the landscape. The conventional process is to run roads across the area and subdivide residential allotments off them. Dwellings are then built on the lots, with specified set-backs from front, rear, and side boundaries. A more innovative approach is to work road placement, landscape characteristics, and dwelling location and form simultaneously. This then provides sites for dwellings and a building envelope within which the dwelling must fit and where it can obtain good aspect, prospect, and access, with suitable surrounding spaces. The boundaries of the lots are then determined. This approach has been tried in the development of Golden Grove, owned by the South Australian Land Trust on the outskirts of Adelaide.

Finally, the place of land use planning in corporate planning should be mentioned. In the last few years, corporate planning and management systems have been widely adopted by local councils and by state government departments and agencies. Land is a basic resource input into these constructs and land use planners frequently take part in these processes. Several land use planners have become town clerks or achieved other senior policy development and administrative positions by becoming involved in corporate planning. Some land use planning operations have become structured and enriched by using some of the terms and techniques of corporate planning. Perhaps the ultimate expression of corporate planning in the land use domain lies in the operations of the National Capital Development Commission in Canberra, where institutional imperatives, organizational structures, resource allocation, land use planning, and urban development are closely aligned (Powell, 1978).

FUTURE THRUSTS

Close Association of Land Use Planning with Urban and Rural Development Policies

A continued close association of land use planning with general urban and rural development policies has been a consistent theme. Max Neutze's book, *Urban Policy in Australia*, deals with urban policy and the distribution of welfare in terms of national population distribution, housing policy, transport policy, urban services, urban planning, and land development. He also reviews the urban dimensions or implications of general government policies and identifies statutory planning as one important means of coordination (Neutze, 1978). In this discussion, he suggests six land use planning issues that are of consequence in urban development: controlling scattered development, determining the form of urban extension, guiding the rehabilitation and redevelopment of inner residential areas, affecting the location and employment and services, enhancing environmental quality, and reserving, preserving, and conserving (Neutze, 1978, 172–91).

These associations and relationships, often of singular subtlety and complexity, will continue to develop in the future. An indication of this is the increasing effort to align housing policies, land use planning, and environmental management at both the local and regional level.

Development of Intergovernmental Relations and Processes

Land use planning has a host of interdependencies. With commonwealth, state, and local governments being involved in these, intergovernmental relations and processes will continue to be a major consideration of the future. At present it is state and local government relationships that are most formally defined in land use planning, through the planning systems developed by each state. The New South Wales legislation, in Part III Environmental Planning Instruments, has sections dealing specifically with state environmental planning policies, regional environmental plans, and local environmental plans. The form and relationships of these is a matter of continuing evolution, even confusion. Despite attempts to divorce strategic planning from local land use control, this has proved difficult to do as it is impossible to attach each operation to one particular arm or level of government.

In a more specific vein, the relationship of local land use and development controls to strategic urban development and housing policies, exemplified in the urban consolidation debate, will be an important focus for intergovernmental action.

Commonwealth Presence in and Focus for Land Use Planning

One important arena of intergovernmental action in land use planning is that where the commonwealth government is involved. There is no focus for this in the commonwealth government. Rather a range of theaters exists for narrowly defined action. During the Whitlam government of 1972-75, the Department of Urban and Regional Development and the Department of the Environment and Conservation provided some focus, but these departments were rapidly emasculated and dismantled in the succeeding years.

In 1981 the Senate referred the matter of land use policy to its Standing Committee on Science, Technology and the Environment, with particular reference to "the development of a coordinated national approach to land use policy." Much of the difficulty in this arises from the very different perceptions as to what are the concerns of national land use policy. In late 1983, the Royal Australian Planning Institute made a submission to the committee. It noted the importance of intergovernmental relations in national land use policy and the desirability of building on existing institutions and processes. It therefore suggested two advances. One is to develop the existing Standing Committee on Soil Conservation into a Land Resources Management Committee with an expanded role, powers, and functions. The present Standing Committee on Soil Conservation is a permanent technical committee of commonwealth and state officers who report to the Australian Agricultural Council formed in 1934 and comprising state and commonwealth ministers. The institute's first proposal was meant to deal with rural land use. The second recommendation was that the commonwealth take the lead and also establish an effective secretariat to service annual meetings of state and commonwealth ministers of planning and associated meetings of planning officers. These meetings had been initiated by the Department of Urban and Regional Development in 1973 but had lacked commonwealth involvement of any substance since 1976. The Royal Australian Planning Institute submission suggested that this should help revive national dimensions of policy about the pattern of settlement and urban-regional land use. It remains to be seen how the Inquiry on Land Use Policy will report on this matter, but it constitutes a matter for further resolution.

Issues Still Requiring Resolution

Much of the 1970s saw Australia in a fairly expansive mood. Land use planning reflected this in its preoccupations and methodologies. The recession of the late

1970s and early 1980s brought high unemployment, difficulties in providing affordable housing, and a shortage of capital funds for urban development. Important social trends continue to develop, particularly regarding the kinds of family and household groupings that provide the basis for use and tenure of dwelling stock. Inner suburban areas have been particularly affected by these trends. Future thrusts in land use planning still need to address some of these issues. One example is the need for development of joint ventures between public and private enterprise of the kind tried in South Australia through the Housing Trust and envisaged for the Land Trust. Projects of this kind could do much to resolve questions as to the degrees of control and intervention by government and the place of regulatory as opposed to entrepreneurial action.

Local Standards and Controls: The Variety and Cost of Housing

The issue of amenity, standards of development, and cost of development is a continuing one. Many Australian cities suffered from a rash of poorly designed and speculative flat building in the late 1960s and early 1970s. To some extent, the present standards and controls can be seen as an overreaction against that kind of development. However, these land use planning measures have been shown to affect adversely the variety of the dwelling stock provided, the range of locational choice for residents, and the cost of development. This issue will continue to preoccupy much local planning. It also raises the possibility of more extensive use of performance standards against which to measure development proposals. Evolution in this regard is represented by the new residential codes for Perth adopted recently as a Statement of Planning Policy in Western Australia.

Land Resource Management

A future thrust is the expansion and evolution of land resource management as part of land use planning, particularly in rural areas. A national program of soil conservation was modestly funded in 1983, but much more progress is needed. Opportunities exist to strengthen the thrust of land resource management. Reconstruction of some of Australia's agricultural and pastoral activities is taking place, particularly in areas where Australia does not hold a natural comparative advantage. The River Murray, Australia's only significant river is considerably polluted, but is still the major source of water supply of Adelaide. The management of this river system, in terms of safeguarding water quality and fighting increasing salinity and pollution, has important land use planning connotations. Economic, environmental, land, and water resource management considerations intertwine.

Research and Education

A final matter for future resolution is research and education for land use planning and urban development. Amid the complexities and changes in cities now apparent, new research and educational initiatives and thrusts are needed. A new challenge is the need for decisions and policies that have both structural and situational dimensions (AIUS 1982; Paris 1983). The concepts, methods, and skills to do this still remain to be developed. The situation has changed from that of a decade ago when research and some educational programs led planning practice and urban practices. That relationship needs to be reasserted.

BIBLIOGRAPHY

Australian Advisory Committee on the Environment. 1974. *Land Use in Australia*, Canberra: AGPS.
Australian Institute of Urban Studies. 1982. *Urban Consolidation and Adelaide*. Canberra: AIUS.
Australian National Commission for UNESCO. 1978. *Urban Management Processes*. Canberra: AGPS.
Bolton, G. 1981. *Spoils and Spoilers: Australians Make Their Environment, 1780-1980*. Sydney: George Allen & Unwin.
Bowman Margaret. 1979. *Australian Approaches to Environmental Management: The Response of State Planning*. Hobart: Environmental Law Reform Group.
Bunker, Raymond. 1971. *Town and Country—or City and Region?* Melbourne: Melbourne University Press.
Bunker, Raymond. 1977. Capital Cities. In D. N. Jeans, ed. *Australia: A Geography*, 386-411. Sydney: Sydney University Press.
Commission of Inquiry into Land Tenures. 1976. *Final Report*. Canberra: AGPS.
Committee of Inquiry into Housing Costs, 1978. *The Cost of Housing*. Vol. 1. Canberra: AGPS.
Department of Environment. Housing and Community Development. 1978. *A Basis for Soil Conservation Policy in Australia*. Canberra: AGPS.
Division of National Mapping. 1979-82. *Atlases of Population and Housing: 1976 Census*. Vol. 1 *Perth*; Vol. 2, *Adelaide*; Vol. 3, *Brisbane/Gold Coast*; Vol. 4, *Newcastle/ Wollongong*; Vol. 5, *Canberra/Hobart*; Vol. 6 *Sydney*; Vol. 7, *Melbourne/Geelong*. Canberra: Division of National Mapping.
Fowler, R. J. 1982. *Environmental Impact Assessment, Planning and Pollution Measures in Australia*. Canberra: AGPS.
Freestone, R. 1983. The Development of Urban Planning in Australia 1888-1948: A Bibliography and Review. In Peter Williams, ed. *Social Process and the City*. Sydney: George Allen & Unwin.
Harrison, Peter. 1975. Atlas of Australian Resources, Second Series. *Major Urban Areas*. Canberra: Division of National Mapping.
Harrison, Peter. 1977. Urban Planning in *Australian Encyclopaedia*. 3d ed. Sydney: Grolier Society of Australia.
Morgan, Travers. 1980. Energy and Land Use. Consultant's report for the South Australia Department of Urban and Regional Affairs. Adelaide.

Neutze, Max. 1977. *Urban Development in Australia*. Sydney: George Allen & Unwin.

Neutze, Max. 1978. *Australian Urban Policy*. Sydney: George Allen & Unwin.

New South Wales Department of Environment and Planning. 1980. *The N.S.W. Planning System*. Sydney.

New South Wales Department of Environment and Planning. 1982. *Residential Development Standards*. Technical Bulletin 15. Sydney: NSW Department of Environment and Planning.

New South Wales State Planning Authority. 1968. *Sydney Region Outline Plan*. Sydney: NSW State Planning Authority.

Paris, C. 1983. *Project 70: Affordable and Available Housing: The Role of the Private Rental Sector in Australia*. Canberra: AIUS.

Paterson, J., D. Yencken, and G. Gunn. 1976. *A Mansion or No House: A Report for U.D.I.A. on Consequences of Planning Standards and Their Impact on Land and Housing*. Melbourne: Urban Development Institute of Australia.

Plumb, T., ed. 1980. *Atlas of Australian Resources*, Third Series, Vol. 2. *Soils and Land Use*. Canberra: Division of National Mapping.

Powell, A. W. J. 1978. *NCDC Corporate Planning*. Technical Paper 27. Canberra: National Capital Development Commission.

Reid, H. M., J. Jones, and D. Wilmoth. 1983. The Development of Urban Consolidation Policies in Sydney. Paper presented at ANZAAS Conference, Macquarie University.

South Australian Land Trust. 1983. *Annual Report*. Adelaide: SALT.

Stimson, R. J. 1982. *The Australian City: A Welfare Geography*. Melbourne: Longman Cheshire.

Stretton, Hugh. 1975. *Ideas for Australian Cities*. Melbourne: Georgian House.

Troy, P. N., ed. 1981. *Equity in the City*. Sydney: George Allen & Unwin.

Westerman, Hans L. 1982. Botany and Randwick Sites Development Bill. *N.S.W. Planner*, no. 1:13.

Contributors

ADIL MUSTAFA AHMAD is associate professor of architecture at the University of Khartoum and head of the department from 1985. His publications examine architectural science, human settlements, and Arab residential design. Since 1977 he has been involved in research covering human settlements in Arab countries, the role of small- and intermediate-sized settlements in development, and popular settlements in Sudan.

RACHELLE ALTERMAN chairs the program in urban and regional planning at the Technion-Israel Institute of Technology. She specializes in comparative planning law, land policy, and the theory of policy implementation. Dr. Alterman has published widely on these topics in U.S., British, and Canadian journals and books. She has been visiting associate professor at the University of North Carolina at Chapel Hill.

EARL M. BROWN, JR. is director of programs of the African Development Foundation in Washington, D.C. Dr. Brown was previously senior development planner, Center for Population and Policy Studies, Research Triangle Institute (RTI), Research Triangle Park, North Carolina. He served as RTI field representative on the Land Use Programming Project, Tamale, Ghana (1979-81) and the Integrated Improvement Program for the Urban Poor (1981-83). He delivered a paper at the USAID Ninth Annual African Housing Conference, Dakar, Senegal, in April 1984. From 1964 to 1966, he worked as a Peace Corps volunteer teacher in Musoma, Tanzania.

RAYMOND BUNKER is senior lecturer in planning at the South Australian Institute of Technology. He has extensive experience in teaching, public administration, and advisory work concerning planning, urban development, and environmental management in Australia. He has also carried out assignments overseas and published extensively.

CLAUDE HENRI CHALINE has been on the faculty of town planning, Institut d'Urbanisme de Paris, since 1972 where he has taught town planning and geography. From 1980 to 1983 he was dean of the faculty of town planning. He is currently professor of city planning at the University of Paris XII. He also has a joint appointment at the Ecole nationale d'administration in Paris where he is professor of regional planning. He is a consultant to UNESCO on the Tunis-Carthage project. Professor Chaline has published many books and articles. His research interests include planning and implementation of new towns in developed and developing countries, urbanization and town planning in large Islamic cities, energy conservation in city planning, and waterfront redevelopment in London, Liège, and Paris.

ROBERT I. CHARD graduated from Oxford University and then worked as a professional town planner in local government in Britain and for town planning consultants in Britain and overseas. He has held teaching posts at Lanchester Polytechnic, United Kingdom, Kadura Polytechnic, Nigeria, and at King Abdul Aziz University, Jeddah, Saudi Arabia. He is a member of the Royal Town Planning Institute.

H. W. E. DAVIES is professor of planning and head of the Department of Land Management and Development at the University of Reading, England. He served as dean of the faculty from 1981 to 1984. He was formerly an associate with Hugh Wilson & Lewis Womersley, Chartered Architects & Town Planners, responsible for the Teesside Survey & Plan, Liverpool Inner Area Study, and projects in Canada, Botswana, and Singapore. He is specialist adviser to the House of Commons Expenditure Committee on Planning Procedures. Professor Davies is also a consultant on urban decline to the OECD and EEC.

IGOR DERGALIN has been professor and head of the Department of Town Planning at the Royal Institute of Technology, Stockholm, since 1972. He was elected dean of the school in 1984. From 1962 to 1972 he was chief planning officer for the city of Stockholm. Dr. Dergalin was professor of planning and housing development at the National Technical University, Athens, during 1980 and 1981. He is a member of the Swedish National Architectural Association, the Greek National Architectural Association and the International Society of City and Regional Planners.

GYÖRGY ENYEDI received his doctorate in Economics from the University of Budapest. He is director of the Research Center for Regional Studies and a corresponding member of the Hungarian Academy of Sciences. He has authored 15 books. Professor Enyedi has been a visiting professor in the United States and in France, president of the International Geographical Union Commission, and an honored member of the Finnish and French Geographical Societies.

KA-IU FUNG is professor of geography at the University of Saskatchewan, Canada. He is the coauthor of *Atlas of Saskatchewan* (1969) and the principal author of *Atlas of Saskatchewan Agriculture* (1978). He has published articles on Shanghai and on China's suburban developments. His recent research interest lies in urban planning and development in the People's Republic of China.

IAN HAYWOOD is a British architect-planner with more than 20 years of professional and academic experience in Europe, the Middle East, and Sudan. From 1979–1984 he was professor of physical planning at the University of Khartoum, where he established the first physical planning program in Sudan.

MORRIS HILL holds the Joseph Meyerhoff Chair in Urban and Regional Planning at the Technion-Israel Institute of Technology where he heads the Center for Urban and Regional Studies. He has been visiting professor at the universities of North Carolina, Harvard, Washington, California at Santa Cruz, London, Cape Town, and Ankara. He specializes in planning theory, plan evaluation, urban renewal, and metropolitan planning, and has published widely.

RICHARD H. JACKSON is a professor of geography and coordinator of the Urban and Regional Planning Program at Brigham Young University, Provo, Utah. He is the author of *Land Use in America* (1981) and numerous articles and reports on land use issues. Dr. Jackson's primary research interests are related to land use and environmental questions posed by the rapid development of the U.S. West, particularly as related to federal regulation of public and private land uses.

HIROSHI MATSUMOTO was recently appointed director of Japan Regional Development Corporation, a national organization responsible for new town development outside the three metropolitan areas. He was formerly inspector general of the Ministry of Construction in Japan and before that vice-director-general of the Land Bureau of the National Land Agency. Since graduating from the University of Kyoto in 1953, he has had substantial roles in policymaking and legislation regarding urban and land administration. He is the principal author of the first White Paper on National Land Use, published in 1974.

NICHOLAS N. PATRICIOS has been a professor of architecture and planning at the University of Miami since 1978 and director of the Urban and Regional Planning Program since 1981. During 1983-84 he served as interim dean of the newly established School of Architecture. He was a visiting scholar at the University of Michigan and University of California, Los Angeles, in 1976-77. Dr. Patricios was professor and head of the Department of Town and Regional Planning at the University of the Witwatersrand, Johannesburg, from 1974 to 1978. He held a groups leader's position in the London borough of Southwark, England, and also worked for a firm of consultants in London from 1965 to 1970. His teaching interests cover land use planning, planning theory, and methods. His research interests include spatial behavior and planning and design for the elderly. He has published widely in national and international journals. Dr. Patricios is a founder member of the American Institute of Certified Planners and a Fellow of the Royal Town Planning Institute.

WILLIAM T. PERKS is professor of urbanism and planning at the University of Calgary, Alberta, Canada. He was for 10 years dean of the faculty of environmental design and led the development of the innovative Calgary program from 1971 to 1981. Professor Perks has had an extensive career in planning consultancy, federal public service and education, and he served for six years as vice-chairman and commissioner of the National Capital Commission. He has been a consultant to several government agencies in Canada and abroad. A frequent contributor to and editor for Canadian and other planning journals, Professor Perks is, with Dr. Ira Robinson, the author of Canada's first reference work on Canadian planning, *Urban and Regional Planning in a Federal State, 1979*. He is a contributor to the *New Canadian Encyclopedia*. Professor Perks currently teaches planning theory, history, and contemporary practice, and he serves on the NCC Design Advisory Committee.

LEO F. POZO-LEDEZMA is a research specialist for the Office of International Affairs of the U.S. Department of Housing and Urban Development, Washington, D.C. He was the program officer for the U.S.-Mexico Agreement for Cooperation in the Field of Housing and Urban Development and also the co-chair of the Working Group on Environment and Urban Development under the U.S.-Mexico Mixed Commission on Science and Technology. Previously he worked as a consultant for the World Health Organization and for the state of Florida. Currently he is a member of the American Planning Association; he has been an officer of its International Division, as well as editor of *Interplan*, its newsletter. He is working on a book on urban and regional planning along the U.S.-Mexico border.

ALBERTO RIVERA is a sociologist, researcher at the Centro de Estudios de la Realidad Economica y Social, and assistant professor at the Universidad Mayor de San Simon, Cochabamba, Bolivia. He has studied at the Universidad Mayor de San Andres in La Paz and the University of Chile. His main research and publications deal with urban problems.

GOLDIE RIVKIN is an urban development consultant whose practice includes clients in both the public and private sectors in the United States and in developing countries. She has taught courses in community infrastructure planning at Middle East Technical University in Turkey and graduate seminars on urban growth management at the American University, Washington, D.C. Her assignments for the U.S. Agency for International Development and United Nations/Habitat have dealt with shelter in several southern African nations, review of human settlements conditions in the developing countries of Asia, and upgrading of spontaneous communities in Peru, Honduras and Panama. She is coauthor of *Community Growth and Water Resources Policy* and has collaborated with M. D. Rivkin on numerous reports, including the major study from which the Tunisia chapter appearing in this book has been excerpted.

MALCOLM RIVKIN is consultant to a wide range of business, institutional, and governmental clients on urban development issues and projects. Sent by OECD as resident adviser to Turkey's Ministry of Reconstruction and Resettlement, he has since carried out assignments for USAID, the United Nations, and the World Bank in more than 15 developing countries. Dr. Rivkin's work for USAID has included design of an urban development strategy for Jamaica, evaluation of shelter programs in Tunisia and Thailand, and housing policy strategy for Swaziland. Dr. Rivkin has directed training programs in shelter and urban development for USAID and the World Bank's Economic Development Institute. He has written extensively on urban issues and has collaborated with G. W. Rivkin on the major study, *Approaches to Planning and Secondary Cities in Developing Countries*.

DEAN S. RUGG is professor of geography at the University of Nebraska. His Ph.D. is from the University of Maryland where his dissertation dealt with a comparison between a U.S. and a German city. Regionally he has specialized in Eastern Europe where he not only worked as a foreign service officer but later carried out academic research.

EBERHARD SCHMIDT-ASSMANN is a professor at the University of Heidelberg. From 1958 until 1963 he studied law in Göttingen and Geneva, obtaining the Dr. iur. (Göttingen) in 1967. He was assistant professor in Göttingen from 1968 to 1971 and from 1972 to 1979 professor at the University of Bochum, where he taught planning law. In 1979 he was appointed professor of administrative and constitutional law at the University of Heidelberg.

DENIS J. B. SHAW obtained the B.A. Hons. in 1968 and the Ph.D. in 1973 from University College, London, specializing in geography. He was an exchange student at Voronezh State University, USSR, 1969-70. Dr. Shaw has been a lecturer in the Department of Geography, University of Birmingham, since 1971. He was an exchange scholar, Moscow State University, in 1974, 1979, and 1983; a visiting professor, University of Manitoba, Canada, in 1977 and 1982; and a guest scholar, Kennan Institute of Advanced Russian Studies,

Washington, D.C., in 1980. He is coauthor of *Planning in the Soviet Union* (1981) and the author of numerous articles on Soviet urban and regional planning and the historical geography of Russian settlement.

K.V. SUNDARAM is a regional planner with the Indian Planning Commission, serving as joint adviser in charge of multilevel planning. He has been consultant to various UN organizations, including the United Nations Centre for Regional Development, Nagoya, ESCAP and F.A.O. He was a Nuffield Fellow during 1978-79 and spent two terms of residence in the Centre of South Asian Studies, University of Cambridge. Dr. Sundaram's major publications include *Regional Development Planning in India: A New Strategy* (1974), *Urban and Regional Planning in India* (1977), *Rural Area Development: Perspectives and Approaches* (1979), *Multi-level Planning and Integrated Rural Development in India* (1980), and *Geography of Underdevelopment—The Spatial Dynamics of Underdevelopment* (1983).

HORACIO A. TORRES is head of the Urban Analysis Laboratory and professor of urbanism at the University of Belgrano, Buenos Aires. He is an architecture graduate from the University of Buenos Aires. He was lecturer and adjunct professor of urbanism and architecture in the School of Architecture at the University of Buenos Aires from 1959 to 1966. In 1967 he was awarded a British Council scholarship in order to undertake planning studies in Britain. He obtained the Architectural Association's postgraduate diploma in planning and spent one year as a visiting associate researcher at the Centre for Land Use and Built Form Studies, School of Architecture, University of Cambridge. He has been a researcher in the National Research Council of Argentina since 1971 and was a visiting researcher in the Centro de Estudios Urbanos y Regionales, Instituto Torcuato Di Tella.

G. C. UNDERWOOD was born in Zimbabwe but attended the University of the Witwatersrand in South Africa where he qualified as a town and regional planner. He has worked for the Zimbabwe Government Department of Physical Planning as a provincial planning officer during which time he obtained experience in rural development. He is now deputy director responsible for urban planning and development.

R. K. WISHWAKARMA is an urban and regional economist on the faculty of the Indian Institute of Public Administration. He is a member of the Indian Economic Service. His contributions are mainly in the fields of urban land economics, urban and regional planning policy, human settlement planning and environment policy, small towns and urban integrated development, and economic base studies and the informal sector. Among Dr. Wishwakarma's publications are the following books: *Land and Property Values: An Analysis of*

Environmental Impact (1980), *Urban and Regional Planning Policy in India* (1981), *Integrated Development of Small and Medium Towns: Critical Areas and Issues for Policy Options* (1982), and *Integrated Development of Small and Medium Towns: Problems and Strategic Policy Issues* (1983).

Index